PENGUIN BOOKS

BEATRIX POTTER

'Rounded, sympathetic and fascinating . . . Potter's legacy is rich and varied, and Lear has done her proud' *Herald*

'Potter's marvellous voice, captured in letters and journals, comes through loud and clear in this new biography . . . Lear gives us much to consider about this unfamiliar and remarkable woman'
Lavinia Greenlaw, *Daily Telegraph*

'Shows Potter in a new light' *Evening Standard*

'Lear's dazzling study of a pioneering life influenced by nature forces us to re-examine every assumption made about Potter. Her own writing shines with wistful appreciation . . . we are left to marvel at the life and work of a true "woman of substance"' Vanessa Curtis, *Scotland on Sunday*

'Curl up with Lear's excellent new biography' *Daily Mail*

'Read *Beatrix Potter* and you sense a woman poised between late-Victorian constraint and the promises, intellectual and amorous, of liberation'
Anthony Lane, *New Yorker*

'Diligent and humorous, Linda Lear is a good match for her subject'
Economist

'The Beatrix Potter depicted in Linda Lear's authoritative biography was undoubtedly heroic' John C.

'Linda Lear's new bio   ery page
is informed by lov   f this
impressively determ   , this
generous and creativ   thetic
biograp   *y Mail*

'Lear has done a terrific job in collating information about a richly fascinating life' Sally Vickers, *The Times*

Linda Lear has always been intrigued by how the lives of artists and writers have been influenced by the natural world. She discovered quite by accident that before Beatrix Potter began her legendary series of 'little books' for children she had been an avid student of natural history and might have had a career in science had such opportunities been available to women. As Lear explored Potter's evolution from amateur scientist to acclaimed author-illustrator and careful steward of the land, she herself became an admirer of Lakeland's farms, fells and sheep. A professor of environmental history, and the author of the prize-winning biography, *Rachel Carson: Witness for Nature*, Lear is an enthusiastic horticulturist and collector of botanical art. She and her husband live in Bethesda, Maryland.

Beatrix Potter

The extraordinary life of a
Victorian genius

LINDA LEAR

PENGUIN BOOKS

PENGUIN BOOKS

Published by the Penguin Group
Penguin Books Ltd, 80 Strand, London WC2R 0RL, England
Penguin Group (USA) Inc., 375 Hudson Street, New York, New York 10014, USA
Penguin Group (Canada), 90 Eglinton Avenue East, Suite 700, Toronto, Ontario, Canada M4P 2Y3
(a division of Pearson Penguin Canada Inc.)
Penguin Ireland, 25 St Stephen's Green, Dublin 2, Ireland
(a division of Penguin Books Ltd)
Penguin Group (Australia), 250 Camberwell Road, Camberwell, Victoria 3124, Australia
(a division of Pearson Australia Group Pty Ltd)
Penguin Books India Pvt Ltd, 11 Community Centre, Panchsheel Park, New Delhi – 110 017, India
Penguin Group (NZ), 67 Apollo Drive, Rosedale, North Shore 0632, New Zealand
(a division of Pearson New Zealand Ltd)
Penguin Books (South Africa) (Pty) Ltd, 24 Sturdee Avenue, Rosebank, Johannesburg 2196, South Africa

Penguin Books Ltd, Registered Offices: 80 Strand, London WC2R 0RL, England

www.penguin.com

First published by Allen Lane 2007
Published in Penguin Books 2008

1

Typeset by Rowland Phototypesetting Ltd, Bury St Edmunds, Suffolk
Printed in England by Clays Ltd, St Ives plc

978-0-141-00310-8

For John

Contents

Acknowledgements

Beatrix Potter was first of all an artist and writer of place who found her personal and intellectual freedom in nature. She later became a conservationist in an effort to preserve the landscape that had inspired her art. Her generosity left an indelible imprint on that part of the English countryside known as the Lake District. This biography was undertaken as an exploration of the life and times of a woman who is a household name on several continents, but whose personal life and significant scientific and environmental accomplishments remain largely unknown. Her life was not without tragedy, but she was one of those rare individuals who is given a real third act. Beatrix Potter made the most of this gift, and it is this coda that I have found the most revealing of her essential nature. Potter was a woman of her time, yet she produced art and story that are timeless. She was emotionally resilient, capable of reinventing herself, and saved from the ordinary by her creative genius. Ultimately, her early longing for useful work and her later passion for preservation give definition to her life's course.

My research has taken me to many of those places which were imprinted upon her inner eye, shared in her art and left to us by her stewardship. I have followed her from London to Hertfordshire, to the coastal towns of the south, to Scotland, Wales, to the Greater Manchester area, and finally to the Lake District. It has been my good fortune to find many of the houses in which she spent time and to wander about the countryside that so delighted her and which she immortalized in her work. I am grateful to all those who have accompanied me in one way or another on this journey.

I have consulted numerous archives, libraries and collections. I wish to thank Joyce Irene Whalley, former Curator of the Linder

Bequest, and Emma Laws, Frederick Warne Curator of Children's Literature, Victoria and Albert Museum, London; Eileen Cox of the Dunkeld Cathedral Archives; Jane Anderson, Blair Castle Archives, Pitlochry; John Hodgson, John Rylands University Library, Manchester; David Taylor and Richard Bond, Manchester Central Library; Guy F. Holborn, Librarian of Lincoln's Inn; Sarah Dodgson, Keeper, Archives, Books and Collections, Athenaeum; Simon Blundell, Librarian, Reform Club; Enid Bassom, former co-editor of the *Beatrix Potter Society Newsletter*; Michael Harvey, National Museum of Photography, Film & Television; Peter Buxton, photographer, Birnam; Margaret Mardall and Ann Wheeler, Charterhouse School; Robin Darwall-Smith, Archivist, Magdalen College, Oxford; Cecily Green and Helen Jones, Society for the Protection of Ancient Buildings; Isabelle Hernandez and Hazel Cook, Kensington Library, Local Studies; Louise Todd and Linda Bowen, National Trust, London and Grasmere; Susan Benson, Girlguiding Archivist, Cumbria South Archives, Cumbria Record Office, Barrow-in-Furness; Susan Dench and David Bowcock, Cumbria Record Office, Carlisle; Richard Hall and Kath Strickland, Cumbria Record Office, Kendal; Geoff Brown, Secretary, Herdwick Sheep Breeders' Association; Terry Fletcher, Editor, *Cumbria Magazine*; Anna Lou Ashby, Inge Dupont and McKenna Lebens, Pierpont Morgan Library and Museum, New York; Sybille A. Jagusch, Children's Library Center, Library of Congress, Washington, DC; Lolly Robinson, *The Horn Book*, Boston, Massachusetts; Diane Williams and Cathy Farrington, Milton Academy, Milton, Massachusetts; Dan Haacker, Milton Public Library; Staff of Miller Library, Colby College, Waterville, Maine.

The following curators and archivists facilitated lengthy research visits with expert assistance: Ivy Trent, Librarian, Cotsen Children's Library, formerly in Los Angeles; Anne Stevenson Hobbs, formerly Frederick Warne Curator of Children's Literature, Victoria and Albert Museum, London; Karen Lightner, formerly Beatrix Potter Curator, Rare Book Librarian, Free Library of Philadelphia, Pennsylvania; Liz Hunter McFarlane, House & Collections Manager, and Hazel Gatford, former Collections Assistant, Hawkshead & Beatrix Potter Property, National Trust; Susan Payne, Robin Rodger and

Michael Taylor of Perth Museum and Art Gallery; Linda Powell, Michelle Kelly, Beth Gabb, Ian Rollins, Barbara Crossley and Tanya Flower of the Armitt Trust Library of the Lakes Discovery Museum @ The Armitt, Ambleside.

Many individual scholars and experts granted interviews and shared material that influenced my thinking about Potter's life and work. I wish to thank Brigadier John Heelis, Brian Alderson, Reita Wilson, Peter Hollindale, Selwyn Goodacre, Laura Stevenson, Kara Sewall, Pam Lancaster, Dudley Chignall, Carol Halebian, Nonya Stevens Wright, Anthony H. Gaddum, Herbert G. Sokinger, Judge George N. Hurd, Jeannette Peverly, Nancy Dean Kingman, Helen Twombly Watkins, Jessie Kenyon, Helen Jackson, Geoff Brown, Christine Clough of The Friends of Gorse Hall, Jack Bredbury and Ken Howard of Stalybridge Unitarian Church, Glynis Reeve Greenman, David Duncan, Joy Sharp, Yumiko Mitsudo, Elaine R. Jacobsen, Marc Samuels Lasner, Margaret Stetz, Justin Schiller, Greg Gilbert, and Lord Rochdale of the Lingholm Private Trust Ltd.

The following individuals aided my understanding of the Lake District and of Beatrix Potter's life there: Joan Duke, Eileen Jay, the late Elizabeth Battrick, Beverly Maggs, Willow Taylor, Jenny Cutcliffe, Louise Taylor Smith, John Birkett, Jean and Dan Birkett, Glenn and Dorothy Wilkinson, W. R. Mitchell, Christopher Hanson-Smith, John A. Nettleton, Gilbert Tyson and Gordon Tyson. Special thanks go to John R. Cawood, Esq., whose understanding of land records and the history of property conveyancing in the Lake District guided me through the maze of land purchases, legal terms, and local traditions. His knowledge and generous advice have been essential.

These scientists and historians guided me through the minefields of specialization: the late Mary Noble and Roy Watling, Royal Botanical Gardens, Edinburgh, in mycology; David Allen, Wellcome Trust for History of Medicine, University College London; Brian Gardiner, Linnean Society. Marc Rothenberg, the late Patricia Gossell and Paula DePriest of the Smithsonian Institution, and Sandra Herbert, my colleague at the University of Maryland, Baltimore County, all contributed to my understanding of the historic protocols and proceedings of the Linnean Society and of nineteenth-century botanical practices. For sharing their expertise in medicine and gynae-cological practice, I am indebted to the kindness of these physicians: Anne Colville, John Nunn and Harold Francis. Eddie McDonough of Astley Tyldesly generously shared his extraordinary knowledge of animal husbandry, fell sheep and the history of country life.

I am grateful to Roger Cutcliffe, formerly head of the biological section of the Process Investigation Department of Glaxo's penicillin factory in Ulverston, and former Beatrix Potter Society Chairman, for his expertise on penicillin and the history of its discovery, and to discussions about Potter's research with the late Mary Noble and with Kevin Brown, Trust Archivist & Alexander Fleming Laboratory Museum Curator, St Mary's Hospital, London.

Frederick Warne, Beatrix Potter's publisher, and the Beatrix Potter Society opened their unrivalled collections to me and gave me per-mission to quote from their materials. Heartfelt thanks go to Warne publisher Sally Floyer, to Diana Syrat and Ronnie Fairweather who have generously supported this project. Former Collections Manager Elizabeth Booth first acquainted me with Warne's remarkable collec-tions of images, manuscripts and art. Sara Glenn, her successor, has guided me through those collections online. The Beatrix Potter Society has furthered research about the life and work of Beatrix Potter for more than a quarter of a century. Their publications, conferences, tours and archives have been essential. Individual Society members on several continents contributed to my understanding. Many contributed their expertise unasked, and sent me down roads I would never have thought to take. Special thanks to Jane Crowell Morse, honorary vice president and Potter scholar, who accompanied me to my first Beatrix Potter Society Conference in Ambleside, and introduced me to the Society and to her many friends in the Lake District; to Jenny Akester, membership secretary, conference organ-izer and tour guide, for her personal research on my behalf and her support in all aspects of this work. Betsy Bray, US East Coast representative, played a pivotal role at the outset and helped me navigate an unfamiliar network. Susan Wittig Albert joined me in the hunt for evidence when she began her own acclaimed mystery series, *The Cottage Tales of Beatrix Potter*. Her friendship has been an unexpected gift of this adventure.

The Washington Biography Group, its members and its esteemed leader Marc Pachter, Director of the National Portrait Gallery, Washington, DC, again challenged my thinking about Potter's life for eight long years. Our discussions always provided fresh insights and renewed spirits. Cynthia Cannell, my literary agent, patiently and calmly nurtured me and piloted this project from the beginning. Her advice and caring have been unfailingly generous. Margaret Bluman, my editor at Allen Lane, Penguin, has given real joy to these years of labour and shepherded this manuscript with confidence, humour and vision. My enthusiastic editor at St Martin's Press, Michael Flamini, provided energy and perspective at just the right time.

This manuscript has been read in whole and in part by Judy Taylor Hough, R. K. Webb, Cynthia Vartan, Libby Joy, Susan Albert, Roy Watling, John Cawood, Jane Morse, Michele Pacifico, Pam Blevins and Karen Shaffer. Michele Pacifico organized and maintained the research archive, prepared the bibliography, and kept me from losing things. Shep Bostin, Michael Weeks and John Emrich saved me from technological failure. Libby Joy, my research associate in London, has given me the benefit of her immense knowledge of Potter, has kept this biography on course, researched, questioned and edited, all the while enduring my steep learning curve with grace and forbearance. R. K. Webb, distinguished professor in English history, colleague and friend, has guided my understanding of Potter's life within the larger context of English social and intellectual history. Without his critical reading this work would have been impoverished. Finally, Judy Taylor Hough, MBE, Beatrix Potter scholar, Beatrix Potter Society chair, author and editor, opened her collection of unpublished materials to me, and thereby made this new biography possible. In every way, she is the 'without whom' of this effort. In the process she has also become my friend, but she bears no responsibility whatsoever for my errors of fact or interpretation, and certainly none for my invariable mispronunciation of her favourite names and places.

My husband, John W. Nickum, Jr., my esteemed literary escort and my life partner, has patiently endured all the deprivations and deferred dreams that befall the spouse of an obsessive biographer. It was he who first suggested that I write this life. He knows my gratitude and has my heart.

L. L.
Bethesda, Maryland
September 2006

March 13ᵗʰ 1900

2, BOLTON GARDENS,
LONDON, S.W.

My dear Marjory,

You will begin to be afraid
I have run away with the
letters altogether! I will keep
them a little longer because I
want to make a list of them, but
I don't think they will be made
into a book this time because
the publisher wants poetry.
The publisher is a gentleman
who prints books, and he wants

Beatrix Potter to Marjory Moore, age 10, about the difficulties of publishing a book (the *Tale of Peter Rabbit*) and a visit to the British Museum Reading Room. Courtesy of the Morgan Library and Museum.

a bigger book, than he has got enough money to pay for! and Miss Potter has arguments with him. He was taken ill on Sunday and his sisters and his cousins and his Aunts had arguments; I wonder if that book will ever be printed! I think Miss Potter will go off to another publisher soon. She would rather make 2 or 3 little books costing 1/

each, than one big book costing
6/. because
she thinks
little rabbits
cannot afford to spend 6 shillings
on one book, and would never
buy it.   I went to the
Reading Room at the British
Museum this morning to see a
delightful old book full of rhymes,
I shall draw pictures of some
of them whether they are printed
or not.   The Reading room is an

<u>enormous</u> big room, quite round.
with galleries
round the sides
the walls covered
with books,

and hundreds of chairs and desks on
the floor. There were not many people
but some of them were very funny to
look at! And there are some people
who live there always but Miss
Potter didn't see them, although
they are said to
be the largest
people of their
sort in London! Next time miss Potter goes
to the British Museum she will take some
keating's powder! It is very odd there should

fleas in books!

List of Illustrations

Frederick Warne & Co. is the owner of all rights, copyrights and trademarks in the Beatrix Potter character names and illustrations.

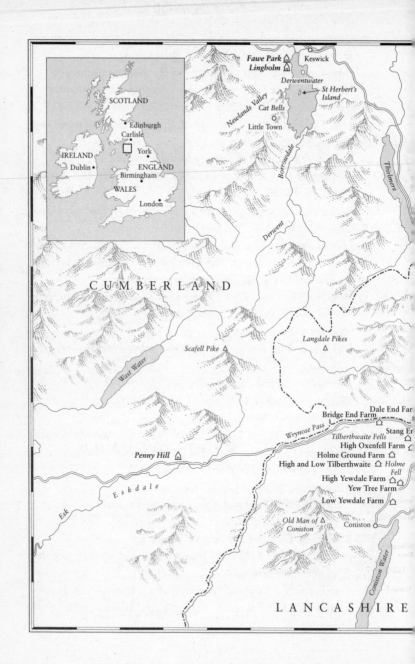

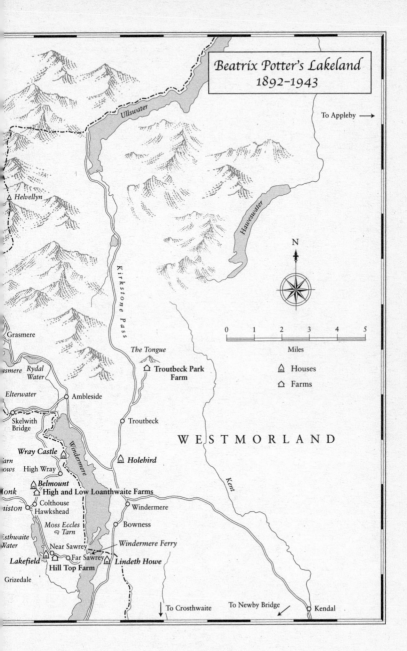

Beatrix Potter's Lakeland
1892–1943

To Appleby →

Ullswater

Haweswater

N

Kirkstone Pass

Helvellyn

0 1 2 3 4 5
Miles

Grasmere

The Tongue

△ Troutbeck Park
Farm

⌂ Houses
△ Farms

asmere *Rydal*
Water

Elterwater   Ambleside

Skelwith
Bridge

Troutbeck

WESTMORLAND

Wray Castle ⌂
     High Wray

Windermere

⌂ *Holehird*

⌂ *Belmount*
⌂ High and Low Loanthwaite Farms

onk
iston
Colthouse
Hawkshead

Windermere

Kent

Moss Eccles
⌒ *Tarn*

Bowness

sthwaite
Water

Near Sawrey
Windermere Ferry

Lakefield   Far Sawrey △ *Lindeth Howe*
△ Hill Top Farm

Grizedale

↓ To Crosthwaite   To Newby Bridge ↘   ○ Kendal

Beatrix Potter

❧ *Ownership* ❧

Near Sawrey, Lancashire

IT WAS A COLD, WET November day in 1918. The frosty air had settled just above the lake. Soon it would be dark. Through the gloom the figure of a woman could just be made out. She was on her hands and knees scrabbling about in the stubble of the harvested cornfield, searching for something. Close up she was a handsome woman with noticeably high colour in her cheeks, deep-set brilliant blue eyes and unruly brown hair pulled back haphazardly from her face. Her somewhat rounded frame was mostly hidden by several layers of outerwear. She wore a long, coarse wool jacket, wool stockings, and serviceable clogs as defence against the chill.

The woman was Mrs William Heelis, the former Beatrix Potter, the acclaimed creator of *The Tale of Peter Rabbit*, and the author and illustrator of over twenty other little books for children. At 52 she was a happily married woman of five years and a successful landowner and country farmer of more than a decade. But just now she was desperately searching for the ring that Norman Warne, once her editor and publisher, had given her a month before he died and which she had worn every day for the past thirteen years as a treasured remembrance. It had slipped off her cold fingers while she was helping the hired men lift the heavy sheaves of bundled corn. She had already untied many on the threshing floor in hopes of finding it there, but now she was back in the field searching one more time before the light completely faded.

Suddenly she saw it, a simple gold ring among the wet stuff they had thrown down for the hens. 'I am glad I was spared that last crowning distress of a most disastrous harvest,' she wrote to Norman's sister a few days later. 'I should have had just one consolation, it was a pretty, quiet sheltered field to lie in, if it had not been found. My hand felt very strange & uncomfortable without it.' The near-loss of Norman's ring reminded Beatrix once again of how sad she had been when she had purchased Hill Top Farm in the autumn of 1905, and how much her life had changed.[1]

Near Sawrey was still a hamlet when Helen Beatrix Potter, a 39-year-old spinster from London, became the unlikely owner of Hill Top. The seventeenth-century farm sits back from the road on the eastern edge of the quiet, peaceful village – a place that looks like artists' country. A few other farms, some scattered whitewashed cottages and the grandly named Tower Bank Arms stood, then as now, fronting fields that slope down to the shore of Esthwaite Water, one of the prettiest of the smaller lakes. Framing this soft hilly country are the Tilberthwaite Fells, and beyond them loom the Langdale Pikes.

Near Sawrey and its sister village, Far Sawrey, are distinguished by their proximity to the ancient market town of Hawkshead. Both sit upon the narrow strip of farmland between Esthwaite Water and the western shore of Windermere, in the township of Claife, now part of Cumbria but until rather recently the northern tip of Lancashire. There was no nationally protected Lake District Park, only a barely identifiable geographic region in the corner of north-west England, made famous in the early nineteenth century by a group of Romantic poets. Their literary celebration of the virtues of rural solitude ironically increased the number of tourists and 'off-comers' who discovered the mesmerizing beauty of the English Lakes. By mid-century the Romantic idyll was over. But in tiny hamlets like Near Sawrey, life went on much as it always had.

'My purchase seems to be regarded as a huge joke,' Beatrix wrote to Norman's brother, Harold Warne, her editor at Frederick Warne & Co. It was early October 1905, just after she had arrived at the farm. 'I have been going over my hill with a tape measure.' But there was little she could do to mitigate the scepticism of her Sawrey neighbours. It was commonly known that Miss Potter had paid nearly twice as much for her thirty-four-acre farm as the previous owner – a fact Beatrix herself would not discover until it was too late to

renegotiate the price. Buying Hill Top Farm had been her first
independent business decision, paid for mostly with her own money.
Her subsequent embarrassment at the inflated price was a painful
lesson. In the future she would do her homework more carefully,
and have a local solicitor to advise her. But nothing could diminish
her joy at owning her own property.[2]

It is impossible to know when Beatrix Potter first came upon Near
Sawrey. It may have been as early as the summer of 1882 when, at
the age of 16, she walked over to the market town of Hawkshead
from Wray Castle on the shore of Windermere. She recorded then,
'Had a series of adventures. Inquired the way three times, lost
continually, alarmed by collies at every farm, stuck in stiles, chased
once by cows.' She had noted the architectural details of Hawkshead's
buildings: the handsome Norman church with its fine oak carving,
and the little Quaker Meeting House at nearby Colthouse whose door
opened with a huge iron key. Several days later, Beatrix joined her
parents and their guest, the orator John Bright, for a drive around
Esthwaite Water. On their way around the lake they certainly passed
through the tiny hamlet.[3]

Over the next decade, the wealthy Potter family frequently came
to the Lake District on holiday. They spent a number of summers at
Lingholm and Fawe Park, two large estates on the western shore of
Derwentwater near Keswick, and some at Holehird, a mansion with
expansive grounds perched high above Windermere. No matter
where the family stayed, Beatrix explored the surrounding countryside. During a holiday in the Scottish lowlands in 1892, an area she
had known and loved since childhood, she was reminded of the little
English village of Near Sawrey. 'I prefer a pastoral landscape backed
by mountains,' she wrote, even after a drive along the scenic Braan.
'I have often been laughed at for thinking Esthwaite Water the most
beautiful of the Lakes. It really strikes me that some scenery is
almost theatrical, or ultra-romantic.' Owing partly to their daughter's
enthusiasm for Near Sawrey, the Potters decided to lease Lakefield
just outside the village in 1896.[4]

That long summer holiday allowed Beatrix to become well acquainted with the village, its cottages, shopkeepers and children,

the countryside around Esthwaite Water, and especially with the neighbouring Hill Top Farm. There was something beautiful, something that pleased her senses everywhere she went. From the garden terrace of Lakefield the fields seem to fold down upon themselves to the edge of the lake. The light was never once the same on the hills opposite. It was a view that always captivated her and one which she would paint in every season.[5]

Beatrix celebrated her thirtieth birthday in Sawrey that summer, noting the passage with some pleasure. 'I feel much younger at thirty than I did at twenty; firmer and stronger both in mind and body,' she wrote, obviously relishing her time there and feeling inwardly renewed. 'A perfect, hot summer day, cloudless' until 'evening when it rolled up like thunder round How Fell'. Walking home after tea with some young cousins, she remarked upon the 'very pleasant evening-light, and village people up and down the road and in the flowery little gardens'. Perhaps this was also the summer she determined to buy property there one day, but whenever it was, her deep contentment in Near Sawrey created an indelible memory.[6]

In 1900 the Potters again came to Lakefield. By then the country house had resumed its Old English name, Ees Wyke, meaning 'house east of the water', although it was more commonly known as Eeswyke, after the inlet close by. One village observer remembered that in 1900 the family came 'with their servants, their carriage and pair, and Miss Potter with her pony and Phaeton'. Their coachman David Beckett and his family took lodgings at Hill Top Farm with Henry Preston and Beatrix frequently walked over to the farm to visit and to sketch.[7]

When the Potters returned two years later, Beatrix had more pressing things on her mind. All spring she had been working with Norman Warne, the youngest son of her publisher, Frederick Warne & Co., who was overseeing the publication of *The Tale of Peter Rabbit*, her first commercially printed children's book. Beatrix had arrived in Sawrey just in time to approve the colour blocks of her illustrations. Letters flew between Beatrix at Eeswyke and Norman Warne in London attending to the details of printing. *The Tale of Peter Rabbit* was published in early October 1902 while the

Potters were still in Sawrey, the entire first printing sold out before publication.[8]

In the autumn of 1905 Beatrix was back at Sawrey. Much had changed in three years. She was the author of five more books for children: *The Tale of Squirrel Nutkin* and *The Tailor of Gloucester* in 1903, *The Tale of Benjamin Bunny* and *The Tale of Two Bad Mice* in 1904, and soon, *The Tale of Mrs. Tiggy-Winkle*, all with Norman Warne as her editor. For a slender moment that spring, after she accepted his engagement ring, Beatrix thought her own story might 'come right'. Then Norman died. But she had earned money on her own, her books were a commercial success, and now she was to be a woman of property: the owner of Hill Top Farm.

The purchase of Hill Top Farm was a turning point: a courageous assertion of personal freedom and emotional independence. Although Beatrix justified it as an investment, her deep attachment to the land and her reasons for wanting to own this property were far more complicated. In 1905 Beatrix was running from disappointment and powerlessness, but she had not forgotten to be curious about what might happen next. She set out upon an unknown course which held at least the possibility of personal fulfilment – a choice inextricably driven by her inherent passion for place – a passion which would ultimately define her life. Sawrey was, as she had known it would be, 'as nearly perfect a little place as I ever lived in'.[9]

The part of the Lake District that Beatrix Potter chose as her own was not only physically beautiful, it was a place in which she felt emotionally rooted as a descendant of hard-working north-country folk. The predictable routines of farm life appealed to her. There was a realism in the countryside that nurtured a deep connection. The scale of the villages was manageable. Yet the vast desolateness of the surrounding fells was awe-inspiring. It was mysterious, but easily imbued with fantasy and tamed by imagination. The sheltered lakes and fertile valleys satisfied her love of the pastoral. The hill farms and the sheep on the high fells demanded accountability. There was a longing in Beatrix Potter for association with permanence: to find a place where time moved slowly, where places remained much as she remembered them from season to season and from year to year.

By 1918 she had found it. Nature, she knew, was not immutable, but nature as revealed in the Lake District, and etched in her mind's eye, was the closest to everlasting as she could come.

⤳ *Roots* ⤵

B EATRIX POTTER NEVER CONSIDERED herself an 'off-comer' in
Sawrey. For much of her adult life she worked hard at shedding
at least the outward vestiges of her upper-middle-class upbringing in
the Kensington area of London and at re-establishing and embellishing her country credentials. It was a matter of great consequence
to her to be identified, not by her accidental place of birth, but rather
by the geographical location of her family's roots. 'My brother & I
were born in London because my father was a lawyer there,' she
wrote once by way of explanation. 'But our descent – our interests
and our joy was in the north country.' From this perspective Beatrix's
purchase of land in Sawrey represented both an independent sallying
forth, and a return to the land of her ancestors – to a place where
she instinctively felt she belonged.[1]

She had always been interested in her family's history, particularly
in the qualities of the north-country stock they came from. She once
wrote to an American friend with considerable pride, 'I am descended
from generations of Lancashire yeomen and weavers; obstinate, hard
headed, *matter of fact* folk . . . As far back as I can go, they were
Puritans, Nonjurors, Nonconformists, Dissenters. Your *Mayflower*
ancestors sailed to America; mine at the same date were sticking it
out at home, probably rather enjoying persecution.' Beatrix did not
have to search far to find evidence of strong character or conviction.
Both sides of her family were distinguished by their Radical political
opinions, Unitarian convictions, extraordinary success in trade, and
a discerning interest in the arts.[2]

When Beatrix was a little girl, obscured and forgotten under the
table skirt with the 'yellowy green fringe' in the library of Camfield
Place, the country home of her paternal grandparents, she absorbed

stories and family gossip which many years later she could recall with unusual clarity and detail. 'I can remember quite plainly from one to two years old,' she wrote; 'not only facts, like learning to walk, but places and sentiments – the way things impressed a very young child.'[3]

The impressionable little girl paid particular attention to the stories told by her adored grandmother Jessy Crompton Potter, once a noted beauty and an accomplished harpist, and now an arresting and spirited older woman. In those recitals of the family's past, the name Crompton was redoubtable. As far as the family legend went, or at least the version that Beatrix embraced, the Cromptons were the source of all that was independent, outspoken, eccentric and worth emulating in the family. 'I am a believer in "breed",' Beatrix wrote to a friend; 'I hold that a strongly marked personality can influence descendants for generations. In the same way that we farmers know that certain sires – bulls – stallions – rams – have been "prepotent" in forming breeds of shorthorns, thoroughbreds, and the numerous varieties of sheep.'[4]

Beatrix's great-grandfather, Abraham Crompton, settled his family of thirteen at Lune Villa, a Georgian house with expansive grounds on the River Lune in Lancashire. He also owned land in the Tilberthwaite Fells near Coniston: fells that Beatrix could later see outlined against the horizon from the upper fields of Hill Top Farm. His property there was known as Holme Ground, which means a place surrounded by water, as indeed it was. Abraham sometimes spent summer holidays there attended by one or other of his children, most often with Beatrix's grandmother, Jessy.

Both Beatrix's father's and mother's families had deep roots in the counties near Manchester, which by the time of Beatrix's birth in 1866 was the second largest city in England and the centre of the textile manufacturing that was fuelled by the Industrial Revolution. The Potters of recent generations came from Glossop, a textile town in Derbyshire, south-east of Manchester. Beatrix's mother's family, the Leeches, were from Stalybridge and Hyde in nearby Cheshire.

Edmund Potter, Beatrix's paternal grandfather, was by far the most accomplished member of either family. His attitudes, passions and talents are important because Beatrix resembled him more than any other family member. She inherited much of his artistic talent, entrepreneurial ability and intellectual curiosity. Edmund was born in 1802 and baptized at Cross Street Chapel, a Unitarian congregation already in the forefront of the Dissenting community. He was brought up rather severely in a hard-working merchant family which valued education. Edmund had a penchant for innovation, held enlightened opinions and kept company with other thoughtful men. Although his eventual wealth qualified him as one of Manchester's cotton oligarchs, Edmund Potter remained a humble man, dedicated to the well-being and improvement of his countrymen.[5]

In 1825 Edmund and his cousin Charles bought a run-down spinning mill in Dinting Vale, a small cotton manufacturing village south of Glossop, on the edge of the open moorland of the High Peak. Theirs was but one of the forty-odd cotton mills in Glossop Dale, where nearly a third of the population was employed in the textile industry. They proceeded to establish a hand-printed calico manufacturing business, applying the woodblocks with good dyes to create innovative prints which proved popular. Years later, when Beatrix was absorbed with the selection of endpapers for the de luxe editions of her 'little books', she discovered that the most popular calico pattern Edmund Potter & Company ever produced was a small crossed broom or brush pattern on a blue ground that her grandfather had designed.[6]

Edmund married Jessy Crompton, 'the pretty Radical', in the Lancaster Priory church of St Mary near her home at Lune Villa in 1829. Jessy had independent opinions of her own and inherited her father's Radical belief in the political emancipation of the working classes. Her views would influence her husband's practices and attitudes as an employer, as well as his views on the necessity of educating the lower classes. The match was remarkably congenial. Jessy was adept at managing a large household and in promoting her husband's political ambitions and social connections. She bore seven children within a decade: four sons and three daughters.[7]

The Potters' social life revolved around the Unitarian community in Manchester. They often attended Cross Street Chapel, where the Revd William Gaskell, an eloquent and compelling preacher, was the newly appointed junior minister. Gaskell's wife, Elizabeth, became one of the major social novelists of the century before her early death in 1865. The Gaskells and the Potters raised their families in the same environment and their friendship influenced the next two generations of Potters.

The calico print trade was increasingly unstable owing to fluctuations in demand and the imposition of a tax levied exclusively on printed cotton. The repeal of the tax did not come soon enough to save the fledgling firm. The company went into receivership, and the cousins went their separate ways. Edmund rebuilt his calico business in Dinting Vale as Edmund Potter & Company. With hard work and innovation, he emerged in 1837 not only debt free, but captain of a modernized calico printing business.[8]

When the Manchester, Sheffield and Lincolnshire Railway came to Dinting Vale and Glossop in 1845, Potter's firm was assured a wider market and Glossop became a regional centre of trade. Edmund had wisely moved his family to Dinting Vale several years earlier and into Dinting Lodge, a substantial house overlooking the mill reservoirs.[9]

As an enlightened employer, Edmund was concerned for the welfare and education of his employees, many of whom were children under the age of 13. He built a large dining room in the mill which could serve a hot meal to three hundred and fifty people at one time. He converted part of a nearby mill into the Logwood School, where the children of his workers, as well as the child labourers, could learn reading, writing and basic hygiene. He also built a reading room and library which was kept well stocked with books and newspapers. Edmund Potter believed in the necessity of educating the working classes and the need to repeal the excise taxes on grain, which raised the price of bread, but he had no sympathy for trade unionism. Such beliefs drew him into association with other politically powerful merchant leaders in Manchester who supported the growing movement for free trade.[10]

Edmund also saw the art of calico printing and art education as tools for social improvement. In 1855 he published a pamphlet, *Schools of Art*, arguing for the benefits of art education for the working man.

His own achievements in the science of calico printing and his technological innovations were displayed at the Great Exhibition of 1851 and earned him election as a Fellow of the Royal Society in 1856. From 1855 to 1858 Edmund served as President of the Manchester School of Art, collected a little art himself and frequently lectured on textile design. By 1862 Edmund Potter & Company had become the largest calico printing firm in the world. The Dinting Vale printworks produced more than sixteen million yards of calico a year. That year Edmund contested a by-election at Carlisle and won the seat in Parliament as a Liberal by three votes. He left the family business in the capable hands of his eldest son, Edmund Crompton, and settled in London. Committed to the growth of the Unitarian ministry and to the gospel of free trade, Edmund served as a Member of Parliament for the next twelve years.[11]

In London, Edmund and Jessy settled at 64 Queen's Gate, in South Kensington. They attended the vibrant Little Portland Street congregation led by colleagues from the faculty of Manchester College. Edmund also served as president of the British and Foreign Unitarian Association, the first official coordinating body of the denomination, a position which increased his public stature. He was well connected within the London art and museum community, including the National Gallery of Art and the Kensington School of Art, insisting that the latter provide art education to the lower classes, not just to the sons and daughters of the wealthy.[12]

In 1866 Edmund bought Camfield Place, a country estate of over 300 acres in Hertfordshire, north of London. The grounds of Camfield, laid out a century earlier by the famous landscape designer Lancelot 'Capability' Brown, were planted with cedars, rhododendrons and pink horse chestnuts. In keeping with the fashion of the times, the property included several sturdy summer houses, lovely terraced ponds, and, best of all, a grotto. Camfield would always be associated in Beatrix's mind with precious visits to her dear Grandmother Potter.[13]

Edmund retired from Parliament and moved to Camfield, where he died in October 1883 at the age of 82. In the years immediately before his death Edmund's mind sadly deteriorated. Instead of the brilliant, kindly reformer and energetic Unitarian that he had been, Beatrix remembered him more as a befuddled old man. Jessy continued to live at Camfield and at Queen's Gate in London until her death in 1891. Edmund died an immensely wealthy man, leaving an estate of £441,970, principally to his wife. A great portion of that wealth eventually passed on to Beatrix's father, Rupert, ironically the son least endowed with his father's entrepreneurial spirit or liberal values.[14]

During the period Edmund served in Parliament, the Potters lived not far from the Kensington home of the family of the late John Leech of Stalybridge, 20 Kensington Palace Gardens. Leech died in 1861, but the two north-country families had long been connected by cotton, Unitarianism, and membership in the art establishment of Manchester. John Leech had been every bit as much a Manchester merchant prince and benefactor of the Unitarian cause as Edmund Potter. Only his more flamboyant style and affinity for risk distinguished him. Although his death at the age of 60 deprived him of a comparable philanthropic career in his later years, Leech acted on a wider international stage than Potter, and also accumulated enormous wealth. In part because his granddaughter Beatrix never knew him, but also because he was a man of action rather than reflection, John Leech's contribution to Beatrix's understanding of family character was less vivid and came to her second-hand.

A year older than Edmund Potter, Leech married Jane Ashton, the lively and quick-witted daughter of a wealthy Unitarian cotton manufacturer in nearby Hyde, in 1832. They moved into Hob Hill House, a large brick structure in the middle of the family's textile mills in Stalybridge. Soon Leech, who was known around the Manchester Exchange as 'Ready Money Jack', bought a larger, historic estate on a hill overlooking the town, tore it down and built a new mansion known as Gorse Hall. It included a lake, landscaped gardens, a tennis court, and offered a panoramic view of the distant Pennines. By 1848 the John Leech Company had a fleet of ships sailing the world and was the largest mercantile business in the area.[15]

The Leeches shared with the Potters a deep commitment to Nonconformity and education, as well as to the promotion of science and art in Manchester. John Leech came to London frequently to promote his firm's trading relations and to lobby Parliament. Like Potter, he too collected contemporary British art, including at least one landscape by J. M. W. Turner. When John Leech died, after a long illness, the *Christian Reformer* reported that 'his name was known in almost every part of the world'.[16]

His surviving sons, John and William, worked in the family business and remained in Stalybridge. One of his five daughters died in infancy, the eldest never married, but the other three made good matches. Harriet married Fred Burton, a wealthy cotton manufacturer who built Gwaynynog, an estate near Denbigh in Wales. Elizabeth and Helen married two sons of Edmund Potter, Walter and Rupert. John Leech left a personal estate of more than £200,000, and settled a generous legacy of £50,000 on each of his daughters.[17]

During her long widowhood, Jane Leech turned her attention to the Unitarian community and the working people of Stalybridge. She gave the pioneer Unitarian congregation permission to make the old Leech home, Hob Hill, into a free school which soon became the centre of the Unitarian reform and educational efforts in the town. During the cotton famine that began in 1862, when mills were forced to close because of the lack of imported raw cotton from the United States, the Hob Hill School offered night classes for workers in thirty different subjects. Mrs Leech and her daughters, Elizabeth and Helen, taught cookery, needlework and housewifery. She established kitchens to feed all the mill workers in Stalybridge, not just those in the Leech mills, and organized an annual bazaar for the support of the Sunday School. At the time of her death in 1884, the school served more than four hundred girls and infants.[18]

As a child Beatrix went less often to Gorse Hall to see Grandmamma Leech than she did to Camfield Place, although her journal records frequent luncheons and teas at both grandmothers' London homes. But when Jane Leech died, Beatrix, not quite 18, felt her loss acutely. Her memories of Gorse Hall, like those of Camfield, were vividly sensory; having to do with the smell of the old house and the quality of light there. She recalled 'the pattern of the door-mat, the pictures on the old music-box, the sound of the rocking horse as it swung, the engravings on the stair, the smell of the Indian corn' and feared it would all be changed. 'I have now seen longer passages and higher halls,' she confided in her journal. 'The rooms will look cold and empty, the passage I used to patter along so kindly on the way to bed will no longer seem dark and mysterious, and, above all, the kind voice which cheered the house is silent for ever.'[19]

During Jane Leech's funeral at Dukinfield, Rupert Potter, Leech's son-in-law and Beatrix's barrister father, was seated near his own father's old pew. As a boy, he had often sat studying a memorial inscription engraved on the south transept wall that began with the Latin phrase *'Cur viator fleas sepultum?* – traveller, why weep for me in my grave?' After the service he wickedly confided to his daughter that the inscription had always made him think of 'dog fleas'. His confession amused Beatrix and became something of a family joke.[20]

As the second son of a rising mill owner, Rupert Potter was born during the time when his father was fighting his way out of bankruptcy and times were hard. His teenage years at Dinting Vale were more privileged, but Edmund, honoured and remote, had little time to spend with his family. Crompton, the eldest by three years, inherited the entrepreneurial ambitions of his father, and although the two brothers had much in common, they were too often in competition as young men to admit admiration.[21]

At 16 Rupert followed Crompton to Manchester College. One of the last of the lay students to matriculate there, Rupert joined some of the leading students and teachers of Unitarian thought. One illustrious member of the college faculty, the Revd William Gaskell, Rupert already knew well. Cross Street Chapel was closely connected with the college, and students had easy access to Gaskell who served as Professor of English History and Literature at the College. James Martineau, younger brother of the famed educational reform writer Harriet, and the Revd John James Tayler, two of the most celebrated theologians of the Unitarian tradition, were also Rupert's teachers. Martineau was Professor of Mental and Moral Philosophy and Political Economy. Tayler taught ecclesiastical history and Rupert soon became a regular at Tayler's services at Upper Brook Street Free Church. Martineau's influence on Rupert's character was profound and lifelong.[22]

Rupert was a good student at Manchester, excelling in the Greek and Roman classics and in ancient history, in which he took prizes in 1849. Rupert and Crompton both inherited their father's interest in the fine arts, attending lectures at the Royal Manchester Institute, and enjoying exhibitions in London. As adults, both collected art, though on a vastly different scale. From his college days on, Rupert was fascinated by the new art of photography, a subject which had also intrigued his father, but he did not have the opportunity to take it up in any serious way until the mid-1860s.[23]

Rupert took a London University degree in 1851, the first member of his family to do so. Although Crompton had matriculated at Manchester, he did not finish. After three years he entered the family business at Dinting Vale and, in the same year as Rupert finished his degree, Crompton was made a partner at Edmund Potter & Company. Rupert's two younger brothers, Walter and William, also followed their elder siblings to the college. Walter took a degree in 1853 from London University and perhaps shared quarters with Rupert at University Hall for a time, but both he and William returned to Manchester to work. Rupert rejected a career in business and instead chose to study law, a choice that met with his father's approval.

There is an unexplained gap of two years between the end of Rupert's studies at Manchester in 1851 and his appearance at Lincoln's Inn in 1854. Evidence suggests that Rupert gave serious consideration to studying for the ministry. But lay students of Rupert's generation were increasingly choosing careers in the professions, and the law had become an attractive alternative for many wealthy parents. For whatever reason, Rupert was temperamentally wise to strike out differently. While he was scientifically curious and artistically able, he was not disposed to decisive action or energetic leadership. He was deliberative, fond of abstractions, uneasy with both intellectual ambiguity and economic uncertainty, and inherently conservative. He loved books, politics and argument. The law suited him.[24]

Rupert's law student days in London were spent at Lincoln's Inn. He was admitted on 17 January 1854 and became a pupil of Hugh McCalmont Cairns, a leading member of the Chancery bar, Member of Parliament, Solicitor-General and in 1868 Lord Chancellor. Since Rupert had already set his sights on the Chancery Division of the High Court, Cairns was probably his only pupil master. His association with Cairns was one from which he derived professional benefit.[25]

Rupert's apprenticeship in law at Lincoln's Inn was not all devoted to serious study. A surviving sketchbook from 1853 includes humorous caricatures of his fellow students and life at the Inns of Court. There are also precise pen-and-ink sketches of animals, including a bear in an overcoat smoking a pipe, a dog at a spinning wheel and, most curiously, a flight of ducks over a marsh including one wearing a bonnet, an image which later struck the imagination of his daughter and was the precursor of another more elaborately bonneted duck she would one day make famous. The sketchbook and other evidence of Rupert's artistry indicate that he enjoyed drawing and that he was skilled at it. He particularly enjoyed copying engravings and book illustrations, and he had an affinity for caricature.[26]

Rupert Potter was called to the bar on 17 November 1857. He occupied chambers at 8 New Square, Lincoln's Inn, from 1858, moving in 1862 to 3 New Square, where he is continuously listed as occupant until 1892 when he would have been 60 and when he presumably retired. The annual Law Lists describe him as a barrister specializing as an equity draughtsman and conveyancer. This type of specialized legal work had to do with the transfer of property and the establishment of trusts, and as such his business was before the Chancery Division of the High Court. Rupert also practised before the Lancaster Chancery Court in Manchester and Liverpool, courts which specialized in conveyancing matters. As a barrister with north-country connections, he would naturally have business with this court. Potter gained considerable expertise in this area of the law, as demonstrated in a book on the subject he published in 1862 analysing legislation then pending in Parliament.

Equity law and conveyancing normally did not involve the barrister in litigation. Furthermore his career would certainly have been impacted by the reorganization of the judicial system about 1876 when the Court of Chancery was abolished as an independent entity.

These particularities of the law help explain the nature of Potter's legal career as well as the rather casual schedule he kept as a barrister in his later years.[27]

Rupert's practice has been the subject of speculation, and, with no case record, it has been accepted that he did not actively practise law, leading a life of cultured idleness and living on inherited wealth. But this view must be amended. First, at least one case in which Rupert appeared as counsel reached the Law Reports, and presumably there were others in which he was a participant and which were not published. On the basis of this record, as well as the nature of the case, and the rarity of cases which identify counsel by name, one must conclude that by the time of Beatrix's birth in 1866 Rupert had achieved some professional reputation.[28]

Secondly, Rupert did not come into any of his inheritance until after his father's estate was settled in 1884. His share was large, but not overly so given the size of his father's estate, and it was not enough to support him in a life of total leisure. In fact, Rupert's final inheritance from his father came in pieces: a more substantial portion upon the death of his mother in 1891, and the remainder when his elder sister Clara died in 1905. Finally, Rupert, like his father before him, made a variety of equity investments, about which his daughter reports him frequently anxious. These, combined with his other sources of earned and unearned income, made him extremely wealthy by the early 1890s.[29]

As a young barrister Rupert pursued an active social life in London, using his father's connections. Shortly after he came up to London he was elected to membership in the Reform Club. It was a natural choice for the son of a prominent Liberal and advantageous for cultivating clients and finding agreeable society. In 1860 Rupert was nominated to the Athenaeum, the most intellectually elite of all London clubs. Sir Charles Eastlake, President of the Royal Academy, Director of the National Gallery, President of the Photography Society of London, and a trend-setter in the art world, was one of his proposers.

Rupert's desire to move into such prestigious intellectual and artistic circles reflects his family's considerable social connections, his own professional standing, and perhaps a certain naivety about social mobility. But it indicates that Rupert was ambitious for himself despite any detriments derived from his north-country birth or his background in trade. There was, however, a fourteen-year waiting list at the Athenaeum between Rupert's entry into the candidates' book and the time a vacancy appeared to which he could be elected. By April 1874, when his name came to the head of the waiting list, his original proposers had died. Their successors, however, were equally distinguished and more reflective of Rupert's own associations. Rupert was elected to the Athenaeum by 243 votes to 5, his supporters' sheet having about thirty-eight signatures, considered an average number. By this time Rupert's politics were decidedly more conservative. The Athenaeum rather than the Reform became his club of choice, a preference also driven by his interest in photography and his participation in the London art scene.[30]

When it came to marriage, Rupert showed an equal mix of ambition and pragmatism. Although he was anxious for entry into London society, he turned to his north-country roots for a bride, seven years younger, whose background and wealth matched his own. Rupert and Helen Leech were married on 8 August 1863 by Rupert's former Manchester College classmate, the Revd Charles Beard, at Gee Cross Chapel. The 24-year-old bride came with a handsome legacy from her father, and looked forward to the prospect of a genteel life in London society. Since her mother still maintained a family home in London, Helen was not without connections of her own.

Of all the members of Beatrix's family, Helen Leech Potter's history and personality is the most obscured and the most controversial. Nothing is known about her childhood and education. Only Beatrix's reporting of Leech family conversations in her journal hint at Helen's relationships with her siblings, her parents or her in-laws. According to family gossip, Elizabeth Leech Potter surpassed her younger sister in both beauty and disposition, and was the family's favourite. Raised in considerable luxury, Helen was educated in the arts of household management and prepared for a life in society.[31]

Helen joined her mother in activities that supported the Unitarian community in Stalybridge during the cotton famine, but her participation in philanthropic work reveals nothing about her commitment either to Nonconformity or to improving the lot of the poor since it was expected of young, single women of her background. Beatrix writes of the family attending church but most often she associates religious observance with her father and his family. As a married woman, Helen's only known charitable involvement in London was the curious transcription of many volumes of unspecified literature into Braille for an association for the blind.[32]

Helen Leech brought to her marriage in 1863 a particularly colourful, elaborately designed bedcover. It was probably a wedding gift from family and friends to which Helen, with her artful needle, may well have contributed a portion. The large bedcover features the initials of the bride and groom and their wedding date centred around a wreath of flowers and leaves. A diamond-shaped centre section featuring appliqué patches of mostly diamond blocks lends a three-dimensional effect. The coverlet's survival testifies to the value Helen placed on it, and to her daughter's later appreciation of its workmanship.[33]

Helen also enjoyed painting and drawing. Several extant landscapes show a pleasing perspective, more than Sunday afternoon skill in brushwork, and a good sense of colour, if a bit too much motion. Her obvious enjoyment of drawing, painting and needlework do not set her apart from most upper-middle-class Victorian women, but they indicate that Helen shared her husband's art enthusiasms and that she too had artistic talent that added to the sum ultimately inherited by both her children.[34]

Photographs of Helen as a young mother show her grimly unsmiling and properly undemonstrative, as indeed do most photographs of the period, which required one to remain completely immobile for interminable minutes. She embraced the style and decorum demanded by her wealth and social aspirations, to which was added a measure of stiff reserve, or perhaps the reflection of an unhappy disposition. Her dark hair was severely parted in the middle, pulled back tightly, and elaborately wrapped on the back of her head in the fashion made popular by Queen Victoria, whom she resembled both in stocky stature and prominent feature.

There is no record of Helen's social activities, other than her daughter's comments on the daily ritual of making social calls. Just how successful she was in her own society is a matter of speculation. Like her husband, Helen was burdened by a distinctive Lancashire accent and by her membership in the Nonconformist community, both detriments to moving up into the genteel society that she, at least, seems to have aspired to join. The Potters entertained in London during the season and, following the ritual of the social calendar, invited friends to join them on holiday, first in Scotland and later in the Lake District.

The Potters' social ambitions in London required that they minimize their family's north-country origins, while at the same time they made use of its social connections. This attitude was not unusual for the second generation of merchant wealth, but Helen's rejection of her family background seems less forgivable because it was accompanied by an often stinging disapproval of those she marked as inferior. Whether Helen was a snob by nature or whether it was an attitude she adopted as a Victorian norm, she felt herself and her family superior to those who worked in trade and to those professionals who were not in the same social class as her husband. Her pretentiousness was perhaps no greater than that of similarly situated Victorian women, but her attitudes contrasted poorly with those of her generous mother and mother-in-law. In any case her social hauteur was not an endearing quality.

From her daughter's maturing point of view, Helen was a difficult, controlling woman who demanded time and attentive service from everyone around her. Her insecurities and biases limited the experiences that were allowed to both her children, subsequently narrowing their social horizons. That said, Helen doubtlessly suffered from the oppressive confines of family, the endless boredom that afflicted many Victorian women who were circumscribed by the range of approved activities, and the paternalism of upper-middle-class society. At least in part, Helen Potter's pretentiousness was a reflection of her personal powerlessness, to which might be added her lack of education and intellectual interests.[35]

Helen's page in a family 'favourites' album drawn in 1873, ten years after her marriage, provides another glimpse. In it she drew small coloured pictures of the things she liked and disliked at the time. She described dancing, music and the company of a sociable gentleman as favourites. The seashore was her choice for a holiday. But more revealing is a drawing that suggests that she had unusually severe dental problems. To be sure, smiling was not the fashion, and being constantly photographed by her husband was an arduous affair at best. But could it be that Helen's sour, unsmiling, demeanour in nearly every extant photograph was in part an effort to hide prominent, even protruding teeth?[36]

We know little of Helen's network of female friends and relationships and thus are deprived of information about another important aspect that sustained the lives of Victorian women. Helen Potter has been portrayed as a disagreeable, self-centred woman who did more to impoverish her daughter's life than enhance it. There is certainly truth in this interpretation. But it is also possible that Helen Potter has been understood primarily through the eyes of a precocious adolescent, an unusual daughter with eclectic interests that Helen did not understand, share or condone. Her marriage to Rupert seems to have been more enduring than truly companionable. It is possible, too, that Helen was bored as well as neglected by a husband whose interests kept him out of the house, in the club or behind the camera, and who certainly preferred the company of his artistic companions to social rounds with his wife.

Rupert and Helen first settled into married life in London in Upper Harley Street, then a fashionable area of Marylebone. When Helen became pregnant with Beatrix in 1865 they sought larger, more fashionable quarters, eventually selecting a house in the rural area of Kensington off the Brompton Road. Bolton Gardens was a newly built enclave of large, granite-faced four-storey homes on both sides of the road, each with a small garden in the front and a larger one in the rear. Each house had its own mews with stables for horses, and housing for carriage and livery behind.

Bolton Gardens was an appropriate neighbourhood for aspiring upper-middle-class professionals from mercantile backgrounds who were doing well and viewed themselves as a rising elite. It also appears to have been an enclave of distinguished Dissenters, among whom the Potters would have felt socially comfortable. Helen Potter brought a below-stairs staff of two sisters, Elizabeth and Sarah Harper from Stalybridge, as cook and housekeeper. A Londoner, George Cox, was hired as butler. Albert Reynolds, his wife and school-age sons, and a boarder, David Beckett, who was the groom, completed the Potters' initial household.[37]

A daughter, Helen Beatrix, was born at 2 Bolton Gardens on Saturday, 28 July 1866, in the twenty-eighth year of Queen Victoria's reign. News of her arrival was announced in *The Times* with customary formality. Nearly six years later, on 14 March 1872, a brother, Walter Bertram, joined her in the nursery on the third floor. This 'unloved birthplace', as she later called it, would be Beatrix's home for the next forty-seven years.[38]

2

～ *Exposures* ～

T HERE WAS NOTHING TO OBSTRUCT the view from the third-
floor nursery window over the rooftops of South Kensington
all the way to the tower of the new Natural History Museum. Nor
was there anything to restrict the physical or intellectual freedom of
the little girl who occupied the nursery at 2 Bolton Gardens. Contrary
to myth, the dormer windows had no iron bars in front of the sash,
nor were there bars on the upper story of any of the Bolton Gardens
houses facing the Old Brompton Road. Their existence, however,
has been accepted as both fact and as a metaphor characterizing
Potter's psychological formation in most accounts of her childhood.
The reality of life lived out on that third-floor nursery in the 1870s
and 1880s was far more complex and much more vital than previously
supposed.[1]

Between early childhood and coming of age, the nursery evolved
from nanny's domain to schoolroom, art studio and botanical laboratory. Along the way it became home to a virtual museum collection
of live pets and dead specimens, anthropological samples and microscopic studies of plants and insects. Potter's childhood and girlhood
was certainly solitary if measured by friendships and social interaction
with her peers, but in terms of exposure to the world of art, literature,
science, fantasy, travel and natural history, it was a rich and enviable
one.

From her earliest days Beatrix was nurtured in two extraordinary
landscapes. Camfield Place, her Potter grandparents' home, was culti-
vated and managed. Dalguise, the holiday house in Perthshire, Scotland, was untamed and chimerical. Both environments stimulated her
interest in natural history, and gave permanent impression to her
artist's eye.

Beatrix was born the year that her Grandfather Potter bought Camfield. Her earliest perceptions of the natural world and of nature's beauty came first from the sights and sounds of the expansively planted grounds with its groves of pink flowering chestnuts and the colours of the surrounding rural countryside. Memories of birdsong and flowers, the routines of country life, farm animals, the pleasures of fresh milk, warm eggs and cosy fires were indelibly recorded. Holding hands with Grandmamma seated on the sofa beside her before dinner, Beatrix was supremely content. Life at Camfield as she recalled it was a 'perfect whole, where all things are a part, the notes of the stable clock and the all pervading smell of new-mown hay, the distant sounds of the farmyard, the feeling of plenty, well-assured, indolent wealth, honourably earned and wisely spent, charity without ostentation, opulence without pride . . .'[2]

She loved old houses even then: exploring the back stairs and the hidden passage ways at Camfield that connected the old house to the new, just as she loved the musty smell and the dust motes floating in the slant of light that penetrated the cellar windows of Grandmother Leech's house, Gorse Hall, in Stalybridge. 'I wonder why houses smell so different,' she wrote after a visit there. 'On thinking of a place the first recollection is the smell and amount of light.' Inquisitive and fearless, she scoffed at superstition and exaggerated claims of terror surrounding both houses, spread by older cousins, and had no hesitation about investigating such terrain by herself.[3]

Camfield was 'the place I love best in the world', she wrote in her journal. It was beautiful to her in all seasons. She seems always to have remembered landscape details in colour. Typical was her reminiscence of Camfield in 1891: 'The autumn frost spreads a ruddy glow over the land . . . Miles upon miles of golden oak wood, with here and there a yellow streak of stubble, and a clump of russet walnut trees behind the red gable, and thin blue smoke of a farm . . . In summer the distant landscapes are intensely blue.'[4]

Quite possibly she was a babe in arms when she was introduced to a starkly different landscape: one that was equally lush in its own right, but distinguished by wide, flat rivers, and grassy green straths which yielded unexpectedly to dark, mysterious larch forests with damp, mossy floors. Forested hills often hid streams which splashed over ancient rocky outcroppings before flowing out into the valley. The Scottish countryside around Perthshire combined landscapes where reality and fantasy were often indistinguishable. Once again it was Grandfather Potter who made this countryside accessible to her.

An avid fisherman, Edmund Potter took a shooting estate in the remote Highlands near Alness in Easter Ross. Henry Roscoe, newly married to Edmund's youngest daughter, Lucy, remembered that in addition to sport, they amused themselves with photography in which both Lucy and Rupert were much interested and at which both excelled. Rupert continued the tradition of Scottish holidays, in 1870, when Beatrix was nearly four, staying at Tulliemet House, an estate in the eastern forests of the Tay. The following summer they moved south, to Dalguise House on the western shore of the river, not far from the ancient cathedral seat of Dunkeld, where the fishing was exceptional.[5]

Dalguise House, a rather stark estate with beautifully landscaped gardens, was begun in 1714 and enlarged in the early nineteenth century, making it more suitable for holiday entertaining. The Laird of Dalguise, John Steuart, although an absentee owner, kept the estate well stocked with game and its many outbuildings in good condition with capable managers. The summer of 1871 was the beginning of a decade of summers Beatrix spent at Dalguise – a place which immediately became home to her heart. The Scottish landscape provided a feast for her eye, nourishment for her imagination and freedom for her spirit. It was this landscape against which she would compare all others, and upon which she would base her aesthetic value of nature.[6]

Beatrix loved Dalguise from her very first visit. When she was about six she wrote a letter to her father, who was already in Perthshire fishing, asking him: 'If you see anything pretty will you please send me a picture of it and then I will send you a letter back, and send word how the dogs are and if it is fine and nice at Dalguise.' Rupert indulged his little daughter with details of Dalguise: 'My dear B., . . . I will write you a letter before I go to bed to tell you something about Dalguise. I said to McIntosh [the gamekeeper] "what

sort of a little dog is Sandy" & he said I should see & he whistled
& out came a brown dog with such long hair & such queer sharp
ears that I did not know him at all [here Rupert drew a pen and ink
sketch of a little terrier] – he is something like this & very full of
fun – but he has not got such a fine tail as Tiny(?) had & he cannot
beg & is rather greedy, so we must teach him manners.' Rupert then
went on to report on the status of Beatrix's 'pretence garden', which
had been trampled by the cows over the winter, and the animals he
had seen. 'I saw a little bunny on the lawn no bigger than your
bear ... but he will be a big bunny soon I am afraid & will be
mischievous.'[7]

Looking back on a decade of holiday summers in Scotland, it
seemed to Beatrix that her happiest moments were those spent at
Dalguise. There she got extra attention from her father, the opportunity to have as many pets as she wanted, to collect butterflies, identify
birds, make friends with farm animals, explore the countryside, and
draw and paint whatever she saw, whenever she wanted. 'I remember
every stone, every tree, the scent of the heather, the music sweetest
mortal ears can hear, the murmuring of the wind through the fir
trees,' she recalled later. 'Even when the thunder growled in the
distance, and the wind swept up the valley in fitful gusts, oh, it was
always beautiful, home sweet home ...'[8]

During these long summer holidays the Potters entertained family
and friends, especially those who liked to fish and who would endure
Rupert's endless photography sessions. John Bright, the elder statesman among the Quakers, and William Gaskell were Beatrix's particular favourites and came regularly. Bright loved to fish and Gaskell
enjoyed the scenic countryside. Some of Rupert's many photographs
show Gaskell, seated in a lawn chair with his arm affectionately
around the pretty young child. Little Beatrix must have reminded the
kindly minister of his own daughters. She responded to his genuine-
ness with affection. For Christmas 1874 she knitted him a scarf. In
his note thanking her, Gaskell wrote: 'Big as I am I know I could
not have done it one-tenth as well. Every time I put it round my
neck – which during this weather will be every day – I shall be sure
to think of you.'[9]

Sir John Everett Millais, the Pre-Raphaelite painter, who by the 1870s was one of the most successful society painters in England, with his wife, the former Effie Ruskin, was another regular at Dalguise. Millais frequently asked Potter to assist him in his portrait and landscape painting by photographing his subject or scene, thus creating an aide-memoire for the painter to work from when his model was unavailable. Although Millais frequently teased the shy Beatrix and made her blush, she listened to his conversation and observed his painting with increasing critical appreciation. There were visits from other distinguished friends and, in between, various Potter and Leech relatives who came to enjoy the countryside. All were recorded by Rupert's camera either on the lawn beside the stately stone column surmounted by a unicorn or on the steps in front of the house.[10]

Beatrix also got to know a variety of local Perthshire people over the years. Charlie McIntosh, the tall, lanky, enormously shy postman-naturalist, walked the rural route from Dunkeld to Tulliemet, Kitty MacDonald, the tiny woman from Inver who took in their laundry, and Mr Wood, the local entomologist, who knew that Beatrix and Bertram liked to draw. One hot summer afternoon Wood stopped by with a present 'out of his hat', of 'buff-tip caterpillars collected on the road . . . but they had got loose amongst his venerable grey locks'. There were trips to tradesmen and merchants, all of whom Beatrix observed carefully. Some, like the well-known photographer A. F. Mackenzie and his wife, became family friends. The station-master John Kinnaird, who greeted them at the railhead at Birnam, was particularly colourful. Unlike the winter months in London, where every activity was carefully regimented and supervised, Beatrix had plenty of opportunity at Dalguise to socialize with her family's guests, or to go off by herself.[11]

Beatrix's first nurse was a Scot – for they were thought simply the best nurses to be had, and no wealthy Victorian family could be without one. Nurse Ann Mackenzie from Inverness was a Calvinist, presumably dour and intolerant of permissiveness, which was, of course, the point. Recalling Nurse Mackenzie, Beatrix later wrote rather uncharitably: 'I remember when I was a child lying in a crib in the nursery bedroom [at Camfield] under the tyranny of a cross old nurse – I used to be awakened at four in the morning by the song of the birds in this elm [opposite the kitchen window]. I can feel the diamond-pattern of that old yellow crib printed against my cheek, as I lay with my head where my heels should be, staring backwards over my eye brows at the plaster heads on the chimney piece, and a large water-colour alpine scene which I regarded with respectful awe.' But it was this same 'cross old nurse' who put Beatrix to bed with stories of fairies and the Scottish good folk, and sang the rousing hymns of the famous eighteenth-century Nonconformist composer Isaac Watts, the cadences of which lingered long in her hearing, and were later imitated in efforts at hymnody. As Beatrix later acknowledged, Nurse Mackenzie bequeathed 'a firm belief in witches, fairies and the creed of the terrible John Calvin (the creed rubbed off, but the fairies remained)'.[12]

Mackenzie immersed her charge in the rich folklore of the Scottish Highlands. During the summer holidays at Dalguise they walked about the countryside discovering the hidden and the magical about them. Beatrix began to explore alone, comfortably certain that the countryside was filled with fairies, and lost in her own imagination. Her later governesses had only to build upon the already rich repository of fantasy and folklore, nature study, and love of drawing that Nurse Mackenzie uncovered.[13]

The books that Nurse Mackenzie read to Beatrix in Scotland contained large amounts of folklore, rhyme and adventure. The good nurse was probably unaware of the still volatile debate as to whether fairy stories were good for young children, or else she had made up her mind that they were harmless, since she provided Beatrix with a sample of everything, but fantasy was heavily favoured. Along with stories from the Old Testament, John Bunyan's *The Pilgrim's Progress* and Harriet Beecher Stowe's *Uncle Tom's Cabin*, Beatrix recalled as favourites *Aesop's Fables*, the older fairy tales of the Brothers Grimm, and newer ones by Hans Christian Andersen, and particularly the Waverley novels of Sir Walter Scott. She also enjoyed Charles Kingsley's *The Water-Babies: A Fairy Tale for a Land-Baby*, a fantasy written in reaction to those who insisted that stories for children must teach a moral value. Surrounded as she was by these fables and rhymes, it is not surprising that they would be the subject of some of her earliest illustrations or that later in life certain landscapes frequently reminded her of scenes from her favourite childhood books.[14]

Beatrix loved to draw and paint. Her talent was obvious from a young age and her parents encouraged her. Beatrix had observed that her parents carried sketchbooks when they went out in the countryside and she imitated them by making her own out of rough paper that she fastened together with string. Her earliest sketchbook, inscribed 'Dalguise 1875', contains a careful study of a dozen or so caterpillars drawn in watercolour. Each page is divided into two columns: one gives a physical description, the other observations on their habits. She made extensive records of birds' eggs and butterflies. The fine wood specimen cabinet that occupied a corner of the schoolroom at Bolton Gardens was filled with the children's collections of moths, butterflies and insects, all properly mounted and identified as to genus and family.[15]

Beatrix was interested in recording what she saw around her. Her sketchbook includes a farmer with a cow, a house at the foot of a mountain, a bridge over the river, all unembellished and realistically rendered. Beatrix also delighted in drawing the fanciful. A sketchbook that dates from 1874 and 1875, when she was eight or nine, includes drawings of rabbits on ice-skates wearing jackets, hats and scarves. As a child growing up in London, Beatrix would have had many opportunities to observe people ice-skating and perhaps to try it herself. But they could also have been inspired by watching members of the Dalguise Curling Club.[16]

In addition to sketching from nature, both Beatrix and Bertram enjoyed drawing and copying from various drawing books popular during the period. Rupert's influence is clear in his children's love of copying animals and sketching from book illustrations. When both children were young, he sketched animals to amuse and to instruct them. He owned a number of Vere Foster drawing books from which he sketched and which Beatrix later enjoyed on her own. For her part, Beatrix approved her father's sketching, though much later she criticized his lack of understanding of what was required to paint a picture. On the back of one drawing that he had made for her as a child and which she kept until her death, she wrote proudly: 'note the direct work & "touch".'[17]

Much of Potter's juvenile work was copied. Some came from outline drawings in the manuals on birds, flowers and mammals. But she also made sketches of buildings, trees, baskets and a water butt. Her particularly vivid flower drawings of 1876 were probably copied from Foster manuals on 'Foxgloves', 'Narcissus' and 'Daffodil', or from the popular *Art of Flower Painting* by James Andrews. These and several of her other copying efforts were also deemed worthy of preservation by her parents.[18]

As the children grew, Rupert encouraged them to study birds. At both Camfield and Dalguise they could listen to their songs, explore the woods, and find their nesting places. For her tenth birthday, in July 1876, Rupert gave Beatrix Jemima Blackburn's *Birds Drawn from Nature* (1868), a gift that delighted her and one that sharpened her eye for nature as well as art. 'I remember so clearly – as clearly as the brightness of rich Scotch sunshine on the threadbare carpet,' she wrote in 1891 after meeting the famous Mrs Blackburn in person,

the morning I was ten years old – and my father gave me Mrs Blackburn's book of birds, drawn from nature, for my birthday present. I remember the dancing expectation and knocking at their bedroom door, it was a Sunday morning, before breakfast. I kept it in the drawing room cupboard, only to be taken out after I had washed my grimy little hands under that wonderful curved brass tap, which, being lifted, let loose the full force of ice-cold amber-water from the hills. The book was bound in scarlet with a gilt edge. I danced about the house with pride, never palled.[19]

That same year she made a fine copy from Blackburn's 1871 narrative poem *The Pipits*.[20]

Beatrix's early summer holidays at Dalguise coincided with her delight in picture books and her earliest efforts to read. Her childhood encompassed both the Arts and Crafts and the Aesthetic movements in art and design. At mid-century there had been an explosion of interest in children's books both as a literary genre and as a venue for stylish artists. Children's book illustration was considered high art and children's books became part of Victorian fashion, like architecture and home decor. Well-to-do parents took delight in buying artistic books for their offspring. The Potters, as consumers with their own artistic enthusiasms, were no exception. Toy books, brightly coloured booklets with stiff covers that contained a nursery rhyme or fairy tale, were enormously popular when Beatrix was young. Often they were illustrated by first-rate artists, which made them especially desirable. The pioneers of the picture book, the so-called 'triumvirate' of Edmund Evans, the virtuoso colour printer who so skilfully reproduced their images from woodblocks, were Walter Crane, Kate Greenaway and Randolph Caldecott. Beatrix absorbed the techniques of all three artists, and all influenced her eye, but she was particularly fond of Caldecott's work. It was an opinion she shared with her father, who later collected Caldecott.[21]

What is known about Beatrix Potter's childhood reading comes primarily from letters she wrote later in life. She recalled enjoying Mrs Molesworth's stories about real children, illustrated by Crane, and remembered particularly one called 'Carrots', about a red-headed boy. It is likely she knew Molesworth's 'The Cuckoo Clock', and 'Reel Fairies', about a child who invented fairy characters from cotton reels in her mother's sewing box. Crane, Greenaway and Caldecott all adopted costumes of the early nineteenth century for their characters, a convention which Beatrix seems to have absorbed. All three artists, as well as Evans' skilful engraving, influenced her tastes.[22]

Beatrix had access to the popular work of the English illustrators Richard 'Dicky' Doyle, Hablot K. Browne, famous as 'Phiz', the illustrator of Dickens's novels, and Gustave Doré, whose drawings frequently appeared in *Punch* and the *Illustrated London News*. In light of her father's friendship with John Everett Millais it is tempting to speculate that Beatrix may also have enjoyed his illustrations in *Little Songs for Me to Sing*, published the year before her birth, which featured a little girl who looked remarkably like the young Beatrix. Later on, she also enjoyed *St. Nicholas*, an American children's magazine that published fine fiction, lavishly illustrated by the best American artists.[23]

Before she was eight years old two books had made a particular impression. She was four-and-a-half when she was given Edward Lear's *Book of Nonsense* with his fanciful illustrations and memorable rhymes, including the much-loved 'Owl and the Pussy-Cat'. She was six or seven when her mother decided she was old enough for Lewis Carroll's *Alice*. Professor John Wilson, a barrister friend of Rupert's, provided her first copy, conferring first with Helen Potter as to 'whether I was old enough – or whether the book was too old? which was the same thing ... I became immediately so absorbed with Tenniel's illustrations that I don't remember what they said about "Lewis Carroll".' Later she made her own illustrations for *Alice's Adventures in Wonderland* as well as for several of Lear's rhymes. There are Carrollian inflections in Potter's private prose writing and, more notably, in her storybook characters. Whether by conscious imitation or by chance, Potter, like Lear and Carroll before her, also amused herself by writing letters to young children.[24]

As a child Beatrix also enjoyed what she later referred to as 'trash ... goody-goody, powder-in-the-jam' books. 'I liked silly stories about other little girls' doings,' she remembered. Most of these were didactic stories, written by an older generation of women writers, that emphasized rationality over fantasy. She could hardly have avoided Anna Barbauld, a woman of the Unitarian persuasion, whose *Little Stories for Little Children* and *Hymns in Prose for Children* were still popular. Her books were noteworthy because of their small size, designed specifically for young children, an aspect which later became an important consideration in Potter's concept of book design. Grandmother Potter had an edition of Sarah Trimmer's *History of the Robins*, with woodcuts by Thomas Bewick, that Beatrix inherited. It was intended to instruct children in the humane treatment of animals and featured talking birds. Mrs Trimmer was an ardent Evangelical, who as editor of the *Guardian of Education* at the turn of the century continued Barbauld's campaign against fairy tales. Beatrix had it as an early primer and later remembered hating its moralism, but had no objection to its anthropomorphism. At Gorse Hall, Grandmother Leech had a set of Miss Edgeworth's *Tales*. She was especially fond of Edgeworth's *Simple Susan*.[25]

Although later in her life Beatrix remembered having only a few books, 'Miss Edgeworth and Scott's novels', that memory, like her poverty of toys, is probably exaggerated, for her appetite for books was large, especially after she started reading for herself. When she had exhausted her own supply, she no doubt went in search of books in her father's library. Her recollection of learning to read, however, was quite specific. 'I learned to read on the Waverly [*sic*] novels,' she recalled in 1929. 'I was let loose on *Rob Roy*, and spelled through a few pages painfully; then I tried *Ivanhoe* – and the *Talisman* – then I tried *Rob Roy* again; all at once I began to READ (missing the long words, of course).' Thanks to Nurse Mackenzie and her parents, this rich diet of art and literature contributed to a lifelong delight in rhythm, cadence, wordplay, humour, dialect and dialogue: all nourishment for her imagination and the creation of her own literary style.[26]

In addition to providing the backdrop for Beatrix's earliest drawing, reading and illustration, Scotland worked its magic on her artistic imagination by educating her eye and refining her perspective of nature. By the time the Potters began to spend their summers in Perthshire, Rupert was seriously engaged in his new hobby of photography. He had taken it up sometime before his marriage with some seriousness. The holidays in Scotland provided the settings of many of his earliest photographs and soon became a favoured subject for his art. As testament to the seriousness of his engagement with the camera, he was elected a member of the Photographic Society of London in 1869 and contributed photographs to its annual exhibitions as early as 1873. Rupert was not an innovator, but a solid practitioner.[27]

Beatrix often went along with her father on his photography outings around Dalguise, happy for his attention. She enjoyed helping him, absorbing the rudiments of photography and composition. These summer outings began a father's loving pictorial record of his daughter's childhood, and she was certainly his most forbearing sitter. The ongoing relationship between photographer and subject bound them emotionally and intellectually as the years passed. There is no doubt that Rupert was the most important influence in his daughter's life.

Soon Beatrix also became a proficient photographer, using the camera in much the same way as her father, to record something she wished to draw later. She discovered for herself that the view through the camera's lens provided a different way of seeing nature and of recording reality. It was a perspective that she incorporated almost unconsciously in her art and underscored her lifelong penchant for artistic realism.[28]

In addition to their long summer holidays, there was the required annual evacuation of Bolton Gardens for several weeks each spring while the house was aired and cleaned from top to bottom. When the children were young and Edmund Potter was alive, they often went to Camfield in the spring, but as they grew older, their preference was to holiday at one of the south coast resorts in Devon, Cornwall or Hampshire.[29]

In London, life was much more structured. Victorian homes like the Potters' functioned on an unwavering schedule. There was a mind-numbing punctuality to the daily rituals of the household, beginning in the early morning and ending when the lamps were lit and the curtains closed at dusk. Rupert left the house, either for his chambers or to attend to business elsewhere in the city, at the same hour each day, and usually spent the afternoon at one of his clubs. He was frequently out of town, probably going to the Manchester area either on family or legal business. Helen directed the household staff, set the daily schedule, and was then driven out in the afternoons in the carriage to pay her social calls.

Until she was about six, Beatrix was attended by Nurse Mackenzie. They took daily walks in Kensington Gardens. Sometimes these included 'Sandy', the brown Scotch terrier who had come from Dalguise who was Beatrix's first, much-loved dog, or a Springer spaniel, 'Spot'. The usual cutlet came up to the nursery at lunchtime along with a pudding; occasionally it was served on a china plate onto which Rupert had reproduced a bird he had copied from one of his many books of natural history.[30]

Beatrix remembered being decked out in clothing that was 'absurdly uncomfortable; white pique starched frocks just like Tenniel's *Alice* . . . and cotton stockings striped round and round like a zebra's legs' and high-buttoned black boots which were much in the fashion then. Rupert's photographs of her at about four years old show a very pretty child with thick, naturally wavy light-brown hair that fell to shoulder length and was kept back from her face by a hair ribbon, 'black velvet on Sundays, and either black or brown' on weekdays. It was 'fastened with a bit of elastic looped over a button behind the ear'. The fastening hurt and frequently gave her a headache.[31]

Beatrix recalled only two toys she ever cared about: 'a dilapidated black wooden doll called Topsy', probably named after the character in *Uncle Tom's Cabin*, and 'a grimy, hard-stuffed, once-white, flannelette pig' which belonged to Grandmamma Potter and was kept in a locked drawer of her secretaire at Camfield. Beatrix entertained herself with resourcefulness and without apparent unhappiness. She was shy but not uncomfortable in the company of adults and on those occasions when she was invited downstairs she was a keen observer of character and social nuance.[32]

After Walter Bertram, known as Bertie, was born in March 1872, Beatrix's life became more lively. She was nearly six then and a loving sister from the outset. Although it would be some time before brother and sister became true companions, their mutual affection was assured. The new baby also meant that Beatrix had more time with her father. Rupert took a good-natured, caring interest in both his children. As he had with Beatrix, he went out of his way to write to the young Bertie about things that would interest him when he was away from home. Helen's involvement with her young children is more difficult to characterize because we have less evidence of it, and much of that reflects her over-protectiveness and presages her later rigidity. Since her domain was the house and social schedule, Helen had little to do with her children's early lives when the nurse was in charge. She sometimes felt imposed upon by Rupert's rather impromptu schedule, and the stress of managing her household, which, in all fairness, was often in transition from one holiday place to another, depending on the season.[33]

When Bertram was old enough to toddle about after his sister, Rupert and Helen were forced to tolerate a growing collection of animals and reptiles that the children brought back from their adventures, and to travel back and forth on holiday with them as part of the family retinue. They were certainly aware of these collections, indeed it would have been difficult to ignore them, even if the occasional species was smuggled up the back stairs. Nothing escaped the children's artistic efforts, from wild flowers to the dead game that were returned after the day's sport to Dalguise, and sentiment was not tolerated. Rabbits were caught, tamed, sketched, painted. When their animals died, they were boiled and their skeletons preserved. The bones were then articulated, measured, drawn, labelled, and preserved.[34]

The third-floor nursery menagerie included, at various times, rabbits (Benjamin Bouncer and Peter), a green frog called Punch, several lizards, including Judy who was a special favourite, water newts, a tortoise, a frog, salamanders, many and different varieties of mice, a ring snake, several bats, a canary and a green budgerigar, a wild duck, a family of snails, several guinea pigs and later a hedgehog or two. Bertram's tastes ran to the less domesticated: bats, a kestrel and a mean-tempered jay. Some treasures, like Sally, a snake, were store-bought, and some suffered inadvertent misfortune. 'Sally and four black newts escaped overnight,' Beatrix reported. 'Caught one black newt in school room and another in larder, but nothing seen of poor Sally, who is probably sporting outside somewhere.' Such domestic adventures required considerable patience on the part of the adults, and testify to their considerable indulgence.[35]

The family's strong identification with Unitarianism accounted for a certain social isolation. Although the Potters' wealth qualified them as upper middle class, their regional background and religious affiliations excluded them from social acceptance among the more fashionable London society. Beatrix was probably alluding to this sense of exclusion when she commented that in London society the Millais family was in a 'different light, we in none at all'.[36]

Nonetheless the Potters seem to have had a comfortable, if narrow, circle of friends and associates that they entertained, and a steady stream of house guests and family. Certainly Rupert had social connections from his law practice and his clubs, and Helen went out almost daily to call upon Kensington friends, to leave her card, and to have tea. When the Potters entertained at Bolton Gardens, they appear to have done so in good style. Mr Cox, the butler, set a perfect table with 'cocked hat table napkins, immaculate silver and precision of cutlery'.[37]

Bolton Gardens was an enclave of prosperous professionals, businessmen and rising government officials. In the early years the Potters' immediate neighbours at number 1 were Sir Louis Mallet and his family. Mallet was a free trade authority who later sponsored Rupert for the Athenaeum. On the other side, in number 3, was the noisy Herbert Saunders family. Saunders, who was later appointed Queen's Counsel, and his wife had seven children below the age of 11, and six servants. The Saunderses were topics of comment because they had difficulty keeping their servants in line, and frequently held some sort of prayer meeting in their home. Curiously, Beatrix never gives any indication that there were young children living next door during a great part of her childhood, and clearly she was not encouraged by her parents to interact with them. When the Saunderses vacated number 3, the Honourable Mrs Henry Trench, a widow, and her unmarried daughter took their place.[38]

The John Paget family lived across the Old Brompton Road, at 28 The Boltons, a slightly older enclave of prosperous families. Mrs Paget and her three daughters used the same milliner as Mrs Potter, and, apparently through the children who delivered hats to both houses, Beatrix got to know the Paget family. Beatrix reports borrowing 'the sultan of Zanzibar', one of the eldest Miss Paget's 'swarms' of guinea pigs, to sketch in 1893 with disastrous results.

This PIG . . . this wretched pig took to eating blotting paper, pasteboard, string and other curious substances, and expired in the night. I suspected something was wrong and intended to take it back. My feelings may be imagined when I found it extended a damp – very damp disagreeable body. Miss Paget proved peaceable, I gave her the drawing.[39]

All three Paget daughters, however, including 'Miss Nina', about whom Beatrix writes with fondness, were between ten and twenty years older than she; women closer in age to her mother than to herself. Miss Rosalind was a certified midwife and nurse at London Hospital. She was one of the founders of the Royal College of Midwives in 1881. Beatrix describes her as 'something of a ghoul' in her enthusiastic preparation for a cholera epidemic in 1893 that never materialized, but she clearly admired her dedication.[40]

Mr Paget was a barrister of distinction who had acted as secretary to several Lord Chancellors, and had subsequently served as a magistrate in police courts, including that for West London. Paget and his family socialized with some of the most distinguished men in science and medicine. One frequent guest was Sir William Flower, who had begun his career in medicine, but was in the 1880s and 1890s the distinguished Director of the Natural History Museum in South Kensington. William Rathbone was also a frequent guest and a distant relative. Rathbone, a Unitarian philanthropist from Liverpool, had, among many other accomplishments, founded the London National Association for Trained Nurses in 1874, later the District Nursing Association, which helped bring nursing care to the rural areas of England. Beatrix was busy making sketches of Miss Paget's fine guinea pigs and did not pay these worthies much attention, but she would later value her association with the Paget family.[41]

The Potters regularly attended Unitarian services on Sunday, and, like their parents on both sides, were conspicuous in their membership. Before the children were born, Rupert and Helen had attended Little Portland Street Chapel, where Rupert's beloved mentors John James Tayler and James Martineau were co-ministers. Little Portland Street was much favoured by both grandmothers as well. After Martineau retired, the Potters frequently attended Essex Street, Strand, the first openly Unitarian chapel, which from 1774 was a place of resort for the well-connected and liberal religious types of London. When Beatrix was in her late teens, the family sometimes attended services at the Free Christian Church in Notting Hill Gate, a thriving congregation on the edge of Kensington. Quite fortuitously, the Essex Street congregation moved to Kensington following wealth and fashion, and merged with the one at Notting Hill in 1887. At all these churches Beatrix would have heard both good and bad preaching and fair-minded debate of the major social issues of the day.

As a child full of imagination and delight in the fanciful, she longed to participate fully in traditional church festivals and holidays. In the Potter household, however, Christmas was acknowledged rather than celebrated. This was apparently more an expression of Rupert's theological views than Helen's, and it was an unusual custom even among Unitarians at the time. Although Christmas was just another day, Beatrix, who loved celebrations all her life, found ways of participating on her own terms. She sent and received Christmas cards, especially New Year cards, which she enjoyed designing and creating from a young age. She also drew charming menu- and place-cards for holiday dinners, including at least one for Christmas breakfast, although these little cards depicted secular and seasonal themes usually featuring one of her pets. Her journal reflects her understandable gloom on most Christmases when her feelings of isolation were often reinforced by dreary weather. Occasionally she was invited to the homes of friends where Christmas was celebrated with all the trimmings. The Pagets were one such family. 'How pretty Miss Paget's tree used to be with the little doll angel up on the top,' Beatrix recalled wistfully many years later.[42]

The Dissenting tradition of Unitarianism did, however, have certain advantages. From it Beatrix acquired an inner self-reliance, a distinctly pragmatic approach to life, and a tendency towards rebelliousness. From childhood on she exhibited a reticence towards dogma and an aversion to creeds of any sort. The culture of Unitarianism contributed to her compatibility with the 'application of reason' as a method of intellectual enquiry. The Unitarian emphasis on the sanctity of the individual conscience, the importance of rational discussion and the application of science as a legitimate means of social improvement indelibly influenced her. Shortly after her eighteenth birthday in 1884 she observed:

All outward forms of religion are almost useless, and are the cause of endless strife. What do Creeds matter, what possible difference does it make to anyone today whether the doctrine of the resurrection is correct or incorrect, or the miracles, they don't happen nowadays, but very queer things do that concern us much more. Believe there is a great power silently working all things for good, behave yourself and never mind the rest.[43]

By 1896 Beatrix seems to have grown increasingly uncomfortable with the compromises required of a religious tradition that differed significantly from orthodox Christianity. Her intellectual rebelliousness is evident in her frustration with what she interpreted as Unitarian equivocation. 'I shall always call myself a Unitarian because of my father and grandmother,' she wrote heatedly in her journal, 'but for the Unitarians as a Dissenting body, as I have known them in London, I have no respect. Their creed is apt to be a timid, illogical compromise, and their forms of Service, a badly performed imitation of the Church.' However, services at Essex Street often amused Beatrix and almost always provided her with an unrivalled opportunity to observe human behaviour. Appreciating this, she dutifully attended and endured, or ignored, the theology.[44]

'Thank goodness, my education was neglected,' Beatrix wrote to an American friend in 1929. 'I was never sent to school . . . it would have rubbed off some of the originality (if I had not died of shyness or been killed with over pressure).' And then she added, on reflection: 'I fancy I could have been taught anything if I had been caught young; but it was in the days when parents kept governesses, and only boys went to school in most families.' The curriculum offered by schools that were open to female students was decidedly inferior to what a well-educated governess could provide a precocious student. While her education was tailored to her interests, it was certainly not 'neglected' and was, by her own choice, rigorous, in part because so much of it was self-directed. 'I have always found my own pleasure in nature and books,' she announced.[45]

When Beatrix left Nurse Mackenzie's supervision at the age of about six, her formal education was begun under a Miss 'Florrie' Hammond, to whom she became deeply attached. Miss Hammond remained until 1883 when Beatrix was nearly 17, and Bertram went off to boarding school.[46]

Beatrix learned basic reading, writing and arithmetic, studied Latin
with real pleasure, was later taught French by a separate tutor, and
eventually wrote quite fluently in that language. Her last tutor, Miss
Annie Carter, was employed most particularly to teach her German.
Beatrix enjoyed ancient history and poetry, treasured the writing of
Sir Walter Scott, and delighted in rhymes and vernacular verse. As
she got older she saw more of her parents and absorbed current
political events, coloured by her father's conservative political attitudes, and was attentive to the social gossip that he brought home
each day from his clubs. But her compulsion to draw intruded
everywhere, as in 1883 when at a small dinner party she busily painted
a pineapple that was soon to be consumed, barely completing her
sketch in time.[47]

Her flower paintings of the 1870s and 1880s followed the tradition
of Victorian women flower painters who often worked as illustrators
of botanical texts and magazines. Some, like Jane Webb Loudon,
whose illustrations were published in popular mid-century periodicals
like the *Ladies' Magazine of Gardening*, mixed botanical illustration with
scientific study and instruction. Because flower painting and drawing
had long been considered an acceptable female accomplishment, many
women artists pursued flower painting as an opportunity to engage in
a serious study of botany, even moving into optics and photography.
Beatrix also copied out trees, of which she was particularly observant
from an early age, zoo animals, exotic plants, birds and fish. Landscapes appear in her earliest sketchbooks, and by 1884 she was
painting the rural panorama that unfolded before her at Camfield.[48]

Her interests in natural history, science and art coalesced in her
menagerie of pet animals, who were the surrogates for the human
friends she lacked, as well as the objects of her scientific study. 'I
once had a mouse which must have been cross bred . . .' she recalled
much later.

I used to let it run about in the evenings & when I wanted to catch it I
flapped a pocket handkcf. in the middle of the room – or rooms – when
it would come out & fight, leaping at the hdcf. I think . . . it was that
same mouse which got into trouble with the authorities by biting out a

circular hole in a sheet on my bed! I had many mouse friends in my youth. I was always catching & taming mice – the common wild ones are far more intelligent & amusing than the fancy variety.[49]

Rabbits were also favourite subjects. She had a pet rabbit at Dalguise and was making serious studies of rabbits by 1880. With the acquisition of Benjamin Bouncer about 1890, and his successor, Peter Piper, she had a model always at hand. Both rabbits were drawn in every imaginable position and attitude. She observed how they rested, how they nested or hibernated, and the characteristics of their play. With her increasing understanding of their behaviour and her growing adeptness with the dry brush, these rabbits were soon lifelike, waiting to be immortalized as 'Benjamin Bunny' and 'Peter Rabbit'. But not before she had absolutely mastered their anatomy and physiognomy.[50]

Miss Hammond allotted a generous portion of the school day to drawing and painting, but most of Beatrix's artistic efforts were unsupervised and she was essentially self-taught. At the age of 10, Beatrix's sketchbook includes a copy from Mrs Blackburn's narrative poem *The Pipits* and a fine copy of 'Mrs Bond calling the ducks' from Walter Crane's *The Baby's Opera*, both taken from books in her father's library. Copying provided discipline and required close observation, both characteristics of her approach to art. From the beginning she laboured over human figures and faces, and never drew them as well as Bertram. Miss Hammond realized that Beatrix had an exceptional gift for drawing and painting, as well as an unusual appreciation of nature and an unusual ability to observe it. In November 1878, when Beatrix was 12, Miss Hammond recommended that the Potters engage a drawing teacher.[51]

For the next five years Beatrix took lessons with a Miss Cameron, grateful for the additional opportunity to paint and draw, but with diminishing enthusiasm for instruction. At 13 she sat for the first of two examinations for the Second Grade Art Student's Certificate, at the Science and Art Department of the Council on Education at the National Art Training School on Exhibition Road. Her first examinations in 1880 were 'freehand' and 'model', which merited an 'Excellent'. The following spring, 1881, she completed the examinations in 'geometry' and 'perspective' with the same assessment. At the end of her lessons with Miss Cameron in 1883 Beatrix acknowledged: 'I have great reason to be grateful to her, though we were not on particularly good terms for the last good while. I have learnt from her freehand, model, geometry, perspective and a little water-colour flower painting.' She was then nearly 17 and she had acquired distinctive opinions of her own on what constituted good and bad art; she was particularly appreciative of good draughtsmanship. 'Painting is an awkward thing to teach except the details of the medium,' Beatrix reflected. 'If you and your master are determined to look at nature and art in two different directions you are sure to stick.'[52]

Art was a central part of life in the Potter family. They had always been on the periphery of the contemporary art world either as patrons, collectors or practitioners. Rupert occasionally invited Beatrix to accompany him on his visits to Millais's studio. Millais was careful to include her in their discussions, advising her on how to mix her paints, and took a kindly interest in her progress. Listening to them, Beatrix absorbed some of the problems encountered by a working artist. Rupert, on the other hand, had little understanding of the practical difficulties of painting. From Beatrix's perspective he could 'draw very well, but he has hardly attempted water-colour, and never oil'. She credited her father with being a man of good taste and artistic experience, who 'sees all the failures and not the difficulties'. Beatrix surmised that being around Millais so often 'would make a man hard on other painters'; 'other' included his daughter. 'It prevents me showing much of my attempts to him, and I lose much by it,' she confessed. Although Beatrix preferred Millais's early Pre-Raphaelite work such as *Ophelia*, his interest and reassurance meant much to her. 'I shall always have a most affectionate remembrance of Sir John Millais, though unmercifully afraid of him as a child,' she wrote when she heard of the painter's death in 1896. 'He gave me the kindest encouragement with my drawings . . .' 'Plenty of people can *draw*,' Millais once told her, 'but you and my son John have observation.' It was an encomium she privately cherished for the rest of her life.[53]

Acknowledging Beatrix's obvious ability, Rupert sought recommendations on more advanced instruction for his daughter from a number of friends, including Lady Eastlake, wife of the Director of the National Gallery and President of the Royal Academy, who was a long-standing family friend. Accordingly, Beatrix began a series of twelve expensive twice-weekly painting lessons with an as yet unidentified Mrs A. in the autumn of 1883.[54]

Beatrix, sceptical of the enterprise from the beginning, had a decided preference for watercolour rather than oil, but she tried to be open-minded and take advantage of the opportunity, particularly since at Mrs A.'s the pupils would sketch from models and learn various techniques of oil painting. 'Of course, I shall paint just as I like when not with her,' Beatrix wrote, with a bravado she did not feel, already nervous that her originality might be somehow compromised.[55]

By just the third lesson she confessed: 'I don't much like it, which is rather disappointing. Wish it did not cost so much, is the money being thrown away, will it even do me harm?' She struggled with her guilt at not enjoying the opportunity, but was increasingly frustrated that she could not work on her own. She worried a good deal about the effect that working in oils would have on her watercolour techniques.

It is a risky thing to copy, shall I catch it? I think and hope my self-will which brings me into so many scrapes will guard me here – but it is tiresome, when you do get some lessons, to be taught in a way you dislike and to have to swallow your feelings out of considerations at home and there. Mrs A is very kind and attentive, hardly letting me do anything . . . I do wish these drawing lessons were over so that I could have some peace and sleep of nights.[56]

Beatrix's objections centred primarily on her instructor's colour palette and technique of underpainting, which she instinctively disliked. But in rebelling against Mrs A.'s methods, Beatrix was challenged to move ahead in her own experiments with light and colour, and to develop her own style. Like many creative people, Beatrix made the most progress when she had something to push against, and on a certain level she recognized this. Lessons with Mrs A. ended at the year's end with no regrets on Beatrix's part, and the hope that her parents would drop the idea of any further instruction. By 1883 she was learning far more by visiting galleries and looking at art.[57]

Rupert took an active part in Beatrix's art education and was, if nothing else, exuberant in his opinions of artists and critics. Beatrix was now included in dinner conversation about exhibits and galleries they had seen and the latest trends. The family enjoyed the work of contemporary Aesthetic Movement artists like Dante Gabriel Rossetti, J. A. M. Whistler and William Holman Hunt. Although Beatrix deferred to her father's opinions in public, she had definite views of her own and slavishly followed no one. At first she catalogued each exhibit she had seen, writing extensive comments expressive of her iconoclastic point of view. Later she seems only to have noted those she judged particularly good or bad.[58]

For some time Rupert Potter had been enthusiastic about the work of the contemporary children's illustrator Randolph Caldecott. Exactly when he acquired the first three coloured drawings from *The Three Jovial Huntsmen* (1880) is unknown, but Beatrix enjoyed copying his pictures, unconsciously absorbing his light-toned palette, economy of line and use of white space. Much later she admitted that she had 'tried in vain' to copy Caldecott. 'I have the greatest admiration for his work – a jealous appreciation; for I think that others, whose names are commonly bracketed with his, are not on the same plane at all as artist-illustrators.'[59]

The first painter to impress Beatrix, however, was J. M. W. Turner, whose pictures she saw first at Grandmother Leech's home in Palace Gate. Turner was, in her view, 'the greatest landscape painter that has ever lived'. In January 1883, at 16, she accompanied her parents to the Winter Exhibition of Old Masters at the Academy. It was an event she had looked forward to with great anticipation and she was not disappointed. 'I never thought it would be like this,' she wrote breathlessly afterwards. 'I never thought there *could* be such pictures. It is almost too much to see them all at once.' There were works by Reynolds, Gainsborough and Van Dyck, and paintings from the Dutch, French and Italian schools. She proclaimed Titian's *Caterina Cornaro, Queen of Cyprus* her favourite. The exhibition 'raised [her] idea of art', but it also overwhelmed her. 'Was rather disheartened at first,' she confided, 'but I have got over it.'[60]

Beatrix was always interested in the work of other women artists and took particular note of their subject matter and their drawing techniques. She commented approvingly that the paintings by Angelica Kauffmann showed 'what a woman has done', and she was favourably impressed with the pictures of Lady Louisa Waterford and Rosa Bonheur.[61]

Reading back over her elaborate but somewhat naive exhibition notes several years later at the mature age of 20, she was embarrassed. 'It is rather appalling to find one was such a goose only three years since.' But she also reflected with honest pique that 'it was a singular thing, when I had always shown a taste for drawing, that I should have reached the age of seventeen without being taken to see any collection of pictures [Old Masters] . . . 'Her belated introduction at the Winter Exhibition of 1883 nourished a voracious appetite to incorporate what she liked into her own efforts, and to further educate her eye. She made up for lost time by visiting as many exhibitions and galleries as she could. On 3 March she was back at the Academy again. This time the experience seems to have inspired rather than overwhelmed, for she wrote prophetically: 'I *will* do something sooner or later.'[62]

It was an optimistic boast for one in adolescence. As she endured the mood swings typical of these years, the future seemed bright one moment and dark the next. Like most young women, Beatrix needed a confidante. Much as she loved her younger brother, and close as they were, Bertram at 11 was absorbed with challenges of his own. Beatrix's role in the family was unsettled as well. She was still close to her father, but in all probability her relationship with her mother was increasingly difficult. Beatrix was not the pliant, conforming daughter that Helen had expected. Without close friendships with other young women her age, Beatrix was left with her pets and her art. But in her journal, in a secret code of her own invention, she poured out her thoughts and observations, both trivial and momentous. For fifteen years, from 1881 to 1897, what we know about Beatrix Potter comes almost exclusively from her private revelations.

3

❧ *Transitions* ❧

Harking back to a tradition often employed by young ladies to indulge their private feelings, Beatrix began a diary, or journal, sometime about the age of 14 – a time when she had begun to be critical of her life and her parents, and needed a secret outlet. 'I am up one day and down another,' Beatrix wrote in the spring of 1883. 'Have been a long way down today, and now my head feels empty and I am nothing particular. Will things never settle? Is this being grown-up?' Unlike most young women who have kept diaries, however, Beatrix Potter wrote hers in a cipher of her own devising: one that consisted pretty much of a letter-for-letter substitution, written in an ever smaller and smaller hand, sometimes in ruled exercise books, but just as often on any scrap of paper conveniently to hand.[1]

Beatrix seems not to have spoken of her journal in later life, and only one extant letter written five weeks before her death refers to its existence. In it she explains that she was 'apparently inspired by a united admiration of Boswell & Pepys . . . When I was young I had already the itch to write, without having any material to write about . . . I used to write long winded descriptions, hymns(!) and records of conversations in a kind of cipher shorthand, which I am now unable to read even with a magnifying glass.' From the vantage point of 1943, she regarded her adolescent efforts as 'exasperating and absurd compositions'. But her later assessment is neither an objective evaluation, nor an honest explanation of her reasons for keeping it.[2]

That she had literary pretensions at 14 is certain. Potter was well read and already had an ear for dialogue and dialect. She loved a good story, possessed an idiosyncratic sense of humour, and recognized the virtues of first-hand social commentary. She was also a keen listener, and was becoming politically aware at a time of profound social change in England. Her once Liberal father was, by the mid-1880s, well on his way to becoming an intractable Tory. By 1881 William Ewart Gladstone, the 'Grand Old Man' of the Liberal Party, had entered his second term as Prime Minister, the franchise was expanding to include almost all adult males, and questions of Empire, Home Rule for Ireland and trade unionism increasingly disrupted the quietude of proper Victorian households like the Potters'.

Diarists, especially adolescents, who go to the trouble to write in code do so to keep their thoughts and opinions private. In Beatrix's case it seems reasonable to conclude that her code writing was at least initially devised against the possibility that her mother might read it. Certainly Helen Potter would have been offended by her daughter's retelling of family gossip and her expression of independent opinions. By Victorian standards, Potter's journal is intimate, confessional and rebellious. She expresses her despair over ever finding something useful to do, voices her fears for the future, vents her frustration with her parents, and describes her furtive self-assertions with uninhibited pleasure. 'No one will read this,' Beatrix wrote with self-confidence after venturing a scathing criticism of a Michelangelo painting in 1884. She was very nearly correct.[3]

Potter's journal was also an important laboratory for her irrepressible creativity. It served as a literary sketchbook where she could sharpen her eye, improve her story-telling, and even experiment with various forms and styles, in some cases clearly imitating writers she admired like Edward Lear, Lewis Carroll, Jane Austen and Fanny Burney. Writing in code had the added benefit of taking much longer and requiring more attention to structure and syntax. It changed the mundane task of reporting what appeared to be rather routine events into a more important, clandestine enterprise. Like the modern obsession with solving crossword puzzles, writing in cipher engaged her mind each day and gave her a secret sense of creative accomplishment.[4]

The journal encompassed the years when her vision of the future stretched rather endlessly from boredom to uselessness. It fulfilled a need not only to express herself, but to have something over which she, who was powerless in every other way, exercised absolute control. The journal ends quite abruptly in 1897 when her artistic and intellectual energies were fully engaged, but, even more significantly, when her extended adolescence had ended, and, as an independent adult, she no longer had any emotional need for it.

Beatrix Potter's adolescent aversion to change often complicated her life, but it enhanced her powers of observation and her unusually vivid memory of the places she loved. She was always aware of her physical surroundings: the tiniest details of the interiors of houses where she stayed, the old furniture, the arrangement of household spaces, the shapes and forms of farm buildings and the peculiar natural features of the landscape. This acuity was reinforced by her constant sketching so that she distilled the essence of rooms, sheds and gardens into mental images. But places were also important to her emotionally and provided a certain psychic stability in a life that had featured a degree of uprootedness. 'Home' for Beatrix was a place in nature and not necessarily coincident with a physical address. As a young girl she endured the family's springtime perambulations, for however they turned out, she was assured of visits to Camfield, and for fifteen years, the long summers at Dalguise.[5]

The first real adult tragedy Beatrix confesses is a loss of place when, in the spring of 1882, she learned that summers at Dalguise would end. Her sadness was not simply the physical loss of a beloved place, but her recognition of the attendant loss of childhood. '[T]he memory of that home is the only bit of childhood I have left,' she lamented. 'It was not perfectly happy, childhood's sorrows are sharp while they last, but they are like April showers serving to freshen the fields and make the sunshine brighter than before.'[6]

Later that summer Rupert found a fitting replacement in what was then the northern tip of Lancashire, in the English Lakes. Beatrix writes simply, 'Papa took Wray Castle.' About two weeks later the family, along with their carriages, horses, staff and assorted pets, arrived at Wray Castle, 'a well known pile' on the western shore of Windermere, about two and a half miles east of the village of Hawkshead. The only similarity between Dalguise and Wray was the lushness of the surrounding landscapes. While Dalguise was a large, but mostly unpretentious country estate, Wray was a faux medieval castle complete with portcullis, castellated roofs and turrets with arrow slits in the towers. Mock ruins were added after completion 'for a touch of realism'.[7]

The castle had been built in 1845 by a Liverpool surgeon named James Dawson, who used up a sizeable portion of his wife's family gin fortune on the enterprise. The good doctor had in mind a house that could withstand the inclement weather of the Lake District, but somehow got carried away in an outburst of Romantic enthusiasm. Beatrix assessed the Castle factually: 'They say it took £60,000 to build' and 'seven years to finish. The stone was brought across the lake. One old horse dragged it all up to the house on a kind of tram way. The architect, one Mr Lightfoot, killed himself with drinking before the house was finished.' (One can understand why, especially when Mrs Dawson apparently took one look at her new home and vowed never to set foot in it.) The Castle had a panoramic view of the western shore of Windermere. It included some 800 acres of land, a fine specimen of Douglas pine, and a mulberry bush reputedly planted by the poet Wordsworth.[8]

Edward Preston Rawnsley, Dawson's nephew, inherited Wray in 1875. Two years later, when the living at St Margaret of Antioch, the church at Wray-on-Windermere, became vacant, Edward offered it to his unemployed cousin, Hardwicke Drummond Rawnsley, an energetic 26-year-old priest and activist who had been serving the poor in Bristol. Rawnsley settled in at Wray and began a lifelong love affair with the countryside. When the wealthy Potter family came for their three-and-a-half-month holiday in July 1882, they were greeted by the young Vicar, a man who was to have lasting impact on all their lives, as well as on the lives of many still unsuspecting dalesmen of the Lake District.[9]

Rawnsley was handsome, approachable, literate and impassioned about the scenic beauty of the Lake District. He had been a student of the great art critic John Ruskin, at Balliol College, Oxford, and was deeply influenced by Ruskin's philosophy of nature and art. After Oxford he joined with the Unitarian social activist Octavia Hill, working in the slums of London. In the process he became convinced of the benefit of access to open spaces and clean air for the urban poor. When he settled at Wray, Rawnsley kept in frequent touch with his mentor Ruskin at Brantwood on Coniston Water. An organizer rather than a philosopher, Rawnsley soon found his own way of furthering Ruskin's efforts to preserve the unspoiled landscape and cultural traditions of the Lakes.[10]

Rupert Potter was charmed by the young priest. The two had common intellectual and aesthetic interests. Rawnsley was a keen photographer and a collector of literary autographs, as was Rupert, and he had already published two books and a seemingly endless outpouring of essays and verse. Rawnsley had recently returned from a sabbatical to Egypt, Sinai and Palestine. He was working on an archeological inventory of a Roman villa discovered at nearby Ravenglass, had just completed the first of his many writings on Lakeland traditions, and was preparing a paper on the subject for the Wordsworth Society. A man of high confidence and tremendous vitality, one could not help but be caught up in his passions.[11]

Rawnsley noticed Beatrix sketching the Castle library and interior corridors, came upon her painting outdoors, and recognized her obvious talent. Beatrix had met no one else quite like him. He eagerly engaged her in conversation about natural history, and shared his extensive knowledge of geology and archeology and his love of the Lake District.[12]

There were no Unitarian congregations in that part of Lancashire, and St Margaret's church and the Vicarage were just across the woods from the Castle. Always interested in folk traditions of the places she visited, Beatrix attended the Harvest Festival at Wray church that summer with interest. Rawnsley had induced his parishioners, mostly hill farmers, to march in procession from the village to his little church bearing with them the fruits of their harvests as well as the tools of their trade for blessing and thanksgiving. They came with their hay rakes, forks, ploughs and other time-honoured implements of the harvest. It was part of his delight in the lives of the common people, and of his intention to celebrate their labour as well as the beauty and bounty they all shared. Rawnsley's wife, Edith, was also artistic and loved crafts, and their son, Noel, barely two years old, provided his own diversions. Beatrix was happily drawn into their activities.[13]

Not long after the Potters returned to London, Rawnsley took up the cause of preservation in earnest. The immediate issue was a proposal to construct a railway to connect the Honister slate quarries in the Newlands Valley with the already existing railway line at Braithwaite, running tracks through Borrowdale along the pristine western shore of Derwentwater. Rawnsley sprang into action, forming a 'defence fund' to oppose the scheme. His organization succeeded in killing the project. The campaign brought Rawnsley into contact with others opposed to vandalizing the land, and from this time on the country Vicar was a nationally recognized figure in a growing preservation movement. In the spring of 1883 Rawnsley proposed the formation of a Lake District Defence Society whose object was the prohibition of 'injurious encroachments upon the scenery . . . from purely commercial or speculative motives'.[14]

Rawnsley had been offered the living at Crosthwaite, an ancient parish at Keswick, near Derwentwater, and one of the most beautiful in the area. The poet laureate Robert Southey, among other distinguished writers, is buried in the churchyard, and from every vista there are spectacular views of the surrounding mountains, including the peak of Skiddaw. The Bishop of Carlisle knew his man when he wrote to Rawnsley: 'the post which I offer you is as near heaven as anything can be.' Thus it was from Crosthwaite that Hardwicke Rawnsley directed the campaign to protect the Lake District for the next thirty-four years, and it was where Beatrix Potter would next encounter him three summers later when the Potters rented Lingholm, an estate on the western shore of Derwentwater.[15]

The spring of 1883 was equally momentous for Beatrix. After her exciting introduction to the Old Masters at the Winter Exhibition, she privately hoped that she could devote herself to her painting. Her private art lessons had ended, and in late March Miss Hammond announced that she had taught Beatrix all she knew and would be leaving after the spring holiday. Bertram, now 11, had his last Latin lesson with his tutor and would soon enter The Grange in Eastbourne. A photograph of Mrs Potter and the children on the beach at Ilfra-

combe in April shows them bundled in coats and hats against un-
seasonably cool temperatures, attempting to enjoy a picnic. In a letter
to her absent father, Beatrix confirmed both the unseasonable weather
and the unsatisfactory view from the hotel, but expressed her pleasure
in watching the sea birds. Both Beatrix and Bertram were enthusiastic
in their collecting efforts, returning to London with several unusual
lizards – 'Judy', a beautiful bright green female, and 'Toby' – to add
to their schoolroom menagerie.[16]

With impeccably poor timing, Helen Potter announced the day
before Bertram was to leave for Eastbourne that she had arbitrarily
engaged a new governess for Beatrix. This lady, a Miss Annie Carter,
only three years older than Beatrix, would tutor her in German, and
be a lady's companion. Beatrix was understandably furious with her
mother's peremptory decision. Three months shy of her seventeenth
birthday, she felt betrayed, her powerlessness painfully reinforced. 'I
thought surely we had got into all the difficulties now, but here is
another. A nice way, a lively [way], to begin with a new governess
. . . Only a year, but if it is like the last it will be a lifetime – I can't
settle to any thing but my painting, I lost my patience over everything
else. There is nothing to be done, I must watch things pass.'[17]

Miss Carter took up her tutoring duties as scheduled. Surprisingly,
Beatrix found her new governess good company. Although close in
age, Carter had experiences Beatrix could only dream of. She had
lived in Germany, travelled about as a student, and had been economically independent for some time. Beatrix was an excellent student of
languages, partly because of her good ear, but also because of her
attention to the nuances of language and her interest in words. She
progressed well in German, and discovered she was increasingly fond
of Latin. Just before the summer holiday Beatrix confessed: 'finished
Dr Arnold, am doing Virgil, like it so much.'[18]

Bertram's departure for boarding school and the arrival of Miss
Carter required certain emotional readjustments, but the deaths of
her Uncle Crompton, Grandfather Potter, Grandmother Leech and
her old friend William Gaskell, all in less than a year, propelled
Beatrix into adulthood with a new sense of loss: now of loved ones,
as well as of loved places. Edmund Crompton Potter, the managing

partner of Edmund Potter and Company of Dinting Vale, and eldest
Potter son, had been in poor health for some time. His doctors
recommended lengthy visits to the seaside at Brighton from which
he benefited temporarily. Rupert faithfully attended his brother, both
at Rusholme House, Crompton's home in Manchester, and at Brighton, where Crompton died on 6 May 1883 at the age of 52. Rupert,
Helen and Beatrix journeyed to the Gee Cross chapel in Hyde where,
in a shower of spring snow, Crompton was interred in a new crypt
a few yards away from the Potter family vault.[19]

Beatrix's journal provides only the barest details of her uncle's
funeral. But she describes her father's intense interest in the value
and disposition of his brother's art collection, particularly his Millais
pictures and his rare collection of *cloisonné* ware.[20] Crompton's funeral
was prominently reported in the *Manchester Guardian*, where he was
praised as a patron of the arts and an educational reformer. Rupert
seemed surprised by his brother's political and artistic prominence.
Beatrix commented 'there is a good deal in the papers . . . about
poor uncle Crompton. A good deal about him and our family which
papa did not know himself. I don't feel at all "distinguished",
"yet." '[21]

Although Crompton had hoped that his 18-year-old nephew
Edmund Potter, Walter's orphaned son, would join the management
of Potter's printworks, the factory at Dinting Vale was now overseen
by Crompton's executors. It was effectively the end of the once great
family business. 'The Works are only equalled in one other firm in
the world,' Beatrix wrote. 'Pride is a bad thing, and this family has
made more than enough money out of them . . . but still it is a pity
to think of their going.' The printworks passed out of the active
management of the Potter family in 1892.[22]

Beatrix celebrated her seventeenth birthday in July 1883 at Woodfield, a country house near Hatfield, not far from Camfield. Grandfather Potter had not been well, and Rupert felt it wise to remain
nearby. Woodfield was a pleasant place with a large pond well stocked
with perch and beautifully landscaped gardens. There were horses,
several cows and pigs about. Beatrix was especially delighted with
the large variety of birds. She reflected rather ominously, however,

on turning 17: 'I, seventeen. I have heard it called "sweet seventeen", no indeed, what a time we are, have been having, and shall have.' Sadly, her prediction proved accurate.[23]

Beatrix and Bertram enjoyed fishing in the ponds at Woodfield, where Beatrix passed the time usefully studying the habits of newts. She compared their underwater breathing habits with those of land-newts, frogs and toads, surprised to observe that newts squeaked, and remarking: 'it is as queer as to hear a fish make a noise.' The several paintings Beatrix made in 1883 of her brilliant green lizard Judy underscore her curiosity about reptiles and amphibians and their habits. She also caught a small scaly lizard, and with Bertram bought a little ring snake. 'It hissed like fun and tied itself into knots in the road when it found it could not escape, but did not attempt to bite . . .' As in Scotland and at Windermere, where she enjoyed the local sheep and cattle shows, Beatrix visited the dog and poultry fairs near Hatfield, but mostly it was a summer of marking time.[24]

When Grandfather Potter died on 26 October Beatrix notes the date of his death without comment. His body was taken by train to Manchester and was buried in the churchyard at Gee Cross in the family vault barely five months after the death of his eldest son. Neither Beatrix nor Bertram was present.[25]

Manchester newspapers as well as the Unitarian press noted the Potter patriarch's passing, praising his public service and his nearly legendary success as a manufacturer, benefactor and promoter of arts education. A lengthy obituary in the *Christian Life* concluded, 'In his death, Manchester may lament the loss of one of her sons who was a steady friend of education and progress, and whose well-directed scientific and commercial ability made him a credit to his class.'[26]

Edmund Potter's will was very advanced for its time, providing further evidence of his business acumen and, perhaps, Rupert's legal advice. His estate was valued at £441,970, an immense fortune for any man, but particularly a self-made one. Rupert received £60,000 outright. The greater part remained in trust to his widow, Jessy.[27]

More losses followed. In June, while on a visit to their friends the Wilsons in Oxford, Rupert was informed of William Gaskell's death. On this occasion Beatrix wrote openly of her feelings, recalling her childhood affection for Gaskell. 'Dear old man, he has had a very peaceful end. If ever any one led a blameless peaceful life, it was he. Another old friend gone to rest. How few are left. There has always been a deep child-like affection between him and me. The memory of it is one of the past lights bound up with the old home.'[28]

Gaskell's death triggered a reverie of her childhood at Dalguise. She recalled the minister in his grey coat and old felt hat sitting in the warm sunshine on the doorstep there and herself as a little girl 'in a print frock and striped stockings' bounding to his side with a 'bunch of meadowsweet. He just says "thank you, dear", and puts his arm round her. The bees hum round the flowers, the air is laden with the smell of roses. Sandy lies in his accustomed place against the doorstop . . . Shall I really never see him again?' Gaskell's death allowed Beatrix to grieve for her other loved ones, and for the un-welcome changes of the past two years: the loss of Dalguise, and Gorse Hall, the inevitable loss of Camfield in the months to come, and most of all, the loss of childhood innocence. Answering her own question, she continues:

but he is gone with almost every other, home is gone for me, the little girl does not bound about now, and live in fairyland, and occasionally wonder in a curious, carefree manner, as of something not concerning her nature, what life means, and whether she shall ever feel sorrow. It is all gone, and he is resting quietly with our fathers. I have begun the dark journey of life. Will it go on as darkly as it has begun? Oh that I might go through life as blamelessly as he![29]

Exactly a year after Grandmother Leech's death, Beatrix records the unexpected death of her 21-year-old cousin, Edmund Roscoe, the only son of Rupert's sister Lucy and Henry Enfield Roscoe. Teddy, as the young man was known, was a popular and able student at Magdalen College, Oxford. He died from complications of a ruptured appendix. For the Roscoes, Teddy's death understandably 'changed the current of their lives'. Beatrix, only two years younger than her cousin, had not much good to say about him, or about her Aunt Lucy, to whom she ascribed Teddy's flaws of character. She was undoubtedly reflecting the view of at least one of her parents, rather than much personal knowledge of her cousin; even so, her remarks demonstrate real callousness. She expressed no sympathy for her aunt and uncle's loss.[30]

The Roscoes were the objects of a good deal of backbiting in the Potter household in the mid-1880s. On learning of Uncle Harry's knighthood, Beatrix wrote derisively, 'how it makes us laugh . . .' It is hard to know the origin of this ill-will: how much was merely in response to what they considered Henry Roscoe's pretentiousness, and how much derived from Rupert and Helen's resentment of his professional prominence, his real achievements and his enhanced social status. Henry Roscoe came from distinguished and quite wealthy Liverpool Unitarians, and his appointment as one of Edmund's executors reflected the regard in which he was held by the family patriarch. It did not help that Lucy was Rupert's youngest sister, and had undoubtedly been her parents' favourite.[31]

Beatrix also mourned the passing of some of her favourite animals. The green lizard Judy from Ilfracombe had brought 'a great deal of pleasure', while the loss of a whole 'Bill family' of garden snails was 'an awful tragedy. I am very much put out about the poor things, they have such a surprising difference of character.' Punch, the little green frog, survived extensive travels with Beatrix for five or six years and had become quite a fixture in her life. 'How time does go,' she wrote, 'and once past it can never be regained.'[32]

The loss of so many family members depressed Beatrix. On the first anniversary of Grandfather Potter's death she wrote: 'if the next year takes away as many dear faces it will bring death very near home. How strange time is looking back! A great moving creeping something closing over one object after another like rising water.' At the end of 1884, after leaving Camfield, anticipating yet another unhappy Christmas in London, Beatrix confessed: 'I do wish we lived in the country . . . I wish for many things, and yet how much I have to be thankful for, but these odious fits of low spirits would spoil any life.' On Christmas Day Bertram was home from school, sullen and sick with a bad cold. Beatrix too was depressed, and more than a little maudlin, asking, 'I wonder how they all feel underground?'[33]

Beatrix Potter's 'odious fits of low spirits' were not unusual in a young woman enduring an unsettled time in her life. There was a degree of neurasthenia endemic to growing up in a socially insecure Victorian household where the spectre of uselessness was all too real. But the loss of Dalguise, her brother's companionship, her old governess, her beloved grandparents, and her enforced companionship with two hypercritical parents were cause enough for depression. Beatrix's situation was further compounded by unspoken disappointment at having her own needs unacknowledged and worse, ignored.[34]

Much of her despair was aggravated by her mother's controlling behaviour, which emphasized Beatrix's dependence and powerlessness. 'Have been very unsettled this week, first mamma said I should go to Manchester, then that I could not, then I was to stop at home with the girls, then it was decided I should go to Camfield, but now I am to go to Manchester tomorrow.' Beatrix usually enjoyed travelling, even in the exclusive company of her hard-to-please parents. Escaping London was pleasure enough.[35]

She was delighted with her first visit to Manchester, riding the trams, seeing the good-looking Lancashire girls about the city, and touring old Potter-family places with her father. But she was virtually ignored when it came to the dispersal of her grandmother's personal effects. Beatrix describes the scene with her mother and Aunt Harriet as 'so ridiculous and melancholy that I shall never forget it'. Beatrix admired a cameo brooch and bracelet, and her grandmother's silk brocade wedding dress. But Harriet claimed the Leech wedding ring and wedding dress herself. 'I thought at first they would have given it to me . . .' Beatrix wrote with deep disappointment. 'I should not have ventured to ask for either, but that they spoke of giving it to the servants! It is extraordinary how little people value old things if they are of little intrinsic value.' She was given an 'old green silk dress' which her grandmother 'wore as a girl' that delighted her and must have been becoming.[36]

The disposition of Jane Leech's estate became even more contentious when William Leech challenged his mother's right to divide and pass on her marriage settlement among her two daughters. The

dispute ended up in court several years later, where Rupert successfully challenged the suit, but meanwhile it caused great agitation in
the family. For one thing Helen was forced to travel back and forth
to Manchester, prompting Rupert to consider renting Dalguise again
for the summer holiday. Beatrix wrote unhappily early in May, 'I am
afraid there is a chance of going back to Dalguise. I feel an extraordinary dislike to this idea, a childish dislike . . . the thoughts of that
peaceful past time of childhood comes to us like soft music and a
blissful vision.' Instead they went first to Edinburgh, a city Beatrix
had always longed to see, and then on to Dunkeld for a brief visit.
Breatix wrote apprehensively, 'O Home, I cannot bear to see it again.
How times and I have changed!'[37]

Her fear of giving up her childhood is understandable since she
was then just shy of her eighteenth birthday with no prospects
whatsoever of an independent adult life. Childhood was beyond her
clinging, but the future was ominously void. Under these circumstances it was natural that she did not want to see Dalguise now
changed or acknowledge herself an adult. In what is one of the rare
confessions in her journal Beatrix wrote:

The place is changed now, and many familiar faces are gone, but the
greatest change is in myself. I was a child then, I had no idea what the
world would be like. I wished to trust myself on the waters and sea.
Everything was romantic in my imagination. The woods were peopled
by the mysterious good folk. The Lords and Ladies of the last century
walked with me along the overgrown paths, and picked the old fashioned
flowers among the box and rose hedges of the garden.

Half believing the picturesque superstitions of the district, seeing my
own fancies so clearly that they became true to me, I lived in a separate
world. Then just as childhood was beginning to shake, we had to go,
my first great sorrow. I do not wish to have to repeat it, it has been a
terrible time since, and the future is dark and uncertain, let me keep the
past. The old plum tree is fallen, the trees are felled, the back river is
an open hollow, the elfin castle is no longer hidden in the dark glades
of Craig Donald Wood . . . I knew nothing of trouble then.[38]

Dalguise was as dilapidated as she had feared and the journey bittersweet. 'A forlorn journey . . . The place is the same in most ways. It is home.' But the village of Dunkeld reaffirmed her joy at the natural beauty she remembered. 'Man may spoil a great deal,' she wrote, 'but he cannot change the everlasting hills, or the mighty river, whose golden waters still flow on at the same measured pace, mysterious, irresistible.'[39]

In July Beatrix celebrated her eighteenth birthday in London with Bertram, who was home for the summer. 'What funny notions of life I used to have as a child!' she wrote. 'I often thought of the time when I should be eighteen – it's a queer business.' Bertram, now 12 years old, had acquitted himself well at Eastbourne and was at the top of his class. Beatrix, however, was privately worried about her younger brother's character. After visiting him that spring she had written: 'I wonder how he will turn out? Sometimes I am hopeful, sometimes I am feared. He has an absorbing interest [in natural history], which is a very great help in keeping anyone straight. The best upbringing has sometimes failed in this family, and I am afraid that Bertram has *it* in him. Heaven grant it is not so, but I am afraid sometimes.' The '*it*' was never named, and only in retrospect does it seem that Beatrix suspected a weakness in her brother's character that eventually led him to alcoholism.[40]

The family spent the rest of the summer at Bush Hall, near Camfield. The house on the River Lea provided excellent trout fishing. It was a rambling, old, red-brick affair with low rooms and long passages that Beatrix loved exploring. A little carriage and pony provided the opportunity for Beatrix to learn to drive, and she discovered an unlimited amount of white clay under the river bank that was perfect for modelling. She busied herself painting landscapes. 'Most landscapes are in bits, stuck together with more or less skill,' she observed, 'a cloud, a field, a tree, which may be good separately, but are not fitted together in the least.' Sounding like a disciple of Ruskin, she continued: 'The way our landscape painters fail most is in failing to grasp their subjects widely enough, that was the great power of Turner . . . There is such complete unity in nature, nothing out of place or without a use.'[41]

Turner and the Old Masters were much on her mind during these years when she was forming independent artistic judgements. Concerned at the rumoured dispersal of Old Masters from Blenheim Palace, she wrote: 'There will be few great collections left in England soon. All the best works of Old Masters leave the Island. The Government is too stingy to buy them, and in the market they are bought cheap for foreign museums . . . or for rich Americans, which is much the same as far as their return is concerned.' Her preservation instincts were also aroused when she saw some fine old oak furniture at an antiques shop in Oxford. An oak cupboard like the one at Wray Castle she 'particularly admired (with a wish to possess) . . . If ever I had a house,' she wrote, 'I would have old furniture, oak in the dining room, and Chippendale in the drawing room. It is not as expensive as modern furniture, and incomparably handsomer and better made.'[42]

But it was John Millais that Beatrix had first-hand opportunity to observe. Rupert was busy assisting Millais, photographing sitters or backgrounds. Millais had received a commission to do a second portrait of the Prime Minister, William Gladstone, a man who was increasingly the object of Rupert's political ire. After the first sitting, Millais asked Rupert to make a photographic portrait of Gladstone for him to work from. Ironically Rupert's photograph was of such quality that he had it published and sold it as a carte-de-visite. Beatrix went happily with her father to see Millais's newest paintings on exhibition in November 1884, but came away more impressed by his early work.[43]

Her favourite painting by Millais was *Ophelia*, which she pronounced 'probably one of the most marvellous pictures in the world'. With exceptional insight Beatrix observed that the singular quality of the Pre-Raphaelite style was the absence of shadow. 'Focus', she wrote, 'is the real essence of pre-Raphaelite art, as is practised by Millais. Everything in focus at once, which though natural . . . produces on the whole a different impression from that which we receive from nature.' When another Pre-Raphaelite painter Holman Hunt's long-awaited work *The Flight into Egypt* created artistic fireworks at the Fine Arts Gallery in the spring of 1885, Beatrix praised the care and attention to detail Hunt had taken, rather than just dashing something off – a veiled criticism of Millais's current work. In a clear statement of independence from her father, who disliked the picture because he said he could not understand it, Beatrix rejoined: 'I had rather a picture I can't understand than one with nothing to be understood.'[44]

The Potter and Millais families occasionally socialized in London. The Potters attended a society ball given by the Millais family at their palatial home, where Oscar Wilde and his wife drew much attention, and they were also invited to Carrie Millais's fashionable wedding at St Mary Abbots church in Kensington. Beatrix's visits to Millais's studio at Palace Gate with her father over the years had afforded her a rare opportunity to study the painter's evolving body of work. She used these visits to absorb all she could of his handling of light, subject and techniques of applying paint. She was flattered by Millais's occasional remarks about her own work, but she did not deceive herself that they bestowed special distinction. Such unparalleled access to a successful painter might have induced shameless fawning in another aspiring artist, but Beatrix never lost her critical independence, liking some of his paintings while rejecting others.[45]

With her own art lessons mercifully behind her, Beatrix was understandably anxious for time to practise her art by herself.

It is all the same, drawing, painting, modelling, the irresistible desire to copy any beautiful object which strikes the eye. Why cannot one be content to look at it? I cannot rest, I must draw, however poor the result, and when I have had a bad time come over me it is a stronger desire than ever, and settles on the queerest things, worse than queer sometimes. Last time . . . I caught myself in the back yard making a careful and admiring copy of the swill bucket, and the laugh it gave me brought me round.[46]

Although Beatrix was visited by fits of self-doubt about her painting and frustrated with obligations that diverted her from practice, she was aware that her experiential education in the galleries of London constituted an important part of her artistic apprenticeship. The galleries were a sort of collective atelier; her education limited only by her capacity to observe. As a consequence of this exposure, she was prompted to experiment with a wide variety of media: oil, watercolour, modelling, block and transfer printing and etching, and unafraid to choose a diversity of subject matter. But by 1885 Beatrix had clearly chosen watercolour and was rapidly perfecting her dry-brush technique.[47]

Her father took her to the French Gallery at the Tate, and to charity art exhibitions in private homes because, as Beatrix confided, 'he is curious to see the insides of great houses' as well as the art collections. The watercolours of Frederick Walker which they saw at a small gallery she approved as the most beautiful she had seen and 'exceedingly true to nature . . . Not but nature has more feeling and beauty than man will ever comprehend, but unfortunately when one says . . . of a picture that it is natural, it generally happens that the painter has picked out the commonplace.'[48]

Now nearly 19, Beatrix enjoyed more social activities. She frequently walked to the newly opened Natural History Museum in South Kensington to sketch. She went to the Royal Globe Theatre to see Charles Hawtrey's popular adaptation of *The Private Secretary*, but enjoyed the drive to the theatre through the Westminster area even more. It was the first time Beatrix had taken this route, passing Horse Guards, the Admiralty, Whitehall and the Strand. She went several times to the International Inventions Exhibition in South Kensington, a sort of trade show, and like her Potter grandfather approved the general scientific knowledge offered to the working classes at such exhibitions. She also enjoyed evening concerts featuring the dance music of Eduard Strauss.[49]

At a time when the nation in general, and London in particular, was plagued with labour unrest, widespread unemployment and the frightening dynamite plots that accompanied the demands of Irish Home Rule, Beatrix's approval of Mechanics Institutes and public exhibitions was a remarkably liberal position. 'It will be a great pity if there are no more,' she wrote, 'they are a great resource for people of our station, and infinitely healthier than the music halls and low theatres.' She complained of all the bawling babies and unpleasant tobacco smoke at such public gatherings, however, and for the first time she complained of her health, noting her lack of energy. 'How is it these high-heeled ladies who dine out, paint and pinch their waists to deformity, can racket about all day long, while I who sleep o'nights, can turn in my stays, and dislike sweets and dinners, am so tired towards the end of the afternoon that I can scarcely keep my feet? It is very hard and strange, I wonder if it will always be so?'[50]

Such comments suggest that Beatrix had not been well. Between 1882 and 1885 she mentions having bad colds, feeling fatigued and not sleeping well. But in the spring of 1885 she reveals she had been chronically ill the past year, once describing herself as 'still middling and suffering from neuralgia'. In March she wrote, 'Had my few remaining locks clipped short at Douglas's. My hair nearly all came off since I was ill.'[51]

Beatrix had suffered from a systemic infection. Headaches, fever, colds, sleeplessness and neuralgia sapped her energy and certainly contributed to her general lethargy. The customary practice for hair loss due to a febrile illness was to cut the remaining hair short. Beatrix had taken some pride in her long, thick hair, which she notes had been within four inches of her knees the previous summer. So while she writes nonchalantly, even humorously, about her hat blowing into the large fountain pool at the International Exhibition where she had gone with her father, it must have been an enormously embarrassing event. 'I always thought I was born to be a discredit to my parents,' she wrote, '. . . it is one of the peculiarities of my nature that when there *is* anything to be shy about, I don't care in the least, and I caused a good deal of harmless amusement.' But, she adds forlornly, 'If only I had not been with papa, he does not often take me out, and I doubt he will do it again for some time.' She was still frail at the year's end, for when Bertram returned from school with a light case of measles, Beatrix was shipped off to Camfield so she would not be exposed, and only returned to London just before Christmas.[52]

Her hair had not grown very long by mid-June when the Potters gave a large party, apparently in honour of Beatrix's approaching nineteenth birthday. Even so, Beatrix was an attractive young woman,

not classically beautiful, but arresting nonetheless. Her shorter, naturally wavy hair framed her face becomingly, emphasizing its pleasing
oval shape and her wide-set blue eyes. She was petite, slim, and
small-waisted, with erect posture. She had pretty hands with long,
graceful fingers. Although not a formal 'coming out', the gathering
was clearly meant to mark Beatrix's entry into adulthood. Beatrix
wrote of it simply as 'The Party . . . first since ten years, and for my
part may it suffice for ten more, when many of us will be gone.'
There were about a hundred guests and even Beatrix considered it a
success. 'I enjoyed myself,' she reported, 'and, contrary to my own
and parents' expectations, behaved well.'[53]

The birthday party was followed by other trappings of adulthood:
the end to her formal education and the departure of her governess.
'My education finished 9th July,' Beatrix wrote.

Whatever moral good and general knowledge I may have got from it,
I have retained no literal rules . . . I have liked my last governess best
on the whole – Miss Carter had her faults, and was one of the youngest
people I have ever seen, but she was very good-tempered and intelligent
. . . The rules of geography and grammar are tiresome, there is no
general word to express the feelings I have always entertained towards
arithmetic.

Miss Carter had announced that she would marry Edwin Moore, a
civil engineer, the following year. The couple settled in Bayswater,
and on Christmas Eve 1887, Noel Moore, the first of eight Moore
children, was born. Soon after his birth the Moores moved to a house
on Baskerville Road, overlooking Wandsworth Common. Beatrix
visited Annie and her growing brood frequently as Mr Moore was
often abroad for extended periods.[54]

Other family changes followed the Potters' summer holiday in
1885 at Lingholm, an estate near Keswick on the shore of Derwentwater. Rupert received a shocking letter from Crompton's widow
announcing the engagement of beautiful Kate Potter to a no-name
former army captain, a sometime 'stockbroker', Fletcher Cruickshank.
Beatrix's comments about Kate's decision reflect her parents' social

conventions and disapproval, but show how deeply ingrained these attitudes were in the family. Beatrix was also challenged by Kate's perhaps frivolous, but nonetheless independent decision. 'This sounds a silly business if nothing worse,' Beatrix wrote. 'Aunt Mary has not a particle of sense, but I can't understand the girl not having more self-pride or ambition.'[55]

Rupert Potter's reaction to his favourite niece's engagement was not lost on Beatrix. Rupert was appalled that his nieces were allowed to marry so far beneath themselves. 'If he had a beautiful daughter like Kate,' Beatrix writes of her father, 'there is no doubt he could marry her very well, he is intimate with all the rich and respectable Unitarians' families, or if ambitious, he could easily take her into fashionable society.' Beatrix concluded philosophically, 'If this is what beauty leads to, I am well content to have a red nose and a shorn head, I may be lonely, but better that than an unhappy marriage.' Barely three weeks later, Beatrix notes the engagement of her double cousin, the orphaned Edith Potter, without comment. But Edith's intended, William H. A. Gaddum, came from a highly respected, wealthy Manchester merchant family. Undoubtedly Rupert and Helen quietly disapproved of his connections to trade. In October came the news that Blanche Potter, Crompton's younger daughter, was engaged to her cousin, Charlie Wrigley. Helen took the occasion to lecture Beatrix severely on her disapproval of such inter-family liaisons. 'Mother is sorry that he is her cousin, and enlarges on that subject to me so continually that I begin to think she desires particularly that I should be acquainted with her views on it.' She added with regret, 'an unnecessary precaution at present'.[56]

Beatrix's social commentary reflects not only changes and fissures between relatives, but a deepening social conservatism which mirrored the very real social and economic unrest of the times. Economic misery followed the serious agricultural depression of 1873. Prices and incomes dropped, rents could not be paid and domestic violence increased. The difficult political question of Irish Home Rule dominated all the elections. The Liberal majority returned in the general election in the autumn of 1885 was unstable and short-lived. When a large demonstration of unemployed labourers spilled onto the streets of London in February 1886, there was widespread property damage. Soldiers were called out and many well-to-do people fled the city. Helen Potter listened nervously for sounds of the mob outside Bolton Gardens in the evening, while Rupert talked about 'going to the Colonies, Edinburgh, [or] quiet provincial towns': threats he had uttered routinely over the last decade. However, he had good reason to fret about the future, particularly as his large portfolio of foreign investments was highly volatile, he had little income from real estate, and, like others of his class, his domestic returns depended upon commercial stability.[57]

By the mid-1880s Rupert had rejected whatever vestiges of his father's enlightened views he had once assumed. His increasing political insularity was juxtaposed to the spectacular political rise of his brother-in-law, Henry Roscoe, and the topic of bitter comment. In the wake of his son's death, Sir Henry Enfield Roscoe, FRS had decided to stand as a Liberal candidate from Manchester in the general election of 1885. Although his political ambitions were much ridiculed in Beatrix's household, Roscoe did the unthinkable, winning the only Liberal seat in Parliament from Manchester. Beatrix commented sourly on the outcome: 'Uncle Harry's position is most extraordinary . . . I fancy he has got rather more of a position than he bargained for.' But clearly Henry Roscoe, 'statesman of science' and liberal advocate, had become a worthy successor to Edmund Potter.[58]

With his election to Parliament, in addition to his knighthood the previous year, his distinguished work in chemistry at Owens College, Manchester, and his well-known expertise in water treatment and industrial pollution, Uncle Harry was by far the most distinguished member of the Potter clan. And he was poised for further distinction. Rupert's disdain also included his youngest sister Lucy Roscoe, who had not only made an impressive marriage, but also had achievements of her own. Lucy had won a gold and two silver medals from the Photographic Society of London as a younger woman, and about 1888 had one of her photographs selected as the best photograph by an English amateur photographer for inclusion in an American publication. Rupert, dallying on the edges of the intelligentsia, must have been inordinately envious of both his brother-in-law's status and his sister's recognition in his own field of artistic endeavour.[59]

On New Year's Eve 1885 Beatrix reviewed the past year with disappointment, and not much optimism for anything better in the next.

How awful it seems at the end of a year to think it has actually passed into space never to return! Gone except its memories! Much bitterness and a few peaceful summer days. Oh life, wearisome, disappointing, and yet in many shades so sweet, I wonder why one is so unwilling to let go this old year? not because it has been joyful, but because I fear its successors – I am terribly afraid of the future. Some fears will inevitably be fulfilled, and the rest is dark – Peace to the old year, may the seed sown therein bear no bitter fruit.[60]

For the better part of the next year and a half, Beatrix endured progressively acute bouts of chronic fatigue often accompanied by low-grade fever. Although it was never diagnosed with certainty, she was most likely suffering from rheumatic fever. There were nearly eight months in 1886 when she did not write at all in her journal. 'Part of the time I was too ill, and since then the laziness and un-settledness consequent on weakness have so demoralized me, that I have persevered in nothing for more than a week at a time except toothache.' In the spring of 1887, on a family trip to Grange-over-Sands on Morecambe Bay, she experienced severe pains in her feet which got progressively worse and moved up her limbs. The family returned to London three weeks later where Beatrix was bedridden, with 'little fever' but a 'great deal of rheumatics. Could not be turned in bed without screaming out.' At the end of June 1887 she was 'amazed to find [her]self in summer, having last seen the trees in winter'.[61]

She insisted that she had not missed much, but there had been changes that she preferred not to dwell upon. In the autumn of 1886 Bertram had been sent off to Charterhouse, a fine school in Surrey, about thirty miles south-west of London. It was a school traditionally favoured by the sons of barristers and solicitors, army men, and the civil service, and was regarded as prerequisite to a place at Oxford or Cambridge. Like other public schools of the late nineteenth century, the subculture at Charterhouse favoured the emotionally stalwart and the physically robust. Quite likely Charterhouse was a very poor choice for a young man with artistic talents and introverted personality. The following April Bertram became ill and returned to London without taking his exams. 'It also is useless to speak more,' Beatrix reported cryptically, 'for the thing is done and can never be undone.' Bertram was sent back to Eastbourne for the autumn term. Although Rupert was reluctant to give up public school for his son, Beatrix, who had some sense of how desperate Bertram had been, was thankful the experiment was over.[62]

While Beatrix was convalescing, she took pleasure in drawing her schoolroom pets. Bertram had left a pair of long-eared bats in her care, which she had enjoyed sketching but which became difficult to keep. She released one and chloroformed the other, rarer specimen, afterwards taking precise measurements of all the bones in its wings and legs, and stuffed it according to Bertram's directions. He also sent her a chrysalis of a privet hawk moth as a gift, which she drew in several stages of development.[63]

Beatrix used Bertram's old microscope to draw the details of her specimens. She drew the trivial and the extraordinary: a ground beetle in pencil and watercolour, artistically presented on the page under different magnifications; a wonderfully hairy jumping spider, magnified to show the colouration of its body, but endowed with an inner energy, and several varieties of her favourite butterflies and lizards. Such drawings suggest that her observation of the natural world and the relationship between nature and art was becoming more sophisticated. The scientific accuracy of her microscopic work also reflected a new confidence and maturity. She painted a fine weasel at Camfield, capturing the sinuous body under a glossy, thick coat. Her observations of animals coincided with similar qualities in people she knew. 'How amusing aunt Harriet is,' she wrote once, 'she is more like a weasel than ever, and her tongue – it exceeds all description.'[64]

One of Beatrix's best drawings is a woodmouse that she sent to a friend as a Christmas present in 1886. There were many sketches of a 'Miss Mouse' otherwise known as 'Xarifa', the dormouse, a creature that she loved to draw. In October 1886 'Xarifa' died in Beatrix's hand. 'Poor little thing,' Beatrix wrote sadly. 'I thought at one time she would last as long as myself . . . I think she was in many respects the sweetest little animal I ever knew.'[65]

The tone of Beatrix's journal changes markedly after December 1886. Thereafter she reports fewer bouts of depression, and less fear of the future; undoubtedly the result of her improving health. By 1891 she was writing about the art world as someone confident in her own critical abilities. She regarded her family with some emotional distance, and occasionally with a worldly ennui. There had been a new female literary influence evident in her life as well. Sometime in 1890 Beatrix read and was much impressed by the literary life of Fanny Burney, whose early diaries had just been republished. In May, Beatrix began writing quite polished letters to a fictional friend she addressed as 'Esther', adopting the name of Burney's younger sister, to whom Burney also addressed herself in her diary. Beatrix calls Fanny Burney 'her heroine' and correctly absorbed their similarities of education, social upbringing and ability to paint skilful verbal portraits.[66]

There were also external forces propelling her in new directions. One was the pragmatic desire for some expendable income. She received a psychological and practical push from her brother and also from Uncle Harry. Less easy to document but no less certain was the influence of Hardwicke Rawnsley.

Rawnsley, the Anglican priest, and Roscoe, the Liberal Unitarian scientist, approached the world very differently. But both were men of deeply held passions and inordinate curiosity, and both were students of nature. They challenged Beatrix to move forward toward emotional independence with a renewed sense of possibility. When the Potters rented Lingholm over the course of several years, Beatrix renewed her friendship with the Rawnsleys. During those summers Rawnsley had ample opportunity to encourage Beatrix's art and her scientific illustration, and to share his enthusiasm for geology, archaeology and the special grandeur of the Newlands Valley just west of Derwentwater.[67]

After his election to Parliament, Roscoe was a frequent guest at the Potters' table in Bolton Gardens, as well as at Camfield. He and Lucy lived at 10 Bramham Gardens, within walking distance of the Potters' house. Henry also had the opportunity to observe Beatrix's artwork over a crucial period. Both he and Lucy admired the Christmas cards and place-cards Beatrix made for the family in 1889. Beatrix recalled that 'the cards were put under the plates at breakfast and proved a five minutes wonder'. Roscoe was aware that Beatrix and Bertram both 'had a desire for coin' in order to purchase a printing machine that cost £16 and that they were short of that amount by £6. He suggested that her cards were of such quality that 'any publisher would snap at' and encouraged her to offer some for sale.

Suggestion was one thing, execution quite another. Forced to take matters into her own hands, she prepared six designs for cards using 'that charming rascal Benjamin Bouncer our tame Jack Hare', as her model. Bouncer, known as Bounce, thus assisted in Beatrix's first venture into commercial art. 'I may mention', she explained after the fact, 'that my best designs occurred to me in chapel – I was rather impeded by the inquisitiveness of my aunt, and the idiosyncrasies of Benjamin who has an appetite for certain sorts of paint, but the cards were finished by Easter.'[68]

She sent them to a list of five publishers that she and Bertram had compiled, beginning with the firm of Marcus Ward, but they were promptly returned. Bertram, home from a recent Continental adventure and busy preparing for entrance exams for Oxford, was 'inclined' to the firm of Hildesheimer & Faulkner, and so delivered his sister's drawings to the publisher himself. The following day came an envelope with a cheque for £6 and the request to the 'gentleman artist' for more sketches.

My first act was to give Bounce (what an investment that rabbit has been in spite of the hutches), a cupful of hemp seeds, the consequence being that when I wanted to draw him next morning he was partially intoxicated and wholly unmanageable. Then I retired to bed, and lay awake chuckling till 2 in the morning, and afterwards had an impression that Bunny came to my bedside in a white cotton night cap and tickled me with his whiskers.[69]

Uncle Harry offered to take Beatrix, poised for commercial success, to the offices of Hildesheimer & Faulkner to show them her new designs. It was in fact Beatrix's first business meeting and Uncle Harry seems to have tried his best to stay in the background and let her negotiate for herself. Beatrix's account of the meeting shows a remarkable attention to detail and to the business of publishing. She gauged what Mr Faulkner liked and disliked, though not always agreeing with his taste. She took note that he wanted designs that referred to the seasons which he did not have in his current albums, and that he also had an ambition to publish a children's book, showing her a sample of what he thought agreeable. 'His one idea seemed to me to be fiddles and trousers. Now, if there is anything hideous, it is trousers, but I have conceded them in two guinea-pig drawings.' Uncle Harry found nothing 'vulgar' in Mr Faulkner's samples, although Beatrix divined correctly that it was humour he wanted rather than artistic realism.[70]

Beatrix was 24 when her designs were published, first as Christmas and New Year cards, and then as illustrations to a set of verses by the prolific versifier Frederic E. Weatherly, a barrister from Bristol. They appeared in a seven-page, gilt-edged booklet bound together by a pink silk cord titled *A Happy Pair*. It sold for 4½d., and gave the illustrator's name as 'H.B.P.'[71]

Flushed with success, Beatrix sent some further watercolour sketches to another London publisher on her initial list, Frederick Warne & Company. Warne returned them with a letter stating that while they were no longer publishing 'Booklets', they found her designs pleasing. Their letter left the door ajar as to a future interest: 'if at any time you have any ideas & drawings in book form: we should be happy to give them our consideration.' It was a beginning.[72]

While one part of Beatrix's world was expanding, another was contracting. In early September 1891, Jessy Potter died at Camfield in her ninetieth year. She was buried in the Potter vault at Hyde, next to her beloved Edmund. Such was the esteem in which Jessy Potter was held within the Unitarian community that a rare obituary appeared in the Unitarian paper, the *Inquirer*, which praised her services 'in the cause of religion and liberty'.[73]

Beatrix had unabashedly adored her grandmother, not only for her charm, beauty and openly affectionate nature, but for her energy, her resilience and especially her rebelliousness. Beatrix thought her 'as near perfect as it is possible here'. With her passing, Beatrix moved into adulthood, determined to discover something meaningful to do with her life.[74]

4

❧ *Experiments* ❧

'Now of all hopeless things to draw,' Beatrix wrote one late October evening in 1892, 'I should think the very worst is a fine fat fungus.' She was referring to her meeting that afternoon with the shy but erudite Charlie McIntosh about her botanical drawings, but also to the irony of finding herself a would-be painter of 'funguses'. The Potters had come to Birnam, a village near Dunkeld, in late July for another long Scottish holiday. Beatrix had been trying all summer to gain an interview with McIntosh, their former postman at Dalguise, who was a highly regarded naturalist, in the hope that he would suggest ways she might improve her work. Theirs was to be a most 'singular acquaintance': a unique scientific collaboration that had far-reaching consequences.[1]

By the early 1890s Beatrix's interests as an artist and naturalist had converged on fungi and, to a lesser degree, on fossils. Such enthusiasms were typical of the Victorian craze for natural history which, beginning earlier in the century, affected everyone from aristocrat to artisan. Women in particular were drawn to the study of insects, shells, ferns, fossils and fungi, and to their naming, classification, collection and frequently their illustration. Like many of her contemporaries, Beatrix was first drawn to natural history as a way to relieve the boredom that beset affluent Victorians, and for the measure of personal freedom it brought. Certainly her initial efforts were amateur, but she enjoyed drawing under the microscope and she had certain undefined artistic ambitions that accompanied her exploration of the natural world.[2]

Collecting, mounting and looking at specimens under the microscope was considered worthwhile entertainment for families of the Potters' class. Debates over identification and proper microscopic techniques were commonplace, enlivened by such guides as P. H. Gosse's popular *Evenings at the Microscope* (1859) and other influential manuals. Beatrix had inherited Bertram's microscope when he went off to boarding school, and while it did not have a particularly good lens, probably no higher than 200 × magnification, she enjoyed viewing and drawing a variety of living and non-living specimens at close range.[3]

While she was recovering her health, she spent time at the nearby Natural History Museum studying the insect displays. Soon insects, spiders, butterflies and moths were subjected to her intense scrutiny and patient rendering. Her microscopic drawings were not only scientifically accurate, but arranged on the paper with a pleasing sense of space. Even her paintings of unattractive creatures, or just pieces of them, had beauty and energy, even personality.[4]

The Potters encouraged Beatrix's precocious talents as a naturalist illustrator with books that would inspire and guide: in addition to Blackburn's *Birds Drawn from Nature*, Grandmother Potter gave her a beautiful gilt-edged edition of John E. Sowerby's *British Wild Flowers* (1882) with its own black-velvet-lined presentation box. It contained some ninety hand-coloured plates by one of the finest botanical illustrators of the day. Its influence on her flower painting was immediate.[5]

But natural history was a public Victorian passion as well as a private one. In 1888 Beatrix had sufficient confidence in her observations of the hawfinches around Camfield to include them in a letter to *The Times*. Her information on the birds' habitat added to that of ornithologist William Yarrell's *A History of British Birds* (1871–85), volumes which were also in the Potter library. Although Beatrix's letter was unfinished, the fact that she thought her observations worthy of publication indicates a high level of confidence.[6]

The public dialogue was carried on in a flood of magazines and journals intended for a wide readership. The Potters subscribed to *Hardwicke's Science-Gossip*, a short-lived, but highly respected journal known affectionately as *Science-Gossip*, published monthly as an illustrated medium for 'the exchange of information for students and lovers of nature'. It featured short essays and articles on various general subjects such as wasps, the hummingbird hawkmoth, geology, entomology and microscopy, as well as short notes and a section for public enquiries and expert responses. The mycologist M. C. Cooke was one of the editors of *Science-Gossip* during the time that Beatrix had access to it. His accurate pen-and-ink drawings, notable for their hints of texture and habitat, illustrated many of the articles on fungi. The demise of *Science-Gossip* in 1893 mirrored the decline of the science generalist and the amateur naturalist.[7]

Beatrix's interest in drawing and painting mushrooms, or fungi, began as a passion for painting beautiful specimens wherever she found them. She never saw art and science as mutually exclusive activities, but recorded what she saw in nature primarily to evoke an aesthetic response. She was drawn to fungi first by their ephemeral fairy qualities and then by the variety of their shape and colour and the challenge they posed to watercolour techniques. Unlike insects or shells or even fossils, fungi also guaranteed an autumn foray into fields and forests, where she could go in her pony cart without being encumbered by family or heavy equipment.[8]

Her first known fungi watercolours were done in the summer of 1887 at Lingholm. Two survive from this date. There were more the following year: a common white helvella (*Helvella crispa*) which she drew in its grassy habitat, a wood hedgehog (*Hydnum repandum*) and a common chanterelle (*Cantharellus cibarius*). In December, she painted a wood blewit (*Lepista nuda*) and a russet shank (*Collybia dryophila*) at Camfield. In both, she included their leafy substrate to illustrate context. Beatrix provided no Latin names for these early drawings, suggesting that she did not know them, and had selected them for their visual appeal.[9]

In 1886 Rupert purchased an expensive two-volume set of the Revd John Stevenson's new opus on British fungi, *Hymenomycetes Britannici (British Fungi)* from his London bookseller. It was an odd and expensive reference work for Rupert to buy for himself and some months later he generously offered it to the learned but impecunious McIntosh, whose need of reference books was well known around Birnam.[10]

The Potters chose the picturesque village of Birnam for their summer holiday in 1892 after successive years at Derwentwater and Windermere undoubtedly because it offered good fishing and fine landscapes. Birnam was very near Dalguise, but Heath Park, the house the Potters rented just outside the village, was so different that Beatrix expressed no sadness at returning to the area. In spite of its grand name Heath Park was a modest villa distinguished by a pair of six-sided spire-like turrets. It was situated on just one acre, facing out over the steep hillside, along with three other similarly styled houses, at what Beatrix thought might be optimistically described as 'a convenient remove' from the railway station. In fact, the house was immediately above the Birnam station.[11]

Rupert was delighted with the constant activity below, and with the coming and going of the trains which he supervised at night from his bedroom window. It took some doing to cram the servants into their quarters, and the horses, phaeton and pony cart into the stable. The house was also difficult to reach. 'We have unluckily a very steep narrow lane to get down first, under the railway, and hanging over the Inchewan Burn.' To make matters worse, the Burn was the playing ground for the local children, one of whom 'invented a charming game of "bolting the pony" under the railway arch'. Notwithstanding such assaults and inconvenience, the Potters settled into a predictable routine. Rupert went out fishing or photographing and after arranging the house as best she could, Helen occupied herself shopping in Dunkeld and making calls on old friends. Beatrix made daily excursions with her pony, traversing the Tay Valley where she took photographs with her father's old camera and sketched.[12]

Heath Park offered a redeeming view of the Birnam green and the distant meandering Tay. A short climb further up the Birnam hill behind the house allowed splendid views of nearby Dunkeld. The house and the garden were in considerable disrepair, but Beatrix discovered a good supply of gooseberries for her rabbit, Benjamin, when he became sufficiently brave to explore his new surroundings. As a precaution she took him out in the garden on a leather dog-lead, which provoked amused comments from the staff.[13]

Beatrix's detailed account of her holiday in Birnam reveals just how extensively she explored this area of the Tay Valley with her pony and trap, or the phaeton. Her very first trip was to Inver to visit Kitty MacDonald, their old washerwoman at Dalguise, who was by now 83. Beatrix described her still 'waken, and delightfully merry . . . She is a comical, round little old woman, as brown as a berry and wears a multitude of petticoats and a white mutch. Her memory goes back for seventy years and I really believe she is prepared to enumerate the articles of her first wash in the year '71.'[14]

The 26-year-old woman who emerges from these journal pages is not only alive to the natural environment about her, but eager and interested in the lives of the ordinary people of Perthshire. She observes people with the same acuity as she observes non-human nature, treating them with almost sociological detachment, keenly aware of language and accent, always on the look-out for the telling physical detail. She gathered her samples in spare verbal portraits, but most are leavened with kindness and humour. Physically active, delighting in her freedom outdoors and intellectually engaged, Beatrix was only occasionally oppressed by her mother's demands or annoying familial duties.

Her travels took her to both sides of the Tay Valley, through luxuriant forests, and into dry, rocky hill country. The hard-working Scottish hill farmers intrigued her, and she filed away in her memory what she observed as she travelled about, noting particularly the changes in the physical environment. She had an unparalleled opportunity to observe the agrarian economy: the quality of the land, how the farmers enriched the soil and irrigated their farms, what crops they counted on as staples for the long winter months, the livestock they raised and the wildlife they hunted. Beatrix commented especially on the condition of the livestock, the customs of breeding, and the odd practice of de-horning cattle. She enjoyed finding the elusive roe deer and was fascinated by the peculiar habits of the red squirrel. She observed the damage to trees done by gnawing rabbits, writing: 'I confess reluctantly, strengthened by observation of the revered Benjamin, [that rabbits] are not game at all, but absolute vermin as regards eating.'[15]

In addition to perfecting her photography, Beatrix continued to produce illustrations for greetings cards or booklets. Shortly after arriving in Birnam, she discovered a tame jackdaw belonging to the tenants who lived on the road behind Heath Park. She made a pen-and-ink drawing of it, turning the curious little black bird into a beady-eyed chimney sweep carrying a set of long-handled brushes. She sent the drawing to Ernest Nister, the German firm of fine art printers in London, who had previously purchased some of her drawings on commission, but had not yet paid her. She produced a fine landscape of a group of beeches, titled *A Beechwood near Inver, Dunkeld*, as well as at least four fungi paintings.[16]

Beatrix had been trying to speak with Charlie McIntosh, 'that learned but extremely shy man', all summer. Her efforts to engage him had been frustrated by his shyness and by Victorian prohibitions against calling on him when she was visiting Inver. Beatrix had known McIntosh since she had been a child of four. She remembered how it had been 'an amusement to hop from puddle to puddle on the strides of Charlie's hob-nailed boots. I forget how many thousand miles he walked, some mathematical person reckoned it up.' In fact, it was about 200,000 miles. The next postman had a tricycle, but Beatrix had grasped McIntosh's uniqueness, writing: 'modern habits and machines are not calculated to bring out individuality or the study of Natural History.'[17]

McIntosh was raised in a musical family, learned the fiddle and the art of wood carving, and was drawn to natural science as a boy. After minimum but good schooling, he went to work in the Inver sawmill where, in 1857, he suffered the loss of all the fingers on his left hand in an accident. With such a disability his job choices were limited and by default he became a rural postman, though with persistence and talent he continued to play the cello, directed the choir at the Little Dunkeld parish church, and was superintendent of the town band. But he was always self-conscious about his maimed hand and kept it hidden as much as possible.[18]

His natural history was self-taught, but his mother encouraged his interest in ferns, urging him to give his beautifully displayed fern collection to the Birnam Institute, which brought his abilities to professional notice. His long walks delivering the mail gave him ample opportunity to observe the flora and fauna, to note geological formations of the Tay Valley and the marks of flood and drought. It was seldom that McIntosh returned from his daily postal rounds without what he called a 'poochfu' o' weeds', and it was in studying and identifying these that he made significant discoveries.[19]

McIntosh had done some research for the founder of the Perthshire Society of Natural Science and in payment for his contributions he was given special borrowing privileges at the Society's library. Access to the latest reference books, the Stevenson volumes and J. M. Berkeley's *Outlines of British Fungology*, enlivened his interest in fungi. Despite the loss of his fingers McIntosh was able to make sections and slides and to draw under the microscope. Soon his humble cottage at Inver was the destination of notable botanists and mycologists who were undoubtedly surprised by McIntosh's easy collegiality. When the 'Perthshire naturalist' found someone who shared his interests, he was a devoted and selfless mentor.[20]

One day near the end of October, Beatrix and her father stopped by A. F. Mackenzie's photography studio. After they left, Mackenzie, ever the intermediary, sent up a book of dried ferns collected by McIntosh for Beatrix to look at, and 'ingeniously' arranged for McIntosh to call at Heath Park to retrieve his book, thereby giving Beatrix an opportunity to show him her fungi drawings. Beatrix recalled her earlier impressions of the postman naturalist:

When one met him, a more scared startled scarecrow it would be difficult to imagine. Very tall and thin, stooping with a weak chest, one arm swinging and the walking-stick much too short, hanging to the stump [of his hand] with a loop, a long wisp of whisker blowing over either shoulder, a drip from his hat and his nose, watery eyes fixed on the puddles or anywhere, rather than the other traveller's face.[21]

McIntosh appeared at Heath Park at the appointed hour 'with his soft hat, a walking stick, a little bundle, and very dirty boots . . . He was quite painfully shy and uncouth at first, as though he was trying to swallow a muffin, and rolling his eyes about and mumbling.' She recounted in her journal, 'I would not make fun of him for worlds, but he reminded me so much of a damaged lamp post. He warmed up to his favourite subject, his comments terse and to the point, and conscientiously accurate.'[22]

Among the drawings that Beatrix showed McIntosh that October afternoon were the two she had drawn at Lingholm. 'I happened by lucky intuition', Beatrix explained, 'to have drawn several rare species.' One of them McIntosh had also discovered for the first time that summer in a wood at Murthly, and 'another, like a spluttered candle', was similar 'to one he had found just once in the grass at the road-side near Inver tunnel'. 'He was certainly pleased with my drawings,' she reported happily, 'and his judgement speaking to their accuracy in minute botanical points gave me infinitely more pleasure than that of critics who assume more, and know less than poor Charlie.' Deeply impressed with his knowledge, and grateful for his evaluation, Beatrix concluded, 'He is a perfect dragon of erudition, and not gardener's Latin either.'[23]

During their hour-and-a-half visit, Beatrix and McIntosh discussed a variety of points about fungi: how they grew, their habitat, classification and proper nomenclature. McIntosh 'became quite excited and spoke with poetical feeling about their exquisite colours'. They also discussed techniques for drawing under the microscope, agreeing to an exchange of talent: he to send her fresh specimens in the post and she to return a drawing of them. After he had shown her his remarkable one-handed drawings, Beatrix gave him her sketchbook with fungi drawings that he had so admired.[24]

A box of specimens arrived from Birnam quite soon after she returned to London. She sent her first fungi drawings to McIntosh in early December, telling him, 'it is a real pleasure to copy them, they are such lovely colours', but she had become more curious about their taxonomy and wanted to learn proper botanical techniques of illustration. Sensing a willing student, McIntosh supplied each specimen with its scientific name and Beatrix worked at becoming more proficient at nomenclature and classification.[25]

In December Beatrix described an unidentified fungus that had sprouted on the same piece of broom where an *Agaricus velutipes* had previously grown. 'Miss Potter wonders,' she wrote with unusual formality, 'whether it grows out of doors at this season or whether it is brought out by the heat of the room?' She included a microscopic sketch of the finger-like *primordia* of the new fungus, showing where it had appeared on the broom, its scale and its characteristics. McIntosh had also sent some mosses. They were harder to draw because they had to be done under magnification. She would not return drawings of those, though she made some excellent ones for herself. But she took exception to the 'horrid plant like a white stick with a loose cap which smells exactly like a dead sheep!', and also suggested that McIntosh mark the rarest plant in each box so that she could draw it before it got damaged or too mouldy.[26]

In London, Beatrix's study of fungi was limited to what was available at the Natural History Museum. She spent a great deal of time there looking at the portfolios of drawings and printed plates in an effort to learn the taxonomy, but it was not easy. The most important reference book available was James Sowerby's monumental work, *Coloured figures of English fungi or mushrooms* (1793–1803), a work of over four hundred hand-coloured plates. Otherwise she had only the museum's limited collection of fungi preserved in alcohol, or a sort of pickling brine in small glass bottles, and a few dried specimens. She found these so badly labelled as to be all but useless.

Beatrix was already frustrated that there was no one at the museum 'to give any information'. They did not have the reference books she wanted, and they 'take no interest whatever in funguses at large'. 'Some day,' she promised McIntosh, she would 'ask at Kew Gardens whether there is anyone who knows more about the names'. In the meantime she made do with what was accessible and by the time the Potters returned to Dunkeld the following summer, she had become familiar with the basic literature on fungi classification and was prepared to take issue with the Kensington museum staff over the identification of some of their *Boletus* and *Hygrophorus* specimens.[27]

The Potters were elegantly situated for the summer of 1893 on the bank of the Tay in Dunkeld at Eastwood, a large dower house owned by the Duke of Atholl but subleased to them by a minor laird named Atholl McGregor. The large house was set in the woods with gardens at the back that rolled gently down to the river's edge, and looked across to the Great Oak of Birnam. In contrast to the detailed journal

Beatrix had kept the previous summer, there are almost no entries for this one. Beatrix and McIntosh evidently continued their collaboration, perhaps going to look for fungi together, for some of his favourite places are noted on her drawings. She shared her drawings, discussed her identifications, and benefited from his guidance. In all, Beatrix painted sixty fungi specimens that year, many of which are marked 'Eastwood, 1893'.[28]

Three of those paintings are of the rare pine cone fungus, *Strobilomyces strobilaceus*, 'old man of the woods'. Sometime in July, Beatrix discovered what she knew to be a rare fungus in the grounds of Eastwood. McIntosh tentatively identified it as *Strobilomyces strobilaceus*. But since he had never seen it in the field before, he sent the specimen off for further verification. It was indeed very rare. It had first been recorded in Scotland at Drummond Wood in Crieff in 1889. Beatrix painted the now somewhat shrivelled specimen on 11 August. Less than a month later, after some hot rainy weather, Beatrix found the rare 'old man of the woods' again at Eastwood and, knowing what it was, made two paintings of it, at least one of which she painted *in situ* on 3 September. On the back of one drawing, which she gave to McIntosh, Beatrix made a little sketch of the garden at Eastwood and put an 'x' where she found the fungus, presumably so he would know where to look for it again.[29]

However exciting it was to find such a rare fungus, Beatrix was not totally absorbed by scientific illustration. She had heard from Annie Moore that same week that Noel was sick in bed and she wanted to send him a letter. Not certain what to write about, she made up a story about her new rabbit, Peter Piper, 'bought at a very tender age, in the Uxbridge Road, Shepherds Bush, for the exorbitant sum of 4/6', whom she had brought to Eastwood. Beatrix took Peter everywhere with her, just as she had Benjamin, drew him from every angle, taught him to do tricks, and was totally devoted to him. Noel knew Peter well and a letter about Peter's adventures was tailor-made to cheer him.[30]

And so it was that on 4 September, the very day after discovering and drawing the rare pine cone fungus, Beatrix sat down in the sunshine on the lawn at Eastwood and wrote a picture letter about a disobedient young rabbit called 'Peter'. 'I don't know what to write to you,' Beatrix told him, 'so I shall tell you a story about four little rabbits whose names were – Flopsy, Mopsy, Cottontail, and Peter.' The hero of her picture letter was her own rabbit Peter, but the villain of the story was 'Mr McGregor', the owner of the garden, whom Peter first encounters 'round the end of a cucumber frame' where McGregor, on hands and knees, was 'planting out young cabbages'. Although McGregor is clearly doing physical labour, he is wearing a tabard, a sleeveless waistcoat buttoned up the front, and on his head is a deerstalker cap, with peaks at front and rear and earflaps tied with a ribbon and bow at the top of the head. The tabard and deerstalker are apparel that a minor laird would wear to show his status. Mr McGregor has a thin face, a long white beard, and wears rimless glasses. Just the day before, Beatrix had undoubtedly seen Charlie McIntosh on his hands and knees, with a single peaked cap on his head, looking at a rare fungus in the grass, through rimless spectacles, his long white wispy beard flowing about. The physical features of the fictional Mr McGregor are too similar not to have been drawn with McIntosh in mind, while his name and dress conformed, with poetic licence, to that of the Potters' landlord, Atholl McGregor, who would have been about the property, given that the Potters were due to leave Eastwood the following Thursday.[31]

Perhaps because there was a new baby at the Moores' household that July and because Beatrix did not want little Eric, who was now nearly five, to feel left out, she wrote a picture letter to him the following day. It too took its adventure from her specific observations of the natural world around her at Eastwood on the River Tay. 'My dear Eric,' she wrote, 'Once upon a time there was a frog called Mr Jeremy Fisher, and he lived in a little house on the bank [drawing of frog in a little den under three broad leaves] of a river. You can see what a little house it is because there is a dock leaf hanging over the roof. One morning Mr Fisher looked out & saw drops of rain . . .' Poor Jeremy catches a prickly stickleback instead of the tasty minnow that he hoped for, and ends up eating 'roasted grass-hopper with lady-bird sauce'. Beatrix conspiratorially tells little Eric that frogs consider this 'very good indeed, but I think it must have been nasty'.[32]

The ironic coincidence of Beatrix's activities at Eastwood in September 1893 would not be recognized for nearly a century. But in the space of two days she had found and painted a rare and important mycological specimen and created two fictional characters that one day would be world-famous. Both were products of her skill as a naturalist, her acute observation of people and places, her creative imagination, and her sure sense of audience.

During the winter of 1893 McIntosh and Beatrix continued their mycological collaboration. She now had her own set of the Stevenson volumes, which she was studying assiduously. 'I wish I had had the book sooner,' she told him, 'for most of my drawings might have been made more accurate, without extra trouble, if I had understood anything about the distinctions. Dr Stevenson's book is rather stiff reading but I understand it sufficiently to find it extremely interesting.' Although she lacked confidence that she would ever master fungi classification, she was pleased that she had learned how to correct her drawings when necessary by washing them out. A good judge of her own work, Beatrix confessed to McIntosh that her weakest point was drawing the gills.[33]

Beatrix's self-critique gave McIntosh an opportunity to offer specific advice on how to improve her illustrations without offending her. His very formal reply of 10 January 1894, addressing her as 'Miss Potter, Madam', indicates that McIntosh took the role of mentor seriously. 'Since you have begun to study the physiology of the funguses,' he writes, 'you seem to see your drawings of them defective in regard to the gills, but you can make them more perfect as botanical drawings by making separate sketches of sections showing the attachment of the gills; the stem if it be hollow or otherways, or any other details that would show the characteristics of the plant more distinctly.'[34]

This was precisely the sort of advice Beatrix needed. Her next drawings show details of the gill attachment. Longitudinal sections of stem are sketched off to the side or a step behind the main illustration. In some drawings there are also notations of both young and developing fructification. These illustrations lose nothing as aesthetically pleasing pictures. Her colours are translucent, yet uncannily true to nature, and her fine brushwork gives the individual fungus both texture and weight. The spatial arrangements of the fungi, whether painted with substrata or as pure botanical objects on the page, are somehow lively illustrations of nature's handiwork, rather than cold objects of natural history.[35]

Charles McIntosh not only provided just the right level of expertise and objectivity to allow Beatrix to advance in her skills, but he also gave her the professional validation she longed for. Over the next two years her interest in fungi grew to a passion. Between 1894 and 1895 Beatrix made seventy-three fungi drawings.[36] After incorporating McIntosh's suggestions she drew numerous sectional views under magnification. In the process she became more observant of the fructification and curious about the role of spores in reproduction.

Her growing self-confidence is evident in a letter she wrote from the Scottish Borders in the early autumn of 1894 after receiving another parcel of specimens. 'If Dr Stevenson were not infallible,' Beatrix writes, 'one would say [*A. paedidus*] was more like the description of *decastes*. I have made some very bad guesses but had chosen the right names for *Hygrophorus*.' Stevenson was indeed fallible. Potter's painting of this fungus, done in September 1894, has recently been identified as an example of the species *decastes* as she supposed. Reflecting on her activities that summer she noted in her journal: 'My photography was not very satisfactory, but I made about forty careful drawings of funguses, and collected some interesting fossils, one of which I find labelled at the Museum, *Auraucarioxylon* from Lennel Braes, a lucky find since I know nothing about it.'[37]

For the next two years geology and palaeontology nearly rivalled Beatrix's interest in fungi. It is safe to say that her interest in natural history was such that nothing on the ground escaped her notice. Although the public enthusiasm for natural history created a congenial climate for her activities and discoveries, it was her observant eye and her desire to know a thing by drawing it that set her apart and marked her as an exceptional student and illustrator of nature. But even Beatrix's enthusiasm had limits. Staying at the Osborne Hotel in the south coast town of Torquay in the spring of 1893, she discovered her bed infested with bugs. After an uncomfortable night sleeping with Keating's powder in her hair, she was of the opinion that 'it is possible to have too much Natural History in a bed'. She also found that it was 'possible to see too much of Ada Smallfield', her mother's loquacious friend, whose social airs Beatrix found irritating. After a day of Miss Smallfield, Beatrix conspired with her father to take a 'reviver' from Miss Smallfield's company in order to explore Kent's Hole, a cavern near the shore just outside Torquay. Beatrix records the furtive scene in her journal: 'We slunk out after breakfast, Miss Smallfield who was not an early bird was seen to throw open a window on the third floor, but we got away through the bushes. We afterwards lost our way which was a judgement . . . Papa who had been in the Peak Cavern was not much impressed, but I who had never been in a cave was extremely interested.'[38]

In June 1894 Beatrix was allowed a holiday that widened her social horizons and brought her real happiness. She was invited to visit her younger Hutton cousins, Caroline and Mary, at their home at Harescombe Grange, Stroud, in Gloucestershire. Their father, Judge Crompton Hutton, was related to Beatrix's grandmother Jessy Potter. Like the Potters, Crompton and his wife Sophia Holland were Unitarians from the north. Crompton was a County Court Judge in the Manchester area, but he preferred to live closer to London, travelling north to hold court for a period of weeks each month.[39]

Now approaching her twenty-eighth birthday, Beatrix records the astonishing fact that she 'had not been away independently for five years'. Even so, she was nearly denied the opportunity by her mother, who worried that she did not have the physical stamina for the journey. Thankfully, cousin Caroline, three years younger and very decisive, prevailed and gathered Beatrix onto the train. By the time the two cousins reached Stroud they had talked themselves out about the universal and the particular. Caroline, fiercely independent and every bit as opinionated as Beatrix, was also beautiful and as full of energy as idealism. Beatrix had not met anyone quite like her and admired her enormously, even if they did not always agree.[40]

Beatrix was at Stroud little more than a week, but the adventure was, as she reflected afterwards, 'like a most pleasant dream'. Caroline, whom Beatrix described as 'a pickle', turned out to be excellent company, once they had resolved their various political, religious and social differences. As a young woman in love with ideas, Caroline was more intellectually fearless and uncompromising, while Beatrix was more analytical, and as a consequence, less ideological. Caroline was an outspoken Darwinian and Beatrix remonstrated with her about the unintended consequences of her views. Beatrix suggested that Darwinism was cold comfort for those less able to deal with uncertainty, but admitted, 'truth is truth'. Imagination and empirical observation provided a more interesting reality for her than either theory or dogma.[41]

Beatrix and Caroline explored the Gloucestershire countryside nearby, tracked the badgers' marks and claw-walks and collected fossils in the quarries. But far more intriguing than any of these activities was the opportunity the visit afforded Beatrix to observe relationships among the Hutton family. Beatrix had rarely seen a married couple so outwardly devoted to each other and so easy together. She liked Mrs Hutton immensely, writing with unusual warmth, 'I don't think I ever became so completely fond of any one in so short at time . . . I cannot imagine a disposition more sweet.' Beatrix proved herself good company. Judge Hutton, who was older than her own father, soon dubbed her 'Busy Bee'. In spite of his intense questioning about her family's domestic arrangements, Beatrix found she liked him. She was, however, nearly undone when Hutton asked her if her mother brushed her own hair or if the Lancashire servants did it. 'Now fortunately I did not say so,' Beatrix wrote later, 'but my mother's hair takes off.'[42]

Beatrix found her cousin's 'only flaw' was her energetic expression of pseudo-feminism. She thought it 'unwise on the part of a nice-looking young lady to proclaim a pronounced dislike of babies and all child cousins', as Caroline boldly did. Later, Beatrix wrote presciently: 'Latter day fate ordains that many women shall be unmarried and self-contained, nor should I personally dream to complain, but I hold an old-fashioned notion that a happy marriage is the crown of a woman's life.' The visit to Stroud provided Beatrix the rare opportunity of sharing beliefs and even feelings about life and the world with a woman of her own age and class. She was exhilarated by it and looked forward to seeing Caroline again. It was, as she hoped, the beginning of a lifelong friendship.[43]

Beatrix's visit to the Huttons also had the effect of deepening her interest in geology, especially in fossils. Mrs Hutton, Caroline's mother, was a renowned collector of Liassic period fossils, especially insects and fish. Mary Hutton, Caroline's younger sister, was already a serious collector. The three young women enjoyed several forays to the well-known quarries around Harescombe Grange. The fossils Beatrix found and painted were of sufficient interest that she went to some lengths to identify them.[44]

By the summer of 1894 Beatrix had acquired copies of James Geikie's *Outlines of Geology* as well as Andrew Ramsay's basic manual *The Physical Geology and Geography of Great Britain*. Geology and palaeontology were enormously popular pastimes, and since the Potters took their spring holidays at seaside towns in Dorset, Devon and Cornwall for three consecutive years from 1892, fossil hunting along the coast was something they enjoyed as a family. Bertram, too, was interested in geology, especially rock formations, and brother and sister enjoyed collecting at Pendennis Point near Falmouth on the Cornish coast, where they stayed in 1894.[45]

Although Bertram was often part of these spring holidays, his activities are rarely recorded by his sister. After being admitted to university, Bertram was proposed for membership in the Athenaeum, an appropriate choice for an aspiring artist. He matriculated at Magdalen College, Oxford in the autumn of 1890, to read classics with Alfred Denis Godley. He took a Third in Classical Moderations in 1892, and read only for a pass degree in the summer of 1893. As a self-described landscape painter and etcher, Bertram clearly preferred the social life at Oxford to that at Bolton Gardens: he stayed for another year, and then went abroad.[46]

In 1894 Bertram joined the family during their summer holiday near Coldstream, the last holiday the Potters would spend in Scotland. Beatrix found the Scottish Border country a place of unexpected beauty. From Coldstream south the River Tweed marks the boundary between Scotland and England, and the wooded valley along the Tweed provided matchless vistas of the green Eildon Hills nearby and the ominous Cheviot Hills beyond. Their house at Lennel was just beyond the bridge and village of Coldstream, not far from the little crossroads of Branxton where the climactic battle of Flodden Field had decided the fate of James IV and Scottish nationalism in the sixteenth century. In such a place, full of wild natural beauty and history, Beatrix celebrated her twenty-eighth birthday, though for a day she thought she was a year older than she really was.[47]

Coldstream was a fisherman's haven and the reason Rupert had chosen to rent Lennel, a large but somewhat dilapidated brick house, from the Hamilton family. There was an overgrown garden, which Beatrix persisted in weeding, though it was invaded by rats and piebald rabbits and full of broken bottles. There were also three cows, a calf, a donkey, two rather headstrong collie dogs, and assorted poultry overseen by a peripatetic gardener whom Beatrix termed 'a curiosity'. 'I like this place very much, there are so many places to drive to see; several old castles,' Beatrix told Eric Moore in a picture letter, 'but my Mamma does not like this house, because it is very dirty.'[48]

At the start of their Lennel holiday, when fungi were less abundant, Beatrix was absorbed by geology. She was rewarded by finding fossilized fish teeth straight away. Having spoken to a local antiquary, she went out several times to examine a stone-pit, noting the marks left by the glacier which had pressed the boulders on either side into hard homogeneous strata. Fascinated by the formations, she made several efforts to photograph the stone-pit, determined to prove that the kame, the ring of stones surrounding the top of the pit, had been thrown up by ice and not water. Intrigued by all the evidence of glacial activity, she remarked: 'Whether it is that one has not previously considered geology, or that there is a sense of the awful power in the track of the ice, I don't know, but I think the view looking from the spurs of the Cheviots across the wide strath to the Lammermoors [*sic*] is magnificent.'[49]

She found a fine fossil specimen at Burnmouth on a cinder-walk just below the railway station and, employing McIntosh's suggestions on scientific illustration, made a painting of it showing the stone from various angles, how it looked both split and whole, indicating the different planes of the stone. Close to the end of their stay at Lennel, Beatrix looked for fossils on the river's edge while Bertram fished. 'I have found out which stones to split,' she wrote, 'and how to use a cold chisel.' She also spent time trying to find the exact location of the Battle of Flodden Field and was rewarded for her efforts by the discovery of an archaeological fragment while walking in a grassy field near Piper's Hill, where she believed the King had been killed. 'To my great pleasure I picked up a very thin, rusted strip of iron about the size of the palm of my hand . . . It might indifferently be an old kettle or a fragment of armour, but I was quite satisfied.'[50]

Happily, by mid-August, with rain and hot weather, the country-side around Coldstream became 'a ideal heavenly dream of the toadstool eaters'. Beatrix had been waiting for such a moment. She discovered a grassy area deep within the nearby Hatchednize Woods where 'the fungus starred the ground apparently in thousands, a dozen sorts in sight at once'. There she found more than twenty different varieties in a few minutes and 'joy of joys, the spiky *Gomphidius glutinosus*, a round, slimy, purple head among the moss'. She took it up using her old cheese knife and saw its distinctive veil. 'There is extreme complacency in finding a totally new species for the first time,' she wrote, fresh with the pleasure of discovery. Beatrix visited Hatchednize Woods several more times and was always rewarded with 'a quantity of funguses'. Her fungus hunting took her and pony Nelly deep into the countryside. Noting the quality of the light, especially at sunset, she found the landscape unexpectedly beautiful. Without anyone knowing, she bravely explored new roads, and although she was once quite lost, she found her way back before being discovered. 'I never was in such a delightful country for driving with a pony, I know fifteen [roads] besides crossroads.'[51]

On a hot day in late September Beatrix and her father took the train to the town of Kelso and from there a carriage to Smailholm Tower, a barren, rocky, sixteenth-century fortification where Sir Walter Scott had explored as a sickly child. His imagination had been set afire by the ballads and stories he had heard while living at the nearby farm of Sandyknowe. Coming as a pilgrim in homage to one of her literary heroes, Beatrix was rewarded with discoveries of her own: a white and a gigantic red *Hygrophorus*. While her father was 'photographing every view but the right one' from inside the Tower, Beatrix busied herself sketching a *Cortinarius* growing on bleached horse dung in the bog near the farmhouse.[52]

More warm, rainy weather at the end of the month brought out even more fungi. In all, she made at least forty paintings. On 30 September she wrote: 'Was overtaken with funguses, especially *Hygrophorus*. Found a lovely pink one. They begin to come in crowds, exasperating to leave.' And a day later: 'I got over a hedge in to Birgham wood, a paradise of funguses', including a large group of 'crisp yellow *Peziza* . . . and a troop of gigantic *Cortinarius*'. She sent one nearly eight inches wide and weighing almost a pound to McIntosh along with several paintings.[53]

There were, however, drawbacks to her fungus hunting. She was often plagued by ticks, once admitting that she had an 'average of seventy bites, but sometimes beyond counting'. Even her pony objected to the flies. Beatrix wrote to Eric Moore describing how her pony wore a pair of 'white ear caps', drawing them to explain how the tassels brushed the flies away. She also drew the sheep wearing little caps that tie under their chins against the fly bites. Always interested in livestock, the condition of the land and the farms, Beatrix wrote, 'They are such fine sheep & the farmers live in big houses & are very well off. They are carrying the corn now & making stacks. I think I never saw such fine big fields.'[54]

But that summer there was the additional problem of her unhappy mother, whom Beatrix now referred to as 'the enemy'. Ever controlling, Helen often refused to order the carriage in the morning or make up her mind when she wanted it. 'If I say I should like to go out after lunch,' Beatrix complained, 'I am keeping her in, and if she does not go and I have missed the chance of a long drive, it is provoking.' Beatrix clearly enjoyed her independence at Lennel, but she was also lonely. She had wanted to invite her Hutton cousins, Caroline and Mary, to visit. But Helen refused to allow them, citing the disreputable condition of the one spare bedroom. Beatrix saw this for the convenient excuse it was, writing: 'I would so very much have liked to have Caroline, and I am afraid they rather expected to be asked,' confessing to being in a very bad temper at the decision. On her last morning at Lennel, Beatrix reflected that they had been 'sojourners in a strange land, I with a feeling of not committing myself, and my mother with a most hearty aversion and prejudice to the whole affair'. Hoping that she might return to the Borders some-day, perhaps with a more agreeable companion, Beatrix complained, 'It is somewhat trying to pass a season of enjoyment in the company of persons who are constantly on the outlook for matters of complaint.'[55]

The Borders, however, had made an indelible impression and so had her growing personal independence. She loved the little streams she discovered with her pony and cart, noticing that they had 'no joyous boisterous rush like Highland Burns, but there is a happy peacefulness about them'. The abundant corn, cattle and sheep and the prosperous land seemed a marvel to her – a testament to the few herdsmen and farm labourers that were in evidence. As a hunter of toadstools, she had found a magical realm. 'I am sure,' she wrote, 'driving for miles among these lonely cornfields and deep silent woods, and on the grassy slopes of the still more quiet hills, I have thought the whole countryside belonged to the fairies, and that they come out of the woods by moonlight into the fields and on to the dewy grass beside the streams. There are not many hedgehogs, which are fairy beasts . . . and how without the aid of the fairy-folk of fosterland could there be so little mildew in the corn?' The autumn, she noted poetically, was the 'pleasantest season of the year, none the less pleasant for being the end, as the last breath of sweets is sweetest last'.[56]

Her Shakespearean illusion was no accident, as one of her accom-plishments at Lennel was committing four acts of *Henry VIII* to memory. She memorized about six Shakespeare plays that year, repeating them randomly as mental practice, keeping account of her progress in an exercise book. She began this during a period of sleeplessness and depression, discovering that the concentration required to memorize was diverting and provided mental exercise. Beatrix not only loved the language of Shakespeare and the Old Testament, but was fascinated with the mind's ability to recall some-thing once thoroughly learned.

Packing up her summer's treasures, Beatrix was 'very sorry indeed to come away, with a feeling of not having half worked through the district, but I have done a good summer's work. The funguses will come up again and the fossils will keep. I hope I may go back again some day when I am an old woman, unless I happen to become a fossil myself, which would save trouble.' Beatrix could not have known how well the field work she had done in the Borders would prepare her for the scientific challenges that lay ahead, nor how the cadences of Shakespeare would inform her literary perspective.[57]

Back in London she was given an unexpected opportunity to draw some Roman and post-Roman artefacts from the Bucklesbury excavations. They were common everyday objects: metal and bone tools, potsherds of various sorts, toilet utensils, craftsmen's artifacts, needles and fragments of Roman leather sandals. Some had been excavated in 1872 from the silts of the ancient Walbrook stream that ran under the National Safe Deposit Company's building near Queen Victoria Street in the City of London; others came from the historic Roman settlement at Southwark, south of the River Thames. They were lent to Beatrix through the auspices of a gentleman connected to the NSDC company, in whose collection they belonged. Allowing someone to 'borrow' ancient artefacts in order to draw them was a common practice in Victorian times. How long Beatrix kept the objects is not known, but it was long enough to do more than thirty watercolours over the winter of 1894, some of which are among her very finest work in scientific illustration.[58]

Now at the height of her powers as an illustrator, she explored these common household articles with an elegantly curious eye. Because she was an amateur interested in archaeology, she arranged her objects on the page with imaginative abandon, mixing types, juxtaposing shapes, exploring the different textures of rust, leather, and metal, giving each a tactile quality, yet drawing them with such accuracy they could almost be photographs. Sir John Millais once made the distinction between those that could merely draw and those whose drawings had 'the divine spark' of observation. These paintings have that spark, as well as a pure translucency that marks the influence of the Pre-Raphaelites both on Potter's palette and use of light. They testify to her discipline and her desire to merge the scientific and the beautiful, revealing the truth of both. Beatrix's interest in the ordinary archaeological implements of long-ago craftsmen is reminiscent of her earlier delight in the tools carried by the farm folk at the Thanksgiving harvest festival Hardwicke Rawnsley had organized at Wray in 1882. Most of Potter's art was never far removed from the everyday and the commonplace. Decoration, design and architecture fascinated her as expressions derivative of forms found in nature. Although Beatrix frequently disparages John Ruskin in her journal, his insistence on close observation of nature was also the hallmark of her best work.[59]

In the spring of 1895 Beatrix records going twice to Burlington House in London to see an exhibit of 'things from Silchester'. The excavations of the Roman settlement near the present-day town of Reading had unearthed coins and a good deal of figured Samian pottery. Some was decorated with an attractive running-scroll pattern. Other pieces had unusual human figures similar to those she had seen on pottery shards from the Bucklesbury dig. These she also rendered in exquisite dry-brush technique, highlighting the texture as well as the design.[60]

Although quarrymen made her nervous, quarries were nature's fossil museums. On holiday at Holehird at Windermere in 1895, she bravely climbed Nanny Lane above the village of Troutbeck to collect coral fossils from the Applethwaite beds and at Sour Howes quarry. Two paintings of the coral fossils found at Applethwaite are examples of her extraordinary ability to show dimension, mass and texture. Blessed with an exacting eye and excellent vision, Beatrix painted the beauty of nature unadorned, but her final product is always softened by the aesthetic arrangement on the page.

Beatrix valued fossils primarily as interesting collections, rather than as objects for systematic study, but she wanted to identify what she found. She wondered once, after a frustrating day in the Natural History Museum, whether 'geology names the fossils or the fossils geology'. In July 1895 she spent some time with Mrs Hutton's friend, the elderly fossil enthusiast Mr Lucy, showing him her fossils and her Roman paintings. Beatrix wanted 'nothing but a little encourage-ment', but Lucy was interested only in theoretical problems. He admired her drawings, but admonished her to be more selective in her collecting; advice she rejected outright, defending her catholic taste. 'I do not feel under any obligation to confine my attention to a particular formation . . . I beg to state I intend to pick up everything I find which is not too heavy.' But after clambering about in a potentially unstable quarry in Swanage a year later, she decided it was 'better not to expect or worry much about geology . . .'[61]

Beatrix Potter could have become expert in any number of fields of natural science: archaeology, botany, ornithology, mycology, geology or entomology; each held a certain fascination for her. Of all the Victorian passions for natural history, only astronomy failed to attract her, though in Swanage she had been fascinated by the brief flight of a night-time meteor. 'I was much impressed by it,' she wrote, 'a strange visitor from the outside of the world. I do not often consider the stars, they give me a *tissick* [make me breathless]. It is more than enough that there should be forty thousand named and classified funguses.' In describing the meteor's appearance she showed an understanding of the basic laws of physics and both its practical and impractical applications. 'Force', she wrote, 'is said to be interminable. I sometimes reflect what may happen when Peter Rabbit stamps, which is one of the most energetic manifestations of insignificance which has come under my notice.' She was always fascinated with how things worked and how the specific fitted into the greater whole, crossing academic disciplines with total abandon. In a proclamation of exemplary Victorian self-confidence, she wrote in 1896: 'With opportunity the world is very interesting.'[62]

Beatrix's skills as a scientific illustrator were given surprising employment in late 1895 when she accepted an unusual commission for twelve entomological lithographs to accompany the science lectures at Morley Memorial College for Working Men and Women, then established in the Victoria Theatre (the Old Vic) in a seamy section of the Waterloo Road. The commission came from Caroline Martineau, then the principal of the school, herself a scientist and the author of several science books for children, who had heard of Beatrix's artistic abilities through her cousin James. Beatrix had rushed to judgement when she had first been introduced to Constance and Caroline Martineau as an 18-year-old. Then she had accompanied her father to visit his old mentor, the Unitarian theologian James Martineau, at his Gordon Square home in Bloomsbury and described Martineau's spinster cousins as 'dry and acid to a degree, which is at once startling and amusing'. But time and maturity had altered her opinion. The commission associated her with two remarkable social activists.[63]

Caroline was a close friend and associate of Emma Cons, an enterprising reformer who had founded the community restoration project in the old theatre as the Royal Victoria Hall and Coffee Tavern. By 1889, it had expanded into a part-time educational institution for working men and women. Emma Cons and Caroline Martineau had both been valued lieutenants for the housing reformer Octavia Hill, and both were members of an important group of social activists that gathered loosely around the Christian socialist theologian F. D. Maurice, and P. H. Wicksteed, the pastor at Little Portland Street Chapel, which two generations of Potters had attended. Beatrix's talents as a science illustrator had been noticed among the Unitarian community. Her commission came out of Caroline's desire to provide accurate illustrations of insect anatomy to accompany the college entomology lectures.[64]

Beatrix appears to have begun work on the lithographs in the autumn of 1895, for the following January she reports studying the entomological 'Index' at the National History Museum and looking at the cases of identified insects, 'being in want of advice' about labels. Once again she was thoroughly frustrated with the museum. 'I worked into indignation about that August Institution. It is the quietest place I know – and the most awkward. They have reached such a pitch of propriety that one cannot ask the simplest question . . . The clerks seem to be all gentlemen and one must not speak to them. If people are forward I can manage them, but if they take the line of being shocked it is perfectly awful to a shy person.' Ultimately she concluded that 'the insect-case is nothing but labels and contrasts . . . an extreme example of museum labelling run mad'. Nothing there could help her design a set of integrated drawings. By June 1896 Beatrix had selected the firm of West, Newman at Hatton Garden to produce the lithographs and took Bertram, who was keenly interested in the project, along with her. She also consulted her former art teacher Miss Cameron. In the end, Beatrix doubted whether her lithographs would be of any educational value.[65]

Two surviving lithographs show various anatomical details of a single insect. One illustrates the anatomy of a privet hawk moth: caterpillar, chrysalis, magnified wing scales, and details of the head and legs; the other is a highly magnified sheet web spider, a *Linyphia triangularis*. In both, different body parts are designated by letters and the levels of magnification are indicated. These extraordinarily effective scientific illustrations reveal that by 1896 Beatrix's horizons had expanded both scientifically and socially. She was conversant about printing and publishing establishments, and her abilities as an illustrator were more widely appreciated than her journal suggests. It is also clear that by the mid-1890s she knew curators in various departments in both the British Museum and the Natural History Museum, had engaged them in conversation and had opinions about their expertise, and that they, in turn, had noticed her artistic ability.[66]

Through the Potters' Unitarian circle Beatrix had also been introduced to Sir William Flower, the director of the Natural History Museum, whom her voluble father engaged in conversation at social occasions at the Pagets, though he had not thought to include his daughter. Initially Beatrix hoped to speak to Flower about her lithographs, as he was a physiologist. She was both irritated and depressed when she failed to get him to recognize her at the museum, and even at the Pagets he did not speak to her. After an ignominious evening there she wrote, 'I wonder if people know the pleasure they may give a person by a little notice. Not that I think that Sir W. Flower is very [un]kind, but absent minded. He knows me occasionally, but generally not at the Museum, and I always thought perhaps if I happened to meet him at the Paget's he would speak to me. Must confess to crying after I got home, my father being as usual deplorable.'[67]

Rosalind Paget suggested that Flower's failure to recognize Beatrix at the museum was not indicative of his absent-mindedness, but because she had on a hat. But Beatrix apparently missed her point. Flower was an outspoken conservationist and vehemently against the use of feathers in millinery. He had embarked on a campaign for the conservation of rare birds and Beatrix's bonnet was undoubtedly stylishly decorated with feathers. 'I should like to know what is Sir W. Flower's subject besides ladies' bonnets,' Beatrix wrote in frustration, unaware of her offence.[68]

It may also have been through the Pagets that Beatrix met Dr Henry Woodward, the leading authority on the Palaeozoic period, who was Keeper of Geology at the British Museum and editor of the *Geological Magazine*. Woodward, who had four daughters of his own, was more approachable than Flower. Whether or not the two families knew each other at this time, it was undoubtedly Dr Woodward that Beatrix sought out at the museum to help identify her fossils.[69]

Sometime around 1894, she met Woodward's daughter Gertrude, also an artist and scientific illustrator, who was employed part-time at the museum where she drew palaeontological specimens for the museum's catalogue and for her father's many publications. Gertrude was roughly five years older than Beatrix, but the two women had much in common and became good friends. Gertrude and Beatrix met quite often at the museum during this period when Beatrix was busily drawing fossils. Gertrude introduced her to her younger sister Alice, also a watercolourist, who had once done scientific renderings, but by 1894 was a successful children's book illustrator. Given their mutual interests in art, story and publishing, it is unimaginable that children's books, printers, publishers, paper, paints and techniques of scientific illustration were not topics of conversation whenever Beatrix and the Woodward sisters were together.[70]

Perhaps with Alice's success in mind, in May 1894 Beatrix offered some illustrations for a booklet, 'A Frog he would a-fishing go', to the firm of fine art printers, Ernest Nister, who had bought a few of her earlier drawings. They were loosely taken from her September 1893 picture letter to Eric Moore about a frog named Jeremy Fisher. Beatrix thought they could be put in a booklet, but was told 'people do not want frogs now'. However, the firm offered to buy the frogs and several miscellaneous drawings, just in case. Beatrix accepted their offer for the single drawings, but stood firm on a price of 25*s*. for the frog group. When Nister continued to bargain, she asked for the return of her artwork. Both parties compromised, but Beatrix succeeded in getting her price of 22*s*. 6*d* for nine frog drawings. Ultimately they were published to illustrate a set of verses by someone else in one of Nister's Children's Annuals called *Comical Customers*.[71]

Throughout the summer holidays of 1895 and 1896 in the Lake District, Beatrix was absorbed in her study of fungi. She was both drawing and photographing them, adding to her growing visual catalogue of various genera and species. Hampers and paintings were posted to Charlie McIntosh in Inver and letters were exchanged regarding identification, environmental conditions and site locations. In 1896 alone, Beatrix made fifty-two fungi drawings, and an increasing number of microscopic studies. Exactly what she planned to do with her fungi paintings at this point is unclear, although her botanical recording alone was both a sufficient and worthwhile objective. She may have had in mind painting a representative sample of fungi, but her collecting and painting was by no means systematic. But certainly she hoped for a practical outcome, perhaps illustrating booklets or even a text on mycology, should she discover some publisher who would buy them. Having money of her own had become increasingly important, both as a symbol of self-worth and as a measure of economic independence. Shortly before a particularly bleak Christmas in 1895 she wrote: 'One must make out some way. It is something to have a little money to spend on books and to look forward to being independent, though forlorn.'[72]

But sometime between the wet summer of 1895 at Holehird on Windermere and the spring of 1896, Beatrix ceased being interested in fungi solely as an aesthetic pursuit. She had gathered young forms of the *Boletus granulatus* in a wood of 'scotch fir and larch', noting in her letter to McIntosh, who was studying the source of the larch canker, that they were 'very slimy & had yellowish milky drops on the spores and stem'. Using her new microscope, she drew the spores of toadstools that formed on tiny club-shaped cells called *basidia*. Could these spores germinate, she wondered? How did they live over the winter, and in what form did they reappear? Few mycologists at the time had given that question any thought. Beatrix speculated that the spores must germinate. Investigating that premise, she quietly

made the transition from collector and illustrator to amateur mycologist. Once again she needed a mentor, and, in particular, she needed
to talk to the mycologists at Kew.[73]

5

~~ *Discoveries* ~~

THE ROYAL BOTANIC GARDENS AT Kew, or 'Imperial Kew', as it was known in some Victorian circles, was not then a garden where the public was welcome to admire floral displays, ponder rare cycads, or stroll the winding paths of a historical landscape. Indeed the public was barely tolerated within Kew's gates, and admitted only on specific days and for limited times. Kew was then, and is now, primarily a scientific institution dedicated to research in taxonomy, anatomy, cytology and conservation. It was then, but is no longer, an enthusiastic agent of imperial expansion, central to discovering and developing the natural resources of the Empire. Kew's directors since its founding in 1841 understood their mission was not only to further botanical research, but also to shape commerce through the acquisition and propagation of economically viable crops.[1]

Throughout the nineteenth century, as the world's environment deteriorated, an increasingly large part of Kew's resources went to documenting existing plants, reducing the rate of their destruction, conserving what they could. Although Kew botanists were by mid-century part of the upper echelon of the English science establishment – which included the British Museum, the Natural History Museum and, to a lesser extent, the Oxford–Cambridge university axis – Kew's pragmatic usefulness to the Empire set it apart. The professionals at Kew moved in a different political orbit from the others. By the end of the century, both the new science of botany and the professionals who directed the economy in plants were resident at Kew.[2]

Kew's professional staff was a tight circle of scientists, related by family and patronage. William Turner Thiselton-Dyer assumed the directorship in 1885. An expert on the tropical plants of Africa, he promoted research in plant physiology and pathology and strength-

ened the Gardens' importance to the Empire. He turned the languish-
ing Jodrell Laboratory at Kew into the best botanical laboratory in
Europe. In his spare moments, Thiselton-Dyer indulged a penchant
for landscaping at Kew that included chivvying the Princess Royal
off the grass when necessary. Scholars wishing to do research at Kew
made application to the director's office for a ticket of admission.
These were given for specific periods or for specific projects. Student
research tickets to the Library and Herbarium were also available for
limited periods upon recommendation from two scientists of standing,
and approval of the director.[3]

Thiselton-Dyer (he began hyphenating his name in 1891) was also
the first director to have a degree from Oxford. His ambition was
nothing less than to 'reorder the British system of colonial botanic
gardens' and to make Kew the centre of the 'new botany' in service
to a reinvigorated imperialism. He was a slight man, with a thin face,
prematurely white hair, a small moustache and goatee, and the manner
of a martinet. Very much an authoritarian and an autocrat in style
and personality, he favoured uniforms for the staff as a mark of
professional status and a means of imposing order. He even had an
inspector's uniform made for himself with epaulets, gold buttons, and
a gold-crested military-style hat. The journeymen-gardeners were
compelled to wear blue serge suits with grey flannel shirts and turned-
down collars. The garden staff included three women, recruited
under pressure in 1896 from the Horticultural College for Women at
Swanley in Kent, who were compelled to labour in brown knickerbockers, woollen stockings, waistcoat, jacket and peaked cap, a
costume guaranteed not to distract their male colleagues.[4]

The other important player in the interlocking world of Victorian
botanical science was the Linnean Society of London, the premier
society for the promotion of natural history. It was founded in 1788
as the repository for the collection of the great Swedish naturalist
Linnaeus, and occupied the handsome Burlington House in Mayfair.
The Linnean was the first specialist scientific learned society founded
after the Royal Society. Its mandate included maintaining a research
library, holding meetings to benefit its elected fellows, and publishing
scholarly papers. It attempted to hold the amateur naturalist, the

gentleman scholar and the emerging professional in a social institution promoting their common interests.[5]

Society protocol was strictly observed. Until 1904 all scholarly papers were delivered to the president, who, in turn, laid them before the elected fellows to decide which should be presented at the general meeting of members and invited guests. Customarily, invited papers were read by the general secretary of the Society, or sometimes the president, who exercised the right to edit those papers as he saw fit. A summary or short précis was then laid before the membership to be read and commented upon by those who were interested in the topic. The decision to publish a paper was made by the Council of Fellows after comments were received from the membership and two designated referees. Very few of the papers that were read at meetings were ever published. Society meetings were held strictly to one hour, and usually no more than one paper would be presented. Frequently meetings also included a brief presentation of exhibits or the demonstration of experiments. Membership of the Linnean was exclusively male, and only men were allowed to attend meetings, to have access to the library or to subscribe to Society publications. Although the question of the admission of women was raised periodically, it had almost no support until 1905 when women were reluctantly allowed to become members.[6]

Through a combination of cultural and political forces coalescing at the end of the nineteenth century, these elitist institutions of learning increasingly defined themselves as organizations exclusively for the promotion of the professional scientist. The professionalization of science in general, and of the natural sciences in particular, was part of an effort to exclude those without formal education, and to elevate a scientific elite. Amateurs and those generalists without degrees or formal training, particularly women, were increasingly excluded from this new scientific dialogue.[7]

These trends filtered down to public places such as museums, zoos and gardens where natural science was displayed. Department heads, known as 'keepers', within museums like the Natural History Museum, the British Museum and at Kew jealously guarded their increasingly specialized turf. Beatrix Potter broke in upon this swirling amalgam of scientific change, redefinition, elitism and misogyny; a naive, curious, but determined amateur mycologist intent on gaining a hearing for her theories of symbiosis and hybridization. Considering the success that other women botanists had enjoyed in both illustration and publishing before her, Beatrix's experience raises questions that are at least as much to do with gender and the politics of professionalism as with the merits of her scientific experiments or the presentation of her theories.[8]

During the autumn and winter of 1895 Beatrix spent an increasing amount of time drawing fungi under the microscope. Her objectives had changed from simply assembling a collection of watercolours and photographs to discovering how fungi reproduced. Certain that she could germinate some spores herself, she wanted to study the environment in which they germinated, discover whether or not conditions were the same for each species, what the spawn of each consisted of, and whether or not she could reproduce it more than once. She never articulated a final purpose for her experiments, other than the pleasure of discovery.

Initially Beatrix had wanted to go to the Royal Botanic Gardens at Kew to speak with someone about the classification of some fungi that puzzled her. Frustrated with the lack of expertise displayed by George Murray, the Keeper of Botany at the museum, she sought someone who knew more. By 1896, however, her confidence was such that she wanted specifically to ask the Kew cryptogamist and Principal Assistant of the Herbarium, George Massee, if he knew how fungi reproduced and, more importantly, if he had ever germinated the spores of any of the higher fungi himself. But in order to get an appointment with Massee, she needed a recommendation from a well-known scientist, and a student ticket.[9]

It is curious that after so many years of research and drawing at the Natural History Museum no one on the staff had offered to provide her with the recommendation for Kew, or that Beatrix had not herself asked either Murray or the librarian in the botany department, Miss Annie Lorraine Smith, who was herself interested in mycology, particularly lichens. Either one could have easily put her name forward. Clearly this favour was one Beatrix would have asked of Sir William Flower if she had ever been successful in speaking with him. She felt the museum atmosphere intellectually stifling, and she was admittedly shy about initiating conversation, but she did not seem to know how to go about it. 'I wonder why I never seem to know people,' she wrote, not long after being rebuffed by Flower. 'It makes one wonder whether one is presentable. It strikes me it is the way to make one not.' As a consequence Beatrix was forced to seek a sponsor and references elsewhere.[10]

The most logical person to effect her desire for a student ticket was her distinguished uncle, the chemist Sir Henry Enfield Roscoe. Now retired from parliament, Roscoe had been named Vice Chancellor of the University of London, and was busy supervising important new research in public sanitation at the Lister Institute. Although Roscoe was not himself a botanist, he came from a family of renowned botanists and botanical artists. His grandfather, William Roscoe, among other accomplishments, was the first president of the Liverpool Royal Institution, a founder and promoter of the Liverpool Botanical Garden, and, like Edmund Potter, a merchant patron of the arts and sciences. He was also the author of a renowned volume of botanical illustration, *Monandrian Plants of the Order Scitamineae* (1824–9), and the author of the popular children's verse, *The Butterfly's Ball and the Grasshopper's Feast* (1807), which Beatrix admired. It is hard to imagine she was not also familiar with the elder Roscoe's botanical work, as his biography had been in the Leech library at Gorse Hall.[11]

Uncle Harry, as he was known, quite naturally took an interest in Beatrix's scientific painting just as he had taken pleasure at her earlier efforts at selling her holiday cards. She had asked her uncle about getting a ticket to Kew several times, but Roscoe, however well intentioned, was busy. In February 1896, when Rupert was stricken with kidney stones, an ailment that he had endured for some years, and which required quantities of morphine to relieve, Roscoe called on him almost daily. So when Uncle Harry was laid up with the gout late that same month, Beatrix returned the kindness, and once again asked for a recommendation to Kew. Afterwards she wrote in happy anticipation, 'Says I, he will give me a note to Mr Thiselton-Dyer.' But once again, Roscoe forgot.[12]

In March, however, Uncle Harry invited the Potters to visit his country home, Woodcote, a rather remote estate but in pretty country near Horsley in Surrey. Beatrix was enormously pleased as she had not been invited there before. 'To Woodcote,' she wrote, 'to stay with the Roscoes, which I enjoyed much, being splendid weather and the visit too short for friction.' While at Woodcote, Beatrix found the exotic-looking black fungus known as witches' butter (*Exidia glandulosa*) on a dead piece of log encrusted with lichens, and made a painting of it. In this congenial setting she also made several microscopic drawings, and enjoyed discussing microscopy with Uncle Harry, who advised her on laboratory techniques and gave her equipment not easily available to the amateur. Beatrix found Woodcote a conducive place in which to work, and looked forward to returning.[13]

Finally, in May, after another house call on Rupert, Roscoe had a 'sudden fit of kindness of conscience' and proposed taking Beatrix to Kew himself the following day to see the director. The next morning the two set out by train for Kew where Beatrix intended both to get a student research ticket and to show the director her drawings. 'I think he [Uncle Harry] rather wanted to see Mr Thiselton-Dyer,' Beatrix wrote later, 'but he was most exceeding kind.'[14]

The enterprise was burdened by poor choices from the outset. Beatrix, an amateur who had never contributed so much as a note to a botanical journal, belonged to no field-club, and was totally unknown to the Kew Herbarium staff, began her quest for information at the top: a move not conducive to enthusiastic response from the professional staff. Moreover, she came on the arm of Sir Henry, one of the most highly regarded of British scientists, but a man not without significant political and scientific enemies, who was undoubtedly oblivious to the adverse effect his sponsorship might have on his niece's desire for an objective assessment of her research. All Beatrix wanted was a student ticket so that she could look at materials in the Herbarium, and time to show her illustrations of the germination of the spores of the agarics to Massee. But as Sir Henry's niece and protégée, Beatrix was presented as no ordinary student. Roscoe introduced her to five of the most important botanists at Kew, one of whom Beatrix describes looking as if he had 'been dried in blotting paper under a press', before finally finding Massee.[15]

Beatrix thought George Massee a 'very pleasant, kind gentleman, who seemed to like my drawings'. He was an attractive man with soft, open features and masses of dark curly hair, who had been the first president of the British Mycological Society and was now second in command of the Herbarium. He was a protégé of the prolific cryptogamic botanist and contributor to *Science-Gossip*, M. C. Cooke, and had been somewhat tainted by that association after Cooke fell out of favour at Kew. Massee was naturally something of a rebel and a romantic. His appraisal of Beatrix's drawings must have been cursory, for she reports no other comment than a polite one.[16]

Beatrix and Uncle Harry returned to the director's office where Thiselton-Dyer received them. Beatrix described him as 'a thin, elderly gentleman in summery attire, with a dry, cynical manner, puffing a cigarette, but wide awake and boastful'. She showed him her drawings and thought he was 'pleased' with them, though she did notice that he was 'a little surprised', but he made no substantive comment. He authorized her student ticket, after which he proceeded to ignore her completely. Since Uncle Harry was suddenly afraid they would miss the train, the three marched off across the Gardens to the station, Roscoe and Thiselton-Dyer in the lead, talking animatedly, while Beatrix trailed behind, indulging in a forgotten peppermint, noticing as she tagged along two of the young women gardeners in 'knickerbockers tying up flowers'.[17]

Beatrix later insisted that she was not resentful that the director did not speak more to her, since she was already tired, but took satisfaction when she 'shot in one remark which made him jump, as if they had forgotten my presence'. They had, of course. Although she was then near her thirtieth birthday, a fully mature woman who had brought scientific drawings to discuss, she got the 'amusing feeling of being regarded as young'.[18]

Beatrix's version of events is a notable exercise in Victorian denial. Her coded account gives the impression that she passively acquiesced in the gentlemen's dismissal of her, as well as in their trivialization of her scientific drawings. She had most assuredly been ignored, but she had also been patronized and infantilized. Her response had been to assume the typical Victorian air of frailty, a sort of instant neurasthenia. Her written account focuses on the little victories of the outing: she had been introduced at 'Imperial Kew', and she had acquired a coveted student ticket! 'I got home without collapse,' she wrote, 'a most interesting morning'.[19]

A month later, Beatrix returned to Kew on her own, specifically to see Massee. She was aware of his diminished reputation, noting that 'it is rather the fashion to make fun of him', an attitude she could only have picked up from the staff at the Natural History Museum, but she thought it refreshing to have a conversation with anyone who has ideas, 'even if they are not founded on very sufficient evidence'. She found Massee enthusiastic about the 'funguses he was growing in little glass covers'. He boasted to her 'that one of them had spores three inches long'. Beatrix found his experiment inconsequential, but not his effort or dedication, writing: 'I opine that he has passed several stages of development into a fungus himself – I am occasionally conscious of a similar transformation.'[20]

On 26 June Beatrix returned to Kew again to show Massee more drawings. He suggested that she confine herself to examining one division of fungi, and recommended the *peʒiʒas*, or cup fungi, as they had not been drawn as much as the agarics. It was good advice, but given for the wrong reason as neither Massee nor Beatrix knew then that the agarics were among the most difficult and unpredictable division to germinate, a quality much lamented by later mycologists.

Talking with Massee at Kew was far preferable to working with the reticent staff at the museum, but Beatrix continued to go there to work on the insect lithographs she was making for Morley College. The printing was going well, but her drawing was impeded by the inability of the entomologists to give her any real assistance. Beatrix judged them not even 'half sharp', and provided a classic description of the new breed of museum professional, describing them as 'less well informed than an ordinary person on any subject outside their own, and occasionally to regard it with petulance'. So far, she was unimpressed with the natural science establishment.[21]

The summer of 1896 – the summer Beatrix turned 30 – the Potters spent at the large country house of Lakefield (Eeswyke) on the shore of Esthwaite Water, just outside the village of Near Sawrey. Although it was still too dry to find many fungi around Sawrey, she felt the sensation of pending discovery when she spied the 'dark hairy stalks and tiny balls of one of the Mycetozoa' on a flat chip of wood. She was working intensely on the problem of germination and had come away with a new Beck's microscope with 600 × magnification and a new camera. When the rains came, bringing up even more fungi, Beatrix was ready for them.[22]

She wrote to Charlie McIntosh from Lakefield in late August asking him to send any large *pezizas* he could find. McIntosh evidently complied, as there are over thirty drawings of cup fungi extant from this summer holiday. Beatrix was successfully germinating spores by then and, with all the confidence of the expert that she now was, she noted in her journal dispassionately, 'The larch peziza came into flower. I took it very calmly being so firmly persuaded it would come.'[23]

Four days later she made a study of one cup fungus, the *Pocolum* species on the petioles of oak leaves, and another on driftwood near Esthwaite Water. She drew these under a microscope, clearly showing the cylindrical cases containing the spores. That night she reported, 'Had further ideas about fungi. It stands to reason, all such as grow on fresh manure for a few weeks in summer must have some other form to take them over the winter months.' She now surmised that fungi with fruiting bodies, like mushrooms and toadstools, must have some sort of underground form. Beatrix showed something of her intellectual métier, continuing: '(I have much pleasure in contradicting Mr G. Murray re *Ascobolus*, whether I grow it or not, I stick to it.)' It was clear to her that this underground form must be the means by which fungi 'get from log to log without cups to spore'. Beatrix hypothesized that 'all the higher fungi have probably a mould', and that if there were individual moulds, all of which could be sprouted with time and patience, there were 'enormously more moulds than have been specified'.[24]

Undoubtedly she shared her observations with McIntosh, as well as the fact that she was successfully growing this underground form, the mycelium. She was so engrossed in her research and in the safe transportation of her 'precious fungi' back to London at the beginning of October that she barely recalled the journey. Similarly she had to force herself out of her preoccupation with fungi to enjoy a brief visit to the Huttons at Stroud, noting only that the beautiful Caroline did not have a particularly fine singing voice: 'The Gods do not give all their gifts to one.'[25]

Before she left Sawrey, Beatrix wrote to Roscoe telling him about her theories of fungi reproduction, clearly anxious to show him her drawings. Aunt Lucy obligingly invited Beatrix to Woodcote for the weekend where she could have her uncle's undivided attention. Afraid that her parents would object, Beatrix 'escaped out of the house' quite early and walked up and down the street in front of the Roscoes' home in Bramham Gardens until the household was awake. On the train to Surrey, Beatrix explained her theories, trying to make Uncle Harry aware of their novelty and asking his advice as to how to approach the botanists at Kew to discover if anyone there had managed to germinate the spores of the gill fungi as she had. Although Roscoe was rather slow to understand exactly how novel her theories were, he realized her need to know if anyone at Kew had done it. He 'invented a fishing letter' to Massee asking for a reference to anyone else who might have been cultivating spores. 'He was not sanguine,' Beatrix reported, but she copied out the letter as instructed. Roscoe also wisely counselled his protégée to make sure she knew the literature on the subject, since 'you have to discover a great deal that has been done before, before you find anything new'.[26]

In two days she had a reply from Massee referring her to Oskar Brefeld's daunting twelve-volume study, *Botanische Untersuchungen über Schimmelpilze* (1872–96). Beatrix knew about Brefeld's work, but had not read it. The thought of doing so nearly 'annihilated her', but she was, after all, fluent in German, as was Roscoe, and by bedtime she had found humour in the prospect of finding out what the Germans had done.[27]

The next morning she went off with her pony to Kew 'in a state of damp resignation'. But it took only minutes to discover that 'Massee knew very little about it'. Under her questioning, Massee admitted that he did not think Brefeld had grown the mushroom mould. Massee was, however, clearly sceptical about what Beatrix's slides actually showed, and, knowing that she was an amateur working in less than ideal conditions, disputed her conclusions on that basis. Beatrix dismissed his concerns, certain that she could germinate the spores again, and confessed, 'I contradicted him badly.'[28]

Roscoe was delighted with Beatrix's account of the meeting. But as far as Beatrix was concerned, he became much too hopeful. Roscoe now understood that some important scientific points were at stake and relished the thought of disparaging the haughty Thiselton-Dyer. 'He is under the delusion no one has grown them except me and Dr Brefeld,' Beatrix wrote, feigning humility because she too had the same notion. Roscoe now urged her to write up her findings as a paper for the botanists at Kew.[29]

Beatrix realized that the kitchen of Bolton Gardens was not an ideal environment for germinating spores, nor as free of contaminates as a proper laboratory. In an effort to eliminate contamination as the basis for Massee's scepticism, she called at the Society of Preventive Medicine on Great Russell Street in Bloomsbury to ask for help from Uncle Harry's former associate, the chemist, Joseph Lunt. An assistant there showed her the best techniques for making sterile slides and probably suggested the nutrient formula which she subsequently used as a medium. After her best ⅙th inch lens had rolled off the table into the hearth, she went to R. & J. Beck, the store in Cornhill in the City which specialized in fine optics, and bought a new ⅛th inch lens to draw the germinating spores. Following Roscoe's direction, she then spent the week writing out her findings and got them typed up. On 3 December she went again to Kew, firmly intending to deliver them to Thiselton-Dyer in person.[30]

In her letter to the director, Beatrix explained that her uncle wished him to look at some of her fungi drawings, and hoped he might read her paper. The text of Beatrix's letter is important in understanding what happened next. It is unclear whether she left the letter and paper before she had an anxiety attack and bolted, or if she brought them back to Kew several days later. Presumably Roscoe either wrote the letter himself or offered the language, but Beatrix concurred in its content.

Sir H. Roscoe sent me to ask whether you would be kind enough to look at some of my fungus drawings which he is interested in. I do not quite like to give the paper to Mr Massee because I am afraid I have rather contradicted him. Uncle Harry is satisfied with my way of working but we wish very much that someone would take it up at Kew to try it, if they do not believe my drawings. Mr Massee took objection to my slides, but the things exist, and will be all done by the Germans. It is rather a long paper to ask you to be kind enough to read.[31]

Regardless of what Beatrix's drawings demonstrated, the issue was now taken between Sir Henry and Thiselton-Dyer and his staff at Kew. The unfortunately worded and politically inept letter slighted Massee, appealed over his head to the director, and challenged science at Kew. Roscoe, the chemist, is 'satisfied' with his niece's botanical slides, and Potter, the amateur, has contradicted Massee, the professional. As if this were not offence enough, the letter impugns English botanists by suggesting that the far-sighted Germans, like the famed chemist R. W. Bunsen with whom Roscoe had worked in Heidelberg, will inevitably prove her theory correct. The professionals at Kew were put on notice by an amateur investigator. Sadly, the worth of her subsequent work had little to do with the ensuing scientific storm.[32]

According to her own account, Beatrix got to the director's office, where she waited uncomfortably for about fifteen minutes, intimidated by Mr Baker's curious glances, and then, overcome with shyness, she 'incontinently fled'. She realized that she had lost an important opportunity at Kew, admitting: 'I am sorry I had not courage to face the Director, it was very warm and draggly.' But her confidence had been undermined even before she set out for Kew that morning. 'I wish I had not showed it to my parents,' she confided. 'He [her father] went through it with a pencil, making remarks upon the grammar. He has bought me that very expensive book [Brefeld] which I have not opened because I wanted to tell Mr Thiselton-Dyer I have not read it. Also I am sure it will put me out in invention.' Undoubtedly Rupert was trying to improve his daughter's project, both by buying her the Brefeld volumes and editing her paper, but his timing was poor. Her parents were aware of what she was about at Kew, and at least tacitly approved her research, without understanding its importance.[33]

Beatrix's failure of nerve is all the more unfortunate because several days earlier she records that she has 'found the idea of the lichens' and had 'another IDEA(?) about hybrids'. Beatrix's use of the term 'lichens' is important, for clearly she was now confident that there could be many kinds of moulds. Some produced a lichen which she believed was a hybrid: a dual organism composed of a fungus and an alga, and that there could be many forms of this hybrid. Beatrix also speculated that a symbiotic relationship necessarily existed between them.[34]

Most nineteenth-century botanists dismissed lichens as Linnaeus had, as 'poor peasants of the plant world'; lower plants that were thought to be either simple mosses or unusual fungi. Only the Swiss botanist Simon Schwendener thought otherwise. In 1869 he proposed a 'dual hypothesis', suggesting from his study of the taxonomy of lichens that they were all hybrids, composed of a liaison between a fungus and an alga, except that he believed one was a parasite on the other. Most botanists treated Schwendener's theory with contempt, thinking it impossible that a hybrid organism could function as an integrated whole. At the time Beatrix was experimenting, calling a botanist a 'Schwendenerist' was a term of abuse and derision.

Hybridization was, in fact, the subject of fierce debate by the end of the century. Most English botanists scoffed at the idea of a 'useful and invigorating parasitism'. Even M. C. Cooke, Massee's mentor, had only derision for such a suggestion. Beatrix, who had read at least some of Schwendener, was not entirely convinced, doubting that one organism was parasitic. Although she did not know how stable hybrids might be, she suspected they existed as complete and independent organisms.[35]

On 7 December Beatrix found new courage. She returned to Kew prepared to stay as long as necessary. She was again kept waiting. While the clerks worked around her, she read the newspaper. The director finally 'bounced in, very dree he was, and in a great hurry', clearly prepared to dismiss her at the soonest possible moment. He must have been taken somewhat aback by her energetic exposition of her findings. 'I was not shy, not at all,' she wrote. 'I had it up and down with him. His line was on the outside edge of civil, but I took it philosophically.' Thiselton-Dyer patronized her, indicating that the subject was 'profound', but her opinions inconsequential; 'mares' nests', he pejoratively called them. Dismissing her drawings without even looking at them, he tried to pass her off to Henry Marshall Ward, the newly appointed Professor of Botany at Cambridge. Beatrix was furious. 'I informed him that it would all be in the books in ten years, whether or no, and departed giggling.'[36]

In high colour after this encounter, Beatrix marched over to the Herbarium ready to take on Massee, only to find to her astonishment that he 'had come round altogether and was prepared to believe my new thing, including Lichens'. He was trying quite 'ineffectually' to grow *Bulgaria inquinans*. Taking pity on his efforts, Beatrix gave him a slide of *Agaricus velutipes* that she had successfully germinated many times. With extraordinary perceptiveness on the consequences of professional specialization which had led to this moment, Beatrix concluded, 'I don't think he has a completely clear head . . . but it is extraordinary how botanists have niggled at a few isolated species and not in the least seen the broad bearings of it. He would never have found out the bearings of the lichen.' Massee, however, was clear-headed enough to caution Beatrix not to talk about her discovery until she had it worked out with more samples. Potter's encounters at Kew, first with Thiselton-Dyer, then with Massee, constituted not only a personal triumph, but a valid challenge by an amateur generalist to the insularity of the professional specialist. It testified to her intellectual fortitude as well as her scientific achievement.[37]

When Beatrix saw Uncle Harry at the end of the week he was waving a letter from Thiselton-Dyer which he described as '*rude* and *stupid*', and which he refused to let her read, calling the director 'a little rough-spoken'. Beatrix feigned innocence as to why the director would have been offended by her visit. But she was probably correct in surmising that his letter 'contained advice that I should be sent to school before I began to teach other people'. In her view the director was 'a short-tempered, clever man with a very good opinion of his Establishment, and jealous of outsiders'. But it is hard to believe that she was so naive as to assume that Thiselton-Dyer would be happy to have such information as she attempted to deliver or to imagine he was obligated to consider her findings without denigrating them. Yet she seems unaware of just how audacious she had been. She had stood up to Thiselton-Dyer and in essence told him that his views, and those of his staff, were not only incorrect, but would be publicly ridiculed in time. There would be consequences.[38]

Sir Henry Roscoe was as stubborn and as quick to take offence as Thiselton-Dyer, though not as pompous or autocratic. He was annoyed that his protégée and her research had been given such a rude and cursory hearing by the likes of a mere agricultural botanist. Roscoe questioned his niece closely about her experiments and the import of her conclusions, asking her repeatedly if she was '*quite* sure'. Beatrix was impressed that he took the time and trouble to understand exactly what she had discovered and why it was significant, and did her best to answer his questions. She grasped some of the politics involved, but probably did not appreciate the political capital Roscoe would risk on her behalf when he promised 'he would see it through'. 'It [Thiselton-Dyer's letter] was the very luckiest thing that could have happened,' she wrote later, 'for uncle Harry was just sufficiently annoyed at the slighting of anything under his patronage to make him take it up all the harder.'[39]

Since the experts at Kew had seen fit to dismiss her conclusions, Roscoe's plan was to offer them to a wider audience, no less than the Linnean Society of London. Confessing to an attack of 'flightiness', a façade of amusement Beatrix often employed to hide her anxiety, she realized the turn of events cast her and her research in a central role. It is likely that this was more than she had bargained for. Leaving Uncle Harry to his plotting, she went to her Hutton cousins in Putney Park to gather a new quantity of fungi. But she also diplomatically sent two slides of *Bulgaria inquinans* to Massee, hoping he would share them with the director, and silently prayed that her precious student ticket would not be revoked because of her insubordinate behaviour.[40]

Christmas morning 1896 found Beatrix at Bramham Gardens refining her paper under Uncle Harry's supervision. Beatrix was impressed that he was taking 'an immense amount of trouble in trying to understand the botanical part, and showing me how to mend my Paper'. She was certain that most fungi were capable of forming a mould, like yeast, which she believed to be a hybrid. She had now read her way through the twelve volumes of Brefeld, who confirmed her theory of germination, but she could not 'discover in his unwieldy volumes' whether he had actually germinated spores himself, or if he was just speculating that it could be done.

Roscoe loaned her Louis Pasteur's volumes explaining the appearance of the mould *penicillium* and *Aspergillus glaucus*, another common mould. Pasteur's experiments were easier to follow, but he did not realize that there were hundreds of moulds, or that some of the fungi would have combined with an alga and hence be distinguished by the presence of chlorophyll. She found Pasteur's work fascinating. 'Brefeld', she observed, 'has a mass of facts . . . and theories which may or may not be correct, but which don't piece on to the experiments however.' And just such a concise, integrated explanation was precisely what Uncle Harry was trying to help Beatrix produce. 'I see what he is trying to teach me in mending mine,' Beatrix wrote after comparing Pasteur to Brefeld. 'Pasteur is all in one piece. Brefeld is as discursive and unstable as – as *Dacromyces deliquescens*.'[41]

Beatrix underestimated just how hard Roscoe would make her work. They spent all Christmas Day together and the day after. Uncle Harry made notes showing her what needed more verification and how the argument should be presented. For someone who had no training in scientific methodology or documentation, the necessary scholarship was daunting. But Beatrix was willing, even enthusiastic about the challenge. 'I cannot sufficiently thank uncle Harry . . .' she wrote. 'I shall keep those pencil marks when I am an old woman.'[42]

For the next month Beatrix worked at her microscope, checking references and refining her argument. Her experiments were not without moments of levity, however. Curious about the fungal properties of dry rot (*Serpula lacrymans*), which McIntosh was also studying, Beatrix had some specimens delivered to Bolton Gardens in a brown paper bag. Realizing her parents would disapprove of such potentially destructive material in the house, she buried it surreptitiously under a stone in the garden until she had time to study it. 'How I should catch it,' she wrote, 'my parents are not devoted to the cause of science.' Indeed few home owners then or now would have welcomed such invasive material. But her interest in the progression of dry rot, the spread of larch canker and the relationship between the appearance of a mould and the proximity of certain species of trees in a forest was also an important observation for forest science and one in advance of most other botanists of her day.[43]

Wanting to make sure that she had not overlooked anything that George Murray at the museum might know about lichens, she took one of hers, albeit an old specimen, to the museum one afternoon to ask him to identify it. After examining it Murray told her it was not a lichen at all, but another jelly-like fungus. Rather than contradict him, Beatrix enquired about his views on Schwendener's theory and why it was that whenever there were lichens, there always seemed to be algae close by. Neither Murray nor Miss Smith was in sympathy with the idea of symbiosis, and Beatrix's suggestion that a symbiotic connection might exist ended the discussion. Beatrix was amused by their reaction, noting Murray's 'contemptuous' attitude toward 'old-fashioned lichenologists'. But she acknowledged her own stubbornness: 'Upon the subject of chlorophyll, and symbiosis I am afraid I am unpleasant.' This visit to the Natural History Museum convinced her that no one else was 'at it'. She was correct, no one was.[44]

Early in January 1897 Beatrix went back to Kew. She was so anxious about the renewal of her research ticket that when she saw the director at a distance, she hid behind a bush. In the Herbarium, however, she discovered that Massee was now growing one of her best moulds. The two had a cordial, but vague, discussion of lichens. The encounter confirmed her suspicion that the Kew botanists were approaching the problem of lichens by way of plant morphology, and that their 'cut and dried' theories prevented them from seeing the thing in a new way. Including Roscoe as a co-conspirator, she wrote: 'We as outsiders express a pleasing, fresh irreverence for the leading botanical authorities, it really does seem very impertinent, but the things are there. It may just be that one sees them because one has an open mind, not in a groove.'[45]

Beatrix and Bertram visited Uncle Harry at Woodcote over the holidays where Roscoe suggested that Professor Ward, the Cambridge botanist, should read her paper even though he might find her thesis as heretical as Thiselton-Dyer had. Roscoe also warned her about the possibility of other scientists 'poaching' her conclusions and submitting them as their own. Beatrix's reaction was naive but generous, for she had come to like Massee. 'I do not in the least suspect that mild gentleman . . .' she wrote, 'but if he casually put them into his books I should wish to have an acknowledgment.'[46]

A few days later Beatrix shared her theory with McIntosh. After asking for some specific fungi, she explained,

I am doing some curious work with fungus spore, trying to draw up a paper with the assistance of my uncle Sir H. Roscoe. Have you ever suspected that there are *intermediate* species amongst *Agarics* and *Boleti*? We are strongly of the opinion for certain good reasons, that there are mixed fungi – that is to say – either growing actually upon a mixed network of mycelium, or else hybrid species which have originated in that way. I do not express any opinion which way, only that they *are* intermediate. Of course such an idea is contrary to the books, except for lichens but I should be curious to hear whether you have had difficulty in naming any of the sorts which I suspect.

She ended her letter asking the question which she should have posed at the outset: 'Do you know anything about lichens?'[47]

McIntosh responded quickly with what must have been a lengthy and important letter on the larch disease. Beatrix replied that she had found the new fungus, the hybrid, again, but that she was frustrated that she did not have enough lichen spores to experiment with. She needed to germinate more spores and to establish chlorophyll lines to prove that a lichen could survive by itself. In all fairness to Beatrix and to Schwendener, the exact nature of the symbiotic relationship remained in doubt for nearly a century more.[48]

Uncle Harry made no further changes in her paper beyond exclaiming that there was one point he could *not* understand. But Beatrix was ready to defend her conclusions. Her last word on Thiselton-Dyer's behaviour was unrepentant. She suspected he was 'something of a misogynist'. Observing the women gardeners at Kew in their ridiculous dress, Beatrix felt that his denigration of her science was not unrelated to her gender. Still smarting from his high-handed treatment, almost the last entry in her journal reads: 'it is odious to a shy person to be snubbed as conceited, especially when the shy person happened to be right, and under the temptation of sauciness.' And with that outspoken opinion, Beatrix Potter's fifteen-year journal ends, but not the controversy over fungi, lichens, hybrids and symbiosis.[49]

Beatrix continued germinating spores of the agarics and studying the resulting moulds over the next six weeks. She kept exact records of the germination process, getting up through the night to check her specimens, and at one period drawing the germinating basidiomycetes spores every six hours at 600 × magnification. Near the end of February McIntosh sent her two parcels; one included some spores of hepatics which Brefeld thought derived from lichens. After germinating some of these, Beatrix summarized what she knew and where she was still in doubt.[50]

The thing which causes so much contradiction is that I succeeded in sprouting the mushroom spore, which I supposed is what it is meant for; but it seems that no one else is admitted to have done it, and therefore no one except my uncle & one gentleman at Kew will believe that any of my slides are right. I have grown between 40 & 50 sorts of spore, but I think we shall probably only send in A. velutipes, which I have grown twice and Mr Massee has also grown according to my direction at Kew . . . I am just as much sure of the mushroom but unless I can get a good slide actually sprouting it seems useless to send it to the Linnean.

More realistic than she had been about the possibility of scientific 'theft', Beatrix cautioned her Scottish mentor, 'I should be obliged if you would *not* mention it to anyone concerned with botany, until the paper is really sent, because without meaning to be uncivil they [by which she surely meant Massee, Murray and Smith] are more inclined to grow the things themselves than to admit that mine are right.'[51]

Beatrix had realistically assessed the impediments to her success. Her working conditions in the kitchen of Bolton Gardens were primitive at best. She may have used Petri dishes occasionally, as several drawings show the mould or moss growing inside one, but it is obvious she had difficulty keeping her slides clean. In several of her microscopic drawings errant mould cells are clearly present. Beatrix realized that the possible contamination of her slides seriously undermined her conclusions. But she had gone beyond stopping. When Massee succeeded in sprouting several of her spores, he conceded that her results were probably more accurate than he initially thought. Forthwith he appears to have become her conduit, if not her champion, to the Linnean Society and submitted her paper to the general secretary who recorded it as paper number 2978 on 18 March 1897.[52]

The general membership of the Society met at seven o'clock on Tuesday evening, 1 April 1897 with President Albert C. L. G. Gunther in the chair. The business of the meeting was the reading of a paper, 'On the Germination of the Spores of *Agaricineae* by Miss Helen B. Potter', and the presentation of several exhibits by five distinguished fellows, including Thiselton-Dyer and George Murray. Since women were not allowed to be members or to participate in the meetings, Beatrix was not present. Her paper was most likely offered by Massee. Afterwards, together with any slide drawings as exhibits, it was 'laid on the table' where it could be examined. Although there is no specific evidence that slide drawings accompanied her paper, one may safely assume they did since they were crucial to her argument, and her paper could hardly have been taken seriously without them. The decision to publish any paper was made by the Council. But Beatrix's paper was never taken nearly that seriously.[53]

'Laid on the table' had the specialized meaning in Linnean Society parlance of the time of 'received but not seriously considered in open forum'. In short, while Beatrix's paper was read at least in part, no substantive notice was given to it. This was certainly not Massee's fault, indeed that he had got her paper on the agenda was remarkable in itself. But like other women at the time who attempted to gain a hearing for their scientific research at the Linnean, Beatrix's theories were never seriously considered.

Not surprisingly, a week after its presentation, the Minutes for the Council Meeting of 8 April 1897 record that a proposal on behalf of Miss Helen Potter to withdraw paper No. 2978 'On the Germination of the Spores of the *Agaricineae*' was sanctioned. Massee would have been the proper person to request the paper's withdrawal on her behalf.[54]

It was not until September that Beatrix reported her Linnean adventure to Charlie McIntosh. 'My paper was read at the Linnean Society, and "well received" according to Mr Massee, but they say it requires more work in it before it is printed.' She felt no need to tell him that she had withdrawn it, for that would have been the normal practice. What Massee told Beatrix after the meeting, and what he meant by 'well received but requires more work', is unknown. Clearly he handled a delicate situation sensitively without hurting her feelings. Her decision to withdraw her paper can be explained simply as a reflection of her desire to do further work on it. She undoubtedly suspected that some of the hyphae she had drawn were moulds and not basidio spores, as this had been a continuing problem. Accuracy then, rather than despair or pique, explains her action.[55]

Over the next two years Beatrix produced nearly seventy more microscopic drawings. In her last extant letter to McIntosh of September 1897 Beatrix wrote, 'I am trying to work out the moulds = [*sic*] conidia forms, of the mushrooms; exceedingly difficult to grow. I find no difficulty in sprouting the mycelium of any fungus but the "spawn" is so very difficult to run. If I am right it will be possible to work out which of the Boleti are hybrids, but it will take many years at the present rate!' There is nothing in this letter to suggest that she had lost interest in the problem. But her estimate of the difficulty and of the time it would require was accurate.[56]

Potter's coded journal, her correspondence with McIntosh, and her efforts to gain a hearing for her theories from the scientific professionals had ended by the autumn of 1897, but the question of how the adventure affected her or what became of her Linnean paper continues to fuel speculation and controversy. There is no evidence as to how much longer Beatrix worked on the problem of germination, when she last used her ticket at Kew, or if she had further association with Massee. Most intriguing of all, her paper 'On the Germination of the Spores of *Agaricineae*', either as it was presented or any later revision, has never been found. Most likely it was destroyed inadvertently and is beyond recovery.[57]

The Linnean Society did not reject Potter's paper because they never seriously considered it. The paper was properly communicated and properly withdrawn. Suggestions that Beatrix abandoned her research in despair, that Thiselton-Dyer or Murray pressured her to withdraw it, or that the outcome would have been different had someone with more prestige than Massee sponsored her, miss the fact that Beatrix was too insignificant a player for the botanical establishment to be concerned with. To have noticed her would only have called more attention to her unwelcome and unproven theories, and perpetuated the intrusions of Sir Henry. The establishment scientists simply discounted her research and ignored her conclusions. They were later proved wrong. That they were antagonistic to her as a woman and as an amateur goes without saying, and their bad manners account for the Linnean Society's official 'apology' for the sins of historic sexism a century later.[58]

When Beatrix began painting fungi seriously in 1892, encouraged by McIntosh's enthusiasm, she may well have had the idea of making a collection of one or several species, thinking that in time these might be used as illustrations for a book on fungi by some expert mycologist. But by 1897 she was aware that most of her paintings were of species found in Scotland and not representative of fungi of the British Isles. In January she agreed to McIntosh's request to exhibit some of the paintings she had sent to him over the years at an upcoming natural history meeting in Scotland, but she wished they were 'better worth lending'. In March, about the time she would have been putting the finishing touches on her Linnean paper, she wrote a picture letter to young Walter Frederick Gaddum, known as 'Jim', the five-year-old son of her cousin Edith, explaining, 'I have been drawing funguses very hard, I think some day they will be put in a book but it will be a dull one to read.' This was a plausible, but vague objective, as she knew of no one other than Massee or McIntosh who might write such a book.[59]

Beatrix took pride in her work, and certainly wanted an acknowledgement of it, but there is no evidence that she had any ambition to be recognized by the scientific community as a mycologist, or that she wished for a life devoted to scientific enquiry. By comparison to her contemporaries, women like Margaret Gatty, Marianne North or Eleanor Ormerod, even her cousin Mary Hutton, who were energetically devoting themselves to natural science or to the illustration of it despite inherent gender prejudice, Beatrix's efforts, while remarkable, show nothing of the same level of commitment. Beatrix attempted to obtain a hearing for her scientific observations at a time when the line of demarcation between amateur and professional scientist was newly drawn and jealously defended. She was not singled out for mistreatment. Her experience was the norm, not the exception.[60]

In most ways Beatrix Potter's foray into professional mycology was completely accidental. She loved painting fungi and she was curious about how they grew. Charles McIntosh was content to help her with identification and taxonomy so she could be more accurate in her illustration. It is hard to imagine that Beatrix would have gone so far into the study of mycology without his encouragement, his baskets of fresh specimens from Scotland, or his patient teaching. Without him she would have remained simply a painter of beautiful 'funguses'. It might well have ended there too if the experts at Kew had not been threatened by the questions of a bright amateur, and if her competitive and adversarial uncle, her other mentor, had not taken personal umbrage and thrust her into a world where no woman of her background and qualifications could possibly have been successful. Roscoe led Beatrix to the inner circles of the scientific establishment, where she acquitted herself well, but it was never a place she herself aspired to be. That she had the 'mind of a professional scientist and biologist', as one modern writer has claimed, may be overstating, but without question, Beatrix Potter was a brilliant amateur.[61]

If Beatrix had defined a goal for her life by 1898 it was essentially what it had always been: to find something useful to do with her talents, and to gain a measure of economic and personal independence. She had explored scientific illustration and research and found that, however intriguing, it could not satisfy that end. Pragmatic as she was, she moved on with events, shaping those she could. But she retained from her experience a certain cynicism about professional science.[62]

Beatrix appreciated Roscoe's mentoring. When Roscoe and Lunt published their popular chemistry textbook *First Steps in Chemistry* in 1899, Beatrix celebrated the occasion with a wonderfully amusing, intricate drawing of little mice working diligently in a laboratory filled with test tubes. Her painting, entitled 'A Dream of Toasted Cheese', featured a learned, bespectacled avuncular mouse perched on a Bunsen burner reading the new textbook, while in the lower left corner she made reference to the compound NH_3 (ammonia gas), writing: 'The peculiar pungent smell of this compound is noticed if we heat a bit of CHEESE in a test-tube.' Uncle Harry included it in his autobiography, acknowledging his talented niece as the artist.[63]

Time has been far kinder to Beatrix's scientific efforts than her contemporaries were. When she tied up her portfolios of fungi paintings with ribbons many years later, she could not have known that her conclusions about the symbiotic nature of lichens and the hybridization of fungi would later be proved and accepted. Nor could she imagine that her watercolours are considered so accurate that modern mycologists refer to them still to identify fungi. Her ephemeral hope that her drawings might some day illustrate a book by an expert mycologist was realized in 1967 when W. P. K. Findlay, a past president of the British Mycological Society, used fifty-nine of them in his volume for the 'Wayside and Woodland' series of natural history. No doubt it would have pleased her, but it was, as she feared it might be, a dull book to all but the experts.

Beatrix was not completely absorbed by mycology between 1892 and 1896, for in these same years she energetically produced a wide variety of fantasy illustrations of favorite stories and rhymes. She illustrated *Cinderella*, *Alice's Adventures in Wonderland*, Joel Chandler Harris's *Nights with Uncle Remus* and a variety of rhymes like Edward Lear's 'The Owl and the Pussy-Cat'. She produced drawings for

Charles Perrault's 'Sleeping Beauty' and for the tale of 'Puss in Boots'. And there were illustrations for other stories from *The Arabian Nights* and *Aesop's Fables*, experimenting with different media and techniques. She made countless drawings of her rabbit Peter and when she became tired of rabbits, she drew mice – voles, dormice, wood mice and little white mice – and caricatured guinea pigs. On holiday travels she sent picture letters to the Moore children, including drawings of the story of 'The Owl and the Pussy-Cat', and from Lingholm in Keswick in 1897, a letter about squirrels that go down the river on little rafts.

She had not given up the idea of publishing booklets or greetings cards. 'The Squirrel's Gift', probably painted in 1895, for example, cleverly shows two red squirrels on a log with the front view and the back view exactly matching so that it could be opened up. Other card possibilities, like guinea pigs in a basket, had moveable parts, and she experimented with toy pictures like one called 'Benjamin Bunny & Son, Greengrocers' that featured bin lids that open to reveal animals hiding underneath.[64]

Her letters to children, cards and fantasy illustrations, even more than her microscopic fungi paintings, suggest where Beatrix Potter's creative energy would take her next. But even her delight in fungi was never exclusively scientific – they too could dwell in the realm of magic and fantasy – and one particular memory linked them and her to the village of Near Sawrey, a foreshadowing of the full circle her life would take. In November 1896, as she was about to leave Sawrey, she wrote:

I think one of my pleasantest memories of Esthwaite is sitting on Oatmeal Crag on a Sunday afternoon, where there is a sort of table of rock with a dip, with the lane and fields and oak copse like in a trough below my feet, and all the little tiny fungus people singing and bobbing and dancing in the grass and under the leaves all down below, like the whistling that some people cannot hear of stray mice and bats, and I sitting up above and knowing something about them.

I cannot tell what possesses me with the fancy that they laugh and clap their hands, especially the little ones that grow in troops and rings amongst dead leaves in the woods. I suppose it is the fairy rings, the myriads of fairy fungi that start into life in autumn woods.[65]

6

❧ *Fantasies* ❧

BEATRIX WAS LATE IN REBELLION, even for a Victorian daughter. A desire for money and the measure of emotional and financial independence it might bring her propelled her out of an extended adolescence and artistic apprenticeship, and shifted her focus from fungi to fantasy. She was sustained in this creative transition by her pragmatic approach to life, an abundance of curiosity, and a sense of humour that found amusement in the absurdity of everyday events. Much of her creative energy derived from a remarkable visual inventory of past experiences and an extraordinary memory for detail. By 1903 Beatrix Potter had emerged as a writer and artist who was not only expert in the art of story-telling and illustration, but who had confidence in her intuitive sense of how she might market her creations. Artist and entrepreneur emerged as one.

Although most of her artistic focus in the 1890s had been on natural science in one form or another, Beatrix was alert for ways in which she could market her fanciful drawings of her pets for greetings cards or as small booklets. Her choice of subject depended very much on the animals that she had at hand and those that matched her text. While her animals were anthropomorphized by human costume and activity, she deliberately set them in a real place and in real, rather than imagined, nature. Typical were her illustrations of the rhyme, 'Three little mice sat down to spin', drawn about 1892 and intended as a booklet. Mice were always among her favourite subjects. But in these sepia illustrations, the setting and activity is extraordinarily accurate. It includes in miniature the paraphernalia of spinning; the looms, the bobbins, the distaffs and the interior of a low-roofed spinning room. The bentwood chairs the mice sit on had been in her favourite bedroom number 4 at Camfield Place. Beatrix produced six drawings, and a coloured title page, but she never finished the booklet. She painted variations of these spinning mice, as well as sewing mice, dancing mice, dining mice, mice at tea, mice playing cards, and a superb bespectacled gentleman mouse reading the *Day's News*.[1]

Her work was experimental and her output prodigious. Creatively, Beatrix was always moved to interpret a familiar story in her own way. In 1893, the same year as her picture letter to Noel Moore about her rabbit Peter, she began a series of eight illustrations of Joel Chandler Harris's *Uncle Remus* stories, finishing the last one in 1896. The adventures of that trickster 'Brer Rabbit' had been family favourites and it was a natural text for her to choose.

The impact of Harris's talking animals on contemporary writers both in Britain and America was enormous, not only because of his cunning but likeable rabbit protagonist, but also because of the cadence and virtuosity of the colloquial dialect, the pacing of the stories and his subversive humour. *Uncle Remus* proved to be 'the great bridging text between the beast fable and animal fantasy'. Like her contemporaries Rudyard Kipling, Kenneth Grahame and A. A. Milne, Beatrix was enthralled by these apparently naive animal fables set in the context of everyday human life. As she studied Harris's art, she was fascinated by the way he turned the ordinary into the extraordinary. It reinforced her choice of familiar settings for her own illustrations.[2]

Each of her drawings from *Uncle Remus* features a single vignetted scene, surrounded by a border of realistically drawn rabbits, with a bit of text off to the side or bottom. Beatrix was fascinated by the language of *Uncle Remus*. Such words as 'rabbit tobacco', 'puddle-ducks', and 'Cottontail' found their way into her vocabulary. So too did adapted cadences such as 'lippity-lippity', a subdued version of Harris's 'lippity-clippity, clippity-lippity'. Beatrix relished the un-expected twist in his tales; how the weak triumphed over the strong through cleverness, cunning and luck, only to be sometimes fooled themselves. The ironic pleased her and the trickster elements of the subversive mischief-maker 'Brer Rabbit' challenged her inventiveness. When she came to write and illustrate her own tales, *Uncle Remus* was her reference point in the creation of a world where animals and humans overlap.[3]

Beatrix was also impressed by the art of Edward Lear, whom she had long admired, not only for his limericks, but as one of the great natural history painters of her day. His *Book of Nonsense* (1846) had been one of her childhood favourites. 'The Owl and the Pussy-cat', which Lear had composed as a gift to the sick daughter of a friend in 1867, she especially admired. Beatrix first appropriated Lear's cadences in 1883 when she illustrated the 'the pig with a ring in his nose', who lived on the idyllic island where the 'Bong tree grows'. She would elaborate his rhyme in several versions.

But it was in her picture letters to the Moore children, and to her various young cousins, that Beatrix practised her art of illustrated story-telling, using her own impressions and experiences as the subject of story and picture. She experimented in these letters with the intricacies of matching drawings to the text, and with the structural elements of story-telling: narrative, language, voice, pacing and humour. Her sense of the absurd is fully in evidence, and she appropriates Harris's technique of embellishing the ordinary. These picture letters to children, upon which the very best of her later books are based, served as the medium for Potter's artistic transition between natural science and fantasy, between the sociological insights of her journal and her stories for children. Since these picture letters are about real life and often about her real pets, they are also the bridge between Beatrix's private and her public art; between her old life and the new one she was creating. Perhaps more clearly than any other medium, these picture letters provide the earliest evidence of her unique genius as artist and story-teller.

Most of her picture letters describe her holiday activities: the weather, the pets she has with her, the animals she sees, farming practices, family gossip and local lore. Each letter was suited to the age and interests of the child, revealing her instinctive ability to match story to audience. She shows her enthusiasm for the natural world and shares her opinion on livestock, fishing, museums, seaports and harbours, and the foibles of her family. Often they address subjects of natural history or archaeology that she knew would challenge them. They highlight her observation of minute but salient details and her ability to explain complicated ideas in a way that would appeal to small children. Her picture letters to Noel and Eric Moore, in particular, become more sophisticated in subject matter as they grow older. In one of her last letters to Noel about the construction of ships and an imaginary battle between mice and frogs in 1900, when he was 13, Beatrix chided him: 'It seems to me you must be getting too old for picture letters!'[4]

Potter's earliest known picture letter was written to Noel from Falmouth in the spring of 1892. After telling him about her trip, sketching the train and palm trees of Cornwall, the harbour and the ships, she writes: 'we went across the water to a pretty little village where the fishermen live. I saw them catching crabs in a basket cage which they let down into the sea with some meat in it & then the crabs go in to eat the meat & cannot get out [drawing].' She continued, 'this is a pussy I saw looking for fish. These are two little dogs that live in the hotel, & two tame seagulls & a great many cocks & hens in the garden,' sketching each. Years later Beatrix would use harbour scenes and boats from these family holidays in the coastal towns of the West Country as backgrounds in her books.

In August 1892 Beatrix wrote to Noel, then four, about bringing Benjamin on the train from London in his basket, of how she took him out in the garden at Heath Park on a leather strap, and about his surprise encounter with a wild rabbit amongst the cabbages. 'It sat up on its hind legs and made a little grunting noise, but Mr Bunny was eating so fast he did not take any notice . . . then he was so much surprised that he ran away.' A second picture letter, to Noel's three-year-old brother Eric, describes her little mouse who was so tame it would sit on her hand and eat hemp seeds.[5]

Two years later Beatrix wrote to Eric Moore again from Falmouth about a ship, the *Pearl of Falmouth*, on which she saw a white pig with a curly tail. Reminded of Lear's rhyme of the owl and the pussy-cat, she told Eric:

I daresay it enjoys the sail but when the sailors get hungry they eat it. If that pig had any sense it would slip down into the boat at the end of the ship & row away [drawing]. This is the captain & the boatswain & the ship's cook pursuing the pig. The cook is waving a knife and fork [drawings]. He wants to make the pig into sausages . . . This is the pig living on Robinson Crusoe's Island. He is still rather afraid of the cook . . . [drawing]. This is the same pig after he has lived ten years on the island, he has grown very very fat & the cook has never found him.

Several years later Beatrix returned to Lear's rhyme in a letter to Noel and another to her young cousin Molly Gaddum. In Molly's letter she illustrated her own version of the marriage of the owl and the pussy-cat. 'It is very odd to see an owl with hands, but how could he play on the guitar without them?'[6]

In April 1895 the Potters visited Salisbury where they saw Stonehenge for the first time. Near Abbotsbury they toured the swannery where Beatrix was fascinated by the decoy system the monks had designed to lure wild ducks through a series of hurdles into ever narrowing covered hoops ending in a bag where up to seventy ducks could be trapped. She wrote Noel a letter featuring a double-page illustration of the duck trap and explaining the mechanics of the device and the habits of the wild life. It was perfect for a bright nine-year-old boy who loved animals and was clever enough to figure out from her illustration how the trap worked.[7]

She told the children about all sorts of real animals that she saw doing strange things. From Holehird on Windermere, she wrote to Noel about a poor frightened donkey pulling an organ who was put on the ferry boat with an apron tied over his eyes. She wrote to Eric about the dogs she saw in Mr Ginnet's circus, illustrating the letter with pictures of the dogs dancing and turning somersaults, the prancing horses and the clown who made the horse do tricks. 'It was a very odd circus,' she wrote with characteristic realism, 'last time I had the pleasure of seeing the circus Mr Ginnet possessed a red bull which he rode, but I fancy he has made it into beef.' Beatrix was especially fond of the circus and returned to it in a later fantasy.[8]

Often she put herself into the letters. From Weymouth on the Dorset coast in 1895, Beatrix wrote to Noel about the 'rocks, & fossils, very old shells in the stone'. Her letter included a little picture of the three Potters walking along the beach looking for fossils. In 1896 she wrote to Noel about her pleasure at being in Sawrey.

It is such a pretty place, and we have a boat on Esthwaite Lake [drawing herself in a rowing boat with the tall rushes and water lilies] . . . I sometimes sit quite still in the boat & watch the water hens. They are black with red bills and make a noise just like kissing . . . One evening I went in the boat when it was nearly dark and saw a flock of lapwings asleep, standing on one leg in the water. What a funny way to go to bed [drawing of birds]! Perhaps they are afraid of foxes, the hens are [drawing a fox carrying off a bird].

In a probable reference to the farmer, a Mr Preston, who farmed Hill Top at the time, she told Noel: 'He is a funny old man, he feeds the calves every morning, he rattles the spoon on the tin pail, to tell them breakfast is ready but they won't always come, then there is a noise like a German band [drawing the farmer calling the calves and the hens going up a wooden runway into the coop for the night].'[9]

A year later, she wrote to Noel from Lingholm about a trap she and Bertram made for catching minnows: 'my brother tied a bit of string to it, put some bread inside and watched [drawing of the trap with bread inside]. The minnows came all around snuffing and at last one old fish found the way in at the end, and all the others followed. I should think there were 50 or 60 inside.' Beatrix never forgot how much little boys like to hear about nasty things such as the man who threw rotten pears and snails into his perry (fermented pear juice). In 1898, just before leaving Lingholm, she told Noel about the young hawk Bertram had been given and how they cared for it. 'We put it in a cage at first, which was a pity, because it spoiled its tail, but we did not know how to fasten it . . . Then we put little straps on its legs [drawing], I cut them out of an old glove, they have to be tied in a peculiar way, so as not to hurt . . . I don't know whether he will really be able to train it to catch birds for him out of doors; the difficulty is to teach them to come back when they are called [drawing]!' Bertram's hawk died and was replaced by a barbary falcon.[10]

Some of her picture letters were simply amusing. When Noel had a case of the mumps she began her letter with a picture of a pathetic little rabbit sitting in a chair all bandaged up about the chin. She told him about her pony who was so stiff he had to have mustard plasters on its hind legs, drawing a picture, and explaining that she could not come to Wandsworth because she would have to run away from the mumps, drawing a group of little 'mumps' with large, swollen heads and little short legs running after a fleeing woman with a large umbrella. She told how Bertram had nearly been blown away when a stiff breeze came up suddenly and almost carried him and his large canvas up into the air. 'I expect he will be blown away some day like a big kite [drawing of Bertram flying over the hills holding on to his picture]!'[11]

Beatrix wrote equally amusing letters to the Gaddum children and to the younger Moore girls, but she especially enjoyed writing to the boys because they were interested in nature and in how things worked. They also appreciated a story with adventure or humour in it. Perhaps the boys reminded her of Bertram and the letters she had once written to him. She practised thinking as both a writer and illustrator as she created these letters, including in them the same sort of sharp-eyed detail about the world around her and what amused her as she had in the pages of her journal. The picture letters, like the journal, were a visual record of her experiences as well as bio-graphical commentary. Both provided training for her future craft, and functioned as the archival sources for many of her books.

The Potters travelled less frequently in the three years between 1897 and 1900 than they had before; perhaps an indication of Rupert Potter's unpredictable health. But when they did go on holiday, Beatrix, now in her early thirties, was often responsible for the travel arrangements. Her mother's expectations of her daughter's participation in the management of domestic affairs at Bolton Gardens had also increased. Most of the time Beatrix managed her duties efficiently. She protected her time by remaining out of reach on the third floor, fully occupied with her own work. But it could not have been easy for her to withstand her mother's efforts to control her time, or to keep from becoming emotionally hobbled by her over-protectiveness. According to Bertram, Helen Potter was 'the sort of woman who would have you pushed in a perambulator until you got out and said you would rather walk'. Beatrix's success in retaining any independence, especially in London, underlines the pleasure she took from her creative work. But no matter how diplomatically she juggled her time, her enlarging interests and activities inevitably led to a clash of expectations within the family.[12]

Earning money from the sale of her cards and from her commission at Morley College had been a boost to her self-esteem. Although the idea of illustrating booklets or doing something in commercial art had begun in earnest in the mid-1890s, earning money became more urgent after she realized that her botanical illustrations would not fulfil her desire for immediate income. Her desire for some financial independence was reinforced by a change in her relationship with her father, and by her reacquaintance with Hardwicke Rawnsley in the summer of 1897.

Rupert had always been an exacting personality, but father and daughter had long enjoyed a common interest in art and photography. When Rupert's health began to deteriorate in the late 1890s family life became more difficult. He suffered from kidney stones, insomnia and pulmonary difficulties. He was overweight and frequently in pain, for which he took increasing amounts of narcotics which did little to improve his disposition. Further agitated by the policies of the Liberal government regarding the expansion of the franchise, the Irish Home Rule question and rights of working men, Rupert was anxious and irritable. His opinions about art as well as politics ossified. Since Bertram was most often away in Scotland painting, Beatrix bore an ever-increasing share of both her father's demands and his dyspepsia. There had been the suggestion that Rupert should go abroad, perhaps to the Low Countries, for his health. Distressed at the prospect of an extended European tour, Beatrix made a private visit to her father's physician, Dr Aiken, explaining to him that she could not tolerate living in an isolated hotel in a foreign city with her discontented parents. She apparently impressed the physician sufficiently as the idea was dropped.[13]

In fairness to Rupert, Beatrix had not the usual social ambitions of an unmarried woman. She showed little interest in society or in meeting eligible young men, being immensely shy, but also despising the process. This distaste undoubtedly increased as she got older. Rupert's estimate of her prospects diminished as he saw that his efforts at matchmaking were unappreciated. Finding eligible introductions for his daughter was not an easy task in the 1890s, but in Beatrix's case there were two particular hurdles: the restricted society to which the Potters belonged, and Helen Potter's unrealistic requirements.

Although Rupert was well known among Unitarians in London, outside this small Nonconformist community his associations were limited to his clubs and to the art world. In spite of their considerable wealth, the Potters moved in a narrow range of society in London, and were not themselves successful outside that circle. Had they remained in Manchester, where they had an extensive family network in the mercantile and political community, there might have been suitable introductions. But Helen and Rupert had chosen to leave the north and reaped the consequences of social isolation in London.

Undoubtedly the Potters would have been pleased had both their children married well and there must have been considerable family pressure on Beatrix to keep up with her Leech and Potter cousins. Ethel Leech, daughter of Helen's eldest brother, had married Sir William Hyde Parker. Through his London clubs, Rupert knew many fine families, especially intellectuals and professionals, who might offer eligible young men. But Helen had a different criteria of suitability. A husband for Beatrix had to offer the one thing that Potter wealth could not buy: family name and inherited land. The issue of religious tradition might have been bridged, as it was for increasing numbers of Nonconformists around the turn of the century, but Helen's social ambitions narrowed the field considerably.[14]

Beatrix was certainly not against marriage; quite the contrary. But as she grew older she realized that her opportunities were limited. Too shy and too conservative to embrace the social and political freedoms promised to the 'New Woman', she remained both dutiful and devoted, but like other women of her class, that loyalty came at an emotional cost. As she increasingly moved in her own orbit, her encroaching spinsterhood was an additional incentive to achieve something on her own.[15]

In 1897 the Potters chose to come back to Lingholm, the estate overlooking Derwentwater near Keswick that they had first rented in 1885. They returned for the next two summers, and again in 1901 and 1904. The large, rather stark, fieldstone house sits high above the lake set off by a long drive, a great expanse of lawn, formal gardens and wide terraces. The rear of the house had elaborate borders designed by Colonel George Kemp, later Lord Rochdale, with terraces set at just the right level for a surprise view of the lake between the trees, spilling down gently to the woods that run along the lakeshore. The woods, then and now, have an extensive collection of prize rhododendrons planted by generations of Rochdales, and remain home to colonies of red squirrels. The rocky shoreline of Derwentwater is dotted here and there by reedy marshes, all providing ideal material for sketching.

When Beatrix arrived at Lingholm, she was for the first time in some years without a specific project or mentor to direct her energies. Finding herself at a sort of intellectual crossroads, she welcomed the energetic Revd Hardwicke Rawnsley, now Vicar of the nearby Crosthwaite parish church in Keswick, back into her life, finding his passion for preservation of natural beauty in the Lake District of compelling interest. Rawnsley, only fifteen years older than Beatrix, was still an altogether appealing figure with his blue eyes, full moustache and ginger beard. He had the shortish, stocky build of an athlete and there was about him a kind of physical and intellectual robustness. He looked deceivingly like one of those simple, old-fashioned parsons with his flat black hat and white tie, although in summertime the black hat was replaced with a dapper straw one. But Rawnsley was hardly a 'country parson'. A man of flashing intellect, robust curiosity and restless energy, he had been made an 'honorary Canon' of Carlisle cathedral in 1893, an acknowledgment of his contributions to the diocese and to the wider community.[16]

Rawnsley's successful opposition to the railway planned through Borrowdale brought him into collaboration with the eminent jurist Viscount Bryce, Sir Robert Hunter of the Commons Preservation Society, as well as his old friend Octavia Hill, who championed the preservation of open spaces for the working poor. The Lake District Defence Society which Rawnsley had founded in 1883 at Wray had grown into a robust organization, supported by the most influential landowners. Rawnsley had offered it as a working model for national preservation, and along with Hunter and Hill, they had successfully founded the National Trust for Places of Historic Interest or Natural Beauty in 1895.[17]

The National Trust was based on the radical legal premise that a non-profit entity could hold title to land or buildings as trustee in perpetuity for the use and enjoyment of the entire nation. The legislation establishing the Trust was a landmark in the British preservation movement. The Trust was officially a charity, entirely supported by individual membership and donations of property. Rawnsley became secretary of the new organization, a post for which he was ideally suited and which provided him the perfect pulpit from which to champion the unique mission of the Trust.

Rupert Potter joined enthusiastically as one of the first Life Members of the National Trust. He enjoyed discussing the legal intricacies of acquiring undeveloped land and properties and, since his legal experience had been in the area of trusts and estates, Rawnsley sought him out and valued his advice. Rawnsley was a frequent visitor to the Potters at Lingholm that summer, often accompanied by his wife Edith, who was involved in efforts to preserve local crafts and craftsmen. Beatrix listened to his impassioned arguments for preservation and his ideas for special appeals to save a vulnerable rural culture, not just romantic vistas and fine architecture.[18]

Rawnsley's attitude towards preservation was often controversial. He did not trust the local fellsmen to make good choices about the future development of their native landscape, knowing that they would often find a commercial venture worthy of destroying an 'empty vista', out of ignorance, for short-term financial reward or merely to relieve the boredom of rural life. It was a point of view that Beatrix agreed with. She could not but be influenced by his attitudes about preservation and rural life, and by his belief in the crucial role of the National Trust. She shared his view that the Lakeland environment should be saved for the benefit of all, and not just the wealthy few. His political and social commitments, so different from her father's, broadened her world-view as well as her attitudes about the environment. Under Rawnsley's tutoring, Beatrix's under-standing of the culture of Lakeland expanded over the following summer holidays.[19]

Rawnsley's interests in preserving the distinctive Herdwick sheep made a particular impression on Beatrix. She had always been inter-ested in livestock, noting the different breeds of cattle and sheep she saw on her travels, especially in Scotland. But under Rawnsley's influence she became aware of the precarious future of the Herdwick and of their unique suitability to fell farming. Two years later, in September 1899, Rawnsley and his son Noel were instrumental in establishing the Herdwick Sheep Association, dedicated to preserving this breed of coarse-wool, fell-bred sheep which had been a fixture of the high fell farms for centuries.[20]

The ever-restless Rawnsley was also a prolific writer of books about the natural history and culture of Lakeland and its literary associations. He was a journalist, a proselytizer and a talented versi-fier, who could compose a sonnet for any occasion. Around 1897 Rawnsley also published *Moral Rhymes for the Young*, a collection of didactic verse for children. With such mutual interests, it is little wonder that Beatrix found him a valued friend and a different sort of mentor.[21]

Beatrix's art had always been place-specific, but these summers at Lingholm offered her an extraordinary choice of landscape. She painted views of Borrowdale near Derwentwater and the dramatic vistas across the lake. St Herbert's Island was just opposite the Lingholm shore, with Walla Crag often a misty presence in the background. The great mass of fells known as Cat Bells looms over the lake, and the green Newlands Valley runs off to the west. In the early summer the rhododendrons around the estate burst into a rainbow of pastel shades, and in autumn the hillsides were ablaze with burnished colour, contrasting dramatically with the grey stone walls and the bare slopes of the upper fells. It was an artist's paradise, with few houses or structures to interrupt the pastoral view.

On rainy days Beatrix painted the everyday things around her: flowerpots, antique furniture, the interior halls and staircases. She once used the inclement weather as the backdrop for an unconventional view of Lingholm; with one side and the roof line of the grey stone house cast up dramatically against the opaque, rainy sky with the distant mountains shrouded in mist. She called it simply *Rain*. When she tired of the pastoral, Beatrix went into the market town of Keswick. Many of its houses and buildings are recognizable in the sketches she made of the market square. Although she found Keswick 'an awfully dull, cold town', it was a change of pace to make quick sketches of people shopping and conversing. Beatrix never drew the human figure well, but these sketches, done almost impressionistically, succeed where her more studied attempts often fail.[22]

As she sketched around the countryside and wrote picture letters to the Moore children, she had no particular idea in mind as to how her landscapes and little stories might be used, but her former governess Annie Moore did. By 1899 there were six little Moores, the two older boys, Noel and Eric, and four girls, of whom the youngest, Joan, was born in 1896. Over the years Beatrix had written a good many letters to the Moore children, but she had not visited them in some months. When she was finally able to go to Wandsworth, in early January 1900, Annie Moore suggested that some of her picture letters could be made into interesting books for little children. She thought they might sell. Beatrix was taken by the idea.[23]

The Moore children had kept all her letters, Marjorie tying hers up with a yellow ribbon. Beatrix asked if she might borrow them back to make copies and consider which one would be most suitable for a book. She selected the letter she had written to Noel from Eastwood in 1893 about Peter Rabbit, copying it out onto folded sheets of paper. The original letter was too short to make a proper book, so she added some text and some new black and white illustrations which expanded the story of the rabbit's adventure in Mr McGregor's garden and made it more suspenseful. These changes also slowed the narrative down, added intrigue, and gave a greater sense of the passage of time. Then she copied it out into a stiff-covered exercise book, and painted a coloured frontispiece showing Mrs Rabbit dosing Peter with camomile tea.[24]

Beatrix sent her book, now titled 'The Tale of Peter Rabbit and Mr McGregor's Garden', to at least six publishers, some suggested by Bertram, others by her friends Gertrude and Alice Woodward, and one or two recommended by Hardwicke Rawnsley. But in rapid succession her manuscript was returned by each of the six, including Frederick Warne & Co. in Covent Garden, who nearly a decade earlier had shown some interest in her artwork. Some publishers wanted a shorter book, others a longer one. But most wanted coloured illustrations which, by 1900, were proving both popular and affordable.

'You will begin to be afraid I have run away with the letters altogether!' Beatrix wrote to Marjorie Moore in March. 'I will keep them a little longer because I want to make a list of them, but I don't think they will be made into a book this time because the publisher wants poetry.' Beatrix illustrated her frustration with little drawings showing 'Miss Potter' arguing with a gentleman holding a big book, and another showing her walking out of the shop with her book, leaving the publisher standing empty-handed at the door. 'The publisher is a gentleman who prints books,' she explained, 'and he wants a bigger book than he has got enough money to pay for! and Miss Potter has arguments with him . . . I wonder if that book will ever be printed! I think Miss Potter will go off to another publisher soon! She would rather make 2 or 3 little books costing 1/- each, than one big book costing 6/- because she thinks little rabbits cannot afford to spend 6 shillings on one book, and would never buy it.' Here Beatrix drew a sketch of Mrs Rabbit in front of a bookshop giving two little bunnies a coin from her purse. Discouraged but determined, Beatrix went off to the British Museum to study a book of old rhymes. 'I shall draw pictures of some of them,' she told Marjorie, 'whether they are printed or not.'[25]

Beatrix had very specific ideas about how she wanted her 'little rabbit book' to look and how much it should cost. She was also accustomed to dealing with card and annual publishers like Ernest Nister, who almost certainly was one of the six to whom she first sent her manuscript and with whom she was now arguing. Once again Beatrix threatened to withdraw her manuscript, but this time the tactic did not work, and the manuscript was returned. In a postscript to a picture letter to Freda Moore in April from Tenby in

South Wales, Beatrix wrote with obvious exasperation, 'Miss Potter is sitting upon her book at present & considering! The publisher cannot tell what has become of it.' The accompanying sketch shows a woman sitting rather awkwardly on a large book on a sandy beach staring resolutely out to sea.[26]

Although it had been seven years since Potter had conceived and illustrated her letter about Peter, her revisions of it in 1900 reveal how far she had progressed in the art of story-telling, how well she understood her audience, and how knowledgeable she was about the children's book market. The late Victorian and early Edwardian publishing world was enormously competitive. In the 1890s important art presses such as William Morris's Kelmscott Press and J. M. Dent's Everyman Library, who published the work of Aubrey Beardsley, had given greater consideration to book format and to producing mass-market books for young children. Dent, for example, brought out a successful line of tiny fairy tales and nursery rhymes in his 'Banbury Cross' series, some illustrated by Beatrix's friend Alice Woodward. In 1895 a twelve-book series known as the 'golliwog' books became a publishing phenomenon, beginning with *The Adventures of Two Dutch Dolls and a Golliwogg*. These were large-format books featuring doggerel verses faced by colour illustrations in bright poster style, set off by large white areas. The 'golliwogs' were followed in 1897 by a series for little children known as the 'Dumpy Books for Children', a creation of Grant Richards, an enterprising young publisher well connected to the highbrow literary world. Both series proved enormously popular and profitable.[27]

In October 1899 Richards published *The Story of Little Black Sambo*, a small picture book for very young children which featured a few words of text opposite brightly coloured pictures in a fashionable colour cover. *Sambo* was the work of Helen Bannerman, a Scottish woman living then in India with her surgeon husband and small children. Bannerman's story derived largely from the golliwog books and the tigers of Rudyard Kipling's *Jungle Books*. But *Little Black Sambo* became a runaway best-seller, going through four printings in as many months. Its success clearly inspired Beatrix to make up a dummy book (sheets folded together to show size, shape and form) of 'Peter' just five months later. As she evaluated the market, it seemed to her that an original and beautifully illustrated tale might sell as well as Bannerman's derivative one. She adopted Bannerman's small-size picture-book format rather than that of several other popular styles both because she preferred it for small children and because she believed it would sell. As Beatrix recalled later, 'After a time there began to be a vogue for small books, and I thought "Peter" might do as well as some that were being published.'[28]

Beatrix knew that her work was original, but she could not have gauged just how generically different her tale of a mischievous rabbit in human clothing was. From a book editor's point of view, her story was too long, her narrative lacked proper pacing, there were no coloured illustrations, and the black-and-white outline pictures were too different from the familiar ones influenced by Morris or Beardsley. When no offers to buy her book were forthcoming, Beatrix decided to publish it herself – exactly as she wanted it.[29]

Armed with recommendations from the Woodward sisters, she withdrew her savings from the bank, and paid a call on Strangeways & Sons, a printer in Tower Street, London. Sometime in early September 1901, she ordered a printing of 250 copies of what was now simply *The Tale of Peter Rabbit*. She had the zinc blocks for the black-and-white illustrations made by the Art Reproduction Company of Fetter Lane, and the engraved coloured frontispiece printed by Hentschel of Fleet Street. She ordered 500 copies just in case she might want to reprint it. The printing and engraving cost about £11. On 16 December 1901, the privately printed edition of *The Tale of Peter Rabbit* was ready for distribution to family and friends. But by then Beatrix found herself with an unexpected dilemma.[30]

Canon Rawnsley had originally recommended several publishers to whom Beatrix had sent her manuscript. During the family holiday at Lingholm in 1901 she discussed her efforts to attract a commercial publisher and her plan to publish it herself. Rawnsley offered to make one final effort on her behalf, tempted perhaps by her report that one publisher had wanted poetry. He turned Beatrix's text into what can only be described as rather dreadful didactic verse, and submitted it, along with Beatrix's illustrations and half her revised manuscript, to

Frederick Warne & Co. Warne's had already rejected Potter's earlier version, but took note of Rawnsley's proprietary interests in the manuscript as well as the fact that a private edition was underway for which there existed blocks and an engraved coloured frontispiece. It may well be that Rawnsley's rhyming version was so bad that it made Beatrix's straightforward narrative look even better. For whatever reason, Warne's asked to see the rest of Potter's manuscript, enquiring particularly why Potter had not done more illustrations in colour. Rawnsley turned the publisher's query over to Beatrix. But her terse reply hinted at an unyielding disposition: 'I did not colour the whole book for two reasons,' she wrote, 'the great expense of good colour printing – and also the rather uninteresting colour of a good many of the subjects which are most of them rabbit-brown and green.'[31]

Warne's interest in Beatrix's book had been renewed in part because of her insistence on the book's size and format. To remain competitive in the broadening children's literature market, Frederick Warne & Co. needed a book to compete with Bannerman's *Little Black Sambo*. But Potter appeared resistant to the idea of coloured illustrations. The 'bunny book', as the Warne editors now referred to it, had appeal, but the artist-writer was unknown and publishing it would be an expensive gamble. Moreover, it was their view that the latter portion of the story 'does not appear . . . to carry out the promise of the earlier part'.[32]

Warne thanked Rawnsley for his efforts, but explained that 'it is absolutely necessary that the pictures should be coloured throughout. Miss Potter seems to think the colour would be uninteresting, so that as we differ so materially on this point and also as it is almost too late to produce a book for this season, we think it best to decline your kind offer, at any rate this year.' The editors had, however, taken the trouble to offer suggestions for improvement, recommending that the number of illustrations be cut from forty-two to thirty-two, all in colour, and marked which ones might best be eliminated. They politely told Rawnsley that while 'there were many good ideas' in his rhymes, they preferred simple narration 'which has been very effectively used in a little book produced last year entitled "Little

Black Sambo . . ."', and waited to see what Potter's response might be.[33]

The tactful letter from Warne's to Rawnsley made Beatrix realize that the tone of her earlier letter had been a mistake and that she was dealing with no ordinary 'Grub Street' publisher. Warne's were treating her professionally and, she had to admit, they had more knowledge about the children's book market than she. Although she would have to cut the book down considerably if she accepted their terms, she realized that by incorporating their suggestions she might have both a privately printed edition and a trade publication with the potential of commercial success. In a letter now lost, Beatrix told the publisher she was amenable to their suggestions and sent a few more coloured illustrations for their review, along with a copy of her privately printed edition.[34]

Warne's then asked L. Leslie Brooke, one of their most successful picture-book illustrators, to give his opinion of her drawings, as Brooke had an unerring sense of how children reacted to art. Brooke took them home with him one evening and returned the next day with an enthusiastic endorsement. His recommendation happily coincided with the publication of Bannerman's second book, *The Story of Little Black Mingo*, and the imminent publication of more golliwog books, and J. M. Dent's series, the 'Bairn Books'. The small picture-book market was booming and by acquiring Potter's 'bunny book', Warne's could be a competitor in it.[35]

The firm of Frederick Warne & Co. had been founded in 1865. Although Frederick Warne inherited some good titles from his previous partnership with Routledge, he liked to say that his success came from buying the British rights to *Uncle Tom's Cabin*. But in fact Warne built up a large list of world literature, and had successfully published the work of such illustrators as Edward Lear, Kate Greenaway, Randolph Caldecott and Leslie Brooke. In addition, the firm had a reputation for fine books on natural history. This line was further enhanced when Edward Step, a keen botanist and entomologist, joined the editorial staff about the time that Potter began her relationship with them. His early titles in the 'Wayside and Woodland' series set a new standard for practical natural science handbooks for the general reader.[36]

Frederick Warne retired from active management in 1894, turning over control of the business to his three sons, Harold, Fruing and Norman, before his death in 1901. The offices were in the Chandos Building on Bedford Street, off the Strand. Harold was the managing partner, Fruing was primarily responsible for sales, while Norman, the youngest son, handled production and some sales. The two older Warne sons were both married. Norman, who was 33 when he met Beatrix in 1901, lived with his unmarried sister Amelia, known as Millie, and his widowed mother in the family house in Bedford Square in Bloomsbury. In her negotiations over the publication of *The Tale of Peter Rabbit*, Beatrix almost always dealt with Norman Warne. Their letters began quite formally, mostly having to do with the terms of a contract and the ownership of copyright, but by the time final terms had been agreed upon, their form of address had progressed from 'Madam' and 'Sir', to 'Miss Potter' and 'Mr Warne'.[37]

Beatrix was adamant that the price of her book be kept as low as possible. She also made it clear that she was now negotiating for herself, telling the publisher, 'I do not know if it is necessary to consult Canon Rawnsley; I should think *not*. Speaking for myself I consider your terms very liberal as regards royalty.' Initially she agreed to an edition of 5,000 copies with only coloured pictures selling for 1*s.* 6*d.*, giving her a royalty of 3*d.* on each. It would amount to a total royalty of approximately £20. 'I am sure', she wrote, 'no one is likely to offer me better . . . and I am aware that these little books don't last long, even if they are a success.' She was more intent on the issue of reprint rights, questioning Warne carefully about who would own copyright and what her rights were should they not choose to reprint. She candidly expressed her uneasiness about her father's inevitable review of any contract. 'I have not spoken to Mr Potter, but I think Sir, it would be well to explain the agreement clearly, because he is a little formal having been a barrister.' Beatrix may have been 35 years old, but as an unmarried daughter, she could not enter any legal or financial agreements without her father's consent.[38]

Negotiations dragged into the following year and it was eventually agreed that ownership of the blocks would be transferred to Potter should there be no subsequent editions. Finally a contract was signed in early June 1902. The delay did not bother Beatrix, nor did the consequent reduction in royalty per copy. Her correspondence throughout these months reflects her willingness to comply with the publisher's suggestions and a growing enjoyment of the whole process. Rupert Potter undoubtedly accompanied his daughter to the Warne office to review the final contract. Apprehensive about their meeting, Beatrix cautioned the publishers:

If my father happens to insist on going with me to see the agreement, would you please not mind him very much, if he is fidgetty [*sic*] about things. I am afraid it is not a very respectful way of talking & I don't wish to refer to it again, but I think it is better to mention beforehand he is sometimes a little difficult; I can of course do what I like about the book being 36. I suppose it is a habit of old gentlemen; but sometimes rather trying.[39]

While all these negotiations were taking place, Beatrix was happily distributing copies of her private edition of *The Tale of Peter Rabbit* to enthusiastic readers. She usually inscribed the copies to relatives and family friends, writing in one: 'In affectionate remembrance of poor old Peter Rabbit, who died on the 26th of January 1901 at the end of his 9th year ... whatever the limitations of his intellect or outward shortcomings of his fur, and his ears and toes, his disposition was uniformly amiable and his temper unfailingly sweet. An affectionate companion and a quiet friend.' Beatrix was a natural marketer, exhibiting none of the inhibitions and shyness that plagued her in other social circumstances, and adept at impressing her would-be publisher that their version would also be an equal success. She reported to Warne, 'It is going off very well amongst my friends & relations, 5 at a time; I will spread it about as much as I can, especially in Manchester. Had you decided *not* to go on with it, I would certainly have done so myself, it has given me so much amusement.'[40]

She was also quick to pass along a potential commercial interest: 'I showed it this morning to some ladies who have a bookshop in Kensington who wanted to put it in the window, on the spot; but I

did not venture to do so – though I would have been much interested.'
Seizing on the potential Christmas market, she wrote to a family
friend: 'I am sending with this 2 copies of a funny little book which
came home from the printer's last night. I think I may say I have
shown considerable spirit in bringing it out myself! . . . If you should
hear of anyone who would care for two or three copies at 1/ and 2d
postage I should be glad to part with a few; but I am afraid everyone
will have bought their grandchildren's presents by this time.' To
another friend who had ordered five copies, Beatrix generously threw
in a sixth, writing: 'I am amused to hear that you like the rabbit book
. . . I daresay you can think of someone to give the extra copy to.
I think my mother told you ½ which is the cost price as far as I
can reckon.' A month earlier she had reported appreciation from a
well-regarded source: 'I do not know if it is worth while mentioning
– but Dr Conan Doyle [the creator of Sherlock Holmes] had a copy
for his children & he has a good opinion of the story & words.'[41]

Quite soon she had given away or sold out her the first printing
of 250 copies; she ordered 200 more since she had printed extra copies
of the coloured frontispiece. The new edition had one or two changes
in the text and the date of February 1902 printed on the title page. It
too was soon sold out. In late April 1902, as she prepared to travel
with Bertram in the Scottish Borders, she could not resist telling
Norman Warne, 'The book seems to go on of itself, I had requests
for 9 copies yesterday from 3 people I do not know.' During their
holiday she prevailed upon Bertram, who drew human figures far
better than she, to help her with the figure of Mr McGregor. 'My
brother is sarcastic about the figures,' she wrote to the publisher from
Scotland, 'what you & he take for Mr McGregor's nose, was intended
for his ear, not his nose at all.' She had even more trouble with the
illustration of Mrs McGregor serving the pie containing the remains
of Peter's father. It took several tries to get a younger, more appealing
woman, but as it was never really successful it was dropped from
later editions.[42]

Beatrix and Bertram spent two weeks in Roxburghshire working
compatibly together on their respective art. Despite their difference
in age, the two had always been close, but Bertram's dependence

on alcohol was now silently acknowledged. While they enjoyed being together, it is not clear what confidences they shared, or whether Bertram confided his plans to marry. Six months later, on 20 November 1902, Bertram eloped with Mary Welsh Scott and was married in Edinburgh. Bertram had met Mary in Birnam, in Perthshire, where he frequently spent his holidays after leaving Oxford, taking rooms with Mrs Emily Hutton in the house behind Heath Park. Mary Scott was one of Hutton's nieces, who helped with summer visitors. The story is told in Birnam that Bertram saw Mary's photograph in the dining room of the boarding house one summer and fell in love with her before they ever met.[43]

Beatrix later described Mary as 'a large, fresh-faced woman'. She was about three years younger than Bertram, the daughter of a wine merchant in the Border town of Hawick, where she had once worked in the textile mills. Their civil ceremony was witnessed by John Purves, a writer friend of Bertram's, and by Mary's sister Lizzie. Bertram listed his profession as landscape painter and gave his address as Throsk House in Stirling, where the couple lived until 1903 when Bertram bought Ashyburn, a farm near the idyllic village of Ancrum in the Scottish Borders. Keeping the marriage a secret from his family, Bertram and Mary settled down to a life of farming. Mary was devoted to him and, although they had no children, they were by all accounts very happy.[44]

For the next eleven years Bertram lived out a terrible lie, dutifully spending some portion of his summer holidays with his parents and sister, and making perfunctory visits to Bolton Gardens at appropriate intervals. In April 1906 Bertram's candidacy for membership in the Athenaeum came up for the ballot. His substitute proposers were as prominent as his first ones: his esteemed Uncle Harry, Sir Henry Roscoe, in place of James Caird, and the Rt. Hon. Charles Booth, the highly successful Unitarian businessman and shipowner who financed and directed the sociological survey of London's working class, in place of Millais. Bertram's ballot was signed by his father, by Charles Mallet, Margaret Roscoe's husband, and by the poet and family friend Lewis Morris, among others. His election was carried by 162 to 2, an adequate number of signatures. Bertram listed his occupation as painter and etcher and his address as 2 Bolton Gardens. In light of Bertram's later behaviour, it seems that Beatrix was initially ignorant of his marriage, and, like her parents, assumed he was farming alone in Scotland. At some point she discovered his secret, or was told, but she kept his confidence until Bertram revealed it himself in 1913. In the interim, Bertram supported his sister's literary and artistic efforts whenever he could.[45]

Even though Beatrix was travelling with her family during much of the spring of 1902, she participated in all the details of the printing and publishing. She had trouble redrawing the rabbits because she had to use a new young rabbit and both the anatomy and perspective were different from Peter's. She worked tirelessly to get the proper word in the proper sequence, with just the right cadence and with just the right number of words on a page. Illustrations were drawn and redrawn until she was satisfied. She had opinions about the hue and intensity of colour on the blocks, the colour and texture of the paper, and of course the size and style of the print and the colour of paper for the bindings. The proofs were done by the highly regarded printer Edmund Evans, but were not ready until after the Potters had left London for their summer holiday at Eeswyke in Sawrey, where they were sent for her approval. She made more changes, moved some words, and corrected some punctuation errors. She wrote to Norman Warne, 'I hope the little book will be a success there seems to be a great deal of trouble being taken with it.'[46]

Even before publication in early October 1902, the first printing of 8,000 copies was sold out. By the year's end there were 28,000 copies of *The Tale of Peter Rabbit* in print. In fact it proved nearly impossible to keep *Peter* in print. By the middle of 1903 there was a fifth edition, sporting coloured endpapers. Beatrix used the occasion to drop two illustrations, Peter going 'lippity-lippity', and his return to the big fir tree. A sixth printing was required within the month, and in November Potter wrote incredulously, 'The public must be fond of rabbits! what an appalling quantity of Peter.' A year after publication there were 56,470 copies in print and even though her royalty on each copy was reduced to about 1*s*. 4*d*., Beatrix had achieved her goal of having some money of her own.[47]

At one time Beatrix credited *Peter Rabbit*'s success to the fact that it was a story initially written for a real little boy. But she was also quick to acknowledge that she wrote chiefly to please herself. 'I think I write carefully because I enjoy my writing, and enjoy taking pains over it. I have always disliked writing to order; I write to please myself.' But like many masterpieces of art, the creator often has very little sense of why the public seizes on one particular work or another.[48]

Beatrix Potter had in fact created a new form of animal fable: one in which anthropomorphized animals behave always as real animals with true animal instincts and are accurately drawn by a scientific illustrator. The gap between animals and humans in Potter's work is so narrow that we scarcely notice the transition between the two. Beatrix had been observing rabbits, both their anatomy and their behaviour, for many years. She knew how they moved, how they slept, how they used their mouths and paws, and how they cleaned themselves. She had drawn their postures of attack and submission. She knew they were both curious and easily startled, bold and cowardly in turn, but more often than not put a good face on any inadvertent mishap. Peter Rabbit's nature is instantly recognizable to anyone who has been around a rabbit, and readily endorsed by those who have not, as true to nature, because her portrayal speaks to some universal understanding of rabbity behaviour. Peter's bravado at entering Mr McGregor's garden is believable both as rabbit-nature and as child-nature. His gastronomic gluttony is equally recognizable as well as vicariously amusing, building the tension which comes from knowing that pleasure is never the long-term state in nature. Peter's fright at near-capture and his desperate efforts to find his way out of unfamiliar territory are true of any cornered animal or human. Potter's insertion of humour and surprise at Peter's choice of a damp watering can as a hiding place, the ephemeral safety of a potting shed, and his pleas for help from other creatures either wiser than he or potentially dangerous are also choices that are true of both rabbits and humans. Peter's utter relief at finding himself safely home, his abject admission of over-eating, but his unrepentant curiosity, have perfect integrity. In *The Tale of Peter Rabbit*, Potter achieves a seamless harmony between animal and human nature. It is an imaginary tale for children that leaves no doubt that such a rabbit as Peter exists in nature now, and has existed in nature forever.

The setting of *Peter Rabbit* is as much a part of its success as the action of the story. Gardens had always fascinated Beatrix. Throughout her journal she comments on gardens and the plants and flowers that pleased her. She especially enjoyed drawing trees. When she began illustrating rabbits inhabiting human dwellings and going about human activities, she frequently pictured them gardening. In 1891, for example, she made a detailed pen-and-ink study of 'The Rabbits' Potting Shed' when the family was at Bedwell Lodge. It was replete with pelargoniums and fuchsias in clay pots, with a collection of gardening tools – rakes, hoes, brooms, spades, forks and a large watering can. She recreated that shed in 1902 as Mr McGregor's potting shed. His garden had been in Scotland, but in the published book it became a composite of the gardens Beatrix loved: Camfield, Lakefield, Lingholm, the garden at Tenby in South Wales, and especially her Aunt Burton's garden at Gwaynynog. 'The garden is very large,' she wrote after a visit there in 1895, 'two-thirds surrounded by a red-brick wall with many apricots, and an inner circle of old grey apple trees on wooden espaliers. It is very productive but not tidy, the prettiest kind of garden, where bright old fashioned flowers grow amongst the currant bushes.' In *Peter Rabbit* all these gardens are blended into the idealized and universal garden, the first that many children are ever introduced to. It is a garden particularized by adventure and always recognizable as 'Mr McGregor's' garden.[49]

Potter's success in her first book was as both writer and illustrator. Although the story was always of central importance, there is in *Peter Rabbit* a perfect marriage of word and image. The precision of her drawings of plants and animals, gardens and woods, embellishes the text and carries the story forward to the next page with a flawless continuity of time and place, fantasy and reality. The illustrations always enhance, rather than distract from or dilute the text, even when a rather sophisticated adult word is introduced. And no matter how beautiful the illustration, the landscape is real, the animals are anatomically accurate, and the plants are planted correctly. It is a triumph of fantasy rooted in fact.[50]

When it was published by Warne's in October 1902, *The Tale of Peter Rabbit* was sold in all the best bookshops in London, and soon in shops around the country. It first appeared in a Warne catalogue in early 1903, where it was given top billing on the list of new books and favourably compared to *Uncle Remus*. '*Brer Rabbit* has always been a nursery favourite and the features of Bunny physiognomy have seldom, if ever, received a more harmonious and dainty exposition.' After this first advertisement, however, *Peter Rabbit* needed no further comparison.[51]

7

~~ *Ideas* ~~

THE SUCCESS OF THE PRIVATELY published *Peter Rabbit*, and the decision by Warne's in December 1901 to produce a coloured edition the following year, galvanized Beatrix into a period of happy creativity. Norman Warne soon discovered that he had an author with a nearly endless supply of ideas for stories and rhymes for picture books. What was not immediately clear to the young editor, however, was how desperately Miss Potter wanted to succeed as a writer and illustrator, or the amount of time and energy she was willing to invest in making it a reality. Between the summer of 1901 and Christmas of 1902 Beatrix proposed at least three new books, in addition to suggesting a story about frogs that might also make 'a pretty book', a term she frequently used to indicate an idea that had captured her imagination.

During the summer holiday at Lingholm in 1901 she had sent a long picture letter to Norah Moore about the adventures of 'Squirrel Nutkin' and the colony of red squirrels that abounded in Cumberland. It was an elaboration of an earlier letter written to Noel, also from Lingholm, about some American squirrels who travelled down a river on little rafts using their tails for sails. Beatrix copied Norah's picture letter out in an exercise book before she sent it off, thinking a squirrel story might be a good idea. All that summer she sketched red squirrels scampering about the grounds at Lingholm. She painted the local landscape, seeing it as potential background, particularly the area around St Herbert's Island which in her story became 'Owl Island'.[1]

At the same time Beatrix continued to work on another story based on a tale she had heard on a visit to Harescombe Grange, probably in 1897, about a poor tailor in the town of Gloucester. By Christmas 1901 she had finished it, copied it out in a stiff-covered exercise book and illustrated it with a dozen watercolours. She gave it to Freda Moore, who had been ill, as a Christmas present. 'And the queerest thing about it', Beatrix wrote to the ten-year-old girl, who was fond of fairy tales, 'is that I heard it in Gloucestershire, and it is true! at least about the tailor, the waistcoat, and the "No more twist . . ."' Her tale was a fairy story with a 'happy ever after' ending. The mice were the surrogate good fairies, and Simpkin, the cat, took the role of the wicked stepmother, albeit one who repents in time. Beatrix explained to Freda she had heard the story 'from Miss Caroline Hutton, who had it of Miss Lucy, of Gloucester, who had it of the tailor'. Once again Beatrix was adapting real life to fantasy.[2]

The real tailor of Gloucester, one John Prichard, had been commissioned to make a suit for the new mayor to wear on an important ceremonial occasion. Prichard had not finished the suit when he closed his shop one weekend, only to return on Monday to find the garment finished but for one buttonhole. Pinned to the waistcoat was the explanation, 'No more twist.' As a shrewd businessman, Prichard used his good fortune to advertise that his waistcoats were made at night by the fairies. The story quickly became the stuff of legend about the town.[3]

Beatrix asked the Huttons to point out the tailor's shop when they drove to town and, even though it was a very hot summer day, she sat down on a doorstep nearby and began to sketch the street scene, returning the next day. Her street scenes, however, were not summer but winter ones, with snow covering the streets and shops, and the action of the story taking place on Christmas Eve. As a regular visitor to the Huttons in subsequent years, Beatrix added illustrations. She used the interiors of cottages, furniture, mantelpieces, crockery, and once inveigled the Hutton coachman's son into posing cross-legged on the floor, busy with his sewing. Just as she had been intrigued by the implements of gardening and had made a careful inventory of the potting shed at Bedwell Lodge, where the family had stayed in 1891, Beatrix was now intrigued by the tools of the tailor's trade. Sometime later, she created an excuse to visit a local tailor in Chelsea for a bogus button repair, so she could observe the interior of his shop, noting the scissors, thimbles and tape measures, the brass bowl of water, the snippets of fabric and thread, buttons of all sizes and shapes, and the colourful bindings and trims that litter a tailor's shop. Some months later she returned to the same tailor's shop and was allowed to do some further sketching of the interior.[4]

The story of the tailor, or the 'mouse book' as Beatrix called it, was a long one and included many of her favourite rhymes, which were recited by Christmas carollers, and especially by the little birds and mice who, according to tradition, can talk in the magical hours before the dawn of Christmas Day. In a note at the end of Freda's story Beatrix explained that some of the rhymes were Scottish versions and some came from J. O. Halliwell's collection of verse. *The Tailor of Gloucester* is unique among the Potter oeuvre, for it is set not only in a particular town, but also in a specific historical period: 'In the time of swords and periwigs and full-skirted coats with flowered lappets – when gentlemen wore ruffles, and gold-laced waistcoats of paduasoy . . .'[5]

Since *The Tale of Peter Rabbit* would not be published until the following October, it was too soon to think of offering Frederick Warne a second book. Instead Beatrix decided once again to publish *The Tailor of Gloucester* herself. Her decision was based on her desire to continue publishing her own work, but also because she was fairly certain that Warne's would insist on cutting out many of her favourite rhymes. Beatrix borrowed the manuscript back from Freda and redrew some of the pictures, even shortening the text. She took it again to Strangeways & Sons, ordering 500 copies, and had sixteen blocks made by Hentschel at a cost of £40. The format was the same small size as *Peter Rabbit*, this time bound in pink paper boards, with a cover drawing of three little mice busily making coats. The title page was marked December 1902.[6]

Although she was working on two stories at the same time, Beatrix wrote to Norman Warne before leaving for the summer in Sawrey proposing a book of illustrated nursery rhymes in the style made famous by Randolph Caldecott and Walter Crane. She had been collecting and illustrating rhymes for some time, but she was anxious to interest Norman Warne in another book. 'It may sound odd to talk about mine & Caldecott's at the same time,' she wrote, 'but I think I could at least try to do better than Peter Rabbit, and if you did not care to risk another book I could pay for it.' Admitting to Norman that she 'very much enjoyed doing the rabbit book', she did not reveal how long the summer stretching ahead would be without the promise of another book. Beatrix explained only: 'I would go on with it in any event because I want something to do . . . I did not mean to ask you to say you would take another book.' A week later she wrote again from Sawrey, offering to send him some of the illustrations she had 'on approval', adding: 'This is a convenient place for subjects to draw, & it seems a pity to miss the chance of going on with them.' Working on two, even three, different story ideas at the same time appealed to her, and the idea that Warne might be interested in publishing another book kept her spirits high.[7]

Back in London in the autumn of 1902, Beatrix was a regular visitor to the Frederick Warne offices in Bedford Street. She came in the family carriage, which waited outside until her business was concluded and took her directly home. There was always a chaperon, either the elderly Elizabeth Harper, the cook, or some other household servant, but occasionally she was accompanied by her friend and fellow illustrator, Gertrude Woodward. Beatrix and Norman Warne were never alone in each other's company. But in spite of these barriers, Beatrix's letters reveal that a friendship was developing as they worked on ideas for books and grappled with the complex problems of printing. In November she had given him a version of the squirrel book. Although he liked the idea, he thought it was too long and included too many riddles. She had also proposed a story about a frog for the second time. A more familiar tone is apparent in her letter to Norman on 6 November: 'I should like to do Mr Jeremy Fisher too some day, and I think I could make something of him, though I am afraid your remark that the story is very *interesting* must have been sarcastic!'[8]

In December, Beatrix sent Norman a copy of the privately printed *Tailor of Gloucester*. She had previously explained its origin, but now had misgivings about the whole thing. 'I thought it a very pretty story when I heard it in the country, but it has proved rather beyond my capacity for working out. All the same it is quite possible you may like it better than the squirrels; things look less silly in type.' Wondering if she had been wise to publish it herself, she wrote two weeks later, 'I undertook the book with very cheerful courage, but I have not the least judgment whether it is satisfactory now that it is done, I'm afraid it is going to fall rather flat here.' Two days later, Norman replied with only moderate enthusiasm. He wanted to see how well the privately printed edition was received, but hoped in the meantime that Beatrix would work on the squirrel drawings. Her idea for a book of rhymes was laid aside – at least for the time being.[9]

A month later Beatrix was busy marketing her latest privately printed tale. She sent a copy of *The Tailor of Gloucester* to Mrs Wicksteed, their former neighbour and the widow of the prominent Unitarian minister, explaining:

I find that children of the right age – about 12 – like it best; the smaller ones who could learn off the short sentences of 'Peter' find this one too long; . . . I am trying to make a squirrel book at present, I have got a very pretty little model; I bought two but they weren't a pair, and fought so frightfully that I had to get rid of the handsomer – and most savage one. The other squirrel [called 'Twinkleberry'], is rather a nice little animal, but half of one ear has been bitten off, which spoils his appearance!

Beatrix sent the new book to the grandchildren of the Pre-Raphaelite painter Edward Burne-Jones, and again told how she was busy drawing a little squirrel and would make a new book about him. 'I have made him a house of a soap box,' drawing a picture of it, '& hung it inside a big bird-cage.' That way, Beatrix explained, she could observe the squirrels' activities and sketch them at any hour.[10]

The Tale of Squirrel Nutkin shares something of the same immediacy of story-telling as *Peter Rabbit*, a quality which comes from beginning life as a picture letter for a real child. *Nutkin*, however, is not only a story about the consequences of disobedience and rudeness, but differs from *Peter Rabbit* in that it is a 'story of place', being set quite specifically and identifiably on the shores of Derwentwater. Basing her narrative line on the story she had first told Noel about the squirrels using their tails as sails, she embellished it with the local tale about red squirrels that mysteriously appeared on St Herbert's Island just when the nuts were ripe. She embellished it with a number of her favourite riddles and rhymes. *Nutkin* falls into the tradition of *pourquoi* tales as it explains how Nutkin's tail came to be shorter than those of all the other squirrels. It has a sense of a folk tale because it also shares the secret of what squirrels say when they chatter, and why they sometimes throw nuts at each other and at humans.

The published story further differs from *Peter Rabbit* in that Nutkin and his friends do not wear clothes, but are only minimally anthropomorphized by their human-like behaviour. The squirrels live in their accurately drawn natural habitat, but Nutkin dances on his hind legs, while the other squirrels and Old Brown, the owl who rules Owl Island, behave like real animals. Potter comes closest in this book to the kind of natural history writing that was popular at the turn of the century, where the story is a vehicle for conveying knowledge to young readers about wildlife and animal behaviour. Viewed in this way, *Nutkin* succeeds. But Nutkin himself is not as sympathetic a character as Peter for he is unapologetically rude to Old Brown, and he is lucky to escape with just a shorter tail. Although Norman tried to minimize the number of riddles, the compromise, unlike that achieved in the *Tailor*, is less satisfactory. While the narrative is amusing, the quality of the writing and the narrative pace are diminished by so many interruptions.[11]

Perhaps the most enchanting part of *Nutkin* is in the beautifully detailed drawing of a real island that can still be identified by reference to these backgrounds. In addition to making sketches from both sides of the island, the shore at Lingholm, and even the view from the fells on the opposite side of the lake, Potter took photographs of many of the same views. There are several black-and-white photographs of Old Brown's tree, which stood for many years after on St Herbert's Island. Its gnarly holes, large, sturdy, almost menacing roots and branches, and rough textured bark are clearly visible in her photographs, as well as the ferns and detritus of the forest floor. Her photographs and paintings are nearly perfect mirrors of one another.[12]

Beatrix understood that real nature has a hard edge and *Nutkin* is a violent story. She does not shy away from depicting it, knowing that it is faithful to life, and that ruthlessness and violence are always popular with children. There is a surreal element in this story as well as the first evidence of Potter's sense of the sardonic; an attribute that is rarely included in children's books, or rarely done well, and which links her to Jane Austen whose understated humour she admired.[13]

In the end, Warne decided to publish both *The Tale of Squirrel Nutkin* and *The Tailor of Gloucester* in 1903, although there was a great deal of discussion about how much the latter had to be shortened. 'I am very glad I came again to Bedford St,' Beatrix wrote to Norman before departing for Wales in February; 'it seemed a pity to have different opinions about it, after having agreed so pleasantly about the rabbit book.' From Denbigh, where she was staying with the Burtons at Gwaynynog, she wrote happily, 'I am quite satisfied with the agreements; my cotton-spinning uncle thinks the per-centage very good; & I think the same.'[14]

Beatrix finished the drawings for *Nutkin* first, remembering just in the nick of time to add the dedication, 'A Story for Norah'. She did not settle into making the necessary revisions for *The Tailor of Gloucester* until late May after she returned to Gloucester for more sketching. But it was at Melford Hall, in Suffolk, the grand home of her cousin Ethel, Lady Hyde Parker, that she found the perfect model for the old-fashioned fireplace in the tailor's shop. When she was in London, her writing took her increasingly away from Bolton Gardens. She went to the Warne office in the Strand several times a week to review blocks and designs. Some days she was at the London Zoological Gardens sketching owls, trying to improve upon her drawing of Old Brown. She frequently visited the costume department of the South Kensington Museum refining the illustrations for the *Tailor*. In March, Beatrix made the happy discovery that she could ask the curator to display some of the eighteenth-century costumes in the collection in an empty office where the light was better. 'I have been looking at them for a long time in an inconvenient dark corner of the goldsmith's court, but had no idea they could be taken out of the case.' Her status as the author of *Peter Rabbit* was such that an assistant was subtly assigned to see that Miss Potter had whatever she needed from the collection. The first things she asked for were the beautifully embroidered dresses, coats and vests that were later to become the hallmark of *The Tailor of Gloucester*.[15]

There was other good news. Warne's had decided that the two books should have a de-luxe edition bound in a more elaborate fabric. Beatrix immediately sought out fabric samples from E. Potter & Company, her grandfather's calico printing company in Dinting Vale, which could print in any desired shade of colour, or cloth. After looking at a great many samples which were unsuitable for one reason or another, she chose a flower pattern art fabric with scattered pansies. She later described these two books as 'bound in a flowered lavender chintz, very pretty', and took pleasure in this serendipitous connection to her grandfather's old firm.

Endpapers in full colour were also introduced in both these books. Beatrix had been unenthusiastic about the idea, and said so bluntly, but she obediently designed a freshly coloured delicate chain that linked the characters from each book around the edges of the page; at least one character would hold the appropriate book with its title. In time new characters were introduced to endpapers as each book was published. Warne's were delighted with Beatrix's design and with the marketing potential the endpapers offered, as new characters could be introduced before the next book was published, hinting at the title to come.[16]

But there were unexpected setbacks: colours were wrong – too green or too red – and more seriously, a mistake by Hentschel's in making the blocks for the *Tailor*. Ignoring Beatrix's wishes, they removed a critical black line around the vignetted plates. Beatrix had relied on the line, especially in the illustrations of the town in winter, to make the snow in the foreground stand out as white. After her protest, a new block of the gateway was made and the line restored around the others. Although Beatrix was sad about having so many of her favourite rhymes and verses cut, she trusted Norman's judgement. She did not, however, understand why he objected to her illustration of the rats carousing at a Christmas Eve party under the mayor's shop. Years later she wrote, 'one of them [was] drinking out of a black bottle. For the life of me, I could not see why Mr Warne insisted on cutting it out?'[17]

Norman brought back bad news from his trip to Warne's New York office. Somehow they had failed to register the copyright for *Peter Rabbit* in the United States. Pirated editions, from which Beatrix would receive no royalties, began to appear in the spring of 1903, and there was nothing anyone could do to stop them. 'I was very sorry to hear about the American edition,' she wrote to Norman. 'I trust they have not got hold of a copy of the mouse book [*Tailor*] also; but perhaps the private edition is not worth stealing.' The enormous financial damage resulting from this oversight only became evident with time, but the lesson was not lost on Beatrix who had worried much earlier about copyright for other reasons. The necessity of protecting her intellectual property was reinforced during the Christmas season, when Rupert Potter bought a toy squirrel at the Burlington Arcade in Mayfair marketed as 'Nutkin'.[18]

The Tale of Squirrel Nutkin was published in August 1903 and became an instant success. 'I am *delighted* to hear such a good account of Nutkin,' she wrote to Norman. 'I never thought when I was drawing it that it would be such a success – though I think you always had a good opinion of it.' She asked for more copies, sympathizing with him that 'it must be a troublesome business to distribute 10,000'. Beatrix began receiving amusing letters from delighted young readers that Norman forwarded to her from Bedford Street. 'I shall always have a strong preference for cheap books myself – even if they did not pay,' she wrote to him; 'all my little friends happen to be shilling people. I do dislike the modern fashion of giving children heaps of expensive things which they don't look at twice.'[19]

The Tailor of Gloucester was published in October, in ample time for Christmas. In a presentation copy Beatrix wrote, 'This is my own favourite amongst my little books.' Over the years her opinion never wavered. Although Beatrix was always in love with the past, the *Tailor* was the only costumed romance she ever produced. In 1919 she wrote to the wife of the President of Magdalen College, Oxford: 'It has always been my own favourite . . . I used to stay with some cousins on the edge of the Cotswolds, overlooking the vale of Severn; they told me the story of the tailor; and I added the mice & the old fashioned coats . . . The Tailor never caught on like the others, but he is far the best.'[20]

The *Tailor* remains a public favourite, associated with the Christmas spirit, beloved because of the charming mice in their eighteenth-century finery, their heroic assistance to the poor, sick tailor, and the magic that the setting, the story and the illustrations weave. It has some of Potter's most beautiful and most elaborate illustrations, breathtaking in their detail, particularly that of the Mayor's embroidered waistcoat, which has since been identified and is still part of the costume collection of the Victoria and Albert Museum. But Beatrix always preferred her own privately printed edition to all others because 'it contains more of the old rhymes (including the Christmas wedding day) . . .'[21]

Her enthusiasm for the *Tailor* was soon confirmed by an unexpected source. Beatrix wrote to Norman just after Christmas with obvious pleasure, 'Did you ever happen to see a review of the *Tailor* in *The Tailor & Cutter*, the paper which the mouse on the bobbin is reading?' She had given a copy to her old Chelsea tailor, who in turn, had shown it to a traveller from the trade journal telling him how Beatrix had sketched his shop. The 'beautiful' review, as Beatrix called it, appeared appropriately on Christmas Eve. It read:

. . . we think it is by far the prettiest story connected with tailoring we have ever read, and as it is full of that spirit of Peace on Earth, Goodwill to Men, we are not ashamed to confess that it brought the moisture to our eyes, as well as the smile to our face. It is got up in choicest style and illustrated by twenty-seven of the prettiest pictures it is possible to imagine.[22]

The three 'little books', as they were now called, had changed both Frederick Warne & Co. and Beatrix Potter. Warne's had found their answer to Mrs Bannerman and acknowledged their happiness with the successful new writer on their list. And Beatrix had never been happier. Her work gave her satisfaction, and success gave her a new self-confidence. She had achieved what she had longed for: a little money of her own and a certain measure of independence. For the first time she got up in the morning with something purposeful to do. She had publishers to visit, proofs to approve, places she needed to visit to sketch, small but meaningful affairs to manage. She desperately hoped that the books might continue, for she had so many ideas.

But every time a holiday loomed, Beatrix felt a certain panic that there would be no more books to consume her energies and offer a diversion from family demands. Facing the prospect of another long summer away from London, Beatrix wrote to Norman before she left for Keswick in July 1903 proposing another project.

I had been a little hoping too that something might be said about another book, but I did not know that I was the right person to make the suggestion. I could send you a list to consider, there are plenty in vague state of existence, one written out in a small copybook which I will get back from the children and send to you to read. I had better try to sketch this summer, as the stock of ideas for backgrounds is rather used up. I would very much like to do another next winter.

She ventured the opinion that both *Tailor* and *Nutkin* were complicated stories compared to *Peter* and suggested that the next 'Little Book' ought to be 'more simple'.[23]

She was surprised when her letter was unexpectedly answered by Harold Warne, as Norman had already left London on an extended selling trip. Harold invited her to come in to the office to discuss her ideas. This was not at all what Beatrix had in mind, for she wanted only to see Norman Warne. She hastily explained that she could not come and tried to cover her disappointment. 'If I had not supposed that the matter would be dealt with through the post, I should not have mentioned the subject of another book at present. I have had such painful unpleasantness at home this winter about the work that I should like a rest, while I am away. I should be obliged if you will kindly say no more about a new book at present.'[24]

Realizing later that she had been too quick in her reply, Beatrix wrote again suggesting to Harold that she might 'make out a rough outline of the stories . . . & post it to you from Fawe Park, Keswick. I should not propose to work on any story while away, but if I knew what was likely to be chosen it would be a guide for sketching.' She closed with a thinly veiled plea to have her letters forwarded to 'Mr Norman Warne'.[25]

Beatrix had become one of the most important authors on the Warne's list. Aware from his initial meeting with Rupert Potter that Beatrix's parents were demanding, Harold Warne gently encouraged her to send something for Norman to review on his return. Beatrix agreed. 'I think I will send the rabbit story as well when I have copied it out, perhaps Mr Norman Warne might be amused to look it over when he comes back.' When Norman returned, they agreed that one of the two new stories should be *The Tale of Benjamin Bunny*, a sequel of sorts to *Peter Rabbit* in which Peter and his cousin Benjamin boldly return to Mr McGregor's garden in search of Peter's lost coat and shoes. The choice of a second book remained undecided. Norman suggested that it might be something in a larger format, similar to that of the popular *Johnny Crow's Garden* by L. Leslie Brooke which Warne's had recently published.[26]

By early September, Beatrix was looking forward to returning to London, although she admitted that 'autumn is far away the best time at the Lakes'. She had been working hard and had painted a great many backgrounds. Fawe Park had proved an ideal setting for another 'bunny book'. It was a large, comfortable country house estate, beautiful but less formal than Lingholm, and more to Beatrix's liking. Its real appeal lay in its gardens and gardeners. Three sides of the house were landscaped in beautifully terraced gardens running down to the lake. Some, close to the house, were formal beds, but down the hillside, enclosed and hidden away from the road by a high brick wall, there was a kitchen garden with greenhouses, cold frames and a potting shed, as well as an orchard with espaliered fruit trees and arbours.

Beatrix probably began drawing the gardens just for their interest and colour without any plan for how she might use them. But soon she added these as backgrounds to the Derwentwater sketchbook she had begun. Once again she was fascinated with the details of the gardens – the baskets and crocks in the potting shed – with lettuces and how their leaves looked when first up, and with onions, drawing them both in and out of the ground in watercolours of striking beauty. She drew the garden wall, the overhanging pear tree and the cold frames and greenhouses in great detail. She worked all summer painting backgrounds, using another female rabbit she had brought along as her model. She confessed to Norman, 'I think I have done every imaginable rabbit background, & miscellaneous sketches as well – about 70! I hope you will like them, though rather scribbled.' Rupert once again took photographs of Fawe Park, its interior and the grassy shoreline, just as he had at Lingholm, but there are no extant photographs by Beatrix though it is likely that she used photography again to aid her recording of the gardens.[27]

Norman left on another selling trip in early November, shortly after *The Tailor of Gloucester* was published, and Beatrix was again frustrated by his absence. 'I am afraid I am not making a good start yet with the rabbit book,' she explained to Harold Warne. 'I have been rather bothered but I hope it will come right; when will Mr Norman Warne be coming back?' She had a cold, she explained, and longed for time in the countryside in pleasant weather to do more sketching. 'I wish I could get the new books settled,' she wrote, obviously frustrated by the delay. Three days later Norman returned and Beatrix made arrangements to call at the Warne office to discuss the next book before leaving for a week in Hastings on the south coast. From there Beatrix sent Norman a copy book containing three stories: one about a cat, in which she used sketches of cottage interiors in Sawrey; one about a long-haired guinea pig; and another featuring a pair of mice she had brought home with her after a visit to Harescombe Grange the previous June. Before she left to spend the Christmas holidays at Melford Hall, she promised Norman she would 'try the new stories on the children there'.[28]

Beatrix's new happiness and its source had not been lost on her parents. Before the summer holiday at Fawe Park, they complained she was working too hard, straining her eyes, spending too much time sketching, inattentive to her domestic responsibilities, out of the house too often, or a combination of all these. There had been criticism, adverse comment and 'painful unpleasantness'. Beatrix returned from Fawe Park in September unchastened, yet ever the dutiful and deferential daughter. Now at the end of the year, she was happily committed to working with Norman Warne on another two new books for 1904. Observing this extended partnership, and their daughter's pleasure in it, the Potters were justly alarmed.

8

❧ *Realities* ❧

BEDFORD SQUARE WAS ON THE other side of London's busy West End from Bolton Gardens, not distant geographically, but in style and substance the Warne and Potter households were worlds apart. The well-known Square on the western edge of Bloomsbury was distinguished by its rows of impressive Georgian brick houses, each with its wrought-iron balcony to the first floor windows. Nearly adjacent on the east was, and still is, the imposing British Museum, and beyond that, Russell Square, north of Holborn. Until 1893 Bedford Square had been sealed off by gates, a quiet oasis where tradesmen entered on foot. It was a neighbourhood of distinguished scientists and jurists, architects and authors, professionals and merchants, as well as assorted high-level Crown appointees.[1]

Although the Warne house had a certain architectural formality and the requisite dark Victorian furnishings, light and air streamed through the lace curtains at the library windows just as abundantly as the echoes of spontaneous laughter from the visitors who seemed always to be about. There were servants, but no butler. The large and active Warne family and their friends made it a point not to let the recently widowed Louisa Jane Warne be too long without company. Although Millie and Norman lived at home, the Bedford Square house was the spontaneous gathering point for the whole family. When Frederick Warne was alive, the large dining room table was nearly always filled with people at the midday meal. After his death, the atmosphere remained one of ease and freedom, of good conversation and ready celebration, a place where children were especially welcome.

Mrs Warne came from an old established Channel Islands family. She was a soft-spoken, interesting and observant lady in lace cap and ribbons, who had taken an active interest in her late husband's publishing business and was now doted on by her whole family. Norman was her 'baby' and undoubtedly her favourite. He was also everyone's favourite uncle or cousin, and he in turn was genuinely fond of his nephews and nieces. He played sports, especially tennis, cycled and swam with the boys, enjoyed catching moths with his brothers, dressed up as 'Father Christmas' during holiday parties, and roared with delight when the children discovered that it was 'only Uncle Norman' behind the beard and costume.[2]

Norman was reserved in his own way, thoughtful rather than effusive, enjoying the intellectual challenges attendant on acquiring and publishing a superior line of books. Now in his mid-thirties, he worked long hours and was not particularly interested in the 'ladies', although his mother had not given up the hope of more grandchildren. Photographs show a tall, slender, attractive man with a receding hairline, wide-set hazel eyes framed by arched brows, a long, straight nose, a full moustache, and a strong chin. The family is said to have thought he resembled the novelist Robert Louis Stevenson.

Norman Warne not only knew a great deal about book design and production, he was also mechanically skilled and enjoyed carpentry. He had devised a makeshift workshop in the basement and there produced bird houses, display cases for his moth collection, toys and even doll's houses. 'I really think I shall have to start building a new doll's house if you dress such a lot of dolls,' he promised one of his little nieces. But when he finally got around to it, the most elaborate doll's house was built for his niece Winifred Warne for Christmas 1903.[3]

Millie Warne, a decade older than Norman and eight years older than Beatrix, was a slender, almost frail woman with a pretty oval face and deep-set eyes. She was almost as shy as Beatrix herself, but was unpretentious and often amusing. She was also fond of the outdoors and of gardening. After they had met several times, Millie and Beatrix became easy friends. Occasionally Beatrix was invited by the Warne brothers to come to Bedford Square for holiday celebrations. Parties at Bedford Square were really for the children, and everyone played games.[4]

Beatrix, now 37, was a handsome woman, and although still shy, refreshingly straightforward. She had a slightly rounded figure, and was always memorable with her pink cheeks, her easy flush and her bright blue eyes. Her hair still came loose from its pins in occasional wavy wisps around her face. She preferred tailored clothes without much ornamentation, and she was rarely without her large, black umbrella, though she could be properly suited out in fine fabrics, lace jabots and elaborate millinery if the occasion demanded.

When not absorbed with her work on *The Tale of Benjamin Bunny*, and while she was awaiting Norman's decision about the subject of the second book for 1904, Beatrix turned her ingenuity to creating a Peter Rabbit doll. She was clearly unhappy with the 'knock-off' German rabbits advertised at Harrods, the big department store in Knightsbridge, and aware that 'there was a run on toys copied from pictures'. After the Nutkin doll appeared in a local shop before Christmas, Beatrix took action. 'I am cutting out calico patterns of Peter,' she told Norman. 'I have not got it right yet, but the expression is going to be lovely; especially the whiskers – (pulled out of a brush!). I think I will make one first of white velveteen painted . . . fur is very difficult to sew.' Referring to the notebook of stories she had left with Norman earlier, she continued: 'I cannot tell what to do about those stories, it would certainly be more amusing to do the one with toys . . . At present I intend to make dolls; I think I could make him stand on his legs if he had some lead bullets in his feet!'[5]

A Peter Rabbit doll with his signature blue coat and black shoes was ready for the public on 15 December and Beatrix sent it to Norman to give to one of his nieces. 'I hope the little girl will like the doll,' she wrote. 'There is some shot in the body & coat tail, I don't think it will come out until the legs give way, children some-times expect comfits out of animals, so I give fair warning!' She took photographs of her creation and, in order not to be caught out again, registered the design at the Patent Office in Chancery Lane on 28 December 1903. She received Patent No. 423888.[6]

She later referred to her merchandise somewhat derisively as her 'sideshows', but this was said disarmingly as she took a serious interest in it, and was quick to take advantage of the marketplace.

She knew instinctively the kinds of derivative toys and accessories that might flow from her stories. At first Beatrix had to keep prodding Norman to 'do something about the dolls', but although he, too, was intrigued by the possibility of such collateral merchandise, it was left primarily to Beatrix to find a manufacturer. Undeterred, she did her own market research. She insisted that the dolls be made in Britain – a requirement which proved unexpectedly difficult as most of the soft toys then on the market were produced more cheaply in Germany and imported without tariff. Her efforts to find a domestic manufacturer marked the beginning of her scepticism about the benefits of the free trade policy her Potter grandfather had advocated so ardently.[7]

The search for a proper rabbit manufacturer went on for several months. 'I find that Harrod's [*sic*] rabbits are *very ugly*,' Beatrix told Norman in April after inspecting the store's selection for workmanship and colour. She found a fur rabbit at Porters, a nearby shop in South Kensington that she knew well, but hesitated to proceed without Norman's approval. 'Do you think it would be worth while to let them make a sample one? Telling them carefully that the doll is copyright. It is a shop I have known for many years, I think I could get at the maker's name by perseverance, they are civil people. I enjoyed going about the rabbits. I did not say who I was, Mrs Porter "knew Peter Rabbit" & I thought seemed rather keen on the dolls idea.' By the end of the year, she reported confidentially, 'The rabbit dollies are in great force at Whitely's.'[8]

Beatrix's instinct about the market for derivative merchandise was much in advance of her publishers' and right on the mark. Not long after she registered her prototype for a Peter Rabbit doll, she was approached by a Mrs Garnett, a woman whom she knew only slightly, who had made a 'frieze' for her children's nursery out of Peter Rabbit drawings. It had proved so popular with her friends that she wanted to show it to a wallpaper manufacturer. Although she was taken aback by Garnett's 'artless appeal' to profit from her ideas, Beatrix agreed the idea of wallpaper had merit. 'I should think it would make a very popular nursery paper,' she told Norman. 'Of course if it were done at all it *ought* to be done by me – but *I* find it rather awkward to say so. I think I could do it rather well – if it were not too much trouble. The idea of rooms covered with badly drawn rabbits is appalling.' After this, Beatrix took control of the derivative market. Getting the colours right and determining the proper elevation of the figures proved more difficult than she had first thought but by early 1905 Beatrix confidently told Norman, 'Mr McGregor is magnificent on the frieze.' Soon she was redesigning it in different colours and wondering if Liberty's, the prestigious fabric shop, might produce it. Although it took some time to find the right manufacturer, Peter Rabbit wallpaper was part of an eventual programme of 'spin-offs' from Potter's books.[9]

Never short of new ideas for merchandise, Beatrix enjoyed thinking about how children might respond to the story or the character in another medium and was artistically challenged by the adaptive process. She liked being involved in the details of negotiations for various products, insisted that the quality of the original art be maintained in any adaptation, and maintained final approval for new merchandise. Beatrix also had an idea for a Peter Rabbit board game. She understood from the outset that while the other book characters might eventually be used as models for merchandise, Peter would always be the most sought after, so that any game had to centre around him.

In a letter to Norman at the end of 1904 Beatrix enclosed a sketch of a game board and a list of rules for playing *The Game of Peter Rabbit*. It was a square-to-square chase game with the object of keeping Mr McGregor from landing on the same square as Peter, thereby capturing him. 'I think this is a rather good game,' she wrote with pleasure. 'I have written the rules at some length, (to prevent arguments!) but it is very simple, & the chances are strongly in favour of Peter.' She needed feedback from real children, however, and asked Norman if he would 'cut out two little wooden pawns, to represent Peter and Mr McGregor, and try the game with some child at Christmas.' Remembering a game called 'Go-Bang' that she had played as a little girl, she wanted to make the map of McGregor's garden larger and mount it on hinged pasteboard that folded in half. 'It is too late to do anything with it this season,' she acknowledged, 'but I think it is a game that children might find exciting, if they were fond of the book.'[10]

Exhibiting the kind of artistic innovation which would have made her calico-designing grandfather proud, Beatrix usually knew exactly how she wanted something produced. In the case of the board game, she wrote, 'I have tried it with the corks; it wants coloured wooden solid persons, like the old fashioned "Noah."' At Norman's suggestion, she made alterations to the garden map aware that if a child were playing the game with adults, the child would want to be 'Peter'. But first she asked Norman to copyright the game, and even before the board or the moves were perfected, he dutifully registered it at Stationers' Hall. Potter's merchandising efforts would bring lucrative licences, producing an eventual royalty windfall for both Frederick Warne & Co., who held the copyright, and for the clever creator.[11]

Beatrix responded to Norman's appreciation and his growing recognition of her artistry and professionalism, try as she might to hide it under the guise of the well-to-do amateur. As they discussed the evolution of her books and the step-by-step process by which they were designed and produced, she realized that his tactful criticism almost always improved her work. She was grateful for that, as well as for his practical advice. In fact there seemed little that Norman could not invent or improve. Beatrix's pet mice, 'Tom Thumb' and 'Hunca Munca', were a case in point.

She had rescued the two mice from the kitchen at Harescombe Grange in 1903 and tamed them. They proved interesting subjects, but her home-made cage allowed only limited visibility of their activities and was too fragile. Aware of Norman's carpentry skills, Beatrix asked him to make her a new box for Hunca Munca, the female mouse, who was an especially good artist's model as well as a sweet pet. Beatrix wrote to Norman, referring to him as 'Johnny Crow', a nickname that his nieces and nephews had given him. 'I wish "Johnny Crow" would make my mouse "a little house",' Beatrix asked, 'do you think he would if I made a paper plan? I want one with the glass at the side before I draw Hunca Munca again. Mine are apt to be ricketty [*sic*]!'[12]

Just before the new year, Norman presented Beatrix with a new mouse house featuring not only a glass front, but a ladder to an upstairs nesting loft. The mice were happily installed and Beatrix could now watch them go about their activities unimpeded. Knowing that Norman would be out of town soon, Beatrix wrote again with some urgency about the still undecided second book for 1904. 'If neither the cat nor the mice would do, one *might* fall back on the rhymes – "Apperly [*sic*] Dapply". I think you will see the difficulty with the mice from what I have sketched already, but I could make a nice *little* book of them.' The cage, her sketches, and the miniature scale of domesticity the little house presented had given her the idea that the mice were the perfect residents for a doll's house like the one she had admired in Norman's basement workshop. And so it was decided that the second book, tentatively titled 'The Tale of the Doll's House and Hunca Munca', would be about the two mice, and that it and *Benjamin Bunny*, a sequel to *Peter Rabbit*, would be in identical small book format.[13]

The large doll's house that Norman had built for Winifred was a three-storeyed affair with a brick paper exterior, a grey slate roof with gables, a turret and a flagstaff. It was a splendid reproduction of a proper Edwardian villa, and fully furnished. Around Christmas-time, Norman installed it at Fruing Warne's house in Surbiton, south of London, so the little nieces could move their dolls in.

By February, Beatrix had planned a story featuring her fine little mouse, Hunca Munca. She wanted to use Winifred's doll's house as a model for one in the book, but it was now inconveniently some distance away. Norman arranged for Beatrix to come to Surbiton for lunch and do her sketching. Beatrix would have been delighted to accept, but Mrs Potter intervened. Although control of the carriage was the initial sticking point, as far as Helen Potter was concerned there had already been too much visiting at the Warne home and office. Aware of the almost daily letters between her daughter and Norman, she sensed that her daughter's relationship with the Warne family, and with Norman in particular, was becoming more than just professional. She did not like its direction, nor did she like the Warnes, who were a family 'in trade'. There was unpleasantness and Beatrix was forced to decline Norman's invitation to Surbiton.

'I was very much perplexed about the doll's house,' Beatrix wrote to Norman in an effort to apologize for what she was afraid would be misinterpreted as rudeness on her part. 'I would have gone gladly to draw it, and I should be so *very* sorry if Mrs Warne or you thought me uncivil. I did not think I could manage to go to Surbiton without staying [to] lunch.' Clearly conflicted as to what she could offer as explanation and berating herself for failing to stand up to her mother, Beatrix continued, 'I hardly ever go out, and my mother is so "exacting" I had not enough spirit to say anything about it. I have felt vexed with myself since, but I did not know what to do. It does wear a person out.' Concerned that her inability to sketch the doll's house might compromise the entire project, Beatrix reassured Norman, 'I will manage to make a nice book somehow . . . I think I can do it from the photograph . . . but it is very hard to have seemed uncivil.'[14]

If Norman sensed the real reason for Mrs Potter's opposition, he hid it well, and did his best to provide Beatrix with what she needed. He took more photographs of the doll's house, and found two dolls at a shop in Seven Dials on the edge of Soho for her to use as models. He was also looking for some plaster food and a stove. 'Thank you so very much for the queer little dollies, they are just exactly what I wanted,' Beatrix wrote to him. 'I will provide a print dress & a smile for Jane; her little stumpy feet are so funny. I think I shall make a dear little book of it, I shall be glad to get done with the rabbits.' The dolls, Lucinda and Jane, were not to scale for Winifred's doll's house, but even so they proved perfect models. Sometime later, Norman also provided a policeman doll, borrowed from a reluctant Winifred.

But Norman persisted in his efforts to get Beatrix to Surbiton, suggesting perhaps Mrs Potter could come to lunch as well. Beatrix's explanation of why this plan would not work was nearer the truth. 'I don't think that my mother would be very likely to want to go to Surbiton,' she told Norman, 'you did not understand what I meant by "exacting." People who only see her casually do not know how disagreeable she can be when she takes dislikes.' Beatrix's frustration and her helplessness to change the situation were transparent, but so too was her loyalty and sense of duty. 'I should have been glad enough to go. I did not know what to do.'[15]

Ever resourceful, Norman sent Beatrix some doll's house furniture and a box of doll's house food on platters. 'I received the parcel from Hamley's this morning; the things will all do beautifully,' Beatrix replied happily, 'the ham's appearance is enough to cause indigestion. I am getting almost more treasures than I can squeeze into one small book.' The furniture and the food inspired some of her best illustrations, including a back view of Hunca Munca mercilessly chopping away at the indigestible plaster ham! Regardless of parental obstacles, *The Tale of Two Bad Mice* was not only turning out to be an enjoyable collaborative adventure, but was also providing the subtext of a love story.[16]

Beatrix worked on the book in high spirits, enjoying the details of the interior of the doll's house as well as Hunca Munca's antics. 'I stopped her in the act of carrying a doll as large as herself up to the nest, she cannot resist anything with lace or ribbon; (she despises the dishes),' she reported. Norman supplied Beatrix with interior and exterior views of the doll's house. Their enjoyment of working together on the book, even in this bifurcated way, was obvious and infectious. They shared the sorts of small personal details that deepen a relationship. 'The inside view is amusing,' Beatrix wrote after looking at the photographs, 'the kind of house where one cannot sit down without upsetting something, I know the sort! I prefer a more severe style . . .' In due course the book was finished. Beatrix dedicated it to Winifred Warne: 'for W. M. L. W. the little girl who had the doll's house.'[17]

The Potters were away from London a good part of the spring, first to the Burtons at Gwaynynog, in Denbigh, and then to Lyme Regis on the Dorset coast. Beatrix took Hunca Munca, who was 'very discontented in the small old box', and her pet hedgehog, Mrs Tiggy-winkle, 'carefully concealed – my aunt cannot endure animals!' She told Norman she had been 'drawing the stump of a hollow tree for another hedgehog drawing; there is not much sign of spring yet but the moss is very pretty in the woods'. The idea for a book about Tiggy-winkle was taking shape, even though Norman was not convinced such an unusual animal would make a popular children's story.[18]

While at Gwaynynog Beatrix enlisted her uncle, Fred Burton, who collected antique furniture, to help her select a handsome Sheraton bureau with impressive joinery that she could use as a bookcase. Before she left London she had received a sizeable royalty statement. 'I was very much amused about the money,' she wrote to Norman. 'I do happen to have been making myself an expensive present.' But she also had other uses for the money, explaining, 'I am going to send one of the little [Moore] girls to college some day, either "Norah" of the squirrel book or "Frida" [*sic*], but there is time enough yet. Their mother was my governess.' Both investments reflect Beatrix's north-country values: fine old furniture and education for women. Although Beatrix did not support the contemporary women's rights movement, her Unitarian tradition had long advocated higher education for women.[19]

In April the Potters visited the charming town of Lyme Regis on the Dorset coast for a fortnight. Beatrix enjoyed fine weather and good sketching. She made several drawings of the town, the main street, its shops and houses, and enjoyed some long but lonely walks. She appears to have been the secretary of a postal drawing society and received some sketches from one of the society members while she was on holiday. Much earlier Beatrix had belonged to a drawing society, but now, as a well-known illustrator, it is interesting that she continued an involvement. She was known to the members by her real name, and obviously took her role seriously, seeing to it that members' portfolios were received and reviewed promptly. While she was still in Dorset, Norman sent a ledger showing unexpectedly brisk sales of *Nutkin*. Beatrix replied, 'it seems a great deal of money for such little books . . . It is pleasant to feel I could earn my own living.' Her original desire for financial independence was now being fulfilled quite beyond her expectations, but it is likely that she already had other ideas of how she wanted to invest her profits.[20]

The spring of 1904 was a busy one. Beatrix was finishing two books, working on a rabbit doll, creating other merchandise, and always thinking about the next book. Warne's suggested she might illustrate the work of another writer whose book they wanted to publish. But Beatrix declined their offer, not only because she wanted to husband her time for her own books, but because she enjoyed being recognized as the illustrator of her own work. 'With regard to illustrating other peoples books,' she told the publisher, 'I have a strong feeling that every outside book which I did, would prevent me from finishing one of my own. I enjoy inventing stories – any number – but I draw so slowly & laboriously, that there are sure to be favourites of my own left undone at the end of my working life-time, whether short or long . . . I will stick to doing as many as I can of my own books.' She did, however, agree to design the Warne catalogue for the winter of 1904. 'I should be delighted to try to make a design on approval for the book-list. I don't know if I should succeed but I can try,' she wrote modestly. 'I think the usual price for that sort of thing is about £2 if you think that reasonable.' She was also designing new endpapers for *The Tale of Two Bad Mice*.[21]

About the time *Nutkin* appeared, Beatrix began sending miniature letters to some of her young friends. These tiny letters were frequently conversations between animal characters in her books that continued the story or offered amusing new anecdotes about their activities. They allowed Beatrix to carry on conversations with the children who, although growing older, were still interested in her fantasy animals and what happened to them after the story ended.[22]

Each tiny letter was folded in such a way that it became its own envelope. Each was addressed and had a small stamp drawn in red crayon. There were no drawings in these miniature letters, simply a few brief sentences from one character to another. Sometimes the letters arrived with their own red tin British postbox. Others, like those to the Moore children, came in a miniature mail-bag inscribed 'G. P. O.' [General Post Office]. Beatrix did not stop writing picture letters, especially when she was on holiday, but these miniature letters could be done quickly. They became more complex as the books and cast of animal characters grew, and were often quite amusing.[23]

An early letter from Squirrel Nutkin to Old Brown read: 'Dear Sir, I should esteem it a favour if you will let me have back my tail, as I miss it very much. I would pay postage. yrs truly Squirrel Nutkin. An answer will oblige.' Another to 'Mrs Tom Thumb, Mouse Hole', was written after *The Tale of Two Bad Mice* was published. 'Miss Lucinda Doll requires Hunca Munca to come for the whole day on Tuesday. Jane Dollcook has had an accident, she has broken the soup tureen and both her wooden legs.' A letter to Mrs Rabbit from Tiggy-winkle, the hedgehog laundress, offers an apology for too much starch. 'Indeed I apologize for the *starch* & hope you will forgive me. Indeed it is Tom Titmouse if you please 'm, he does want his collars that *starchy*, my mind does get full of pins!' Frequently the miniature letters told something of Miss Potter's activities, or hinted at what the next book might be.[24]

By the middle of June, both *The Tale of Benjamin Bunny* and *The Tale of Two Bad Mice* were nearly finished. Beatrix spent a great deal of time going over the page proofs, making corrections, while resisting the changes suggested by the copy editor. 'I wish the printer could set Hunca Munca on one line,' she wrote, 'at all events on this page where first mentioned.' ' "Leant against" instead of "stood" and "conversed," children like a fine word occasionally.' She had very particular reasons for her choice of language; sometimes it was rhythm and cadence, sometimes it was the sound of a word, or just something that amused her. She had an intuitive sense about what children liked. Endings and beginnings of books were always very important and she took great trouble with them. For *The Tale of Benjamin Bunny* she specified, 'I would like the book to end with the word "rabbit tobacco" it is a rather fine word.' It was also a word drawn from *Uncle Remus*.[25]

The Tale of Benjamin Bunny and *The Tale of Two Bad Mice* were published simultaneously by Warne's in September 1904. The action of *Benjamin Bunny* takes place in Mr McGregor's garden, which is no longer a Scottish vegetable garden, but modelled on the garden of Fawe Park at Derwentwater. Reflecting the Lake District location as well as the author's familiarity with the area, the dedication reads: 'for the children of Sawrey from old Mr Bunny.' Although *Two Bad Mice* has an upper-middle-class Edwardian doll's house as its 'house-within-a-house' setting, it too has a reference to Sawrey, for

Lucinda and Jane Doll-cook buy their groceries at Ginger and Pickles shop in the village. Her genuine interest in the village children was evident a few months later when she heard there had been an epidemic of scarlet fever in Sawrey and that the school was closed. She asked Norman 'for books to be sent to the little people at Sawrey', but insisted 'there are to be no letters of thanks!'[26]

Eager for news of how the latest books were being received, Beatrix wrote to Norman from Keswick, 'Are you printing a large edition of Benjamin, does it seem to be liked?' She need not have worried. Once again her rabbits proved irresistible. Warne printed 20,000 copies of each book, and within a month, *Benjamin Bunny* had to be reprinted. To her chagrin, Beatrix realized that 'Muffettees' was spelled incorrectly; an error that was not corrected until the third printing.[27]

Benjamin Bunny not only sold well but merited a review in *The Times Literary Supplement*, which although not altogether approving, indicates the level of critical attention Potter was receiving. In the reviewer's opinion the story was weak:

Among the little books which have become as much a manifestation of autumn as falling leaves, one looks first for whatever Miss Beatrix Potter gives, for Miss Potter is the author and artist of 'The Tale of Peter Rabbit.' In her new book we meet again with Peter Rabbit, and also with Mr McGregor; but although there is no diminution in the charm and drollery of the drawings, Miss Potter's fancy is not what it was. The story is inconclusive. Next year we think she must call in a literary assistant. We have no hesitation in calling her pencil perfect.

Beatrix found the review 'amusing'. She also enjoyed a good report in the *Scotsman*, but wisely decided that it was 'a mistake to attend to them at all'. Warne had printed another 10,000 copies by the year's end.[28]

The *Times Literary Supplement* reviewer was not off the mark, for none of the subsequent rabbit books ever appealed to Potter in quite the same way as the story of Peter had. Neither of the rabbit sequels began as a picture letter to real children and for that reason they lack a certain vitality. Both *Benjamin Bunny* and the later *Tale of the Flopsy Bunnies* grew out of 'left-over illustrations' from *Peter Rabbit* and are what Beatrix considered 'made to order' books. The weaker story line also reflects her lack of enthusiasm for continuing the *Peter Rabbit* saga: it was surely this lack of energy the reviewer sensed. Even her miniature letters about Benjamin and his family, mostly composed after *Flopsy Bunnies* was published in 1909, reflect a certain boredom with the further lives of the rabbit characters.[29]

But in *Benjamin Bunny* Beatrix had successfully written a 'bunny book' that would appeal to younger children. The plot was less complicated than the previous tales and, almost inevitably, more didactic. At the time the book was conceived, she had few alternatives for the backgrounds since by her own admission she had run out of ideas and consequently had to spend time making new sketches of rabbits in gardens. She was also consciously catering both to the public's demand and to her publisher's desire for another commercial success, while suffering some of the familiar pains of trying to write a sequel to 'an original work of genius'.[30]

The unique quality she brought to *Benjamin Bunny*, in addition to a contagious delight in place, was a thorough understanding of rabbit anatomy and behaviour. Benjamin Bouncer, her model for *Benjamin Bunny*, had been her first pet rabbit and her insights into rabbit nature are remarkable. After walking Benjamin one afternoon at Heath Park in Perthshire in 1892, Beatrix had observed:

Rabbits are creatures of warm volatile temperament but shallow and absurdly transparent. It is this naturalness, one touch of nature, that I find so delightful in Mr Benjamin Bunny, though I frankly admit his vulgarity. At one moment amiably sentimental to the verge of silliness, at the next, the upsetting of a jug or tea-cup . . . will convert him into a demon . . . He is an abject coward, but believes in bluster, could stare our old dog out of countenance, chase a cat that has turned tail . . . Benjamin once fell into an Aquarium head first, and sat in the water which he could not get out of, pretending to eat a piece of string. Nothing like putting a face upon circumstances.[31]

The *Times Literary Supplement* reviewer was also correct in calling attention to her 'pencil perfect' drawings. The beautifully miniaturized backgrounds of the vegetable gardens, as well as the drawings of the rabbits themselves, are some of her finest paintings of this period. Over and over, Beatrix tells her editors that she can make a 'pretty book of it' – and that promise is most often fulfilled in the details of setting and place. She once remarked that it did not matter how large or small the area given her on a page, she could not restrain herself from filling it. This attention to detail – to what is true to nature – is what sets her illustration apart and also what carries a book in which the story line may wander. Her pleasure in sketching at Fawe Park – its charming, helter-skelter kitchen garden, the red-brick garden wall on which old Mr Bunny pranced, the tiny ferns poking out of its crevices, the rose bush espaliered on the top, the red foxgloves, the onions, broad beans and lettuces, and the clutter of flowerpots, frames and tubs in the greenhouse – is reflected on every page. As fine as the rabbits are anatomically, Potter's studies for the red carnations, and her several drawings of the onions that Peter and Benjamin bring home to appease Mrs Rabbit, are each a perfection of botanical illustration. The onions and the carnations are rendered in a fluent line of sepia ink with a transparent wash. Although the flowers and vegetables are incidental to the main action of the story, they stand out because of their detail, their sense of movement, their liveliness and their translucent colour. The repeated bright red of the carnation, the foxgloves and the red pocket handkerchief that Peter repeatedly drops are calculated to catch a child's eye in a book that is once again predominantly rabbit-brown and garden-green. It was indeed a 'pretty book'.[32]

For the greater part of 1904, however, Potter's creative and emotional energy was focused on the text and illustrations for *The Tale of Two Bad Mice*. This book reflects her pleasure in her deepening partnership with Norman Warne, as well as her delight in debunking some of the rigours and restrictions of middle-class domesticity. *Two Bad Mice* is certainly one of Potter's most light-hearted creations. For all the havoc that the mice wreak, their vandalism is miniaturized and thereby more amusing than serious. Beatrix called *Two Bad Mice* a 'girl's book' because of the doll's house, its elaborate furnishings, the invading mice and their imitations of housekeeping. This second mouse book has the same detail that makes *The Tailor of Gloucester* so memorable, but it has more action and more humour. Beatrix enjoyed drawing the characters and developing a story that provided her with the vicarious experience of totally improper behaviour. The picture of the tiny mice releasing all the feathers from the feather bed is analogous to having the pillow fight she never would have dared in real life.[33]

The story came from a sketchbook inscribed 'Hastings, Nov. 26th–Dec. 3rd'. She and Bertram had gone to Hastings for a week's holiday in 1903. Unfortunately, the weather was quite wet, and Beatrix, who had hoped for outdoor sketching, was forced inside. There is no indication that Beatrix had any of her pet mice with her that week, although she certainly may have. But she had always loved drawing mice, and easily dressed them in clothing of all sorts – frilly cotton dresses, aprons, mob caps, period trousers and elaborate waistcoats. For *The Tale of Two Bad Mice*, Beatrix's charming drawings of a mouse family are interpreted for the proper Victorian decor offered by Norman's doll's house, and given a rebellious sort of twist.[34]

When Beatrix saw the advance proofs of 'Hunca Munca's book' in late September 1904, she felt confident that 'it will be a nice little book', and she told her editor, 'It is a pleasant change from the interminable rabbit stories.' A reviewer in the *Bookman* agreed, noting that 'these mischievous mice are not entirely bad and in the twenty-seven water-colour drawings they look both innocent and loveable'. The reviewer approved Miss Potter's 'Chelsea-china like books' that were 'Messrs Warne and Co.'s annual marvels . . . to an adoring nursery-world'.[35]

Beatrix and Norman had tentatively agreed that one of the books for 1905 would be the book of rhymes, in a new larger format. In May 1904 Norman went abroad, and Beatrix visited the Huttons at Harescombe Grange in early June. After they had both returned to London, Beatrix was again anxious to get the subject of both books settled before leaving for the summer. She longed to do a book of nursery rhymes, but the idea was always pushed aside in favour of an original tale. Norman was less enthusiastic about a rhyme collection for several reasons: verse was already a well-represented genre at Warne's and, aware of Beatrix's fondness for rhymes, he anticipated another struggle to contain her enthusiasms. Most of all, Norman was trying to wean Beatrix from a reliance on riddles and rhymes, believing that her original stories were superior. Now Norman reluctantly acceded to Beatrix's desire to do the Appley Dapply book. The second book for 1905 remained undecided.[36]

The Potters arrived at Lingholm on Derwentwater in late July, staying until the end of October. 'I have made some more rhymes for the new book but I have not done much drawing yet,' Beatrix wrote to Norman in early August. '[I]t would be a great pleasure to get settled to work again . . . I tried to look over into the Fawe Park garden the other evening & got all over tar. He [Benjamin Bunny] might well have had that adventure in addition to his other scrapes!' A month later Norman provided her with a plan for the rhyme book and a large dummy book to lay it out. 'The plan of it which you suggest is just *exactly* what I should like,' Beatrix wrote. 'If my rhymes are good enough, I don't think I should have much difficulty in filling that number of pages! & I would rather try to make it a real pretty book than try to have more royalty.'[37]

Beatrix had suggested earlier that she might also revise a story she had invented some years earlier about her hedgehog, Mrs Tiggy-winkle. Over the years she had several pet hedgehogs, usually named Pricklepin or some variation thereof. In 1902 she made some especially fine paintings of one to illustrate the rhyme 'Old Mr. Pricklepin', using pencil, pen and ink and watercolour. Years later, she still considered this painting 'about the best drawing I ever made'. She also had a good many backgrounds of the Newlands Valley in the Derwentwater sketchbook she kept in 1903. To ease Norman's scepticism about the appeal of a book featuring a hedgehog, Beatrix explained, 'I think "Mrs Tiggy" would be all right; it is a *girl's* book; so is the Hunca Munca, but there must be a large audience of little girls. I think they would like the different clothes.' Sometime that summer, Norman agreed to the hedgehog book, and Beatrix began revising her original story and adding drawings in pen and ink.[38]

Beatrix later claimed that she had begun a hedgehog story as early as 1886. It had its origins in her recollection of Kitty MacDonald, the little laundress of Inver, who had so fascinated Beatrix during her summer holidays at Dalguise. She probably first elaborated the story of Lucie of Little-town and Mrs Tiggy-winkle, the hedgehog clear-starcher, during the summer of 1901 at Lingholm. The immediate catalyst for the story was her introduction to the Carr family through their mutual friend, Canon Rawnsley. Carr was the Vicar of New-lands, the parish church at a crossroads at the head of the beautiful Newlands Valley, west of Derwentwater. The Vicar's daughter, Lucie, was just a year old when Beatrix first met her, and she was quite taken with the little blond child. Lucie came to play with Mrs Tiggy whenever her parents came to tea at Lingholm and, after watching her, Beatrix put her into the hedgehog story. For Christmas that year she sent the Carrs a copy of the privately printed *Peter Rabbit*, inscribing it: 'For Lucie with love from H. B. P., Christmas 1901 – I should like to put Lucie into a little book.'[39]

Beatrix tried out her story of Mrs Tiggy-winkle and Lucie on Stephanie Hyde Parker, her cousin Ethel Hyde Parker's daughter, who was then about three. However, she did not write the story down until the following summer at Sawrey – and even then, it was a story without pictures. Beatrix intended it for Stephanie, as the opening paragraph in the original exercise manuscript reads, 'Now Stephanie, this is the story about a little girl called Lucie; she was smaller than you and she could not speak quite plain . . .', but in the end she dedicated *The Tale of Mrs. Tiggy-Winkle** to Lucie.[40]

Although *The Tale of Mrs. Tiggy-Winkle* did not evolve from a picture letter, it was also a tale true to nature: a story set in a real place, about a real washerwoman, a real hedgehog named Tiggy-winkle and a child, Lucie, from Little-town in the Newlands Valley. When Beatrix began revising and illustrating the book in November 1904, she drew upon the watercolour sketches of the Newlands Valley for

---

* The real animal and the character in the book Beatrix spells 'Tiggy-winkle', while the book title is 'Tiggy-Winkle'. The same applies to Jemima Puddle-duck and Johnny Town-mouse.

backgrounds. These finished and remarkably beautiful landscapes underscore the fact that Potter was a painter of place, not just a composite and idealized place, but an identifiable place that is transformed by her art into the ideal and the universal. Much of this book's ultimate success comes from the accurate depiction of the natural setting that underlies the animal fantasy. The vistas of the Newlands Valley are recognizable even today, although Beatrix took artistic liberties and moved parts of the real valley to suit her narrative.

The fells surrounding the valley had been deeply veined with copper and lead. In medieval times, these mines had been among the richest in north-west Britain, but by the nineteenth century they were mostly abandoned because the depth required for shafts down into the fells made it too expensive to extract the ore. When Beatrix explored the area during her summer holidays at Lingholm in 1901 and at Fawe Park in 1903, she noted the abandoned mineshafts, some marked by small doors set into the hillside. She sketched a scene on the western slopes of Cat Bells where there was a little door covering the opening into the Yewthwaite Mine, as well as a prominent crag known as Castle Rock above the abandoned Castlenook Mine. Later she put Mrs Tiggy-winkle's cosy little kitchen behind one of those doors. Above Little-town, a short distance up the Keskadale Beck was, and still is, the small, whitewashed Newlands church. A smaller building, the Newlands School, rebuilt by the parishioners in 1877, adjoined the church. It was there that Lucie and her little sister Kathleen later went to school. Beatrix climbed the path beyond Little-town to sketch a spectacular view of the valley with the lake and Cat Bells in the distance, adjusting her artistic perspective to include the Newlands church just below and changing the name of the hamlet to Little-town.[41]

Beatrix explored even the remote parts of the Newlands Valley, where she was especially interested in the high fell farms, such as Skelghyl, Low and High Snab, Gatesgarth, and Seathwaite near Buttermere; delighting as much in the sound of their names as in the farm life. Three pages of Beatrix's Derwentwater sketchbook are filled with descriptions and sketches of the various sheep markings used at these farms, confirming her interest in sheep and the traditions of Lakeland sheep farming that she shared with Rawnsley. Her notes describe the distinctive smit marks and ear crops that she observed at each farm. In Beatrix's story, Mrs Tiggy-winkle also washes the woolly coats of lambs from Skelghyl, Gatesgarth and Little-town, explaining to Lucie that the lambs' coats are '*always* marked at washing!'[42]

The action in *The Tale of Mrs. Tiggy-Winkle* revolves around Lucie's search for her lost pocket hankerchiefs and 'pinnie', finding them at last beautifully washed and ironed in Mrs Tiggy-winkle's fell-kitchen laundry. This part of the story also has a basis in fact. In August 1904 the Carrs came to Lingholm for tea, and little Lucie, now about four, decked out in her best frock, left without her party gloves. Beatrix wrote Lucie a picture letter that included drawings of a mouse in a party dress with blue ribbons and a blue pinafore, and sent back the child's gloves. Beatrix also wrote a short poem about the incident which she intended to include in the rhyme book. It began, 'I found a tiny pair of gloves/When Lucie'd been to tea,/ They were the dearest little loves − /I thought they'd do for me −.' Lucie's picture letter is an unusual one, in that it is one of only two known picture letters done in colour.[43]

For the remainder of her Lingholm holiday in 1904, Beatrix worked on a variety of pen-and-sepia-ink sketches as backgrounds for the hedgehog book. 'Not exactly useful subjects,' she told Norman, 'but to get my hand into the way, I find it very interesting to do, & I think pretty good results.' One lovely sketch she called 'The Greta [river], Near Portinscale, Keswick' reflects her success with this technique. She had also been collecting more rhymes; 'most extremely odd ones some of them!, but of course,' she assured Norman, 'if they strike you as too fanciful they can easily go. I think it ought to make a nice book.' Confessing that the family holiday had been long enough, she added, 'I am hoping very much to go away myself again the next week; our summer "holiday" is always a weary business & Keswick pulls me down in August; though quite delightful in autumn when there is a bit of frost. The colours are most beautiful now the fern has turned.'[44]

When Beatrix returned to London in late October, however, she was too distracted by family matters to go off sketching. Her Aunt Harriet was ill in Wales, and it is likely that her parents were again objecting to the time she was spending on her books. In early November she confessed, 'I have not begun on the hedgehog-book yet I am ashamed to say; but I think it is not a bad thing to take a holiday; I have been working very industriously drawing fossils at the museum, upon the theory that a change of work is the best sort of rest! but I shall be quite keen to get to work on the books again.' She made plans to call at the Warne office the following week, after she returned from a brief visit to Gwaynynog.[45]

That meeting, however, was postponed by a variety of inconveniences; some physical, some fabricated. 'I am afraid I have not got on much, I was very disappointed that I could not call at the office,' she wrote, without explanation. Beatrix wanted Norman's reaction to her pen-and-ink drawings and planned to try again the following week. 'It sometimes gives me a fresh start to have the drawings looked at. I will try to call on Thursday afternoon . . . I think the book will go all right once started. I have been rather upset & very distressed about one of my aunts who is dying, but I hope she will be soon released. I don't suppose there is any hurry about the books but I would have been glad to get settled to work.'[46]

But November continued uncooperative, both to the progress of the hedgehog book and to the relationship between author and editor. Another meeting was abandoned because of thick fog; another because of 'muddles . . . with the servants'. Mrs Potter expected Beatrix to resolve the servant problems. '[They] make me rather tied,' she confessed to Norman, and 'there are so many things I wanted to ask about, it is very disappointing. I will try & get on with my work.'[47]

Beatrix finally began drawing her hedgehog in late November. Mrs Tiggy was usually a very compliant subject, but she had her moments. As Beatrix described the problem to Norman, 'Mrs Tiggy as a model is comical; so long as she can go to sleep on my knee she is delighted, but if she is propped up on end for half an hour, she first begins to yawn pathetically, and then she *does* bite! Never the less she is a dear person; just like a very fat, rather stupid little dog.

I think the book will go all right once started.' Her drawings of Mrs Tiggy are indeed some of her most endearing, as is the character of the hedgehog washerwoman, with her white frilled cap with prickles sticking through, her print apron and striped petticoat. She was, as Beatrix wrote in the last line, 'nothing but a HEDGEHOG' but as dear in illustration as she was in real life.[48]

Beatrix's attention was briefly diverted to the subject of nursery wallpaper, this time featuring Benjamin Bunny, and to necessary improvements to *The Game of Peter Rabbit*. She kept Norman informed on her progress on *Tiggy-Winkle* every few days, delighting in his encouragement. 'The hedgehog drawings are turning out very comical,' she reported. 'I have dressed up a cotton wool dummy figure for convenience of drawing the clothes. It is such a little figure of fun, it terrifies my rabbit; but Hunca Munca is always pulling out the stuffing. I think it should make a good book, when I have learnt to draw the child.' Lucie of the book proved especially difficult to draw, and the more Beatrix tried the worse it seemed. She told Norman she was going to visit her cousin, Alice Burton Davies at St Asaph, near Gwaynynog, in the spring. Conveniently, Alice's little girl was about the right age for her to use as a model, and Beatrix hoped having a real child to draw would improve things.[49]

It was apparent by year's end that the rhyme book would not be ready for 1905, so once again there was the question of a second book. Warne's wanted two books each year, not only for commercial advantage, but because of the way Beatrix worked and the length of time it took her to do the illustrations. Beatrix had also discovered she liked to work on two books at once, starting the second after she was well into the first. It was a method designed not only to vary the subject of her sketching and give her hand and eye a change, but also to have something else to think about. In early February 1905 Beatrix sent Norman the text for two stories: one about a frog named Jeremy Fisher, and another longer tale about a dog and cat. Explaining that the dog and cat story was 'funny, but *very* greedy', she reassured her editor that 'there is one thing in its favour, children like conversations'. 'I'm afraid you don't like *frogs*,' she admitted, 'but it would make pretty pictures with water-forget-me-nots, lilies, etc. I should like to do both & I think I could, if the longer one were part black & white which takes very little time to process.' While Norman considered the options, Beatrix finished *Tiggy-Winkle*.[50]

By late February, some of the drawings of *Tiggy-Winkle* were ready for the block-maker and for Norman's review. 'Would Thursday afternoon be convenient to you to look over the hedgehog drawings, if I can arrange to bring them? I have finished a good many and should like to have them processed because I have used a different white . . . I have redrawn the birds & mice, it looks much better.' The story was moving along well except for Beatrix's persistent difficulties in drawing Lucie.[51]

In spite of her deadline, she enjoyed moments of spontaneity. A letter from Hugh Bridgeman, her first from a young American reader, merited a response. The boy had written to say how much he had enjoyed *Two Bad Mice*. In her reply Beatrix told him about her new hedgehog book, and about Hunca Munca. Her letter reveals how much she liked inventing stories as well as illustrating them. 'I like writing stories,' she told the youngster; 'I should like to write lots and lots! I have ever so many inside my head but the pictures take such a dreadful long time to draw! I get quite tired of the pictures before the book is finished . . . I think *you* will like the next book but one, because it has got a dog in it.'[52]

9

❧ *Losses* ❧

THE POTTERS SPENT A FORTNIGHT in Colwyn Bay and St Asaph in north Wales in late March 1905. The trip was designed so that Helen Potter could be near her ailing sister Harriet as well as take the family away from spring house-cleaning. Beatrix's story about a 'pussy cat who gives a tea party for a little dog' would be the companion book to Mrs Tiggy and she was anxious to make a start on it. It was to be in a larger format, just as the rhyme book would have been, but only ten of the drawings would be in full colour, the rest in pen and sepia ink.[1]

'If convenient to you I will call on Friday afternoon to go over the plan of the new book,' Beatrix wrote to Norman before leaving London, 'and I could bring away the proofs then, & you could print out any alterations required.' She was busy sketching Duchess, a Pomeranian, using as a model a little dog she borrowed from a friend. The magpie, Dr Maggotty, she drew from birds at the Zoological Gardens. In a small sketchbook, Beatrix made careful notes concerning the anatomical structure and colouring of the bird's feathers. 'Brown black eye, nose a little hookier than jackdaw, less feathered.' The bird's tail, she observed, was over half the bird's total length; parts of its feathers were 'very blue', and other parts 'green'.[2]

Like the story of Mrs Tiggy, *The Tale of The Pie and The Patty-Pan* was set in a real place, the village of Near Sawrey, where the Potters had spent the summers of 1896, 1900 and 1902. Beatrix had enjoyed sketching the three small Lakefield cottages just below the Kendal road, particularly the interior of the cottage owned by a Mrs Lord, with its pots of red geraniums on the window sill, the cosy stone-floored entry and carved oak furniture. She also sketched various village shops, the post office, whitewashed cottages, cottage doors, tiger lilies and snapdragons – almost anything that struck her fancy. Her sketches brimmed with her pleasure in country life and in the picturesque beauty of Sawrey.[3]

In some, she had drawn an outline of a cat and had an idea for a 'cat story' set in Sawrey. She wrote it out during the wet and rainy holiday week in Hastings in 1903. It was called 'Something very very nice' and is replete with domestic details of a tea party. Her original version was an amusing and rather short, simple story. She put it aside when *The Tale of Two Bad Mice* was chosen as the next book. When she returned to the cat story in the spring of 1905, she felt the original needed a stronger plot. She rewrote the story, keeping the dog and cat, Duchess and Ribby, as the central characters in the tea party, and elaborating the setting.

Once *The Pie*, as she called it, was selected as the second book for 1905, Beatrix made steady progress on the drawings and by May they were ready for Norman to see. Letters flew between them, often crossing each other as both artist and editor worked to match text to illustrations, blocks to proofs. Beatrix wrote to Fruing Warne on the black-edged stationery of a family in mourning on 2 May, 'I think I had better bring the drawings on Wednesday afternoon on the chance that Mr Norman Warne could look them over, I think it promises to make a pretty book.' Harriet Burton had died at Gwaynynog and Beatrix was leaving for Wales. She had been very fond of this acid-tongued aunt, whom she had once likened to a weasel. She found Harriet's outlook on life amusing, even a bit daring, and she enjoyed visiting Gwaynynog, even though her pets had to be smuggled in.[4]

On 25 May Norman wrote to Beatrix before she left: 'I think you have two dummy books of "The Pie & The Patty Pan" could you spare me one of these for a time? as I want to be quite clear about the size of the plates before going on with the blocks.' He had looked at her drawings and was not satisfied with two plates of Duchess, the dog. He explained to Beatrix: 'There seems to me to be too much bend about her nose & the division between the legs should be made clearer; my brothers find the same fault, so I think I will keep these two plates back & get you to look at them once more before making the blocks.' The following day he wrote to say that the illustration of the two animals at tea still looked unfinished. 'I like your brown pen & ink sketches very much & I think if you carry out the outline pictures for the Pie and the Patty-Pan in this spirit, there will be no difficulty in reproducing them in brown ink . . . we can go over them again together when we see how those I am putting in hand come out.'[5]

Beatrix continued to struggle with her drawing of Duchess, at one point resorting to sending a photograph of the original Pomeranian to prove to Norman and Fruing that her model had the same thick and heavy ruff as the one she had drawn. It was not the first or the last time she would resort to photography to validate her artistic accuracy. The plates of the cat were turning out well, which made Beatrix feel that perhaps the dog was just too black.

In early June Beatrix began to worry about the approaching summer holidays, wanting to get both *Tiggy-Winkle* and *The Pie* finished before Norman went away. 'I don't think I have ever seriously considered the state of the *pie*,' she wrote, 'but I think the *book* runs some risk of being over-cooked if it goes on much longer! I am sorry about the little dog's nose. I saw it was too sharp, I think I have got it right.' Several days later a deeper apprehension was apparent when she confided, 'I wish another book could be planned out before the summer, if we are going on with them, I always feel very much lost when they are finished.' And at the month's end she wrote with more urgency, 'I do so *hate* finishing books, I would like to go on with them for years.'[6]

Beatrix had good reason to be anxious about continuing projects, for it was becoming increasingly difficult for her to visit the Warne office when Norman was there. Although she does not give specifics, there had been more unpleasantness at home about her frequent trips to Bedford Street, the inconvenience to Mrs Potter's schedule and perhaps even open disapproval of the relationship. On 18 June Beatrix wrote apologetically, 'I will bring the drawings again tomorrow unless prevented, *still* in doubt . . . I had not time to stop to ask about another book on Friday, and you were busy the time before. I should like to have some other work in prospect when these are finished. I have given up the idea of going away [for sketching], but I remember that you usually leave town at the beginning of July.'[7]

While finishing touches were given to both books, there was the ongoing matter of merchandising. A manufacturer for both Peter Rabbit and Benjamin Bunny nursery wallpapers had been found. Now Norman wanted Beatrix to consider a 'pincushion' doll of Mrs Tiggy. It would be a change of pace for her, and she was tired of redrawing plates. 'The pincushion is a splendid idea,' she wrote to him. 'I should like to begin one at once – all the more so because I ought to be doing something else – as you very properly remark! It would be most pleasing to use large black pins for the eyes and nose. Mrs Tig is scattering pins all over the place, she moults about a third of them every season, they are simply stiff hairs. Perhaps I can try a model some evening.'[8]

But Beatrix was still unhappy with the drawing of Lucie, and reluctant to let it go. 'I wish I had drawn the child better,' she complained. 'I feel sure I could get into the way of it, only it is too much of a hurry.' The text of *Tiggy-Winkle* was not quite to her liking, either. She explained to Norman: 'I do not think the rhyme is right grammar – it is the "no" that throws it out – If it were "Smooth & hot – red rusty spot never here be seen – oh!" that would be all right. She is supposed to be exorcizing spots and iron stains, same as Lady MacBeth(!), the verb is imperative . . . I used to know my Latin grammar but it has faded.' But Beatrix had convinced her editor and the changes were made.[9]

Before leaving for the summer holiday Beatrix needed some of 'Johnny Crow's' expert joinery. 'It is Hunca Munca's travelling box that is shaky,' she explained, 'it seems a shame to ask for joinering when it is such fine evenings, but perhaps it would not take so long to mend, I have so very much pleasure from her other little house.' Norman, too, had recently lost one of his aunts, and Beatrix added her condolences. It was the only time she revealed her feelings about the death of Harriet Burton, to whom she would soon owe a great deal. 'I was sorry to hear of your loss,' she told Norman, 'for I shall miss my own old aunt sadly in Wales.'[10]

In late June it seemed likely that the Potters would return to

Derwentwater and Lingholm for the summer; if they did, Beatrix planned to continue work on the rhyme book. She called Norman's attention to one rhyme in particular that she wanted to illustrate: it featured a botanical form she knew by heart. '"Nid Nid Noddy, we stand in a ring,"' she told him, 'I meant it for mushrooms dancing in the moonlight with little faces peeping underneath their caps. I will try to sketch out some ideas, perhaps you would let me know when you are back in August & able to consider them.'[11]

The Tale of Mrs. Tiggy-Winkle was finished at last in early July. 'I enclose the remainder of Tiggy regretfully,' Beatrix wrote to Norman. 'I began that story in Aug. 86, & I am just beginning to be able to do it – and without undue "slaving"!' Although this book had required a different kind of collaboration from *Two Bad Mice*, Beatrix and Norman had enjoyed working on it. Her beautiful water-colours of Derwentwater, as well as her little hedgehog, and even her struggles with the figure of Lucie, had drawn them closer. Beatrix dedicated *Tiggy-Winkle* 'for the real little Lucie of Newlands', inscrib-ing her copy, '"For little Lucie with much love from Beatrix Potter and from dear 'Mrs Tiggy-Winkle' . . ."' Two days later she wrote to Norman again about *The Pie and The Patty-Pan*. 'I am very glad you liked the remaining drawings, if the book prints well it will be my next favourite to the "Tailor."'[12]

Rupert Potter had procrastinated too long about where to go on holiday. By the time he decided, Lingholm had been rented. So instead of leaving for the north around 20 July, the Potters made alternative plans to rent an estate called Hafod-y-Bryn ('The summer place on the hill'), in Llanbedr, Merionethshire, a small village on the west coast of Wales, where there was both fresh- and salt-water fishing. This part of Wales was new to the Potters. The house stood on high ground with some twenty acres of garden and woodlands overlooking Cardigan Bay. It had been built by Samuel Pope, QC, from Manchester, who had come to London about the same time as Rupert, and had been a fellow member of the Reform Club. Although Pope died in 1901, Rupert knew that the estate was available.[13]

Beatrix had assumed they would leave for Wales before the end of the month. She planned to call at Bedford Street on Saturday,

22 July, to select the proper dummy for *Appley Dapply*, since there was some discrepancy in margin size. But she also needed Norman's comfort as she had not seen him since Hunca Munca's tragic death. Beatrix had probably been playing with the little mouse when the accident happened, and she felt terribly guilty. 'I have made a little doll of poor Hunca Munca,' she explained to Norman. 'I cannot forgive myself for letting her tumble, I do so miss her. She fell off the chandelier, she managed to stagger up the staircase into your little house, but she died in my hand about 10 minutes after. I think if I had broken my own neck it would have saved a great deal of trouble.' Obviously distraught, Beatrix ended her letter pleading, 'I should like to get some new work fixed before going away to Wales. I am feeling all right for work, but very worried.'[14]

Reading between the lines, Beatrix must have suspected that Norman would formally ask her to marry him before she left for the summer holiday. On Tuesday, 25 July Beatrix either saw or was sent the proofs for *Tiggy-Winkle*, and was much distressed by their spottiness. She suspected the problem had been caused by the inter-action between the hot weather and the hydrochloric and nitric acid, but there was no time now to re-engrave the plates. She sent Norman her summer address in Wales as of Thursday, 27 July. On that same Tuesday Beatrix did indeed receive a letter from Norman formally asking her to marry him. Then 39 years old, she accepted his proposal.[15]

When Beatrix revealed the news of Norman's proposal and her intention to accept him, the household at 2 Bolton Gardens must have nearly come undone. The Potters vehemently disapproved of their daughter marrying a publisher, a man without professional accomplishment by their standards, and objected to a union with a family 'in trade'. His was precisely the sort of family and social status they had worked to distinguish themselves from. Beatrix did not question her parents' right to object, but she believed their opposition to Norman was patently hypocritical and unreasonable. 'Publishing books', she said quietly to Caroline Hutton, whose confidence she sought, 'is as clean a trade as spinning cotton', a direct reference to the profession of her maternal grandparents. Helen Potter found the proposed liaison particularly abhorrent. Whatever Rupert's private views were, he supported his wife's opposition.[16]

The next ten days were spent in acrimonious debate over what should be done – the crisis was so serious that the Potters' departure to Llanbedr was postponed. Although Beatrix may have wished that Norman had proceeded more cautiously, once the deed was done she understood that her future happiness was at stake. She dug deeply into her Crompton spirit, her newly won self-confidence and her devotion to Norman, and found the courage, despite considerable guilt, to oppose her parents. At some point, Beatrix and Norman exchanged rings as tokens of their betrothal. But Beatrix acceded to her parents' demand that there would be no official announcement. While she would wear Norman's ring in public, the engagement would remain a secret from all except the immediate family. After this compromise was agreed to, Beatrix's decision to marry Norman Warne was probably never mentioned again. As far as her parents were concerned, there was no betrothal. For Beatrix and Norman, the agony of uncertainty had begun.[17]

Meanwhile Norman had returned from his sales trip to Manchester quite ill. Beatrix had sent a messenger with the dummy book and proofs of *The Pie* to the Bedford Street office while Norman was away, but Harold, unable to find the parcel, became alarmed, thinking the proofs were lost. Beatrix fled from the poisonous silence at home to the comfort of her elderly former governess's house in West Hampstead, in north London. Writing from Miss Hammond's address on Sunday, 30 July, she informed Harold she would come to the office the next day, even though Norman would not be there. 'I shall bring Miss Florrie Hammond with me,' she explained. 'You will not think me very cross if I say I would rather *not* talk much *yet* about that business though I am *very glad* you have been told.' Although not all of Norman's family may have been pleased at the proposed union with the older and rather idiosyncratic Miss Potter, some of Norman's nieces had already been instructed to call her 'Aunt Bee'.[18]

Beatrix's letter to Harold Warne reveals a greater concern. 'I do trust that your brother is not going to be very ill,' she wrote. 'I got scared before he went to Manchester, wondering if he had been drinking bad water. I shall be able to ask you after his health, as Miss Florrie is not quite "all there" & stone deaf!' Terribly anxious about Norman, as well as how the uproar would ultimately resolve itself, she confessed, 'It is a very awkward way of happening; I think he is going a little fast now that he has started.' Although she wished events were not rushing on so uncontrollably, she graciously ended her letter with more confidence than she felt: 'I trust it may come right in the end. Thanking you all for your kindness.'[19]

Beatrix's letter of the 30th from Miss Hammond's is the last she posted from the London area. Her exact whereabouts the next few days are difficult to determine, but she visited the town of Amersham in Buckinghamshire, where she painted two extant watercolours on Thursday, 3 August. This suggests that the Potters did not leave for Wales until Friday the 4th at the earliest. In the interim the painful struggle of wills going on inside 2 Bolton Gardens, hidden from the world, was hopelessly deadlocked.

It was not entirely unusual for an adult woman of nearly 40 to oppose her parents' wishes regarding such an important issue as marriage, but it was a near-revolutionary act for a daughter as dutiful and respectful as Beatrix. There is no evidence that Bertram was involved, but his views must have been solicited as he joined the family in Wales for at least some part of the ensuing holiday. Since Bertram, however, had not yet found the courage to confront his parents about his own marriage nearly three years earlier, Beatrix's brave decision to marry Norman put him in an uncomfortable position. If Beatrix knew then about her brother's status, and she probably did, she said nothing. But she was unshakeable in her decision to accept Norman's proposal. Before she left for Wales, Beatrix had given Norman an engagement present: a drawing in grey wash and pen and ink of Cinderella's pumpkin carriage going to fetch her from the ball. The drawing was one of several done a decade earlier when she had been illustrating fairy tales and fables. In Beatrix's version, the pumpkin carriage is drawn by three pairs of rabbits, with mice as coachmen and other small animals carrying lanterns and sedan chairs. The town is swathed in moonlight and the street scene is a medieval-looking town with more tiny mice peering out of the windows at the fine coach rushing through the street. It is a drawing of an escape, with the hope of a happy ending, and a perfect engagement present to Beatrix's 'Prince Charming'.[20]

Over at 8 Bedford Square, Norman had been ordered bed rest on 29 July, five days after he had proposed to Beatrix. What preliminary diagnosis his physician made at the time is unknown, nor how alarmed his family was initially, although the doctor apparently indicated his illness was serious. Norman had promised Beatrix he would send for her if their separation become too difficult. They had last seen each other on Saturday, 22 July. Whether they saw each other before Beatrix left for Wales is unknown, but Beatrix never saw Norman alive again.[21]

In order to keep herself occupied in Wales and to share her activities and thoughts with her intended, Beatrix began a 'holiday diary', making the first entry on 12 August. That day, she recorded her delight in the summer sea and a swimming beach where she had visions 'of bare legs, & a little green crab . . . I am sure the crabs & shrimps join hands & caper about when the tide is coming in and the children have gone home.' She added some shells to her shell collection, found good places for sketching, took interest in Bertram's purchase of some Japanese double-tailed goldfish, and took Tiggy into the kitchen garden where the ageing hedgehog caught some spiders and a small snail. She rebuilt her rabbit hutch. The pages of Potter's diary are filled with the sort of natural history that had always intrigued her: habits of the goldfish, varieties of butterflies, catching and sketching grasshoppers and watching sea birds. She was fascinated by the large beds of sea lavender and the blue-grey sea holly, noting their changing colours in the afternoon light. As always, she noticed and remarked upon the sheep and the handsome, sleek black Galloway cattle with long horns. She especially enjoyed the view over a barley field that she painted on the evening of 17 August, noting that 'it is a beautiful colour, nodding & waving in the wind'.[22]

On 20 August she drew a picturesque drain pipe 'with a trimming of leaves & moss projecting from the garden wall' and made the acquaintance of a wood toad, 'nearly as large as a tea-pot', whose bulk was damming the water in the pipe and to whom she fed some woodlice. She later likened him to their late host Sam Pope, who was a very large man, thinking the toad looked 'dreadfully like him . . .' She recorded her observations of nature that day: the garden insects, butterflies, and some aggressive grey and brown ants who 'stood on their hind legs with their nippers open'.[23]

That day, 20 August, was also Louisa Jane Warne's eightieth birthday. Back in Bedford Square, Norman's mother wrote to her granddaughter Jennie: 'I wish dear Norman was getting better, but it is very slow work. He is so weak and cannot take anything but milk, he keeps very cheerful for all that but he can scarcely stand. Harold is coming . . . to-day to see the Doctor, but we fear it will be very slow recovery.'[24]

But Norman Warne died in his bedroom at 8 Bedford Square on the afternoon of Friday, 25 August, with his mother, sister Millie, and two brothers at his bedside. He was barely a month past his thirty-seventh birthday. His simple will had been drawn up hastily that morning, dividing his small estate between his brothers, Millie, and his nephew Fred Stephens. The cause of death was lymphatic leukaemia: a difficult condition to diagnose in those days. His decline had been extraordinarily rapid. Edith Warne Stephens recorded her brother's death that day in her family journal, *Immortelles:* 'Dearest Norman joined his Daddy.' It was exactly a month since he had asked Beatrix Potter to be his wife.[25]

Beatrix's holiday chronicle stops abruptly on Tuesday morning, 22 August, when she went up on the hill to pick blackberries, and was not taken up again until 29 August, the day of Norman's funeral and burial. Where precisely she was when she wrote of her activities during the days just before Norman's death is unclear, although it is likely she wrote after the services. Norman was buried in the Warne family tomb at the fashionable Highgate Cemetery in London. The crypt rested among those of other literary notables: George Eliot, Christina Rossetti, Herbert Spenser and Karl Marx. Beatrix attended the service along with the Warne family and friends.[26]

Her diary entry for Tuesday, 29 August, 1905 reads: 'This was all I had written but I remember it all so well & what I meant to write.' She recounts how she had gone into the woods on the morning of

24 August to write letters, but reveals that she had just received a letter, perhaps from Harold or Fruing Warne, that made her think that Norman was very ill. After lunch she took her rabbits, Josey and Mopsy, down into the cellar where she 'got rather depressed & *most mercifully* I wrote to my dear old man – the letter he got the last morning. I soon wrote myself quite merry again, & it is a silly letter all about my rabbits, & the walking stick that I was going to get for him to thrash his wife with – but he didn't read it, so it was good enough. I am so thankful I wrote it.'[27]

She got her sketching things and went down to the village to post her letter, enjoying the fields, sketching several on her way. After tea that same afternoon she went out again to draw the barley field in the waning light. 'I sat on a big stone with my back against the wall. Down below, sloping steep, was the little field of red-gold barley, – golden & green – for the rain had brought up the clover, & there was a lighter patch beside each stook where they had been shifted.' She remembered how the valley had looked with the black poplars, 'how their trunk & branches stood up, first across the farm, the marshes, the sea & the sky, holding the landscape together'. She watched a train travelling south and wished 'vaguely I was in it', for her bags were packed. But that train was the last one of the day. So she sat there, watching the sunset. The night was 'so still; not a breath of wind, and so peaceful & beautiful in a grey light . . . The sea was in a soft haze, pearly grey & indistinct except at one point under the sun . . . I remember thinking about Turner's pictures & thinking how profane it seemed to be to try to draw anything so beautiful with my dirty little paint box. I remember thinking the evening was as still as death – and as beautiful – as I was looking at it there came out through the mist over the sea just for a few seconds – a gleam of golden sunshine . . . ? Her diary ends: 'In the evening there shall be Light.'[28]

It was not until the morning of 25 August that Beatrix received the telegram the Warne family had sent, telling her that Norman was dying and asking her to come to London. In her postdated diary entry she reflects, 'I am *quite* [heavily underlined] glad now I was not in time, I should only have cried & upset him . . . They did not send the wire to Llanbedr till the next morning . . . It was merciful to me anyhow, for I do not think there was another night train after that one I was looking at [on the 24th].' Forced to cut short their holiday by many weeks because of Norman's death, the Potters probably left Wales on the 27th, arriving back in London in time for Beatrix to view Norman's body before burial.[29]

'I thought my story had come right with patience & waiting like Anne Eliott's [*sic*] did,' Beatrix wrote to Millie Warne months later from Bath, the setting of Jane Austen's novel *Persuasion*. 'It was always my favourite and I read the end part of it again last July, on the 26th the day after I got Norman's letter.' She had held fast to that ephemeral hope of happiness. But Anne Elliot's fulfilment was fictional, and Beatrix Potter's loss was terrible and real. Bereft of her own story's happy ending, with dreadful silence at home, and no one except Norman's immediate family with whom she could share her grief or be comforted, Beatrix fled London for Wales.[30]

Once again her movements are hard to follow. After a week, maybe longer, Beatrix emerged at Gwaynynog, where she joined her unhappy uncle Fred Burton, also in mourning. Beatrix loved this house with its carved oak panelling, its fine antique furniture and its romantic, untidy garden where she had so often sketched. Harold Warne sent the re-proofed plates for *Tiggy-Winkle* on 5 September. Beatrix pronounced them better than the first set which had so displeased Norman. Pushing through her grief, Beatrix wrote: 'It will be a trying thing to come for the first time to the office, but there is no help for it. I have begun sketching again; I am badly behindhand with my stock of summer work but I shall be able to make it up if there is a fine autumn.' She planned to work on the book of verses and 'the frog "Mr Jeremy Fisher". I know some people don't like frogs! but I think I had convinced Norman that I could make it a really pretty book with a good many flowers & water plants for backgrounds.'[31]

Soon the atmosphere at Gwaynynog proved too depressing, and Beatrix escaped to the seaside by herself. 'I am moving from this terrible address on Saturday to lodgings,' she wrote Harold, promising to send a new address. Her plans were quite specific: she would be away from London for two months, but would come back to the Warne office after a month 'to see dear Millie again' and to discuss the progress on the new books. 'I feel as if my work and your kindness will be my greatest comfort.'[32]

The following day Beatrix wrote a loving and lively picture letter to Norman's niece, Winifred Warne, calling herself the 'Peter Rabbit Lady', telling about her rabbits, Josey and Mopsy, and Mrs Tiggy, all of whom had travelled with her to Gwaynynog. 'I have got my hedgehog here with me too; she enjoys going by train, she is always very hungry when she is on a journey. I carry her in a little basket and the bunnies in a small wooden box, I don't take any tickets for them.' Drawing pictures of Mrs Tiggy dressed as she was in the book, she tells Winifred how Tiggy disdains to eat shrimps, preferring worms and beetles instead, but suggesting that the little girl could invite Mrs Tiggy to tea as 'she will drink milk like anything out of a doll's tea-cup!' She then sketches the real hedgehog drinking out of a teacup, and signs the letter, 'with a great many kisses from your loving friend'.[33]

True to her word, Beatrix was back in London by the 25th. She went to Norman's grave at Highgate with Millie to see that the family headstone had been properly replaced, and arranged for some new plants, seeking Mary, Fruing's wife's, advice about the suitability of Japanese anemones. Beatrix was invited to stay at 8 Bedford Square while she was in town, and she gratefully accepted. The opportunity to be at the Warnes' house with Millie and her mother pleased and comforted her. She did some watercolour paintings of the interior rooms of the house, including Norman's bedroom, which she undoubtedly intended as a gift for Mrs Warne. Before she left Bedford Square she wrote to Mary, thanking her warmly for a photograph of the children that she had sent. 'I should have liked it . . . even if they had been strangers, but I have heard Norman talk so often about the children that they seem like little friends.' Explaining that she was leaving again for Wales on the 27th and would not return until the end of October, Beatrix wrote: 'I cannot tell you how grateful I have felt for the kindness of all of you, it has been a real comfort & pleasure to stay in this house.' As a token of her gratitude, Beatrix sent Millie a special Christmas present in December: a copy of the watercolour sketch of the barley field at Llandbedr she had done the evening before Norman died. 'I try to think of the golden sheaves, and harvest,' she told Millie, 'he did not live long but he fulfilled a useful happy life. I must try to make a fresh beginning next year.'[34]

After leaving London, Beatrix returned to Gwaynynog briefly, and from there travelled north to Sawrey. Harriet Burton's estate had been probated in early June and Beatrix had received a small legacy from her aunt. Having learned earlier that spring that Hill Top Farm was for sale, Beatrix had begun serious negotiations with Frederic Fowkes to purchase the farm acres from his larger property, planning to use her new inheritance and the royalties from her books, a sum that now amounted to approximately £1,075. It was a purchase Norman must surely have known about and approved; a dream they shared of owning a small farm in the English Lakes. Norman was dead, but this part of her 'story' Beatrix refused to relinquish. As long as she lived, Hill Top would be a memorial to that hoped-for storybook ending, and the place where she would reinvent herself yet again.[35]

10

❧ Stories ☙

AS BEATRIX POTTER COPIED OUT her deeds and walked the boundaries of her fields in early October 1905 at Near Sawrey in Lancashire, she was aware of the irony in her ownership of Hill Top Farm. It had come about because she had dared a few small rebellions as an otherwise dutiful daughter of a family who had rejected their roots in the north and turned their backs on the origins of their wealth.

Now, at the age of 39, Beatrix was mysteriously on the brink of liberation. She was the author of six popular books for young children and, by any measure, successful. She had used her profits, along with the legacy from her Leech aunt, Harriet Burton, a woman who was proud of her association with merchant life, to make an investment in Lancashire land, thereby returning to the countryside her ancestors had embraced. Most ironic of all, Hill Top Farm would have been shared with a husband in trade, a man whom her parents had scorned, and whose sudden death made her more determined than ever to control at least this aspect of her life and to make a success at farming – even if it had to be from a distance.[1]

The happy challenge provided by Hill Top Farm – the necessity of overcoming her grief and getting on with her life – inspired a remarkable outburst of creativity. She produced thirteen stories over the next eight years, including some of her best work. In the course of this creative effort, Beatrix Potter was transformed into a countrywoman.[2]

Hill Top was a working farm of 34 acres, 36 perches, with a late-seventeenth-century farmhouse, outbuildings, orchard and enclosures. It had been part of a much larger property that had come onto the market in the early spring and was purchased in May by a local timber merchant. He immediately sold all but the farm lots on to Frederic Fowkes, an enterprising landowner who lived at Waterside, on Esthwaite Water, and who owned most of the land between Colthouse and Sawrey. Almost certainly John Cannon, the interim tenant at Hill Top, alerted Beatrix to the farm's availability, but it was well known in Sawrey that Beatrix wanted to buy a farm. Beatrix began negotiations with Fowkes, and, once it was clear that her London solicitors would approve her contract, Fowkes bought the remaining farm on 25 September for £1,375 and sold it to Beatrix on 15 November for £2,805.[3]

Beatrix arrived in Sawrey just as the air took on an edge of autumn crispness in the morning and the hillsides gleamed gold in the twilight. She wanted to copy out her deeds and check their accuracy, fully educated as to the minutest details of boundary fence and property line. It was also a task, like so many others, that appealed to her sense of realism, as well as to her nascent understanding of the proper stewardship of the land. With the terms of the sale approved, Beatrix began negotiating with Fowkes for an additional field known as Buckle Yeat Croft on the north side of the Kendal road which would connect her two fields on that side, thereby making her holdings nearly contiguous. This field was conveyed to Potter on 11 December 1905 for a discounted price of £250, renegotiated by her father's solicitors after she discovered the handsome profit Fowkes had made on the sale of Hill Top.[4]

The farmhouse was occupied by John Cannon, his wife, and their two children, Ralph and Betsy. Beatrix took lodgings with the village blacksmith, Satterthwaite, and his wife, who lived at the top of Market Street in a cottage called Belle Green, intending to stay until the end of the month. Cannon was not from the Sawrey area, and while he had handled things adequately Beatrix was uncertain whether or not to keep him on.[5]

Up at dawn, she studied her property inside and out, sorry when she was driven inside at last by the early dusk. After assessing the necessary repairs to the farmhouse and outbuildings, Beatrix asked Cannon and his wife to stay on. That decided, the first order of business was to appraise the condition of the farm animals and the land. Cannon took her out in the trap to look at the various fields and pastures. Beatrix was amazed to discover that pigs, which Cannon bought only with verifiable pedigree, were an important part of farm income. 'The pigs are mostly sold – at what the drapers call a "sacrifice"; they seem to me to have devoured most of my potatoes before their departure,' she explained to Millie Warne about two weeks after arriving in Sawrey. It seems 'the whole district is planted out with my pigs; but we still take an interest in them because if they grow well we shall "get a name for pigs." Such is fame!' She went along with Cannon to the police station, a requirement of any farmer who 'traded', so that the accuracy of the farm scales could be certified. She discovered that the Hill Top scales were out of register and the farm had been undercharging for butter.[6]

Beatrix was anxious to begin physical improvements to the farm-house and to improve the areas of the farm that had been neglected since Henry Preston's death. The only garden left at Hill Top was a small walled kitchen garden opposite the front door. Beatrix had the track moved away from the house, creating a large area for the new garden, and laid out an access path to the front door along the line of the old drive, ending at a small wicket gate in the wall beside the Kendal road. She hired a quarryman to lay out new walks and bedding areas for flowers and vegetables. They put down a Brathay flagstone path, which matched the four slabs of local slate that made up the front entrance porch, and used smaller flags set on edge to mark out the beds. But before she could do much more to improve the gardens, she had to solve the problem of proper living quarters for herself and the Cannon family, as the farmhouse was too small for them both.[7]

Travelling about the neighbourhood, Beatrix studied the old farm-houses, noting those that had been successfully expanded. She decided to enlarge the house to make two separate living spaces. A new two-storey wing would replace the former one-storey kitchen. The roof line would be altered by adding a gable. The former kitchen would move into a detached building where it would be supplied with a water pump. The Cannons would live in the new wing, and Beatrix would have the old farmhouse to herself. Before she left

Sawrey she had decided on the design and hired various craftsmen.[8]

When Beatrix bought Hill Top, a staircase wing and adjoining larder had already been added at the rear of the house, as well as the kitchen on the farmyard side. Her design sketches show how closely she had observed Lake District architecture and how sensitively she altered her old structure, wanting to make only minimal changes. When it was finished in 1906 the new wing had a pentice roof across the front, sheltering the door. The exterior was finished in a grey pebbledash to unify the new with the old. Observing Lakeland custom and tradition, Beatrix had a plaque made and placed on the front of the addition with her initials and the date.[9]

Beatrix did not return to Sawrey again until April 1906. In the interim she had supervised the sale of her aunt Clara Potter's estate at Queen's Gate, and her dear hedgehog Mrs Tiggy had died. The years of keeping Tiggy in an unnatural environment had taken a toll on the little animal, and Beatrix would not allow her to suffer. 'She has got so dirty & miserable I think it is better not to keep her any longer,' she told Millie Warne in February. 'I am going away for a few days so it is best to chloroform her first. She is not fit to be anybody else's hearthrug . . . she has always been such a scrupulously clean little animal.' She finished her picture of Tiggy, then probably buried her in the back garden of 2 Bolton Gardens.[10]

When she arrived in Sawrey on 4 April, again lodging at Belle Green, Beatrix was disappointed with the lack of progress on the addition, and the bare and unfinished look of her farm. 'I thought my property was looking extremely ugly when I arrived I was quite glad you weren't there!' she told Millie, with whom she was now regularly exchanging letters. 'The new works though doubtless an improvement are painfully *new*. Instead of the old winding road – with a tumble down wall covered with polypody [creeping fern] – there is a straight wide road & a very bare wall. Also heaps of soil everywhere & new railings, they would show less if they were tarred.' She knew that the moss would grow up fast and that things would look better in time, but she was 'vexed' to discover that some of the work had been done incorrectly. She hired a man to make a flat bit of lawn, but somehow 'the word "tennis" had been mentioned' and

Beatrix returned to find a much larger, flatter garden lawn than she ever dreamed of. Rather than pay the man more to correct his work, she asked Cannon to plant it all in potatoes until she had time to design new beds. But she was pleased that the little fruit trees she had planted would soon be in flower.[11]

Beatrix took the opportunity to explore her new farmhouse from top to bottom. There were some surprising discoveries. The worst was a serious infestation of rats. The best was discovering one four-foot-thick wall with a staircase inside it. 'I never saw such a place for hide & seek, & funny cupboards & closets,' she told Millie, with stories already forming in her mind. 'It really is delightful if the rats could be stopped out!' She had Mrs Cannon pull the mattresses out into the yard for airing and sew them up before the rats could nest inside. 'We must try & keep them out next autumn, they got in before I had had the holes cemented. It is indeed a funny old house, it would amuse children very much, especially the farm yard part of it.'[12]

Beatrix left Hill Top after barely a week, not in the best of tempers. She took a crowded train from Windermere to Brighton on the south coast and joined her parents at Worthing for the rest of the spring holiday. She did some sketching at Chichester, finding it 'very quaint & pretty', and wrote to Winifred Warne about a dog she had met at the greengrocer's shop. He was called Nip and knew how to beg for coins and buy chocolate for himself. 'I think Nip spends most of the day buying and eating chocolate, he is most dreadfully fat!' Beatrix wrote. She hand-coloured the illustration of Nip and sent the letter, signed 'Aunt B', along to Millie to give to Winifred. But it was impossible to do any proper sketching and she was anxious about her work. 'I shall be very glad to get home, I feel as if I were getting so behind hand with the second book [*The Story of A Fierce Bad Rabbit*], & there is no room to work here – I am writing this on the wash stand!'[13]

Although Beatrix had hoped to get back to Sawrey in May, she did not return until July. She finished *The Tale of Mr. Jeremy Fisher*, the last of the books she had planned out with Norman. The story began life as a picture letter to Eric Moore, written from Eastwood,

Dunkeld, on 5 September 1893, sent the day after the letter to Noel about Peter Rabbit. *Jeremy Fisher* was based upon several pet frogs that Beatrix had kept and whose habits she had observed. The natural behaviour of frogs, toads and newts was easy to adapt to fantasy. Her letter to Eric provided a story line that was sure to amuse a child and give opportunity for both artistic and literary embellishment.

Jeremy's home was originally a little house on the beautiful River Tay in Scotland, where he passed the time fishing. Beatrix had sold some of her early frog drawings to Ernest Nister as illustrations for 'A Frog he would a-fishing go'. With foresight, she bought back the frog drawings and blocks from Nister after *Peter Rabbit* was published in 1902, so that when she revised the frog story for Warne's, there was no question who owned copyright.[14]

Beatrix had wanted to do a frog story for some time, because it was amusing and offered the opportunity for the naturalist illustrations she delighted in. She changed the setting from Dunkeld to Sawrey and, recalling her love of Randolph Caldecott's style, made Jeremy a Regency-period dandy with fine jacket, galoshes and pumps, who sailed elegantly on a water-lily leaf. Beatrix indulged her sense of humour as well as her thorough knowledge of amphibians and insects. Jeremy's friends are perfectly outfitted gentlemen: Sir Isaac Newton, the newt, wears a black-and-gold waistcoat beneath his long tailcoat and cravat. Mr Alderman Ptolemy Tortoise is regal in his chain and gold medal of office, his ponderous shell resembling a heavy macintosh, although as a vegetarian he brings his string bag of salad along to Jeremy's 'nasty' feast of roasted grasshopper with ladybird sauce. The story of a fisherman down on his luck reminded Beatrix of the 'fish stories' her father's friends had told in Scotland, as well as her brother's travails with rod and reel. She also recreated the gentlemen's club atmosphere absorbed from her father's reports of evenings spent at the Reform and the Athenaeum.[15]

Beatrix's letters in the spring of 1906 contain very few references to the progress she was making on the book, but she knew she had found the perfect venue for her elaboration of Eric's picture letter. Her delight in sketching the natural beauty of both Esthwaite Water behind Hill Top and Moss Heckle Tarn, a small manmade lake high above the village of Near Sawrey, later called Moss Eccles Tarn, is obvious from her many watercolours of both places. Moss Eccles Tarn was already noted for its colonies of water lilies, and even the name 'Sawrey' is said to derive from the Anglo-Saxon word for shore reeds, jagged and saw-toothed, just like the ones that grow so abundantly around Esthwaite. The text and illustrations for this story are some of the most balanced and compatible of all her writing. Nature is described and illustrated truthfully: beautifully tranquil as well as unpredictably aggressive.[16]

Whether Beatrix was amused or annoyed by Fruing Warne's suggestion that the frog's coloration was inaccurate, she settled the question by bringing the live frog to Bedford Street in a jam jar. *The Tale of Mr. Jeremy Fisher* appeared in July 1906 and was, as she had convinced Norman that it would be, a 'very pretty book'. Its carefully coloured botanical backgrounds of water plants, a frog with anatomically correct turned-out feet, a trout that any self-respecting fisherman would enjoy snagging, and a rather frighteningly rendered water-beetle who tweaks Jeremy's dainty toes, all made it a delight to look at as well as to read. It was dedicated 'For Stephanie from Cousin B', since Ethel's daughter had been passed over previously. For the next book in the series, Beatrix was planning a story featuring Tom, a kitten who lived at Belle Green, but first there were three stories for very young children to finish.[17]

For these stories Beatrix experimented with a panorama format of fourteen pictures on one long strip of paper which folded into a wallet tied with a ribbon. *The Story of A Fierce Bad Rabbit*, about two rabbits and a hunter, had been written especially for Harold Warne's daughter Louie, who thought that Peter had been too well behaved and wanted a story about a truly naughty rabbit. *The Story of Miss Moppet*, about a mouse and a cat, proved more of a challenge, owing to the feisty kitten Beatrix borrowed from one of the masons who was working at Hill Top when she was there in July. It had turned out to be a difficult model, being 'very young & pretty and a most fearful pickle'. The panorama books, although popular with readers, were ultimately unsuccessful, because shopkeepers found them difficult to keep folded.[18]

Anticipating another long summer holiday with her parents at Lingholm, Beatrix found comfort in Millie Warne's frequent letters and in several visitors. 'I should be glad if you can find time to write occasionally – even if there isn't much news to write about, it is cheering!' Beatrix told her. She enjoyed a visit from Gertrude Woodward, her good friend from the Natural History Museum. While Gertrude was there, Beatrix captured a swarm of bees that had been blown out of a tree near the quarry on her property. Delighted with the prospect of raising bees, she bought a box hive which Mr Satterthwaite fixed up. 'No one in the village has lost them,' Beatrix reported, '& I don't mean to inquire further afield!' The old Ees bridge, a local landmark at the bottom of Graythwaite Lane, had to be pulled down. Beatrix wrote to Millie a few weeks later to say that she had obtained an order for stone from her quarry to rebuild the old bridge. 'I don't think I shall make much profit, not being there to look after things, but I shall like to see my stone in the bridge. I have hired a very good quarry man & insured him in case of accidents; but it is an easy one to work.' It was her first venture in local preservation.[19]

After the usual struggle moving the household from London for the summer, Beatrix reported that her parents were well settled and she expected a visit from Bertram. She tried to work on a much neglected book about Tom Kitten, her first about Sawrey, but the attic at Lingholm was stuffy, and she missed 'the sheltered open air & the gardening' at Hill Top. 'I am wishing most heartily that I was back at Sawrey,' she told Millie. It was over twenty miles, as the crow flies, between Lingholm and Hill Top Farm. Since there was no direct public transport, it was not easy to get from one place to the other. Still, Beatrix found it hard to stay away. 'I think I must go over again before the mason finishes to make sure the work is all right,' she told Millie, adding, 'also I don't want to be at home at the end of this month' – the first anniversary of Norman's death. Millie reported in mid-August that Mary Warne had produced a son – named after Norman. Beatrix knew Norman's mother would be pleased that 'there is a little son & heir at last for the business', adding sadly, 'I wish we could have kept our own dear old boy but one must take things as they come.' She sent Millie some white heather to take up to Norman's grave. The following year she sent some southernwood, an artemisia known as 'lad's love', which she hoped Millie would plant at Highgate. Beatrix never forgot the anniversary of Norman's death, and was faithful in tending his grave. If she was in London around the end of August, she went herself, often taking a plant from the countryside.[20]

Back in London, Beatrix spent three nights with Millie and her mother at the end of August. She planned her trip in part so that she would not return to London with the family at the end of September, but instead would spend as much time at Sawrey in October as possible. 'If I come back with them to London,' she explained, 'either I will begin a cold – or the cook will give notice or something will prevent me going back to Sawrey, & I want so much to have a good month there, to garden & get extra fat before winter.'[21]

She reported on the progress and setbacks she had found at Hill Top in August, especially delighted with her new garden. 'I have been planting hard all day – thanks to a very well meant but slightly ill-timed present of saxifrage from Mrs Taylor at the corner cottage. She brought out a large newspaper full! It is not all planted yet.' Beatrix was also learning the protocols of dealing with the local tradesmen. 'I had rather a row with the plumber – or perhaps I ought to say I lost my temper! – the men have been very good so far, if he won't take orders from a lady I may pack him off & get one from Kendal.' She was provoked that in her absence the same plumber had 'put up a pipe at the opposite end of the kitchen to where I wanted it'. There were more heated exchanges and Beatrix despaired that it might never be made right. She was learning that her gender was frequently a disadvantage in negotiations with local artisans, who were unaccustomed to taking direction from a London lady, but if she showed herself knowledgeable as well as resolute, she usually got their cooperation. A bit later Beatrix wrote to Millie, 'there are several rows going on! but I am not in any of them at present – though much inclined! I think I shall attack the county council about manure, I am entitled to all the road sweepings along my piece, & their old man is using it to fill up holes, which is both illegal and nasty.'[22]

Beatrix's letters to Millie chronicle her rising spirits as she worked on her farmhouse, especially enjoying laying out a large flowerbed. She had discovered a 'rather good pink rose on the farmhouse, very scraggy and neglected but making new shoots'.

Although she went to a nursery at Windermere for some bushes – syringa, rhododendron and 'a red fuchsia', reputed to be perennial – she did not have to go far to find plants that pleased her. 'I am being inundated with offers of plants!' she told Millie. 'It is very kind of people; and as it really is the right time to thin & replant, I don't feel such a robber of the village gardens.' She got some splendid phloxes from the quarryman, planted them between the laurels, and put the lilies between the azaleas. She planted out a saxifrage that had taken over several pots and she put cuttings of rock plants on top of the garden wall – 'I have got cuttings of "white" rock which have crimson & purple flowers,' she wrote with pleasure. From an old lady at Windermere who had an overgrown garden, Beatrix got a bundle of lavender slips: 'if they "strike" they will be enough for a lavender hedge.' Edith Gaddum sent over a hamper of plants, including Japanese anemones and sweet williams. 'It is nice to have plants from places one knows of or with some associations,' she had written to Millie from Wales. 'I am going to get some of the wild daffodil bulbs which grow in thousands here.' Admiring the Satterthwaites' garden, Beatrix took some of their discarded honesty (*Lunaria annua*) from the garbage heap, reassured by Mrs Satterthwaite's opinion that 'stolen plants always grow'. Delighted with her horticultural treasures, Beatrix told Millie, 'I have had something out of nearly every garden in the village.'[23]

But Beatrix had also discovered her farmhouse roof had no ridge poles to keep the slates in place during a storm or high wind, and she had fallen through the back kitchen ceiling. 'I don't think I ran any risk,' she explained to Millie with more equanimity than she must have felt at the time. 'It went down wholesale so it was not scratchy to my stockings, & the rafters were too near together to permit my slipping through. The joiner & plasterer were much alarmed & hauled me out. I was very much amused. It was a very bad ceiling, I was intending to have it patched up so it did not matter.'[24]

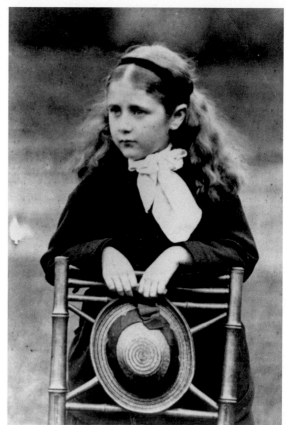

1. Beatrix aged about five. A very pretty child, much photographed by her father.

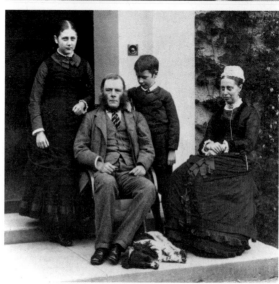

2. The Potter family at Dalguise House, about 1881, their last holiday at the Perthshire house Beatrix once considered 'home sweet home'.

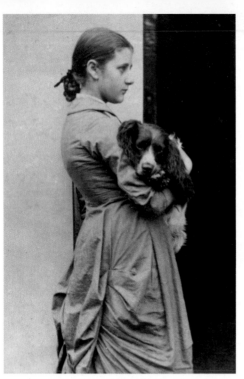

3. Beatrix at Dalguise House, with her spaniel 'Spot'.

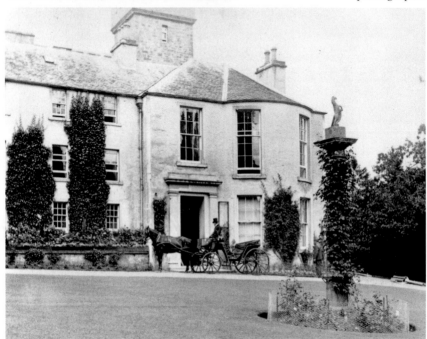

4. Dalguise House in Perthshire. The country estate where Beatrix spent eleven happy summers is distinguished by its unicorn-topped pillar, a favourite backdrop for Rupert Potter's photographs.

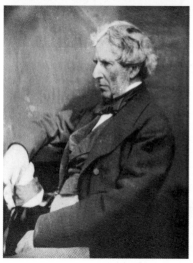

5. Edmund Potter, FRS, MP (1802–83), Beatrix's talented entrepreneurial grandfather, photographed by his daughter Lucy about 1859.

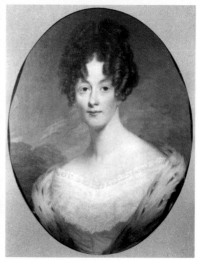

6. Jessy Crompton (1801–91), the beautiful Radical who married Edmund Potter in 1829, was idolized by her granddaughter for her character and spirited independence.

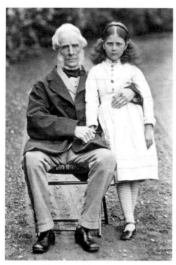

7. Beatrix, wearing the velvet ribbon that gave her headaches, and the striped stockings that reminded her of a zebra's legs, at Dalguise House with her Unitarian friend, the Revd William Gaskell.

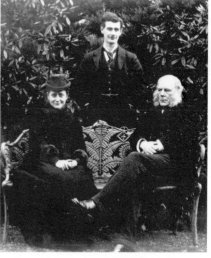

8. Beatrix, Bertram and Rupert Potter at Heath Park, Birnam, Perthshire, 1892, perhaps the same holiday on which Bertram first met his future wife, Mary Scott.

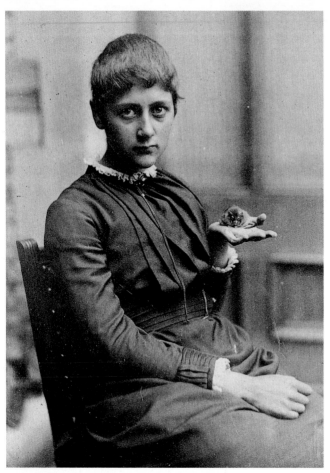

9. Beatrix with Xarifa, her pet dormouse, 1885. Beatrix later endorsed this picture 'Age 19 – much out of health. Hair cut short!' Xarifa achieved fame later as a leading lady in *The Fairy Caravan*.

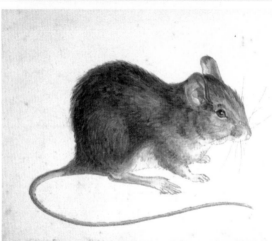

10. Woodmouse (*Apodemus sylvaticus*), drawn as a Christmas gift in 1886. Beatrix used feathery brush strokes to highlight the texture of the fur. She enjoyed painting mice when she grew tired of painting rabbits.

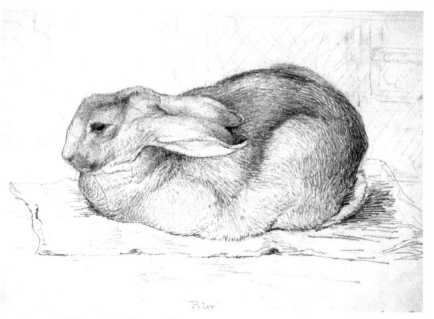

11. Peter Rabbit, 1898. The real Peter Rabbit was 'bought at a tender age' in 1892 and taught to do tricks. When Peter died at the age of nine, Beatrix memorialized him as 'An affectionate companion and a quiet friend'.

12. Study of Judy the lizard, 1884. Another pet that brought Beatrix a great deal of pleasure and which she painted with skill.

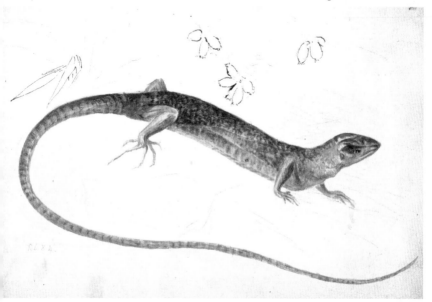

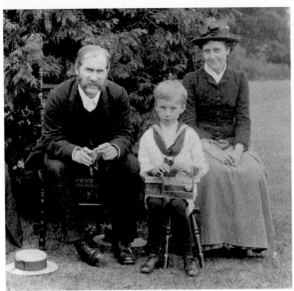

13. Beatrix, her Lake District mentor, Hardwicke Drummond Rawnsley, and his son, Noel, photographed by Rupert Potter at Lingholm in 1887.

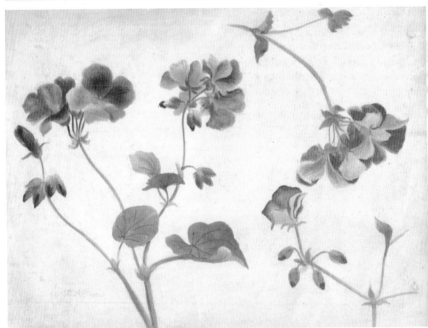

14. 'Sprays of Regal Pelargonium, including Buds' (*Pelargonium x domesticum*), 1886. Painted at Camfield Place. Beatrix gave this beautiful watercolour to Miss Hammond, the governess who encouraged her interest in art and remained a lifelong friend.

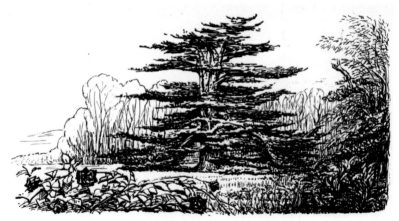

15. Cedar at Birds' Place, Camfield Place. A pen-and-ink rendering of a cherished old cedar at her grandfather's estate. The drawing speaks to Beatrix's lifelong fascination with trees and her careful observation of how they grew. She used it as the headpiece to chapter VII of *The Fairy Caravan*, published in 1929, writing: 'In the middle of the mossy grass plot stood the glory of the garden – the cedar.'

16. 'Leaves and Flowers of the Orchid Cactus' (*Epiphyllum phylanthus*), 1886. A little-known watercolour of one of Grandmother Potter's much admired orchid cacti, painted at Camfield and given to Miss Hammond in 1887. Beatrix enjoyed this plant and grew several varieties at Castle Cottage. (Collection of Charles Ryskamp.)

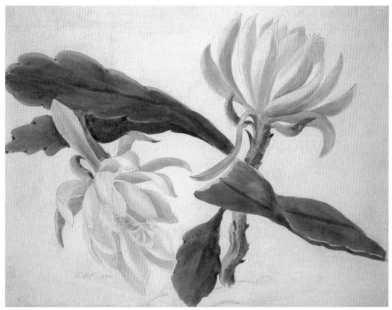

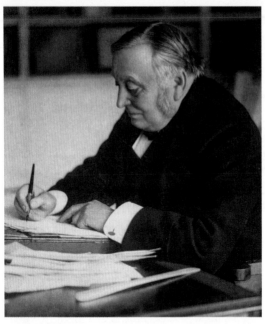

17. Sir Henry Enfield Roscoe, the chemist, Beatrix's multi-talented uncle and scientific promoter.

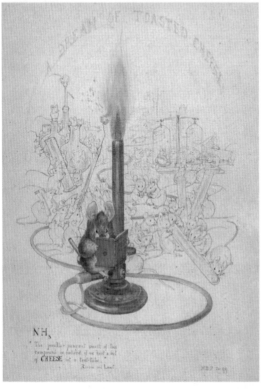

18. 'A Dream of Toasted Cheese', 1899. Beatrix drew these mice cavorting in a chemistry laboratory as a gift for her Uncle Harry, and he proudly published the drawing in his autobiography.

Beatrix was delighted when Cannon bought sixteen Herdwick ewes so that there would be lambs at Hill Top the following spring. She wanted to help bring down fern from the moor which was used as bedding for the sheep: 'I think I will go up next time with the cart & help the children to rake it, it is such nice dry crackly fern.' In mid-October she celebrated the near completion of the interior improvements by lighting her first fire in the library. 'I laid the fire & lit it myself & it went straight up directly & gives a great heat.' She was also pleased with 'the old fashioned high hob pattern' on the mantel. It was all just as she wanted it.[25]

Beatrix was also enjoying the traditions of her new neighbourhood and entertaining a few guests. She attended the harvest festival at St Peter's church in Far Sawrey, enjoyed another visit from Gertrude Woodward and entertained Nurse Bond, the woman who took care of Beatrix's former governess Miss Hammond. The latter was now old and suffering from rheumatism, but insistent that her nurse enjoy a holiday. 'We got a walk before it began to rain,' she told Millie, 'we went along the other side of Esthwaite & looked at the charcoal burning in the wood, such funny mounds, banked up with turf, like a smouldering vocano.'[26]

In October the rats had returned with reinforcements: '2 big ones were trapped in the shed here,' she reported, 'besides turning out a nest of 8 baby rats in the cucumber frame opposite the door . . . Mrs Cannon calmly announced that she should get 4 or 5 cats! imagine my feelings.' Beatrix acquiesced when Mrs Cannon later reported seeing a rat 'sitting up eating its dinner under the kitchen table in the middle of the afternoon'. In spite of such infestations, Beatrix relished her life at Hill Top. She was able to stay most of the month, telling Millie, 'I feel so very well, & eating so much I am almost ashamed of my appetite. Moreover I am absorbed in gardening. I am in course of putting liquid manure on the apple trees!! It is a most interesting performance with a long scoop.'[27]

When she returned to London, Beatrix missed her farm. During the Christmas holidays she walked around Bedford Square where the Warne family had lived, noting sadly that the shutters were up at number 8, and wishing she was at back in Sawrey. The physical beauty of the place, as well as the hard physical work and mental concentration required of her, made her grief bearable. Hill Top Farm and the quaint village of Near Sawrey had become an integral part both of her life and her imagination. Her gardens, her house and her animals – even the rats – were to figure in the books she produced over the next several years. 'I want to do a picture book someday of the village in the snow,' she told Millie. 'I had a nice little letter of thanks from little Betsy Cannon at the farm, signed "yours respectfully," is it not a beautiful word?!'[28]

For Christmas 1906 Beatrix had given Winifred Warne an illustrated story called 'The Roly-Poly Pudding', which featured her old pet white rat Samuel Whiskers and his wife, Anna Maria, now imagined as residents of Hill Top. While *Tom Kitten* would be set predominantly in the Hill Top garden and farmyard, with a few interior views of the farmhouse, the village duck pond, and the distant fell sides, 'The Roly-Poly Pudding' featured the interior of the farmhouse. She began it during the summer of 1906, intending it as a companion to *Tom Kitten*, but its publication was delayed because she lacked finished background sketches. Potter quite consciously used these Sawrey tales to celebrate her new identity as the owner of Hill Top Farm, even including herself in one of the illustrations. They all bear evidence of her growing involvement in village life and her pleasure in being at her farm, even if she could snatch only a few weeks each year from her family obligations.[29]

The Tale of Tom Kitten, a story about manners and civility, was published in September 1907. Tom's mother, Tabitha Twitchit, was named after one of Mrs Satterthwaite's cats at Belle Green. The book was dedicated to 'all Pickles – especially to those that get upon my garden wall'. 'Pickle' was a word that pleased Potter. She used it to identify free-thinking, exuberant people, like her cousin Caroline, or mischievous kittens and small children, who could not contain their enthusiasms and romped in her flowerbeds or apple orchard. Tom's misadventures in quite ridiculous bib and tucker are set off by loving illustrations of Hill Top's flower garden, imagined with the riotous abundance that she hoped it would have someday. The drawings detail some of the specific trees, flowers, shrubs and butterflies she had described in her letters to Millie over the summer. They are among the best of her work and give the book a special visual delight. Somewhat later she added a gaggle of farmyard 'puddleducks', which brighten up the story and give it an unexpected twist. *Tom Kitten* resembles *Nutkin* in its explanation of animal behaviour. Ducks are frequently seen with their heads underwater; Potter suggests in this story that they are looking for the clothes they have stolen from Tom Kitten and his sisters.[30]

The farmhouse interiors are precisely rendered. The entrance porch with its large Brathay slate walls, the stone-flagged floors, oak panelling and deep-set windows were all original. She also included some of the small furnishings she had added: a beautifully rendered flowered washbasin, the caned chair where Tabitha washes her kittens' faces, the new clock in the hall, the wall mirror, all faithfully illustrated. The white wicket gate at the end of the new walk is there, as is the lush fern-covered stone wall where the three kittens dance in various stages of undress, and from which they uncertainly watch the surly and slightly malevolent ducks with 'very small eyes' who are on their way to usurp the kittens' discarded clothes. The views looking out from Hill Top over the fields are as true to nature as the flower garden. There is the gate at the end of Smithy Lane, and a view of Stoney Lane winding up the hillside toward Bank Wood, with the ubiquitous dry-stone walls marching over the fields and up the fells.[31]

The real farm stock at Hill Top, including ducks and hens, increased rapidly after 1906, and their care occupied much of Beatrix's attention. By the summer of 1907, in addition to the sixteen Herdwick sheep and Kep the collie, the first and favourite of Beatrix's farm collies, there were six dairy cows, including an excellent milking cow called Kitchen. 'They have got funny names,' Beatrix wrote to Harold Warne's daughter Louie in July. 'I have got two lovely pigs, one is a little bigger than the other, she is very fat and black with a very turned up nose and the fattest cheeks I ever saw; she likes being tickled under the chin . . . I call her Aunt Susan.' Dorcas, the smaller pig, was not as friendly and squealed loudly when Beatrix caught her by the ears. 'But Aunt Susan is so tame I have to kick her when she wants to nibble my galoshes.' Probably during that same summer, Beatrix sketched some of her barnyard animals in an exercise book with the idea of designing a painting book for children. The following year eight new pigs arrived, bringing the herd at Hill Top to fourteen, and Beatrix knew that some little pig would have to go to market. At Christmas 1908 she bought a 'beautiful cow from another old woman', who gave her a shilling for good luck. John Cannon had spent all the pig money on sheep so the farm now boasted ten cows and thirty-one sheep.[32]

Beatrix was learning a great deal about farm animals, including how to care for the sick ones. With Mrs Cannon's help, Beatrix nursed a sick calf, giving it medicine out of a hollow horn, called a drench, which she inserted into its mouth. After an emergency dose of brandy, the calf recovered, but the carthorse developed a toothache that also required attention. In August 1907 Beatrix told Millie she had been out early in the morning 'photographing the lambs before they depart! oh shocking! it does not do to be sentimental on a farm. I am going to have some lambskin hearthrugs.' As realistic as Beatrix was about the purpose of raising livestock, she occasionally found that being a farmer was not easy. The Hill Top Farm animals featured in her imaginative stories for children, but they were also the source of her income in the real world of fell farming and when necessary they were eaten.[33]

Improvements to outbuildings and fields – building the new barn and milking parlours, laying water to the new kitchen, putting in field drains, and moving the farm track – took longer to complete than she had hoped, but the renovations, including indoor plumbing in the farmhouse, were finished by October 1907. 'The new barn is very satisfactory,' Beatrix reported to Millie. 'I have come just in time to see the finishing & fittings, there is a large loft above & a stable for calves & bullocks below. The farm has done very well.' She celebrated quietly. For the next two weeks she enjoyed clear weather when Esthwaite Water was like a mirror. 'I think a still autumn day is almost the most beautiful time of year,' she wrote, 'but when there are such heavy hoar frosts at night it is always a chance whether the sun conquers the mist, or whether it turns to rain.'

Next Beatrix turned her energies to the inside of the farmhouse.[34]

The first room to be sorted out was the front kitchen, or hall, as she called it. She kept the fireplace as it was because she wanted to sketch the old hearth for the 'Roly-Poly Pudding'. But she put out more of her small personal treasures, as well as some of the old oak furniture she had begun to collect. 'I have got a pretty dresser with some plates on it & some old fashioned chairs,' she explained to Millie. She put out a cherished warming pan, uniquely designed to hold hot water rather than coals, that had belonged to her beloved Grandmother Potter, '& Mr Warne's bellows which look well'. Soon she added a fine carved oak cupboard. A Schofields grandfather clock, inlaid with walnut, graced the half-landing on the stairs. Farmhouse chairs and a gateleg table completed the oak dining room. A pen wiper, a kettle holder, and later a framed collection of photographs of children she had never met, but who wrote to her and were now friends, as well as some of the gifts they sent, were put in the hall: especially the small bag made of woven grass that little Louisa Ferguson and her mother sent from Wellington, New Zealand. Her happiness made Beatrix almost giddy: 'When I lie in bed,' she wrote to Louie Warne, 'I can see a hill of green grass opposite the window . . . and when the sheep walk across there is a crooked pane of glass that makes them look like this [drawing of weirdly misshapen sheep], and the hens are all wrong too; it is a very funny house.'[35]

Beatrix was slowly but surely creating the new patterns of her life, unconsciously becoming as attuned to the seasons and rhythms of the farm year as she had become to those of the publishing world. She was always attentive to the details surrounding her books. *Peter Rabbit* had been translated into French and German, and now Warne's were seeking publishers, but Beatrix was not always happy with the quality of the translations. 'That French is choke full of mistakes both in spelling & grammar,' she told Harold, finding it rather 'flat' and 'too English'. She was more pleased with how *Tom Kitten* had turned out. 'Some of the pictures are very bad, but the book as a whole is passable, and the ducks help it out.'[36]

Beatrix spent Christmas afternoon 1907 with Millie and her mother at their new home in Primrose Hill, near Harold Warne's house, enjoying the warmth and affection she found in their company. It had been a harsh winter and there was a lot of illness. Beatrix herself had a bad cold. She had called in the doctor in the hope of forestalling bronchitis or any more serious upper respiratory infections, to which she seemed especially susceptible. While she recuperated she worked on the sketches for *The Tale of Jemima Puddle-Duck*, which would accompany *The Roly-Poly Pudding* as the books for 1908. She was also making clay models of book characters for statuette makers. She insisted on an active role in selecting licensing agreements for this merchandise. In April 1908 she accompanied her parents on their customary springtime holiday to the south coast, this time to Sidmouth, but her mind was on her lambs in the snow at Hill Top with little green to eat, and on Mrs Warne's health. The kindly old woman had developed bronchitis, and despite Millie's heroic nursing efforts, died on 25 April.[37]

Beatrix was devastated. In a letter of condolence to Millie, written the following day from Sidmouth, Beatrix confessed, 'I don't feel as if I know how to write to you in your dreadful loss. I wish you had Norman to help you . . . But we must try to feel it is all ordered . . . Nothing could be happier and brighter than the memory we shall always have of your dear Mother. There could not be a more brave cheerful old lady, but it is rather early to talk dry common-sense.' Beatrix's letter includes a rare invocation of the hope of divine comfort. 'I pray that God may give you strength and peace,' she wrote. 'I have kept feeling I ought to come [to the funeral], I have felt nearly worried to pieces.'[38]

Beatrix returned to work on the story of a barnyard duck, Jemima, whom she imbued with certain autobiographical characteristics. Beatrix chose the name 'Jemima' almost certainly to honour the famous ornithological painter and illustrator Jemima Blackburn, whose *Birds from Nature* (1868) she had been given for her tenth birthday, and whom she had been honoured to meet in 1891. *The Tale of Jemima Puddle-Duck* appeared in July after several heated discussions with Harold about its dialogue and cover illustration. Jemima, the story of the naive duck in poke bonnet and shawl who wanders off to find a safe place to lay her eggs, was 'a farmyard tale' for Ralph and Betsy Cannon, the children of Potter's farm manager. It was a story inspired in part by their mother, who held the view that ducks were poor sitters and was thus in the habit of confiscating the duck eggs and giving them to the Hill Top hens to incubate, but also by Beatrix's amusement at her farmyard ducks. Both children and Mrs Cannon appear in the story, as do other Hill Top animals, especially the heroic collie, Kep, who rescues Jemima from certain culinary catastrophe at the hands of the elegantly mannered 'sandy whiskered gentleman'. The story features Hill Top's new barn and outbuildings, the wrought-iron gate Beatrix put in front of the kitchen garden, the rhubarb patch, the entrance porch of the farmhouse, the façade of the Tower Bank Arms in the village, as well as imagined aerial views of the countryside around Near Sawrey, and some beautifully rendered pink foxgloves in bloom. *Jemima* was an immediate success and inspired more merchandise, eventually including a popular soft 'Jemima' doll.[39]

The Roly-Poly Pudding, published finally in October 1908, took its story line from the invasion of rats at Hill Top when Beatrix first bought the property and her ongoing battles against them. It was dedicated to an actual pet rat, long deceased, Mr Samuel Whiskers, and the dedication appropriately read, 'In Remembrance of "Sammy", The Intelligent pink-eyed Representative of a Persecuted (but Irrepressible) Race. An Affectionate little Friend, and most accomplished thief.' It had black-and-white line drawings as well as full-colour plates and was a longer, more involved story than any of her previous tales. The story features Tabitha Twitchit and her poor son, Tom Kitten. Tom is imprisoned by the enterprising rats, Samuel and Anna Maria, who plan to make him into a pudding using 'borrowed' ingredients from the farm kitchen. Some children wondered if the artist used a live model 'trussed up with string, like breast of lamb with stuffing', so realistic is her drawing of Tom Kitten waiting helplessly to be rolled in pastry.[40]

Beatrix's adventures renovating the old farmhouse are incorporated into this tale, as are the architectural details of the house, its thick walls, the secret tunnels the rats had made behind the chimney, and its many cupboards, as well as the kitchen roof through which she had fallen. The hall of Hill Top and its furnishings are detailed in the colour illustrations. The range and the remnant of the large chimney-hood appear in several pictures, as does the half-landing, the upper hall and stair carpets, the claret curtains, the grandfather clock, the raised-panelled front door and the old timbers of the attic. The Hill Top interior is drawn with such accuracy that it soon became universally recognizable as what an old English farmhouse should look like, in much the same way that Mr McGregor's garden came to stand for all vegetable gardens.

Beatrix quite bravely drew herself into the story, where she can be seen standing at the end of Smithy Lane next to the Ginger and Pickles shop. There is a picture of Farmer Potatoes near his barn, to which Samuel Whiskers and Anna are racing with their wheelbarrow loaded with 'borrowed' bundles. Beatrix had taken a photograph of her near neighbour John Postlethwaite and copied from it for her book illustration. John Taylor, the village repair man, also appears, as John Joiner, the carpenter dog. *The Tale of Samuel Whiskers* is Beatrix's tribute to the old farmhouse in much the same way as *Tom Kitten* and *Jemima* celebrate her garden and farmyard. The inclusion of the details of the interior of Hill Top and the view of the countryside from the Hill Top roof indicates that this book is a very personal one, clearly a celebration of her liberation from her parents' house to one of her own.[41]

By the early autumn Beatrix wrote to Harold Warne with the idea of getting started on several new books. Her energy was high and she had some stories she wanted Harold to consider. She sent the text of 'The Faithful Dove', a tale set in the town of Rye and written some years earlier and for which she had plenty of sketches. She also included a sequel to *Benjamin Bunny*, even though she was tired of drawing rabbits. 'I must try and do another rabbit book,' she had written to a young fan, William Warner, 'all the little boys and girls like the rabbits best.' This one was about Benjamin's family of Flopsy Bunnies. Another story was about the village shop in Sawrey. 'I should like to get rid of one of them,' Beatrix told Harold. 'When a thing is once printed I dismiss it from my dreams! & don't care what becomes of the reviewers. But an accumulation of half finished ideas is bothersome.' *The Tale of the Flopsy Bunnies* and *The Tale of Ginger and Pickles*, the story about the village shop, were chosen as the books for 1909.[42]

Her letters to Harold Warne were now characterized by a new self-confidence and an increasing frustration with his erratic management of the publishing company, particularly his haphazard payment of her royalties and his inattention to her growing market in merchandise. There were too many unanswered enquiries about books and illustrations, too many unsettled licence agreements, and even agreements for her own books which remained unsigned. She had explained that she needed regular payment of royalties in order to continue improvements at the farm, pay bills and plan for future expenditures. In November Beatrix told Harold that she planned to buy another field in Sawrey and would need money for the deposit, while she financed the balance. But in early March 1909 Beatrix had to ask again, explaining that she needed a cheque, as arranged 'on 15th', because 'there are one or two sales coming on & may be some bargains'.[43]

Sometime later Beatrix discovered that Warne's had received a reasonable offer to produce Peter Rabbit dolls a year before, but Harold had not even bothered to answer the letter of enquiry. 'I should very much prefer to manage the dolls myself, in future,' Beatrix wrote to Harold. 'I must ask you *not to make any fresh arrangements* without letting me know, I am seriously provoked about things being in such a muddle.' It was a strong rebuke but elicited only 'an enormous letter' of justifications and explanations which irritated Beatrix even more. 'I made *no* complaint about the management of my books,' she told him, '. . . you are incorrigible as a correspondent.'[44]

Beatrix went to the farm briefly in February 1909 where she worked hard on the drawings for the *Flopsy Bunnies*, kept indoors by cold weather and snow. She had chosen the garden of Gwaynynog as the setting for this episode of disobedient and gluttonous bunnies who return to the rubbish heap in Mr McGregor's garden. Unlike the earlier bunny books, the more formal Gwaynynog garden with its archways, beds and long vistas gave her simple plot a floral and horticultural abundance that captures the reader's attention quite as much as the sleepy bunnies suffering the 'soporific' effects of too much lettuce.

The garden at Gwaynynog held a special place in Beatrix's affections. She wrote about the garden again, probably during a summer visit in 1911, in an unfinished fairy tale, 'Llewellyn's Well', which includes her description of the garden's pleasures.

The garden lay behind the house, inside a mossy red brick wall. It was filled with apricots, apples and pears; and peaches in their season.

In Summer there were white and damask roses, and the smell of thyme and musk. In Spring there were green gooseberries and throstles, and the flowers they call ceninen [daffodils]. And leeks and cabbages also grew in that garden; and between long straight grass alleys, and apple-trained espaliers, there were beds of strawberries, and mint and sage. And great holly trees and a thicket of nuts; it was a great big garden.[45]

Gwaynynog was also an ideal garden whose various aspects Beatrix replicated in miniature both at Hill Top and later at Castle Cottage. In 1912 and again in 1913, shortly before Fred Burton died, Beatrix also painted several fine airy landscapes around Gwaynynog, capturing once again her love of that green countryside.[46]

The *Flopsy Bunnies* was finished in March, and would be published in July. In April she wrote to Millie from Woodcote, where she had gathered some 'dear little white violets under some nut bushes', thinking of Mrs Warne's final illness the year before, and of course, of Norman. 'There are some yellow butterflies flitting about, I think Norman & Frue used to come up on the common between here & Shere to get butterflies. It is very pretty country and curiously quiet . . .' Her parents were spending the spring holiday at the Lowood Hotel in Windermere while Beatrix went off to see her new lambs. But she had other personal business in Sawrey as well.[47]

11

～ *Diversions* ～

B Y THE SPRING OF 1909 Beatrix had published fourteen books which were now considered 'nursery classics', and which were paying her substantial royalties. She received additional income from merchandise licences based on her books. There were wallpapers, china tea sets, figurines, and soon a Peter Rabbit painting book and Jemima Puddle-duck doll, as well as wooden jointed rabbits. Beatrix took an active interest in all this merchandise and the licences for it. Commenting perceptively on a model for the Jemima doll, Beatrix wrote to Harold Warne, 'The young lady has done the legs particularly well, and made the bonnet very neatly, also the tail. If she had less stuffing in the head below the chin it would allow a more graceful neck; but the shape really doesn't matter so long as it is funny!'[1]

Beatrix had become a canny businesswoman. She used her royalty income not only for physical improvements to the farm, but to increase her herds of livestock, native Herdwick sheep, dairy cows and beef cattle, and to buy additional land. She wanted to protect her existing boundaries and expand her farm, particularly when land came on the market which was contiguous to her existing property or was offered at an especially attractive price.

When Beatrix bought Hill Top and Buckle Yeat Croft in 1905, her father's firm of solicitors in London had acted for her. Only after the fact did she discover that she had been very poorly represented. In 1908 she sought the advice of W. H. Heelis & Son, a well-regarded local firm of solicitors with offices in nearby Hawkshead and Ambleside. It was an established firm, thoroughly familiar with the sometimes quirky traditions of property transfer in the Lake District. The Hawkshead office consisted of two partners, William Dickenson Heelis, and a cousin, William Heelis, formerly of Appleby, the county town of Westmorland. The latter had joined the firm ten years earlier and was known around the area as Appleby Billy to distinguish him from his cousin, who was called Hawkshead Willy. It was to the Appleby-bred solicitor that Beatrix went for assistance in buying more property in Near Sawrey. Heelis was then 38 years old. He was a tall, quiet, rather handsome man with an athletic build and an easy manner – some thought he resembled the poet Wordsworth, although he had rather larger ears. In December 1908 Beatrix had approached the local bank for a loan to buy some closes of pasture and woodland which were offered at a good price near Far Sawrey, a move that had the advice and support of her brother Bertram. But she also consulted with William Heelis, whose firm arranged for the conveyancing of the title. When Castle Farm came on the market the following spring, William Heelis acted as her solicitor.[2]

Castle Farm and its farmhouse, known locally as Castle Cottage, is opposite Hill Top and above the Kendal road. Its fields bordered Potter's Buckle Yeat Croft and extended some distance to the north-east up Stoney Lane. Castle Farm consisted then of just over twenty acres. It included a farmhouse, outbuildings, a barn and a small dwelling house. The view from Castle Cottage looks out across Post Office Meadow directly to the Hill Top farmhouse. The farm was conveyed to Potter on 12 May 1909 for £1,573. It was a very good buy at the price, and was already tenanted, but the buildings needed some major improvements, particularly the laying of a water supply to the property. On Heelis's recommendation Beatrix continued the existing arrangements, and went about the necessary improvements. The addition of Castle Farm with fields contiguous to Hill Top provided an important buffer to Potter's primary property, and added greater grazing capacity. But it also extended her property directly into the village of Near Sawrey, making her a more visible landowner in the local area. With the purchase of Castle Farm, William Heelis became Beatrix's principal legal adviser, and unofficial property manager when she was away in London.[3]

The purchase of Castle Farm provided even more reasons for Beatrix to celebrate her participation in village life in her next book.

Ginger and Pickles was a story based on old Mr Taylor's shop in Smithy Lane where everyone came to make their purchases, to visit and to gossip. Beatrix had written the story first in a penny exercise book as a Christmas gift for Louie Warne in 1908. She put a crowd of familiar characters into this story to please Louie, but it also turned out to be a clever marketing device. Tom Kitten, Moppet and Mittens, the dolls Lucinda and Jane, even the policeman from *Two Bad Mice*, Peter Rabbit and his family, Jeremy Fisher, Mrs Tiggy-winkle, Jemima Puddle-duck, Samuel Whiskers and Anna Maria, all visited the village shop and its proprietors, Ginger, a yellow tomcat, and Pickles, a terrier. Since the shopkeepers are the natural predators of some of their customers, tension is built up as to whether or not they can keep their predatory instincts in check long enough to make sales. Unlike Tabitha Twitchit's shop, Ginger and Pickles gave credit, a concept which Beatrix explains in the story. Eventually poor management forces the shop to close, causing some disruption and inconvenience to village life.[4]

The story is not particularly complex, although it deals with such basic business matters as making a profit and keeping accounts. Potter's drawings are especially rich in texture and detail and the book as a whole is vividly coloured. The animals wear bright clothing and the interior views of the shop are elaborately detailed and cleverly lit, with sunlight streaming though open windows and doorways. The tale was initially published in large format, to highlight Potter's love of detail, but later it was republished in the now traditional small size.

Beatrix finished work on the proofs during a long summer holiday in 1909. The Potters had taken Broad Leys, a large, comfortable estate with charming gardens near Bowness on Windermere. It was, however, some distance from the Windermere ferry, a long walk for Beatrix to and from Hill Top. It was becoming more and more difficult for Beatrix to sit relatively idle in London, dealing with servant problems or holiday arrangements, when there was so much to do at the farm, especially at harvest time when the hay needed to be got in and the bracken cut for winter bedding. Despite the distance she was required to travel each day, she spent a good deal of time at the farm, and managed to finish *Ginger and Pickles* in late August. It was published in October.[5]

'The "Ginger & Pickle" book has been causing amusement,' Beatrix reported to Millie. 'It has got a good many views which can be recognized in the village which is what they like, they are all quite jealous of each others houses & cats getting into a book.' She had dedicated it to old Mr John Taylor, who had been bedridden for some years and who had wanted to be put into a book. He once told Beatrix he thought 'he might pass as a dormouse'. Sadly, Taylor did not live to see his characterization as an elderly dormouse, or Beatrix's dedication.[6]

Beatrix later sent a copy to Mrs Bunkle, the Sawrey schoolmistress who owned the yellow-haired Tommy Bunkle, alias Ginger, explaining that sometimes she had to bow to necessity in her art, even at the expense of nature. 'His colour is so unusual, I thought it was rather a shame to cover him up with clothes in the pictures, but unfortunately there is a demand for comic animals in coats, and *trousers*. I generally refuse to supply trousers on any terms; but it is an unfortunate fact that animals in their own natural pretty fur coats don't sell so well as dressed up – and one has to consider the bills at this time of year' – a clear reference to her recent purchases of farm property.[7]

Beatrix managed to squeeze in two nights at the farm before leaving the north to accompany her parents back to London. Her 'chief occupation', she told Millie, 'is contemplating an important drain (clean water!) which ought to drain about half my farm and doesn't! ... I am going up on the hill after dinner to help rake bracken, I think it is the pleasantest "harvest", it is not so hot as the haymaking.' Beatrix was back in Sawrey again unexpectedly in October to attend to more drainage problems, hampered as usual in her business dealings by unpredictability of funds from Warne's. She spent another week there in late November, a time of year she particularly enjoyed.[8]

There had been an early frost which made farm work more difficult, but did nothing to subdue her delight. She wrote to Millie, 'It has been glorious weather but I shall be rather glad of a thaw ... I managed to get some fruit trees moved today. The colours are most lovely in the sunshine, all the leaves are off the trees, but the copse wood and fern on the hills keep their colour all winter . . . The woods look crimson. I managed to do some sketching yesterday in a sheltered place.' She had two Persian kittens and about twenty white pullets which had come into full feather and which she hoped would become good layers. A hen she brought from Sidmouth had turned out to be especially productive but, like Jemima, 'she always gets over the fence and lays her egg in the garden, in a hole in the wall'. Beatrix was still preoccupied with repairs. 'This morning I went to Hawkshead in the trap to see about the fire insurances', no doubt meeting with William Heelis about their 're-arranging'. She had sold her two largest pigs, sad to break up the family, but pleased that they brought a good price, 'their appetites were fearful – 5 meals a day and not satisfied'. To Millie she confessed, 'was rather over done with the head yesterday, the poor little cherub had such a sweet smile, but in other respects it was disagreeable. It is rather a shame to kill them so young; one has no sentimental feeling about a large bacon pig.' Clearly content with her life as a farm woman, she told Millie, 'I have no particular plans of coming back, if I am not required at home & the weather keeps fine I may stop another week.'[9]

Pigs were much on her mind because it had also been decided that one of the books for 1910 would be about pigs (*The Tale of Pigling Bland*) and the other about a little wood-mouse (*The Tale of Mrs Tittlemouse*). 'I have got them planned out,' she wrote to Harold Warne a month later, 'but no drawings finished yet.'[10]

Unpredictably, Beatrix's attention was diverted from both her sketching and her farming by the mercantile and rural-life issues at stake in the run-up to the first of two general elections held in Britain in 1910. She had always been interested in politics, indeed, it would have been difficult to grow up in the Potter household and not absorb the issues and the personalities of late-Victorian and Edwardian politics. Beatrix's flirtation with politics had begun back in 1902 when she registered a patent for a Peter Rabbit doll, but was unable to find an English manufacturer who could compete against the cheap foreign doll. She had been dismayed to find the shops filled with unauthorized imports.

By 1910 merchandise was a large part of Potter's royalty income, and the British government's adherence to free trade was having an adverse impact on her business interests and the protection of her copyright. It did not help that part of her problem lay on the immediate doorstep at 10 Bedford Street, where Harold Warne's desk was piled high with unanswered letters from toy manufacturers and other would-be vendors, or that she still smarted over the pirated editions of *Peter Rabbit* that continued to flood the market in the United States. When free trade and unfair copyright laws became issues in the general election, Beatrix became politically active.[11]

Although she had absorbed the litany of free trade from her Potter grandfather and his friends, by 1909 Beatrix believed that the extension of the franchise had changed the weight of the argument, and that tariff reform was necessary to correct the imbalance. She undertook her own campaign for fair trade, or protectionism, which by January 1910 consumed her in painting and printing up posters, and writing leaflets in support of the Unionist campaign for tariffs. To one of her young fans she wrote, 'I am so busy over the Election my fingers are quite stiff with drawing.'[12]

One of her handmade posters read 'Poor Camberwell Dolly is Dead' and featured a doll, once a familiar part of the south London toy trade, leaning limply against a gravestone on which was printed, 'Here lies the Camberwell Wax Doll killed by Free Trade with Germany.' Beatrix called these posters her 'Camberwell Beauties', alluding privately to the butterfly with white-edged wings first observed in Camberwell in 1748, but by then as extinct as the English doll. Her other poster displayed a recognizable Peter Rabbit doll made in Germany, carrying an expensive price tag. The poster read: 'Made in Germany'. Beatrix's fair-trade posters reflected the current anti-German protectionist sentiment pervasive in England at the time, as well as her own commercial self-interest. 'These posters are bold practice, I must have made 60.'[13]

Beatrix was realistic enough to know that copyright protection and doll manufacturing were not issues that would persuade farmers to abandon free trade. The government's rationale for a horse census was another matter, as conscription of horses was an important issue among farmers. 'It is useless to talk to farmers about *dolls*,' she wrote to her printer, 'But if there *is* a subject which enrages us – it is meddling with our horses! (*I* am a one-horse farmer, amongst other trades.)' For this audience Beatrix created a separate leaflet, titled 'The Shortage of Horses', printed by the firm of Edmund Evans. It was a much more closely reasoned statement addressing the present shortage of horses in rural areas, and the very real prospect of conscription of horses in wartime. 'No doubt we should be paid for our horses,' Beatrix wrote, 'but what about our ruined crops?' However, the connection between horse conscription and free trade was a stretch. When the leaflet appeared, it was signed 'Yours truly, North Country Farmer.' Beatrix insisted that 'It must not be let out the horse leaflet is written by a *female*.' Evans printed over a thousand, and Beatrix, with the help of Miss Hammond's niece Margaret, known as Daisy, spent days stuffing and addressing hundreds of envelopes. She sent it to the printers of agricultural show catalogues, country papers, and advertisers of farm equipment.[14]

It was disappointing to Beatrix, who of course could not vote herself and disapproved of the women's suffrage campaign, that the January 1910 general election returned a Liberal government. The vote in the Lake District was closer. 'I am much rejoiced to see the results of the neighbouring Windermere & Kendal elections,' she wrote to Harold Warne. 'I promise faithfully to return to pigs & mice next week.' This was the first and last time Beatrix would be involved in national politics, but only the beginning of her interest in local matters.[15]

Beatrix admitted that she was 'over busy', rushing off to Sawrey whenever she could get away from family obligations. Finally at the end of July, after much ado about finding a suitable holiday house and making special arrangements for lodging the coachmen, Beatrix and her parents arrived at Helm Farm in Bowness. Helm Farm was a charming whitewashed farmhouse with an old stone barn attached at the back. It stood atop a steep hill above the lake, which made horse and foot traffic to and from Bowness arduous. The inconvenient access left the Potters less inclined to go out than usual and consequently made it more difficult for Beatrix to spend time in Sawrey.

'I don't like leaving my parents for any length of time,' she wrote to Millie in late August, 'they are both very well in health, but they do not like this place . . . It is a fine view, but *such* a hill!' Rupert had not been well just before leaving for Windermere, and Beatrix worried, knowing that she would have to go back to London if her father's health deteriorated.[16]

She squeezed out every available moment at the farm, gardening and looking after the haying, but had little time or energy for books. 'I cannot screw anything out of my head at present!' she told Millie. 'I have done a little sketching when it does not rain, and I spent a very wet hour *inside* the pig stye drawing the pig. It tries to nibble my boots, which is interrupting. I don't think it ever answers to try & finish a book in summer, it makes me short of material afterwards if I do not sketch.' She hoped to return to Sawrey later that autumn. For the first time in seven years there would be only one book for the year.[17]

The Tale of Mrs. Tittlemouse was originally written out in a small leather-covered notebook as a New Year's gift for Nellie Warne, Harold's youngest daughter. Mrs Tittlemouse, who was first introduced as the heroine of the Flopsy Bunnies, is a story of a very fastidious country wood-mouse with a long tail. She lives in a bank under a hedge, and her housekeeping is put upon by a variety of careless callers with dirty feet, some of whom come hoping to be fed. Mrs Tittlemouse becomes so upset with her uninvited visitors that she threatens to 'go distracted' and shuts herself up in the nut-cellar until they leave, and she can get her little house cleaned up again to give a party for other equally tidy wood-mice.

This was a story that called upon Beatrix's acute observation of the habits of a variety of insects and amphibians, and her experience drawing them. She includes bees, a beetle, a ladybird, a butterfly and a spider, as well as Mr Jackson, a large toad. In at least one version of the story Beatrix included woodlice, an earwig and a centipede among the uninvited guests. But Harold objected to having woodlice in a children's story. Beatrix argued for keeping the word 'slaters', the generic word for woodlice, but later acquiesced to the much more innocuous description of them as the 'creepy-crawly people' hiding behind the plate racks. Like the more fantastical *Jeremy Fisher*, Mrs Tittlemouse's insect visitors reflect Beatrix's microscopic understanding of their anatomy, coloration and behaviour. She painted her insects with accuracy but also with humour. The toad, she knows, moves crab-wise on land and only goes to find water for spawning in the spring. She also knows that toads are inordinately fond of honey and can smell it out. The fat spider who seeks shelter in the rain is very much like the spiders with hairy legs and jointed appendages that she drew under the microscope in the 1890s, as is the entomologically identifiable butterfly who lands on the sugar cube. Beatrix delighted in the drawings of the insects and in the details of Mrs Tittlemouse's house, which has a cosy quality, not unlike the interiors she was creating at Hill Top. She had observed many such serious nest-making mice over the years, and all of Mrs Tittlemouse's visitors had come at one time or another to call at Hill Top Farm.

Beatrix was pleased with the bound copies she received, certain that the book would be 'popular with little girls'. *The Tale of Mrs Tittlemouse* was published at the end of July. A rare note to one of the Moore daughters from Rupert Potter reveals that, despite his poor health, he still took pleasure in his daughter's talents. 'I think I am rather proud of my daughter's freshness of humour which has never yet become dull,' he wrote. It was a touching comment on the sometimes tempestuous relationship between father and daughter.[18]

In early October Bertram came to Bolton Gardens for a rare visit and Beatrix jumped at the opportunity to leave the field to him. It had been 'a trying season' and she was wanting a change. Rupert had become very irascible, complaining of his stomach. But when nothing serious could be found, Beatrix decided to stay away as long as possible. Most of the harvesting chores at Hill Top had been finished before she got there, but there were still apples to be gathered and stored, and there was always gardening to do. She did some sketching, but mostly worried about sheep sales – buying and selling – and the price of mutton. She had a hired a man to dig the garden while she divided perennials, and there was a new brood of chickens. 'I have got some white pullets which amuse me, they are such pets,' she wrote to Millie, 'they will all try to jump on my knee at once if I sit

on the doorstep, and two or three will allow me to pick them up &
stroke them like a parrot. Their feet are rather dirty.' It was clear
that the pig book had been put aside.[19]

In mid-November Beatrix made another impromptu 'bolt for it' to
Hill Top. She wanted to get her tax papers completed, a task which
undoubtedly took her to the Heelis office in Hawkshead. In spite of
a light snow, she was very glad she had come, cheered by how pretty
the farm looked in winter. Beatrix had taken an interest in the local
Grasmere games, a sporting tradition of long standing held in the
beautiful lakeside village of Grasmere, where wrestling and hound
trailing were especially popular. She had attended some of the games
in August, perhaps in the company of William Heelis, who was an
avid sportsman. She was especially intrigued when one of the temporary farm hands helping with the Hill Top harvest brought out a
puppy he was training for the trail hound competition the following
year, and demonstrated how the dog could track. Delighted with the
demonstration, Beatrix watched the puppy following the aniseed scent
his master had laid around the farm from a nearby hill. 'The leaves
are all off, it is very wintry looking, but I do not feel cold at all,' she
told Millie. In fact, Beatrix seemed to catch cold only when she
returned to London – understandable, given its smoky air and contagious diseases, and where her life was increasingly stressful.[20]

Rupert Potter was now nearly 80 and Helen was in her seventies.
Beatrix was effectively managing two households, Bolton Gardens
and her farm, as well as arranging the several holiday trips the family
made each season. The year 1910 marked a falling off of the intense
creative activity that had sustained her since Norman's death five
years earlier. 'I did not succeed in finishing more than one book last
year,' she wrote to a friend on New Year's Day 1911. 'I find it very
difficult lately to get the drawings done. I do not seem to be able to
go into the country for a long enough time to do a sufficient amount
of sketching and when I was at Bowness last summer I spent most
of my time upon the road going backwards & forwards to the farm
– which was amusing, but not satisfactory for work. It is awkward
with old people, especially in winter – it is not very fit to leave them.'
Her creative work and the hard physical energy she expended at the

farm had been the key to warding off depression. But it was a slippery slope she clung to every winter in London. It was becoming harder and harder to escape to Sawrey, and once there, work on the farm kept her from sketching.[21]

In 1911 she managed to 'squeeze out' *The Tale of Timmy Tiptoes*, the least satisfactory of her tales. She probably agreed to do it for all the wrong reasons: to satisfy demand from Warne's for another book, for the money, and to court her growing American audience. The story featured a couple of grey squirrels (*Sciurus carolinensis*), an American import to Great Britain which began to flourish at the turn of the century, and an American chipmunk resembling the common eastern variety (*Tamias striatus*). Beatrix may have seen grey squirrels in the Sawrey woods, but it seems unlikely they had reached the Lake District by then. She did most of the squirrel drawings either from models at the zoo or from reference books at the Natural History Museum, and she had no live models of chipmunks. Because Timmy Tiptoes and Chippy Hackee are not drawn from nature, their images have a certain artificiality that her other animal characters do not have. They seem more like 'stuffed animals', particularly in facial appearance, than live ones. The squirrels' solution to the problem of over-eating holds the tale together and the book sold well, but it seems marred by its mixed environment, including the surprising appearance of an American black bear. The awkwardness of both story and image reflects how difficult it was for Potter to write about nature that was outside her knowledge or that she had not directly observed.[22]

She put more energy into finishing *Peter Rabbit's Painting Book*, the first of three such successful ventures. It contained pairs of outlined drawings of animal characters from her earlier books, with a short text under each pair. Beatrix had definite ideas about how the pictures in the painting books should be done. In the front of the book, she wrote brief instructions about the five colours a child needed and explained how to mix Antwerp blue with burnt sienna to make dark brown. She also included the admonition, 'Don't put the Brush in your mouth. If you do, you will be ill, like Peter.' Both the painting book and *Timmy Tiptoes* were published in October. During the summer Beatrix suggested to Harold Warne that they should sell loose sets of outline drawings separately from the painting book. She tried out her new marketing idea on the two youngest Moore girls, Hilda and Beatrix, and their mother sent their painted pictures back to Beatrix so she could see the happy results. 'People don't buy two or three copies of the book . . .' she reasoned to Harold, 'but I quite think they would nearly all buy extra prints, & children might come again for more from their own pocket money if they were done for 3d or 4d . . . I should certainly like some for myself as soon as you have any.' Harold accepted her suggestion, and single sheets were printed with the full text under each and were sold in an envelope in sets of twelve for 4d. The painting book had wide appeal and was immensely successful.[23]

Imperceptibly, the balance of Beatrix's creative energy had shifted. By 1911, she was more happily focused on Hill Top and her life as a countrywoman in the village of Sawrey than on meeting the seemingly insatiable demand from Warne's for books. But farming required capital, and Beatrix never forgot for an instant that the books were the key to maintaining and expanding her properties. Knowing that Harold Warne was in Jersey on holiday, Beatrix wrote to Fruing about her delinquent royalties. 'I am *not* short. I am *not* of opinion that the circulation of the books is smaller than it ought to be, or any other of Mr Warne's etcs. His letters are enough to drive anybody mad. I only want to know as a matter of banking arrangements whether the next cheque is going to be inside August, or whether it means September 15th . . . The difficulty of getting cheques at the time promised has sometimes rather perplexed and alarmed me . . .'[24]

There were other diversions. A new king, George V, would be crowned in June. In February Beatrix had been appointed to the committee on local coronation celebrations in the village, where tempers ran high. 'There was such a row over the appointment of a committee that I don't know how it will end,' she wrote to Millie. 'The chairman wanted 7 members & we emerged with 14, and several of the leading inhabitants left out; it is a regular mess! I am on the committee & a determined person; but unfortunately non-resident.' Beatrix did what she could, including allowing some of the celebra-

tions to be held on Bull Banks, one of the larger pastures below
Oatmeal Crag, on Castle Farm.[25]

But the real reason for her winter visit to Sawrey was real estate.
William Heelis had told her that two small pieces of land bordering
Hill Top would soon come on the market. Beatrix and William
tramped through the snow in the cold, making certain of the property
lines and fences. Together these small strips would regularize the
complicated boundary on the western side of Hill Top, close to
Sawrey House. It would also enable her to construct a 'good turnable
fence of wood wire or stone' on her property which would give her
more control over a public access. Once again, Heelis acted as her
agent, acquiring the two portions from Thomas Baines for £20.[26]

Beatrix was able to make only two other visits to Hill Top that
spring. In early April she found it very cold with frequent blizzards,
but no snow lying on the ground. 'There are a good many polyan-
thuses [hybrid primrose] but everything is pinched and shrivelled,
except the violets which happen to be at the foot of a wall,' she
reported. 'There are quantities of lambs, extremely lively & pretty,
and two calves have arrived since I came yesterday.' She was pleased
with her flower gardening, and hopeful that the crown imperial lilies
Mrs Warne had given her years before might yet bloom at Hill Top.
Back again in the middle of June, during Whitsuntide holiday, she
happily busied herself singling a potential bumper crop of turnips to
be used later as cattle feed, but privately she worried about the effects
of an extended drought in the area. 'The drought is dreadful on this
light hilly soil, it is difficult to decide whether to move the hay, or
let it wither up still worse.' Such questions were crucial for fell
farmers who worried about the survival of their livestock in bad
weather.[27]

The Potters rented Lindeth Howe for the summer of 1911. It was
a large nineteenth-century house, with garage, cottages and extensive
gardens, in an elite area of Windermere known as Storrs Park. The
house was once again on the top of a hill, not quite as steep as the
one at Helm Farm, but still a hard walk up from the ferry. Beatrix
went over to Sawrey about four days a week. 'I go there on the
Coniston coach in the morning & come back after tea . . . The lake

and woods look lovely in the evening, when I get down to the ferry,' she told Millie. But the daily travel took valuable time away from both farm work and her sketching.[28]

The summer weather was lovely but rather warm, and although the drought had been serious, Beatrix's two pump wells 'held out'. The flower garden had suffered most but she was very pleased with her crop of fruit, especially the apples. Her attention was diverted for several days by a Boy Scout encampment in the field just beyond the farmhouse. Beatrix told Louie Warne all about the camp in an amusing picture letter. 'This is a camp of boy scouts – This is my house! & my apple trees, & me in my garden [drawings] . . . I find tents just above my chimnies [*sic*] and scouts all over everywhere, especially on the walls [drawing].' Beatrix struck a deal with the Scout commander that the boys could take the small apples from two designated trees and some very hard pears. But as she explained to Louie, she expected him to send two boys for the apples and got '*20* scouts & 1 trumpet' instead (drawing). The picture letter shows the Scouts with apples stuffed in their shirt and shorts pockets. 'Three cheers for the *old* lady!(!)' they had called out. 'The "old lady" has dismissed the scouts with strict injunctions to *cook* the pears.' But minutes later a Scout reappears to ask for a '*bucketful*' of sugar to cook the pears with (drawing). 'I think it prudent to conduct the scout to "Ginger & Pickles," as sugar is cheap,' she told Louie. Although she fussed about her apple trees, the Scout encampment was the beginning of many more to follow, of both Boy Scouts and Girl Guides, and of Beatrix's pleasure in accommodating the young people on her land.[29]

Beatrix had also discovered a new piece of legislation proposed as an addition to the Protection of Animals Act, 1911, to which she objected both as a farm woman and an employer of young farmhands. The proposed Act prohibited anyone under 16 years of age from being admitted to or participating in the slaughter of an animal at a knacker's yard. The Act came into effect in 1912 and carried a fine of up to £10. Beatrix drafted a letter of protest sometime that autumn, probably intending it for *The Times*. She argued that while it was unwise to allow young children to be present at a pig killing, since 'there have once or twice been serious accidents, where they have tried to imitate the scene in play', she insisted that a farm lad of 15½ was certainly able to assist 'at the cutting up'. Recalling her own childhood, Beatrix opined, 'The present generation is being reared upon tea – and slops.'[30]

These diversions were minor, however, compared with Beatrix's participation in the local campaign mounted against the construction of an aeroplane factory at Cockshott Point on Windermere and the use of hydroplanes on the lake, both of which began in the winter of 1911. Here was a cause she could not ignore, for both personal and environmental reasons, and one she felt passionately about. Like her earlier petitions against free trade and the horse census, the campaign against what she called 'the beastly fly-swimming spluttering aeroplane careering up & down over Windermere' involved a letter-writing campaign and publicly aligned her with Hardwicke Rawnsley in another fight for the protection of the lakes.[31]

'It is an irritating noise here, a mile off; it must be horrible in Bowness,' Beatrix explained to Millie. 'It seemed to be flying very well; but I am extremely sorry it has succeeded, if others are built – or indeed this one – [it] will very much spoil the Lake. It has been buzzing up & down for hours today, and it has already caused a horse to bolt & smashed a tradesman's cart.' Potter was no Luddite protesting against modern technology for the sake of the old ways. The hydroplane was a hazard to boating, fishing and the quality of life around the lakes. It frightened animals aboard the ferry boat, interfered with hunting and fishing, and caused accidents. Its exhaust and gasoline polluted the lake, and the noise level, whether the plane was flying overhead or taking off and landing on the lake, altered a cherished quality of life in the lakes – solitude and tranquillity.[32]

A letter from Beatrix Potter appeared in the 13 January issue of *Country Life* magazine titled 'Windermere and the Hydroplane'. Quoting from Cowper's *History of Hawkshead* on the history of the Windermere ferry and its centrality to all commerce between the Kendal district of Westmorland and the northern part of Furness, Beatrix argued that 'a more inappropriate place for experimenting with flying machines could scarcely be chosen . . . The first consideration should be given to the question of danger to existing traffic – the traffic of steamers, yachts, row-boats and Windermere Ferry.'[33]

The public debate over aeroplanes on the lake had begun a week or so earlier when *The Times* published a letter from Canon Rawnsley, who wrote as secretary of the National Trust, but also as one who cherished the inherent peace of the unique environment. 'The value of the shores of Windermere as a resort of rest and peace', he wrote, 'is seriously imperilled and . . . residential property will be thereby deteriorated.' E. W. Wakefield, a principal of the Lakes Flying Company who proposed the aeroplane factory, responded with an appeal to science and the need for military testing, as well as the importance of the hydroplane for surveillance. But Rawnsley and his committee knew that Wakefield also had plans to start local hydroplane passenger services between Bowness and Grasmere.

Beatrix's next letter to *The Times* exposed Wakefield's hidden agenda, predicting that a factory at Bowness and continued flying at low level 'will turn Windermere into a pandemonium of sound'. She argued that the proper place for testing hydroplanes 'is upon the sea'. 'Canon Rawnsley says modestly that he does not desire to be a "spoil sport". I respectfully maintain that work, business and the undisturbed customary use of centuries should be set before idle amusement.'[34]

After another week of exchanges, *The Times* printed a leading article stating that 'the National Trust are using influence in support of the effort which Canon Rawnsley and the local protest committee are making to preserve Windermere from being used as an experimental ground for the hydroplane', and reported that the opponents were lodging protests with the Home Secretary. Beatrix's letters to *The Times* and to the various publishers to whom she circulated her petitions were signed 'H. B. Potter', and those to the locals, 'H. B. Potter, farmer'. By August, the protest committee had forced the Home Office and the Board of Trade to open a public inquiry into the matter of hydroplanes on Windermere.[35]

The experience provided Beatrix with new insight into the constituencies of the Lake District and conservation politics. Remembering Rawnsley's view that residents of the Lake District were not always able to act in the best interests of preserving their environment,

Beatrix was not surprised by the opposition's argument that they supported the aeroplane factory because the presence of more airmen in the local villages would be good for business. Economic gain for many of them was, understandably, a higher good than natural beauty and tranquillity. Beatrix was also chagrined to discover that most of what she termed 'the aristocrat' publishers of London would not sign her petition, whether they recognized her name or not. 'I find radicals much more willing than conservatives,' she wrote to Harold Warne, 'which may be a good omen.' She got fourteen firms to sign her petition, but was more impressed by the signatures of '34 doctors & nurses at the London Hospital, of whom 31 have visited the Lakes, collected by a nurse who had been to Sawrey'. In April Beatrix reported gleefully, 'the roof of the hydro hangar has blown in, & smashed two machines . . . I hear one broke down & actually blocked the ferry the other day. It is quite monstrous to allow them in such an unsuitable place.' By the end of the year Wakefield's plans to build the aeroplane factory had been abandoned and soon after the hydroplanes left Windermere.[36]

Her work on the winter scenes for *The Tale of Mr. Tod* was further delayed by the necessity of going to Stalybridge, the home of her maternal grandparents, to open the Golden Jubilee celebration of the Stalybridge Church and Sunday School Bazaar. Rupert had officiated at the opening of the Bazaar in 1900, and 'as there seemed no one left of the family', Beatrix felt obligated. She anticipated selling quite a lot of books there, but was shocked to discover that the school officials expected them to be donated gratis. Beatrix made up the wholesale price. It was a big spring event for Stalybridge, with printed programmes announcing that 'Miss Beatrix Potter of London' would open the Bazaar. A similar notice in the Unitarian *Inquirer* quoted Beatrix as saying 'Of Stalybridge (church) I know little; of Hob Hill (school) I have heard much.'[37]

Beatrix had been working on the text of *The Tale of Mr. Tod* since the previous November. It was a longer tale than her other books and based in part on a tale from *Uncle Remus*. She had copied it out from an old notebook, changing the setting to the Sawrey countryside, even placing the fox's earth 'at the top of Bull Banks, under Oatmeal

Crag', fields on Castle Farm that she had explored extensively. For this tale there would be more pen-and-ink sketches than watercolours; an indication not only of her bifurcated time in sketching at the farm, but also a reflection of her desire to work in other media.

Soon after receiving the text of *Mr. Tod*, Harold Warne had written questioning the name 'Tod' for a fox. He also suggested that this longer book should begin a new series with an entirely different format from the shorter 'Peter Rabbit Books'. Beatrix was indignant. '"Tod" is surely a very common name for fox? It is probably Saxon, it was the word in ordinary use in Scotland a few years ago, probably is still amongst country people. In the same way "brock" or "gray" is the country name for badger. I should call them "brocks" – both names are used in Westmoreland [*sic*].' She also objected to the idea of a new series simply because '*I* find it so difficult to continue to make "fresh" short stories' and there had been no falling off in sales of the little books.[38]

The early spring of 1912 found Beatrix emotionally unsettled. There were severe strikes in the country; one by the coal miners adversely affected the countryside, causing economic hardship in the village of Sawrey. She had not been to Hill Top in two months and longed to get away from Bolton Gardens, but could make no plans. Her father had been 'out of sorts, but won't have the doctor'. Finally in early April she left London. 'The country doesn't show much sign of spring yet,' she wrote to Harold from Sawrey. 'Yesterday was very fine, but I spent it at the selling off of an unlucky (& deserving) neighbour . . . nobody had come to the sale from the outside driving distance.' The weather was mild and there were a 'quantity of lambs – nearly all twins. But the pig has only six pink cherubs.' She was able to do some background drawings for *Mr. Tod*. In July she came again for a meeting of a committee on footpaths to which she had been elected. Historically, access to footpaths across private lands had been a controversial issue. Hardwicke Rawnsley was a long-time advocate of open footpaths and his views once again influenced hers. Potter's election to this committee signified her deeper involvement in local affairs, not only as a large landowner in Sawrey, with herds of cattle and flocks of sheep, but as someone with recognizable expertise about boundaries and rights of way, and as an advocate of open access to fields and fells.[39]

Although most of the colour blocks for *Mr. Tod* were finished, she had still to correct some of the fox's anatomy and so spent time in the Natural History Museum looking at photographs and reference books, trying to distinguish the anatomical lines of the true English red fox (*Vulpes vulpes*) from other species. She took the precaution of asking Harold Warne if he objected to the name 'Bull Banks' where Mr Tod had an earth. 'One thinks nothing about bulls and tups in the farming world; but after you objected to cigars it occurred to me to wonder. "Bull Banks" is a fine-sounding name, but I could just as well call it "Oatmeal crag."' No one at Warne's objected. Telling Millie that 'spring had been a scramble', she reported that her father was still 'out of sorts' but hoped that he would be better out of London. The Potters had decided to go back to Broad Leys in Windermere in July, a house that was also inconvenient to the ferry and hence to the farm. 'I must make the best of it,' Beatrix wrote with resigned acceptance.[40]

The Tale of Mr. Tod was finished before Beatrix left for Windermere. She dedicated it to Francis William Clark of Ulva, the two-year-old son of her dear cousin Caroline Hutton who had married Francis William Clark, the Laird of Ulva, and was living and farming on a small island off the coast of Mull. The opening paragraph of the new story was one that she was particularly proud of, since it got away from the familiar setting of 'once upon a time'. It also highlighted her mood and her approach to this last book set at Sawrey. Her original manuscript began: 'I am quite tired of making goody goody books about nice people. I will make a story about two disagreeable people, called Tommy Brock and Mr Tod.' The principal characters, the badger and the fox, were both villains, although Beatrix's sympathies seem to lie with the fox in the endless struggle they waged with each other – perhaps because badgers were known predators of hedgehogs. But Harold Warne objected to the opening and suggested some sweeter alternatives. Beatrix knew a good beginning when she saw one and altered it only slightly. 'If it were not impertinent to lecture one's publisher,' she told him, thoroughly exasperated with his literary timidity, 'you are a great deal too much afraid of the public for whom I have never cared one tuppenny-button. I am *sure* that it is that attitude of mind which has enabled me to keep up the series. Most people, after one success, are so cringingly afraid of doing less well that they rub all the edge off their subsequent work.' In the end, they reached a compromise; Beatrix agreed to drop 'goody goody books' and substituted 'well-behaved' for 'nice'.[41]

The forty-two pen-and-ink sketches in *Mr. Tod* are deliberately framed by heavy lines, making them resemble woodcuts. They give the violent story a primitive quality suited to the atmosphere of primal enmity. Potter chose this style because it suited the mood of this longer, darker tale, where moonlight was a motif. All along, her chief interest had been with language and with more complex plot and character development, and with 'more reading'. While *Mr. Tod* is a dark book, set in Sawrey's bleak winter with views of Esthwaite Water in several sketches, Beatrix cleverly incorporates Peter and Benjamin, Old Mr Bunny, and the Flopsy Bunnies, ensuring its appeal to readers of her other tales. The fox and the badger are both primarily, though not invariably, nocturnal animals, and she accurately captures their mutual gastronomic preference for small bunnies. Badgers (*Meles meles*), with their labyrinthine setts, would have been as familiar to Beatrix as rabbits and farm animals. But badgers in the wild are not like the disreputable character she creates in Tommy Brock. They are extremely clean animals and excellent housekeepers, maintaining their setts immaculately, and badgers do not smell.[42]

As some of Potter's previous stories had been 'girl books', *The Tale of Mr. Tod* appealed perhaps more to boys. The enmity between Brock and Tod was instinctual and their physical battle rages from the kitchen floor out over the rocks and crags with 'dreadful bad language! I think they have fallen down the stone quarry.' The fighting scene was as real as the tension over whether or not the Flopsy Bunnies would ever be rescued. Six-year-old Harold Botcherby's response to the story must have been typical of that of other boys. He wrote asking Beatrix about the outcome of the battle, wondering if the two enemies were still fighting. Beatrix, not at all adverse to carrying on with the story, responded to young Harold, describing the end of the fight and detailing the injuries to each, but telling young Botcherby that, sadly, Mr Tod and Tommy Brock 'are still quarrelling'. 'Tommy Brock', she said, was 'a nasty person. He will go on living in Mr Tod's comfortable house till spring time – then he will move off into the woods & live out of doors – and Mr Tod will come back very cautiously – & there will need to be a big spring cleaning!' Botcherby, who grew up to be an artist himself, must have been delighted with her visually graphic reply.[43]

As Beatrix had predicted, the summer at Broad Leys proved difficult, although it was briefly enlivened in August by a visit from Norah and Joan Moore, who came in time to care for a hatch of little chicks in the incubator. 'I don't know when I remember such a summer,' Beatrix wrote to Millie. 'My hay was nearly all got in before the rain, but . . . it is sad to see other peoples haycocks rotting.' She went to the farm three or four days each week, walking the long way back to the ferry at the end of the day, and frequently getting caught in the rain. Beatrix tried to put an amusing face on her growing exhaustion: 'Today I came by road instead of by steamer, in state, in the farm gig with a swill tub on the back seat. We have rather a crowd of little pigs.' One can only imagine how Mrs Potter reacted when she witnessed her daughter's arrival in such a conveyance.[44]

There had been tragedy too – a serious outbreak of foot-and-mouth disease, the first since Beatrix had farmed Hill Top. Fortunately, the farm was just outside the area where the livestock were quarantined so Beatrix's own herds were unaffected, but the local markets were closed and other commerce inconvenienced by police orders affecting livestock movements. There was understandable anxiety in the neighbouring agricultural community. A pickpocket had been working in the village of Near Sawrey, and then came the accidental death of a young farmer who had a wife and three little children. 'He was a bad husband,' Beatrix explained to Millie near the seventh anniversary of Norman's death, 'but somehow that seems to make it more shocking. I think it is a comfort to have pleasant memories, if nothing else.'[45]

The physical wear and tear on Beatrix, as well as the extra effort of finishing the book, was evident by the time the Potters left Windermere in September 1912. She had never had such an exhausting summer. 'I have done no sketching – alas –' she confessed to Millie, 'partly the weather, & partly fatigue. I have kept very well & managed the going backwards & forwards; but it takes it out of me.' What she did not confess to Norman's sister was that she was also harbouring an agonizing secret.[46]

In June William Heelis, her devoted and respected Hawkshead solicitor, had asked Beatrix to be his wife and she had happily accepted him. But she did not immediately tell her parents, knowing once again that they would vehemently disapprove. When she did confide in them, probably late in the summer, there ensued another long and bitter contest of wills, not unlike the violent battle between badger and fox that she had described in *Mr. Tod*. Under prolonged siege, Beatrix's health broke down.

12

❦ *Satisfactions* ❦

BEATRIX HAD FALLEN IN LOVE with William Heelis in much the same way as she had with Norman Warne: slowly and companionably. Although Norman's early death robbed her of a happy marriage, Beatrix was in many ways unusually lucky in love for a woman of her class and time. She had been able to get to know Norman as a person as well as an artist and tradesman, to discover his temperament over time, and to see him at work and at play with his family, even with the encumbrance of chaperones. Similarly, she was able to meet and work with William Heelis, though this time without chaperones, first as a business and financial adviser in Hawkshead, then to get to know him in the community while working together on community matters. By the time William proposed to her, Beatrix was comfortable with his character and his temperament. This depth of understanding was highly unusual for a couple at a time when middle- and upper-class marriages were commonly arranged on the basis of suitability of family, and meetings between the betrothed couple were severely circumscribed.

The two men in Beatrix Potter's life had much in common both physically and temperamentally. They were both tall and thin, quiet and reflective, and accomplished at their particular craft. Both were athletic, and both had a certain inherent sweetness in their personalities. In the same way as she had come to love Norman, Beatrix discovered the satisfaction and security that came from William's knowledge of the Lake District and its customs, and she relied on his advice about her properties in the same way as she had trusted Norman's expertise in publishing.

Both Norman and William came from large families, which was attractive to a woman raised essentially as an only child. William was the youngest of eleven siblings, seven boys and four girls. Both men were younger than she, William by nearly five years, but that disparity bothered no one except one or two of his older sisters. Beatrix had loved Norman for his imagination and his humour, and she similarly delighted in William's love of nature, his knowledge of the country-side and his zest for being out in it, whether he was fishing, shooting, golfing, bowling, boating or country dancing.

William Heelis had been a much sought-after Hawkshead bachelor – so the more intriguing question to the Hawkshead locals was what he found attractive in this 46-year-old Londoner, undoubtedly destined to be a spinster dutifully looking after her elderly parents. He was obviously fascinated by the wealthy London lady who had shown a great independence of spirit in buying a small hill-country farm and in insisting on becoming part of a country village. It may have been her intense blue eyes and her obvious intelligence that initially attracted him. She had unexpected flashes of humour and understatement, a quick wit and a subtle rebelliousness, but Heelis was certainly impressed by her determination to learn about country ways and to carry on a life of her own as far as she could find time to create one. He must have found Beatrix refreshingly forthright, and was secure enough to admire a woman who was both informed and opinionated. He respected Beatrix's literary success, but must have been more amazed by the watercolours she made of the places he knew and loved too. He knew nothing of the publishing business, or of children's literature, and it is likely that she did not talk about her books or her past.

As the two walked boundaries and tramped the fields of Near Sawrey in all sorts of weather, studied deeds, determined rights of way, laid on water to fields, expanded farmhouses and outbuildings, discussed tax rates and land values, and corresponded over such issues year after year, they had time to share their stories, to become comfortable with each other and to fall in love. There were no doll's houses or mice to act as intermediaries, but there were farms, fields and fell sides.

And so it was that Beatrix was confronted with an important decision in the autumn of 1912. Should she strike out for her own happiness, for she clearly loved William and wanted to marry him? Or should she bow to expectation and duty – to be sure an old-fashioned notion of filial piety, but nonetheless one she deeply embraced? Shrewdly, but also characteristically, William did not push, respecting her devotion to her elderly and increasingly frail parents, while quietly supporting the idea that she could marry and still remain a dutiful daughter. When Mrs Warne died in 1908, Beatrix's letter to Millie had revealed one of her own deepest longings: 'You will all your life have the comfort of remembering you have been the most devoted daughter . . .' Beatrix wanted that assurance too, and now she worried that she would feel guilty and selfish leaving her parents in their old age to embrace her own happiness.[1]

There were other, albeit minor, impediments to their marriage beside guilt and parental disapproval. William came from a long line of Anglican clergymen, doctors, land agents and solicitors – all respectable professionals. His father, the Revd John Heelis, had been the Rector of Kirkby Thore on the main road from Appleby to Penrith. His grandfather Edward had been the Rector of Long Marton, an unusually well-endowed parish. Two of his brothers were country parsons; two others were also solicitors. His law partner and cousin in Hawkshead was a leader in the Anglican community and an active member of St Michael and All Angels church there. Beatrix was a Unitarian, from a family of outstanding Dissenters. She had grown uncomfortable with any sort of organized religion, preferring a simple Quaker meeting above any. Her family on both sides had been in trade, and while her father had been a barrister, he had longer acted the gentleman of leisure. Ironically, some members of the Heelis family found her family's connections to commerce and their Nonconformist background difficult to accept. They were not initially delighted with William's choice.

Beatrix was a difficult woman for some traditionally raised women to relate to. She was socially indifferent, even eccentric. She cared little for fashion or society. She was also very wealthy, a woman of substantial property, already enhanced by William's knowledge and skills, and a writer and artist who was earnestly making herself into a countrywoman. She dressed as a farmer and could be found walking to and from the ferry, dressed in a practical, workmanlike way, happier caring for her farm animals, working in the garden, reviewing livestock at the local agricultural shows, than offering tea. As village gossip had it, sometime before their engagement, Mrs William Dickenson Heelis, William's Hawkshead partner's wife, once met Beatrix on the Kendal road, 'with pattens on her feet and a shawl over her head carrying a butter basket with flowers in it', looking just like a simple woman from the village. She was astonished to learn later that she had just met 'Miss Potter'.[2]

At some point during the summer, Beatrix and William decided that she must tell her parents she wished to marry. Their reaction to this news was precisely what Beatrix had feared it would be. Their objections were the same as they had been to Norman: a country solicitor was beneath their daughter's merit – she came, as her parents reminded her archly, from a family 'of the Bar and Bench'. Their other objection was harder for Beatrix to deal with: if she married, who would look after them?

Beatrix repeated her strategy of seven years earlier, quietly per-severing, doggedly patient with their objections, offering ways to appease while still insisting on eventually marrying William. And as before, their struggle of wills was carried on in secret – more like subversive warfare and just as debilitating. Beatrix returned to London in late September, bringing along her little dairymaid who wanted to see the big agricultural show at Islington. It provided a brief respite from the stifling atmosphere at Bolton Gardens.[3]

She got away to Sawrey in October and once again in November. She was a judge at the trussed poultry contest at the local agricultural show in November, and she stayed on at the farm for a week of very cold weather. Once back in London, she came down with an influenza that turned into bronchial pneumonia. Her heart, never particularly strong after her bout of rheumatic fever, was affected, and she was ordered to bed.[4]

She was very ill. In early March, still too weak to write letters herself, she dictated a letter to Harold Warne explaining, 'I have been resting on my back for a week as my heart has been rather disturbed by the Influenza. I am assured it will recover with quiet.' A week later, still unable to sit up, she seemed more optimistic. 'The doctor has been & he is so much pleased with my progress that I am going to keep flat a few days longer. My heart now feels quite comfortable.'[5]

Superficially, life went on at 2 Bolton Gardens as though nothing had happened. As spring approached, the Potters made plans to go to Windermere for Easter. Beatrix had improved enough to do some work on the 'pig story'. She sent Harold the text of *Pigling Bland* from Hill Top in early April, thinking it a 'rather pretty' book, and requested galleys so she could plan out the drawings. 'I am very glad to have got here,' she told him, 'it is cold but bright; I am well but not able to walk up hill yet.' But two weeks later she was laid low again by emotional stress, as well as the physical energy needed to carry on farm work and travel back and forth to Windermere every few days. 'The weather has been extremely bad, & I have had a bilious turn,' she explained to Harold. 'I seem to take a long time to get strong again. I have been drawing pigs, but cannot do much till I see where the plates fall.' Her sense of humour was still evident, however, when recounting her failure at turkey raising. 'The last ill-luck is that a rat has taken *10* fine turkey eggs last night. The silly hen was sitting calmly on nothing, Mr S. Whiskers having tunnelled underneath the coop, & removed the eggs down the hole!' By the end of the month she had yet to receive the galleys from Harold.[6]

Beatrix was still at Hill Top at the end of April, anxious to stay there as long as she could, telling Harold that she was recovering more slowly than she had hoped. 'I am decidedly stronger & look perfectly well, but I was completely stopped by a short hill on trying to walk to the next village this afternoon. I believe perserving slow exercise is the best cure, I do not think there is anything wrong with my heart now. I am always better on fine days when I can work in the garden.' She thought she could get the plates for the pig book done if she could stay and work at the farm. 'I am quite sure I am best out of London, & as my parents have come to an hotel for a holiday (& spring cleaning) I hope they will be satisfied for me to stay here a little longer.' She acknowledged, however, that 'one of my front teeth is coming out' and that she would have to come back to London, both for the dentist and to get some books.[7]

So long as Beatrix was at Hill Top, she was healthier and happier, and drew reassurance from William. William would ride his motorbike over to Hill Top on Sunday afternoons and, if the weather was pleasant, they would take long walks together. Although Beatrix had accepted his proposal, she could not decide when they could reasonably marry, and was nearly reconciled to the idea of postponing it indefinitely. They had, however, agreed to remodel the farmhouse, Castle Cottage, on Castle Farm, and even to install plumbing there. When they married they would make that their primary residence in Sawrey. The old farmhouse at Hill Top would continue as Beatrix's private quarters for her writing and painting. She was loath to alter it further, and she knew from experience that its walls and small rooms offered little privacy from the tenant's family.

William had learned that some of the fields belonging to the Sawrey House Estate, the property bordering Hill Top Farm on the west, stretching some distance beyond the near shore of Esthwaite Water, would soon come up for sale. The poor management, unrepaired fences and indifferent maintenance had troubled Beatrix, so that if the opportunity came to buy these fields, including the deep well on the property, she would not hesitate. The possibility of such an advantageous purchase kept the two happily working together while they waited out the storm of opposition at home, and Beatrix dealt with her guilt.[8]

Once again Beatrix sought advice from her independent-minded cousin Caroline Hutton Clark, now happily married and herself a young mother. She repeated her parents' objections that a country solicitor was beneath her family's status, and shared her conviction that she could not leave her parents old and alone. Caroline's reply must have been profoundly encouraging. Clark recalled in an interview years later, 'I advised her to marry him quietly, in spite of them,' and to give up her old-fashioned ideas of filial duty. While Beatrix could never have eloped, Caroline's support stiffened her spine. But in the end, it was Bertram's unexpected advocacy which broke down much of the Potters' opposition to William Heelis.[9]

Bertram arrived at Bolton Gardens for one of his infrequent visits sometime in May, while Beatrix was still recuperating at Hill Top.

He was immediately drawn into the contest and his opinion solicited. Perhaps as much to unburden himself of years of secrecy as to assuage his own guilt at not speaking up to support his sister in 1905 when she had wanted to marry Norman Warne, Bertram told his flabbergasted parents that he had married Mary Scott, a 'farmer's daughter' from Scotland, more than eleven years earlier, and that they had been perfectly happy all these years without their blessing. Beatrix, he told them, should be allowed to marry whom she wanted and to have an independent life.[10]

However brave Bertram's confession was, he was still not able to be completely candid about his wife's background, undoubtedly thinking that the shock of his secret marriage was quite enough for his parents. But the depth and passion of the Potters' prejudices must have persuaded him not to reveal that Mary was the daughter of a wine merchant in Hawick. Had he elaborated, he would have made his sister's selection of a country solicitor look favourable by comparison. Happy as Beatrix must have been to have her brother's support, once Bertram returned to Ancrum she would still be left with the guilt of abandoning her parents in their final years. But Bertram's belated confession and advocacy had broken down the united family front that the senior Potters had been confident of mounting.[11]

By July 1913 Beatrix could write from her farm, 'I am feeling much stronger now, & very much interested in farming matters; today there is a promising hatch of turkeys – and John [Cannon] & I are seriously discussing the question of buying a pedigree bull calf!' She had received a cheque from Warne's that had significantly lifted her mood, and she was making some progress on the story of Pigling Bland. 'I took so very long to get over my illness,' she explained to Evans, her printer. 'I had my heart bad for weeks & could do nothing. I am alright now; but it might have been wiser to give up the book, before they took orders for it.' Evans had asked if Beatrix was interested in buying a small interest in his printing company, and she had confided that she was saving her money to build 'another room or two onto my house'. She neglected to tell him just which house she had in mind.[12]

By the time the Potters returned to Lindeth Howe at Windermere for the summer they had given their reluctant consent to her inevitable marriage to Heelis, but urged her to postpone it – indefinitely. However, Beatrix was now free to make her engagement public. One of her first letters was to Millie Warne. Beatrix received immediate congratulations and good wishes from her dear friend, who assured her that Norman would have wanted her happiness, as did she and her family. Beatrix responded, confessing, 'I have felt very uncomfortable and guilty when with you for some time – especially when you asked about Sawrey. You would be only human if you felt a little hurt! Norman was a saint, if ever man was good, I do not believe he would object, especially as it was my illness and the miserable feeling of loneliness that decided me at last.' Beatrix shared her misgivings. 'I certainly am not doing it from thoughtless light-heartedness as I am in very poor spirits about the future. We are very much attached and I have every confidence in W. H. but I think it can only mean waiting, and should never be surprised if it were for the time broken off.' Beatrix had been in London for ten days at the end of June and she had gone up to Norman's grave at Highgate. 'The grass is neatly cut & the little veronica plants are growing; it looked as if it wanted some very small-growing flower between them.' She had tea with Harold's wife Alice and the children, reporting: 'Louie played a piece remarkably well, good style and expression. Now I cannot thank you enough for all your kindness and your mother's.'[13]

Although Beatrix was stoically prepared for more battles, the Potters made no further overt efforts to obstruct. But Rupert's health continued to deteriorate at Windermere. As she later told Fanny Cooper, 'He was very poorly – but really it was his own doing, he nearly turned himself inside out with strong medicines . . . The doctor could do nothing with him. At last he got so weak we got a nurse.' Nurse Bryant was something of a tyrant but, with careful diet and no further narcotic purges, Rupert improved. The summer moved on, with Beatrix still spending a great deal of her time and energy travelling the half-mile from Lindeth Howe to the ferry, then walking two and a half miles more from the ferry to Hill Top (and most of that was uphill).[14]

She sent off eight watercolour illustrations for *Pigling Bland* at the end of the month, including one of the grocer and horse which she copied from a photograph. In late September she returned to London to see about printing. 'I was very ill last spring,' she wrote to a young friend. 'I thought it was the last of "Peter Rabbit", and since then I have been drawing dozens of pigs!' *The Tale of Pigling Bland* had fewer watercolours and more black-and-white illustrations, and a good many last-minute additions. It came directly out of Potter's farming experience and was set at Hill Top with views of the interior of the farmhouse as well as the farmyard. It recalled the little black pig that Beatrix had insisted upon buying, despite Cannon's objections, in her early days at the farm. She had kept it in a basket by her bed and bottle-fed it until it was able to live on its own. The little black pig became her pet and followed Beatrix around the farm, inside the house and out. The story also evolved from the sale of two very fat and very hungry pigs Beatrix had let go with some trepidation in 1909, and from her extraneous sketching during various visits to her pigs in the sty. She had mentioned a 'pig book' in a miniature letter to Andrew Fayle as early as 1910, telling him that Peter Rabbit would appear in it as well, as he does on the last page, when the rabbits watch the two pigs joyously escaping.[15]

In her 1913 story, the little black Berkshire pig becomes the 'perfectly lovely' Pig-wig who is rescued by Pigling Bland, one of the two pigs sold to market. Beatrix herself appears in the story, handing the necessary travelling papers to Alexander, the other pig going off to market. It is in many ways a love story, although Beatrix denied this, but it is also a captivating tale filled with rhyme and ironic humour. There are clear biographical touches, some humorous, as in the toothache that plagues Pigling Bland, so that he could eat no peppermints, and some more serious, such as the admonition that 'if you once cross the county boundary you cannot come back', certainly an acknowledgement that marriage would dramatically change her life. Like Pig-wig, Beatrix was about to be rescued from her confining existence, daring only occasionally to hope that she would escape any last-minute threats to freedom.

Pigling Bland is a tale with an ominous beginning, a happy ending and a middle full of danger and dalliance. But in the end, Pig-wig and Pigling Bland are seen escaping to live 'over the hills and far away'. Their route takes them over a quite recognizable Colwith Bridge and beyond the distinctive signpost that stands at the fork in the road just behind Hill Top – a landmark she and William passed on their Sunday walks. Their destination was near Little Langdale, a tiny village in the foothills of the majestic Langdale Fells. '"That's Westmorland," said Pig-wig. She dropped Pigling's hand and commenced to dance.' It was an expansive landscape, full of possibilities for a new life. It echoed Potter's own love of the vast open spaces of the fell country, and her desire to make a place for herself in it.[16]

She had written the story out as she typically did, in a paper-covered exercise book, and dedicated it to Farmer Townley's two little children, Cecily and Charlie, as 'A Tale of the Christmas Pig'. While she was recuperating, and once she had the dummy book to paste her drawings into, she began to shorten the text, feeling that it should be a story for smaller children than the readers of *Mr. Tod*. She scrambled all summer to finish it, her mind clearly elsewhere, finally sending most of the drawings to Warne's in late July. Even then there were last-minute additions to the galley proofs. She had forgotten to draw in Pig-wig's peppermint in one picture. 'I only got rid of the revised proofs last week,' Beatrix wrote to her friend Gertrude Woodward in late September, 'it is disgracefully late. It has been such a nuisance all summer.' *The Tale of Pigling Bland* was published in October, only days before her wedding. Beatrix later denied that the picture of the two pigs arm in arm looking at the sunrise was a portrait of herself and her betrothed. 'When I want to put William in a book,' she wrote to a young friend, 'it will have to be as some very tall thin animal.'[17]

The struggle between parents and daughter over when she would marry William continued at Lindeth Howe until the end of September. Beatrix had made a good offer on the Sawrey House Estate property, and would close on it at the end of the year. Construction at Castle Cottage went forward, plagued by slow contractors, bad weather and the usual unpredictability of payments from Warne's. 'I am not short but I am spending money on building,' she told Harold in mid-September, still at Lindeth Howe, 'and I ought to cut my coat according to my cloth! When one knows there is money overdue one is tempted to spending.'[18]

The next phase of the crisis was, predictably, a domestic one. Rupert's health improved so much at Windermere that Helen Potter decided Nurse Bryant had become superfluous. She refused to have her return with them to London. At the same time Helen also decided to rearrange all her household help; clearly another attempt to tie Beatrix to Bolton Gardens. Beatrix knew that, left on his own, her father would be ill again, and that she would be expected to help with his care. 'We are in the most awkward fix,' she complained to Fanny. 'I feel I am deserting my post. But I am of nothing use [*sic*] compared with the nurse – I have never been in the way of doing little things for him, and he won't pay the slightest attention to me – we *both* lose our tempers.'[19]

Predictably, after returning to London, Beatrix fell ill again with a nasty cold. Her illness made her realize that she had to act or the cycle would endlessly repeat itself. 'That decides the matter,' she told Fanny. 'I am going to get married! *I* can't keep well in London, and my father is under no obligation to live in town.' She hoped that in the end her parents would lease a house at Windermere, where she could keep an eye on them for at least part of the year. 'Then it would be all right, for they like him now they have got over the shock, & he is very nice with old people & anxious to be friendly & useful ... He is 42 (I am 47) very quiet – dreadfully shy, but I'm sure he will be more comfortable married – I have known him six years; he is in every way satisfactory, well known in the district and respected ... My father didn't much appreciate the match at first, but I tell him if I had chosen a wealthy man with a place of his own – I should have to have given up my farm which I am so fond of.' Beatrix candidly revealed to her cousin, 'When I got engaged last June I was quite of the mind to wait ... but there was a good deal of bother – they were very silly they would not let Mr Heelis come to the house for ever so long – and I think the opposition only made us more fond of one another – he has waited six years already! ... We have every prospect of happiness – if it pleases Heaven – I was engaged once before to someone who died . . . which is one reason I wish to get it over, I don't seem to believe in it.'[20]

By early October Beatrix and William had made their decision. 'I think we shall get married very quietly & go away for a holiday, & then I shall come back here & make a desperate effort to see them settled with some proper attendant,' she wrote. 'I was feeling the going away very much,' she confided to Gertrude Woodward, whom she had asked to be her witness at the ceremony, 'but William has actually been invited up [to London] for a weekend soon – they never say much but they cannot dislike him.' Beatrix reported that there had even been some light moments between her parents and William at Windermere: 'A wasp which got "inside everything" & must have made Wm lively for once! Also he has asserted himself upon the subject of hens & put down Mr Simpson our new neighbour, to the satisfaction of J. C. [Cannon].'[21]

The marriage of Helen Beatrix Potter to William Heelis took place in London on Wednesday, 15 October 1913. Since Beatrix was marrying an Anglican, Rupert and Helen insisted that the brief ceremony take place at the elegant and socially prestigious St Mary Abbots in Kensington, a parish church near to Bolton Gardens. It happened that St Mary Abbots was also the church that Rupert's sister Lucy and Henry Roscoe had chosen for the marriage of their daughter, and where Sir John Millais's daughter had been married. St Mary Abbots is a parish with a long and distinguished history, dating to medieval times. Rebuilt in 1872, the church has a large, almost cathedral-like, vaulted interior, a long nave and dramatic transept. The high altar before which Beatrix and William stood is of highly ornate gilt with Italian mosaic panels of the four Evangelists and an alabaster reredos. Behind the altar are large and elaborate stained-glass windows depicting the life and death of Christ. It was a setting completely out of character for both Beatrix and William, and while it must have been a concession of sorts to her parents, it was an odd wedding for the granddaughter of two stalwart Unitarian families, as well as for the son of the Rector of the country parish of Kirkby Thore.[22]

Rupert Potter took the conventional photographs of Beatrix and

William the day before the wedding in the back garden at 2 Bolton Gardens. Beatrix is shown standing next to William, who is seated comfortably in a garden chair. She is wearing a distinctive tweed suit, made from Herdwick wool, with a long skirt and matching jacket, a dressy blouse, with a high-necked lace jabot, and a wide-brimmed hat trimmed elaborately with flowers and lace. William is appropriately attired in a lounge suit.[23]

Rupert ordered the carriage for the next morning at ten o'clock, and drove with Beatrix and her mother to the church. There is no indication of what the bride wore for the ceremony. The Revd Paul Maxwell Arnold conducted the service. Rupert and Helen witnessed their daughter's marriage and signed the parish register, as did Gertrude Woodward and William's cousin, Lelio Stampa, a don at Oxford whose mother had been a Heelis. There were apparently no other guests, nor is there record of any wedding breakfast. The son of the Potter's longtime coachman recalled the wedding as a 'very secret affair'. He attributed this to the bride's fame and her fear that strange people might show up at the church. More likely, the ceremony had been hastily arranged to coincide with William's London visit, and Beatrix's desire to be married quickly and quietly.[24]

Beatrix Potter was finally Mrs William Heelis. The newly-weds returned to Sawrey, probably the next day, for a brief honeymoon. Beatrix Moore, Beatrix's god-daughter, remembers that Beatrix and William called on her mother before leaving London. All were amused to discover that the newly-weds were to collect a new white bull when they arrived at the railroad station at Windermere. When John Cannon met them with the bull in tow, he addressed Beatrix as 'Miss Potter', and was instantly instructed that she was 'Mrs Heelis now'.[25]

The marriage announcement in *The Times* identified William as of 'Hawkshead Hall, Ambleside, youngest son of the late Revd. John Heelis', and Beatrix as the 'only daughter of Rupert Potter . . . and granddaughter of the late Edmund Potter, M.P., F.R.S. of Dinting Lodge, Glossop, and Camfield Place, Herts.' The *Westmorland Gazette* offered more unusual details. The writer had obviously never been inside St Mary Abbots, but he had done his homework and knew the sort of local colour that would interest his readers: 'In the quietest of quiet manners two very well-known local inhabitants were married in London. None of their friends knew of the wedding, which was solemnized in the simplest form, characteristic of such modest though accomplished bridegroom and bride.' It went on to say: 'Mr Heelis comes of one of the most athletic and sporting County families. He himself is one of the best all-round sportsmen in the Lake District. There is hardly a finer shot in the countryside. He is a keen angler. The bride is a successful exhibitor at local agricultural shows of shorthorn cattle and her name is known now all over the country for those charming books for children which have become so deservedly popular.'[26]

Upon arriving back in Sawrey, Beatrix and William stayed for a brief time in a furnished bungalow above Castle Farm. It was remembered that Beatrix went up and down the Kendal road offering pieces of wedding cake to her village neighbours, a traditional gesture that would have been in keeping with her desire to be part of the community. Whether this is true or not, she did send wedding cake to several friends, including little Margaret Hough, who had written to congratulate her, and somewhat awkwardly to Millie Warne. A week after becoming Mrs Heelis, Beatrix wrote to Millie, enclosing a clipping of the marriage announcement in *The Times*, and a piece of cake. 'I am sending you belated cake, which I hadn't courage to do before! Thank you so much for your kind letter, you did exactly what I should have wished [about Norman's grave]. I am *very* happy, & in every way satisfied with Willie – It is best now not to look back. But I can assure you I shall *always* remain yrs very aff. Beatrix Heelis.'[27]

13

❧ *Partnerships* ❧

'I FEEL VERY DUMPY WITHOUT my husband,' Beatrix wrote from Bolton Gardens barely three weeks after her marriage to William, 'it was hard luck to have to leave.' She had returned to London to calm the domestic crisis of changing servants. Beatrix had settled comfortably into marriage, 'the crown of a woman's life', as she had once described it and now happily knew it. She was understandably distressed by her forced separation from her new husband. To another friend she wrote conspiratorially, 'It is rather too soon to have to leave the disconsolate Wm. People are sure to say we have quarrelled!'[1]

During this first post-nuptial visit to London, Beatrix spent considerable time going through personal possessions in her old third floor schoolroom, cleaning out drawers and dressers. The sorting process resurrected painful memories of her engagement to Norman Warne. She had been looking unsuccessfully for a small gold pin that Norman had given her, but instead found a packet of letters from him that were 'so upsetting' that she could not go through them. 'There are things I scarcely know what to do with – like his pipe – I scarcely ought to be keeping them,' she confided. But she did keep them. Norman's umbrella remained in its place at Hill Top, and she continued to wear his engagement ring on her right hand.[2]

'I wish I were out of London & back in Sawrey,' she complained to her cousin Edith, 'I *never* knew 10 days go so slowly! . . . Willie is coming for me on Saturday thank goodness.' She also complained that 'Nobody remembers to call me Mrs Heelis' in London. There was no time to visit Millie, but Beatrix did not hesitate to ask her friend for a special wedding present: a copy of *Mrs Beeton's Cookery for All*. A 'nice useful present that I shall always use & remember you by . . . & write my name in it!' she directed. When the cookbook arrived, Beatrix was amused to discover that 'Mrs Beeton had grown so stout'. Proud of her newly acquired domesticity, she reported, 'I already take exception to her direction to fry bacon in a cold pan. Wm. prefers blue smoke before the bacon is laid on the frying pan. There are probably more disputes over bacon & plain potatoes than any other eatable. I can do both – (and very little else!).'[3]

By Christmas-time, Beatrix boasted of further culinary progress. She and William were cooking ordinary 'messes – "mingled with really elegant suppers". Wm. took a turn at pastry "a la Mrs Beeton"' and they did 'roasts and veg. really well . . .' Beatrix had acquired enough confidence by spring to attempt a local herb pudding she fancied William would enjoy, a dish of 'nettles, & various spring leaves, it is very good when properly assorted'. She added with deep happiness, 'I feel as if I had been married for many years.' She had also discovered that her skills with a needle were employed, as 'Mr Heelis walks through the toes of his stockings so it is lucky I like darning!'[4]

For their first married Christmas William took his bride back to his family home in Appleby and introduced her to his large family. Beatrix was understandably nervous, but nonetheless pleased to be part of the large Heelis gathering. It felt somewhat odd to be away from her parents, but they had 'never kept up anything different to a usual Sunday'. Christmas at Battlebarrow House introduced Beatrix to a true Dickensian Christmas holiday. The countryside about Appleby opened into the fertile Eden valley. It was a lush contrast to the more rugged fell sides that characterized Sawrey. Blanche and May, the two older Heelis sisters, both spinsters, presided over the festivities. Every available Heelis relation gathered for the occasion. The Stampa cousins, George and Lelio, and their wives and children came. James Nicholson, who had married William's sister Grace, and their five children were all there, as they lived nearby in Kirkby Thore. Alec Heelis, the eldest Heelis brother, who at one time had been Mayor of Appleby, and his wife Aday were the hosts. Alec and Aday had given William and Beatrix a dozen place settings of cutlery

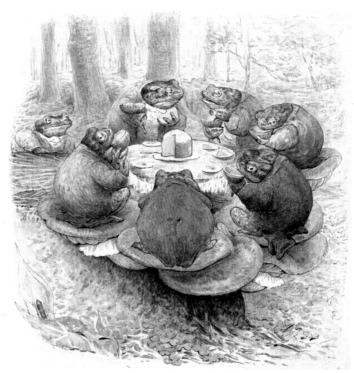

19. 'The Toads' Tea Party', 1902?
Beatrix's interest in fungi and
toads is transformed in fantasy to
illustrate the rhyme 'If acorn cups
were tea cups'. The tansy cake
stands on a toadstool table and the
stools are part of a bracket fungus.
The drawing was intended for the
1905 book of rhymes.

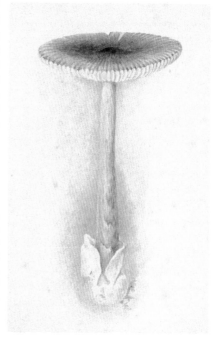

20. Grisette (*Amanita vaginatus*),
1893, painted at Eastwood and
undoubtedly given to Charles
McIntosh. Although Beatrix
does not show sections of this
mushroom, her mastery of
technique captures both the
texture of the gills and its
delicate colour.

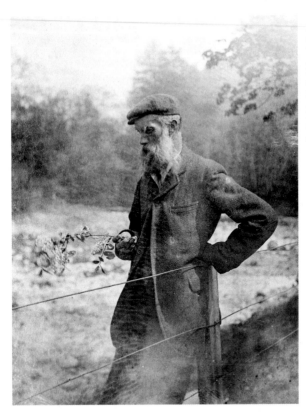

21. Charles McIntosh of Inver, the Perthshire naturalist who was Beatrix's mentor in drawing and identifying fungi and her first scientific collaborator.

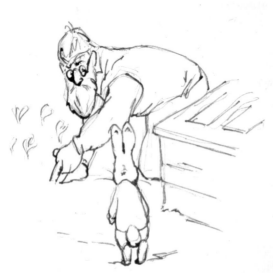

22. Peter Rabbit and Mr McGregor, the latter perhaps modelled on the learned but shy McIntosh.

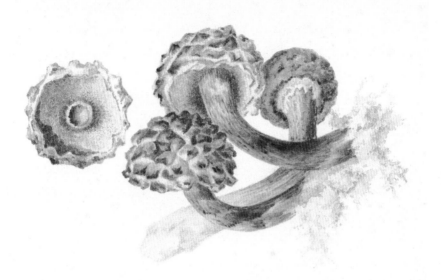

23. Old Man of the Woods
(*Strobilomyces strobilaceus*),
3 September [1893],
Eastwood. Beatrix drew a
map on the reverse to indicate
to McIntosh where she found
and painted this rare fungus.

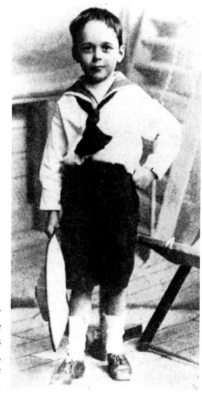

24. Noel Moore, the little boy
to whom the famous picture
letter about Peter Rabbit was
written on 4 September 1893,
the day after finding the rare
mushroom at Eastwood.

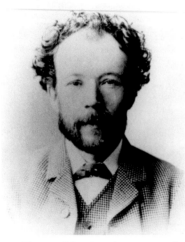

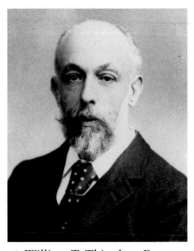

25. George Massee, the cytogamic botanist at Kew. His reputation was on the wane, but he was finally convinced that Beatrix's theory of symbiosis had merit. He gave her entrée to the Linnean Society so that her paper 'On the Germination of the Spores of *Agaricineae*' could be considered.

26. William T. Thistelton-Dyer, director of the Royal Botanic Gardens at Kew, whom Beatrix described as having a 'dry, cynical manner', was not inclined to give standing to amateur mycologists, especially if young and female.

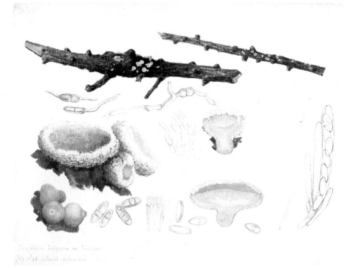

27. Larch canker (*Lachnellula wilkommii*), Esthwaite, 1896. Beatrix has drawn the ascospores, speculating in a letter to McIntosh as to the progression of the fungus on a fallen larch branch.

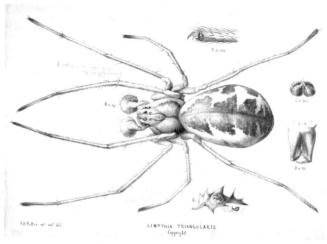

28. Sheet Web spider (*Linyphia triangularis*), 1896. One of a set of educational lithographs prepared for Caroline Martineau and Emma Cons for classes at the Morley Memorial College for Working Men and Women. The spider is drawn at different magnifications detailing its entomological structure.

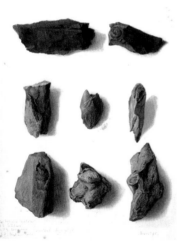

29. Eight fossils, including corals, from the Applethwaite beds, Troutbeck, 1895. Like other nineteenth-century naturalists, Beatrix photographed and then painted the fossils she collected. Laying them out on the page with artistry, she rendered the fossils with realism showing both detail and texture.

30. A street of shops leading down to the sea, Lyme Regis, Dorset (1904). Beatrix drew several versions of the shops lining the steep street where she went on holiday, providing in each a detailed rendering of the old seaside town.

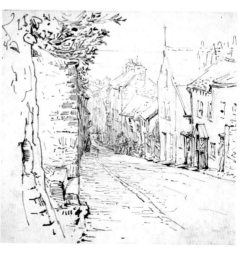

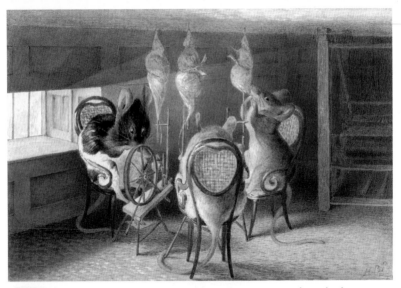

31. 'Three little mice sat down to spin', *c.* 1892. One of a series of unpublished drawings for an illustrated booklet. The Bentwood chairs, similar to one in her bedroom at Camfield, reflect her love of good design. The loom, spinning wheels and distaffs were familiar to the granddaughter of a textile merchant.

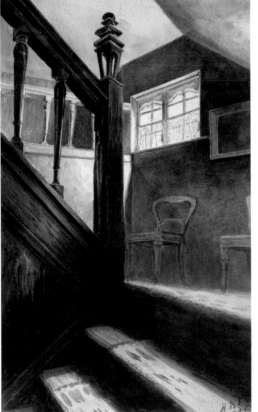

32. Staircase at Bedwell Lodge, 1891. Shortly before the death of Jessy Potter, the family stayed near Hatfield at Bedwell Lodge, an architecturally interesting house with a fine panelled staircase and newel posts that provided Beatrix with an opportunity to experiment with light and perspective.

33. Welsh dresser, Gwaynynog, 1903. Beatrix painted this fine oak dresser, dated 1696, at the home of her Burton relatives at Denbigh, Wales, where she frequently stayed. She also admired her uncle's taste in mahogany.

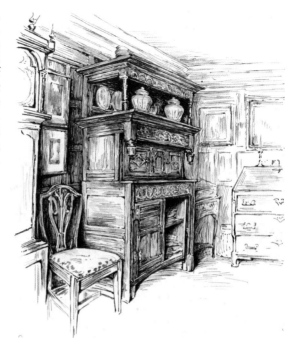

34. 'The Rabbits' Potting Shed', 1891. The Bedwell Lodge potting shed in Hatfield was replete with geraniums, garden tools and flowerpots. Beatrix used the background as a model for Mr McGregor's potting shed in *The Tale of Peter Rabbit*.

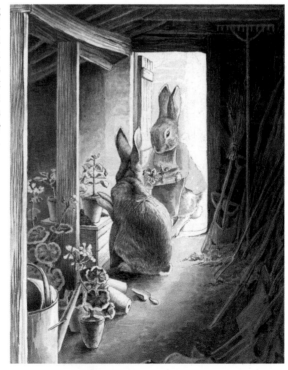

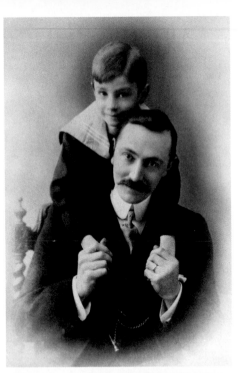

35. Norman Warne, 1898, Beatrix's publisher at Frederick Warne & Co., her first love and, briefly until his death, her fiancé.

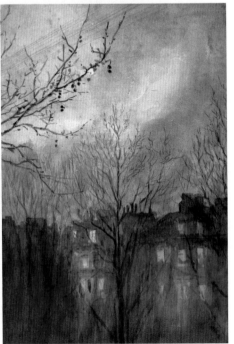

36. 'A November day', c. 1905, a sombre rendering of Bolton Gardens at dusk as seen from Beatrix's schoolroom window. It reflects her attitude towards her 'unloved birthplace' and her mood after Norman Warne's death in August 1905.

as a wedding present. Beatrix privately regarded the gift as ostentatious, thinking half that number quite sufficient. That first Christmas Beatrix and William began a popular tradition of bringing a Hawkshead cake, a confection of puff pastry full of raisins and sugar, as their contribution to the festivities. Beatrix had always liked celebrations, even though she was shy about conversation. She was inherently curious about people and enjoyed observing the customs and activities of a gregarious family, especially watching the children.[5]

Beatrix had something else to celebrate at the end of a most momentous year. On 30 December she concluded the purchase of the sixty-six-acre addition to Hill Top Farm she had wanted. It included fields which had been part of the Sawrey House Estate. Pleased to have her western borders regularized, the greater part of this purchase included parcels on the other side of the Kendal road accessed by Market Street and Stoney Lane, particularly eighteen-odd acres of what was then known as Moss Heckle Intake and the western part of Moss Heckle Tarn. Beatrix and William considered the tarn, the boggy intake and the southern paddocks especially desirable properties. She paid £1,225 for the whole, and had the satisfaction of resolving her quarrels with the owner of Sawrey House. Beatrix went about quietly stocking the tarn with trout for William, who loved to fish, and repaired the small tarn boat they kept there.[6]

At last her own person, Beatrix Heelis began to settle into the partnerships that were to shape the rest of her life. Her country solicitor husband and his family, her farms, the Sawrey community and the predictable rounds of country life which she embraced more ardently each year provided the context within which these partnerships were sustained. Beatrix began her new life as Mrs Heelis with a quiet confidence in who she was and what she was about, but she scarcely had time to enjoy it before events overtook her.

On New Year's Eve Beatrix set out once again for London, where her father's health continued to deteriorate. During the spring of 1914 she was back and forth to London several times a month, leaving little energy for farming or for creating new stories. In early March she wrote to Millie, 'I was up [in London] not long ago, but was too much worried about my father, to go anywhere. He has failed very much since Christmas and the doctor does not seem at all sure what is the matter with him.'[7]

As a realist Beatrix knew her father's illness could 'only have one end . . . It is a miserable state.' In an effort to relieve Rupert's intense pain, his physician, Sir Alfred Downing Fripp, reluctantly decided to operate, but Rupert died on 8 May of stomach cancer, with his wife and daughter at his bedside. Beatrix wrote to Harold, 'We are very thankful it is over, as we feared he might drag on for weeks longer – he went suddenly at the end. I suppose he was just worn out.'[8]

Beatrix ended her vigil with a severe sore throat. When William arrived, they took rooms at a hotel across the road where Beatrix could get some rest. A week later she wrote to Millie from Sawrey, 'I have been by no means well . . . I choke & cough, & Wm hops out of bed & applies all manner of poultices and pilasters, perhaps too many contradictory sorts.' She was already worrying about what to do with her mother, who could not be left alone. The couple had been so constantly together and with few outside interests. It was 'A trying, tiring time'.[9]

Rupert Potter left a will with three codicils and an estate valued after probate at £132,757, or the equivalent of about £7 million today. To his daughter he specifically bequeathed the phaeton cob harness, stable furniture and accessories, and all his cameras and camera equipment. To Bertram, he left his guns and fishing rods, tackle and equipment, and the large silver salver that had been given to his father by the grateful creditors of Edmund Potter and Company. Rupert was generous to his household staff, past and present, and left a generous bequest to the Essex Street Chapel in Kensington.

Rupert named Helen, Beatrix and Bertram as his trustees. He gave his children £35,000 each, leaving the rest of his estate in trust for his wife, together with Bolton Gardens and the mews properties. After Helen's death, the trust was to be divided equally between Beatrix and Bertram. The bulk of his wealth came not from real property, but from very conservative investments in stocks and bonds. Some had been inherited from his father, but many of the best investments were those he had made in railways, especially American companies, and in municipal, corporate and government bonds in countries around the world. As a conservative investor, he had used his wealth to create wealth, believing the future lay in transportation and urbanization. Beatrix, who acted as executrix on behalf of her mother and brother, sold about £12,000 of securities to cover the estate duties and small legacies. On 4 August, a month after settling his estate, Britain declared war on Germany. Beatrix was grateful her father had been spared the anxiety of war.[10]

Beatrix and William did not move into Castle Cottage until well into the new year and renovations were still incomplete. Although Beatrix deemed it 'an awful mess', she was glad to be there. She had lived in three separate houses since her marriage and was understandably anxious to get settled. Mrs Mary Agnes Rogerson, whom Beatrix had hired as housekeeper in 1911, did her best to get the newly-weds settled. 'The new rooms are nothing like built yet,' Beatrix wrote to a young friend, '& the old part has been all upset with breaking doors in the wall & taking out partitions. Those front rooms . . . are one long room now & the staircase is altered, & we are going to have a bathroom – in the course of time . . .'[11]

Beatrix had little energy for work on a new book. But one of her short stories appeared in *Country Life* magazine on 25 October 1913, just ten days after her marriage, and under her married name. It was part of a feature called 'Tales of Country Life'. The magazine's editor, Anderson Graham, had selected 'Fairy Clogs' from several stories Beatrix had written about local life a few years earlier. The stories were rather dark and dealt with the harsh and sometimes tragic aspects of life in the north. They also included her early experiments using country dialect. 'Fairy Clogs' tells of two little children who are blown across the ice on their iron clogs following the dancing fairies. Beatrix often wrote down a story she had heard or retold a vignette in dialect and, like Harris's *Uncle Remus* tales, she tried to capture in them some of the unique qualities of ordinary folk life.[12]

Before her father's death, Beatrix had begun a story she called 'The Tale of Kitty-in-Boots'. She explained to Harold Warne that it was about 'a well-behaved prim black Kitty cat, who leads rather a double life, and goes out hunting with a little gun on moonlight nights, dressed up like puss in boots'. By March she had made several drawings, including one for the frontispiece. It showed Miss Kitty holding the gun quite expertly, the result of having used William to model the correct posture. Since the story was slightly derivative of Charles Perrault's fable 'Puss in Boots' and there was a convention against using traps in animal stories, Harold and Fruing responded with only moderate enthusiasm. In March Beatrix had told Harold, 'I'm afraid it's all I can offer this spring – so make the best of it!' But when summer came, she had added little to it.[13]

Early in June Beatrix went up to London to work on her father's estate, answer letters of condolence, and to have 'all my top front teeth out!!' Since her parents had already taken Lindeth Howe in Bowness for the summer, Beatrix spent three weeks later that month helping her mother and the London household get settled into the country house. 'I have tried to get on with the book, but there are no plates finished yet,' she complained in mid-July. 'I am interested in the drawings again – in the sense of getting my mind on it, and feeling I could make something of it – if only I had time & opportunity.' She regretted that she had not done more during the winter, but confessed that her enthusiasm had been dampened by the Warnes' lack of enthusiasm. 'It is very difficult to keep up to a fixed level of success,' she explained. Harold Warne had 'The Tale of Kitty-in-Boots' set up in type and Beatrix pasted it into a dummy copy, but only the frontispiece was ever completed.[14]

Reluctant to go back to London after the war broke out, Helen Potter took a year's lease on Beechmount, an unfurnished cottage on the western edge of Sawrey, had some furniture sent up from Bolton Gardens, and installed her coachman and his family in Buckle Yeat cottage. Beatrix persuaded Rupert's only surviving sister, Aunt Polly (Mary Potter Wrigley) to keep Helen company for a time, renting an unfurnished cottage for her next to Beechmount. Beatrix made the best of the situation, telling William that it was 'highly complimentary to *him* that these old ladies take refuge in the neighbourhood'. Privately she admitted that she was a bit thinner, since her mother and aunt kept her 'on the trot'.[15] When Rupert's estate had been distributed and the taxes paid, Helen bought Lindeth Howe after it came on the market the following September, 1915. She sent for the rest of her furniture and belongings from London, installed a caretaker in Bolton Gardens, and moved her retinue to Bowness. Warne's had no book by Beatrix Potter for their 1914 Christmas list, the first time since *The Tale of Peter Rabbit* was published in 1902. Beatrix tried a bit of drawing in the winter but could not stick to it. 'My eyes are gone so long sighted & not clear nearby,' she explained to Harold Warne, but probably a lack of enthusiasm rather than impaired vision was closer to the truth.[16]

The Great War of 1914–18 changed the nation and the countryside for ever. After the harvest had been gathered in 1914, a growing number of farmers encouraged their youthful workers and the youth of their own families to enlist. Beatrix's harvest had been good, but she was worried about the mandatory conscription of farm horses. 'All one can do at present is to forbear spending more than possible & cut down some wood, as there is going to be no coal.' Like other rural residents, she anxiously watched the numbers of troops moving out on the railways that autumn, worried about German spies rumoured to have infiltrated the shipbuilding docks at nearby Barrow, and fretted over the security of the Thirlmere–Manchester reservoir. 'The war is very horrid,' she wrote to Millie; 'W. put down his name as a special constable & old volunteer reservist; but so far has not had any job. There seems no place for "*volunteers*", it is enlistment or nothing . . . A great many lads have gone away.' Several of William's nephews had volunteered, and so had Bertram, but to Beatrix's relief, he failed the medical. By the end of the year there were already 'sad losses amongst local officers' who had been sent to the front from the Sawrey area.[17]

Beatrix worried about all the young men she had known, particularly upset that 'many fine lads from this part went to Gallipoli' – an expedition that had resulted in enormous loss of life. She thought it must be a relief to families to have their loved ones safe in hospital instead of fighting such battles. The winter of 1915 brought heavy snows to Sawrey which increased her concern for the sheep on the fells, but did not lessen her appreciation of the physical beauty of the snow. 'The snow was lovely, weeks of it crisp and dry in bright sunshine.' But, she told Fruing, 'Somehow winter seems more appropriate to the sad times, than the glorious summer weather, though we were thankful to have it for getting the crops.' For the first time since they had married, William and Beatrix did not go to Appleby for Christmas 1915, unwilling to leave Helen Potter alone for the holiday. Like many other rural farmers, Beatrix had a 'stay at home' life during the early part of the war. She realized her eyesight was changing and that she needed glasses which could only be fitted in London, but for many reasons, London was a place she had no wish to go.[18]

Beatrix had a lot on her mind as the nation went to war. It was not only the declining agricultural markets that troubled her, but the persistent anxieties about her publishing income, as the promised accounts from Harold Warne had never materialized. About the time of her marriage, Beatrix had made arrangements in her will that in the event of her death, the copyrights in her books would remain with the publishing company. Now she began to wonder if that assignment had been wise. When the war broke out, she had agreed to forgo payments since business was volatile. Still she could not help making a plea for 'the accounts' or enquiring of Harold, 'What has become of all the little side shows we discussed last spring? note papers? almanacs?' She heard nothing. By May 1915 her patience, however admirable, was at an end. She had serious concerns about the company's management and its future. She wrote to Harold, 'I really must say I don't like going on indefinitely without some sort of accounts, you did not send any statement as you talked of doing, after the New Year. The last I can lay my hand on is for 1911!! . . . I am a healthy person, but think what it would be like for unbusiness if I happened to wind up. If it has got beyond keeping account of, it would be better to say so.' Harold's explanations about cash flows, government restrictions and lack of office help were not sufficient to allay her concerns or diminish her scepticism. But there was little she felt she could do.[19]

Six months later, she turned to Fruing for some enlightenment. 'I am getting seriously perplexed about the accounts . . . I promised not to ask the firm for payments while times were so difficult; but I think you will allow that the failure to send any statements at all is a trial of patience; and the overlapping and unpunctuality had begun *long before the war* ... I am not out of temper; I am very sorry for you all ... But I am tired of the muddle, and it is *not* all due to the war. Neither is it *all* due to Harold; I think it would have been courteous if *you* had sent a line of regret about the half yearly interest.'[20]

Beatrix had deliberately not shared her concerns about Warne's management with William, who had little patience for bad business practices. She felt 'a repugnance to his intervening in any business between me and your family', she confided to Fruing. But now Beatrix was prepared to force some changes. Telling Fruing that she wanted new copyright arrangements, she warned, 'I shall have to take some steps about it – not in any unfriendly spirit, but to put the matter on a more businesslike footing. For one thing I should instruct my London solicitor to alter my will; I cannot leave this muddle to go accumulating.' Fruing's response to her threat is lost, but the stalemate continued. The following spring, Harold sent Beatrix a cheque for back royalties, but no accounts.[21]

Even with wartime restrictions, there were some happy compensations to country living – which Beatrix called 'mild dissipations'. The Heelises had hosted two dances – 'hops' – for the school children and the farm servants. 'My word how they did dance quadrilles like spinning tops! I never saw more cheerful parties, and some of the old singing games are curious & pretty,' she wrote happily to Millie. Although she did not dance herself, Beatrix loved watching the dancers, especially William. She could be found in the back of the room, tapping her toe in time to the music, occasionally making a note about a verse or rhyme that pleased her. Beatrix enjoyed the rare merriment and made no complaint about spending all the next day 'scrubbing the dining room'.[22]

Beatrix had become an upland fell farmer in a period of rapid rural and agricultural change. Even before the war broke out, agricultural prices were falling as wheat, wool and meat were undercut by imports. As prices fell, the cost of maintaining soil fertility increased and the use of fertilizers declined, drainage was neglected and erosion increased. Labour shortages caused by war recruitment did not begin to impact north-country farms until the spring planting season in 1916. The rising cost of labour encouraged a greater use of farm machinery, particularly for ploughing, harvesting and binding hay.

When the war started, women first moved into the more attractive and remunerative posts as shop assistants or delivery girls, or went to work in the munitions factories. Land work was viewed negatively by most women, and there was a widespread belief among farmers that women were incapable of performing dirty jobs, using horses or working in bad weather. But in 1916 the Women's National Land Service Corps was established to promote the use of female labour and to offer those who joined some form of training, despite initial scepticism. *The Times* reported the inaugural meeting of the Service and followed this with a leading article, 'Women Workers: Demand and Supply'. It urged farmers not only to hire women to work on the land, but to offer them adequate wages.[23]

Beatrix had given the employment of women serious consideration. To her amusement William had hired a little office girl to help replace the three clerks from the law firm who had enlisted, leading her to wonder 'what will become of all these lady clerks after the war'. Like many of her fellow farmers, Beatrix doubted the commitment of women who applied to work through the WNLS. 'I think there will have to be more [women] on the land in the future,' she wrote to young Augusta Burn, 'but in my opinion they will be ladies,' not the 'sham "lidies" turned out by the board schools [who] are so despicably afraid of dirtying their hands'. But she was realistic about planning for wartime shortages. 'I have worked very hard, poultry & gardening on top of housekeeping,' she continued, '& I never felt happier & better health; but I don't know how long I can hope to keep it up at 50!'[24]

Beatrix and the Cannon family had been struggling with the farm work that spring. One son had already enlisted, and she anticipated that Willie Cannon, who was both ploughman and horseman and hence exempted from military service, would enlist after the ploughing was finished. Although John Cannon was resigned to manage as best he could, Beatrix was concerned because he was not robust and she knew they would be short-handed by summer. In March 1916

The Times ran several leaders about the employment of women on the land. Since Beatrix had firm opinions about women's ability to do farm work and the kind of training and clothing they required, she wrote a letter on the subject of 'women on the land', which *The Times* published on 13 March under the pseudonym of 'A Woman Farmer'.[25]

Her letter noted the high wages offered for women in the munitions factories, complaining that they drew skilled and trained farm girls from the land into unskilled jobs at wages no farmer could afford. She lamented that the WNLS had stooped to recruiting young women by touting 'theatrical attractions of uniform and armlet'. Identifying herself as someone who had farmed for years and loved it, she proclaimed herself ready to employ the 'right sort of woman', to fill the shortage of farm labourers. Unable to resist adding her views to the ongoing debate over appropriate farming costume, Beatrix noted that 'French women and North country girls have found it possible to work in a short petticoat.'

As it happened, Beatrix's letter to *The Times* was read by a woman with some farming experience. Miss Eleanor L. Choyce's enquiry was forwarded to Beatrix in Sawrey, where it received intense scrutiny and a thoughtful reply. Beatrix's description of both herself and Hill Top remarkably summarizes her experience as a country woman and her outlook on life in middle age. Relieved that Miss Choyce sounded like a mature woman, Beatrix wrote candidly that she and her husband had been impressed with her credentials, and asked for a photograph and references.[26]

Beatrix explained that she did not depend on her 120-acre farm exclusively for a living and that she could pay a 'proper wage'. Hill Top then consisted of nine arable acres, 'the rest meadow hay & hill pastures, 2 horses, 9 or 10 cows, young stock (rear many calves), 60 sheep, 47 being lambing ewes'. She described herself as '50 this year – very active and cheerful', but feared that she and her farm housekeeper would be overworked, and needed help 'with the garden & haymaking' for the coming summer. 'I have farmed my own land for 10 years as a business (before & since marriage) and I have got it into such good order it would be a pity to let it go down.' Beatrix described the farm and her work: 'I have poultry, orchard, flower garden, vegetables . . . Mrs C. I & this girl all help with hay, & I single turnips when I can find time, & look after some intake land on the fell.'

Concerned to give an accurate picture of domestic arrangements and a clear understanding of the household, Beatrix explained that her husband was a solicitor and 'as there are all sorts of people in the world I may say he is a very quiet gentleman, & I am a total abstainer!! . . . We live very quietly in a cottage separate from the old farm house . . . It is best to speak straight out; the great difficulty with a stranger woman is the boarding. I can see Mr Heelis does not want a lady living here [Castle Cottage]' but she hoped to find a woman who could live in the front part of the old farmhouse (Hill Top) for the summer and who would be a 'careful occupier' and take care of the 'old oak' furniture. She described the village and the reticence of village people to embrace strangers, confessing 'I don't go out much, haven't time; & the little town seems nothing but gossip & cards. I'm afraid our own special sin is not attending church regularly; not loving the nearest parson; & I was brought up a dissenter.' She hoped Miss Choyce would not think her rude for asking for references and ended her long letter with a brief self-portrait. 'I am very downright; but I get on with every body. I can make jam, while there is sugar; but should be glad to learn more cooking!' She did, however, have one initial reservation about Miss Choyce, which in typical fashion, she laid out bluntly: 'Your letter is very earnest; I wonder if you have a sense of humour!'

Eleanor Louisa Choyce, or 'Louie' as her family called her, was only ten years younger than Beatrix. Not only was she a lady and a proficient farm worker, but she was also a woman of some musicality and proved to be excellent company. Miss Choyce was between positions. She had most recently been the governess to a wealthy family in Gloucestershire. The youngest child had just gone off to boarding school and she was looking for something different. Intrigued by the letter printed in *The Times*, Choyce offered her credentials to 'A Woman Farmer'. Beatrix checked her references and was only slightly worried that Miss Choyce's previous farming experience would be 'rather wasted in this post'. Miss Choyce accepted the position and arrived in Sawrey in late April 1916. Almost immediately she was diagnosed with measles, though Beatrix kept insisting it was influenza with a rash. After two weeks of virtual quarantine, an unlucky beginning to any employment, Louie settled companionably into Hill Top Farm.[27]

Louie was a rather large-boned woman with a 'cheerful rosy face' and an easy manner. She fitted into the Heelis entourage quite comfortably, delighted with Beatrix's garden and with the farm. Beatrix was also taking care of the garden at Eeswyke that summer. In a letter to her mother, Louie described the huge azalea bushes there and of walking some distance with Beatrix to gather broom tips, foxglove leaves and barberry. 'Mrs Heelis isn't a bit of a driver . . .' she reassured her mother. 'I simply do like her exceedingly.' Louie's descriptions underscore the unpretentiousness of the Heelis household, and provide an observant portrait of Beatrix Heelis: 'she is quite out of the common . . . short, blue-eyed, fresh-coloured face, frizzy hair brushed tightly back, dresses in a tweed skirt pinned at the back with a safety-pin . . . Mr Heelis is a quiet man, very kind. They believe together in the simple life.'[28]

It was a busy spring and both women worked exceedingly hard. Miss Choyce probably left sometime in the early summer after all the planting was finished, with high praise from Beatrix, and the expectation that she would return the following spring. Beatrix need not have worried that she had employed a 'sham lidy'. Her investment was, as it turned out, in a farming friendship which would last the rest of her life.[29]

Hill Top Farm now boasted a sizeable flock of chickens, turkeys and some ducks which produced income but also provided food on the farm. Rationing and wartime shortages meant that even rabbits were raised as farm stock, but Beatrix confessed, 'I don't half like having them killed.' She was sometimes ambiguous about her flock of turkeys as well. They brought a fair price, but she did not look forward to the 'horrid slaughter'. 'Poor dears,' she wrote, 'they are so tame and tractable, but they *do* eat.' Beatrix was generally quite philosophic about the inevitability of animal death, but the loss of her favourite farm collie Kep was particularly hard. His passing added to the gloomy mood of winter and of wartime.[30]

There had been other losses unconnected with the war. Henry Roscoe, Beatrix's well-intentioned mentor and devoted uncle, had died unexpectedly at Woodcote, and early in the new year came news that Hardwicke Rawnsley's wife, Edith, had died after a long and painful illness. Rawnsley decided to retire as the Vicar of Crosthwaite, announcing he could not continue without the help and comfort of his wife of thirty-eight years. He moved to Grasmere, taking Allan Bank, famous as Wordsworth's house, where he and Edith had planned to live. From there Rawnsley continued his efforts to raise money for the National Trust, which had been severely hampered by the economic strains of wartime. Beatrix, who had kept in touch with Rawnsley about various country matters, was saddened by Edith's death, writing to him: 'I am sure you will believe it was not carelessness that prevented my writing before with sympathy from us and my mother . . . really, I did *not* know how to write.'[31]

Beatrix had been married to William for three years when Edith died. Some members of Rawnsley's family later speculated that Beatrix had been the love of his life, but there is no evidence for this. Barely eighteen months after Edith's death, Rawnsley married his secretary, Eleanor Simpson. Beatrix had known Eleanor for some years and maintained a cordial relationship with her from the outset. Her friendship with Hardwicke continued as it had always been, centred on issues of country life and preservation.[32]

Writing to Millie at the end of the year, Beatrix complained: 'I do seem to have so little time; & my writing time is after supper, with eyes that – like your legs – are beginning to feel anno domini . . . I hardly know what "legs" are, & seldom sit down except to meals.' She bartered farmstuffs at the village shop for an extra bit of sugar, but she was quite cross when Agnes Anne at the shop inadvertently sold William cream of tartar instead of the necessary saltpetre. William had rubbed it into the hams before discovering the mistake. Labour, Beatrix confided to Millie, was now her greatest anxiety. She had managed to put together a 'scratch crew', but had lost all her domestic help. 'I had a woman (lady) help last summer who is coming back, we expect rather a strenuous summer.'[33]

Although Beatrix was preoccupied with her own farm, her attention never shifted far from her responsibilities as a landowner in the parish of Claife. When she purchased Hill Top Farm in 1905 she automatically became a member of the Landowners of Claife, an ancient body created after the enclosure of land to protect the freeholder's rights. In 1912 she had been elected to the Landowner's Community Association as a Representative Freeholder. Frederic Fowkes was the Association's secretary. Even before her election Beatrix had taken a lively part in the group which enforced the repair and upkeep of roads, timber and property boundaries. It is likely that she had been associated with William Heelis as a member of this group, as he had been its legal adviser for some years.

The Association was charged with the maintenance of the public quarry up Stoney Lane, and the equitable distribution of gravel and stone from the lake sites for road repair. The quarry had fallen into disrepair when the war started, and could no longer be safely mined; a condition which Beatrix wanted to remedy. Stoney Lane and the Kendal road had also been neglected. Beatrix had long been a friend of Fowkes's wife Emily, and together they goaded him into holding regular meetings, electing new members, and enforcing the need for commons maintenance. Beatrix's membership in the Association kept her active in village life. Through it she kept herself informed about boundary disputes, property values, upcoming sales, as well as a variety of important preservation issues that came before the group.[34]

Beatrix was also active in the Footpath Association, a group Canon Rawnsley actively championed. Although Beatrix realized that tourists frequently caused damage to stone walls and carelessly left gates open, allowing livestock to roam, she vigorously insisted that landowners not impede access to footpaths on fell land. 'Speaking for oneself,' she told Rawnsley, 'it is always a pity to hear of visitors being turned back from *fell land*. I speak with feeling as a farmer! . . . I have not forgotten the exasperation of seeing a large party of young women steeple chasing [*sic*] over a succession of newly "cammed" walls in pursuit of mushrooms. And a neighbour . . . has two heifers lost since Monday . . . The visitors are perfect terrors . . . and they are least in the way on the fells – if they would shut gates when they come down again.' She added in a postscript, 'I have seen a pretty good one [automatic gate] in Wales, worked with a log, but it won't stay open for a cart unfortunately.' Her attitude towards tourists and walkers was remarkably enlightened, and she was pragmatic about the need to accommodate tourism in Lakeland.[35]

During the war years, William's brothers and sisters and their children provided Beatrix with most of her light-hearted moments. George Heelis and his wife Sybil had two children, Rosemary and Colin, who regularly visited Castle Cottage. William's sister Grace Nicholson, however, had a brood of five, including two younger girls, Esther and Nancy. The younger Nicholson daughters found their new aunt most intriguing. Beatrix took pleasure in nurturing the relationship with her nieces and nephews and relished her new role of benevolent aunt.[36]

She first met the Nicholson children during the Christmas and Easter festivities at Appleby. She particularly enjoyed William's sister Grace. They were close in age and both married to lawyers. They had common interests in gardening, herbs and herbal medicine. Like Beatrix, Grace was responsible for the family's farm, and was especially knowledgeable about horses. Beatrix found her a sensible woman, often using her sister-in-law as a sounding board when she needed someone to listen to her problems. Grace also welcomed Beatrix's relationship with Esther and Nancy, seeing that both girls enjoyed their new and altogether different aunt. Even though Beatrix could be a bit overbearing, Grace knew her advice and her efforts to help were completely well-intentioned.[37]

Esther, then 14, was an eager scholar and a girl of earnest disposition. About 1915 Esther entered St Katharine's School in Wantage, near Oxford, to prepare for a place at the university. Beatrix supported Esther's ambition to become a teacher and quietly contributed to her tuition, making it possible for her to go to boarding school. Perhaps she remembered her earlier desire to help one of the Moore girls go to college, so now she thought to help Esther during wartime.[38]

Nancy, the youngest child, who was also William's god-daughter, was ten years younger than Esther. In 1916, when Nancy was seven, Beatrix and William invited her to come to Castle Cottage for an extended visit. Much to her delight, Beatrix discovered that Nancy not only had a steadfast belief in fairies, but enjoyed inventing stories of her own. Nancy told her aunt about the little people she called oakmen who lived in the trees. Beatrix was enchanted by Nancy's imagination and the two began to exchange stories about the oakmen's adventures. For Christmas 1916, Beatrix gave Nancy a story she had written about the oakmen. It consisted of six pages of text, each illustrated by a watercolour sketch in a loose-leaf binder. The oakmen resembled little gnome-like creatures with green suits and red caps. They lived in the larch wood up Stoney Lane. Each tree had its oakman occupant who peeped out of tiny doors and windows. Sometimes the oakmen met for a tea party which was set out on a toad-table with toadstools as chairs. But the tree-fellers came and cut down their homes, forcing an emergency relocation of all the oakmen to the new woods Beatrix had planted overlooking Moss Eccles Tarn.[39]

'The Oakmen' was one of several fairy tales Beatrix wrote about trees and the imaginary fairy creatures who lived in them. She had always noticed trees, fascinated by the way they grew, sensitive to their mysteriously long residence in the forests, and scientifically knowledgeable about their culture. She drew trees with a natural facility, beginning notably with 'The Three Witches of Birnam Woods', painted in Perthshire when she was 12. Around 1911 she sent a fairy story to two little girls in New Zealand, called 'The Fairy in the Oak'. It is a rather sad story about 'an enormous oak that had stood for centuries' and that 'did not want to leave the place it had grown'. Beatrix's elaboration of tree fairies as oakmen for Nancy Nicholson testifies to her persistent fascination with trees, as well as with the fairies who inhabited them. But her scientific and agricultural interest in trees was equally passionate, and she had a ready pen to write on the subject of timber culture. In the course of farming in the Lake District, she developed particularly strong opinions on afforestation.[40]

In spite of her busy farm schedule, Beatrix had managed to

complete new frontispieces for both *Miss Moppet* and *A Fierce Bad Rabbit* as Warne's were reprinting her panoramic books in the Little Book format. She considered 'The Sly Old Cat', which she had written originally for Nellie Warne in 1906, the best of the lot, but it remained unfinished. With the harvest approaching, Beatrix suggested that Warne's hire Ernest A. Aris, a children's writer and illustrator of some success, but few scruples, to copy her designs for 'The Sly Old Cat' since she had no desire to do so herself. 'You will have to get used to the idea that my eyes are giving way,' she told Harold, 'whether you like it or not – and if I managed to do yet another book it would not be that cat story . . . but I do not draw cats well, & I am away from that sort of background.'[41]

Beatrix's interest in employing Aris had been prompted by some of his cribs which Harold Warne had sent her. Rather than be offended by Aris's plagiarism, she suggested that Warne's hire him. 'His plagiarisms are unblushing,' she told Harold, 'and his drawings excellent.' In fact, she thought Aris drew cats better than she did, but she thought his mice had overly large ears. 'Frankly,' she told Harold, 'it does not annoy me because it is good.' She urged Warne's to offer him a sum for a set of designs. 'I have wished for a long time that you would find some second string – this man to my thinking is just what we want *if* he would draw to order & take suggestions.'[42]

Beatrix had become acquainted with Aris at Windermere some years before her marriage, when he worked briefly in a photographer's studio. Although she took his measure as an opportunist, when Harold did nothing further Beatrix commissioned Aris herself for a set of designs for Nancy's oakmen story, but deliberately concealed her artistic identity, writing in her married name. Without revealing the plot, she sent some rough sketches and instructions on composition and colouring for the gnomes and country backgrounds and asked for him for six drawings.

Aris produced the drawings which Beatrix judged 'uncommonly good'. She purchased the copyright and the drawings, apparently believing that Aris did not recognize her artistic identity. Aris went along with her subterfuge, but he probably knew exactly who 'Mrs Heelis' was from the outset. Nearly a year later, Beatrix asked Nancy

Nicholson to let her borrow back her precious binder with its oakman story with the idea of making it into a book. She began work, but at some point she concluded that Nancy's oakman story was not original, and she abandoned the idea of publishing it. But William was suspicious of Aris, and warned Beatrix that if she did not use the oakman character herself, Aris would.[43]

In November 1917 Fruing alerted Beatrix to another more blatant Aris plagiarism. He had discovered a rabbit named 'Peter' in Aris's latest book, *The Treasure Seekers*. Fruing wanted to lodge a protest both with the artist and his publisher, but Beatrix was strangely defensive of Aris. 'I most certainly object to entrusting "Peter Rabbit" to that objectionable (but amusing) little bounder,' she wrote to Fruing. 'But I do blame his publishers [Gale and Polden] more than himself.' In her opinion Aris was 'the sort of person who will do anything for a few pounds; I was expecting an outbreak of his booklets this winter as he conceitedly said he was overwhelmed with orders . . . I don't take Mr Arris [*sic*] seriously. But his publishers are rogues . . .'[44]

Fruing, however, felt compelled to protest, as Aris had already imitated Jemima in an earlier book (*Mrs Beak Duck*). Aris reacted with hot denial, appealing directly to Beatrix, thereby acknowledging that he knew the identity of 'Mrs Heelis'. With unmitigated ego, Aris explained he could not have plagiarized 'Peter' as he 'had never heard of your book *Peter Rabbit* till now. It is probably one of your early ones.' He had the additional audacity to add in a postscript, 'Perhaps you would be kind enough to give me a signed copy . . . It would be interesting to compare "the two Peters." '[45]

Beatrix's initial response to Aris's plagiarism had been uncharacteristically restrained, which suggests that she had hoped for a collaborator and that she probably regretted her earlier deceit. Although she was ready to entertain the notion that probably 'all rabbits are called Peter now', Aris had gone too far. She wrote now more honestly, 'Your work has considerable technical facility and no originality.' She concluded that without a good deal of explanation from him, 'I regret that I am unable to believe that your statements are truthful. Coincidence has a long arm but there are limits to coincidences.' Aris was only momentarily chastened. He abruptly changed publishers in 1918, after which he produced six more books under the unlikely and rather ludicrous pseudonym 'Robin A. Hood'.[46]

Beatrix's efforts to obtain some relief from the demand from Warne's for new books, and her willingness to explore a sort of partnership with Aris, underscore her weariness with deadlines and her disillusionment with her publisher, who now owed her a great deal of money and had never yet produced any satisfactory accounts. Beatrix had given Warne's permission to raise the price of the little books from 1s. to 1s. 3d. in 1916. But she had used the opportunity to change the indefinite term of the copyright assignment to Warne's, 'in view of the uncertain future for all trade'. Due to the lack of acceptable accounting, she judged the original agreements between Warne's and herself 'virtually a dead letter'. 'It is unthinkable that I should ever quarrel with you & your family,' she told Harold Warne, 'but if there were ever a reconstitution of your business in the uncertain future I think I ought not to be in that indefinitely tied up position, in view of my easyness in the past.' Without a new Potter book in 1916, Warne's had reissued a shortened *Peter Rabbit's Painting Book*. The left-over illustrations were now added to a few new ones to create *Tom Kitten's Painting Book*, scheduled for publication in June 1917.[47]

For most of the spring of 1917 Beatrix was occupied with an unpredictable labour supply at Hill Top and was 'not in particularly good temper'. She now had 160 acres under the plough. But in the very middle of the ploughing season, her best ploughman got his call-up and the weather turned cold and wet. The fundamentals of British farming changed dramatically when agricultural imports were cut off by the successful German U-boat blockade. The sudden demand for increased domestic food production and the cultivation of new, sometimes marginal land – all with the immediate goal of saving the country from starvation – made for a volatile market. Beatrix's efforts at self-sufficient farming and profitable livestock production were made even more uncertain by the imposition of agricultural subsidies, the unpredictably of labour, and her dependency on a plough horse.[48]

'We have a wild day here . . .' she wrote to Harold in March, 'all day wet lambs before the fire – the third dead since breakfast has just expired! There is not an atom of grass & the hill flocks must be in a pitiable state. Mine being fed hay – yet they have no milk.' But at the end of the month, Beatrix's attention was abruptly changed from the problems of farming to those of publishing when Frederick Warne & Co. was rocked by public scandal.[49]

14

⤜ *Salvages* ⤛

H AROLD WARNE AND HIS BROTHER Fruing had been walking near their office in Covent Garden when the police arrested Harold and charged him before the Lord Mayor in Mansion House with 'uttering [passing] a bill of exchange for £988.10s.3d. knowing it to be forged'. On 3 April *The Times* reported an alleged forged bill charge against Harold Edmund Warne, 56, making the crime public.[1]

The forgeries, totalling some £20,000, stemmed from Harold's efforts to siphon money from the publishing company into a small fishing business on Jersey in the Channel Islands, a business he had inherited from his mother. Through mismanagement, he had allowed it to run into significant debt. Now both businesses were in financial ruin. A meeting of Frederick Warne & Co.'s principal associates and creditors was hastily convened. Fruing wrote to Beatrix explaining the situation on 5 April. She had not seen an earlier newspaper report of the arrest and had not been represented at the meeting, even though she was the firm's largest creditor. Although she was stunned by the news, she could not have been completely surprised.

Not yet aware of the extent of Harold's fraud, Beatrix wrote of her distress to Millie:

I would thankfully have sunk my share of the debt to have hushed the matter up . . . I'm afraid it must be a pretty bad job or surely it would have been kept quiet. I have felt for a long time there was a great risk of ending in a smash . . . I am writing to express as well as I can my exceeding sympathy with you and Alice [Harold's wife] in this dreadful trouble – it is *more than sympathy* – fellow suffering.

Considering the nature of Harold's crime and his long history of prevarications, Beatrix's initial reaction was uncommonly charitable: an effort to make the best of a tragic situation for everyone. 'I was always afraid he would go off his head with business worries,' she told Millie, 'but he is such a self deceiving optimist he has apparently done something worse. I don't bear him the least grudge.' But she was deeply hurt by his betrayal. For the next two years, she did what she could to rescue her publisher from ruin, all the while keeping her farms and family viable amidst the anxieties and turmoil of war.[2]

Beatrix particularly dreaded having to tell William about the scandal. She knew he would have little sympathy with Harold's crime, and undoubtedly he had feared just such an outcome for some time. Beatrix regarded her loyalty to the Warne family as a private matter and did not want William to interfere. 'My husband is quite unconscious at the other side of the table,' Beatrix wrote to Millie. 'I *hate* having to tell him ... I don't think I can come to London myself, and to tell the truth I am very unwilling to, for I should not like Mr Heelis to be any way acting [legally involved]? I don't mean that he is a hard man; but he is so different to Norman.' Realistically she warned Millie that she would probably have to involve her London solicitor in order to safeguard her 'share of the copyrights & original drawings from other creditors'.[3]

On 11 April *The Times* published an account of Harold's forgeries and on 26 April he pleaded guilty in the Central Criminal Court and was sentenced to eighteen months of hard labour at Wormwood Scrubs prison in London. Fruing Warne was exonerated of any knowledge of the forgeries and took charge of a company on the verge of bankruptcy – one whose major asset was the published and future work of Beatrix Potter. Beatrix instructed Braikenridge & Edwards to deliver to her the original illustrations of all nineteen of her published books and her two painting books, which she received two days before Harold's sentencing. In June Beatrix went up to the Covent Garden office to see to the safekeeping of her copyrights.[4]

Fruing was forced to sell all the firm's property as well as his personal possessions in order to raise enough money to stop the company's debtors from foreclosing. He sold his house in Surbiton and moved his stunned and uncomprehending family into a tiny place near Richmond Park. Harold's wife, Alice, was forced to sell all her assets at public auction and move her family back to her father's house. Millie rented out her north London house at Eton Villas, and went to live with her sister Edith.[5]

Among Fruing's first acts was to send Beatrix the account statements she had been so long denied. Then he asked for her help to save the publishing house. Treading lightly at first, he asked if she might keep Winifred's doll's house – the one Norman had made which had been featured in *Two Bad Mice* – since he now had no room for it. Although Beatrix was willing, her mother had not seen the newspaper reports of Harold's arrest and disgrace, and Beatrix was not anxious to make her aware of it. 'One doesn't want to start anyone asking questions gratuitously,' Beatrix explained, suggesting the doll's house might be lent to a children's hospital.[6]

Fruing hoped to persuade Beatrix not only to reassign the merchandise contracts and to expand the 'side shows', but also to start a new book. Beatrix was willing to help, even sympathetic, but her continued involvement was contingent on Harold never having anything to do with the business again. 'One thing I am firm about, if I am to go on working for the firm, *he* must not come back.' Trying rather badly to put a good face on things, she told Fruing, 'It *is* dreadfully sad for you and Mary, I do feel sorry for you. But when she gets over the wrench of leaving a pretty home – there will be less housekeeping in a smaller house.'[7]

As a practical matter, Beatrix realized that she needed to help Frederick Warne & Co. survive. After rummaging through her portfolios, Beatrix wondered if it 'would be too shabby' to put together a version of 'Appley Dapply's Nursery Rhymes' for Christmas 1917. '½ a loaf is better than no bread, (and *such* bread too) . . . I find I could scrape together sufficient old drawings to fill a book the size of "Miss Moppet." I would do several pencil outline [*sic*] if you will supply pasted up blank books. I'm afraid this sounds very lazy, but you don't know what a scramble I live in; and the old drawings are some of them better than any I could do now, I suppose the larger ones would reduce all right.' Fruing jumped at the idea even though the rhymes had been passed over several times since she first offered them in 1902. Beatrix selected six rhymes and their illustrations to make a small book to fit the series. 'I hope Apply Dap will be in time to be useful,' she wrote, 'and that it will be as good a season as can be had during this war.'

Appley Dapply's Nursery Rhymes included the endearing little brown house mouse, Appley Dapply, with her freshly baked pies, taken from some of the mice sketches she had used to illustrate 'You know the old woman who lived a shoe?' Beatrix chose a drawing from 1893, old Mr Pricklepin, the little hedgehog modelled on Mrs Tiggy-winkle, and introduced the 'amiable guinea-pig'. In spite of the fact that the drawings had been done at different times, with different margin outline styles, it turned out to be a charming book and sold very well. *Tom Kitten's Painting Book* had appeared in June, while *Appley Dapply* and the revised *Peter Rabbit Painting Book* appeared in October. A second printing of the rhyme book was required a month later. 'I am much pleased with A. D.,' Beatrix wrote to Fruing in late October, 'it makes a pretty little book.'[8]

While it is probably claiming too much to say that Beatrix's contributions saved the firm in 1917, without them Warne's could not have risen from the ruins. As she was the largest creditor and their most valuable artistic property, the firm had to have her cooperation and agreement in order to continue to do business. Beatrix was far too tied up at the farm to travel back and forth to London for creditors' meetings, and since she did not wish to involve William in the financial *post mortem*, she was represented by Braiken-ridge & Edwards, who recommended that the firm be restructured. She agreed that part of Warne's indebtedness to her could be paid in allotted shares and debentures rather than in royalties, but she stood firm on her condition that Harold Warne 'never meddles again'. 'I bear him no grudge,' she told Fruing, 'but I know & remember what a trial he has been, even to me, for many years.' By the end of 1917 the relationship between the firm and Beatrix Heelis had been restored to the point where she felt comfortable enough to return her original drawings to London.

Beatrix was aware that now she would have no relief from Fruing's request for new books, and that both financially and artistically she was committed in ways she had not been previously. Just when she wanted to move on in her country life, she was pulled back in. She did what she could out of loyalty to Norman's memory, her real affection for the Warne family, and gratitude to the firm which had taken a risk on an unknown woman writer and made her famous. But Beatrix had made a pragmatic business decision in sticking with the firm. Had she not, she would have had to physically remove all her printing blocks, find another publisher, and renegotiate licences and copyright – all at a time when she was not producing new work. She also understood that leaving would seriously jeopardize any hope of the firm's financial recovery. In May 1919 a new entity, Frederick Warne & Company Limited, was registered for business, with Fruing as managing director.[9]

Between 1907 and 1917 Beatrix had been the driving force in the licensing of merchandise, such as that with J. I. Farnell of Acton who produced and sold the Jemima Puddle-duck doll. But the war had altered relations with German producers, and Beatrix seized the opportunity to terminate agreements that had not worked to her advantage. She advised Fruing to end the relationship with Levien, a German company which had produced and sold china tea sets which she had never liked, as well as to terminate the agreement with Hughes, another German firm which produced soft rabbit toys. Pressed by the increasing number of pirated products appearing in the shops, Beatrix and Fruing had been negotiating with Grimwades to produce moulded figures based on book characters, as well as a new design for a children's china tea set. But wartime shortages made production difficult. It was not until 1922 that Grimwades china tea sets finally appeared in shops.[10]

But Beatrix took every opportunity to license new items and to increase her income with new merchandise. Handkerchiefs were produced in attractive little boxes by Messrs John Brown & Co., as well as Peter Rabbit slippers. Wooden puzzles and little packets of children's stationery which featured a variety of characters were soon available. Bookcases in white enamelled wood, made to house the entire set of little books, previously only available to bookshops or travellers for display, were introduced to the public and proved popular. Fruing kept Beatrix informed at every turn and, while she commented on every item, shrewdly judging its quality, requesting adjustments when she thought the work inferior or had a better idea, she insisted that Fruing take charge of the administration of the licences.[11]

Saving the publishing firm became a family affair. Mary Warne, Fruing's wife, suggested an alternative version of the old Peter Rabbit board game that Beatrix had designed for Norman in 1904, but which had never been published. Mary's game used all the little book characters instead of just Peter Rabbit and Mr McGregor. Renaming it 'Peter Rabbit's Race Game', she sent a sample for Beatrix to evaluate. Beatrix tried out both old and new versions on Esther and Nancy and reported the results to Fruing in September 1917. Although she preferred her own game as it required more skill, both nieces preferred Mary's version as more elaborate and more like the games that were sold in toy fairs. Mary's version was a 'race between competitors, being separate books' while hers was a contest between characters. 'Dice throws combined with choice of routes would make the best game,' she wrote to Fruing. 'But I haven't either time or intellect to work it out, and I don't really much care: I get so very sick of both versions! The smaller niece preferred yours; but then the little wretch learnt how to throw sixes.'[12]

Beatrix directed the company to produce Mary's game rather than hers. 'I have not sent mine,' she told Fruing, 'for on thinking it over I believe yours is the more likely one – and I hope Mary will have a success with it next Christmas, and please consider it *hers* – Let her use any profit for Christmas presents.' It was a generous gesture, for when the game was finally produced at the end of 1919 it sold well for many years.[13]

Visits from the extended Heelis family lightened what would otherwise have been a very gloomy summer of 1917. In August Beatrix invited Sybil's children, Rosemary and Colin, for a fortnight and begged Sybil to allow them to stay another week. 'I'm sure it is doing them *both* a world of good to run wild for a bit. Colin is improved by school, quite talkative.' She hoped Grace would send the girls so that all the cousins 'overlapped'. When the Nicholson nieces arrived they declared they were staying 'for three weeks!' Beatrix worried about the weather, which had been extraordinarily inclement, '4½ inches of rain last week', but she too wanted them to stay longer so that she could take them to Coniston and then to Windermere on the steamer. 'Nancy is delightful,' Beatrix told Grace, 'we are getting accustomed to hard articles in bed! and think they are enjoying themselves in spite of the rain.' Esther and Nancy stayed till the end of August. 'You needn't thank *us* for having them,' she wrote to Grace, 'it has been a great pleasure – they are both dears. Tell Esther if she ever wants a quiet place to study in, she must remember the farm.'[14]

Beatrix enjoyed writing to Esther and Nancy during the school term. In September she sent Nancy a picture letter telling how she and John Cannon had rescued her prize cow just before it fell off a precipice, backed through a poorly repaired fence by an errant bull. She sent Nancy a copy of the newly published *Appley Dapply*, telling her she had found 'a very young prickle pin last week running about lost on the hill opposite the farm. I carried it home in my pocket, but it died next day, I don't know what was the matter with it.'[15]

Beatrix's letters to the Nicholsons often contained small details of her married life. To her sister-in-law she wrote, 'I flatter myself that I have learnt to make hay, without advice from a party who plays golf till 7 pm on a workable Saturday! It is a little annoying to be lectured when one has been breaking ones back . . .' After the August Bank Holiday, she reported, 'Willie . . . worked every evening at hay & we had a grand hay time, about 100 carts.' 'Tell Nancy', Beatrix instructed, that 'there are *swarms* of rabbits, we had a hunt amongst the cabbages one evening'. In September she wrote to Nancy about Mr Tod, who had got into the yard at Hill Top and killed ten out of eleven birds. 'We have gathered 5 corpses on the hill but there is hardly enough on them to make a pie, the hen is nothing but bones & feathers. Your Uncle Willie went up with his gun but it was too late . . . The cock chickens were ready to kill but I would have preferred to eat them myself and 5 were nice pullets. He has left one cock chicken, I expect it got away into the road.' Beatrix had more success but less drama with her fruit trees.[16]

Beatrix and William visited Battlebarrow for Easter in 1918. Beatrix used the occasion to offer to pay Esther's fees at Somerville Hall if she got a place. James, Grace and Esther were perhaps a bit embarrassed by Beatrix's generosity, but Beatrix would have none of it, writing, 'I hope and trust that no awkward feeling of obligation may stand in the way of Esther's advantage – I don't think it will or ought to do.' Her letter reveals her genuine commitment to family and to country, an emotion she would not normally have articulated. It also expresses her views on the upbringing of children and her unrepentant Victorian standards. 'I have no boy or girl to bring up, to help their country,' she wrote. 'I see all these wretched shirkers & unsound youths & odious self conscious girl workers – and so much of the best gone down. We cannot do too much for the healthy *unspoilt* younger children; they are the hope of the future.' Beatrix's estimate of Esther's potential proved remarkably accurate: 'I never saw more promising material than Esther; she has the brains, balanced by a solid body and unusual common sense.'[17]

In response to Esther's letter of thanks, Beatrix wrote: 'It is pleasant to have made you happy! I have on several occasions through a sense of duty helped several uninteresting persons; now at last I look forward to the pleasure of pleasing myself as well as you.' But she also let Esther know that one day she would be obliged to help Nancy when her turn came to go to university. Teasingly, Beatrix warned: 'If you get plucked over the Greek . . . ??? I wash my hands of you!!' Esther struggled with Greek but she did not disappoint.[18]

Although Fruing Warne had asked Beatrix for another book even before *Appley Dapply* had been published, Beatrix was too busy with farming matters to give much thought to it. Food shortages were rampant and rationing had become an ominous burden; making do kept everyone busy. On a particularly cold day near Christmas 1917, Beatrix had found time to answer a letter from 11-year-old Thomas (Tom) Harding, who lived at Histon Manor, Cambridge. Tom came from a family of zoologists and writers and was interested in her farm animals. Beatrix's response put a good face on farming in wartime. She told the boy,

I have a big farm and a very great deal to do since the war . . . There are 3 horses . . . 14 cows, a lot of calves & young cattle, and 80 ewes & 40 young sheep & some pigs & 25 hens & 5 ducks, & there *were* 13 turkeys . . . Jemima [Puddle-duck] & Rebeccah are white, Semolina is a comical little Indian runner. She made a very deep nest under a nut bush & sat on 11 eggs . . . But alas – Semolina never turned her eggs. The bottom eggs were always stony cold, only the top ones hatched. I called the two children Tapioca & Sago. We have eaten Sago. It was rather dreadful & the stuffing disagreed with my conscience . . . I have lots of rabbits, Belgians – Old Benjamin & Cottontail are pets, but I'm afraid we do have rabbit pies of the young ones.

To Fruing Warne Beatrix confided more personal hardships. She was doing all the cooking, including food for the hens and the dogs. 'Four of us have got through very nicely on 3½ lbs meat . . . a rabbit & pheasant . . . I presume the hens are now to be killed, as they are due to lay again. We are governed by idiots.'[19]

Nonetheless Beatrix had not forgotten Fruing's request for another book. Although she had enough illustrations of rhymes left over, Fruing preferred a story. At the beginning of the year she asked, 'Do you think this mouse story would do? It makes pretty pictures, but not an indefinite number as there is not a great deal of variety . . . A few years ago I amused myself by writing out several of Aesop's fables, this is one that got rather longer than the others.' *Aesop's Fables* was a natural source for Potter's intellect and artistry. Her versions of the fables always reflected the true characteristics of animals. When she altered Aesop, it was in order to more faithfully interpret animal nature within her imaginary world. Beatrix had illustrated such tales as 'The Fox and the Grapes', 'The Hare and the Tortoise' and 'The Fox and the Stork' in the late 1890s, but the fable of 'The Town Mouse and the Country Mouse', which explains why some people prefer the country and some the town, was a natural choice, and very nearly biographical. The charm of her version and setting comes from the sympathetic manner in which she lays out the social and environmental alternatives. Although the sophistication of the city mouse, Johnny, is captured with style and élan, our sympathies are immediately with Timmy Willie who longs for the simplicity of the countryside as Beatrix once had. She sent Warne odd scraps of text and pictures done years earlier, desperately snatching time between sowing turnips, battling an infestation of turnip fly, and the beginning of lambing.

Beatrix pasted up the drawings of the new mouse book in a dummy, ironically made from *The Tale of Mrs. Tittlemouse*. She thought it would make 'a pretty book'. Several titles for the new book were discarded as inaccurate or confusing. In the end, 'The Tale of Johnny Town-Mouse' was selected. The change in title required a commensurate change in the first paragraph of the original manuscript: 'Timmy Willie . . . went to town by mistake in a hamper' was changed to 'Johnny Town-Mouse was born in a cupboard. Timmy Willie was born in a garden.'[20]

As she worked, Beatrix kept a close eye on Warne's financial restructuring. She was anxious about Fruing and aware that he was overworked. Reluctantly she approved the increased price of the little books to 2s., wishing sentimentally for prices to reflect the quality of things in a time now long past. After receiving a surprisingly large royalty cheque in March from the sale of *Appley Dapply* and the painting books, Beatrix wrote to Fruing, 'I am surprised and pleased to hear that the books have done so well in these bad times, I expect people want a cheerful present for children, so they buy them.'[21]

Finally in May she sent six drawings for the new book, 'in desperation – I simply *cannot* see to put colour in them . . . It would have made a good book,' she concluded, 'with sight & cheerfulness to do it.' Her writing and drawing was captured between lost sheep and the normal calamities of farm life. The kitchen boiler had collapsed and the plumber had enlisted in the army. 'I do feel ashamed of my delay over the book,' she wrote to Fruing. 'I have seemed so rushed lately . . . I have just come in after a rough two hours search for some sheep & lambs with a boy – the old man being poorly. We got them; so that is done with. They are beggars to ramble, these hill sheep. I got 2 back from Coniston last winter that were making tracks for Scawfell [*sic*] where they were born.' And then, in a comment which says much about her changed attitudes toward book-making, she added: 'Somehow when one is up to the eyes in work with real live animals it makes one despise paper-book animals – but I mustn't say that to my publisher!'[22]

The Tale of Johnny Town-Mouse is the most autobiographical of Potter's little books. Cobbled together in wartime, it reflects her deep understanding of animal nature, but its subtext is her own happiness as a 'country mouse'. Timmy Willie is carried away by mistake in a vegetable hamper from a garden in Sawrey to Hawkshead, a town only in comparison to the village of Sawrey, where he escapes immediate feline danger, but lands unceremoniously on the dining table of the elegant Johnny Town-mouse who is just then entertaining guests. Differences in manners, physiognomy, diet and ambient noise are remarked upon, parodying human class and culture. Timmy Willie tries unsuccessfully to adjust to his host's accommodation, unnerved by the proximate cat, and snatches a ride back to his Sawrey garden and the peace of the countryside. Although Johnny Town-mouse reluctantly arrives for his promised visit during spring cleaning, he cannot abide either the herb pudding, the frightening farm noises or the deep quiet, and he takes the next hamper back to town. Beatrix offers her opinion of events at the end of the story, as she had in several other tales. 'One place suits one person, another place suits another person. For my part I prefer to live in the country, like Timmy Willie.'

Although some of the drawings are not up to her best work, reflecting her failing eyesight and her bifurcated attention, they are nonetheless enchanting, particularly those set in the garden and the countryside. The story is filled with local colour, as the best of her other Sawrey books were. The carrier's cart, her favourite illustration, is pulled by Old Diamond, one of her farm horses. A young Mrs Rogerson, once a housemaid at Eeswyke, appears as the cook, and there are glimpses of the skyline and architectural elements of both Sawrey and Hawkshead, as well as the village gardens. Johnny himself is a caricature of Dr Parsons, one of William's golfing partners, authentic even to the details of his golf bag and clubs. Beatrix is as interested in the varieties of mice, and their class distinctions, as she is in those of men, and her curiosity about each makes her satire worth savouring.[23]

When Beatrix sent off the last drawings in August 1918 the carnage of war was coming to an ignominious end. With characteristic aplomb, she dedicated her tale 'to Aesop in the shadows'. It was published in December, barely making it into the shops for Christmas. A review in the *Bookman* gave Fruing Warne such pleasure that he sent it to Beatrix, although she claimed she had long since ceased to read them: 'Another volume for the Peter Rabbit bookshelf. Oh, such charming pictures and exciting letter press! . . . Miss Potter need not worry about rivals. She has none. *Johnny Town-Mouse* does even so accomplished an artist and writer as herself much credit.' Given the sadness Beatrix had endured that year, such accolades must have boosted her flagging spirits.[24]

She had finished what she later referred to as 'that unlucky book' under the most difficult circumstances. Her brother Bertram had died suddenly of a cerebral haemorrhage at Ashyburn, just outside the tiny village of Ancrum, on 22 June 1918. Although Beatrix and Bertram rarely saw one another after the war began, they continued to share common interests in farming and in animal husbandry, just as they had earlier embraced a shared delight in natural history and art. It was Bertram who encouraged Beatrix to get a self-binding machine for harvesting corn, and to put together a 'complete outfit of farm machinery'. 'I shall miss my brother sadly,' she confided to Millie the week following Bertram's death, 'we seldom met, but he wrote regularly about farming matters, & we could help one another a bit, by exchange. He sent me a splendid ram last year.'[25]

Bertram and Mary had a fine farm in the Scottish Borders. After Rupert died in 1914, Bertram, who was then financially independent, renounced any intention to return to England. Mary had transformed his sad and lonely life. He had been very happy and proud of her, referring to her as his 'M.P.' But his life was marred by bouts of drinking, and his alcoholism was both recognized and tolerated charitably by his farmhands and neighbours as 'his little weakness'. Bertram, the artist-farmer, fitted in well with the Border country acceptance of the eccentric, and he had found a niche for himself. He hosted an annual football match for his workers at the New Year, spoiled them with higher wages and shorter hours than most and held musical events at the farm for special holiday entertainment. He and Mary had unofficially adopted Mary's niece Margaret, 'Hetty' Hutton Douglas, whom they sent off to boarding school in the Lake District during the war.

Bertram and Charlie Blaikie, a younger man whom Bertram had befriended as a boy and whom he regarded as a son, had gone out early in the morning to work on his fish ponds. Feeling unwell, Bertram started for the house when he was struck down and died a few hours later without regaining consciousness. He left everything to Mary, with generous legacies to Hetty and to Mary's sister Elizabeth, to Blaikie, and to several of his farm workers. Mary was his executrix, but since neither she nor Helen Potter was up to handling the requirements, most of the legal work fell to Beatrix and William.[26]

Beatrix was devastated by her brother's sudden death. She told Hardwicke Rawnsley several months later, 'I don't think I yet realize that Bertram is gone – in his prime and in his usefulness. He had such a fine farm; and although his nature – sensitive and like his father's – and patriotic & upright to a rare degree – made him feel the war very keenly – I do think he found true happiness in hard useful manual work. It is good to remember how much more cheerful & contented he had seemed towards the last.' Beatrix took special comfort from the place where Bertram had chosen to be laid to rest, describing for Rawnsley the picturesque cemetery in Ancrum: 'He is buried like the Grasmere folks in the bend of a stream – a flowery graveyard with a ruined ivy grown church and graves of the covenanters on the banks of Ale Water.'[27]

The week before Bertram died, Beatrix had been upset by the arrival of William's call-up papers. Fortunately his age, 46, and an old 'football knee' placed him in Grade 3, which meant that he did not have to go. There was more than enough for him to do at home.

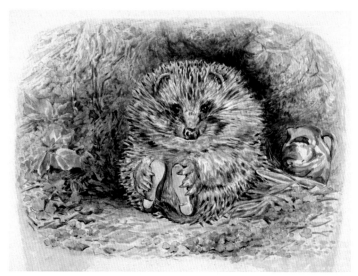

37. 'Old Mr. Prickly Pin',
c. 1902. This hedgehog has
been identified as Mrs Tiggy-
winkle's uncle. Fascinated by
the habits of hedgehogs and
devoted to those she tamed,
Beatrix thought this 'about the
best drawing I ever made'.

38. 'Guinea pigs go
gardening', 1893. These
charming gardeners are
modelled after the guinea
pigs Beatrix borrowed from
her friend Miss Paget, the
nursing reformer. She used
them later in *Cecily Parsley's
Nursery Rhymes* (1922).

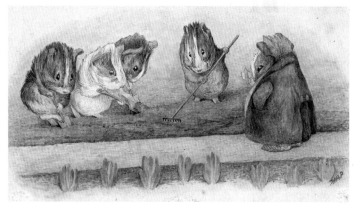

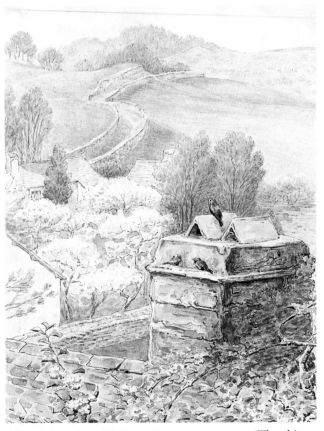

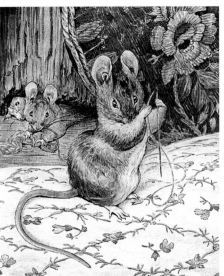

39. 'The chimney stack stood up above the roof like a little stone tower', from *The Tale of Samuel Whiskers* (1908). Beatrix liked the view from the roof of Hill Top, where she could see the stone walls marching up the fells.

40. Mouse threading a needle, from *The Tailor of Gloucester* (1903). This tale was always Beatrix's personal favourite. She copied the elaborately embroidered satin waistcoat from one in the Victoria and Albert Museum.

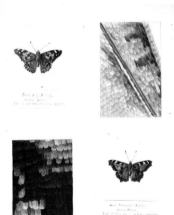

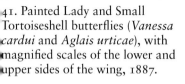

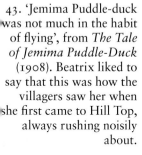

41. Painted Lady and Small Tortoiseshell butterflies (*Vanessa cardui* and *Aglais urticae*), with magnified scales of the lower and upper sides of the wing, 1887.

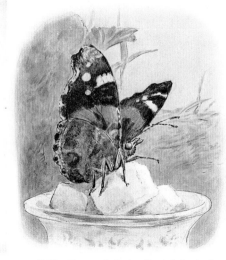

42. 'Miss Butterfly', the Red Admiral butterfly tasting the sugar, from *The Tale of Mrs. Tittlemouse* (1910). Beatrix adapted her interest in natural history to create many characters that appear in the tales.

43. 'Jemima Puddle-duck was not much in the habit of flying', from *The Tale of Jemima Puddle-Duck* (1908). Beatrix liked to say that this was how the villagers saw her when she first came to Hill Top, always rushing noisily about.

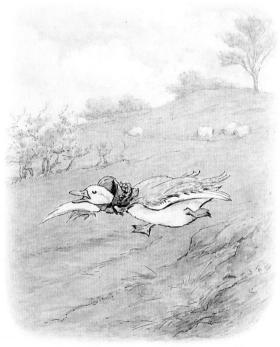

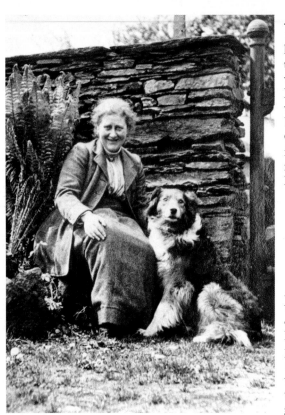

44. Beatrix with Kep, 1913. Beatrix, wearing her familiar Herdwick tweed skirt and jacket, was photographed in her Hill Top Farm garden with her favourite collie by a visiting American, Charles G. Y. King, just four months before her marriage to William Heelis.

45. 'An entrance gate in a wall, with a background of fields and trees', Laund House, Bolton Abbey, a painting included in her 1902 sketchbook. Beatrix was impressed with the trees on the Abbey grounds.

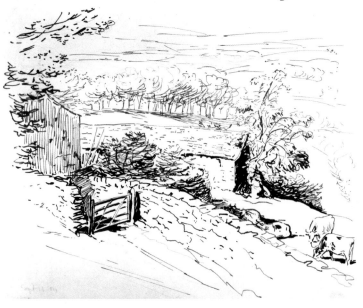

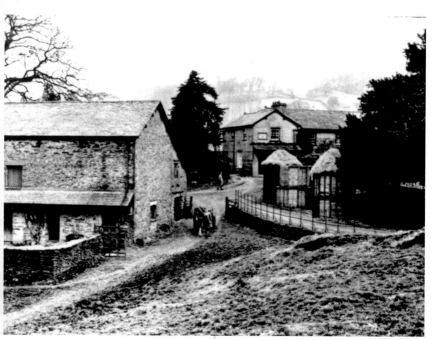

46. Hill Top Farm, 1940. The war years were difficult for farmers. Beatrix adapted to wartime restrictions in crops and livestock, but she was anxious that her sheep and cattle should have enough fodder. She adopted modern harvesting equipment, but refused to have electricity in the farmhouse

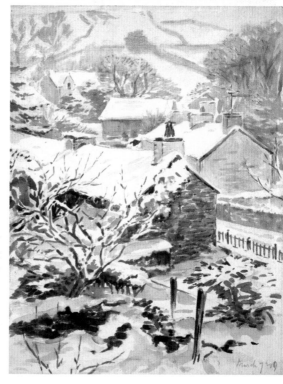

47. Sawrey village under snow, 1909. Beatrix enjoyed painting the landscapes and buildings that she loved under the cover of snow. Intrigued by the variations of light in each season, she gave snow a realistic depth and texture.

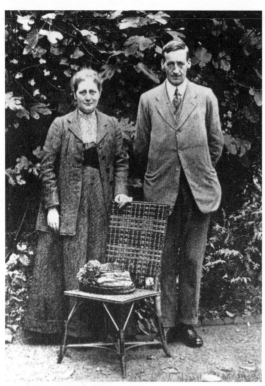

48. Beatrix and William, photographed by Rupert Potter at Bolton Gardens the day before their wedding on 15 October 1913. Theirs was a close and happy marriage of thirty years.

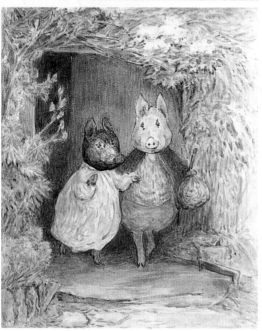

49. Pigwig and Pigling Bland escape. *The Tale of Pigling Bland* was finished just before Beatrix's marriage to William in 1913 and published just after. There is a romantic element to the tale of the little black pig and the shy Pigling Bland, although Beatrix rejected the suggestion that it was autobiographical.

50. Background for the frontispiece for *The Tale of Pigling Bland*. During their extended courtship, Beatrix and William frequently walked by this crossroads behind Hill Top. It represented both a particular moment in her life and the choice between duty and happiness.

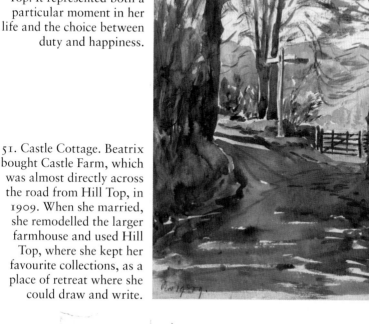

51. Castle Cottage. Beatrix bought Castle Farm, which was almost directly across the road from Hill Top, in 1909. When she married, she remodelled the larger farmhouse and used Hill Top, where she kept her favourite collections, as a place of retreat where she could draw and write.

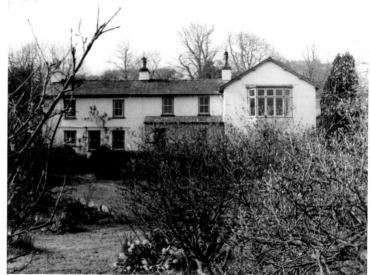

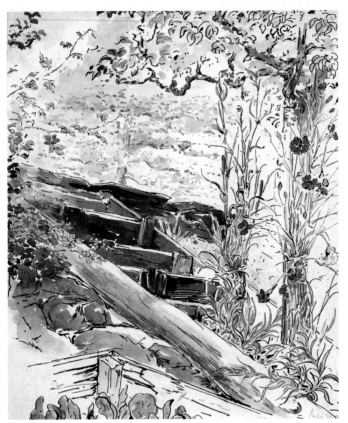

52. Garden steps at Fawe Park, Derwentwater,
1903. Beatrix used these steps, bordered by red
carnations and leading to the terraced garden
at Fawe Park, as a background for *The Tale of
Benjamin Bunny* (1904). She considered it a
'scribble'.

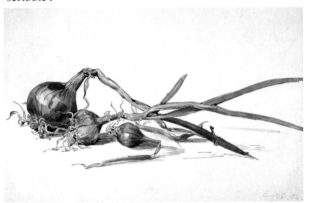

53. Onions at Fawe
Park, Derwentwater,
1903. Beatrix drew
several variations
of the onions in the
garden at Fawe Park

The harvest had begun in promising weather but had quickly changed to terrible storms, floods and rains. The two farm boys came down with measles, and the older lad caught influenza, leaving Beatrix with old John Cannon and two girls. Between storms, she tried to save her apple crop. She was also anxious for her 'old mother', who had been deeply shocked at losing Bertram.[28]

Beatrix was nothing if not resilient, and found humour in her daily life on the farm and in her life with William. She complained to Nancy Nicholson that William was a 'heartless man. I was stung by a wasp – (where I sit down). It was in my bath towel; and when I called out to your Uncle Willie who was safe in bed asleep – he calmly said "It doesn't matter", and went on sleeping.' She always found pleasure and amusement in her real animals. Sarah, the pig, who followed Beatrix about like a dog and tended to be overly affectionate, had been 'ill with eating too many plum stones. I gave her castor oil in porridge . . . The fish man has begun to come again', and the cat Judy 'has just brought a cod's tail into the hall. She is teaching the kittens to mouse . . . Perhaps she wants to teach them to fish . . . It rains and rains and rains.'[29]

To Millie Warne, however, Beatrix's recital of farm events was more sobering. 'The corn is a complete loss in the north. It is mostly oats, but it affects human food because there is such trouble this winter how to feed the animals. I do grudge the good clover which we ploughed up to make room for corn . . . And we have 8 pigs, got in hopes of plenty of grain.' That number included Sarah, whom she confessed she could never eat. But she was hopeful that better times were ahead. 'Isn't the war news wonderful?'[30]

The Allies and Germany had begun to negotiate a peace settlement in November. The Peace of Paris that officially ended the war was a diplomatic event that occurred far from Sawrey. Nearer at hand were food shortages, influenza and rain. Beatrix sensed it was the end of an era; a time when Timmy Willie's country values would be increasingly eroded and change would be everywhere.

15

～ *Opportunities* ～

OUTWARDLY LIFE FOR BEATRIX AND William at Castle Cottage and Hill Top Farm after the war continued much as it had before. Beatrix tended to the business of farming, and William went to his Hawkshead law office. Together they enjoyed taking the boat out on Moss Eccles Tarn in the late afternoon. There were many days like one she later described when 'Mr Heelis & I fished (at least I rowed!) till darkness . . . it was lovely on the tarn, not a breath of wind & no midges.' Their life moved more or less within the accustomed rhythms of farm and family.[1]

Farmers still went out lambing in the middle of the night, the weather remained harsh and unpredictable, and the daily grind of keeping the animals healthy, the milk pure and the harvest gathered went on as before. But the deeper marks of change to rural life in the Lake District were visible everywhere. Tourism returned with a vengeance, providing new sources of income for those lucky farmers near scenic areas who could offer food or lodging. Roads had to be widened to accommodate the crowds of trippers, automobiles and charabancs. Harvesters and threshing machines, once a rarity, were now commonplace, even at Hill Top. Electricity was widely available and accepted, though Beatrix permitted it only in her barns and not in either farmhouse. She wrote by candlelight until William arrived home in the evening and only then lit the gas lamps – there were no exceptions – and housekeepers who objected did not remain long at Castle Cottage. There were water closets at both Hill Top and Castle Cottage, but she obstinately opposed them for her tenanted farms and cottages, where she insisted that earth closets were adequate. She was not so old-fashioned about telephones when they became available, and installed one for her mother at Lindeth Howe, or about motor cars, to which she was simply resigned. 'Some people think it is spoiling the countryside,' she wrote to a young friend, 'but there is no help, for everybody will have a small car or a motor byke [*sic*] presently.' By 1925 the Heelises owned two cars. William used one to go between his two offices in Hawkshead and Ambleside and later drove 'all over the district like a doctor'. Beatrix thought herself too old to learn to drive and so employed one of the farmhands, Tommy Christopherson, who ordinarily was occupied with drains and fences, to drive her in the two-seater.[2]

Technology and mechanization contributed to an increase in land values and added ease for some, but at a price. Rural trades shrivelled and patronage from the old gentry and ecclesiastical institutions evaporated, their places taken by an expanded and increasingly remote government bureaucracy. Poverty was more widespread and more visible. Small farms failed and were put up for sale. Land development flourished all over Lakeland, and old buildings were torn down, rather than repaired. The bonfires that celebrated the armistice in 1918 yielded to a new kind of economic uncertainty about the future of fell farming. Beatrix and William were among many who considered buying land in Canada, somewhere along the St Lawrence River, and emigrating. But the idea was a fleeting one and not terribly practical, given their family responsibilities.[3]

But the post-war years also brought Beatrix unexpected opportunity. She had never adapted quickly or without a certain ambivalence to change, but she was extraordinarily resilient. There were changes at her farms, within her immediate family, and within the Sawrey community which she could not ignore. With typical realism, she asked questions and looked for solutions. She took advantage of the opportunities for wide associations and new friendships and discovered in the process that she was enjoying herself, feeling that she was contributing to something larger than her own self-interest. She also discovered that she was not as invisible in Near Sawrey as she had assumed. For the first time since her marriage, new activities nearly usurped her passion for writing books for children.

Beatrix's relationship with her publisher, Frederick Warne and Company Ltd., was the first to require sorting out. The Warne's restructuring was completed in the spring of 1919 with Beatrix's approval of the financial terms, but to move ahead they needed a new book from her. Her successful adaption of Aesop for *The Tale of Johnny Town-Mouse* and her enthusiasm for this material prompted her to work up an amalgam of fables featuring Miss Jenny Crow and the Fox. She sent a draft of it to Fruing telling him, 'I hope very much this may find favour? As I have (perhaps rashly!) started some of the pictures. Also crow shooting starts on Saturday so I have hopes of both models & pies.'[4]

But Fruing did not like it, and bluntly said so. 'Practically,' he wrote, 'you have adopted the idea of putting together five of Aesop's tales into modern language for children – with the result that your Publisher is disappointed; it is not Miss Potter, it is Aesop.' He suggested instead the 'very brilliant little MS in that Pigeon story' (*The Tale of the Faithful Dove*), a story about a pigeon stuck in a chimney that Beatrix had written for the Warne children in 1908. Beatrix was offended and reacted defensively, explaining she had no time for 'namby pamby pigeons for this season'. Besides, she told him, birds did not lend themselves to 'dressing up' in any case.[5]

Fruing realized he had offended her, but his efforts to placate fell flat. 'The thing that principally concerns & interests me at the present,' Beatrix wrote, 'is a bad drought, the crops are burnt up like August.' Very much put off, Beatrix let it be known that the publisher no longer had much influence with her.

You do not realize that I have become more – rather than less obstinate as I grow older; and that you have no lever to make use of with me; beyond sympathy with you and the old firm, nothing else would induce me to go on at all. You see I am not short of money. I never have cared tuppence either for popularity or for the modern child; they are pampered & spoilt with too many toys & books. And when you infer that my originality is more precious than old Aesop's you *do* put your foot in it![6]

She did a few more drawings, more for herself than for Warne's, for what she now referred to as 'The Tale of the Birds and Mr. Tod'. In August she sent a new idea for the cover but told Fruing, 'you must *not* count on my going on doing books of coloured illustrations. Find someone else.' Thoroughly disheartened by his criticism, and finding it harder and harder both to do close work and to create new stories for younger children, Beatrix had tired of deadlines, pressure and feelings of obligation. She wrote offering only 'very moderate apologies',

I am glad you are having a good season – apart from my misdeeds – which you will have to put up with sooner or later – for you don't suppose I shall be able to continue these d . . . d little books when I am dead and buried!! I am utterly tired of doing them, and my eyes are wearing out. I will try to do you one or two more for the good of the old firm; but it is quite time I had rest from them. Especially as there is still other work that I should like to finish for my own pleasure.[7]

In retrospect, Fruing Warne made a serious misjudgement when he rejected Potter's retelling of Aesop. The new fables were particular favourites of hers and were characterized by her unique way of retelling fine old tales that children never tire of hearing. Beatrix had an unfailing eye for capturing animal nature. Her interpretation was imaginative yet faithful to the foibles of both humans and animals. Although the initial drawings may have been somewhat muddy, she had embellished them with the same distinctive details of Lake District scenery and rural customs that she had put into the best of the Sawrey books. There had been plenty of 'Potter' in 'The Tale of Jenny Crow'.

But her loyalty to the old firm was too strong to abandon them for long. Despite her protests, every so often she rummaged in her old portfolios to see what she might pull together. But the effort only caused her to wonder 'how I ever drew so much and well, while I could see'. To an old acquaintance she confided that her difficulty in producing a new book was not simply her fading eyesight, but a lack of passion for the subject. 'Somehow since the war I have never felt as if I could concentrate my attention on drawing, there is a great deal of work in the illustrations. It is much easier for me to attend to real live pigs & rabbits; and after all I have done about 30 books, so

I have earned a holiday. I have been much amused with two large litters of little pigs which I have been rearing this autumn.' In the autumn of 1920 she suggested once more that she might pull together another book of rhymes from the ones she had gathered as 'Cecily Parsley's Nursery Rhymes', but Fruing remained unenthusiastic, sceptical that they would sell. Liberated from his requests, Beatrix was fully occupied with her farm.[8]

The most fundamental change at Hill Top was the departure of the now frail John Cannon and his family as tenants in the spring of 1919. Beatrix hired John Mackereth, an honest, hard-working man who was knowledgeable about breeding Galloway cattle, as her new manager. The post-war market for cattle had improved, and Beatrix, who had been assiduously raising more Galloways each year, benefited. Shortly after Cannon retired, the great influenza epidemic of 1918, which had rampaged across western Europe, reached the British north and lingered into spring planting time. The village of Sawrey was not spared; neither were her employees, although Beatrix and William escaped that first winter. This particular human epidemic was just waning when foot-and-mouth disease broke out among Westmorland cattle. Beatrix's herd at Hill Top was unaffected, but she, like all the other local farmers, was apprehensive. Cattle movements were completely halted. 'The cattle disease is a great anxiety, and one feels much sympathy for neighbours who have got it,' she wrote to Fruing Warne. 'The finest herd in the district has been slaughtered, 70 head; many of them quite unaffected, and others *recovering*. It [slaughter] may be the wisest course; but the remedy is more alarming than the disease, which seems to be *not* a severe type, but terribly infectious.' Beatrix always thought it strange that the 'scientifics never find an innoculation' against influenza or 'against cattle plague either'.[9]

In between these two epidemics there were seasonal outbreaks of measles among the village children. Normal activities of those adults who were not caring for the sick were curtailed in an effort to minimize the contagion. 'Nearly all the children in the village have had measles, some were pretty bad, if they got cold it seemed to affect their ears,' Beatrix told her niece. Beatrix herself had toothache and then earache. But she was deeply concerned about the waves of disease which periodically ran through the community and about the inadequacy of rural health care when they did. Beatrix decided the Hawkshead district needed a nurse, and not just any sort of nurse, but a Queen's Nurse. She found a congenial ally for this endeavour in her friend and neighbour Emily Fowkes.[10]

Although Emily was a good deal older than Beatrix, they had known each other since Beatrix had first come to Lakefield. Emily's family had been members of the Quaker community at Colthouse for generations, and Beatrix sometimes accompanied her to the Quaker Meeting there. In accordance with the best ideals of the Dissenting tradition they shared, Beatrix and Emily decided to do something about the lack of nursing care.

Beatrix's interest in district nursing, particularly in finding a suitable Queen's Nurse for the area, had several sources. The most immediate was her experience with the influenza pandemic of 1918. In such a crisis there was little health care available to rural communities, especially in remote villages, and few tenant farmers, shepherds or labourers could afford to have a doctor visit them. After nearly twenty years of being a farmer and landowner in Sawrey, Beatrix was well acquainted with the periodic outbreaks of contagious diseases, but by the 1920s she had also had first-hand experience of women who died needlessly in childbirth, and of the elderly who endured illness and death without aid or comfort on the remote fell farms. Beatrix's commitment to secure the services of a Queen's Nurse for Sawrey and her commitment to district nursing undoubtedly drew on her long-standing admiration for the Paget family, her London neighbours in the Boltons, who had been pioneers in district nursing services and midwifery. Rosalind Paget, the younger daughter, had become well known after the war as a Queen's Nurse, and particularly as an advocate for the health care needs of women and children.[11]

The district nurse system was organized around parish jurisdictions, and in rural areas several parishes joined together to form a district committee. But to secure a district nurse it was first necessary to enlist the support of Canon Thomas Irving, Vicar of St Michael and All Angels in Hawkshead, a person with whom Beatrix had little to do, and with whom she disagreed on a number of issues, including the treatment of animals. Luckily, Irving had also concluded after the influenza epidemic that there was a need for a trained nurse and was prepared to support the necessary fund-raising. The next step was to get approval for the geographic area the district nurse would cover, raise the required £160 a year for her salary, establish an endowment fund and find housing. Beatrix, who was a natural behind-the-scenes organizer, contacted Mrs Balm-Jones, a Hawkshead lady of means and political skills, who put together a temporary committee. Beatrix and Emily were surprised to discover real opposition to the idea from many of the older women of the parish who for years had taken on the job of midwife, and saw no reason to be supplanted by a Queen's Nurse. But plans moved forward nonetheless.

Hawkshead, Wray, Graythwaite and Sawrey elected two representatives to form the nucleus of a general committee. Beatrix and Miss Alcock-Beck, another long-time friend from Sawrey, were elected from Sawrey. The District Nursing Association approved the Hawkshead District Nurse Association application in October 1919. The minimum subscription was set at 2s. 6d. Non-subscribers would pay 6d. a visit. The endowment fund was doubled by the end of the year from a variety of endeavours, including jumble sales, refreshment booths at parish functions, and outright donations. Beatrix was elected treasurer of the local committee, and Miss Peacock from the Hawkshead parish became the secretary. The two women decidedly did not get on, but Beatrix controlled the funds and zestfully dominated the early committee meetings. She also had difficulties with the secretary of the larger Hawkshead group, whom she regarded as a gossip and whose visits she found 'unpleasant prospects'. In spite of the petty politics, in December 1919 she got her way. Beatrix wrote to her sister-in-law in some excitement: 'there is at last a prospect of a district nurse, rather old at 49 – but we are going to try her, she has had plenty of experience but principally in towns.' Nurse Filkin received her enthusiastic support, and Beatrix found herself much more publicly involved in directing the charity than she had ever imagined.[12]

The Queen's Nurse was an active, wiry little woman who had served in both the Boer War and the Great War. She moved into a small cottage that Beatrix owned at Hanniken, on the outskirts of Hawkshead, and allowed her to live in rent free. From there she went about her rounds on a bicycle. Although Nurse Filkin worked under the direct supervision of the local doctor, it was the three-village committee which met once a month that saw to the organization of her rounds and raised the money to pay for the necessary medical supplies. But in practicality she reported to Mrs Heelis, who controlled the funds, kept track of supplies and directed her visits. Beatrix was aware that Nurse Filkin had a quick tongue, but she had also observed from personal experience that there 'could not be a kinder hearted woman'. Beatrix was often required to defend the enormously over-worked nurse. After one difficult meeting with Miss Peacock in August 1923 Beatrix wrote to her sister-in-law,

I believe I partly kept my temper but I remember telling her that neither she nor I, being childless, were competent to discuss the conduct of a confinement . . . I can see that the Secretary would prefer a 'homely' half brained woman, but I am firmly against it, especially if the doctors won't employ her . . . This one is a most excellent nurse, but rather peppery and a sharp tongue. She will take any saying from me; but apparently she answers back Miss Peacock and the doctor.[13]

Beatrix won that particular battle with Peacock, but by February 1924 Nurse Filkin had worn herself out. Beatrix, who as honorary treasurer and acting secretary of the local association had raised enough money to put the nursing fund on a sound financial basis, was now charged with finding a replacement. Everyone now saw the 'advantage of having a capable and much-liked nurse . . .'. Beatrix had heard of a Queen's Nurse from Lancashire who, with her young son, might be coaxed back to the area. She now campaigned to convince Celia Edwards to take the post. 'It is a very healthy district; the scattered cottages are what takes time – I understand that you are an active cyclist, and not afraid of wet weather. The bicycle is a

Swift, an easy one to use.' When Edwards decided to apply, Beatrix took the risk of engaging her, 'unofficially', confident she could push her selection through the committee.[14]

Beatrix prepared Celia Edwards well for what she would find in Hawkshead, describing the Hanniken cottage, the local shops, and the various physicians who practised in the district. Nurse Edwards proved a great success and served the district for nearly a decade. Although she was employed by several local physicians, she too relied upon Beatrix for information on who was ill and who needed visiting. Most days Nurse Edwards called at Castle Cottage to get her list updated. After 1925 Beatrix no longer served as an officer of the committee, but she remained a principal, usually anonymous, bene-factor and kept her finger on the pulse of the local committee. In addition to supplying the nurse's cottage, Beatrix dipped into her own pocket to help buy Nurse Edwards a car, a discounted Morris Cowley, so she could manage the high waters around Hawkshead during the winter, and get about the fell farms in bad weather. The nurse always had a Christmas turkey from Hill Top Farm. Among the locals it was well known that 'Mrs Heelis was awfully keen on the district nursing'.[15]

Beatrix's desire to have a Queen's Nurse was not totally altruistic, especially after 1922 when William's brother, Arthur John, one-time Rector of Brougham, became too ill to live on his own and moved into the spare bedroom at Castle Cottage. No one else in the extended Heelis family had been willing to take the Revd AJ in, so Beatrix and William brought him to Sawrey as a more or less permanent lodger. AJ, as he was called in the family, was emotionally troubled and often chronically ill with a variety of digestive and bowel com-plaints. He was not an easy or particularly pleasant patient, and he was also a chain-smoker. Beatrix worried that he would set himself and the cottage on fire. His personal hygiene was such that it was very difficult for Beatrix to care for him. She did her best, but it was a great relief to be able to call on Nurse Filkin or Nurse Edwards when AJ got too sick for her to handle.

Beatrix had no fireplace in the spare bedroom at the cottage and no indoor water closet for him to use, so it was especially difficult to house a sick person in cold weather. During holidays when she had company or needed to travel, AJ went back to his sisters in Appleby or sometimes stayed with friends in Blackpool. But he so enjoyed being with Beatrix that he escaped his sisters and even his friends as soon as he could. He was especially happy when Louie Choyce was there as she played the piano and sang, and the two were equally bad at bridge. For a woman raised in a rigid Victorian household with servants, who had not been adept at nursing her own father, Beatrix's nursing care of AJ was extraordinarily generous. She did it quite willingly out of respect for William and his family, seeing it as her duty. She was uncomplaining, and realistic about AJ's longterm prognosis, telling Louie, 'his heart is weak & he might go suddenly; but myself I think he will last some time, wearing out by repeated illnesses.' Sadly, her prediction was all too accurate, as AJ's descent into invalidism continued until his death three years later in January 1926. By then his care and presence had become a fixture not only of her routine, but of her heart. His death left a gap. She wrote to Fruing Warne, 'Our poor invalid Arthur Heelis has peacefully fallen asleep. It is a release for him & will be a relief when one gets used to it.' But it took her a long time to do so. Six years later she wrote to a young friend, 'I never thought how much I would miss him, when I missed his stick tapping on the bedroom floor.'[16]

The extended Heelis family was also responsible for getting Beatrix involved in the Girl Guide organization. William's eldest sister Blanche had been a supporter of the outdoor programme for young girls, and their niece, Sylvie Heelis, became a Guide leader in Hawkshead after the war. Companies of Girl Guides, generally between the ages of 11 and 15, and their younger counterparts, the Brownies, raised money every year to go camping in the countryside, where they lived in the open and learned outdoor skills. At first Beatrix simply obliged her niece by allowing the Guides to use one of her fields near Hawkshead, but she discovered she derived pleasure from her interaction with them and admired their energetic leaders. The Guide companies exposed Beatrix to young women who shared her curiosity about the natural world, and who were grateful to be out of the crowded, unhealthy cities and to spend a week outdoors in the beautiful Lake District. Until the economic depression of the 1930s made it difficult for companies of Guides to afford an overnight camping trip, Beatrix enjoyed a regular flow of Guides camping on Heelis land, and contributed to their experience with touching generosity.[17]

Local sites were arranged between Beatrix and Joy Brownlow, known as Brownie, the County Camp Adviser. At first, the companies stayed either at her fields near Hawkshead on the western side of Esthwaite or on land closer to Sawrey. In spite of the girls' tendency to leave a litter of hair ribbons and slides in the hay which the sheep could eat, Beatrix allowed them to sleep in an empty barn at Hawkshead when the weather turned inclement. Beatrix and Joy Brownlow began a regular correspondence in the off-season and Beatrix was always pleased when Joy wrote early each year to make sure the Sawrey fields were available. Beatrix watched the girls learn the discipline of successful group living, and discover how to survive outdoors in all sorts of weather. Sometimes she entered into their merriment.[18]

In May 1928, the 1st Chorlton-cum-Hardy Company, which had become one of her favourite groups, came to Troutbeck Park. They invited Beatrix for tea to celebrate one Guide's eighteenth birthday and to stay for a piece of cake. Asked to sign their log book, Beatrix drew a picture of Peter Rabbit sharing a large cake with a blue uniformed Guide. Soon a tradition was established that each company would make a log book for their hostess describing what they had done during their camp. These log books were frequently decorated with rabbits looking much like Peter, sketches of the local wildlife, and photographs of the girls for Mrs Heelis. They recorded the times Mrs Heelis came to tea, or when the Guides recited something for her. The Skylark Guides offered her some physical labour in return for sharing such a beautiful setting. Their log book reads, 'As it was a lovely day, we decided to go and cut bracken for Mrs Heelis.' It includes a photograph of the girls cutting bracken and burning thistles.[19]

In 1931 the Chorlton gang came again, under the leadership of Nora Burt and Kitty Holdsworth, two Guide leaders who had become quite fond of Mrs Heelis. The weather was unusually wet and dismal, and the outing was threatened when one of the girls developed appendicitis. Beatrix called in Nurse Edwards and then lent her own car and driver to Nora to take the young woman to hospital in Manchester. Nora Burt's note of thanks began a friendship that continued for the next decade. Beatrix took a special interest in Nora, who had shown such ability in the emergency and was particularly pleased when the young woman decided on a career in nursing. 'It is always a pleasure to help Guides,' Beatrix wrote, 'and it brings its own reward – for surely it is blessing when old age is coming, to be able still to understand and share the joy of life that is being lived by the young.'[20]

Part of Beatrix's commitment to the Guides sprang from her understanding of what such an experience would have meant to her when she was a young girl and in want of friendships and of doing something useful. 'I wish they had been invented when I was young,' she wrote to a friend. 'All I can do in old age is to lend them camps (and dry blankets!) . . . It is a grand thing to enjoy play and enjoy work, which is what the Scouts & Guides learn to do.'[21]

She frequently gave the Guides autographed copies of her books as prizes for their competitions, and even allowed them to take photographs of her, commenting on one in 1928, 'The camp makes such a pretty picture. I can recognize many of the guides. We had a laugh at ME – I ought to have had my fine new teeth in! I look a good natured old body at all events.' Her active support of Girl Guiding as well as her encouragement of nursing careers for young women like Nora Burt underscore her interest in young people and her pleasure in sharing the countryside with them. As she told a friend in 1928, 'If I have done anything – even a little – to help small children on the road to enjoy and appreciate honest simple pleasures – of the sort that leads to becoming Boy Scouts or Girl Guides – I have done a bit of good.'[22]

Beatrix's pleasure in the Guides and her friendships with the girls, some of whom visited her for years afterwards, contrasts markedly with her reputation among some of the local village children, who were not only afraid of the sharp-tongued Mrs Heelis, but took some delight in taunting her. The Guides were polite and orderly visitors, under the supervision of other disciplined young people. They had also come a long way and even made sacrifices to travel to the Lake District and felt privileged to be on her property. Local children were under no such supervision and often had little desire to learn or to improve themselves. They took the countryside for granted and created their own fun. Pinching apples, climbing on her walls and fences, generally being silly or even rude was simply a normal part of being a country child in a small village. Mrs Heelis, who could be sternly disapproving and was somewhat idiosyncratic in dress and behaviour, was sometimes the object of their teasing and deliberate provoking. Beatrix enjoyed young people, especially bright and imaginative ones, but as a Victorian woman, she expected well-behaved children and would not tolerate rudeness.[23]

About the same time as Beatrix began her activities on behalf of the District Nursing Association and the Girl Guides, she received a letter from her father's surgeon, Sir Alfred Fripp, inviting her involvement in the Invalid Children's Aid Association (ICAA), a national charity for children established in 1888. Fripp's committee wanted to launch a special appeal to better-off children to help fund a hospital bed at the ICAA home at West Wickham in Kent. As Beatrix explained to Fruing Warne, 'he wants the help of Peter Rabbit, with the use of a picture printed on the appeal'. She liked the idea of raising money for a Peter Rabbit bed and asked Warne's to give Fripp something they could use. Beatrix did what she could to help write an appeal letter from Peter Rabbit that had the right tone, and to design a penny stamp collecting card. 'Miss Beatrix Potter' appeared on the letterhead of the ICAA's Peter Rabbit Committee, but in parentheses it identified her as 'Mrs W. Heelis'.[24]

Subsequently Mrs Stanley Baldwin, wife of the Prime Minister, who chaired the Peter Rabbit Fund, asked Beatrix if she would contribute a Christmas card for the charity to use as a 'reward for collectors'. Beatrix thought it a worthwhile venture, and Warne's agreed to contribute the coloured block and produce the card. The first card was ready by Christmas 1924, but was not published until the following year. Between 1925 and 1941 Beatrix regularly produced perhaps as many as two dozen cards, featuring delightful animals, not always rabbits, that helped raise money for four more Peter Rabbit beds and for the work of the ICAA. She also wrote several form letters from herself and Peter Rabbit to thank children who subscribed to the ICAA and who filled out the stamp collecting cards. The most popular ICAA card, which Beatrix drew in 1932 and which was republished several times, featured the 'Rabbits' Christmas tree' with all the little animals dancing around it in a circle.[25]

Beatrix's advocacy of the ICAA through the use of Peter Rabbit and the Christmas cards connected her in another way to the sick and unfortunate around the country. She responded to the opportunity not only because she wanted to help sick children, but because she had suffered from rheumatic heart disease as a young woman, and knew its debilitating effects as an adult. Beatrix was a quietly determined advocate for improved public health, but especially for those women and children who lived in the unhealthy and polluted cities. Ironically her rare public visibility on the letterhead of the ICAA coincided with a successful performance of a dramatic version of *The Tailor of Gloucester* at Steinway Hall in London during the Christmas season in 1923. The publicity from these associations encouraged a persistent case of mistaken identity in the press that Beatrix and William found most annoying.

In January 1924 an article appeared in the *Illustrated Sunday Herald* which referred to Mrs Sidney Webb, 'whom many of us remember as the writer of children's books when she was Miss Beatrix Potter . . .' It was not the first time that the former Beatrice Potter Webb, the Fabian social reformer, and Beatrix Potter Heelis, an ardent Conservative, had been confused, even though their Christian names were spelled differently. Beatrix had ignored the previous insults 'of being mistaken for Mrs S. Webb' rather than elicit further publicity by trying to correct them, but this time the *Herald* article was accompanied by an unbecoming photograph of Mr and Mrs Sidney Webb. It was too much. William was especially upset, telling Beatrix, 'it is adding insult to injury to suggest that Miss Beatrix Potter is married "to such a little animal." '[26]

Beatrix sent a copy of the article to Fruing asking him to request a published correction, and she told Louie Choyce, 'The papers print the untruth prominently, and the contradiction so unprominently that it has no effect to stop the lie. The most laughable part of it was a photograph of Beatrix Potter & her husband – a horrid little fat man with a billy goat beard! Wm. was furious, said it was a libel on *him*.' Beatrix naively hoped the *Herald* was not read by 'the class who purchase my books', but she feared it would be reprinted elsewhere. With characteristic humour, however, she suggested the best correction might be to 'get photographed along with a favourite pig or cow and get it inserted in some more genteel newspaper!' She added a pen-and-ink drawing of herself next to a smiling pig.[27]

There was some irony in this case of mistaken identity, as Beatrice Potter Webb had grown up in a Unitarian household in Gloucestershire, the daughter of a wealthy industrialist, an entrepreneur the equal of Edmund Potter. And although Beatrix Heelis was unaware of it, they were distantly related through Webb's cousin, Charles Booth, the pioneering sociologist and advocate for the poor, who had been one of Bertram's proposers for membership at the Athenaeum. 'Bother Mrs Sidney Webb,' Beatrix wrote to Fruing a month later. 'Mr Heelis was asked in Ambleside yesterday whether his wife had married again.'[28]

The end of the war also brought with it the opportunity for new friendships, although until Beatrix Heelis met the Americans who came to Sawrey to see her, she had not realized how much she craved literary companionship. When Anne Carroll Moore, the Superintendent of Children's Work for the New York Public Library, asked to call on her during the summer of 1921, Beatrix had already a rather good opinion of Americans because of her friendship with the wealthy Miss Rebekah Owen. Miss Owen lived down the road beyond Hawkshead at Belmount Hall, a large Georgian house with extensive grounds and fine gardens. She was an eccentric friend of the novelist Thomas Hardy, and an authority on and collector of his work. She and her sister brought the property through William in 1899 and when they moved from New York City they hoped the writer might visit them in Hawkshead. Beatrix had known Miss Owen since she bought the farm. 'We have an American neighbour & friend,' she wrote to Fruing, '. . . who has proved to us that Americans can be "educated & literary" – in fact Miss Rebeccah [*sic*] O [Owen] – is alarming!' Rebekah, then in her late sixties, wore lipstick and shiny pink nail polish, and was driven about in a handsome car with an Italian chauffeur. Beatrix admired her taste in silver, books, and antique furniture, as well as her erudition and wide literary acquaintance. They shared an interest in horticulture and garden design, and both were active in supporting the collections at the Armitt Trust Library. It was on the basis of her admiration for Miss Owen that Beatrix agreed to meet Anne Carroll Moore.[29]

Moore had been in France during the summer of 1921 visiting children's libraries and contributing picture books so that those libraries devastated by the war might reopen. Once in England she visited the Warne offices and ordered fifty copies each of the newly translated *Pierre Lapin* and *Jeannot Lapin* (*Peter Rabbit* and *Benjamin Bunny*) for the library in Soissons. Fruing, who acted as gatekeeper for Beatrix, reluctantly forwarded her request to call at Sawrey. Moore's letter described her work in France, the French children's love of picture books, and her purchase of Potter's translations. Totally charmed and curious about this American librarian, Beatrix sent Moore a cordial invitation to lunch. 'I like the French translations, it is like reading some one else's work – refreshing.'[30]

Beatrix was curious to meet an intelligent woman who knew something about the genre of children's literature, as well as someone who was appreciative of her work. Although Beatrix was perfectly content in her marriage, she and William did not talk much about her books or her art. He knew little of the material in her old portfolios and even less of her current efforts. In this, as in other ways, Beatrix continued to compartmentalize her life – particularly her past life. But as a consequence she was hungry to talk to someone knowledgeable about both writers and writing for children.

Their lunch was an immediate success. Moore was given a tour of Hill Top Farm and shown the original sketches, drawings and watercolours for some of the little books. Interested in hearing more about the New York library programmes and the children there,

Beatrix asked Miss Moore to stay on for tea and finally to spend the night. Quite spontaneously, Beatrix invited her to choose a painting for the children in New York and allowed her to rummage about in her portfolios. They talked into the evening, and before Moore departed the next morning, Beatrix extended a welcome to return, and to 'send any of the storytellers in your children's libraries. I know they would be coming for the sake of the children and not out of mere curiosity.'[31]

Moore's visit reassured Beatrix that not only was her work still popular, but that it was appreciated and taken seriously. Aside from the occasional review that Fruing passed on to her, Beatrix got little creative affirmation of her work beyond cold sales figures. She had no sense that her books were regarded as anything more than toys. There were no equivalent professional children's librarians in Britain, and she knew no one with Moore's expertise. Still smarting from Fruing's cavalier rejection of 'The Tale of the Birds and Mr. Tod' the year before, Beatrix asked the American librarian what she thought of another book of rhymes similar to *Appley Dapply* and was rewarded with an enthusiastic response.

Energized by Moore's visit and her appreciation, Beatrix went back to work on *Cecily Parsley's Nursery Rhymes*, choosing another eight from her original collection. She told Fruing, 'I thought it was safely too late for the current season when I showed them to Miss Moore. I very much enjoyed talking to her – and there have been some more Americans since. And visitors in prospect for all summer; which is cheerful, but fatiguing.' Knowing that these rhymes were all he was likely to be able to extract from Beatrix that year, and acknowledging Moore's enthusiasm, Fruing agreed that *Cecily Parsley* would be the new Potter book for Christmas 1922.[32]

Beatrix chose two drawings of the 'Guinea-pigs' Garden' and a favourite rhyme, 'Nanny Netticoat', from her 1897 version. By spring she had recopied most of those she wanted to use and sent them off to Warne's. 'I would have got them done this week,' she wrote, 'but I am plagued with visitors & poultry, & a bad drought.' One of those visitors was Louie Choyce, who contributed the rhyme used to illustrate the gardening guinea pigs. Beatrix wrote to Louie after the book was published, 'you will recognize the bluebell wood, up Stoney Lane behind this house . . . Pity there was not room for the "red rose" verse. The other two verses fit beautifully.'[33]

Fruing asked for some curious alterations in the text. At first Beatrix acquiesced in his desire to omit the line in 'Three Blind Mice' about the farmer's wife 'cut[ting] off their tails', but later she insisted that it be restored, finding the rhyme incomplete without it. In the original title illustration Beatrix had shown Cecily Parsley, the little rabbit, brewing cider from red apples to make 'a good ale'. But the ever-cautious editor asked her to change the drink to 'cowslip wine', apparently unaware of its alcoholic content. Beatrix acknowledged her debt to Anne Carroll Moore, sending an autographed copy for Moore's doll, Nicholas Knickerbocker.[34]

Although Anne Carroll Moore did not return to Sawrey for many years, Beatrix welcomed a steady stream of other American visitors, delighted with the opportunity they brought her for adult friendship and a widened sense of the post-war world. The most important of these visitors came as a result of her long correspondence with Mary Gill, a Boston Unitarian who belonged to an organization called Friendly Links, which promoted intellectual exchange between British and American Unitarians. Gill came to Sawrey, along with her sister Rebecca Field, her husband William and their two daughters, shortly after Moore's visit. The William L. W. Field family would be an important link for Beatrix to an unusually distinguished group of artists and intellectuals in the Boston area. During the next decade the Fields were responsible for sending other well-educated and appreciative New Englanders to Near Sawrey.

These Americans were a rather self-selected group: New England Unitarians, well-educated, well-informed, wealthy enough to travel abroad after the war, and often naturalists and artists themselves. They all loved books, had an appreciation of children's literature and illustration, and all had well-mannered, interesting children who were delighted to see where Peter Rabbit lived. Field was then the Headmaster of Milton Academy, a fine preparatory school for boys outside Boston, and the Fields suggested that Beatrix meet the well-known American portrait painter Charles S. Hopkinson and his family. These new acquaintances were each invited to tea at Castle Cottage, allowed to see her portfolios, and in many instances given drawings to take home.[35]

It took a bit of reassurance for Beatrix to see any benefit in Miss Bertha Mahony's request for biographical information in 1925 as she had an 'intense dislike to advertisement'. But she knew that mystery also invited curiosity and was fearful that if she refused, she might once again be mistaken for the wife of Sidney Webb. Mahony, along with her friend and colleague Elinor Whitney, were the founders of *The Horn Book* magazine, a Boston publication devoted to children's books and reading. The magazine, a project of the Bookshop for Boys and Girls in Boston, which the two women had opened in 1916, was the first literary journal devoted entirely to children's literature. Unfortunately, Mahony was not as assertive as Anne Carroll Moore, and Fruing Warne successfully deflected her request to call on Beatrix in 1924. Instead, Mahony sent Beatrix a letter enquiring about the origins of Peter Rabbit, sending some copies of *The Horn Book*, and a request for biographical information for a reference book on children's authors. When Moore reassured her that Mahony's request was legitimate, Beatrix obliged.

Her first biographical entry read: 'Beatrix Potter is Mrs William Heelis. She lives in the north of England, her home is amongst the mountains and lakes that she has drawn in her picture books. Her husband is a lawyer. They have no family. Mrs Heelis is in her 60th year. She leads a very busy contented life, living always in the country and managing a large sheep farm on her own land.' Beatrix added offhandedly, 'I have never been able to understand what is the attraction of the book; but it continues to sell.' This initial and quite tenuous exchange of letters with Bertha Mahony began a remarkable friendship in letters between Beatrix and a most interesting and able American pioneer in children's literature. *The Horn Book* also proved an immensely useful literary vehicle for bringing Beatrix Potter to America.[36]

Changes in her farming friendships also provided unexpected opportunities for companionship. Louie Choyce was always welcome, but her visits were unpredictable. Beatrix missed her company and her physical help, particularly with the garden. Quite unexpectedly in 1922, she learned that Margaret 'Daisy' Hammond, the niece of her former governess, was in some financial distress after the death of her aunt. Beatrix invited Daisy and her companion Miss Cecily Mills to take the front half of the farm dwelling known as 'the Castle' for a six-month trial to see if they liked living in Near Sawrey.

Cecily found work as a day gardener and Daisy kept busy on Beatrix's farms. Both women got around the countryside on bicycles which they parked in Beatrix's wash house. After six months they were comfortably settled and Beatrix was pleased to have their company and their help, particularly in looking after the Revd AJ. They shared the work in the garden, and looked after fruit trees and the growing brood of turkey chicks. William liked the two women and also found them good company. For Beatrix it was like having younger, compatible cousins around.

But the most life-changing opportunities that came to Beatrix in the post-war years flowed from the pervasive influence of her mentor and friend, Hardwicke Rawnsley. His death in May 1920 pushed her to take a more public role in carrying on his legacy and making it her own.[37]

16

✎ *Legacies* ✎

OVER THE YEARS BEATRIX AND Rawnsley had frequently joined together to further the work of the National Trust. She had embraced his ideas on open footpaths, had campaigned with him against hydroplanes on the lakes, and had been a faithful, but mostly anonymous contributor to various appeals from the National Trust in the Lake District. Equally important, Beatrix had thought a great deal about the long-term value of the Trust as a hill country farmer and landowner. She not only approved of saving scenic shorelines from falling into private ownership, but she also agreed with Rawnsley that the Trust should expand its preservation efforts to include the culture of fell farming. With ever more tourist businesses catering to holiday trippers, country life as well as scenic beauty were threatened by division and development. As a result of Rawnsley's prodding, and the failure of many small farms in the post-war period, the Trust slowly began acquiring valley-bottom farms, lands at the head of watersheds and indigenous farmhouses, and in general broadening the definition of preservation.

This initiative was one that Beatrix could support enthusiastically, but she was under no illusions that it could soon make any significant difference, since it was always easier to raise money for dramatic vistas and grand estates than for run-down sheep farms or quaint Lakeland cottages. But Beatrix had also observed that quite often the first thing a small farmer would do when he got into debt was to cut down all the timber and to sell off the farm's sheep stocks, which in many cases meant scattering flocks of valuable Herdwick sheep. Beatrix instinctively widened her definition of Lake District preservation to include the Herdwick as well as timber culture.

She first learned to appreciate the qualities of the Herdwick from

Hardwicke Rawnsley. He wrote eloquently about this unique breed, believing that these particular little sheep, 'with their shy black faces', 'gave life to the mountain side'. Herdwick lambs are all black. As they mature their fleece turns grey and their faces go mostly white. In his essay 'A Crack about Herdwick Sheep' (1911), Rawnsley wrote enthusiastically of their culture, breeding and temperament, making clear why Herdwick were so uniquely suited to the fell environment.[1]

His advocacy was no mere romantic enthusiasm. Rawnsley recognized this breed had special qualities that made them particularly suited to fell farming. They are sturdy, hearty, agile sheep uniquely suited to the rocky terrain of the fells. They can survive the harsh climate on the short herbage of the high fells, and have been known to stay alive buried in snow for weeks, sometimes eating their own wool, sustained by its lanolin content. Among other attributes, the Herdwick graze heather and grass evenly, and keep bracken and scrub under control. But it is the Herdwicks' extraordinary memory to 'heaf' (to return to a certain place or pasture), which they acquire as lambs, that most distinguishes them. In practical terms this heafing instinct means they do not require fencing on the fell, nor extensive shepherding to bring them down to pasture. Their coarse wool makes them unsuitable to raise for the luxury markets, but as a breed the Herdwick were, and remain, ecologically and economically indispensable to the continuation of fell farming.[2]

As secretary of the National Trust, Hardwicke Rawnsley lent his public support to efforts to promote the Herdwick. His son Noel, along with S. D. Stanley Dodgson, an energetic stockman from Cockermouth, promoted the Herdwick as a pure-bred sheep stock when they started the Herdwick Sheep Association in 1899. Rawnsley and Dodgson worked hard to improve the breed, and to get geographically far-flung sheep men to agree on pedigree registration and exhibition standards. By 1916 the Herdwick Sheep Association and several other groups of breeders had coalesced into the Herdwick Sheep Breeders' Association. The first Flock Book was published in 1920, ironically the same year that Hardwicke Rawnsley died.[3]

Rawnsley's efforts to preserve the culture of fell farming played a role in Beatrix's remarkable decision to buy Troutbeck Park Farm in the summer of 1923. A year later she became one of the very few female members of the Herdwick Sheep Breeders' Association, an indication of her commitment to their preservation, as well as to the farming, breeding and shepherding customs that surrounded them.[4]

Troutbeck Park Farm occupies the head of the Trout Beck valley, which runs up into the fells to the north-east out of Windermere, through the quaint seventeenth-century village of Troutbeck. The road rises dramatically to the Kirkstone Pass, the highest road in the Lake District. From the Pass there is a superb view out over the head of the valley with its remarkable Tongue (Old Norse *tunga* or tableland between the two valleys) that joins Hird Gill on the one side and Hag Gill on the other. The picturesque white farmhouse and outbuildings of Troutbeck Park Farm are nestled at the foot of the Tongue on the valley bottom. It was then, and is still, a magnificent property of nearly 2,000 acres; a spectacular farm, one of the largest in the Lake District, with the capacity to support several thousand sheep.

Like the publication of *The Tale of Peter Rabbit* in 1902, Beatrix's purchase of Troutbeck Park Farm began an equally momentous entrepreneurial adventure. Both were creative endeavours, and in both cases her love of the natural world, her delight in country life, her willingness to work hard and her instinctive business acumen were essential to success. But Beatrix could not have undertaken this new enterprise without the knowledge and dedication of her country solicitor husband, William. While she was accepted, even liked, by many of the locals, she would always be an 'off-comer'. By 1923 her wealth, her unpredictable crustiness, even her absorption with farming and her animals set her apart. William Heelis, on the other hand, had a long connection to Westmorland. His familiarity with old district families and their properties, his participation in sports, hunting and country dancing, and his easygoing personality were vital assets. Without William's expertise and political finesse, Beatrix could never have become the successful landowner, farm manager and sheep breeder that she did. The restoration of Troutbeck Park Farm was a joint business venture by two people who shared a love of the countryside, had a passion for its preservation, and supported the mission of the National Trust.

William, always attentive to potential sales of farm properties, had learned that developers were poised to buy the rundown Troutbeck Park, intending to build holiday houses on the bottom land. With his help Beatrix had the advantage over her competitors, and outbid the developers. The purchase of Troutbeck Park Farm was an ambitious effort under any circumstances. The deed for the farm contains twenty-five separately described parcels. She paid £8,000 for the 1,875 acres. The farm was conveyed to her on 28 August 1923. Beatrix became a significant landholder in the Lake district, and the owner of a large and important flock of Herdwick sheep. Her engagement with the restoration of this unique landscape became an absorbing passion, all but replacing her interest in writing books for children. All her creative efforts were directed into farming, breeding Herdwicks, and promoting their importance to the culture of the Lake District.[5]

Troutbeck Park Farm had always been a magical place for Beatrix. Once an ancient Norman deer park, it was home to a variety of bird and animal life, stands of old forest, ruined walls and ancient stone huts and cairns. From her earliest visit to Windermere in 1895, Beatrix had loved to walk out on the Tongue, looking for fossils, sometimes coming just to hear the susurrus of wind, stopping to eat her bread and cheese, taking refuge from the rain in an old barn. She found it 'uncanny; a place of silences and whispering echoes'. She witnessed her first Coniston fox-hunt at the Park, shortly after buying it, watching in amazement as the hounds bravely spilled down over the crags and fells in pursuit of their quarry. That day she had taken off her shoes and stockings and waded through the beck, the only clean place on the farm, to rejoin the hunt spectators.[6]

When Beatrix bought the farm it was under a tenancy agreement to Mrs Leake and her two sons that ran for three more years. The Leakes had allowed the farmland and the pastures to erode and the stream was badly polluted. The lovely white farmhouse and outbuildings were rundown and badly in need of expensive repairs. While William tried rather ineffectively to get the Leakes out of the farm sooner so repairs could be started, Beatrix did as she had at Hill Top, adding land to the perimeters of the farm as buffers against development. Between December 1923 and September 1927 she added seven closes, including several small contiguous farms, spending another £4,000 to insure that her intake fields at the Park were protected. She and William did this gradually, first buying parcels along the road, and then making sure the owners of bordering lands knew that she would buy them out at a fair market price when the current tenants left or died. Her aim was to hold all the land along the road frontages, making any interior property worthless.[7]

From the outset, Beatrix planned to bequeath Troutbeck Park Farm to the National Trust at her death. She made out a new will in which she stated her intention. Deeply moved by the mysterious qualities of the place, and so determined to preserve something of that sense of peace into the future, she added a clause to the terms of the bequest, forbidding hunting by otter hounds and harriers any-where in the Park. However, Beatrix said nothing about her plans to Samuel Hamer, the new secretary of the National Trust. Instead, her first extant letters to Rawnsley's successor detail her concern about other particularly vulnerable properties in the area: the possible sale of land high in the silent Mickelden Ghyll in Langdale for holiday huts, and the potential sale of the Old Bridge House in Ambleside. She argued astutely that although the structure was architecturally without much distinction, saving it would preserve what little was left of old Ambleside and would endear the Trust to the townspeople. Beatrix was cautiously trying to take Hamer's measure before she revealed her intended bequest. Hamer's response to her concerns, now lost, must have met with approval.[8]

Beginning early in 1925, there ensued an almost weekly exchange of letters between the two. Early letters to Hamer trace Beatrix's evolving philosophy of preservation and her sincere desire to educate the new Trust secretary about a variety of threats from development to a unique and fragile environment. 'I usually know my mind,' she confided, 'but I am puzzled. Small purchases are a wasteful way of buying land. Large properties are down in value & unsaleable. What perplexes me is whether it is wisest to pick up little bits, when I have opportunity, or which I can afford; *or to wait*. With the risk of the place waited for being spoilt in the meantime. Such a little can do it; one red tiled bungalow on a spot like Troutbeck Tongue!'[9]

Beatrix had both a vision and specific plans to implement it. It was essential to her long-term goals that the National Trust become a partner at Troutbeck. She told Hamer, 'It is a dream, – or *was* – that I wish all that corner of the district were a reservation, running back against the Haweswater land, bounded by the Kirkstone road. The land . . . is as nearly "plain" = unbeautiful as Lakes land can be, but with judicious planting it could be made interesting . . . [It] seemed to me to be one of the few corners of the district not exploited; and curiously unspoilt.' Beatrix knew preserving such a large swathe of land was likely to be impossible, but her scheme encompassed valleys and watersheds, acknowledging that the purchase of one farm here and one there could not prevent the damage done by haphazard development.[10]

When at last the Leakes were out of Troutbeck, Beatrix decided not to re-let the farm for at least two years because the land and the sheepstock were in such a derelict and unhealthy condition. She wanted a free hand to start over. 'It is a most lovely place and a fine farm,' she assured Hamer, 'but until the mosses & drains are cleared, and the sheepstock is reclaimed by proper management – it is not fit to let.'[11]

It was not until June 1926, a month shy of her sixtieth birthday, that Beatrix finally divulged her intention to bequeath Troutbeck Park Farm to the National Trust. 'From the point of view of the Trust,' she told Hamer, 'the desirable prospect would be that I survive to get the farm on a sound basis, and that I find a well chosen tenant . . . But if I should happen to end while the farm is still in my hands I cannot disguise that I should be leaving a handful for my executors & the Trust to deal with.' She had rejected the idea of extensive afforestation – in part because government subsidies had been reduced, but mostly because she believed it would ruin the landscape and take away important intake land. But she had already planted five acres of larch for replacing fence posts and had determined that the landlord's stock of sheep be set at 1,100, 'all to be pure bred heafed Herdwicks'. Beatrix insisted that there should always be a large landlord stock at Troutbeck as a hedge against a tenant getting into debt and having the heaf stolen or lost. She was naively optimistic about what lay ahead, and it was just as well. 'I have had a good deal of worry and hard work with the Park,' she told the secretary, 'but I have had never for a moment regretted the purchase.'[12]

With much of its fell grazing lands at high altitudes, Troutbeck Park was a perfect farm for the Herdwick. But in order to breed healthy lambs, Beatrix first had to solve the problem of wet fields, stream pollution, bad drains and 'rotten' sheep. When Beatrix bought Troutbeck, there was a nucleus of some eight hundred 'landlord's sheep' on the farm, pure-bred Herdwick, as well as many cross-bred sheep. But much of the flock were 'rotten' with parasitic liver fluke. One shepherd remembered that 'the lambs were dying like flies'. Liver fluke is a variety of trematode flatworm that thrives in damp fields and standing water – conditions that characterized most of the valley land at the Park. Once it has infected one or two animals, the fluke can run through a whole flock. Cleaning up the pastures of Troutbeck Park proved a long and expensive process.[13]

Liver fluke was not the only challenge Beatrix confronted. When she bought the farm foot-and-mouth disease was still affecting the movement of sheep and cattle in the area, and there was a subsequent outbreak of the infection in 1926–7. Nearer to hand, the barns at Troutbeck were infested with rats 'who came out & fought and ate one another'. Although they were thinned with traps and poison, Beatrix worried that the collie puppies might get into the poison. The 'yellows', an acute form of jaundice, was also a recurrent problem, not only for Troutbeck farm dogs, but for dogs all over the Lake District, and it had no cure. A few years later Beatrix discovered that canine distemper was rampant in the derelict dog kennels at the Park. She disinfected them and eventually built a new, larger one. A farm the size of Troutbeck was hard on any working dog, and Beatrix, who was enormously fond of her sheepdogs, did what she could to keep them healthy. On arriving at the farm, her shepherds knew she always went first to check on the dogs.[14]

Beatrix also spent time and money cleaning up the dirty seven-teenth-century farmhouse. While she was about the repairs, she had a room made up for herself, using it initially as a kind of farm office. Later it became a place she could rest after a long walk on the Tongue, draw and write, as well as review accounts. She furnished it with some favourite pieces and eventually she set up a microscope there where she checked sheep dung for parasites. The farmhouse had no good old oak except a floor, but Beatrix improved things by moving in one of her best sale pieces, a large oak cupboard dated 1667, and a heavy gateleg table. She considered these antique pieces ones 'belonging to the house', telling Hamer '[i]t would be safe to "let" them with the house, as Lakes housewives are accustomed to the care of old oak furniture'.[15]

After talking to many people, Beatrix appointed Jimmy Hislop as her farm manager and moved him and his family into the main Troutbeck farmhouse. Owning both a large fell farm in Troutbeck and a smaller lowland farm in Near Sawrey, Beatrix needed managers at each with skills appropriate to the very different environments and animal herds. At Troutbeck she installed both a farm manager and later a head shepherd. Hill Top required only a farm manager. Sometime after hiring Hislop, she designed a new smaller house for the head shepherd which she had built next to the main house. It mimics in design the details of the main house, including cylindrical chimneys and mullion and transom windows, but has its own garth or paddock around. Inside, Beatrix placed a datestone on the fireplace lintel to commemorate her architectural efforts.[16]

Given the precarious conditions of the Troutbeck flock, Beatrix needed to find just the right shepherd – one who was familiar with hefted sheep, and someone who would be careful to keep the sheep stock from being depleted and the heaf lost. After consulting with a number of Herdwick breeders and other farmers, Beatrix asked Tommy to drive her to the Gregg farm at Townend to interview a shepherd there named Tom Storey. The Greggs had been forced to downsize their herd, and Storey was looking for other employment. As the owner of a large high-fell farm, Beatrix now had the opportunity to expand her flock and she wanted to improve her Herdwick breeding stock. She had learned enough about Storey to think that he was the man she needed.[17]

Tom Storey always described himself as 'pigeon-chested' from a childhood pulmonary illness, but he was physically powerful enough. He was rather short in stature, but ruggedly handsome, with bright blue eyes, dimples in his cheeks and a cleft chin. He had the direct manner of the north-country stockman and spoke his mind without hesitation. He had married in 1922 and lived with his wife and two small children, Geoff and Freda, at High Green Cottages in Troutbeck village. Tom vividly remembered his first encounter with Mrs Heelis when she came to see him at Townend Farm.

We'd just finished milking and my boss came into the shippon and said, 'there's a lady wants to see you.' 'Mrs Heelis.' She was quite smart for her age . . . For her age she looked, well a bonny looking woman to tell you the truth. That's what I thought about her. 'You're Tom Storey,' she said. 'Yes.' 'Well, I've come to see you about working for me. Will you go to Troutbeck Park to be my shepherd?' I said, 'Yes, I'll go if the money's right.'

Beatrix then asked him what his wage was and when he told her, she said she would double it. So Tom Storey went to Troutbeck Park, but continued to live with his young family in the village overlooking the farm.[18]

Tom recalled that a new cure for fluke in the form of a capsule had recently become available. He told Beatrix about it and she immediately sent for it. As a naturalist Beatrix had a keen interest in scientific farming, whether it be finding a new castrating knife or a new sheep dip. By 1926 she realized she had little to lose by trying almost any remedy to clear the sheep at Troutbeck. Storey recalled about the same time that a vet in Newcastle developed an injection against the 'drop', or grass staggers, a sudden respiratory attack. Tom tried it on one sheep with immediate benefit. Word got around and soon all the sheep breeders were using it. Beatrix's managers and shepherds always found her interest in science and animal husbandry and her willingness to experiment admirable. It further distinguished her as a woman farmer and sheep breeder. As Storey put it, 'she was very good at sending for new cures, nothing was too good for the sheep'. Whether the new worming capsule was the agent of success against the liver fluke or not, Storey lambed 1,000 sheep at Troutbeck in the spring of 1927. After that, Beatrix was, as he put it, 'set up'.[19]

The successful lambing at Troutbeck was not all due to Tom Storey, however boldly he might have claimed it. Joseph Moscrop, a shy, unassuming, but highly skilled shepherd from the north of Cumberland, near the Scottish border, first came to the Park with his fine dog for lambing in the spring of 1926, working there and at Sawrey. Joseph was then just 40 years old. He was slight of build, but healthy and strong, with an easy athleticism. He was unremarkable in appearance except for a weakness in his left eye. Like many who had lived in the rural countryside from childhood, he was observant of the natural world and comfortable in it. He had been an experienced farm worker before he enlisted in the army. His letters from the Greek front in the First World War to his brother comment perceptively on the birds and vegetation he found interesting.[20]

Joseph usually hired out at the spring hiring fairs around Whitsun, either for six months or a year. He had experienced a variety of farming environments by the time he probably answered an advertisement that Beatrix Heelis had placed at one of the fairs. Moscrop had good references, was familiar with different breeds of sheep and cattle, and was aware of how livestock responded to different soils and grasses. Like most shepherds, he lived at the farm that employed him. Although Joseph was shy by nature, he was not at all afraid to speak his mind. He was a meticulous worker, who saw to whatever needed doing. Joseph never married, though Beatrix wondered in 1928 if he might have a love interest. He was, however, a religious man who quoted easily from the Bible and in later life joined the Lord's Day Observance Society. Perhaps his most distinguishing quality was his deeply positive attitude about life; indeed about whatever it was he was doing. It was his outlook and disposition, as well as his knowledge and love of animals, that drew Beatrix to him.[21]

Beatrix was so pleased with Moscrop's work that she hired him every spring for the next seventeen years. Her terms were always four weeks, with Joseph bringing his own dog, although occasionally he had to use one of hers. And each year, almost as a ritual, the two haggled over wages, with Beatrix usually giving a bit more than she had initially offered; but in hard times Joseph also made adjustments. Their negotiations were important more for the symbolic measure of respect each accorded the other than for the actual sum finally agreed upon.[22]

Their employment relationship soon settled into an easy pattern. Early each year Beatrix wrote to engage Joseph, telling him the date that the tups (rams) had been put to the ewes so he could calculate the roughly five months' time until the start of lambing. In early April she would write again confirming the date she needed him, telling him which dog was working and which was not, and enclosing a postal order to cover half his transportation costs. Beatrix knew that Joseph was a 'diamond in the rough', and valued his friendship as well as his knowledge.[23]

The first spring that Beatrix owned Troutbeck, Moscrop worked alongside Hislop and another shepherd, Ted Wood, who was in charge of grazing. When Tom Storey became head shepherd in 1927, Joseph came again for lambing. When lambing was over, John Mackereth announced that he was retiring after eleven years as manager of Hill Top Farm. Mackereth's primary interest had been in cattle breeding. During his tenure Beatrix had increased her Galloway herd, bred some fine calves, and made money on meat, milk and butter. Beginning around 1919, Beatrix and Mackereth entered some of her Herdwick sheep at the regional sheep shows held every year in August and September. But Hill Top sheep had not had much success in the judging. Mackereth's retirement presented Beatrix with an opportunity to expand her breeding programme at Hill Top.[24]

In June 1927 Beatrix drove out to Troutbeck Park to have another talk with Tom Storey. 'I want to ask you something Storey.' 'Oh, aye?' 'Will you come and work for me and manage Hill Top, Sawrey?' 'I want to show Herdwick sheep, and I've heard you've done a bit.' So, after consulting his wife, Tom and his family moved to Near Sawrey. It was always Tom's considered opinion that to make money Hill Top Farm should not have had any Herdwick sheep, but rather cross-bred sheep for the better meat and wool markets. In fact, the Sawrey countryside was really too soft for the wiry, small-hoofed breed, but as Tom recalled, 'it was her love was Herdwick sheep'. Beatrix proudly entered the new smit mark for her sheep stock at Hill Top in the Herdwick Flock Book. It was the letter 'H' for Heelis.[25]

Since the sheep exhibition season was soon upon them, Tom came over to the Castle Farm to look over her sheep there. As he later recalled, even he was surprised when he recognized a ram there called 'Cowie' that he had picked out at the big Eskdale show when it was a lamb. 'Cowie' had gone on to win at Eskdale four years in a row. He must have been in a group of sheep Beatrix bought from John Gregg. Storey was enormously pleased with his luck in rediscovering that prize ram. But it was typical of his remarkable ability to remember individual animals. Later, with Beatrix in tow, he picked out a few lambs to enter at the local Hawkshead show. Two of them won a first prize. Storey recalled Beatrix's delight: 'She was as proud as a dog with two tails as the saying goes. It was the first time she'd won a first prize. I said I was glad for that and I hoped we'd win a few more.' Tom began a breeding programme at Hill Top that by 1930 was one of the most successful in the area.[26]

Beatrix and her new farm manager developed a mutual respect for one another over the years which went beyond that normally accorded by employer to employee or by farm owner to manager. Storey was unusual in that he apparently had no trouble working for a female employer. This is not to say he did not have a certain male chauvinism, but he respected her. Beatrix rarely gave him a direct order, confident in Tom's knowledge of livestock and their needs, as well as in his ability to manage the planting and harvesting of fodder crops. She often worked, getting in the harvest along with the other hands, but when she did, she took orders from him. Storey was quick to learn how 'Mrs Heelis' liked things done. Habits were established early and continued with little change. Early every morning when Tom brought fresh milk over to Castle Cottage he found Beatrix up and ready for the day. If something special was required, they discussed it then.

But sheep breeding and exhibiting was one area where Tom's chauvinism was hard to disguise. Tom liked to tell of one occasion

early in his tenure when he and Mrs Heelis disagreed. As he remembered it, he had been sorting out sheep in preparation for the
Keswick show when he noticed that some sheep had already had
their fleeces ruddled (marked with an iron-based red powder also
used to dye a fleece so as to hide its imperfections), identifying
them as show sheep. Storey, however, did not think highly of these
particular sheep and was intending to take them back down to the
intake, when Beatrix came in and asked him why he was removing
them. '"Well, she says, haven't they been show sheep?" I told her
they were no good to show and she was quite cut up about it. Well,
now I didn't let her carry on. "If you want these sheep showing, Mrs
Heelis, you'd better have Mackereth back." "I won't show them,
they're not fit to show."' At that, according to Tom, Mrs Heelis
stomped off to the Hill Top kitchen where she burst in on Tom's
wife. 'I'll tell you what it is, Mrs Storey,' she reportedly said, 'your
husband's a bad tempered little devil.' Shortly after that, Tom began
to win prizes with her sheep, and Beatrix apparently never intervened
again.[27]

Stockmen on Bertram Potter's farm in Ancrum, who endured
Beatrix's comments during her annual visits, some of the shepherds
at Troutbeck and some sheep men who competed with her at the
local shows, liked to say that Mrs Heelis did not really know much
about sheep. This was almost always the bravado of men uncomfortable with a woman, and an off-comer. They mistook the eccentric
farmer in her dowdy Herdwick wool suit and wooden clogs, thinking
her a sentimental old woman who loved sheep but did not know
much about them. The normally reticent Mrs Heelis loved talking to
the other sheep farmers, stockmen and breeders, indeed anyone who
knew anything about sheep. She did not care 'a two-penny bit' what
they thought of her or what they thought she knew.[28]

But Beatrix Heelis was an expert in judging the qualities of all sorts
of animals, including Herdwicks. Like her thorough understanding of
rabbits and mice, she knew the proper anatomy of the Herdwick, and
of a good many other breeds of sheep and cattle as well, from years
of close observation, handling and drawing. She may on occasion
have confused individual sheep, but she was a shrewd judge of good

body line, leg, bone type, head and wool. Little by little she earned the grudging respect of most of her fellow sheep breeders. This was not easy. Understandably, it was hard for stockmen to admit a woman to their ranks, let alone accord her any expertise. There was also turf competition between sheep breeders from Westmorland and Lancashire which affected how much credit any breeder was given. Joseph Moscrop was one of the few males who was not threatened by her participation, knowledge or strongly held opinions. He respected Beatrix as an equal in animal husbandry.[29]

Tom readily conceded that Beatrix excelled at drawing sheep. 'One spring she came across and she said "Storey, the next lamb that dies, could you cut its head off for me and skin it back to the shoulder." ' The next day he came to find the sheep's head pinned against a wall in the meadow and Beatrix sitting on a stone sketching it. 'It was really a grand job when she finished it.'[30]

When Storey moved over to Hill Top Farm in the autumn of 1927 Beatrix hired Anthony 'Tant' Benson to replace him as her shepherd at Troutbeck. Benson was a local man who had worked at the Park as a boy. At their interview, he asked her what wage he would receive, telling her he had been getting 25s. a week. Mrs Heelis once again offered him double. 'Tant' was happy to come back. He and his family first lived in the village, as Storey had. But when the smaller shepherd's house was ready, the Bensons moved into that. 'She kept us in coal. She fed five or six dogs. So that wage was as good as 60s.,' Benson remembered. He stayed as shepherd at Troutbeck for fifteen years, but during all those years Mrs Heelis never paid him his wages directly. Instead, when she came to the Park every two weeks with the wages, she went directly into the Benson cottage and left the money with Benson's wife. Beatrix believed strongly that the money should go to the family.[31]

Even for the most experienced farm managers and sheep breeders there was an inherent unpredictability to hill-country sheep farming. Changeable weather and the scarcity of good pasture could play havoc, even with the best of care. A severe snowstorm and freezing temperatures under a bright moon always made Beatrix anxious for her sheep. Although she was quick to adopt the latest remedies against disease, she also respected many of the traditional ways. What saved sheep after a big snowfall on a low-lying farm like Hill Top, where hay and ash were available, was impossible to do for a large fell flock at Troutbeck. Beatrix honoured the old custom of having some 'crop' ash and holly growing near the farmhouses and urged her tenants to do likewise. Both could be cut and given to the sheep in severe winters.

The spring of 1927 was unusually wet and the sheep's wool never entirely dried out. As a consequence, they suffered from skin sores and infections. Damp weather also brought on foot rot, a kind of decomposing horn that resulted in lameness. Hoofs had to be pared and dressed with a variety of solutions. In the 1920s farmers still disputed whether foot rot was infectious, but most took precautions against a potential parasite. Pests and infectious diseases afflicting sheep, indeed animal husbandry in general, continued to occupy Beatrix's attention long after she had solved the immediate problem of liver fluke at Troutbeck. She waged war against 'the fly' or maggot-fly, to which a milking ewe was particularly vulnerable. The fly deposited maggot worms in any skin abrasion and these quickly ate away the flesh of the sheep leaving deep, painful wounds. Beatrix used standard sheep dips of carbolic acid and linseed oil, but these were labour-intensive and only effective for a short time. She also experimented with a variety of fly powders and even invented a kind of trap for the maggot-fly which she tried out on her sheep at Troutbeck. 'I am sure it would pay to tackle the *blue-bottle*', she wrote to a sheep-breeding friend, 'instead of so much dip and supervision of suffering sheep and lambs.'[32]

Personnel problems involved in managing her farms were sometimes more vexing than animal pests. When Jimmy Hislop abruptly gave notice that he was leaving Troutbeck just after Christmas 1927, Beatrix had no choice but to promote young Tom Martin in his place. Much after the fact, she discovered there had been a serious case of sheep stealing at the Park which the timid Martin had not reported until it was too late either to find the sheep or to file a police report. The new dog she hoped to have ready for lambing that spring had not worked, and another she had just been given tended to ramble. She hoped Joseph could find a reliable dog before he came, but the uncertainty made her uneasy. 'Things have "hatched" badly here this spring,' she wrote. 'There are seasons when things go wrong; and they just have to be lived through; like the old inscription "Good times and bad times; all times get over."'[33]

But Hislop's departure gave Beatrix an opportunity to make a fresh start at Troutbeck and to hire a new 'head man'. She put everyone on notice until she could find the right person. It took her the better part of a year. George Walker was a highly regarded stockman who had been managing a large farm for the Greenside (Lead) Mining Company in Ullswater. Beatrix lured him away with the promise not only of better wages, but also the opportunity to manage one of the premier farms in the district. She also interviewed his wife Lucy, as she understood the farm manager's wife was critical to the success of any farm. But with a farm as remote as Troutbeck, she wanted to be sure the wife was not only a reliable housekeeper, but had the necessary skills and abilities to help manage the property and look after the domestic animals. The Walkers and their teenage children Robin and Mary moved into the big white Troutbeck farmhouse early in 1930. Lucy Walker proved as invaluable as George – although she often felt isolated and lonely during the long winters with a wireless that had limited reception at the bottom of the valley. Beatrix refused to allow a more powerful aerial attached to the roof of the farmhouse because it was not in keeping with the historic exterior.[34]

By 1928 the worldwide depression had begun to affect agriculture and food exports. Prices for wool and mutton had fallen sharply. Livestock farmers all over Britain were discouraged, and tenant farmers everywhere were having a particularly difficult time holding on to their land. Beatrix wrote to Moscrop in January 1929, hoping to persuade him to 'resist the hiring fairs' and come to Troutbeck again. 'A lambing time at the Park would not be itself without Joseph,' she told him. She had made improvements to the Park including a brick addition, new kennels, enlarged bunk rooms for the shepherds and miles of new fence. But she confessed she was tired. 'Perhaps . . . it is partly "anno domini" – I am turned 62.'[35]

When Joseph arrived at the Park in April, he brought two new dogs since many of the dogs at the farm had died of the 'yellows'. Beatrix was enormously relieved to have him. But like most fell farms, Troutbeck too suffered a bad season. The wind had turned cold quite suddenly and dried out much of the land, and the lambing ewes were spread out and difficult to get to. There were many tiny, underweight lambs. Even with Joseph's tender care, and the drop or two of gin that he sometimes added to the bottle of warm milk he used to revive distressed and chilled newborns, many were lost. As Joseph later reported to his brother, 'Mrs Heelis had the worst crop of lambs on record, but certainly the best record of calves.'[36]

The agricultural shows that autumn, however, told a different story. When the principal sheep breeders gathered twice a year at the Keswick Tup Fair, in May and October, or at the auctions and local sheep shows held around the district, Beatrix happily joined the Herdwick men and listened to their talk. Her rounded figure, clad in her favourite Herdwick tweed suit – brown felt hat clamped to her head with a black elastic under her chin – soon became a familiar sight at the shows and around the judging pens. Beatrix found certain amusement in the fact that although she was a total abstainer from alcohol, most of the sheep breeders' business meetings were held in pubs or taverns. She dutifully attended, but she rarely stayed for the meal afterwards, concocting some excuse to take Tom Storey off to a tearoom where she felt more comfortable.[37]

Beatrix won 'a number of first prizes' for her Herdwick ewes. 'I think we could have gone to the "Royal", ' she announced proudly, 'as we beat Willie Wilson with lambs yesterday at Ennerdale, and he has held the field a many seasons as Herdwick king. It is lovely weather and our hay & bit of harvest is in, so we are enjoying the "shows" with a clean conscience . . .' Beatrix's account of her prize-winning sheep was modest. Her Herdwick ewes took all the top prizes at the big shows at Keswick, Cockermouth, Ennerdale, Loweswater and Eskdale.[38]

The following year, 1930, Beatrix's sheep took top honours again. 'We had our pretty little Baa's at Ennerdale Show last week, and yesterday at Keswick,' Beatrix reported enthusiastically, during glorious September weather. 'The sheep have been very successful in the female classes; 16 first prizes, and several shows yet to come. Including Loweswater.' All her spare time was taken up in travelling with William from one local agricultural show to another. She explained to a friend in the United States that her sheep 'have got a lot of prizes this year, including a silver challenge cup for the best ewe in the Lake district. I hold it for a year; if I take it 3 years it becomes mine; I think next year is pretty safe, as my younger sheep was never beaten – but 3 years would be a stroke of good luck!' Beatrix's sheep won dozens of firsts, and her Hill Top ewes remained unbeaten for the next nine years. She took home silver tankards, salvers and teapots, but, as an abstainer, she always gave Tom the tankards. Over the next decade Beatrix's Herdwicks won the champion cup several times. Her most famous ewe was called Water Lily. It was one of the progenitors of the prize-winning Hill Top ewes Tom Storey bred. In the *Herdwick Flock Book* for 1929–30 there is a photograph of Tom displaying Water Lily at one of the Cumberland shows. She was a beautiful animal and Beatrix had good reason to be proud of the line of Herdwick ewes she was establishing.[39]

Beatrix kept careful notes in the programme of each agricultural show, noting the top prize winners, as well as an especially good lamb, or a particularly inferior animal. As the economy declined, fewer breeders chose to exhibit at the smaller shows. Even so, it was especially gratifying for Beatrix, at the age of 71, to be asked to be a co-judge at the 1937 Lowick show for all the classes of Herdwick sheep and collie dogs. 'Dear dogs,' she wrote to Louie Choyce afterwards. 'I would have liked to give prizes to half a dozen instead of 3.' But at the important Cockermouth show she had plenty of entries. She won another cup outright and two other prizes for the same ram. No activity engaged her more completely or brought her so much pleasure, although breeding and raising Galloway cattle had become a close rival. The cattle were a passion which she shared with Joseph Moscrop, whose knowledge of cattle was extensive and whose opinions she always solicited when the time came to buy another animal.[40]

In 1935 Beatrix's accomplishments as a Herdwick breeder brought her unique recognition within the very male-dominated sheep-breeding community. Mrs H. B. Heelis was named president of the

Keswick Agricultural Show. 'I guess they think its time I should give some prizes as well as take some, which I am very willing to do,' she wrote, 'so long as I am not expected to make a speech.' Hardwicke Rawnsley would have been proud when, at the Keswick show, where her ewes were again unbeaten, the cup was awarded to her by S. D. Stanley Dodgson of Armaside, son of one of the founders of the Herdwick Sheep Association. Two weeks later she won the challenge cup for the third time at Loweswater, earning the President's Prize. One incident at a Hawkshead show where she had been asked to preside some years earlier always amused her: 'We had speeches at lunch,' she recalled, '. . . and an old jolly farmer – replying to a "toast" – likened me – the president – to the first prize cow! He said she was a lady-like animal; and one of us had neat legs, and walked well; but I think that was the cow not me, being slightly lame.'[41]

With Walker and Benson at Troutbeck Park, Storey at Hill Top, and Moscrop at lambing time, by the end of 1930 Beatrix had assembled a team of managers and shepherds that she could trust. It had taken her seven years of hard work and careful oversight, but in spite of bad winters and declining wool markets, her several farms, many fields and thousands of real animals were doing well. Beatrix had successfully carried on Rawnsley's legacy to preserve the Herdwick. She had saved a unique and important fell farm, and had begun an alliance with the National Trust. But Beatrix's imaginary animals and their London publisher had not fared as well.[42]

17

❧ *Americans* ❧

TROUTBECK PARK FARM HAD CHANGED Beatrix's outlook as well as absorbed her energy. The only new books since 1922 had been *Jemima Puddle-Duck's Painting Book*, and a new edition of *The Roly-Poly Pudding*, retitled as *The Tale of Samuel Whiskers* and reduced to little book format, which was published in October 1926. She worked half-heartedly on a 'Peter Rabbit Almanac', which she put together from some odds and ends in the spring of 1927 at the urging of an American painter from Boston who had come on a visit with his family. But it required more work on the blocks than she had patience for.[1]

Although Fruing Warne kept pressing for another book, Beatrix was far too busy and, in truth, too happy with her farm to oblige. Some years before, Fruing had even made a pilgrimage to Near Sawrey, hoping to cajole her into doing something, but the visit had only put her off. 'It brought back such a nightmare of painful memories that it took six months to forget again,' she told him. Her memories of Norman and her sense of betrayal by Harold Warne's deception had never entirely left her. Although she was fond of Fruing, and had once been of his children, she had never felt him to be a close creative collaborator, and she was thoroughly tired of rabbits. 'It is not the least use asking me to write or draw to order. I neither can nor will.' She admitted she felt 'dried up', and in fact had not done much more than the minimum to protect her financial interests, being more excited by new ideas for merchandise, such as baby blankets and bibs, than writing stories.[2]

In the spring of 1927 Beatrix joined in the National Trust's campaign to rescue Cockshott Point from town development. It was a particularly lovely historic strip of land that jutted out into

Windermere near the ferry, and provided a peaceful view of the high fells across the lake. When the subscription was in danger of falling short, Beatrix had the idea that perhaps readers of *The Horn Book*, and other American friends who seemed so fond of Peter Rabbit, might like to contribute to 'The Windermere Fund'. Ever since she had responded to Bertha Mahony's request for biographical information, Beatrix had been reading *The Horn Book*, which remained much to her liking. The writing was fresh and the journal exhibited good sense in its efforts to educate the public about books for children. Beatrix applauded Mahony's efforts to improve the quality of children's literature.[3]

Her scheme was to offer fifty original autographed drawings, copied from four of the illustrations for Peter Rabbit, for sale at a guinea (£1. 1s.) to help save Cockshott Point. In May she sent the packet of drawings along with an appeal letter to Bertha Mahony, hoping that *The Horn Book* and the Bookshop for Boys and Girls would act as agent for her efforts. The appeal was made by 'Beatrix Potter and Peter Rabbit' under the auspices of the National Trust. Mahony published Beatrix's letter along with a colour plate showing a sample watercolour and an editorial endorsement in the August 1927 issue of *The Horn Book*. Beatrix had written an engaging appeal: 'Peter Rabbit is not begging for himself – and he offers something. "Beatrix Potter" has very much at heart an appeal to raise a fund to save a strip of foreshore woodland and meadow . . . from immenent [*sic*] risk of disfigurement by extensive building and town extension.' Mahony displayed the drawings in the windows of the Bookshop. *Horn Book* readers and Bookshop customers lined up to pay $5 for an original Potter drawing and help save a 'bit of [English] scenery', particularly as Beatrix had described it as 'right in the middle of the most beautiful part of Windermere; and it is near my home'.[4]

By November, Beatrix was able to report to the 'friends from Boston' that the appeal had been successful. 'It is pleasant to know that New Englanders value the old country. The land is safely purchased, and a dry gravel path is being made near the bank of the lake.' There would be a public area for visitors and a park and playing fields for the local young people. But one person to whom Beatrix wrote to thank for her contribution and such a 'nice letter' was not from Boston. Marian Frazer Harris Perry was a well-to-do and well-travelled Philadelphia widow, who subscribed to the appeal and had purchased three drawings. Beatrix explained,

I'm sure I am doing good in trying to save anything I can of our Lake country from being vulgarized; for, as true education advances, the beauty of unspoilt nature will be appreciated; and it would be a pity if the appreciation came too late. We do not wish to interfere with house building in suitable places, but we wish to preserve some portions of wild land unspoilt for the general good, and above all to avoid the erection, of perhaps *one*, unsightly building; which might destroy the beauty of a whole wide landscape.

Beatrix sensed correctly that Mrs Perry, who had visited the Lake District many times, was one of those who 'still believe in Old England . . .'.[5]

Marian Perry and Beatrix continued to exchange letters over the next year and found they had much in common, including the year of their birth. Mrs Perry was the daughter of a wealthy industrial entrepreneur from Philadelphia, a business associate of the financier, J. P. Morgan. She had lived a sedate Victorian life of wealth and ease punctuated by an interest in literature, art and continental travel with her father and two successive stepmothers. Like Beatrix she had been educated at home and, also like her, had been expected to manage a household staff, entertain and care for her elderly parents. Of all the Americans Beatrix met and befriended, Marian Perry was the closest to her in upbringing, experience and personality, though she was by nature more outgoing.[6]

Marian's marriage at the age of 48, to a man who was a contemporary of her father's, lent an additional depth to their friendship. James DeWolfe Perry, the Rector of her church, Calvary Episcopal Church in Germantown, was the father of her best friend and was already retired and in poor health when they were married in 1914. He died in 1927, not long before Marian heard about the Windermere Fund and purchased Beatrix's drawings. Marian, known to her friends as 'Andy', was delighted by the letters she received from Beatrix and was eager to visit her at Near Sawrey.[7]

In February 1929 Beatrix had written to Marian suggesting hotels in Windermere and Grasmere.

I wish I could have invited you to stay here – there's no use mincing matters! I have only a daily servant and how can one invite strangers to sleep in cold weather when one has to get fires and breakfast oneself! During the day I have a good servant, and I shall be delighted to see you and show you my drawings – it is a pleasure to look forward to. Life has been trying lately; burst and frozen water pipes, influenza, and intense frost.

When the two women finally met in April 1929 Beatrix was not disappointed. Her new American friend was a thorough Anglophile. She appreciated the countryside, was interested in farming and knowledgeable about all sorts of books, and had brought Beatrix some books by unfamiliar American authors which Beatrix looked forward to reading. 'I enjoyed the afternoon too,' Beatrix wrote after their visit. 'It's very pleasant to meet appreciative Americans, and to feel that you value old associations and will take care of our treasures, that have to cross the seas.' Marian particularly admired Beatrix's antique oak furniture in Hill Top. Beatrix invited her to come back again. 'If I cannot be in – I cannot, and will say so! And you can send any other very nice Americans . . . Indeed I have never had any of the loud inquisitive type that one reads about.' Marian left Beatrix with the same sense that she had of her earlier New England visitors: that 'they had more understanding and appreciation for old English traditions than the bulk of English people have'.[8]

New American friends like Marian Perry were an unexpected benefit of the Windermere appeal. Beatrix's now well-established connections with Boston-area Unitarians encouraged other families to call upon her. Most made their headquarters somewhere in or near Grasmere or Keswick, and wrote ahead with introductions from the Fields or the Hopkinsons to ask if they might call. Mr and Mrs J. Templeman Coolidge and their sons, Henry, known as Henry P., and Usher, were involved in the Boston art world and were friends of the Hopkinsons. The Coolidges were also Unitarians and Gail Parsons Coolidge had ties to the Bookshop for Boys and Girls. In the late summer of 1927 the Coolidges were staying at Fawe Park in Keswick and wrote to ask if they might visit Hill Top Farm. Mrs Coolidge did not realize that they were at the very place where twenty-four years earlier Beatrix had made the sketches for *The Tale of Benjamin Bunny*. But it did not take long for her eldest son to work out where he was, and to explore Mrs Tiggy-winkle's neighbourhood around Cat Bells and Squirrel Nutkin's owl island.[9]

Gail Coolidge explained how her son considered the little books 'like unto the books that make up the bible', asking if she might bring Henry P., then 13, with her to visit Hill Top. Beatrix was pleased to receive them so long as they gave her advance notice so that she was not in the midst of farm work. She explained, 'the lamb sales are on now – and we are still in the corn and hay . . . I shall be very glad to see your boy, and I think you had better come too, and tell me about Fawe Park. It has a familiar sound.' Beatrix told Mrs Coolidge, 'I am always pleased to see Americans, I don't know what to think about you as a nation (with a big N!) but the individuals who have looked for Peter Rabbit have all been delightful.'[10]

Henry P. was a striking boy, oval-faced, blue-eyed and so much the tow-head blond that his hair was nearly white. He later described himself as 'having a maudlin passion for animals', including mice, rabbits, guinea pigs, cross-bred bantams, pigeons and pure-bred dogs; while his friends, and his younger brother Usher, much preferred tinkering with model steam engines, guns and automobiles. Not only did Henry P. admire the books of Beatrix Potter, he 'knew every creature, every place, and every conversation' contained in them, and he recalled waiting for 'the answer to our letter of introduction in high suspense'. When Beatrix encountered him at the door of Castle Cottage, she must have been as struck by his physical beauty as she was later charmed by his quick intelligence and gentle manner. She correctly gauged him an exceptional young man. She introduced her visitors to the barnyard animals and her collie, and then led them on an expedition through the village of Near Sawrey, ending back at

Hill Top Farm. Beatrix opened the door of the farmhouse with 'an enormous key' and let them into the museum that was '*Tom Kitten's* home'.[11]

Henry P. had a keen eye for detail, a delight in fantasy and a vivid memory. Over sixty years after that first visit to Sawrey he recalled,

As I look back, Mrs Heelis seemed fairly aged – twelve years older than my mother – plump, and rather bent, with rosy cheeks and firm blue eyes in a weather-beaten face. Her somewhat untidy grey hair was carelessly drawn back in a bun. On the whole, I thought she had the familiar air of a shrewd, battered, independent Maine fisherman's wife. Though not very aware of clothes, even I was conscious that she was dowdy.

He remembered that she 'was always jamming on a squashed flat hat to go outside', while his mother 'had on something towering, black and Bostonian'. But for all that, Gail Coolidge was a warm, charming, outgoing woman and she and Beatrix got on immediately.[12]

Like her other American visitors, Beatrix invited the Coolidges to Castle Cottage for tea, and then they were invited upstairs to her study. Henry P. recalled later,

This was a room entirely filled with portfolios of her work. A series of long, deep, baseboard cupboards ran the whole length of one wall, and when she opened one of these to take out two pictures, I saw they were stacked with more portfolios still. The pictures were the middle two in the delightful set of six comprising 'The Rabbits' Christmas Party' – early work for which she professes some scorn. 'You can see how poor my anatomy was,' she said, and seizing a blunt pencil, she bent forward and made a couple of swift curves, doubling the size of the leading rabbit's paws.

When Henry P. and his mother left Castle Cottage that afternoon, Henry had been given two drawings from the 'The Rabbits' Christmas Party', as well as a number of others including a watercolour of Lucie's Little-town farm from *Mrs Tiggy-Winkle* and perhaps an unfinished sketch of Peter in the Fawe Park garden done for *Benjamin Bunny*. Henry P. was also impressed with the numerous background drawings he saw in Beatrix's portfolios and told her so. Although Beatrix considered them 'very scribblesome', she took note of the boy's interest and enthusiasm.[13]

Realizing immediately after the Coolidges departed that the drawings she had given the boy were unsigned, Beatrix wrote to Fawe Park seeking to rectify her omission. 'We tried to call you back! They weren't autographed. So you *must* come again, to get my precious signature – Thanks so very much for your visit –'. When the Coolidges returned, Beatrix enquired of Mrs Coolidge exactly what the Women's Educational and Industrial Union was, how it related to the Bookshop for Boys and Girls and to *The Horn Book*, and why it was that they would support her efforts to save Cockshott Point. Henry P. recalled, 'My mother laughed. "Bless you," she said, "I'm one of the directors!"' Completely reassured, Beatrix confided that while she 'felt disloyal to leave her English publishers and doubted anyone would be interested', she did have some unpublished drawings in her portfolios and some old ideas which might be combined for new stories which might interest Miss Mahony.[14]

Beatrix also told Henry P. and his mother how her much-loved guinea pig Tuppenny had died of old age shortly before their visit. She confided that she sometimes wrote short vignettes about her fell farm, her farm animals and especially about Tuppenny. Before the Coolidges left England, Gail Coolidge made a generous contribution to the Cockshott appeal and purchased at least one of Beatrix's remarkable fungi paintings. On their way back through London she bought two long-haired guinea pigs at Harrods – the department store which sold almost everything imaginable – and had them delivered to Beatrix at Sawrey. Beatrix was delighted with the unexpected gift, and although both guinea pigs turned out to be female, she christened one Henry P. and the other Mrs Tuppenny, grateful to Gail Coolidge for her thoughtfulness.[15]

'Everyone is happy and satisfied,' she wrote to them with uncharacteristic warmth. 'Henry P. is pleased, and so am I – pleased to have given pleasure and drawings to such an appreciative friend of Peter

Rabbit's, and such a very charming young boy. And it is not unpleasing to receive such a substantial return this morning!' referring to the Coolidges' gift to the Windermere fund. Most of all, Beatrix expressed her delight in the qualities she had found in Henry P., telling his mother, 'I can quite believe that when Henry P. was a very very small white headed baby he may have been acquainted with fairies, like I was, if there are fairies in New England.'[16]

Beatrix was energized by the Coolidges' visit, and by Henry P.'s enthusiasm for her work, her animals and the beauty of the countryside she had memorialized. Her Boston visitors set her thinking about writing again. 'Your interest in my surroundings will encourage me to try to work up my desultory chapters this winter,' she wrote to Mrs Coolidge.

It is not easy to explain my feeling about publishing them on this side of the Atlantic. Do you know the old rhyme? 'As I walked by myself, I talked by myself, and myself said to me –' I have always talked to myself (out loud too, which is an indiscreet slightly crazy habit, *not* to be imitated by Henry P.!) and I rather shrink from submitting the talkings to be pulled about by a matter of fact English publisher, or obtruded on my notice in the London Daily.

Beatrix consoled herself that if such stories were printed in an American paper or magazine, 'and were considered foolishness, I needn't see them at all'. But all the New Englanders who had visited Sawrey had been 'singularly sympathetic', which gave her further confidence to write something new. To Beatrix, these Americans seemed to 'appreciate the memories of old times, the simple country pleasures, – the homely beauty of the old farm house, the sublime beauty of the silent lonely hills – and – blessed folk – you are not afraid of being laughed at for [being] sentimental'.[17]

The Coolidge visit not only allayed Beatrix's hesitation in sending her stories to *The Horn Book*, but provided the incentive to revise 'The Tale of Tuppenny' that she had begun in 1903. It was one of three stories she had written at Hastings, but it had been lost in the tragic events of 1905. Beatrix had been at her best then as a writer,

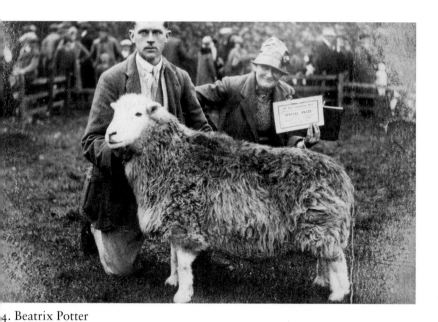

54. Beatrix Potter
and Tom Storey
with their prize-
winning ewe,
1930. Tom Storey
left Troutbeck
Park in 1927 to
become Beatrix's
farm manager at
Hill Top Farm.
There he bred a
line of Herdwick
ewes which took
top prizes for two
decades at the
agricultural shows,
much to Beatrix's
delight.

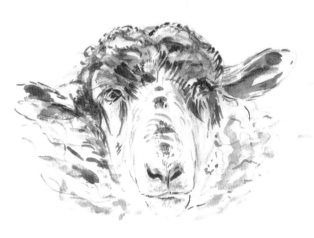

55. Study of a
sheep's head. Beatrix
drew her sheep and
cattle with obvious
pleasure. Her skill
impressed her
shepherds.

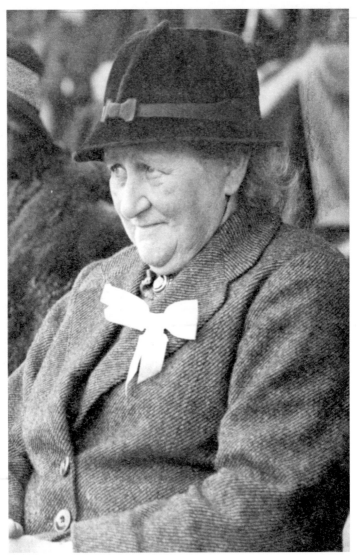

56. Mrs Heelis at the Keswick
sheep show, 1935, dressed in her
best Herdwick tweeds, watching
the judging intently. Her passion
for raising Herdwick led her
to preserve the culture of fell
farming. She was elected president
of the Herdwick Sheep Breeders'
Association for 1944 but did not
live to serve.

57. Beatrix frequently walked out on the Troutbeck Tongue where the quality of the land never failed to lift her spirits and inspire her imagination. The best of the *Fairy Caravan* tales are set out on the Tongue.

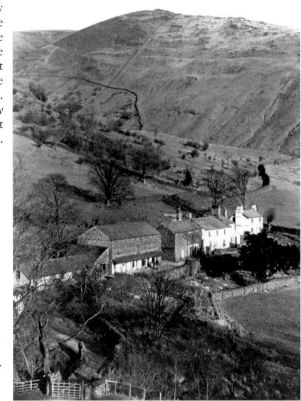

58. View across Esthwaite Water to hills and mountains, 1909. Beatrix considered Esthwaite Water the most beautiful of the smaller lakes and painted it in every season.

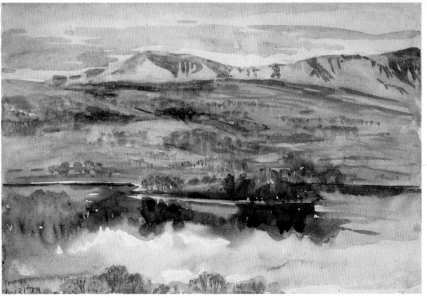

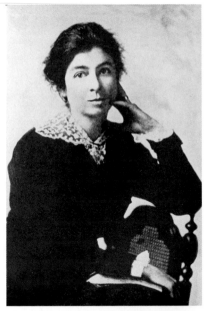

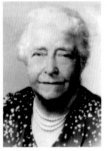

59. (*Above left*) Bertha Mahony (Miller), 1929, one of the founders of The Bookshop for Boys and Girls in Boston, Massachusetts, and the editor of *The Horn Book*. Through her network, many interesting Americans called on Beatrix in Sawrey. Although they never met, Bertha and Beatrix had parallel lives and shared common interests. Bertha promoted Beatrix's work in America.

60. (*Above right*) Marian Frazer Harris Perry, the wealthy Philadelphia widow, was a welcome visitor to the Heelis home and became a trusted friend and frequent correspondent. Like Beatrix, Marian had married late in life. She admired Beatrix's books, but was equally impressed with her accomplishments as a countrywoman.

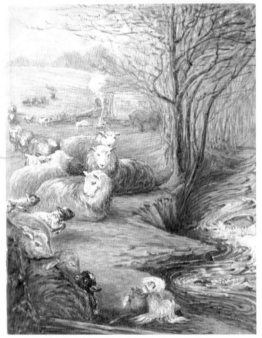

61. The Eller-Tree Camp from *The Fairy Caravan* (1929).

62. Xarifa's tale from *The Fairy Caravan* (1929).

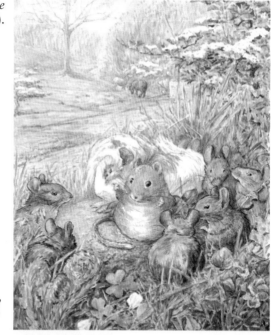

63. Beatrix and a group of Girl Guides, 1932. Beatrix supported the interests of young women who wanted to learn and enjoy the countryside, and allowed them to camp on her land. She enjoyed visiting the girls, listening to their singing and watching them grow.

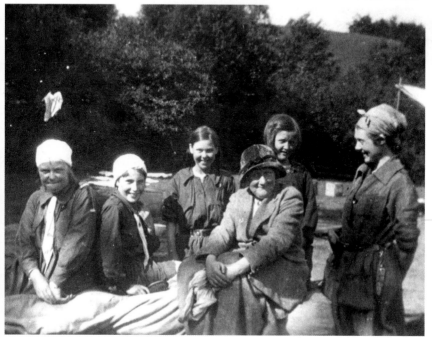

the thing unfortunately spread I think the best contradiction would be to get photographed along with a favourite pig or cow and get it inserted in some more *genteel* newspaper!

I had lately a pig that continually stood on its hind legs leaning over the pig stye, but its hanging up, un photographed & cured now.

64. Caricature of Beatrix and a pig leaning on a fence, *c.* 1924. Beatrix enjoyed drawing her pigs and made a house pet of several favourites. She drew one such caricature of herself and her pig to amuse Josefina Banner and another to mock the annoying confusion between herself and the socialist Beatrice Potter Webb.

65. ICAA Christmas card, 1932. Beatrix contributed an annual drawing to the Invalid Children's Aid Association which the charity sold as a Christmas card to support the invalid children's hospitals. Her signed card for 1932 shows her animal characters dancing around a Christmas tree.

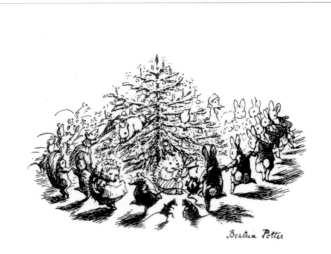

Beatrix Potter

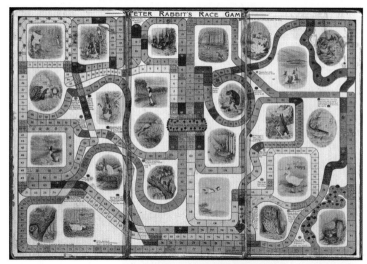

66. The board for Peter Rabbit's Race Game (1919). Beatrix was a natural merchandiser. She devised the first Peter Rabbit game with a board and rules in 1904, but Warne decided not to market it. Mary Warne elaborated this version to help bring the company back from financial ruin.

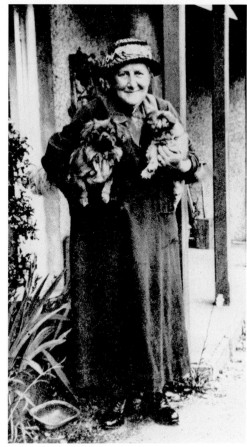

67. Beatrix with her Pekinese, Tzusee and Chuleh, 1943. As an older woman, Beatrix enjoyed these little dogs and found them convenient footwarmers when she was forced to stay in bed with bronchitis.

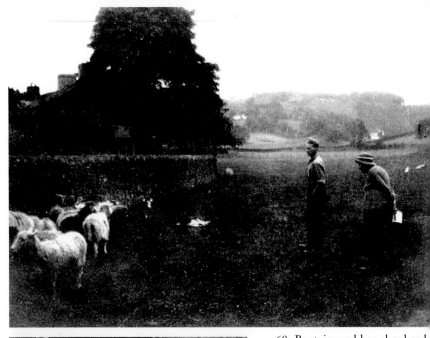

68. Beatrix and her shepherd. Crippled by her surgeries and vulnerable to the cold, Beatrix nevertheless came out to watch her sheep and talk to her shepherds

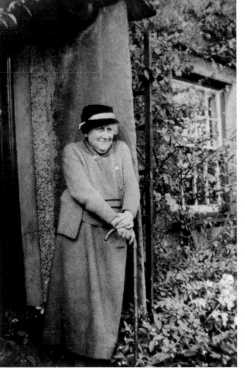

69. Beatrix as an old woman at Hill Top. Whenever she could, she came across the meadow to work on her portfolios or to arrange her treasures at Hill Top. She hoped it would be preserved as she had left it.

but she set it aside after she bought Hill Top in favour of tales that included her new surroundings. During the winter of 1927, when it was clear that her old guinea pig Tuppenny would not last long, Beatrix had pulled it out. Even with her poor eyesight, she thought her quick little pen-and-ink sketches might embellish such a tale.[18]

Beatrix used all her spare time that winter to work on the story of Tuppenny, the long-haired guinea pig who lived in the 'land of Green Ginger' in a 'town called Marmalade'. She put it together with other vignettes about her pets and farm animals, to construct a loose narrative about a group of animals who travel about the Lakeland countryside in a caravan entertaining children as a small circus. In the evenings the animals gather around a campfire and tell each other stories. The stories were drawn from Beatrix's collection of old folk tales and Lake District anecdotes.[19]

She illustrated some of these stories with unused pictures, but she also added new pen-and-ink drawings of her two new guinea pigs. She called the collection, 'Over the Hills and Far Away'. 'I became so much interested in it,' she confided later to Henry P.,

it grew longer and longer, and I kept re-writing earlier chapters. In spring, before lambing time I came in sight of a halt . . . but before I could finish off the series of stories . . . the spring work outside commenced – and various disappointments and annoyances; so that I had no time to 'finish' the adventures of the caravan. Besides being out of tune and cross. The wanderings of the circus company go on and on without end or 'finis'; next winter I hope to write out carefully a sufficient number of varied tales up to a point that is a convenient breaking-off-place. I could have finished it after a fashion; but I like to do my work carefully.[20]

Beatrix was enjoying writing about times long past. Henry P.'s letters seemed to spark her memory. 'I wonder if you will like this piece describing Spring . . . and Birds' Place was so lovely if I could do justice to the recollection . . . I have written some amusing chapters about Paddy Pig's adventures; he lost the caravan by wandering away into a wood, and by the time Pony Billy found him – he was ill through unwisely eating toadstool tartlets.' She enclosed a copy of

Peter Rabbit's Almanac for 1929 in her letter to Henry P., 'which', she explained, 'has fallen flat! People like it, but the shopkeepers did not, so there are not many on sale.'[21]

The possibility of a new publishing relationship in America was coincidentally reinforced by the unexpected visit of Alexander McKay, president of the firm of David McKay Co., a publisher of fine books in Philadelphia. McKay called on Beatrix in Sawrey late in 1927, undoubtedly at Bertha Mahony's suggestion, 'in search of a book that does not exist'. The McKay firm was an advertiser in *The Horn Book*, and Mahony had heard from Gail Coolidge that Beatrix had been writing some new stories. But it was to their mutual friend Mrs Hopkinson, the Boston painter's wife, that Beatrix first reported McKay's visit. 'There has been an alarming visitation' by an American publisher, Beatrix wrote, acknowledging that McKay had asked for a new book. Loath to be disloyal, Beatrix admitted: 'It would vex my old publishers very much, and I don't like breaking with old friends.' But she was nonetheless impressed by McKay's 'very beautifully illustrated books' and by the fact that he had come all the way to Sawrey. 'Possibly', she wrote, 'I may arrange to have published something in America for the American market only.'[22]

Alexander McKay was a very persuasive man, and although Beatrix made no commitments, she was flattered that he had liked her fanciful caravan stories. When Beatrix acknowledged that she was considering giving a book to another publisher, Warne's were understandably unhappy, but the British market for children's books was once again in transition, and Fruing was not well. In the autumn he had pneumonia. His health improved enough for a holiday in February 1928 but then he suffered a fatal heart attack. He was 66. The stress of bringing the family publishing business back from the brink of bankruptcy and the post-war challenges of book publishing had taken their toll. Fruing's son, Norman, had not followed him into the firm, and so Arthur Stephens, Fruing's brother-in-law and a member of the Warne board, became the new managing director. For Beatrix, Fruing's death was the end of a family friendship as well as a long and deeply cherished business partnership. Alexander McKay's visit had been well timed.[23]

By the summer of 1928 Beatrix was earnestly planning out the book which would become *The Fairy Caravan*. The idea for these tales dates from her pleasure in seeing Ginnet's Travelling Circus in Ambleside in 1895. She wrote then: 'I would go any distance to see a Caravan . . . it is the only species of entertainment I care for.' Her tale begins with Tuppenny, the long-haired guinea pig, who ran away from his jeering friends and joined Alexander and William's travelling circus. The circus caravan with its troop of animals travelled over fell and tarn giving performances for the invisible Little Folk. Beatrix's pets and farm animals are among the circus troupe, which is led by Pony Billy and Sandy, a white West Highland terrier, modelled after Beatrix's childhood terrier of the same name. Charles, the handsome rooster, was drawn from Beatrix's favourite cock, who lived to an old age and had never been beaten in battle. But the most engaging character is Xarifa, the sleepy dormouse, who tells Tuppenny stories to keep herself awake. Xarifa's tales include vivid descriptions of identifiable Lakeland places, embellished by legend and lore. There are vistas drawn from Troutbeck, old-fashioned names of flowers, descriptions of birdsong and performances occurring through the magical power of fern seeds which make the animals invisible to the human eye. Even Beatrix's knowledge and fascination with fungi is included.[24]

Beatrix herself appears in several of the tales, as 'Mistress Heelis', including the story of how she once lost her clogs, but most notably in a chapter about Herdwick sheep. The sheep hold conversations about various pastures of merit and tell their own stories based on Beatrix's memory of summertime walks out on Troutbeck Tongue. Tibbie Woolstockit, Maggie Dinmont and Hannah Brighteyes, and of course Hill Top Queenie, one of her prize-winning Herdwicks, go through bad and bright weather and across craggy summits and down fells, aided by faithful dogs. The caravan tales end with a version of Beatrix's beloved old story of 'The Fairy and the Oak', proving her view that 'all fairies are peppery'.[25]

'I will send you a copy of the first chapter of "Over the hills & far away"', Beatrix wrote to Henry P. in June, 'but you must understand there is not so much exclusively guinea pig in the other later chapters after Tuppenny joins the caravan. I don't know what Miss Mahony is thinking of my delays – but I *can not* write if I am out of humour.' The next day she sent the boy a handwritten revised version of 'The Tale of Tuppenny', explaining, 'I have written perhaps six pieces of this length, but there are connecting pieces that I am not satisfied with yet; and I want another fairy tale (partly invented) to round off this collection . . . You see – you and I take our fiction *very seriously*.' She sent the chapter to Bertha Mahony, who promptly bought it for *The Horn Book*, where it appeared as the leading feature in February 1929.[26]

There were good reasons why Beatrix was 'out of humour' in the spring of 1928, most having to do with the demands of managing two very different farms, dealing with the idiosyncracies of her elderly mother and housing problems at Hill Top. After Bertram's death in 1918 Beatrix and William made it a point to go to her mother's home, Lindeth Howe, for lunch on Sunday afternoons. When the war ended, Helen began a ritual visit to Castle Cottage nearly every Wednesday afternoon, arriving punctually in her large carriage dressed entirely in black. Sometimes she came for tea, other times she arrived to find Beatrix, dressed in her sturdy woollens, clogs on her feet, working in the garden or busy with her animals. She stayed precisely one hour. Never more, rarely less. Henry Byers, who as a young man worked for Beatrix as a gardener, later recalled, 'I never saw that old woman smile. She always looked miserable and she never stayed long. You could set your watch by her arrival and departure.'[27]

Wealthy as Helen Potter was, she was quite stingy, especially when it came to Beatrix. The settlement of Bertram's estate had presented unforeseen difficulties since it involved the reapportioning of considerable sums from his will, his father's will and the Leech marriage settlement. Concerned about Mrs Potter's increasing wealth and the death duties her estate would incur, William used the ritual Sunday dinner trying to convince his mother-in-law to increase Beatrix's £300 yearly allowance, suggesting she put £15,000 worth of securities into her daughter's name, and that she give some money to appeals from the National Trust. Helen had no inclination to do either, and selfishly believed that if she gave stock to Beatrix her own spending would be curtailed.

Helen had finally agreed to sell the Potter family home at 2 Bolton Gardens. Beatrix and William spent a miserable week in London in June 1924 trying to clear the place, sorting through fifty-eight years' worth of possessions, deciding what to keep and what to sell. Beatrix sent off three van loads of furniture and personal belongings to her 'imperious old mother' in Bowness. The London house was 'grimy with London soot', but it was a relief to Beatrix to get rid of the place. 'I was never very well or happy there in old times, and I had no affection for the place,' she wrote to her cousin afterwards. She was afraid that her mother would burn important old letters, so she put all the books and old letters into sacks and trunks and hauled them back to Sawrey to go through herself.[28]

Beatrix was unimpressed by new buildings that had gone up in London since she had last been there; a 'jumble of old and new', which she did not think improved the city much. Beatrix had always been a keen observer of architecture and had taken pleasure in drawing churches, cottages and farm buildings. She appreciated good design and was attuned to how a building related to and extended its natural surroundings. In 1925, inspired by her visit to London and by the need to preserve the vernacular architecture of the Lake District, Beatrix joined the Society for the Protection of Ancient Buildings (SPAB), once again following the lead of Hardwicke Rawnsley, who had also belonged to it. Her concern for the preservation of old buildings and good architecture was a natural extension of her efforts to preserve fell farms.[29]

But the most perplexing housing problem was the necessity of clearing her personal treasures out of Hill Top in the autumn of 1928 so that William's nephew John ('Jack') Heelis and his wife would have a place to live. Jack Heelis had joined the Hawkshead law practice, which was in a state of crisis as William's cousin and law partner, W. D. Heelis, had been confined to bed. Jack had impetuously married Wynne Yeadon, and in order to help William, Beatrix had allowed the young couple to move into Hill Top until they could afford a place on their own. Beatrix confided to her sister-in-law that she felt it 'a bit of a wrench', particularly as she had to push out a window, and put in another W C and a bath. 'Henry P will be grieved to hear that I have had to dismantle the dear old house where Tom Kitten lived,' Beatrix wrote. 'I hope at the end of three years I may be able to put my pretty things back; some are squeezed in here, and others lent out amongst friends in the village.' Beatrix liked Jack, but she judged Wynne a poor housekeeper. The newly-weds sat around listening to the wireless, and they did not appreciate the farm cats or the rats that came along with the old house. 'I was maliciously pleased to hear that Sam [Samuel Whiskers] had been upstairs and made himself a nuisance,' she told Gail Coolidge. 'They are quite nice young people; but I regard them as cuckoos. I never thought I would be giving up the old house to anybody.'[30]

But in spite of all these distractions, by the end of the year Beatrix was close to signing a contract with Alexander McKay. McKay had offered her an agreement based on an escalating percentage of royalty, plus an advance of £200, rather than a single lump sum upon delivery. Beatrix worried about some of the financial details, and she was even more anxious that the stories revealed too much of herself, that they were too autobiographical and might be found silly. 'Sometimes,' she confessed to Gail Coolidge, 'I feel I don't want to print the stories at all, just keep them for the private edification of Henry P. and me. I guess we will keep some of them private and unprinted; they are more & more peculiar; I wonder what makes me spin such funny spider webs.' Pleased with the financial terms McKay offered, however, Beatrix took courage and signed a contract for 'The Caravan Stories' on 19 December 1928.[31]

Now committed to a new book for an older audience, Beatrix struggled with the drawings, particularly with the coloured ones. In February she told McKay, 'I am afraid that book is like the curate's egg when he breakfasted with the bishop – "parts of it are excellent!" Some of it is awful bosh; and this colour drawing is – will it process? My eyes have lost the faculty of seeing clean colours.' But even she judged the new pen-and-ink drawings satisfactory, especially those of the sheep, the fell landscapes and the woods in moonlight. In the end, she managed to do all the drawings herself. McKay gave her encouragement and attended to her directions about how she wanted things done. In spite of delays with the art and proofing, the experience proved a pleasant one.[32]

Although Warne's tried to intimidate Beatrix about potential loss of copyright if the book was not published in Britain, she was not easily bullied. But she knew she must register the copyright there even though she had no desire to see the book in print. Acting as her own agent, she contracted with George Middleton, an Ambleside printer, and arranged for one hundred unbound sets of the American edition to be shipped to him. The first eighteen pages, including the preface and dedication, were discarded so that a new set of pages printed at Ambleside could be inserted. To this privately printed edition she added a page on which were sketches of her favourite sheepdogs with their names written underneath. On the title page she used her married name, Beatrix Heelis. William was insistent that she have absolute proof of copyright date in case anyone tried to pirate it. Accordingly the requisite three copies were deposited at Stationers' Hall in London at the same time as the book was published in America. Beatrix gave some of the privately printed editions to her relatives, friends and neighbours, making sure that her shepherds and farmhands got autographed copies. The rest she kept for herself. 'Part of the 100 I intend to hoard,' she told her American publisher, 'taking experience by the disappearance of the first editions of Peter.' Ironically, she also made sure McKay had a copy of the English binding, with an extra line block just in case of any copyright infringement.[33]

The Fairy Caravan was published in the United States in October 1929, and bore a simple dedication, 'To Henry P.' Beatrix wanted the book to 'stand on its own merits' without any sort of publicity or fanfare, and she wrote out two prefaces. Finally she decided on the old rhyme she had first shared with Gail Coolidge, and the briefest of explanations:

> As I walk'd by myself,
> And talked to myself,
> Myself said unto me –

Through many changing seasons these tales have walked and talked with me. They were not meant for printing; I have left them in the homely idiom of our old north country speech. I send them on the insistence of friends beyond the sea.

Beatrix Potter.

To Henry P., Beatrix wrote: 'I hope by this time you have received your copy of Our Book!' Other specially signed copies were delivered to her friends: Mary Gill, Ivy Steel, Anne Carroll Moore and several of the librarians Moore had sent to Sawrey. Copies also went to Bertha Mahony and to Marian Perry. Beatrix approved McKay's printing. 'I like type, paper and all,' she wrote, thanking him, but unable to resist pointing out three typographical errors. 'I hope it will give satisfaction to both of us – And I may add – to my most exacting critics – my own shepherds and the blacksmith. I do not care tuppence about anybody else's opinion.'[34]

The Fairy Caravan sold only adequately in America. Anne Carroll Moore lent it her imprimatur, as did public libraries all over the country. Beatrix particularly liked a review by Alice M. Jordan in *The Horn Book*. Jordan, Supervisor of Work with Children at the Boston Public Library, picked out the qualities that Beatrix herself liked best, writing: 'Full of the spirit of the north country April, sunshiny open meadows, frisking lambs and skimming swallows, here is a book for the springtime when fairy adventures are afoot.' But it had such a specific English setting and folklore that its appeal was limited in America.[35]

Bemused by the local acclamation accorded to *The Fairy Caravan*, Beatrix reported to Gail Coolidge, 'they are all claiming bits, and disputing whose [*sic*] who.' 'It has been a great pleasure to receive such kind *understanding* letters from you and others in America . . . I feel you take me seriously! . . . I am sure the average Londoner would care nothing about Herdwick sheep!' *The Fairy Caravan* had given her a great deal of pleasure. It was a personal book, full of tales that first of all pleased her. 'It would have been rather a pity', she confided, 'if I had shuffled off this mortal coil with most of those chapters inside my head. And it surprises myself that some of the late written chapters are as good as any, for instance the sheep anecdotes, and the woods by moonlight. It seems I can still write and invent.'[36]

Beatrix ordered a dozen copies of the American edition and gave the very first one to Tom Storey. He remembered how 'she came over from Castle Cottage and said, "Here, Storey, this is a copy of The Fairy Caravan I've written, sent from America and I'm giving you the first one."' It was signed and in the back she had sketched her favourite sheepdogs. The inscription reads: 'To Tom Storey in memory of Queenie and the sheep dogs.'

The approval of her shepherds meant more to Beatrix than anything else. 'That chapter [about Herdwick sheep] made my old shepherd [John Mackereth] cry with pleasure; that is appreciation worth having,' she told Henry P.'s mother. Joseph Moscrop was one of those shepherds whose approval Beatrix very much coveted. His copy was from the small stock she had printed in Ambleside. In it she wrote: 'In remembrance of Troutbeck Park and sheep, May 30, 1930.' Moscrop gave The Fairy Caravan a close reading, later writing her a letter about it. 'Now you have paid me the compliment of reading the Caravan with careful attention – not merely skimming, but dijesting [*sic*] the immortal work (!?).' Nothing could have pleased her more.[37]

Beatrix was aware that the places she mentioned and the north-country vernacular that she used would be somewhat mysterious to American readers. For McKay's children, to whom she dedicated the book, she wrote out definitions of terms and identified people and places – a glossary of sorts – in the text and the illustrations. She also sent these 'explains', as she called them, to Henry P. They constitute a primer on Lakeland farming and offer usual insights into Beatrix's daily life in the Lake District. The 'explains' include farming terms, local colloquialisms, places, reminiscences, details about her dogs and other farm pets, old Celtic words for counting sheep, and other terms unique to north-country life. She took particular trouble in the explains about her sheep, telling McKay: 'I have two sheep stocks . . . we keep the old pedigree flock here, on the low ground farm; and the main flock goes on the fells . . . The young sheep and rams are brought down in summer. I am conceited enough to say I am the only person who could have written about the sheep; because I know them and the fell like a shepherd; but the Herdwick men are not articulate.' All in all she was pleased with the way she had woven the tapestry of her memories, her travels over the landscape and north-country lore into a fanciful, entertaining tale, assuring McKay, 'Every anecdote is fact – except possibly: the fairies?'[38]

Charmed by her stories, Alexander McKay, like Harold and Fruing Warne before him, immediately asked Beatrix for another book of country tales. Surprisingly, Beatrix seemed willing to consider it. But she was inclined to 'appease the English public and publishers' with something she could cobble together quickly, 'and make a sequel to the *caravan* the year following, if spared; which would give time for more adequate illustrations.' She felt duty-bound to remind McKay of her publishing history: 'I am not a prolific scribbler. I wrote myself out on the rabbit series.' For material, Beatrix turned to a new story based loosely on Edward Lear's rhyme, 'The Owl and the Pussy-Cat', with liberal amounts from Daniel Defoe's *Robinson Crusoe* and excerpts from various stories of her pet pigs. Her tale was about a country pig sent to town by his overly portly aunts Dorcas and Porcas, who was taken to sea against his will and gratefully rescued from either starvation or becoming table fare by the ship's cat. Pig Robinson eventually finds his way to the Land of the Bong Tree, where he presumably lives happily ever after. *The Tale of Little Pig Robinson*, which would be the last in the Peter Rabbit series, was an early tale; its origins derive from Potter family vacations in the 1890s. Beatrix had sketched it at various harbour towns on the south coast of England. She embellished the story, adding a few coloured drawings, and many more in pen and ink.[39]

When McKay visited Sawrey in December 1929, they agreed on the revised tale of the foolish pig. But out of loyalty, and a guilty conscience, Beatrix also offered the story to Warne's. That may have been good public relations, but it proved more difficult than she anticipated to please both publishers with the same tale. Stephens and McKay liked different drawings and favoured different parts of the story. Revisions and alterations seemed endless, and everyone was dissatisfied at one point or another. Final drawings were delayed when Beatrix went to bed with a bad case of bronchitis. The resulting book was an amalgam both in style and narrative. Her writing lacks the concentrated intensity of her earlier books, and while there are scenes reminiscent of the local Sawrey countryside, there is more fantasy than reality in the tale.

In July 1930 Beatrix learned that the Warne edition would lack many of the black-and-white illustrations, including some which Beatrix considered among her best work. 'I hope you may care to include them in the U.S.A. edition,' she asked McKay, and was pleased when the American edition contained twelve additional black-and-white drawings. William was angry about this decision by Warne's, which he believed violated their contract, but Beatrix was philosophic. 'F. W. & Co have always been inclined to save expenses at the expense of the appearance of the book,' she explained to McKay. Beatrix and her Philadelphia publisher did have one disagreement: it was over a word that was not in the dictionary. Beatrix had used the word 'fatterer' as the superlative of the word 'fat' when of course she knew there was no such word. For her, it was a matter of rhythm and sound, and, as she told him, 'it is expressive! If you don't like it, say "fatter and fatter and more fat". It requires 3 repeats to make a balanced ending.' McKay acquiesced and 'fatterer' remained.[40]

The Tale of Little Pig Robinson was published in Britain and America in September 1930. Warne's published only 5,000 copies and were soon caught short, as the book proved more popular in Britain than in America, and they had to reprint several times. Beatrix told McKay, 'I like the appearance of the book *extremely* – the head & tail pieces give it much more character than the English edition; and it is grand print. It *might* make a hit. It is much more concise and understandable for children than *The Fairy Caravan*.' Although she thought it could be improved by a few more illustrations, she wrote to him, 'I think P. R. looking into a shop window is the best black & white I ever did.'[41]

The unexpected income from her two American publications could not have come at a better time. The worldwide economic depression began to affect agriculture and food exports long before the collapse of the financial markets. Over the past several years the prices for wool and mutton had fallen sharply. Livestock farmers were discouraged and tenant farmers in the north were having a difficult time holding on to their land. Such things were on her mind when Beatrix wrote to McKay in anticipation of a royalty payment from the September publication of *Little Pig Robinson* in America. Asking him to hold off sending the funds, she explained: 'I shall be re-investing something presently, and I will ask for it later on.' She further instructed that payment go directly to Messrs W. H. Heelis & Son, 'who invests clients money for them'. Shrewdly, Beatrix and William were negotiating to buy more land.[42]

18

≫ *Ventures* ≪

O NE BEAUTIFUL AUTUMN SUNDAY in late October 1929, Beatrix
wrote to her young friend Henry P.,

After dinner Mr Heelis & I are going to Coniston. There is a lovely
stretch of mountain and valley to sell there and the National Trust are
trying to buy it . . . I am very interested because my great grandfather
had land there and I have always longed to buy it back and give it to
the Trust in remembrance. I was very much attached to my grandmother
Jessy Crompton and said to be very like her, 'only not so good looking!!'
Perhaps I will be able to help out of this book [*The Fairy Caravan*] – it
would be like a fairy tale, would it not?[1]

Although her remark was offhand, Beatrix and William were already
seriously negotiating to buy Monk Coniston Park, a large, dispersed
property north and east of Coniston, with the National Trust a silent
partner to their efforts. Before their Sunday drive, Beatrix had taken
Samuel Hamer, secretary of the Trust, into her confidence, informing
him that 'J. Marshall has been to the office when Mr Heelis was out,
talking in rather a desperate way about selling. It may be my hand
will be forced at Coniston . . . The rough lands are a very big thing;
but if Jimmy is really desirous to clear out – there might be a bargain.'
Beatrix knew from experience that it was 'better for *one* businesslike
person to buy *all*, and resell part . . . I could lift it . . . but it would
be too big for me to hold intire [*sic*]. Too much money to tie up –
and such a lump of land . . . We shall see what he is up to.'[2]

The following week Beatrix reported on their excursion: 'Mr Heelis
says the purchase is quite sure to go through. He is getting out a
plan – but it is the most perplexing business . . . It is an enormous

scattered piece – we did not attempt to go to Tilberthwaite [a separate area], or to the south end. We went through the Tarns roads (where we met about 15 cars with no room to pass.)' Beatrix found Tarn Hows, the large teardrop-shaped lake long famous for its scenic beauty, 'too theatrical for my own taste; like scene painting. I think the south bank of the Brathay is very pretty.' But she was impressed with the property, advising Hamer: 'The more money you can find, and the more land you can take – the better and simpler in the long run . . . It is a bewildering place. I do prefer a single large valley like Troutbeck. But it appeals to the public to judge by the numbers yesterday.'[3]

Beatrix conservatively estimated that the roughly 700 acres of forest, including some fine larch plantations, would be worth thousands of pounds one day. She urged Hamer to come up as soon as possible and to bring John Bailey, the chairman of the National Trust. '[I]t is a very big thing and worth looking at,' she told Hamer, though she admitted that it might take them more than two days to see it all, and without better maps than she had at present, or the headman's identification of the many enclosures, she could not tell how the estate would divide.[4]

For many years William Heelis had acted on behalf of James Aubrey Garth Marshall, heir to Monk Coniston Park. It was an enormous tract of land that straddled the Coniston and Tilberthwaite valleys, stretching from the head of Coniston Water to Little Langdale. The estate had been cobbled together piecemeal by James Marshall, a wealthy Manchester industrialist. Around his home at Monk Coniston Hall he had installed a pleasure ground: damming the bogs to create Tarn Hows, establishing conifer plantations, and siting picturesque hill farms in the shadow of Holme Fell and the summit of Wetherlam. Marshall's holdings embraced more than seven farms, myriad cottages, numerous quarries, extensive timberlands and open fell land extending down to the town of Coniston. All in all, the estate consisted of nearly 4,000 acres. One of the farms, Holme Ground at Tilberthwaite, had once belonged to Beatrix's great grandfather Abraham Crompton, and the opportunity to purchase this property had pricked her desire to buy and preserve the whole.[5]

William had learned that the asking price was to be somewhere between £15,000 and £18,000. At the lower price Beatrix thought it 'a price to snap'. 'I will say at once I cannot afford to present anything to the Trust, much as it would please me to do so – because this speculation means selling out what is the mainstay of my income and replacing it by rents ... What makes me afraid of being all in, is not so much possible loss of income as being so much more fond of Troutbeck than Coniston ...' She knew she should tenant Troutbeck in her lifetime but admitted to Hamer 'it would break my heart to part with my colly dogs and the galloways and the sheep while I can stagger on ... Apart from a sentimental interest in Holme Ground – and a strong desire to help save a most picturesque region – I have no feeling of affection for Coniston at all.'[6]

Few people could afford to buy the land for farming, but the demand from developers for holiday houses, villas, bungalows and small tourist establishments close to the tarn and with picturesque fell-side vistas was intense. The piecemeal purchase of Monk Coniston would mean the disintegration of traditional hill-country farms, intakes and commons, the loss of livelihood to farmers, tenants and cottagers, and the scattering of livestock, particularly of hefted sheep. Both the National Trust and the Forestry Commission were potential buyers, but neither entity could act quickly or had the immediate cash resources to make an offer for the whole, and therein lay Beatrix Heelis's advantage.[7]

Beatrix promised to get a plan to Hamer on how she might purchase the estate and then sell part of it to the Trust. But she forthrightly explained why the obvious solution – giving the land to them at the outset – was not possible. Although Rupert Potter had been one of the first Life Members of the National Trust, her miserly mother would neither contribute to the National Trust efforts nor loan her daughter the money. 'Tarn Hows is such a favourite walk that on the face of it you might think it was a case for public subscription; but it would not work. My mother is known to be so wealthy that nobody would subscribe to help *me!* She is hopeless.' Beatrix needed to know how much financial help she could expect from the Trust. If Marshall stuck to the high figure, she admitted she would have to 'stand over'. But Beatrix knew how to apply pressure to the Trust, telling Hamer, 'I might reasonably expect to be in a stronger position someday,' but 'Against that there is the risk of his selling to a speculator. Then we would both be sorry when it was too late.'[8]

Two days after the Heelises' Sunday visit, Beatrix decided to make Marshall an offer to buy the whole of Monk Coniston Park. Her scheme hinged on an unofficial partnership with the National Trust. If she were successful in purchasing the estate, the Trust would raise an appeal for half the purchase price, and buy back some 2,090 acres. Beatrix told Hamer, 'You can tell your friends that the matter *is* urgent ... The thing must be done somehow. Mr Heelis is very strongly for it. He thinks it would be a good bargain for both of us, but too dear at £18000 so he may have to haggle.' Negotiations between William and Jimmy Marshall were at a delicate point and as far as Marshall knew, Beatrix was acting on her own.

Over the course of the next week, the deal threatened to unravel several times. Marshall, it would seem, cared little who eventually owned his 'little green farms', so long as he was able to maintain the right to fish for trout in Tarn Hows. Beatrix cautioned Hamer, 'Mr JM does *not* know it is the Trust. He is swayed by the hope of money paid down and the fishing. Let him fish for life!' The next day Beatrix's bulletin to the Trust secretary warned, 'We may all end in a lunatic asylum.' Beatrix enjoyed sending unofficial information to the Trust secretary, punctuating her accounts with her own idiosyncratic opinions. When Marshall came to Castle Cottage with another set of conditions, Beatrix confessed, 'I was listening behind the dining room door ...' 'One [condition] was that he and his step son should hatch trout for two generations (trout or step sons?) in the private water supply of Monk Coniston house which he has sold to a man he has quarrelled with.'

But it was poor William who was doing all the hard work. Negotiating with the childish Jimmy, his socialite wife, their estate agent McVey, whom Beatrix described as 'a fat little man lately promoted from selling furniture', and the Marshalls' London solicitor, required immense skill and even greater patience. Beatrix often made fun of her deliberative husband, but while sometimes frustrated in her desire for faster action, she had great admiration for William's thoroughness. One night even the usually calm William had 'had a panic about the size of the Estate', and nearly lost his nerve. But Beatrix was confident, telling Hamer, 'It is no bigger than the Park but more bother.'

By the end of October, Marshall was anxious to get a deposit from Mrs Heelis. William sent for Ordnance sheets and copied out the whole estate to send to the Trust. After that they could plan for the division of the property. 'Mr Heelis considers it absolutely certain to go through,' Beatrix reported. 'They were so *very* anxious for money they will not be likely to wreck it over fish or rabbits.'[9]

It was a happy circumstance that all these negotiations came at the back end of the year. Troutbeck Park was now running smoothly in the capable hands of George Walker and Anthony Benson. Much of the harvest at Hill Top had already been gathered, and the sheep fairs were almost over. Although Beatrix thrived on the excitement of the negotiations, she now realized she would have to put down the entire deposit amount. 'I have plenty at the bank,' she assured Hamer, 'thanks to the October [sheep] fairs, and we will pay the deposit as soon as possible.'[10]

Nearly every day Beatrix drove out to various parcels that comprised Monk Coniston, calculating which ones she could sell off, the number and condition of the quarries and the amount of usable timber. Her mind was full of how the various farms and cottages could be tenanted and by whom. She relied on Marshall's head man, an ageing Scotch forester who had been at Monk Coniston for a very long time as overseer, to show her the various farms, and she had wisely decided to keep him on. She was happily surprised to find much more timber than she expected.[11]

And so Beatrix embarked upon a 'quixotic venture' in land preservation and management by which she assumed the mantle of her mentor Hardwicke Rawnsley both as public advocate and as land agent. With the purchase of Monk Coniston, Beatrix not only became one of the largest landowners in the Lake District, but also a major benefactor of the National Trust. As manager and agent both for herself and for the Trust, she had the opportunity to implement her ideas on land use and preservation and thus leave an indelible imprint on the future of hill-country culture and farming. Her success in this would never have been possible without her partnership with William. Although they were not always of one mind, they shared the same objective of preserving the landscape and culture they loved, and they agreed that the National Trust was 'the only salvation for the Lake district'. The Trust was, as Beatrix aptly put it, 'a noble thing, and – humanely speaking – immortal'.[12]

Beatrix paid the deposit money, approximately £7,000, on 5 November. Then for the next two months she worked to understand the condition of the estate, its agricultural and livestock potential, its various natural environments and how it could best be managed. The rest of her time was occupied with the thankless but crucial job of identifying wealthy individuals as potential donors, and advising the Trust on the best way to mount a public appeal in the Lake District. But raising money was difficult in the widening economic depression. As she looked back over the year, Beatrix was particularly grateful for the additional income from sales of *The Fairy Caravan*, telling Hamer, 'that *Book* may save my financial situation . . . I have been accustomed to solace myself with two mis-quotations from the Scriptures. "Blessed are they that expect very little for they shall *not* be disappointed" and "The Lord helps them that help (i.e. assist) themselves".'[13]

On 21 January 1930 the Monk Coniston Park estate, consisting of 3,738 acres o rods and 12 perches in the parishes of Coniston, Church Coniston and Skelwith, was conveyed to Helen Beatrix Heelis for the price of £15,000. It was over twice the size of Troutbeck Park Farm. The complicated conveyance document, copied out in William's fine hand, listed over one hundred and thirty-seven separate parcels. Like Troutbeck Park, it was a property of unparalleled beauty, and it was essential to protect it from development.[14]

On 15 February *The Times* carried a signed article by Trust chairman John Bailey, praising the 'generous and public spirited action of Mrs Heelis' in preserving the Monk Coniston estate and in giving the Trust the opportunity of acquiring 2,600 acres of it for the public. He then announced that 'Tarn Hows, Holme Fell, and Yew Tree Farm may be regarded as definitely secured', leaving only the Tilberthwaite portion to be given for a remaining £3,500. Noting that the Trust had acquired many properties in the Lake District in the last thirty years, Bailey wrote that 'not one of them . . . was better worth saving and holding than this glorious stretch of mountain, moor, and tarn'.[15]

Over the next several months Beatrix and William continued their unaccustomed role of fund-raisers, calling on potential donors to the Trust. Beatrix's political and social skills were in evidence as she reported some progress to Hamer, 'I will have a try at Miss Holt again. My Mamma says the Holts are "rolling in money!"' She urged the Trust to make a more concerted appeal through a variety of local newspapers, including those in Manchester and Liverpool – even writing some of the text herself.[16]

Although Beatrix spent some days in bed with bronchitis in February, her almost daily letters to the Trust reveal how accurately she had inventoried the various physical components of the estate. She assessed potential income from rents and expenses for necessary repairs to the infrastructure: roads, quarries, fences, footpaths, postings, parking areas, drains and flood plains. She had inspected all the farms and their outbuildings, untold cottages and huts, and had thoroughly reviewed the timber supply. She knew which plantations needed to be left alone, which could be added to, and what timber could be taken as thinnings for new fences. The working quarries needed special access and consideration, but they also required protection from trespass.

In the evenings Beatrix and William made endless calculations of costs, worried over dozens of boundary lines, and negotiated the troublesome issues of fire and hazard insurance. Their efforts at a sensible management plan were handicapped by a lack of local and regional guidelines and the necessity of finding the answers to such vexing legal questions as pedestrian access. In general, husband and wife divided responsibilities according to their expertise: William keeping the accounts, negotiating boundaries and researching the legal problems affecting their management; while Beatrix interviewed tenants, negotiated wages, refurbished cottages, contracted for endless fence repairs, had new walls built and quarrelled with a particularly strict sanitation inspector over the admittedly unhealthy amenities of the Tilberthwaite cottages and the overcrowding at Stang End Farm.

Beatrix clambered over rock and woods inspecting drains and locating breached walls, but most of her letters to the Trust officials concern the problem of fences, the wrongful cutting of trees by the wagoners, and the 'miles & miles of straggling woods which fence themselves'. No detail seemed too small for her attention. She decided where noticeboards should be placed and where parking should be posted. She had to determine whether the Boy Scouts and the Girl Guides could build campfires and where, and how fell gates could be secured so that animals would not wander out.

The level of detail with which the Heelises dealt, some of which may be calculated from the extant tax records, is staggering. It underscores not only Beatrix's skills in property management and her knowledge of fell farming, but the degree to which husband and wife were partners in the management of this far-flung estate. Such evidence reinforces the conclusion that, without William Heelis's almost infinite knowledge of Lakeland families, his history of property ownership and his steady, careful accounting of thousands of head of livestock, acres of timber, as well as diverse physical property, tenancies, taxes and wages, the whole effort to preserve Monk Coniston could easily have failed. 'I *hate* accts!' Beatrix wrote to Hamer in exasperation a year into her ownership. 'Wm. gave me such a lecture about wages that I was awake nearly all night.'[17]

By the late spring of 1930 the Trust's public fund had grown to the point that only the last little bit was wanting. Poised to begin repaying Beatrix for their portion of Monk Coniston, chairman John Bailey, Samuel Hamer and some of his staff met the Heelises in Coniston and concluded the transaction. The Tarns and Holme Fell had been subscribed for and, after some soul-searching, Beatrix decided to make an anonymous gift of Holme Ground, rather than hold it for her lifetime. Beatrix's half of the estate was roughly 3,000 acres which, according to their agreement, would come to the Trust on her death.[18]

It came as something of a surprise, albeit a pleasant one, that after the Trust had paid Beatrix for its portion, Hamer asked her to continue managing it for them. It was an enormous responsibility. 'I want to thank you again for the mark of confidence implied in looking after the estate at present, it gratified me very much,' she wrote to him. Beatrix was flattered that her skills had been recognized. She was also pleased that as an 'amateur land agent', she could manage her great-grandfather's Holme Ground, even if she no longer owned it. She explained to a young American editor, 'The Coniston estate is being taken over by the National Trust this month [September] . . . – they have asked *me* to manage it for a time, till it is in better order; the farm rents will enable repairs and replanting to be undertaken this winter – interesting work, at other people's expense!'[19]

Even before Monk Coniston came on the market, Trust officials had hinted that they needed a local representative in the Lake District. Beatrix adamantly opposed such decentralization in principle, but particularly feared the Trust might appoint someone with whom she could not work compatibly. For the best part of a month, she sent Hamer almost daily letters elaborating her views on the sort of refined and educated man who might fill the position, detailing her opposition to the selection of a rough local man, or some estate agent who knew nothing and cared less about fell farming. Beatrix's arguments may well have been a factor, as no official agent for the northern counties was appointed until 1932. So Beatrix, now managing the whole of Monk Coniston, continued to deal directly with Hamer and his staff in London for the next six years.[20]

Early in 1931 the assistant secretary of the National Trust, Bruce Thompson, a local man whose family had been in the hostelry business in Bowness and Windermere, wrote to Beatrix asking if he could call on her when he was in next in the area. Thompson was preparing the first analysis of the problems facing preservation in the Lake District from such threats as building expansion, afforestation, quarrying and electricity cables. Beatrix was delighted to share her views. Anticipating that Thompson would have heard criticism of her management style, particularly her difficulties with the sanitation inspector, she wrote, 'It would not surprise me to hear that in some quarters there is a feeling that I have not got on with the "amenities" (overworked word). I have deliberately put practical requirements first; and will give what I think good reasons … I don't care what people think. I could not have believed an estate could be so mismanaged & neglected.'[21]

But overseeing such distant areas and tramping about in bad weather inevitably took a toll on her health. Beatrix confessed to Marian Perry at the end of 1930, 'I have been in bed twice this winter already with bad colds – not serious, but just sufficiently bronchial to make me afraid of bronchitis if I live to be as old as my mother, which is unlikely.' To her cousin Caroline she was more candid: 'My mother is 91 and very well … She is very lucky in having good lungs, no rheumatism and good eyesight. She amuses herself with needlework and knitting. It is annoying that she is so difficult about money – a regular miser in reluctance to spend money, which will simply be wasted in death duties when she has hoarded it up.' Mrs Potter had stubbornly refused to contribute a penny to the National Trust's appeal. Despite Beatrix's feigned indifference to this slight, it must have saddened her and contributed to her crusty cynicism. Urging the Trust to publish the list of subscribers for Monk Coniston in the *Westmorland Gazette*, she noted, 'my mamma *might* feel stirred to send a trifle! – only she has just had the car varnished.'[22]

What made Beatrix Heelis so good at farming and property management seems less a matter of genes than of character. Certainly her shrewdness and flexibility in business dealings and her determination to resolve problems were qualities inherited from her Potter grandparents, but her character had been toughened by battle and honed by first-hand experience in nature. She had the necessary qualifications for doing exactly what she found herself doing at the age of 64. She had a pragmatic understanding of the seasonal variability of climate and a deep appreciation of the fragile fell farm environment, but she also retained a romantic's love of both inclement weather and the rugged landscape. She had a quiet acceptance that things will quite often go wrong, yet she had remarkable patience and optimism. Loving the natural world as she did, Beatrix had long ago accepted that nature was wild, cruel and endlessly beautiful.

Now with Monk Coniston added to the column of land she had rescued from development and preserved from desecration, Beatrix had some prescient sense as she went about her tasks that she had a hand in shaping one small part of the English countryside. She acknowledged as much in a letter to the Trust chairman, John Bailey, writing: 'It seems that we have done a big thing; without premeditation; suddenly; inevitably – what else could one do? It will be happy consummation if the Trust is able to turn this quixotic venture into a splendid reality.'[23]

Beatrix's daily work on her farms, her management of Monk Coniston, her ability to travel and certainly her creative work had been increasingly complicated by the necessity of supervising the care of her frail nonagenarian mother. Although Beatrix had become accustomed to using the telephone, the situation at Lindeth Howe required frequent trips in person to the inconveniently located Bowness estate.[24]

Helen Potter had lived a life of aimless ease in comfort and style at Lindeth Howe after Rupert's death in 1914. She was amused by her little dog and her many canaries, occupied by her needlework, and much fawned over by an obsequious staff. Beatrix always seemed a thorn in her side. She disapproved of her daughter's passion for sheep, her activities on behalf of the National Trust, and her unstylish countrywoman appearance. When she was no longer able to pay calls at Castle Cottage, William and Beatrix redoubled their visits across the lake. In 1931 Beatrix found it necessary to come across several times a week, in all kinds of weather, and in most cases, she had to walk as her mother refused to send her car or inconvenience the maid. Weary from all the effort, Beatrix came down with a serious bronchial cold. 'Mrs Heelis ha[s] not been well,' Lucy Walker reported to Joseph Moscrop from Troutbeck Park in January 1932. 'She has only once been here since Christmas.'[25]

After a difficult winter, Beatrix made the extravagant decision of hiring her mother's former coachman, Walter Stevens, who was without work, to drive her about. She was now cautious for her own health and 'rather afraid of driving in an open car in the wind. I got up to Troutbeck on Tuesday in the lorry, which is warmer than the open car,' she told Joseph Moscrop, 'and I was delighted to see the first calves, 2 bulls ... G. Walker thinks all the cows are in calf this year. Too good to be true; but a good crop I expect.'[26]

When her own health returned, Beatrix was confronted once again with the perpetual staffing crisis at Lindeth Howe. No soon had she hired nurses than her mother dismissed them. 'I hope you and your family are having a Merry Christmas,' Beatrix wrote to Alexander McKay on 18 December, obviously agitated. 'I am *not*. My old mother is refusing to die. She was unconscious for 4 hours yesterday, and then suddenly asked for tea. She cannot possibly recover ... so we hope it will soon be over; but she has wonderful vitality for any age – let alone 93.' Helen Potter died two days later.[27]

Beatrix's words seem harsh, but in the context of her weariness and of the dutiful daughter who had given so much of her time and energy to an ungracious, if not ungrateful, old woman, they betray only her customary realism and the desire to move on. The relationship of mother and daughter had always been awkward, often adversarial. There was duty and respect, but the degree of charity and understanding one had for the other is less calculable.[28]

Helen Potter was buried beside her husband at Gee Cross, Hyde, in Cheshire, on 24 December. In response to a letter of condolence from Hardwicke Rawnsley's widow, Eleanor, Beatrix wrote with more reflection than annoyance, 'My mother's long life was a link with times that are passed away, though still vivid in our memory ... she was wonderfully clear in mind, but ... I am glad she is at rest.' She rarely spoke of her mother in her letters to friends or family.[29]

Beatrix was the sole executor of her mother's estate, which was valued at £74,553. Helen left everything to Beatrix, with bequests to her past and present servants. Beatrix also inherited her deceased brother Bertram's share of dividends and securities, which had been in trust under Rupert's estate during Helen's lifetime. This amounted to £139,500, composed primarily of dividends and securities including municipal bonds, railway bonds and the notes of British Empire countries. An additional £19,359 came to her from the estimated value of 11 Bolton Garden Mews, where the household staff had lived, and later proceeds of the sale of furniture and household effects in Rupert's estate, the sale of Lindeth Howe, and auction proceeds. Small wonder that Beatrix and William had tried in vain to persuade Helen to give her daughter some further allowance while she was alive in an effort to avoid the high death duties, and to make some charitable contributions. Helen left a bequest of £5,000 to her son-in-law William Heelis, whose thankless job it was to close the estate and calculate the tax.[30]

Beatrix approved of the obituary that appeared in the *Westmorland Gazette* which stated 'The passing of Mrs Helen Potter ... caused profound sorrow to a large circle of friends and neighbours in whom she was held in great affection on account of her courtesy and kindness.' However, the subsequent notice detailing the value of her mother's estate and listing the bequests she deemed 'an impertinence'. 'The newspapers respect nothing private these days,' she wrote to Moscrop. 'They don't mention that there is over twenty six thousand to pay in duty.'[31]

Beatrix had been critical of her mother's sedentary life, obviously frustrated that despite her great wealth she seemed not to care about anything or anyone other than that which benefited her own comfort. For all the emotional damage her mother inflicted during Beatrix's brief courtship and engagement to Norman Warne, and later in opposing her marriage to William Heelis, Beatrix seemed to have successfully put it behind her, at least in terms of not letting it interfere with her sense of obligation. Most of the time she put a good face on her mother's selfish behaviour. Only occasionally did she voice frustration, notably when Mrs Potter refused to contribute to the National Trust because she had spent a bit of money on something frivolous, or when Beatrix arrived cold and wet at Lindeth Howe only to be chastised for her baggy clothes and muddy wellingtons. But with her every breath Beatrix expressed her independence, even her rebellion against the life her mother had chosen for herself and would have imposed on her daughter. She intended to be as different from her mother as it was possible to be, and she intended to end her days being active, useful, and, if she were especially fortunate, out and about in countryside she loved. As dutiful and respectful as Beatrix was, implicit in her own life choices was a deep disdain for her mother's life and values. When Lindeth Howe was sold later that spring, Beatrix was at last physically free of a life she had left in spirit long before.[32]

The demands on Beatrix's time as land agent respected none of these life changes. In addition to routine management problems, which included stopped drains, rotting timbers, broken fences and unhappy or unsatisfactory tenants, Beatrix was confronted with such extraordinary challenges as suspicious fire on the fells and sheep theft. In February 1933 night-time fires broke out on Holme Fell in Tilberthwaite. A handful of sheep were burnt as well as about a half a mile of heather and bracken. 'This fire is a wicked thing – incendiarism,' Beatrix reported to Trust officials.

Beatrix was a natural detective, observant of details and eager to investigate. She found one fire spot that could not have been caused accidentally by a child or a visitor. 'I came on this thawed circle and a nasty little stacked up heap of green savin [juniper] branches. I found the bush [drawing of bush] they had been hacked off with a knife.' There were three or four other similar spots where branches had been separately lighted; 'I think there was more than one lad in the mischief.' She also discovered a 'neat new calico bandage for a sore finger. Not a *cut* finger', caught in one of the piles of sticks. Several weeks later, she had no satisfactory solution to the crime but 'suspicion against a young man, resident at the quarry cottages' and proof that there had been a series of manmade fires. Luckily, injury to the sheep had been minimal, and the thawed ground had kept the fire from spreading.[33]

Sheep stealing was a serious matter to all Lakeland farmers and stockmen. In the winter of 1933–4 sheep began disappearing out at the remote Tilberthwaite farms. The farms had been tenanted, but in the spring of 1934 the tenant had 'thrown up and left things in a mess'. Beatrix decided to take the farm in hand herself, renting it back from the National Trust. She moved one of her best farm managers, Thomas (Tommy) Stoddart, and his wife from Troutbeck Park to Tilberthwaite to see if he could bring order to the situation. 'I do not expect a man to do the impossible . . .' she told him. 'If you can get the hoggs heafed on the sunny side of Wetherlam, without *heavy* loss, I will be *well satisfied*.' Her instincts were correct. Stoddart proved an able manager at Tilberthwaite, and by the autumn the sheep stealing had virtually stopped.[34]

Quite remarkably, Beatrix somehow found time, between solving mysteries, showing sheep, getting in the harvest and overseeing operations at Monk Coniston, to do a bit of writing. Although Alexander McKay persistently pressed for another book, Beatrix more enthusiastically took up her pen to comment publicly on topics of natural history and science that interested her. In doing this, she was returning to a habit of contributing to discussions reported in *The Times* that she had enjoyed as a young woman.

She was intrigued by a series of time-lapse photographs published in the newspaper of a toad climbing on top of a large fungus. The photographs elicited several letters, including one on the subject of 'singing' reptiles. A woman in Reigate described her success attracting toads with guitar music. Beatrix responded to the Reigate writer directly, explaining that she had little confidence that scientists would take seriously any amateur's observations or consider the matter of a toad's singing remarkable. Nonetheless she explained that she had 'known for 50 years that the British smooth newt does, very rarely, utter an extremely sweet whistling note'. Beatrix had discovered the newt was also the Highlanders' 'singing fish': a phenomenon which children in Scotland regularly reported hearing in a bog. She had heard her own newt utter a whistling sound when out of its aquarium sitting on her writing table at Bolton Gardens. Later she heard newts 'sing' again in some stagnant water near a Highland barn in Scotland.[35]

Beatrix's letter reveals that she had grown rather more cynical about the responsiveness of professional scientists to the observations of amateur naturalists. Thirty-three years after having her theory on the symbiosis of lichens and fungi rejected by the professionals of the Linnean Society, she characterized their attitude as one of 'contemptuous incredulity', no doubt having Thistelton-Dyer in mind. 'They don't believe that reptiles can "sing" and there is an end of it. Although it is an axiom of science that it is not possible to prove a negative.' Adding that there was little hope that any further evidence would be taken seriously, she wrote philosophically, 'And it makes no difference to the little "singing fishes". I should like to hear them again; but I am growing deaf.'[36]

Another exchange in *The Times* concerned the feeding of buzzards. It provoked a defensive letter from Beatrix to Hamer on the usefulness of buzzards on Trust property. 'I have had large experience of buzzards,' she wrote, 'my Troutbeck shepherds have always *favoured* them, as they clear off field mice which eat a surprising amount of herbage up the fells.' They could not possibly prey on ducks, as the article alleged, and were quite harmless, but she warned against anyone trying to domesticate them. Carrion crows, on the other hand, not only stole chicken eggs, but picked the eyes out of live sheep and lambs. 'The crows are exterminating other birds, buzzards eggs included. I have been very vexed about them, and they are most difficult to shoot.'[37]

Beatrix also turned her daily observations as land agent into short notes on such matters of wasted land, the toxic qualities of acorns and the questionable commercial value of spreading oaks. None of these notes was finished or published, but each underscores her close observations in the field and her command of livestock science and timber culture.[38]

Beatrix's long interest in the properties of dry rot also unhappily intruded into her work as land agent when she discovered this fungus in several Monk Coniston farmhouses and had to make expensive repairs. Her passion for collecting old oak and other vernacular furniture had been stimulated by the need to refurbish her tenants' cottages and the old farmhouses. She kept abreast of the market in old oak, and local collectors and dealers knew she drove a hard bargain when she found a good piece at an estate sale or in an overlooked corner of a farmhouse kitchen. 'I poked into a dark dirty little kitchen and amongst broken chairs & lumber beheld a carved & dated dark oak court cupboard . . .', she had reported to Louie Choyce. 'Unquestionably it is genuine & untouched – except by rats. It did not seem to be wormy. The back was eaten into holes . . . I think it is a very good cupboard, horribly dirty, but it will polish alright.' The cupboard turned out to be a fine example of old country oak and was given pride of place in the Hill Top entrance hall, opposite the kitchen range. A blanket chest in her bedroom was carved with a tulip and pomegranate motif. She put a carved oak bible-box which housed her Bible on top of the chest. Eventually she acquired more than a dozen fine court cupboards and chests. Most of these found homes in her farmhouse kitchens, where she believed these fine vernacular pieces belonged and where they would be enjoyed by Lakeland farm wives, and eventually would be preserved by the National Trust. When Beatrix sent Tommy Stoddart and his wife out to manage Tilberthwaite, she gathered all the old oak furniture she could find, as well as some basic necessities, and had them hauled out to the farm. She sent Tommy's wife an extensive list of the furniture and supplies, adding, 'I have the bath that I was bathed in. Would you like it?'[39]

These old furnishings enlivened all her houses, and especially at Hill Top where she combined them with other 'treasures': Chinese and English porcelain, a collection of Staffordshire earthenware and figurines, Doulton stoneware jugs, Wedgwood jasper and early Mason-ware (ironstone china). There were not many women in Near Sawrey who could afford or who understood such furnishings. But Beatrix enjoyed sharing her enthusiasms with Rebekah Owen, who was herself a collector of fine furniture and antiques. When Miss Owen moved to Italy, Beatrix bought some of her framed family silhouettes and hung them to the right of the Adam-style fireplace in the Hill Top parlour. Her most interesting piece from Miss Owen's collection, however, was a small American Windsor chair, stained a very dark green. Miss Owen told her it had been made by the Shakers about 1800. Beatrix found its simplicity as well as its unusual colour appealing. She placed it next to the fine seventeenth-century tester bed with its ornately carved panels and ceiling that she found at a sale early in her marriage.[40]

Her love of country furniture and country craftsmanship paralleled the popularity of William Morris's traditional designs for the Society for the Protection of Ancient Buildings, and of the Arts and Crafts Movement in general. As a long-standing supporter of the Society,

Beatrix was keenly aware of architectural and design trends, but above all she appreciated craftsmanship as the basis of all good design, regardless of period or style. She deplored poor workmanship and the disappearance of the old crafts. 'Shoddy is king,' Morris had famously declared, a sentiment Beatrix seconded. Her delight in simple handmade furniture also drew from John Ruskin's views on the superiority of designs incorporating forms found in nature and of handmade objects. Hardwicke Rawnsley's Keswick School of Industrial Arts had promoted local design traditions which Beatrix also encouraged. Never a blind follower of any one school, she was always attuned to what was afoot generally in the arts, no matter how remote her county life might appear.

Her love of good mahogany or old oak furniture, her appreciation of the decorative arts and her sense of 'home' and of what spaces of comfort looked like derived from the houses that she had loved as a child. She incorporated that sense of comfort and of art and craft into the interiors of her little books. When she had a house of her own, she furnished it with a mix of artistic styles. In many respects she furnished Hill Top as a set on which she played out her imaginative stories. 'I am "written out" for story books, and my eyes are tired for painting,' she wrote to Bertha Mahony in 1934, 'but I can still take great and useful pleasure in old oak – and drains – and old roofs – and damp walls – oh the repairs!'[41]

Beatrix seized an opportunity to put her interest in country furniture and good craftsmanship to practical use when she oversaw the restoration of the whitewashed Yew Tree farmhouse in 1932 and 1933. The farm was named for a famous yew which once stood on land that had been in the Walker family for at least two hundred years. It was justly famous in the district for the delicate spinning gallery that ran across the front of the barn. Beatrix did not hesitate to spend what was needed to restore the dilapidated house, including most of a new roof. As she reported to Hamer in November 1932, 'I can only say – if I have spent too much – I am totally unrepentant. I consider Yew Tree is a typical north country farm house, very well worth preserving.' She had consulted with the SPAB about its proper restoration and used a preservative on the timbers recommended by their architect-secretary, A. (Albert) R. Powys, whose opinion on such matters she trusted. Beatrix was pleased with the workmanship, especially the masonry which had been done in the 'old fashioned style'. As a witness to its reconstruction, she produced a fine pencil drawing of Yew Tree's barn with its distinctive spinning gallery on 8 July 1932, about the time the farm was once again ready to tenant.[42]

After many interviews, Beatrix selected Thomas Jackson and his wife for Yew Tree. Thomas also became the tenant farmer for the grazing land on Holme Fell and, with Beatrix's financial help, he bought more sheep stock, in order to preserve the genetic strain of Yew Tree's herd, which was the same as the sheep at Hill Top, and thereby created a permanent pool for Herdwick breeding.[43]

Yew Tree Farm had always attracted tourists. To help defray the costs of her restoration, Beatrix turned the parlour of the farmhouse into a tearoom for tourists and walkers. The farmhouse already boasted a press cupboard marked '1685' which had belonged to its earliest owner. She bought some local art and installed some of her more interesting oak and mahogany tables, a dresser, a variety of chairs and other treasures. She framed several autographed letters, including one each from the poets William Wordsworth and Robert Southey which had belonged to her father, and hung them in an enclosed glass case on one wall.

The Yew Tree tearoom opened for business in the summer of 1933, with Mrs Jackson as hostess. Although Beatrix thought Mrs Jackson a bit too 'smush' – or smart – preferring a 'genuine farm kitchen' – Mrs Jackson's teas were popular with tourists and essential to making the farm pay that year. The following summer, when Mrs Jackson was too ill to run the tearoom, the lost revenue reinforced the value of opening Trust farms to tourists as a means of preserving them. 'I think the little white farm houses and green fields in the dales are part of the character of the Lake district,' Beatrix told Eleanor Rawnsley in 1934, 'and I take such a pessimistic view of the future of our local farming . . . that I wish there may be a sufficient representative number of the old farms in the hands of the Trust.'[44]

In opening Yew Tree to tourists and teas Beatrix showed herself a pragmatic preservationist. She consciously hoped to educate the public about the value of old farms and farmhouses, as well as turn a bit of profit. In her mind there was an important distinction between preservation to protect against the building of offensive non-vernacular structures, and preservation which preserved the character of the countryside. At Yew Tree, she intended to preserve both historic building and tradition by showing its relevance and adaptability to modern use.[45]

It was ironic that after once lamenting the export of treasured English art and antiques by rich Americans, it was the *Horn Book* editor Bertha Mahony with whom Beatrix most completely shared her love of old furniture and good design. Beatrix and Bertha had become even closer after 1932 when Bertha married William Miller, the owner of an American furniture manufacturing business specializing in colonial maple reproductions. Bertha, at 50, was about the same age Beatrix had been when she married. The two women now shared not only a love of children's books and old furniture, but the experience of a late-life domesticity.[46]

In her 1934 Christmas letter Beatrix wrote to Bertha in some detail about her own Lakeland furniture collection, and described some of her favourite Chippendale and Queen Anne chairs. 'The local furniture in this district was oak, rather out of fashion in the sale room now, but I collect any genuine pieces I can get hold of to put back into the farmhouses. The court cupboards with carved fronts are the most interesting as they are usually dated . . . The oldest I know is 1639.' Beatrix found the differences between American and British styles intriguing. Bertha sent catalogues from her husband's company so that Beatrix could compare her pieces with the American reproductions. Beatrix was intrigued to discover that the Chippendale and Sheraton chairs and settees made in the United States were more delicate than the robust mahogany chairs with which she was familiar.[47]

Several years later the Millers sent Beatrix two volumes of Luke Vincent Lockwood's illustrated *Colonial Furniture* (1926), which Beatrix studied intently. She made copious notes on the designs which she may well have intended to publish. She incorporated some of these in a letter to Bertha that reflects the depth of her expertise. 'I have a theory only out of my own observations and probably only fanciful,' she wrote. 'I like to think that the craftsmen who carved our old cupboards were influenced by the strap work designs on the Scandinavian crosses, such as the Gosforth cross with its curious mixture of runic design and legend and early Christian symbolism.' She also confessed, 'I have always wanted to write a paper on cupboards for the Westmorland & Cumbrian Archaeological Society. But I am afraid it is one of the things I shall never do. A bad habit of procrastination, want of knowledge, and difficulty about procuring good photographs in dark narrow places.'[48]

Some of these creative outpourings were the result of being house-bound with gastric influenza, or what Beatrix called 'a liver chill', which sent her to bed for six weeks in the autumn of 1933. Beatrix found it 'a great waste of time in one's old age' to be ill. William was also plagued by several colds. A severe one a year earlier had left him very deaf – an unfortunate condition for a solicitor who also served as a magistrates' clerk. A specialist in Liverpool had brought about a 'miraculous cure' by clearing his eustachian tubes, but Beatrix worried that another bad cold would leave him deaf again. All in all, Christmas of 1933 was a dismal one. It came with news of 'the death of one dear old friend [her distant cousin Fanny Cooper], the illness of another still older, the dark damp weather and the remains . . . of a liverchill. I have been out of sorts since early November . . . but it is ingrateful to grumble after such a splendid spring, summer and autumn.'[49]

'You will be as welcome as the flowers of spring!' Beatrix wrote to Joseph Moscrop, as the days lengthened and the snowdrops came out. 'I have had an unlucky winter myself . . .' she continued. 'I was just feeling nicely again, when I tumbled over a board across a sill and put my right shoulder out . . . It was completely my own fault. I knew about the board. I felt very silly, but might have been worse if I had hit my head. I fell into the grip [gutter] in the shippon [cattle shed].' Fly, one of her favourite sheepdogs, had been chewing at the door sill, and Beatrix had put the board across to stop her, but then forgot it was there. Later she discovered she had also pulled a muscle in her forearm. To her friend Louie Choyce, she was more candid:

'Whenever I feel very well again – something goes wrong. I had an awful shaking up when I put my shoulder out.' Her shoulder remained stiff, and it was painful to raise her hand above her head.[50]

By summer Beatrix was feeling better. She and William had taken an unusual holiday weekend. 'We motored through Northumberland, following Hadrian's Wall and road to Chollerford . . . and next day over the Cheviots to my Scotch sister-in-law between Jedburgh and Hawick; it was a fine drive.' Beatrix had always wanted to see the Roman Wall and although they tried to spend every August Bank Holiday with Mary Potter at Ashyburn, this extended outing was especially rewarding. 'That is the only time I have slept out of this house since 2 years,' she told Marian Perry. Beatrix took pleasure in sharing her farming experiences, especially comparing notes on breeding livestock and the latest prices of sheep and wool with Mary and also with her cousin Caroline, who raised cattle on her farms on Mull and at Argyllshire. 'I am still stiff, always over busy, & feeling old,' she told Caroline. 'I do not resent older age; if it brings slowness it brings experience & weight. I am not "on" things; but I pull strings. The regional planning is very interesting just now.'[51]

For the past several years, Beatrix had been actively trying to influence the County Council, which was charged with overseeing growth and planning in the Coniston Valley. Like her earlier work with the Landowners Association, her views commanded attention. She was optimistic about the zoning of private open spaces along lake shores because the large landowners would cooperate. But, as she explained to her cousin, she was less sanguine about small-holdings. The worst zoning was in the valleys. 'If it is zoned for houses with 20–40 acres of land it will stop bungalows; but it may also destroy farms. Our pretty old white washed farm houses in the sheltered valleys are a feature of the district.'[52]

One of her concerns grew out of her desire to preserve the vernacular architecture of the area wherever possible. 'The destruction of pretty old cottages is much more serious – irreplaceable,' she told her cousin. By the mid-1930s there was a shortage of old cottages in the villages for the elderly and for large, low-income families, a condition aggravated by the New Housing Act. This was aimed at town slums, but in practice it mandated that when the County Councils condemned an old country cottage as unfit, it was replaced with fixed-rent council housing. These units were usually two-storeyed houses that Beatrix scorned as 'little hatbox council houses'. The housing and health inspector's policies about which cottages were habitable and which were not were inconsistent and frequently arbitrary. Beatrix, who had once thought seriously of being the Lake District representative for the Society for the Protection of Ancient Buildings, took up her pen in protest on several counts – worried that Near Sawrey cottages could be next and annoyed by the housing inspector's remark that 'all this talk about preservation is piffle'. She vented her frustration to Anne Carroll Moore, who was planning to visit: 'You had better come . . . while there are any left; he says half Hawkshead wants pulling down. The new . . . council house is ugly and flimsy and "high rented" compared with our old thick walls and stone built chimnies. It seems very shortsighted policy when the Lake District depends so much on tourists and visitors.'[53]

In a letter published in *Country Life*, Beatrix decried not only the hardship to a few cottage families who loved their old-fashioned seventeenth-century homes, but the change in Lake District architecture implicit in the council policies. 'The ancient farm houses and cottages were long and low,' she wrote. 'New two-storeyed houses . . . are bound to be taller than the old local type. Two recently built Council houses near Coniston are conspicuous for miles. It is the fashion to decry bungalows . . . but at all events these amateur little houses, built by local quarrymen, do not flaunt their roofs and chimneys in the upper air and sky.'[54]

Beatrix was familiar with the perils of bureaucratic regulations. She had regularly come up on the wrong side both of the housing inspector and of Mr Bolton, the local public health inspector. Several cottages at Tilberthwaite were occupied by many more people than health regulations allowed, but Beatrix was unwilling to turn the tenants out, especially in hard times. Bolton's job required him to inspect all the farm cottages and certify them for occupancy. There is a credible story that Bolton once brought with him a copy of one of her little books when he came to inspect a Tilberthwaite cottage and asked Beatrix to sign it for him. She initially refused, saying she never autographed her books, whereupon the inspector let her know that she could not expect any further 'cooperation' from him in the future. At that, Beatrix is said to have snatched back the book, signed it, and handed it back, warning: 'if you tell anyone about this I will not let you come on any of my properties again.' The certificate for occupancy was promptly issued. Such were the private negotiations required of the Trust's 'amateur land agent' which Beatrix confided to William at day's end, but rarely revealed in her letters.[55]

19

❧ *Passages* ❧

As she moved into her eighth decade, Beatrix and William were enjoying life together as they had not been able to do in many years. After twenty-three years of marriage, the Heelises had settled into a companionable domesticity. Still in good health, they took pleasure from the certain routine of the seasons and the work of their days. Ageing seemed to bother Beatrix very little, and she was busier than ever. 'You ask how I like growing old,' she wrote to her cousin Caroline in February 1937. 'I have felt curiously better & younger this last 12 months! . . . Also do you not feel it is rather pleasing to be so much *wiser* than quantities of young idiots? . . . I begin to assert myself at 70 . . . It is a pity that the wisdom and experience of old age is largely wasted.' Unfortunately, the wider world around them was increasingly unsettled and unpredictable. Beatrix was wary of the military build-up in Germany and disdainful of England's participation in the League of Nations, but for the moment she intended to enjoy the certain and celebrate the familiar.[1]

The year had begun with an unusual domestic crisis. The Heelises had been invited to celebrate her cousin Edith Gaddum's silver wedding anniversary at a party at Brockhole, the Gaddums' estate on the shore of Windermere. But William faced a challenge when it came to gathering the appropriate evening attire. Beatrix recounted his dilemma to her sister-in-law with humorous indulgence. 'We knew his [evening clothes] would not button; and when the matter became serious, it was remembered that they were sent to a jumble sale many years ago! George's are large enough. The figure does not seem to be quite correct in front, G. being even more portly than W, but I am careful not to criticize as Wm. is quite sufficiently perturbed.

I bought him 2 different patterns of ties yesterday; and now he has no collar that satisfies him.'[2]

Beatrix had different problems: 'My long, handsome ancient silk gown *will hook!!* and trains have returned into fashion.' But her hair, or rather her lack of it, was the difficulty. Beatrix's rheumatic fever had left her not only with painful joints, a condition she called 'rheumatics', but with a bare patch on the top of her head. 'I have no hair and no wig,' she complained to Grace, 'do you think I can go in a tam o'shanter!?' Only half-jokingly she briefly considered her father's old barrister's wig, stuck away in a box, but then remembered it had 'little tails'. In the end, she decided to 'rig up a lace cap'. Their efforts rendered them presentable, and the happy gathering was all the more memorable because Edith Gaddum died the following year.[3]

While William enjoyed country dancing all year round, as well as his various sports, Beatrix had few social outlets in the winter. Both Beatrix and William worked over the complicated farm valuations that were due each year, but she relied on William entirely to prepare the farming accounts. She kept busy with the District Nursing Association annual reports, and planned the annual jumble sales to raise money. The Queen's Nurse, Celia Edwards, had been busier than ever, with an expanding territory to cover, the burdensome regulations of the newly enacted Midwifery Act, and babies born inconveniently in snowbound cottages in outlying Coniston. Beatrix and Edwards had become valued friends and so when Edwards decided to retire after fourteen years of service, Beatrix was pleased that she decided to take temporary lodgings close by in Hawkshead. 'We shall all look forward to seeing you as a friend – if not as a nurse,' Beatrix wrote. 'I remain with much love.' A new Queen's Nurse, Mrs Heaton, took up residence at Beatrix's cottage at Hanniken and made her visits in William's old Wolseley Hornet.[4]

Each spring there were also applications from various Girl Guide groups to use her fields for the holiday camps that began at Easter. Her fields, especially at Hawkshead, continued to be popular with the Guides and the Boy Scouts, and few summer weeks went unsubscribed. Nora Burt, her favourite Guide leader from the Chorlton Guides, was in nurses' training and no longer came to camp, but

Beatrix took an interest in her career, as she had in her Nicholson nieces, and they exchanged frequent and, for Beatrix, rather intimate letters. 'It is a real pleasure to me', she wrote to one of the Guide leaders, 'to see young people enjoying the land that I love so well; though I cannot manage to enjoy every square yard of it myself . . . I feel as though the beauty of my own woods and fields might have been a bit wasted if it had not been useful to appreciative campers and holiday makers.'[5]

At 70, Beatrix had given up, if indeed she had ever seriously tried, keeping either a tidy house or her muddles of papers in order. William had his law office at Hawkshead, so the large table in the centre of the hearth room at Castle Cottage was primarily her working desk – though it was used for all sorts of other purposes as well. It was perpetually strewn with letters, maps, land ordinances, books, news-papers, sheep catalogues, flower seeds, clippings, jottings of all kinds and things waiting to be sorted. If a visitor called, a place was created by pushing the piles to another spot. Quite often supper was served on a cleared end. After dinner William and Beatrix enjoyed playing two-handed piquet or a game of cribbage. William was a heavy smoker all his life. His tins of tobacco, cigarette papers and ashtrays, along with the coveted cigarette cards saved for the favourite Hyde Parker nieces and other young collectors, were also near at hand. When electricity came to Sawrey in 1936 Beatrix would have none of it. 'I'll put it in the shippon's [cattle shed],' she told a disappointed Tom Storey, who would have been pleased to have it at Hill Top, 'the cows may like it.'[6]

With the exception of the ritual trip to Ancrum to see Mary Potter, Bertram's widow, the Heelises were too busy with farm and estate work to travel much. William was a poor driver, very cautious, and very slow. He frequently stalled on the hills, obliging his passengers to get out and put stones behind the rear wheels while he tried to put the car in gear. William drove back to Appleby occasionally to see to the needs of his elderly sisters, who remained at Battlebarrow. Grace and James Nicholson also travelled less. Esther was working in New Zealand, and only their niece Nancy stopped occasionally on a holiday from her posts as Norland nurse for young children. But other younger second cousins had taken their place as regular summer visitors.

Stephanie Hyde Parker Duke, her husband, Lieutenant Commander Duke, and their two daughters, Rosemary and Jean, had been coming regularly for several years to spend time in July and August at Castle Cottage. The girls went fishing with William in Moss Eccles Tarn and looked forward to being out in the countryside. Beatrix frequently took them along when she went out to Monk Coniston to check on her farms. Walter, her mother's former coachman, now employed as Beatrix's chauffeur, drove one of her mother's large old cars, affectionately dubbed 'Noah's Ark'. It was not unusual for Beatrix to pick up a sick sheep or two, and put it in the back seat along with the girls to take to the vet or to drop at another farm. The roof leaked and if it rained they had to put up an umbrella inside. 'Noah's Ark' and Walter were well matched in age and disability. Walter, far more comfortable with real horses than with mechanical gears, frequently had difficulty getting the large car and its cargo up the steep Lakeland hills. In such cases, he would lean forward as if urging horses on, forgetting entirely what gear he was in. Beatrix would shout from behind the glass, 'Change gear, Walter, change gear!' and the old car would lurch forward, 'and the sheep would baa', and the little girls would 'laugh and laugh'.[7]

Stephanie, to whom Beatrix had dedicated *The Tale of Jeremy Fisher* in 1906, remained a favourite cousin. By 1936 her annual entourage at Sawrey had expanded to include her Pekinese dog. Beatrix had no use for such pampered creatures, but upon hearing how energetically the little dog had climbed up the steep paths on Helvellyn, she changed her mind, and asked Stephanie to get her one. After a brutal winter, with some of her sheep at Troutbeck Park buried in snowdrifts for eighteen days and so many of her old friends and neighbours in the village gone, she found both pleasure and comfort in the small female peke who arrived just in time for spring. 'We have a queer little animal here,' she wrote to Marian Perry, 'a small female Pekingese, a very "heathen Chinese" for mischief and naughtiness, but engaging and affectionate. The colleys don't like her; she is impertinent.' By summer she had bought another one, this time called Chuleh, so that Tzusee would not suffer being an only child. 'Here we have found mild but harmless amusement from 2 little Pekingese ladies, I always despised foreign dogs; but these are both spirited and affectionate, and less trouble than terriers, as they get sufficient play and exercise in the garden.'[8]

Soon the little dogs and their antics became a feature of her letters: 'Tzusee and Chuleh are going round and round under table and chairs like a hurricane, the puppy chasing the older one.' The two little dogs were thoroughly indulged by both Beatrix and William. Given complete freedom of the house, they even slept on the bed at night. Beatrix discovered their virtues as 'foot warmers' during dark cold winter nights. Although William sometimes made a show of being tough, they became his devoted shooting companions after impressing him with their fearlessness and their ability to catch rats, even some in the Castle Cottage pantry, and quite remarkably, an occasional rabbit.[9]

As the Great Depression deepened in the United States, fewer Americans visited Lakeland and fewer old friends found their way to Near Sawrey. Beatrix missed them. As compensation she wrote more frequently, describing the progress of farming, her sheep and cattle, the harvests and the changes in the countryside as she observed them on her rounds for the National Trust. She especially missed Marian Perry and her niece Betty Harris, now married with a family of her own, with whom she also kept up a correspondence. Like many older people, Beatrix enjoyed recalling those people in her life who had given her special pleasure.[10]

For twenty years, Beatrix had been corresponding with Ivy Steel, the young girl who had once delivered millinery from their mother's shop to the Paget family in Bolton Gardens. Ivy was now married, living in New York, and had a 12-year-old daughter, June, to whom Beatrix also enjoyed writing picture letters. Ivy worked hard at being a good mother, and at Beatrix's suggestion enjoyed taking June to the Bronx Public Library. Beatrix was curious about Ivy and had it in her mind that she would enjoy seeing her and her little girl. She knew that the family had gone through hard times in the Depression and that Ivy had wanted to visit relatives in Scotland. When Beatrix generously offered transatlantic passage for mother and daughter in the summer of 1936 so that they, and their Aunt Jessie, who had been the Paget lady's maid and was still in London, might visit her in Sawrey, Ivy happily accepted.[11]

One day in early August, Beatrix sent Walter and the car to Windermere station to pick up her American visitors. Beatrix had not seen Jessie in seven or eight years. They all met at Castle Cottage, and then Beatrix took them to Hill Top where they were to stay. The visit proved a great success and Beatrix thoroughly enjoyed herself. 'I was very relieved to find I liked "Ivy" as much as when she was a young girl – and I was interested in her girl,' Beatrix reported to Betty Harris Stevens. 'It was the first time I had ever heard the native accent of Bronx. I am tempted to say I hope I may never hear that accent again. She was a dear child. When one got over the accent she compared favourably with the average English child of the same class; obedient, intelligent, and natural manners without forwardness. But the accent was a caution; on her father's side descended from Glasgow Scotch which is even worse.' After their visit Beatrix wrote to Ivy, 'You will be so much more real and dear in future, since I have really seen you and liked you. It has been a real pleasure to me to find you both so loveable.'[12]

There was another, quite unexpected, visitor from Beatrix's past to Sawrey that summer whom she described in a letter as 'a middle aged active man, a clergyman in Kent'. It turned out to be none other than Noel Moore, the little boy for whom she had written the Peter Rabbit picture letter in 1897. 'He called here,' she wrote, 'and said "You will not remember me?" I said "I seem to remember your face."' Much influenced by his mother's strong religious convictions, Noel had taken degrees at Cambridge, studied for the priesthood at Bishop's College, and been ordained in the Anglo-Catholic tradition in 1915. He had served at a parish in the docklands of London's East End, and later at another on the outskirts of London. Beatrix still corresponded with his mother, Annie Moore, and she must have suggested that Noel call on Beatrix while on holiday.[13]

But new friends and new challenges kept Beatrix more involved in the future than the past. Between 1934 and 1936 she purchased several significant properties in beautiful Eskdale and in Little Lang-dale, one of most remote and untouched of the fell valleys. These were areas north and, in the case of Eskdale, significantly west of Monk Coniston. She bought them not only to preserve traditional fell farms and their Herdwick stock, but to prevent town development and particularly the destruction of wild scenery. These farms added over 2,300 acres and nearly a thousand sheep to her holdings, as well as valuable woods and rights of way.[14]

Unlike her purchase of Monk Coniston, Beatrix bought these farms with the intention of managing them personally. But equally important, her move into Eskdale and Little Langdale signalled to the National Trust that Beatrix Heelis's interests in land and fell farm preservation had enlarged beyond one or two self-contained geographic areas. The timing of her purchases was also important, as Samuel Hamer, her trusted ally, retired as Trust secretary at the end of 1934. Beatrix viewed this change in Trust leadership with considerable scepticism. Her purchase of these five farms was, there-fore, also meant to underscore her increased independence from the Trust.

Beatrix's expansion as a landowner, and her success in buying up farm property utilizing William's advance knowledge of the market, caused some local resentment, but by 1936 her expertise as a farm manager was also widely respected. That autumn, Delmar Banner, a portraitist and painter of mountain landscapes who had been renting places in the Lake District for some years, took the sensible course of enquiring about any small parcels in Little Langdale that might be suitable for building a home and studio for himself and his artist wife, Josefina. Unlike other 'offcomers' who wanted to buy land in the Lake District, Banner wanted to be off the road and up high in the fells with a view out over the valley, a request that Beatrix as a fellow artist understood.[15]

Beatrix had been introduced to Banner sometime in 1935. An artist and intellectual of independent means, Banner was also a devout and rigorous Anglican lay minister. He had studied history at Oxford and painting at Regent Street Polytechnic. He came from a family of distinguished musicians and clergymen who had settled in Liverpool.

In 1930 he married Josefina de Vasconcellos, the only child of a talented Brazilian diplomat and an over-protective English Quaker mother. Josefina had been working as a sculptor since the early 1920s and her reputation had been growing steadily. As a wedding present, Josefina gave Delmar the complete set of Beatrix Potter's little books, which he had not known as a child. They found particular delight in *The Tale of Pigling Bland*, and because Josefina had the habit of snorting when she laughed too hard, Delmar dubbed her 'Pig-wig'.[16]

Beatrix had seen some of Banner's landscapes, perhaps at Hawkshead, and had offered some advice as to how to improve them. She thought him talented and liked his work. In early September 1936 she wrote, 'I was a little alarmed to find how seriously you had taken my criticism. But they *are* wonderfully better – breadth, atmosphere; without sacrifice of colour and drawing.' She expressed particular interest in one of his landscapes of Coniston, asking if he might hold on to it for her, explaining, 'A day will come when my old legs refuse to climb stiles and wet lanes, so painted views will have to suffice.'[17]

Beatrix advised the Banners not to buy a remote fell farm since they had no experience in farming, and also expressed her dismay that land values in Langdale were being inflated by the 'misdirected zeal' of 'well meaning outsiders', referring to the National Trust. 'I have the deepest respect and admiration for the National Trust as an institution,' she told them, 'but the present officials are not very satisfying at buying properties. Unsatisfactory. I don't want them meddling in Little Langdale.'[18]

Delmar invited Beatrix to lunch after the big Eskdale Sheep Show in late September, where Beatrix was judging as well as exhibiting Herdwicks. She declined, as she customarily had lunch with the shepherds, and she also cautioned him, 'You mustn't talk to me about anything till after the judging is over on Friday.' But it was Josefina, not Delmar, who came to greet her after the show, introduced by Clive Bulman, a fellow farmer and judge.[19]

Josefina had been around Eskdale long enough to make her own inroads into fell culture, learning the country dances and shepherds' calls. On this particular day she was serving huge plates of food at the shippon to the farmers who had risen before dawn to bring their stock over the valley to exhibit or sell. Josefina was a tall, slender woman with striking rather than beautiful features. She had thick, curly dark hair, unusual green eyes, and large, strong hands. She was wearing a dark blue boiler suit and clogs when Bulman brought her over to meet Mrs Heelis. Beatrix's attire for judging at sheep shows was quite formal compared to her usual farm garb. She had on her best Herdwick tweed coat and skirt, a wool scarf, a felt hat held on her head by an elastic strap under the chin, and clogs on her feet. According to Josefina's recollection, the little round woman with rosy cheeks and sparkling blue eyes sized her up, took in her dirty overalls and clogs, and issued a rare invitation to come to Castle Cottage in two weeks time.[20]

Josefina's recollection of their first visit is marked by an artist's attention to detail and the soft lens of sentimentality that comes from recalling the event and the friendship between herself and Beatrix that followed. Tea was served in the farmhouse kitchen, which had a cheerful fire, dark oak furniture, a large table and red plush Victorian armchairs. The Banners remarked upon a fine Girton watercolour on the wall, a painting Beatrix showed off proudly. There were beautiful tall silver candlesticks on the table and silver-mounted guns in the hall. Josefina recalled they sat on 'very straight-backed chairs, feeling rather like Pigling Bland and on our best behaviour because she was quite over-awing'. Beatrix was very interested in the two young artists and questioned them carefully about their work. Whether it was on this first visit, or some subsequent one, Delmar asked if he could see some of her original book illustrations. She returned from upstairs with bundles in brown paper, some fastened with blue ribbon. The Banners expressed their admiration for her art, but Delmar remembered that Beatrix responded, half to herself, 'Aye, they'll do nobody any harm.'[21]

Beatrix was attracted to this artistic pair by their energy and talent, and by the fact that when they came to the lakes on holiday they worked on the farms they visited and participated in country life. They, in turn, were flattered by her friendship, knowing that she did not make herself available to many, but they did not lionize her. Beatrix studied the work of many artists who came to paint in the

Lake District, but she did not have many close artist friends. When the Banners were in the area, she found their company stimulating.

After buying the watercolour of the Coniston fells she had admired, Beatrix felt free to offer Delmar further advice on his drawing. She appreciated this particular landscape because she thought it reflected a temporary stage in landscape painting when the goal of the artist was to be typographically exact in detail. She explained to him, 'So I seized on that landscape while I could get it, because for better or worse you may possibly not paint like that a few months or years hence.' Having praised his clouds, she went on to suggest that he give some consideration to 'studying trees'.[22]

Beatrix was rightly critical of many professional woodland landscape painters who never 'considered how the branches grow from a tree trunk'. She told Delmar, 'if you study an ash you will see every branch from the main trunk, or the stem of the young sapling, has come out in curves; and curved on and on with the weight of foliage. Other species in contrast grow upward. We can tell every tree in winter without reference to foliage by its mode of growth. So study them some spare moments Mr Banner; they will repay – they are – *in the right place* – as beautiful as rocks. And they have a nobility of growth which is usually entirely over looked.' Several months later, after seeing the work of another fell painter at a Kendal gallery, she wrote to Josefina urging Delmar to get more light into his paintings. 'Your husband has learnt clouds. Light next please. He has the *drawing* that is the foundation.' It was therefore a great compliment when Beatrix acceded to Delmar's repeated pleas to photograph her for a portrait in 1938. She refused to sit for such a thing – no time and no patience. He painted her in her good Herdwick wool coat and felt hat, against a background of the fells and scenes of the sheep show at Eskdale, holding a show programme in one hand, the umbrella that Norman Warne had given her in the other.[23]

Josefina de Vasconcellos Banner, on the other hand, was an altogether different sort of woman from anyone Beatrix had met before. She wrote poetry, loved music and dancing, did woodblock printing, and enjoyed handicrafts of all sorts, as well as being a fine sculptor. Josefina found Beatrix an 'intuitive friend': 'She knew a lot without having to be told.' After seven years with Delmar, Josefina was a desperately unhappy wife. Her marriage had never been consummated, and Delmar had banished her from his bed. Later she would understand that he was a homosexual, and that their relationship would never change. Beatrix sensed Josefina's despair as well as her restless creative energy. In their letters and conversations she may have shared something of her own childhood and Norman's tragic death, but the extant letters provide no details. What is clear is that Beatrix found pleasure in their friendship and much to admire in Josefina as an artist and independent spirit whose efforts to triumph over despair were not unlike her own.[24]

The winter of 1936–7 brought an unusual amount of snow to the Lake District. Beatrix found it 'beautiful to look at, but hard for the mountain sheep when it lasts so long'. But Christmas was cold and wet. At first, Beatrix fretted about the quality of grass for keeping up butterfats in the dairy herd, but she was preoccupied with the widespread economic unrest in the farming world. 'Too much [government] interference; well meant; unavoidable; but unsettling and very expensive.' Wool prices were rising, 'yet', she told Louie Choyce, 'men are wanting to give up sheep farming and turn to *milk*; although the dairy farmers grumble too.' The worst blizzard to the Lake District in a generation hit on 1 March with the highest drifts Beatrix had ever seen.[25]

She insisted on getting out to Troutbeck as soon as roads were clear, only to find that in some intakes the drifts were level with the top of walls. 'I went up the lane above the farm house walking in a narrow trod which the shepherds had trampled,' she told Nancy Nicholson, 'it was curious to look down over a seven foot wall, with snow elbow high on the other hand.' There she watched the shepherds digging the sheep from the drifts. 'We lost perhaps 30, perhaps more, when the drifts disappear . . . Our men got out about 400 . . . mostly no worse.' But there were other consequences from the long spell of snow showers and bitter weather. 'I have lost all faith in the climate,' she complained. 'Good lambing weather is past expecting. There are 3 lambs here; and dead twins this morning. I am afraid there will be many dead lambs, from the fell sheep.'[26]

When Beatrix wrote her customary note to Joseph Moscrop in February asking him to come to the Park for spring lambing, he had surprised her by asking for a raise of a whole pound to £16. Beatrix objected, complaining of the drop in wool prices and the poor return at the fairs. 'I really think you ought to be content with £15 Joseph! You are a hard nut! . . . Think it over.' Even though she thought it a big increase, such negotiation was now part of the give and take that had become a tradition between them, and her objection was more rhetorical than real, while her fondness for Joseph was patent. 'Spring would not be spring time without the smile of Joseph!' she told him. By May, the damage of the harsh winter was evident everywhere.[27]

Late that spring there was a major outbreak of foot-and-mouth disease, and a thousand vets were mobilized to try to contain it. Beatrix was rightly alarmed. She had been expanding her herds of cattle at all of her farms, but particularly at Troutbeck where George Walker had been successfully raising and breeding shorthorns (both beef and dairy). Beatrix was as fascinated by the lineage of animals as she was of people. Although her interest in cattle dates from her summers at Dalguise, by 1937 she had invested time and considerable capital in their breeding, trying to create a line that would be adaptable to fell farming.

Much of her early interest in beef cattle came as a result of her close relationship with Mary Potter in Ancrum, and her annual visits to her in the Scottish Borders. Mary and Bertram had kept some fine specimens at Ashyburn. Perhaps because of her visits to the Borders, and her memories of summers in Perthshire, Beatrix became particularly enamoured of Galloways, a hornless breed associated more with the Scottish Lowlands than the fell farms of Lakeland. Her pleasure in them was akin to her passion for the Herdwick; an appreciation of the animal first for its ancient origins in the rugged coastal environment of Galloway, then for its beauty, its distinctive coat of thick black curly hair, and finally for its adaptability to poor land. Galloways are unrivalled as a grazing breed, utilizing coarse grass and still producing high-quality beef. Beatrix was convinced that Galloways could be successfully raised on her fell farms.[28]

In the late 1920s Beatrix had begun corresponding with C. S. Forrester, a local stockman from Skitby, north of Carlisle on the Borders, in whom she came to have confidence and from whom she bought her first Galloway bull for the Park. She also bought both a black and a white bull, intending to cross them with the Galloways to create a line of Bluegrey, another breed of shorthorn. She was especially delighted with the white bull, and anxious for Joseph Moscrop, who was also an expert on cattle, to see him. 'I like the look of him . . .' she wrote. 'I hope he is lucky. He was a luxury; we have a liking for the Agricultural products, man & beast, of the Northern Border, although expensive.' She was fascinated with the bull's beauty and made several sketches of it, but sadly, she had little luck with it as breeding stock.[29]

Her seriousness about breeding and selling beef cattle is apparent from the increasing numbers listed in her farming accounts, beginning about 1936. These animals were much more costly than sheep, and her experimentation was a serious financial investment, but as war approached, it made sense economically. In 1937 her farm inventory lists 94 cattle, of which 36 were beef, but two years later, she had a total herd of 112, of which 64 were beef.[30]

But raising cattle, like sheep, was a volatile business, and Beatrix's hopes went up and down. In the spring she wrote to Joseph about the availability of heifers at Road Head or any dispersal sales, telling him, 'I am worried about the cattle at Troutbeck Park. I don't think I shall go on keeping a galloway bull, and rearing home bred heifers. The younger cows are nothing like as sound as the original Road head's. Although they are bigger and fine looking – too many have gone wrong at 3rd or 4th calf. A sure sign of Johne's disease . . . I believe heifers are less likely to be infected than young calves. They pick up the microbes as calves, but it does not become a serious state for several years.'[31]

Beatrix's observations about cattle going bad after several calvings were unusually insightful for the time as no one understood the cause of 'Johne's disease', which infected cattle, sheep and goats, and was soon to become a worldwide problem. Even in the late 1930s it had become particularly virulent in England, Scotland and Wales, where commonly sheep and cattle infected each other. Johne's was a wasting disease similar to tuberculosis in its aetiology, and it had no cure. Cattle simply wasted away, unable to digest food. They could be infected in the womb, by nursing, or by contaminated milk, and calves were most susceptible in the first two years of life. It was highly contagious, and vaccines were of little use. It is now suspected that tuberculosis, and therefore Johne's disease in cloven animals, can be spread by the badger, a creature Beatrix had already made the villain in *The Tale of Mr. Tod*, but which she unwittingly protected when she banned hunting by otter hounds or harriers at Troutbeck Park. Despite the risk, Beatrix persisted in her efforts to breed Galloways and increased her herds whenever she found good stock, enjoying the animals and, on the whole, making money by it.[32]

By far the most time-consuming and personally challenging changes Beatrix confronted during these jittery pre-war years had to do with her evolving relationship with the National Trust. The appointment of Donald M. Matheson as Trust secretary in 1935 had been expected. Bruce Logan Thompson, who had been the Trust's northern representative since 1933, was named land agent for the northern district in 1936, the first land agent for the Trust anywhere in England. Prior to his appointment, Beatrix informed the new secretary that she and William would retire from active management of the Trust's portion of Monk Coniston at the end of the year. 'I shall be glad to give him [Thompson] any information which may be useful for the management of the Trust's Coniston estate,' Beatrix wrote. 'This management will be a much simpler matter when the delapidations [*sic*] consequent on 30–40 years of neglect have been remedied.' But it was another year before the Trust took over their half of the estate.[33]

Thompson was then nearly 40 years old, a studious, thoughtful man who had known and admired Hardwicke Rawnsley, and followed him into the Trust. Since at least 1931 Thompson had been a frequent presence in the Lake District, completing his survey of Trust properties in the northern area, and after 1933 overseeing all the Trust properties there other than Monk Coniston. When Thompson was named land agent, he already had an extensive understanding of many of the local problems relating to the Trust, and although he did not have agricultural training, on every other level he knew nearly as much about Lakeland's past and present as Beatrix Heelis.[34]

Bruce Thompson also had the advantage of not being an off-comer, a status that Beatrix could never overcome. He was named after his uncle, Bruce Logan, who had made his fortune in the carriage trade in Windermere; the same gentleman who had generously allowed Beatrix to observe the fox-hunt on the Troutbeck fells in 1924. Thompson had grown up in Bowness and Windermere, where for generations his family had owned the Ferry Hotel. The same year he was appointed land agent he married his wealthy cousin, Mary Rigg, whose family was also in the hostelry business, being proprietors of the famed Windermere Hotel.[35]

Thompson had a deep interest in the history and culture of the Lake District. He had read history and archaeology at St John's College, Cambridge, and was an active member of the Cumberland & Westmorland Antiquarian and Archaeological Society and a trustee, along with William Heelis, of the Armitt Trust Library. He was a handsome, courtly man, with a quiet, self-effacing manner, tending to the philosophic and the intellectual. He was well known in the local villages and immensely well liked by farmers as well as gentlemen. He and Mary raised fell ponies for the National Trust, and they often rode out together to the Trust farms to collect the rent. Tom Storey also knew and liked Thompson, having known both him and his wife before he came to work at Hill Top. Thompson was also a popular leader in the Boy Scout movement, and even when he lived in London, he had frequently accompanied Scout troops to camps, sometimes using Beatrix's land in Hawkshead and at Troutbeck, where she had welcomed them. Beatrix Heelis and Bruce Thompson had much in common, and their paths and passions intersected at important points, but their relationship after 1936 was neither easy nor predictable.[36]

Thompson's appointment as land agent was an obvious, as well as an inspired, choice. Although he lacked Rawnsley's robust passion and combative style, his knowledge and quiet demeanour had their own merits. It is impossible to know, then, why Beatrix Heelis found him so unsuitable as a land agent, but she did. Most likely it was a clash of personality and style, and more than a little jealousy on Beatrix's part.

Beatrix knew from experience that none of the members of the Lake District Estates Committee, to whom Thompson reported, had any substantive agricultural experience, and yet for the first time the National Trust was faced with significant estate work in Coniston: keeping up physical property as well as agricultural land and livestock. On this account she was justifiably concerned that her seven years of back-breaking work for the Trust would be undone by an inept agent and committee that would allow the property, especially the farms, 'to fall back into ruin'. She considered Thompson a dilettante who did not understand the essentials of estate management: the chronic expenses and the constant repairs necessary to 'buildings damaged by tempest; woodlands; drains, occupation roads and paths etc.' This legitimate concern was aggravated by significant differences in style between the two. Thompson was deliberative and thoughtful, whereas Beatrix usually knew her mind and got on with it. She was blunt and forthright, and she appreciated this quality in her shepherds and her farmers, even when it verged on rudeness. Thompson, by contrast, was unfailingly courteous and diplomatic, regardless of how rude or crusty she was. For whatever combination of reasons, Beatrix found little to admire in Bruce Thompson and was never enthusiastic about his appointment, and never wholeheartedly supported him.[37]

Knowingly or unknowingly Thompson challenged Beatrix's real or assumed authority on several levels. His appointment as land agent of necessity took away some of her local independence and altered her status with the Coniston farmers and tenants. It also allowed him to do things that she, as temporary custodian, had not been able to do, and she was understandably jealous of that authority. She complained that he did not listen, and although he was solicitous of her opinion, he sometimes went ahead and did things his own way. Unfortunately Bruce Thompson's sins were those of both omission and commission, and probably there was nothing he could have done, particularly as manager of the Trust's Monk Coniston farms, that would have gained her approval. This is regrettable, for had the two been able to forge a close working alliance, the National Trust's work in the Lake District would have been immeasurably more successful.

Trust officials transferred Monk Coniston to Thompson's oversight in January 1937. Although the Heelises had indicated when they bought the whole of Monk Coniston in 1930 that they intended to give the portion they retained to the Trust as a bequest after their deaths, that gift was by no means assured. Therefore Trust officials walked a tightrope in their management of Monk Coniston, hoping that nothing would be done to offend the Heelises or make them change their mind about the ultimate destination of the larger, and more valuable half of the estate. Beatrix was aware of the power she wielded and was not above threatening to withdraw her gift. So while she continued to manage her Monk Coniston farms, the Trust, in the person of Bruce Thompson, rather awkwardly took over the rest.[38]

From the outset Beatrix adhered to the line that she would give Thompson information, but that she would not offer advice. In January alone Beatrix sent Thompson four long letters laden with specifics on every conceivable aspect of farm management, including equipment recommendations, preferred sources of materials, lists of tradesmen, together with a commentary on their skills, fees and reliability, a history of various problematic drains and fences, and a half-completed planting key. She belaboured the need to use only round wire, 1 cwt No. 9, to repair any fences near flood water because woven wire netting got clogged with debris. She had chosen tenants, fixed rents, approved and organized repairs, and managed timber cutting. Understandably, after nearly seven years it was difficult for tenants and their families to suddenly look to Thompson as their representative landlord, and invariably lines of authority got twisted. Moreover, Beatrix was accustomed to doing things her way. Now she had to endure the effect of Thompson's independent decisions. Areas of potential conflict emerged early and centred around repairs to fences, the planting of new trees and the harvesting of timber.[39]

Throughout 1938 Beatrix's letters to Thompson show an increasing testiness. Commenting on the management of Yew Tree Farm, she wrote, 'I have felt it very awkward and indeed quite wrong to offer any advice that might seem interfering with a new agent. We all have to learn by mistakes; I remember making plenty! I thought, since you mention it, that Holme Fell fence was a costly mistake. It is exactly the sort of wild open fell ground that ought and could be left open to the public . . . I can't imagine why you fenced it?' But a week later, she had remembered herself, writing: 'After further consideration I should like to withdraw any expression of opinion about Yew Tree . . . I am always glad to give you any information which I can about the Coniston estate or about elementary details of estate repairs; but it is manifestly not fair to *either* of us for me to interfere by comments that might amount to advice upon any matter.' But unable to restrain herself, she added, 'My expression of opinion was not intended to cover problematical useless fences . . . In future I think I had better confine myself to minding my own business.'⁴⁰

But barely a month later, Beatrix was horrified to learn that instead of cutting down a single larch tree that had blown over the wall at Tilberthwaite, Thompson had approved the felling of a 'whole group of magnificent old larches' at the foot of Tilberthwaite Ghyll and had the further temerity to sell them to a timber merchant she had specifically warned him against. 'You are right to exercise your judgement in this and other matters; but please be careful that no decisions on *any* matters are attributed to my suggestions . . . I begin to think you are rather a dangerous young man to talk to!'⁴¹

In May Beatrix was sufficiently frustrated to go over Thompson's head to Matheson in London. The particular issue was who would pay for new fencing at Holme Ground where she, as Trust tenant, was grazing cattle. It was a muddled jurisdiction, to be sure, but by now her grievances included a multitude of decisions to which she took exception. 'Mr Thompson's usual excuse for delaying farm repairs is that the Trust "has no money,"' she wrote to Matheson. 'He said this morning that there was "plenty of money" but that "he did not think the Trust is under obligation to fence land that has not been fenced before." . . . Is it the policy of the National Trust to take no interest in its farms? or is it not? I regret heartily that I ever presented Holme Ground to the Trust.' Clearly upset, she continued, 'I have asked Mr Thompson 3 times not to buy the "wry-lock" type of netting, but he seems to have no understanding about anything; and he is not learning either . . . If my cattle hang themselves or get lost you will have to pay for them.'[42]

Thompson had little choice but to write his own letter of explanation. 'I am afraid you may be getting an angry letter from Mrs Heelis about a fence at Holme Ground Farm,' he wrote. Getting to the heart of the difficulty, Thompson acknowledged: 'Because the National Trust are anxious to do everything to please Mrs Heelis I have given instructions for the work to be done. But Mrs Heelis is evidently very indignant with me because I made the mistake of demurring when the suggestion was first put forward.' Matheson must have dabbed at his forehead over the entanglement, but he wrote the next day reassuring Mrs Heelis that the 'National Trust appreciates the importance of good farming'. Beatrix retorted sarcastically, 'An institution which pays neither income tax nor death duties should be in a position to give a useful lead to less fortunate landowners. As regards advice – a man must have judgement to sift the value of advice and of advisors, otherwise it is like the fable of the old man and his donky [*sic*] . . . It is not my affair or wish to interfere with Bruce Thompson; and most emphatically I cannot take any responsibility for anything he may do.' Thompson's additional efforts to placate her did little good, as Beatrix wrote to Matheson a week later about another jurisdictional dispute commenting: 'I am getting very tired of Mr Thompson.'[43]

Perhaps Thompson did not appreciate how emotionally tied Beatrix was to the Tilberthwaite farms, and specifically to Holme Ground, but even if he had been more sensitive, the farms were under Trust management and he had to push on with thinnings and repairs as he saw fit. He had tried his best to accommodate her views, frequently calling on the Heelises at Castle Cottage on Sunday afternoons. But, to his peril, he had severely underestimated her concern with preserving the pastoral landscape, and how the arrangement of trees figured in that effort.

Thompson was genuinely taken aback when Matheson reported he had received a scorching letter about the cutting of timber at Tilberthwaite Coppice. Beatrix had written, 'Although it is probably useless I am writing about your agent Mr Bruce Thompson. There is a keen demand for all sorts of wood, and he may do irreparable damage. It is useless for me to talk to him. A man cannot help having been born dull. Thompson is supercilious as well.'[44]

Thompson's crime, which Beatrix described as 'wicked', was the indiscriminate cutting of scrub wood amongst the rocks in the coppice. 'An experienced agent with any taste for the picturesque would have decided to thin it in patches, deliberately and cautiously.' She further complained that Thompson had no taste at all for the preservation of natural beauty. Admittedly there were plenty of coppices of no interest, 'but the coppices in Tilberthwaite and in Yewdale which clothe the lower slopes of Holme Fell are specially beautiful; glorious in autumn colours, and in winter & spring.' She itemized Thompson's further sins, concluding: 'He seems to have no sense at all. And not capable of learning. Indeed, excusably; because it is impossible to inculcate a pictorial sense of trees arranged in landscape, when imagination is a blank ... My husband & I never drive through Coniston without vexation. There is a great quantity of possible hardwood that might be cleared with advantage, but Mr Thompson is too deficient in experience and taste to be trusted to choose it.'[45]

Beatrix sent a second letter outlining Thompson's deficiencies to the members of the Estates Committee, not having much confidence in Matheson to rectify matters. Privately, the National Trust Estates Committee, chaired by Professor G. M. Trevelyan, found her letter 'a rather exaggerated outpouring of an injured lady's mind', and thought it unfortunate that Mrs Heelis chose to involve herself in such matters as the artistic arrangement of coppice wood. They advised Thompson to go out of his way to consult the Heelises about all Monk Coniston timber matters, and refer all woodland questions to the Estates Committee so that 'any criticism they may make will be directed at the Committee rather than at you'.[46]

Thompson's letters show that he understood that, while the issue of woodlands and natural beauty was genuinely important to Beatrix, the larger issue was one of whose view of natural beauty would be preserved, and who would control it. He told Matheson, 'The whole matter is in itself of small importance but it has led to the revival of former grievances. I have always . . . referred any major woodland problems . . . to you or Heyder [Trust woodland adviser]. Mrs Heelis does not, however, reckon much of you or Heyder or me: none of us is a patch on Hamer.' Without any attempt at self-justification, he continued,

I realise only too keenly how much the Trust wishes to win the approval of Mr & Mrs Heelis and I have this constantly in mind but you probably appreciate that my position isn't an easy one. When I took over the management of the Monk Coniston Estate it was on the understanding that I should have the Heelises behind me. With certain exceptions Mrs Heelis has generally taken the line that she would give me information but not advice. Advice, of course, is just what I would like to have had.

Thompson wisely cautioned his superiors in London, 'you must'nt [*sic*] be surprised if there's a storm now and then'.[47]

Beatrix may have been correct that Thompson and the other Trust officials had little sense of the pictorial when it came to thinning trees, and little sense of the picturesque as a value in landscape preservation. Just as she had lectured Delmar Banner to study how trees grew, she was ahead of her time in urging natural beauty as an important value in preserving an historic landscape. The 'timber question', as she referred to it, was something that she had thought about, as both an artist and a preservationist. Few administrators at the National Trust understood that such seemingly mundane things as thinning coppice on fell sides were integral to the whole question of what sort of landscape would be preserved. In December 1939 Beatrix wrote to Louie Choyce, 'I think ⅓ of the trees in this district could be felled with positive advantage to the landscape, provided they were properly selected, and the remaining trees left in suitable groups.' Beyond such comments, Beatrix seems not to have elaborated further on a subject about which she had very deeply held views.[48]

But her scornful personal remarks about Bruce Thompson in this controversy reflect poorly on Beatrix. The privileges of age, wealth and patronage had made her careless and inconsiderate of others in the preservation community with whom she needed to cooperate.

She had grown intolerant of opinions or methods that differed from her own, and for seven years no one had challenged her. In this case she allowed petty jealousies, mere bagatelles of turf, to get the better of her basic generosity and her profound concern for the future of the Lake District. Had Bruce Thompson been a lesser man, or one who had not shared her ultimate goals, including the preservation of natural beauty, Beatrix's behaviour could have had disastrous results.

Although Thompson's appointment as land agent relieved Beatrix of some estate management duties, she was almost immediately saddled with the care of another property closer at hand. Rebekah Owen had become increasingly unhappy living in England and in the summer of 1937 she decided to move to Italy permanently. Beatrix bought Belmount Hall, Owen's handsome Georgian stone mansion with its twenty-six acres on the outskirts of Hawkshead, in August. Miss Owen made a half-hearted effort to sort and package up her enormous collection of Thomas Hardy's books and her other valuables for auction at Sotheby's, but the old woman was hopelessly disorganized, and left in a hurry, leaving bulging albums of Hardy's correspondence, autographed books and assorted literary detritus locked away in one room of the house.[49]

Beatrix had done what she could to help Miss Owen sort and sift. 'Do you remember I told you about some furniture & china at Belmont [*sic*] Hall?' Beatrix wrote to Marian Perry, whose visit to Beatrix that summer had brought great pleasure to both old friends. 'Miss Owen could not make up her mind to sell and disperse it – she went back to Rome in very poor health, and the place remains locked up. Romantic, but damp! She burnt a lot of clothes and things in the yard before leaving.' Beatrix supervised the shipment of Miss Owen's books, including the bulk of her Hardy collection, to London where most of it was bought by a professor of American literature for the library of Colby College in Waterville, Maine. She took possession of a derelict property with a locked room filled with Miss Owen's personal possessions. She could do little about these, but with the help of her gardening friends, Miss Hammond and Miss Mills, she began the more enjoyable task of restoring Belmount's once splendid old walled gardens. It was a preservation effort of a different sort and one she enjoyed. 'Is chimonanthus fragrans a bush that would grow?' Beatrix asked of Caroline, who knew more about shrubs than she. 'I have witch hazel, and shrubby spiraeas, and syringas.'[50]

But by the autumn of 1938 Beatrix was worn out and apprehensive at the very real possibility of hundreds of evacuees being dispersed into the countryside. 'The seasons have been all wrong,' she complained to Anne Carroll Moore, whom she had seen again that August. 'We did not finish hay till Sept. 19th. There is plenty of it, but not very good. My husband is well – I am not! I have had colds and sciatica and chills one on top of an other.' She confessed to Marian Perry that in addition to not feeling well, she was depressed by the death of old friends and neighbours.[51]

Beatrix was sick enough at the end of October to seek medical attention and was quietly referred by the local doctor to Arthur Gemmell, a highly regarded gynaecologist and surgeon in Liverpool. Beatrix entered Liverpool Women's Hospital on 31 October for surgical repair of what she described to Daisy Hammond as a 'insignificant [urethral] caruncle.' She was to have a complete anaesthetic because 'the place is difficult to get at – right in the opening to the bladder, and . . . it would be too difficult and painful without complete anaesthetic.'[52]

The condition, not uncommon in older women, was particularly painful, and the cause of repeated bouts of urinary tract infections and aggravated bleeding. After the surgery and three days in the hospital, Beatrix spent the next ten days recuperating, somewhat unsuccessfully, at Nurse Edwards's little house in Higher Bebington, Cheshire. She had found the hospital 'comfortable and interesting, and quite amusing' but described the setting in Cheshire as 'noisy without interest . . . Its sad to see the eating up of fields & trees.' She put on a more cheerful face for Nancy Nicholson. 'Your uncle must have written in woe begone style! I abandoned him for eleven days for the first time in more than 25 years!!' Beatrix looked forward to being back in Sawrey, admitting, 'I am a country mouse, like Timmy Willy.'[53]

December found her again unwell and, like everyone else, anxious about England's military unpreparedness and unhappy that America had not been moved to help. 'It is fatal to give way to bullies in the first instance,' she told Bertha Mahony Miller, but even her truculence could not hide her anxiety. 'The shipyards & docks [of Barrow] are only 15 miles away . . . Unless America backs us up – we are done.' Her outlook was made worse by exhaustion and her physical discomfort. 'Enforced leisure indoors does not reawaken literary inspiration. I'm sorry Miss Mahony!' Beatrix wrote to her Boston friend. 'The wells of fancy have run dry! I can think of nothing but forebodings.'[54]

As Hitler's troops began meticulously dismembering Czechoslovakia, Beatrix bravely sent Christmas greetings to her American friends. But her efforts at cheer were mostly futile. 'Things are gloomy here . . .' she wrote to Marian Perry. 'The best hope is that the Germans themselves will become tired of Hitler . . . No one wants war; but this country has been made a fool of.' The weather deepened her dismay. 'We have rain – rain – rain – luckily no snow in the lowlands or we would be deeply buried – never was such a wet year in oldest memory!' But Beatrix had her own particular antidote to foreboding that surrounded her. As she explained to her cousin Caroline, '"Thank God I have the seeing eye", that is to say, as I lie in bed I can . . . walk step by step on the fells and rough lands seeing every stone and flower and patch of bog and cotton grass where my old legs will never take me again.' For now it would suffice.[55]

20

❦ *Challenges* ❦

WHILE NEVILLE CHAMBERLAIN'S government waited to see what Hitler would do next, Beatrix Heelis of Near Sawrey was intently preparing for spring lambing, the return of Joseph and his dog, and the birth of new calves at Troutbeck and Tilberthwaite. She took the rationing of petrol and the other unpredictable shortages in her stride, and focused her energy on her farms and what she could control of the world around her.

The winter of 1938–9 had been 'gloomy, in every way'. Both Beatrix and William had influenza. It spread through the farming community and through each household. Beatrix complained to her cousin, 'I got up the day our maid went to bed; which was some blessing. But I wasted 5 weeks indoors.' At Troutbeck Park, George Walker's good dog Matt was nearly dead from pneumonia, and distemper had spread through the kennels. Johne's disease continued to plague the cattle at the Park, particularly the Galloways. Beatrix knew it was nearly hopeless to try to breed them there, but it was a passion she could not give up. 'It is the old trouble,' she told Moscrop, 'in the soil and pasture. The new heifers are at Coniston. I do not think adult cattle catch the disease.' She also persisted in using whatever vaccine was available, having observed that vaccinated adult cattle did not seem as vulnerable. In her spring letter to Joseph, she once again insisted he take a cut in wages. 'You will please come down a pound Joseph – take it or leave it! Not even King Canute could control the tide – or the slump.'[1]

Meanwhile Beatrix and William, like the other hill farmers, did what they could to prepare for the war that was by now inevitable. Beatrix remembered that in the last war she had missed butter and sugar the most, but it was perplexing to decide what stores to lay in this time. 'I have laid in a hoard of dog biscuits for our two little dogs,' she wrote to Marian Perry, who had wisely decided against her usual European holiday. 'They turn up their snub noses at biscuit, while they can get scraps of meat, or rabbit . . . One must just rub along and see what comes.'[2]

There had been changes in the Heelis family. James Nicholson, Esther and Nancy's father, died, leaving his wife, Grace, in serious financial difficulty. As sister-in-law, there was little Beatrix could do, and she never meddled. She remained in touch with Nancy, encouraging her career as a Norland nurse; happy to hear her news or to have her at Castle Cottage. With characteristic downrightness, Beatrix told her, 'Do not be puffed up, but I begin to think you Nancy are the only one of the bunch with any heart or proper feeling.'[3]

A different sadness came with word from the Borders in February that Mary Potter, Bertram's widow, had died. Although Beatrix was in the middle of clearing out Belmount, she and William set off in wet weather for the funeral at Ancrum, leaving the pekes with the spinsters next door. Beatrix took charge of burying Mary next to Bertram in the picturesque Scottish cemetery in the tiny village. She wrote to Daisy about the funeral, calling Mary 'a nice Scotch body; homely quiet and sensible.' Beatrix now had to help Mary's niece Hetty, and her sister Ina, who stayed on at Ashyburn, settle Mary's estate, which included an enviable collection of Potter family art and furniture, and substantial income in securities. She brought back a few more of Bertram's paintings which they hung at Hill Top.[4]

On 29 March 1939 Beatrix entered the Women's Hospital at Liverpool for a serious operation. She told very few people about her surgery. To Joseph she wrote simply, 'I am going away from home for a few days next week, so I left it with Walkers to fix up the date.' Surgery the previous November had not satisfactorily repaired the caruncle and for several weeks Beatrix had experienced serious vaginal bleeding. She surmised on her own that she was probably in for more than the curetting that Dr Gemmell first suggested, since she realized 'anything in the womb is apt to be the beginning of the end'. 'I have not been well this six months . . .' she admitted to Nora Burt. 'We all have to reach journey's end, and I am a stout cheerful old person so I may get through curetting, – but it is rather like the "writing on the wall" to see haemorrhage.' To Marian Perry, she confided, 'I have felt very tired and aged the last two years. Maybe the surgeon will put me right – but he cannot put me young again.'[5]

Mrs Rogerson, Beatrix's housekeeper, was left in charge of Castle Cottage and the precious pekes, Chuleh and Tzusee, while Beatrix was away. Before Beatrix and William arrived at hospital that Wednesday, Beatrix dictated her will and legacies to her husband, who wrote it all down in pencil in his tiny, fine hand, and she signed it on 31 March. She had also made enquiry as to whether there was a crematorium in Liverpool. She explained to Nora without sentimentality, 'Apart from my poor old husband – I don't care. Its wonderfully sudden & easy, going under with the new way of injection – and how very much more convenient for cremation than Sawrey; then the clean residue would go back to the intake looking up the fell.' Her sheep and her farms were always at the centre of her concern. Before her surgery, she wrote to Matheson, the Trust secretary, just in case William was 'too upset to remember to write', giving formal notice that she intended to give up her tenancy at Tilberthwaite and Holme Ground Farms in the spring of 1940, but asking that this decision be withheld 'for a time till we see whether I survive . . .' She further instructed the Trust to 'purchase a sufficient landlord's stock of sheep – it would be wicked to let them be dispersed a second time after the labour and profitless expense incurred by the shepherd and me, in founding a new heafed flock.' Matheson assured her that her wishes would be carried out. William did remember to give the notice, but did not mention ending the tenancy until after the surgery, bravely telling Thompson, 'I am very anxious but if she gets over the next few days I have every hope of a complete recovery.'[6]

Surgery was not scheduled until Saturday, 1 April, and Beatrix used the time in hospital to write letters to friends to whom she wanted to say a final word. Her letters to Daisy and Cecily, to Marian Perry and to Anne Carroll Moore reflect both her apprehension and her courage at facing what was in 1939 quite dangerous and somewhat primitive gynaecological surgery. It is clear that Beatrix feared becoming an invalid more than death. 'I have failed in strength more than people know this last 2 years. Most times it has been an effort to walk to Hill Top. I am so glad I was feeling particularly well last week; and I have seen the snow drops again . . . [T]he whole world seems to be rushing to Armageddon. But not even Hitler can damage the fells.' She gave Daisy and Cecily a list of instructions, mainly to do with how she wanted furniture and china arranged at Hill Top, should she not survive, voicing her frustration that she had not done more of it herself. She admitted, 'I am conceited about arranging china.'[7]

Clearly concerned about William, she told her spinster friends,

I hope that Cecily and Wm will walk out little dogs on Sundays; they are old enough to face comment! *Could* she learn picquet or could you play 3 handed whist? It would be far best for the poor man to follow Willy Gaddum's example and remarry, provided he did not make a fool of himself by marrying, or not marrying, a servant. The misfortune is that I have acquiesced in such slovenly untidyness and unpunctuality that I am afraid no old maidly lady would put up with it; and he is old to remodel.

Mindful of their loyalty and friendship, Beatrix assured them, 'I have very great confidence in the good sense and kindness of both of you. If I did a kindness in providing a nice house – a lovely house – you provided me with my delightful neighbours.' She closed with instructions about the disposition of her clothes to the Friends of the Poor and some particularly historic costumes to the Manchester Museum.

To her two American friends, Beatrix wrote rather more anxious letters. She told Marian Perry, 'I am in no pain or discomfort, but awfully worried about my husband. You might have noticed I am the stronger minded of the pair, also the money is mine; death duties would make it awkward for him and the servants. He belongs to a family who have the privilege of dying suddenly – in their sleep. I have always hoped to survive!' She was reading *Uncle Tom's Cabin*, recalling how her nurse had read it to her when she was a small child. But she also shared her love for the Lake District, and the comfort she drew from the 'lonely hills'. 'What a pretty country it is at the Lakes is it not? Hitler cannot spoil the fells, the rocks and fern and lakes and waterfalls will outlast us all . . . I want to say how much pleasure I have had from knowing you and other delightful New Englanders.'[8]

To Anne Carroll Moore, whom she had seen more recently than 'dear Mrs Perry', but who would always be more of a professional than a personal friend, Beatrix voiced her anxiety about the sorry state of the world. She expressed her regret that not all the 'Caravan' stories ever 'got hatched', but remained resolute in her decision not to publish more. In 1932 Beatrix had allowed Alexander McKay to publish *Sister Anne*, a rather grisly version of the tale of Bluebeard, which had been among the second group of 'Caravan' stories. It had not sold well. 'I have always felt that the New Englanders understood and liked an aspect of my writings which is not appreciated by the British shop keeper,' she explained to Moore, 'though very possibly children the world over appreciate it, without consciously understanding that there is more in the books than mere funniness. They circulate anyhow; more than 150 thousand [little books] sold last year. Astronomical figures! How ever will the nations pay their debts?' Sending her regards to Moore's doll Nicholas, she wrote, 'good-bye if we don't happen to meet again. Keep on the safe side of the Atlantic. Remember me to all friends.'[9]

On Saturday, 1 April Arthur Gemmell performed a subtotal hysterectomy using a mid-line vertical incision. Whether there was evidence of carcinoma of the uterus at the time is unknown. William kept vigil at the Adelphi Hotel in Liverpool while Beatrix remained very ill indeed. About one week after the surgery, Beatrix experienced severe vomiting, undoubtedly a reaction to the ether/chloroform anaesthesia, and burst the stitches of the incision, requiring more surgery to repair the damage and significantly delaying her recovery. She was in considerable discomfort but tried bravely not to be discouraged. 'As to whether I am thankful I refuse to make any observation before seeing how it lasts,' she told Moore. And to Daisy, she wrote, 'I do not think it is merciful to put an old woman through such an experience.'[10]

After spending a nervous Easter with her in hospital, William went back to Sawrey with his laundry and a heavy cough and cold and a month later Beatrix returned to Sawrey. She felt remarkably well considering, and was happily occupied sorting through Miss Owen's papers, having satisfied herself as to the progress Miss Mills had made on reconstructing Belmount's perennial beds. She complained only of swelling in her ankles and of tiring easily. She had done a bit of weeding, and was looking forward to going to the sheep farms when she was stronger. She was intrigued by the possibilities for bracken control offered by a Holt's bracken breaker, a device for wounding the bracken fronds, and she corresponded with her cousin Caroline about the best time to attack the bracken beds on the farms.[11]

In early July the drought had broken and haymaking had begun. Beatrix was going about with the aid of a stick, happier walking than being shaken about in a car. Her greatest pleasure, however, was finally getting back to Troutbeck Park. She told Marian Perry about it: 'I went to the Troutbeck sheep farm this morning and watched the men clipping, and afterwards had the cattle driven into the "West fold," a fine sight, about 30 black cows with their calves at foot, and a magnificent white bull. He is a lovely beast and so far he is very quiet.' Beatrix's appearance at Troutbeck was warmly celebrated by her farm manager George Walker, his wife, and the farmhands. Lucy Walker told Joseph Moscrop of the visit two weeks later. 'Now you will like to hear of Mrs Heelis. She was up here on her first visit a fortnight gone Tuesday . . . [I]n fact she looked wonderful when she was up here, no doubt she is an old lady with plenty of grit!!! She told us it would be twelve months before she could say if her operation had been a success, if so the doctors told her she could "be good for 10 years".'[12]

But the evening after her visit to the Park, Beatrix experienced violent stomach pains. A few days later, she was taken by ambulance back to Liverpool. The local doctor's initial diagnosis was an appendicitis, but that was most likely incorrect. Beatrix referred to it as 'digestive trouble'. She explained to Miss Choyce that the doctor had chided her for eating too much food too soon, although she thought privately the abdominal pains had come from the extreme changes in temperature from very hot to very cold weather. She stayed in hospital nine days and was given what she described as a 'thorough overhaul'. It seems likely that her incision split open again, since Gemmell would not release her until he had 'observed' the result. She was ordered extended convalescence as she had been very sick and her pulse was rapid. Writing to Nora Burt at the end of July, she wondered if it had been gastric flu, which had been going around the village, a more likely explanation than appendicitis. Nearing her seventy-third birthday, Beatrix realized she was much weaker than she had been in April.[13]

Beatrix never seemed to really mind being in hospital. 'There could not be a pleasanter place to be ill in,' she had written to Miss Choyce after her hysterectomy. 'I have been twice in Catherine Street hospital, and both times I have been heartily sorry to leave!' She was observant of the nurses and enjoyed the company. Her natural instinct for story-telling and her childhood practice of eavesdropping were talents that she employed there with favourable results. She enjoyed listening to the stories told by the other women in the ward, telling her cousin, 'There are 2 other women in the small ward; one very cheerful party who seems to have had vast experience; and another – the wife of a sea-captain-mate or engineer, who is a bundle of nerves. She admits to smoking 300 cigarettes per week . . . The nurses & sisters seem very pleasant.' In April she had been befriended by a 'little Jewess whom I found so interesting to talk to . . .' The two must have continued to correspond, for the woman came to visit Beatrix when she was hospitalized again in July. This time Beatrix was fascinated to learn her views on the Palestine question. Eternally curious about people and the world around her, she used her curiosity in the most trying of circumstances.[14]

Beatrix had been interested in nursing all her life and had great regard for her care-givers. Nora Burt was working as a nurse in Scotland, and had come to visit Beatrix in November 1938. Beatrix wrote warmly to the young woman while recuperating again in July, particularly interested in her work in the Scottish countryside. 'I will not be able for going away,' she wrote wistfully, wishing she could see Scotland again, 'its evidently my job to keep within reach of

Liverpool! though they say I need not expect to have it again.' She confided, 'I suppose I shall recover – its getting a bit wearisome.'[15]

Beatrix's recovery from this secondary illness was slower than from either surgeries. Over the course of the next months she suffered further complications because the vertical incision had weakened her abdominal muscles and the abdominal wall bulged. She wore a wide elastic as a sort of girdle to hold herself in. As the years passed, Beatrix became increasingly stooped. Neighbours attributed this hunched posture to arthritis or curvature of the spine, but it was primarily the result of the failed incision, and the source not only of considerable pain, but real inconvenience in going about or doing any outdoor tasks. Only occasionally did she complain, and then it was usually to despair of ever finding a new, clean piece of elastic to hold herself together during wartime when such things were extremely scarce.

Beatrix's surgeries required some inconvenient domestic adjustments. Nurse Edwards, who frequently clashed with the outspoken Daisy Hammond, came to Sawrey to help care for Beatrix and took over the spare room at Castle Cottage. A hospital bed was set up for Beatrix in the big upstairs sitting room. When Nurse Edwards left, Beatrix needed to find different sleeping arrangements. 'I have always sneered at married people requiring 2 beds! but now don't know what to do,' she wrote to Miss Choyce. 'W. H. is an uneasy bed fellow, in the habit of rolling up the whole of the bedclothes – so much so that the last three winters I have hit on the plan of having a thick separate rug. There is not room for 2 beds in our old bedroom and the spare room is bitterly cold in winter, perhaps it will be better to sleep in the piano. It is a pleasant outlook.'[16]

When war was declared in September 1939 Beatrix was in the midst of gathering the harvest. Sheep fairs, which had barely begun, were quickly cancelled. William was busier than ever. He had been appointed to the County War Agricultural Committee, an important and powerful group and well suited to his talents. He made the rounds of local farms, estimated food reserves and helped make decisions on what crops to grow and how much pasture to plough. He continued serving as a magistrate's clerk and later he took his place as a rather elderly, but altogether willing, reserve policeman, with a 'tin hat'. Beatrix observed that the ploughing committees were 'more sensible than the last war', and was pleased that the district had been designated for stock raising rather than corn growing. Beatrix explained to an American friend, 'Mr Heelis & I are both busy with useful work, but not hard work this time. I am too old to take charge of the pigs & calves this time.'[17]

Although not many farm lads had been called up, enough had volunteered, so that there was a shortage of farmhands. 'The lads want to go,' Beatrix lamented; 'they regard the war as a pic-nic. I only trust and hope they won't be gassed. Hitler is an awful brute; and what a mad mistake to invite the Russians in. I think they are a rotten country.' The early months of the war had little impact on the farm economy. 'So far there is no shortage at all – though butter will be a perplexity,' she wrote to an American friend in November. 'I don't know who will stop us eating our own but I suppose conscience will prick. There are no evacuees in this village. We see a good deal of activity overhead being near the coast, but so far no raids have come so far as the west coast, and every one runs out when we hear a plane.' Beatrix and William were both dismayed by the flood of government forms that greeted them. 'I put down to grow oats & potatoes, and I am being circularised to know why I object to grow an approved crop?' Beatrix bristled; 'If he writes again I shall ask him if he wants the address of rabbit holes? I am licensed to sell milk butter potatoes rabbits and margarine!!!'[18]

Beatrix was better at the end of the year than she expected to be, and complained only of occasional sciatica and of feeling the cold in her bones. She told Choyce, 'I am very well now; but aged. W. H. has *not* been standing up well to the worries of the times.' He was out late in the cold making his rounds as a reserve policeman, checking that houses were properly blacked out. 'I am always thankful to see W. safe back! he has never liked driving at night, even with lights. He has been overworked lately – one clerk is called up; another seriously ill.' To Nora Burt she confessed, 'I am not very comfortable about my husband – we are getting old! Whether he is really unwell; or whether he saw and heard too much about hospitals & operations last April I don't know. He has been laid up twice this winter. A big strong man(?) Takes badly with it.' But she was 'thankful to have fires indoors and food, when one reads of the awful suffering. And no end in sight, the war seems to spread.'[19]

Both William and Beatrix were happy to see spring come in 1940. 'The bluebells are very lovely and the hawthorn blossom like snow on the green hedges and the cuckoo calling; a world of beauty that will survive . . . whatever happens to us.' Their domestic tranquillity had been disrupted once again, but not entirely unpleasantly, by new lodgers at Hill Top. Beatrix learned that her second cousin, Sir William Hyde Parker, Ethel Leech's son and Stephanie Duke's older brother, had been badly injured in a car accident in the blackout, near his ancestral home, Melford Hall in Suffolk. Melford Hall itself, where Beatrix had spent so many lovely days sketching, had been commandeered by the army. After surgery in London, William, also known as Willie, together with his Danish wife Ulla, their son Richard, and infant daughter Elizabeth, were homeless. Ulla, a tall, large-boned blond woman, who had visited Beatrix on several occasions since her marriage in 1931, telephoned asking if she could help them find lodgings.[20]

Beatrix found rooms at a local inn, but Willie was so weak that after a time the innkeeper was uncomfortable keeping them. At that point Beatrix offered them Hill Top. She sent over a big spare bed which was set up in the back sitting room where Bertram's landscapes kept watch. She cleaned out drawers and put away her fragile furniture and collections of china. Ulla understood what Hill Top meant to Beatrix, and went about making a temporary home for her family, while protecting Beatrix's possessions as best she could. 'The Parkers are in Tom Kittens "house". They are dear little children, but I felt it would tire me out in this house . . . Richard, aged 3 is a pickle,' Beatrix told Marian Perry. The Hyde Parkers' residence at Hill Top at least temporarily put an end to Beatrix's fear that it could be commandeered to house evacuees from one of the nearby towns. 'If any more evacs arrive,' Beatrix wrote, 'they will have to sleep on the floor.'[21]

Beatrix wrote to Anne Carroll Moore in May with more optimism about the future than she had felt in a while. 'The war has made little difference to living,' Beatrix wrote; 'there has been no scarcity yet – except paper, which we collect save, and there is a great demand for timber, but mainly fir trees which do not cause any regrettable gap in the landscape.' But she acknowledged, 'of course it would be idle to conceal that we are very anxious – personally in old age – it does not matter much to us, & we will "stick it out" what ever happens.' But it was clear that Beatrix, like the rest of Britain, was bracing for the possibility of a German invasion. The British Expeditionary Force was being beaten back, Belgium had surrendered and France was on the brink of collapse. Relieved in an odd way that she had no 'young ones' herself, she told Moore that she was concerned about Rosemary and Jean Duke. She wanted Stephanie to send the girls to Canada or the United States.[22]

When Beatrix was especially anxious she wrote letters to her family and friends, often several on the same day. She confided to the Dukes, 'It is the aliens I am afraid of. When I am worried I find relief in writing letters – sometimes I post them – sometimes not.' Telling them about her American friends, all 'genuine "New Englanders", the old stock,' Beatrix urged that if worst came to worst, 'send your daughters to finish their education in the States or Canada.' She had already alerted her friends in Philadelphia that they might expect the Duke sisters.[23]

Kenneth Duke was serving as an ordnance inspector in the northern district, and frequently stopped by to see the Heelises and his sister and brother-in-law at Hill Top. He appears to have been uncharacteristically anxious about his daughters' future, and with the best of intentions Beatrix did what she could to help by involving her American friends, but she rather overdid it. She arranged for the girls' lodging and even authorized Marian Perry to hold her American royalty payments during the war so that they would have access to funds. During the dark days of spring 1940 telegrams flew from Sawrey to Philadelphia. Beatrix went to a good deal of trouble and so did Mrs Perry on her behalf. It was Beatrix's way of taking some action in the face of the total helplessness that she found nearly unendurable.[24]

By the middle of July, the most frightening days, after the fall of France and the retreat from Dunkirk, were past. The Royal Air Force with its squadrons of Spitfires and Hurricanes was preparing to defend the country. Beatrix wrote to Moore, 'It is still difficult to realize that we are at war. We have had no raids here . . . As for invasion – we don't know what to think.' By the end of the month she was more hopeful, telling Marian Perry, 'There is a great change of feeling – a complete recovery of confidence compared to that black ten days.' But sadly, her optimism was premature.[25]

In August 1940 the German Luftwaffe began targeting coastal airfields in a critical phase of the Battle of Britain, and a month later daylight attacks switched to London. Beatrix's letters to America were now censored, so she was careful about what she wrote, but she sometimes addressed a comment to the censor himself. There were occasional stray planes going over the fells at night, and sometimes a bomb was dropped in a field but did not explode. The sheep seemed not to mind the noise overhead or the inconvenience of metal shrapnel in the grass. More people were injured in automobile accidents in the blackouts at night than by bombing. The shipbuilding yards at Barrow were continual targets, and there was fear of raids from Ireland, but mainly Beatrix complained that 'people *will not* take cover. I was in a cottage yesterday when a plane flew very low and every child ran out to watch it.'[26]

Once the British military had raised some resistance to Hitler's plans for invasion, Beatrix was less frightened than curious. 'I think I am sustained by a sort of stunned curiosity to see what happens?' she told Mrs Perry. 'I am very cripply, on a stick. Any dream of ending as a comfortable petted semi-invalid is vanished! But it never could have been in any case. I will hobble about till it is ended.' She admitted she too went out hoping to see a 'dog fight', and admired the 'wonderful flying by our own patrols'. 'One thing is certain,' she told Bertha Mahony Miller,

I shall not run far. I will retire into the nearest wood . . . If there is an invasion, I am afraid villages near the landings will be burnt. I look wistfully at my fine old furniture. I have a wonderful old bedstead too

416

heavy to move in a hurry. Nevertheless I went to a sale at Coniston . . . & bought 3 chests and a coffin stool . . . [T]wo of my chests are plain & long, like deed boxes. They might come in convenient in the wood for holding things, dry and solid.[27]

Beatrix's letters to Bertha Miller during the war are among the most revealing. Even though they had never met, their mutual respect and shared interests in children's literature, books and old furniture, as well as the similarities of their domestic lives, had deepened their bond. Beatrix admired Mrs Miller's efforts to raise the level of children's literature. She thought *The Horn Book*, a 'splendid publication; the articles and critiques are so alive; and real criticism, speaking out'. In England, Beatrix thought, 'the review of the new crop of children's books is either indiscriminate, exaggerated praise, or silence'. Beatrix also appreciated that *Horn Book* reviewers did not go in for the 'Freudian school' of criticism which she herself had no use for whatsoever.[28]

In January 1933 the English novelist Graham Greene had published a critical essay in the *London Mercury* describing Potter's influence on his writing, commenting on what he described as her 'selective realism, which takes emotion for granted and puts aside love and death with a gentle detachment . . .' Among other comments, Greene speculated that 'At some time between 1907 and 1909 Miss Potter [with the creation of the perfidious Mr Drake Puddle-duck in *Tom Kitten* and the sinister Mr Tod] must have passed through an emotional ordeal which changed the character of her genius.' Beatrix had been sufficiently aroused by what she considered Greene's ridiculous foray into amateur psychoanalysis to respond to him. She explained she had been suffering from the flu when she wrote *Mr. Tod* and not from any emotional upset.[29]

Such intrusive personal speculation as Greene's deepened her indebtedness to Bertha Mahony Miller, not only for her advice on publishing *The Fairy Caravan*, but also for what she considered the fair and impersonal critical appraisal she gave her work in the pages of *The Horn Book*. Writing to her friend in December 1934, Beatrix had reiterated her wish that 'I could think of something worth while writing for it'. But nothing came of that good intention until Miller wrote in the summer of 1940 recounting her little granddaughter's undiminished enthusiasm for *The Fairy Caravan*, and her desire for more stories about it. Nancy Dean wanted explicitly to know where the caravan was now, and where it was wandering to next.[30]

Beatrix was so moved by the child's pleasure in tales she considered very personal that she took time out in the midst of worries about bombs and evacuees to respond to her.

When we grow old and wear spectacles, our eyes are not bright, like children's eyes, nor our ears so quick, to see and hear the fairies . . . Where can the circus have wandered to? I believe I know! Right away amongst the fells – the green & blue hills above my sheep farm in Troutbeck. Such a lonely place, miles along a lovely green road. That was where I first saw the mark of little horse shoes. There is an old barn there that we call High Buildings . . . and when I was younger and used to take long walks, I used to eat my bread & cheese at High Buildings, or shelter from the rain. That was where the Caravan sheltered in a very wild rainstorm, and Xarifa made acquaintance with the melancholy Mouse . . .[31]

A few months later Bertha Miller, who was planning to write an essay for *The Horn Book* on Beatrix Potter's 'nursery classics', wrote to ask if she would consider adding to the biographical essay on the origins of Peter Rabbit that she had first written in 1929. At the same time, she told Beatrix she wanted to publish 'Wag-by-Wall', a story that originally had been part of the unused 'Caravan' tales. Beatrix read over her previous statement and decided that she had something to add as 'one's outlook alters a little as one grows old'. Candidly, she considered her previous response 'a little petty and egoistical'.[32]

Nancy Dean's genuine enthusiasm for her stories and Bertha's requests prompted Beatrix to reflect again on the years when she had written the little books, something she rarely allowed herself to do. 'I have been asked to tell again how Peter Rabbit came to be written. It seems a long time ago; and in another world. Though after all the world does not change much in the country, where the seasons follow their accustomed course – the green leaf and the sere – and where nature, though never consciously wicked, has always been ruthless.' She had thought about her stories, but she still had no explanation for Peter's continued popularity. 'I have never quite understood the secret of Peter's perennial charm,' she wrote with perfect honesty. 'Perhaps it is because he and his little friends keep on their way, busily absorbed with their own doings. They were always independant [*sic*]. Like Topsy – they just "grow'd".' She explained that the first books were drawn from picture letters to real children. But after those, 'I confess that . . . I painted most of the little pictures to please myself. The more spontaneous the pleasure – the more happy the result.' Drawing on her life experience and her many years as artist-storyteller, she confessed in a sort of valedictory summation: 'I do not remember a time when I did not try to invent pictures and make for myself a fairyland amongst the wild flowers, the animals, fungi, mosses, woods and streams, all the thousand objects of the country-side; that pleasant, unchanging world of realism and romance, which in our northern clime is stiffened by hard weather, a tough ancestry, and the strength that comes from the hills.'[33]

'Wag-by-Wall' was a story that Beatrix had always liked, but could never quite finish. It was a country tale that dated from November 1909 when it was called 'The Little Black Kettle'. Beatrix had left the story unfinished because the verses she had wanted the kettle to sing had never satisfied her. 'I remember', she explained later, 'Sally's story stuck because the kettle was obstinately dumb.' Bertha Miller suggested that the setting be changed to Christmas Eve, and Beatrix liked the idea.[34]

When Beatrix first revised it for the *Fairy Caravan* collection in 1929, Sally Scales had become an old woman named Sally Benson and the story retitled as 'Wag-by-the-Wa'.' A wag was the term for the pendulum of an old wall clock, and 'Wa'' was an abbreviation of wall. Beatrix owned an antique wall clock like the one featured in the story and, like her old oak court cupboards, it had character. 'Wag-by-Wall' was similar in tone to 'The Oakmen', and, like those other country stories, it derived from her experience out in the countryside. These were simply stories Beatrix wrote to amuse herself on cold winter nights.[35]

The story tells of an old widow in her simple cottage with her garden, the bees, the kettle, the clock and the pair of beloved white owls who live in the shed and raise their owlets on the ridge of the roof. But 'good times and hard times – all times go over'. Sally had given what little money she had to her errant daughter when a baby granddaughter was born. But when the money was gone, Sally never heard again from the daughter or knew what had become of the little 'Goldie-locks' child. One dark winter's evening Sally reads a letter from a stranger who had taken in her orphaned grandchild and writes to ask for money to send her to her Grannie. Poor Sally, with only the prospect of the poorhouse for herself, sits long after the fire has died wondering what to do. She has dozed off when, 'There came a rush of soot and stones . . . Several large heavy stones tumbled after; and the white owl on the top . . . Amongst the stones was a black thing which smoked. It was an old stocking tied round the ankle with a bit of string.' Inside are gold pieces and the wag-by-the-wall suddenly changes its song from 'Tic: toc: gold: toes' to 'Tick:er tocks:Goldie:locks'. Sally lives happily to old age with her little granddaughter, the singing kettle, the owls, and the wag-by-the-wall clock. Beatrix sent off her biographical revisions to Mrs Miller at the end of November and promised to write out 'Nancy's Christmas story before the scribbly fit passes'.[36]

But Beatrix had found it hard to steal time away from the demands of the farms to fiddle with the revisions she wanted to make. The Girl Guides had come to camp on her fields near Hawkshead in August 1940, but could not stay in the usual place because it was being used for military supply. Thinking quickly, Beatrix settled the Guides with their dyed green tents in a 'little larch wood' known as 'the heights' above Castle Cottage, where they were perfectly camouflaged. Haymaking was in full swing and although they were shorthanded at Hill Top and Tilberthwaite they managed. 'Uncle Willie is busy inspecting farms for next year's ploughing, not altogether a grateful task amongst neighbours, yet he is a very suitable person to do it because he knows everybody's business, and the conditions of local farming,' she explained to Nancy. Eggs and poultry were in the shortest supply, and hen feed was scarce and expensive. Beatrix and Miss Mills started keeping rabbits in order to make sure that the dogs had a adequate supply of food, and in case of more serious food shortages. 'I don't know whether Miss Mills will have much appetite for rabbit pie,' she wrote to Marian Perry. 'I am thinking about our little dogs; with potatoes & rabbits produced in the garden, our 2 pekes won't encroach on public rationings.' She never forgot about her sheepdogs either, worrying that they would not stand up to their work on such poor scraps. She had some oatmeal ground for them at the mill, whether it was lawful or not. Still anxious about the possibility of invasion from the coast, Beatrix hoped Hitler 'had missed his chance'.[37]

She was particularly anxious about the number of working-class homes that had been destroyed in the bombing of the coastal cities, and now the country villages were 'packed to overflowing' with evacuees. In September a wandering German plane unloaded fifteen bombs on wasteland ten miles off, but, Beatrix wrote cheerfully, she never woke up. 'Wm's habit of snoring is very tiresome. I have put up with it for many years, but it drowns the noise of approaching planes!' From London there came word that her family home at 2 Bolton Gardens in Kensington had been hit in the London bombing in October. Beatrix did not mourn its destruction, commenting once later, 'It is immaterial to give the exact address of my unloved birthplace. It was hit by shrapnel . . . now I am rather pleased to hear it is no more!'[38]

At the end of 1940 Beatrix's farming, especially her cattle-breeding programme, sustained a blow when George Walker, her Troutbeck Park manager, was rushed from the remote farm to hospital in Kendal with a perforated ulcer. Beatrix wrote to Moscrop, 'I saw Mrs Walker & Mary at the hospital on Tuesday in a sad way, but she sounded cheerful last night when she phoned. The doctor is still anxious.' Beatrix had just been to the Park where tupping was in full swing. 'Poor George,' she wrote, 'its a mess – not only am I grieved for him and his family but the *cows!!* He has all written down in a book but I doubt if anyone but himself can understand the book or know one cow from another. I used to know the old original cows but I have lost track of late years.' She told Moscrop about the autumn sales, which started off poorly, but 'prices went up very high at the finish when there was little left'. She had sold about six hundred sheep from Troutbeck alone.

The Tilberthwaite sheep suffered something cruel last spring. The poor things lived through the snow and had plenty of lambs and reared them; it is a *dry fell* – there never seemed to grow any grass in the droughty May & June, they just pined. Tommy Stoddart thinks we lost near a hundred, not so much in the storm, but never picked up in the summer. I have got salt for them. And we have made silage. I have an idea it might be very useful, fed carefully, in a dry spring. Summer & back end have been favourable. A small hay crop, but plenty straw & turnips. And all will be wanted [referring to the submarine blockade of Britain] . . . Sheep are the standby on the fells – and the herdwicks don't need feeding stuffs.[39]

Christmas 1940 was a low one for Beatrix, the first in many years without a single greeting from America. 'Perhaps they are being wasted upon the deep sea fishes!' she complained. But she had been able to tell Joseph that Walker was out of immediate danger, although it would take months for him to recuperate to the point of actively managing the farm. 'Now about the wage Joseph I think you should be satisfied with £20 – but if you ain't – why you have us fast! for we cannot do without you, that's a fact; more than ever.'[40]

Her farm hands knew that Mrs Heelis would have 'everything possible done for a sick animal on any of her farms, so long as there was a chance of its recovery, but once that point was passed she was quite matter-of-fact and unsentimental'. Although Bruce Thompson remembered once seeing her in tears at a village funeral, her attitude towards human death was much the same. 'Don't worry about us!' she told Ivy Steel. 'In this house we are too old to matter.' She lamented the loss of friends and neighbours, as well as local landmarks like the Ginger and Pickles shop and the village blacksmith. 'All that were "old" when I was younger, are dead. To be dead is in the course of nature – and war,' but she considered it more disagreeable to be left behind.[41]

Sometime that spring Beatrix learned that a whole printing of *Peter Rabbit* had been destroyed when a bomb exploded at the binders. Luckily the 'copper blocks & electros' were safe at the printers. The event forced both Beatrix and her publisher to consider an alternative storage place for the irreplaceable blocks and drawings. They finally decided that the original drawings of *Peter Rabbit* would be safer with Beatrix in Sawrey than any place in London. 'No place is safe,' she wrote to Arthur Stephens on their receipt, 'but the chances of any individual house being hit is small in the country.' Beatrix had been trying to convince Warne's to produce a 'a cheap reprint' in black and white for less than the 2s. 6d. that she considered too expensive for 'a little gift book for "infants" or school baby-classes'. She encouraged Stephens to take the opportunity of the lost printing to experiment. 'I cannot see any reason why it should interfere with the coloured edition – and *if* it did so I am afraid *I* would not be inconsolable. I do so dislike that idiotic prancing rabbit on the cover!'[42]

When the Hyde Parkers returned to Suffolk in May 1941, Beatrix was keenly aware that once again she ran the risk of having evacuees settled at Hill Top. The very day they left, she wrote to Louie Choyce with the suggestion that she and her more-or-less invalid brother Tom 'might like to come to Hill Top for a while . . . It would be a great pleasure to me to see you again – and frankly – (selfishly?) – I am concerned about the house & contents.' The Barrow shipyards had been raided again and people were fleeing. Beatrix knew she could not keep an empty house for long. She offered suggestions for their employment and paid their train fares. 'I hope you and Tom will be able to come and "hold the fort" and, if able later to do a little work, there would be opportunity! If I were not married I would go to Hill Top myself & give up this house; but W.H. is placid, he will never believe in scarcity of sugar or marmalade or arrival of evacs. Until they are on the door step!' The problem was solved when Miss Choyce returned to Sawrey that summer. She and her brother lived in the two front rooms, watching over house and garden.[43]

In June 1941 Beatrix wrote to Joseph again, asking him to come back to the Park for clipping instead of going to his usual summer haymaking. 'I was at the Park this morning. George said he was *not* poorly? he seemed *exhausted* by this sudden intense heat . . . but whatever the climate he ought to go easy . . . George looks very tired. He says you are a great comfort to him because he can trust you absolutely, if you say you have looked [at] any stock – he knows *you have* – which he cannot be sure with a stranger.' Upon learning that Joseph was indeed an experienced clipper, Beatrix offered him £70 for clipping and helping with the hay, chiding him for being 'too modest'. Beatrix hoped that life would improve for the Walkers at Troutbeck, but Lucy Walker had undergone surgery on her neck, probably a thyroid or glandular tumour, and, while she struggled valiantly to continue with her farmwork, Beatrix was rightly worried. She made it a point to drive out to the Park at least once every fortnight and saved her petrol ration for the trip.[44]

During the worst of the air raids on the northern coastal cities and naval bases in the summer and autumn of 1941 Beatrix kept up her reports to her American friends. She told Ivy Steel: 'The bombs nearest here fell in fields & a road. I was told that some cows were much alarmed, but a family of geese continued calmly feeding!' But later she reported the 'destruction of a farm house, the whole family killed, including 5 evacuees'. She felt sorry for the evacuees, who had crowded into the countryside for safety, and she was worried about Ivy Steel's Aunt Jessie, who had fled London during the Blitz, but she had also noticed that, like the town mouse and the country mouse, 'all the townspeople go back. At one time there were crowds of evacuees, but they found the country cold & dull in winter. They said they would rather be bombed than bored.'[45]

There was plenty to eat, but some things were short, such as 'peppermints and eggs and oranges'. But Beatrix approved of the strict blackouts and rationing, except for eggs which got broken or turned bad before they were redistributed. Grateful for old friends whom she could rely on, Beatrix was heartened when the United

States entered the war on 8 December 1941, but did not hide her feelings that it came belatedly. She listened to President Roosevelt's speech on the wireless thinking to herself, 'how many "December 7th's" have there been in Europe?' Christmas that year was bright and windless. Beatrix shared her anxieties with Bertha Mahony Miller. 'I was never afraid of house work or outdoor work while I could do it, but I am rather infirm being so badly ruptured. There is plenty to eat and much to be thankful for.' She looked forward to getting 'over winter – without disaster – and see the spring sunshine again'.[46]

In late November Beatrix finally posted off to Mrs Miller 'two old unfinished tales belonging to the Caravan series', 'The Solitary Mouse' and 'Wag-by-Wall', which she intended as stories for Bertha's granddaughter. 'I cannot judge my own work,' she told the editor. 'Is not "Wag by the Wa'"' rather a pretty story . . . ? I thought of it years ago as a pendant to *The Tailor of Gloucester* – the old lonely man and the lonely old woman – but I never could finish it all; and after 9 months occasional nibblings – it seems likely to go into the post – unfinished yet!'[47]

A few months later Bertha wrote asking permission to publish 'Wag-by-Wall' in *The Horn Book*. 'On your own head be it!' Beatrix replied. But she acquiesced, providing she could 'polish' it further. She explained to her friend, 'I think the art of essay writing is to balance the main theme by ruthlessly cutting, no matter whether the incidents sacrificed are pretty or not . . . If you really decide to use it I should like to alter a few sentences.' Beatrix had been copying old loose pages of several stories into one notebook and wanted to 'compress' the story further. 'If the Horn book printed it . . .' Beatrix continued, 'it would have the benefit of safeguarding the copyright, in case Sally [Wag-by-Wall] were worth making into a separate book.' The terms Bertha offered – $50 for serial rights – were satisfactory, but Beatrix wanted to be paid directly rather than forwarding payment through Warne's, explaining, 'They were *not* pleased about the *Caravan*.'[48]

Beatrix wrote to Mrs Miller again the following day with more revisions. 'I told you I think the *Mouse* is *twaddle!*' But she continued to think that '"Wag" is a pretty little story. I should like to print it someday in book form.' Telling Miller that she would receive several lists of corrections, Beatrix likened herself to Mr Turveydrop, a Dickens character: 'I "polish! polish! polish!" to the last revise . . .' But she gave Bertha carte blanche to edit as she saw fit. She was pleased that Bertha was considering some of the 'Caravan' stories for publication, rather than 'those wearisome rabbits'. Confined to the house by a bad cold, sciatica and severe winter weather in March 1942, Beatrix began copying out some of the other 'Caravan' stories, not with a view to their publication, but hoping that they might be preserved 'in a continent that is safer than this little island'. Comparing herself to Anne Carroll Moore's lifetime of achievements, Beatrix felt her accomplishments were meagre, confiding, 'I have just made stories to please myself because I never grew up!'[49]

Friends in America continued to send books and food parcels, uncertain what she lacked on the farm. Much of the butter, bacon and tea Beatrix gave away to neighbours in the village, but she was especially grateful when the packages contained any form of sugar, chocolate or dried seasonings. One parcel from Gail Coolidge contained concentrated lemon juice, which she put away for a time when it would be gratefully used against a bronchial cough. From Americans too came the sort of fan letters that she treasured. 'I have been surprised at the number and friendliness – of the packets of dozens of letters from [the] U.S.A. . . . I don't receive English letters like that; a good many from children, some wanting autographs, some enthusiastic grateful parents . . . But never does anyone outside your perfidiously complimentary nation write to tell me that I write good prose!'[50]

21

～ *Reflections* ～

O LD AGE HAS A WAY of forcing a person back upon themselves. The pace of life slows and brings with it a natural inclination to reflect upon the past. The spring of her seventy-fifth year, 1942, was a difficult one and Beatrix had more time to indulge in introspection than she was accustomed to, most of it prompted by admirers of her work. The winter had been the third one in a row with heavy snowfall. Getting about was difficult and going out to Troutbeck Park was impossible. Beatrix was sorrier by far 'for the sheep than for the Germans', and worried about them growing weak and thin in the snow. She rummaged in her portfolios in the mornings, and sorted books and papers in the afternoon. Much of her time was taken with sending off packets of Rebekah Owen's collection of Hardiana to Professor Carl Weber at Colby College in Maine. She had been fond of Miss Owen and, she told the professor when she took possession of Owen's papers, 'I am an old woman. *I wish to sort her things*.' Beatrix began sending parcels of material to America in July 1941, and continued through November, after which she feared for their loss at sea, and so made up packets to post in a safer time. She found sorting Miss Owen's collection intellectually interesting, a kind of impromptu literary detour. It took her mind off the war and she took pleasure in her continued correspondence with the professor, who was the beneficiary of her good will and of her personal analysis of Thomas Hardy's work.[1]

The past two years had brought interesting new friends into Beatrix's life; people who sought her out because as children they had loved her stories, and as adults they were admirers of her craft. John Kingston Stone, a young New Zealand journalist, came to Sawrey on a trip to England in 1940, begging for a guide to the actual scenes and settings in her books that he was so fond of. Beatrix had agreed to meet him because she sensed that Stone was 'one of the individuals who never grow up, and belonging to the age of Alice and the Water Babies', and so invited him to Hill Top where together they pored over her portfolios. When they came to the famous picture of Jemima rushing down the hill, bonnet askew and shawl fluttering behind, Beatrix told him, 'that is what I used to look like to the Sawrey people. I rushed about quacking industriously!' Stone's love of the English countryside had elicited a long discussion on the National Trust and her hopes for saving the countryside. 'You found *some* of the England that is still unspoilt,' she wrote to him later. 'It is most unfortunate how much has been wilfully destroyed . . . I have tried to do my humble bit of preservation in this district.' She also confided to Stone that she hoped the Trust would preserve Hill Top, telling him, 'I have taken much pleasure in collecting some oddments . . . along with my land; it would be easy to maintain it – separately yet under one roof – with the modern farm house.' She had found Stone a person of such quality that she could not help wishing 'the N. T.'s present secretarial representative [Bruce Thompson] were like you!'[2]

Reginald Hart, another collector seeking information on the origins of each of the tales, appeared in Sawrey the year after Stone's visit. Hart was a keen photographer, a collector of children's books, particularly admiring those of Randolph Caldecott. Like Stone, Hart had done his Potter homework. By profession he was an architect who had been sent by the Ministry of Works in London to work at Blackpool, where he had certain civil service responsibilities for the granting of building permits and the allocation of building materials. Hart not only shared Beatrix's interest in the architecture of the Lake District, but like Stone, he shared her passion for the decorative arts, antique furniture, early pottery and slipware. Hart had written to Beatrix in 1940 hoping to add a photograph of Hill Top to his private collection, which he called 'A Lakeland Enquiry', and he also wanted to take photographs of Hawkshead, correctly identifying it as the setting for the illustrations of *Johnny Town-Mouse*.

When Hart, his wife and three-year-old daughter Alison arrived during the summer of 1940, Beatrix had welcomed them warmly and spent time showing them her collection of Randolph Caldecott's original drawings for *The Mad Dog*, which had been purchased by her father and were hung on the wall upstairs at Castle Cottage. The following year Beatrix sought his advice about building permits and repairs to her farm buildings, and graciously accepted Hart's help in cutting through the bureaucratic red tape. They exchanged information about slipware, the paltriness of Lake District kitchen middens which yielded little pottery of merit, and her efforts to buy a rare old oak refectory table on sale at Bowness. Beatrix was impressed by Hart's photographic skill and enjoyed corresponding with him. During their visit the following summer, Hart took some photographs of Beatrix, of her pekes, and of little Alison and Beatrix playing with them. Hart sent Beatrix copies of the photographs, which pleased her so much she asked for three more copies – to send to friends in the United States. 'I am quite delighted with the photographs of the little dogs – and *Alison* is even more delightful! . . . You have a good lens,' she told him, 'it does not distort . . . Its very good of my lace edged cap (which seems to have hitched forward over my nose) and not too bad of the old woman!'[3]

Although Beatrix never met Samuel Cunningham, he too found favour as a correspondent because of his knowledge and perspective on rural life. Cunningham was a Unionist politician from Northern Ireland with whom Beatrix began to correspond sometime in 1936. He had been a businessman in Belfast and came from old Whig stock; his father, like Rupert, had been a barrister. Cunningham raised several varieties of cattle and had a large dairy herd out in the countryside. He was also a passionate and very knowledgeable gardener. In all likelihood Cunningham wrote to Beatrix about his pleasure in her animal drawings, wondering why she never wrote much about dogs. Beatrix replied that she could only 'describe little rubbish, like mice and rabbits – dogs, sheep and horses are on a higher level'. Their letters ranged over a variety of congenial topics: livestock management, animal pests, farming and the war.[4]

Most of all, Beatrix and Cunningham shared a passion for the preservation of the countryside. In one of the most complete statements of her philosophy of land preservation, Beatrix told him, 'For years I have been gradually picking up land, chance bargains, and specializing on road frontages and the heads of valleys. I have a long way towards three thousand acres . . . It is an open secret it will go to the Trust eventually . . . I own two or three strikingly beautiful spots. The rest is pleasant peaceful country, foreground of the hills, I think more liable to be spoilt than the high fells themselves.' Beatrix found corresponding with these similarly spirited men, Stone, Hart and Cunningham, invigorating. They all shared a passion to leave the world better than they found it, and were propelled forward in hard times by curiosity to see what would happen next. 'I would rather keep going till I drop – early or late – never mind what the work is, so long as it is useful and well done.' 'I am sometimes surprised at myself, being contented,' she wrote to Cunningham. 'I lift my eyes to the hills, and I am content to look at them from below.' Then she added almost to herself, 'I did dream of getting an old pony (or a donkey) but I think I am safer pottering about on my own old legs . . .'[5]

These friendships, the writing she had been doing for *The Horn Book* and the renewed critical interest in her reputation led Beatrix to think about her life's accomplishments. Such reflection was reinforced during a severe case of bronchitis that sent her to bed for over a month in May 1942, and by the receipt of a very large royalty cheque from her English publisher for nearly two hundred thousand copies of her little books. 'Prodigious! . . . The world goes mad on astronomical figures,' she told her publisher, Arthur Stephens. She could hardly imagine such a number of books, but it pleased her.[6]

In May 1942, 'The Lonely Hills', Beatrix's essay drawn from parts of the 'Caravan' stories, appeared in *The Horn Book*. Bertha Mahony Miller had taken her reminiscences about country dancing and her musings about walking out on the Troutbeck Tongue, and melded them into a pleasant reverie on country life, as unwilling as Beatrix to let such tales 'float away out of existence'. The phrase 'the lonely hills' was one Beatrix had always loved and found comfort in. She explained to Mrs Miller that the title, indeed the moral of the essay, was from Wordsworth's poem, the 'Song at the Feast of Brougham Castle (Upon the Restoration of Lord Clifford, the Shepherd, to the

Estates and Honours of his Ancestors)'. The proper wording, she told her, was '[T]he sleep that is among the lonely hills'. 'I have so often thought of those lines, since the silence of the starry sky has been interrupted by aeroplanes, which at first we detested as an intrusion but since the war we delight to see them.'[7]

In her essay Beatrix recalls some of the country things that she loved and found beauty in: the music of the breeze in the hemlocks, the song of the brook running over pebbles, the 'pretty jingling tunes' of the English folk dances. She remembered reverently observing a 'weird dance' of the wild fell ponies to 'music of Piper Wind' in that 'lonely wilderness behind the table-land on Troutbeck Tongue'. Then she had wandered in the 'company of gentle sheep, and wild flowers and singing waters', and 'listened to the voices of the Little Folk'. 'In the calm spacious days that seem so long ago, I loved to wander on the Troutbeck fell. Sometimes I had with me an old sheep dog, "Nip" or "Fly", more often I went alone. But never lonely.' Beatrix described the Tongue as an 'uncanny' place of 'silences and whispering echoes', remembered the black Galloway cattle that seemed like 'dark specks moving slowly', the 'shaggy cows' and the shepherds as they 'drove down a thousand sheep from the high fell for dipping'. Her reverie ends with an evocation of the strength and comfort she found in that special place blurred by rising, swirling mist, the peace the fells offered to all who would look up. 'Memories of "old unhappy far-off things and battles long ago"; sorrows of yesterday and today and tomorrow – the vastness of the fells covers all with a mantle of peace.' It was a fitting essay in a time of war, and a unique reflection from the writer in her old age.[8]

Mahony used three pen-and-ink illustrations from *The Fairy Caravan* within the essay. When Beatrix received her copy in July she was suitably pleased. 'It reads quite presentably I think – though to me . . . a bit dislocated.' She then corrected the footnote which had incorrectly listed Warne's rather than McKay as the publisher of the *Caravan*. But she could not smother the artistic injury she felt in the mismatch of text to illustration. 'Why? – oh why? – did you plant a cedar in the middle of a paragraph about a stunted thorn???' Then she added, 'It is a favourite picture of mine so it does not matter.'[9]

There exists a reflection of an entirely different sort that Beatrix probably wrote sometime in 1942 in an old notebook. At the time there was intense speculation in the press about the discovery of antibiotic properties in the compound leached by the *penicillium* mould (of which there are many). Clinical trials had been going on at Oxford University and there was speculation about their application to a wide variety of human diseases. Beatrix's note fits the context of this public debate. It is a remarkable reflection because it reveals how thoroughly innovative Beatrix's own fungi experiments in the 1890s had been, and how easily, even forty years later, she could apply her own first-hand knowledge of *penicillium* moulds to contemporary research.[10]

Defining *penicillium* as 'an alternative generation – a endorphic form of certain species of fungi whose mycelium – under favourable circumstance – effloresces in a "toadstool"', Beatrix recalls that there has always been 'a – superstition – that houses can be "cancer houses"', and suggests that 'It might be worth while to follow up experiments with *Merulius* [now *Serpula*] *lachrymans* [*sic*] (the dry-rot fungus), & other decayed-wood fungi.' Remembering how she and Charlie McIntosh had once speculated about the properties of witches' broom efflorescence and its potential to infect an entire birch forest, she also suggests that students of cancer research might profitably experiment with 'cultivations of cancerous growths on plants'. 'Has a serum ever been made from witches' brooms? Those abnormal tissue growths on birch trees, resulting from fungoid infection?' she wondered, and speculates about what other applications there might be. Beatrix was clearly not surprised by the discovery of the *penicillium* mould's antibacterial potential, for she had observed it herself many years before.[11]

By the summer of 1942 Beatrix's health had improved and she had even enjoyed a 'bit of haymaking'. Her hill sheep farms, now receiving government subsidies, were paying reasonably well. In spite of anxious news from the Russian front, everyone was more hopeful about the progress of the war. The Girl Guides, with Joy Brownlow, the County Camp Adviser, were coming in July for a 'big holiday camp in the little wood on the "heights"'. Beatrix was looking forward to seeing them again, hoping the weather would improve. Their campsite was well camouflaged from the air by the trees Beatrix had planted long ago. Beatrix had written in the Guide log book the first year they had used it, 'I am pleased to see a camp – new style in a wood. I am glad that this little wood is useful at last. – When I planted it in 1906, I was told that it would not grow because the soil was too rocky and poor – nothing like trying and having patience! It is a well grown wood now and a very creditable camp. Keep on smiling! And growing.' Beatrix even gave one of the girls an axe with the order that she could 'cut down any trees that were in the way'. Some of the Guide groups were from depressed areas of coastal cities that had been bombed. With the strict rationing enforced in 1942, they were obviously not getting enough to eat. Beatrix observed their thin frames when they arrived for camp and privately told Brownie, 'a sheep shall die tonight'.[12]

By far the most exciting Guide camp came a year later, when the Guides who were at the 'heights' on 27 July learned that Mrs Heelis's seventy-seventh birthday was the following day. With Brownie's help, they made costumes from materials collected around the camp, and each Guide dressed as a character from the little books. They held a rehearsal the day before at a 'camp fire' without a real fire. The keeper of camp log book described the excitement of the next morning as the girls put on their fancy dresses and handmade accessories. There was every sort of character: Jemima Puddle-ducks with bonnets made from bloomers and feet from cereal boxes, the Mrs Tiggy-winkles had sewn larch needles into grey blankets to make prickles, there were owls, frogs and little rabbits. The log book writer was herself dressed as a Pigling Bland with pink blanket and gas-mask snout. She recounted the scene: 'Arriving at her house, we proceeded to sing "Happy birthday to you," which is rather difficult when one happens to be a pig and has a gas mask on.' As each girl stepped forward to greet her, Beatrix had to guess who they were.[13]

Beatrix was enchanted and a little overwhelmed. She wrote to Miss Brownlow afterwards, 'the birthday party was such a surprise – I could scarcely rise to the occasion before they had passed. It was such a treat, quite charming. I never had such a birthday before!' She had not recognized the 'Tailor of Gloucester', until she realized it was the 'mayor of Gloucester' wearing the famous red coat. 'I also remember Mrs Tiggy, but was it she who gave me "rinso" [a soap powder]? Highly appropriate! Mr McGregor was very good – they all were – I should like to give them *all* books – but I have not enough.' In a postscript to Miss Brownlow Beatrix wrote, ' "Brownie" *you* can spin a moral that the simplest things can give true simple pleasure.' A note to her publisher the same day requested 'two dozen or so [books] . . . in any selection – I have just parted with my last remaining consignment – a most amusing party of Girl Guides – brownie size – presenting about 40 little animals from the books, in such attire as can be scraped together in camp. I had to give prizes lavishly.'

Responding to a request from Brownie a month later, Beatrix invited 'as many [Guides] as like to come, under control!' to see the 'treasure dolls house (large & small)' at Hill Top. 'I was inside dusting – and sweeping with Hunca Munca's dustpan yesterday and measuring another piece of tapestry that should be hung up . . . It is always a pleasure to see or help Guides.'[14]

Beatrix's Christmas letters to her American friends in 1942 were full of farm news. 'The country has been beautiful with autumn colours – but crops have been a struggle . . . It has been very hard work for everybody; and rather a worry, though interesting and profitable to run a sheep farm in these days. I had more than 3 tons of wool to sell.' She was still raising hutch rabbits which helped make vegetarian days more tolerable, and in all had plenty to eat. Proudly she told Marian Perry that she had saved up enough sugar to make some marmalade from oranges going to waste at a port, and of course she had plenty of apples.[15]

Beatrix was busier at the start of 1943 than she had been for some time. The wartime subsidies to farmers had increased acreage under the plough, and vegetable gardens, potatoes and fodder crops as well as hay took longer to harvest. Like other sheep farmers, Beatrix was apprehensive about what would happen after the war when such assistance ended. She told Bertha Mahony Miller, 'Its doubtful if Herdwick sheep farms can survive another slump *unless* a fresh market can be found for the harsh hard wearing wool. Govt. is buying it *all*, reported to be for kaki [*sic*] and a rumour that the cloth it is going to Russia [for army uniforms]. I wish very much it may be true; and lasting.' To Joseph she was more realistic. 'There's no use pretending that it is equal to other wools; but it is the most useful and waterproof wool for Lakes' climate. And it should do well for the Russians.' For the time being, the high prices allowed Beatrix to buy more cattle from Forrester as well as several properties in Hawkshead to 'prevent jerry building and [to] let at fair rent'.[16]

The winter had been wet as well as cold, and Beatrix felt the cold more than ever. Unable to find new elastic to hold herself together, she was quite stooped, finding it more difficult to get around. She confessed her discomfort to her physician friend, Charlie Cooper.

I had a slight rupture which gradually enlarged, so I cannot move about without the belt, and I get fridged [*sic*] underneath it, especially since there is no broad elastic to be got. I am perfectly comfortable so long as I am strapped up, & I can wash above and below, but not under the belt! I doubt if it could be sewn up, right down the middle on an old operation scar, and at 77 its hardly worth while to experiment. I can still work in the garden & grow vegetables. We are bothered with rabbits.[17]

Luckily there was not the heavy snow of the previous winters. In late March she got out to Troutbeck Park. The dogs there were not well. Some were threatening seizures due to lack of minerals in their diet. Beatrix had gone to the vet for bromide and told Walker to give the young dogs yeast whenever he could find any, and to try boiled potatoes as a change of diet. She reported on conditions at the Park when she wrote to Joseph about lambing time. 'I went to the Park this morning, Mrs Walker was stirring about and fairly cheerful I am glad to say she is quite looking forward to seeing you again as a lodger at lambing time.' The Walkers, in turn, reported to Joseph about their employer's health. 'Mrs Heelis was here on Monday. She looks really well. Her first black calf has arrived today so lambing time will soon come round.'[18]

In March, at the annual general meeting of the Herdwick Sheep Breeders' Association, Beatrix Heelis was voted president-elect for 1944. She would be the first woman ever elected to the presidency of this bastion of male sheep breeders, and she recognized it as a singular honour. In April at the monthly association meeting she was put temporarily in the chair. 'I am in the chair at the Herdwick breeders' Association meetings,' she told Bertha Miller. 'You would laugh to see me, amongst the other old farmers – usually in a tavern! after a sheep fair. We are serious enough; about the future.' Telling Moscrop there was poor attendance because of petrol rationing, she complained about the Association secretary R. H. Lamb's report on prices and wool sales. 'R. H. L. [Lamb]', she wrote, 'is a less agreeable person, – at least I cannot get on with him at Hd Association meetings . . . they put me in the chair; I did *not* drink porter . . . at the White Lion!' She characterized Lamb's report as 'scarcely gracious' for the (government) benefits the sheep breeders had received, and noted that he took all the credit to himself for better prices. But she acknowledged that everyone was edgy about what would happen to wool prices after the war.[19]

Nothing could diminish Beatrix's appreciation of the spring in the countryside or the beauty of her surroundings. 'The birds sing nearly all night,' she wrote to Louie Choyce, who had left Hill Top and was back at her home in Tuck Mill. 'The country is lovely just now, the hawthorns so sweet, the air is full of their scent.' In June she reported, 'The garden here is very gay; white bell flowers everywhere amongst the weeds, and the house covered with roses. The pinks are very full – I have been excited about your cactus, it has had 5 flowers – lovely – very like my old pink cactus, but prettier.' The harvest was large, except for the potatoes which once again were sodden: 'The garden is very overgrown. I can't get at it with the wet.' Nancy Nicholson had left her duties as Norland nurse and was doing an interval of farm work. Beatrix approved of the change for Nancy's physical health and mental well-being. 'We give the work our blessing,' Beatrix told her. '(NB your uncle says you are not to marry a farm man! I say – it depends on the sort of farm man!)' In August the weather had already turned unusually cold, 'very thundery and sopping under the corn ... How the days have drawn in ... I have a bit of cold with the change from heat to chilly nights, but its going. I went to Hill Top & had a good dust last week.'[20]

At Hill Top she spent hours organizing her treasures. Ever since she had dictated her will to William in 1939 she had been remedying her failure to set out her things as she wanted them. It was her fondest hope that Hill Top could be left as it was after her death – a reality and a reflection of her art in the Sawrey tales and a museum of her personal treasures: doll's houses, furniture, old oak, her china displayed precisely as she wanted it, her ornaments arranged, and her portfolios, manuscripts and copybooks all labelled. On the back of paintings and antiques she placed notes giving the details of their provenance, often with a pithy comment and a notation of the price she paid for them.

Beatrix was annoyed when, in early September, she went to bed with another bronchial cough. Severe coughing kept her from sleep at night, and her pulse was rapid. When she felt up to it, she worked at her writing desk on correspondence and attending to farm paperwork. Unhappily, she had to send Tommy Stoddart his wages, rather than taking them up to Tilberthwaite herself. 'The weather is so very bad and I do not feel right yet ... I wonder how many of those bonny little ducklings have lived through?' She worried a good deal about Tilberthwaite. Her several notes to Stoddart speak of her confidence in him, but also of her concern about sufficient places to winter the sheep and cattle since so much grazing land had been ploughed. Her frustration at not being able to get over to Coniston to see to repairs and to evaluate the supply of grass and fodder for herself is palpable. 'I have not been out in the car yet,' she complained to one of the Tilberthwaite tenants in the middle of October, 'I am getting sick of the doctor coming. My heart has been too quick since I had rheumatic fever at 20 – so if I stay at home till it mends to "normal" you will not see me for a bit! I am not short of breath now.'[21]

'I have spent more than enough time upstairs ...' she wrote to Bertha Miller in early November. 'I am out and about now – when the rain stops – which is seldom ... I hope to do a bit more active work yet — and anyhow I have survived to see Hitler beaten past hope of recovery!' She approved Bertha's request to print Reginald Hart's photograph of her with little Alison to accompany 'Wag-by-Wall' in *The Horn Book*, now scheduled for publication in May 1944 for the twentieth anniversary issue.[22]

Nurse Edwards had been in and out of Castle Cottage during the summer. Sometimes she came for weekend relief from midwife duties; sometimes just to check on Beatrix and William. Mrs Rogerson, their elderly housekeeper at Castle Cottage, was not strong, so when Nurse Edwards offered to come and stay through the New Year, they were grateful. 'I am much as usual,' she reported, 'but not so unusually well as in early summer when I felt grand; I am rather "under the weather" — there is scarcely a fine day a week.' She worried about the tups at Troutbeck and about George Walker's health. But being out in the wind made her cough and she knew she could not get to the Park. Unhappily, she acquiesced and sent Nurse Edwards up with the wages.[23]

Her annual Christmas letters to her American friends in November reported an early snow, a lucky harvest quickly got in, and the receipt of welcome Christmas packages with such treats as dried eggs, fruit and tins of lemon juice. To each friend she reported the continued weakness of her heart, but her gratitude that she and William had suffered so little compared to others during the bombing. 'When we think what we have escaped and survived compared with other lands — I don't know how we have got through alive.' At the end of the month she acknowledged her decline to Anne Carroll Moore: 'I may pick up in spring. I was pretty bad.'[24]

Nancy Nicholson came for a visit at the end of November looking fit and obviously enjoying her farm work. Beatrix and Nancy went over to Hill Top together and 'had a rummage around, taking some things there & bringing some back'. Beatrix was thinking about what she wanted to leave to various family members, but wanted to make sure that her precious mycological portfolios were organized so that eventually they could be given to the Armitt Trust Library. She had already given the Library the collection of archaeological drawings she had made in the 1890s and her father's books. But she was also worried about practical matters. Nancy had helped her put a padlock on the door of the china room at Hill Top because Christmas was 'no time to change servants'. She wrote to Louie Choyce to assure her that Mrs Edwards would look after her if she were ill, noting philosophically, 'We all have to grow old; but some of us don't take to stopping in.'[25]

One of her end-of-year letters was to her dear cousin Caroline Clark, with whom she had shared so much of her joy in country life. There was already snow 'to the bottom of the fells' and a north-east wind made her disinclined to put her nose outside the door. She told Caroline that in one of her searches through her drawers at Hill Top she had 'found some exasperating & absurd compositions' written in a cipher which she was now unable to decode. Thinking of Holme Ground and of her grandparents she told Caroline, 'It is some years ago since I have walked on the beloved hills, but I remember every stone & rock – and *stick*. I think it is pleasanter to remember an old stunted thorn or holly than to go to the spot and find it gone.'[26]

Beatrix failed to rally over the next several weeks and her heart weakened. She was aware that she did not have long to live. Her sheep and shepherds were never far from her mind. On 13 December she wrote a brief note to Joseph Moscrop: 'Very far through, but still some kick in me. Am not going right way at present. I write a line to shake you by the hand, our friendship has been entirely pleasant. I am very ill with bronchitis.' Not quite ten days later, on Wednesday, 22 December, Mrs Rogerson was sent to Hill Top to ask Tom Storey to stop by Castle Cottage to see Mrs Heelis that evening. When Tom came into the large bedroom, he was shocked at her condition. Beatrix told him she was dying and asked him to stay on and manage the farm for William, which Tom agreed to do. Either that night, or in a previous conversation, Beatrix told Tom that her body was to be cremated and asked him to scatter her ashes on the intake above Hill Top where she had so often walked and sketched, but to tell no one where he put them. 'I want it kept a secret.'[27]

Beatrix died later that night at Castle Cottage with her beloved William at her side. Many years earlier she had written about the course of human life as she sorted through old bundles of family letters

– records of illness and death. 'They give a distorted impression,' she thought. 'The milestones are all tombstones! But the record of the cheerful jog trot round of life between them is not kept.' Although she had always been somewhat ambivalent about how she wished to be remembered, Beatrix Potter Heelis had left abundant testament of her unique 'jog trot'.[28]

The death notice in the *Westmorland Gazette* read simply, 'Heelis. On Wednesday. Dec. 22, 1943 at Castle Cottage, Sawrey, near Ambleside. Helen Beatrix, dearly loved wife of William Heelis, and only daughter of the late Rupert Potter. Cremation private. No mourning, no flowers, and no letters, please.' Characteristically, she had arranged her departure from this life to be markedly unsentimental and matter of fact. It was her wish so to disappear.

⤳ *Stewardship* ⤲

The Lake District

W ILLIAM HEELIS AND TOM STOREY scattered Beatrix's ashes on the intake above Hill Top as she had bidden. In the eighteen months that remained to William, public curiosity about the exact location seems to have made the grieving and ever-protective husband cautious about leaving the slightest clue. He changed the first clause in his own will, which had originally directed Tom to distribute his ashes in the same place, 'where he and I distributed those of my late wife', to read only, 'at the same place where they were distributed', thereby keeping his participation a secret as well as providing Tom anonymity. Tom Storey kept their secret until 1986 when on his own deathbed he confided it to his son Geoff, who succeeded his Trust tenancy at Hill Top. With Geoff's unexpected death several years later, the secret has properly passed to the ages. It is enough to know only that Beatrix returned to her beloved hills.[1]

William was fully occupied for the next year and a half with the settlement and distribution of her estate, which was valued for probate at £211, 636. 4s. 10d., or roughly £7,000,000 today. Beatrix had never underestimated how burdensome his work would be, paying death duties, securing the royalty figures, and obtaining valuations of furnishings, art, land and livestock, as well as keeping the farming accounts. The meticulous William made sure his wife's wishes were carried out.[2]

One of his thorniest decisions was whether to take a life interest in the properties Beatrix owned personally or to give them over immediately to the National Trust. For this he sought the advice of his brother George Heelis in Appleby and ultimately concluded to take only a beneficial occupation as 'Tenant at Will' at Castle Farm.

He carried on with the farming there and at Hill Top, Troutbeck Park and Tilberthwaite until he could be certain the Trust could take over and manage the farms as Beatrix had in her lifetime. Sensitive and sorrowful, William was carefully watched over by Miss Hammond and Miss Mills, who continued to be the sort of scrutinizing gatekeepers Beatrix would have wanted.[3]

George Walker continued on as Trust tenant at Troutbeck Park, noting that the 'new boss' only came up every two weeks at pay day and was 'a bit harder on money matters'. Walker's devoted wife Lucy died a little more than a year after Beatrix and rests in a peaceful graveyard at the bottom of the Trout Beck valley. William had simply assumed that Joseph Moscrop would come back for lambing at the Park in the spring of 1944 as he had for nearly twenty years. At Walker's urging, he belatedly wrote to Joseph in February, 'I am trying to carry on at the farm as usual but I feel lost without the "Head".' When Joseph responded with his terms for that spring, they included his usual request for an increase in wage. William was unaware of the delicate dance with which Joseph and Beatrix customarily did business. Shocked by Moscrop's request for an increase and clearly hurt by its timing and temerity, William responded too abruptly, 'the wage you ask is impossible!' thereby sadly ending the old and valued connection, probably unnecessarily. Tommy Stoddart and his wife remained as Trust tenants at Tilberthwaite, which continued to support both Herdwicks and Galloways.[4]

The proper disposition of the Crompton family linen from Chorley Hall in which Beatrix and Fanny Cooper had taken such pride was another detail that fell to William. Beatrix had been concerned about it just two days before her death, dictating a letter to Caroline Clark about offering the napkins to the Royal Scottish Museum in Edinburgh. William's enquiry to Caroline elicited her help and some incisive remarks regarding Beatrix's relationship with her parents. She told William, 'I think I knew more of her than almost anyone. She was delicate & her Mother tried to keep her as a semi-invalid far too much.' A few months later Caroline elaborated, 'I do not think her mother was much help to her: it was her brother first, then her father whom she cared for. She was the reverse of strong, & then found great happiness in her farm, & got much stronger – ... Her father was very proud of her and her books but like many fathers of his time, did not realize that she had the right to her own life.' Recalling Beatrix's 'acute sense of fun', Caroline confessed, 'I never knew how much I should miss her.'[5]

In spite of his wish for 'no letters', William was flooded by expressions of condolence, including many from Beatrix's friends in America. His reply to a letter from Marian Perry, with whom Beatrix had carried on the most frequent and intimate correspondence, was typical of his response to these outpourings. 'It is sad to think that her last few years were so interfered with by this awful "war", but she was always cheerful and brave to the end.'

Bertha Mahony Miller faithfully published 'Wag-by-Wall' in the twentieth anniversary edition of *The Horn Book* in May 1944. Later that year, with William's permission, it appeared in book form, accompanied by small wood engravings, very much in keeping with Sally Benson's story.[6]

It was William's particular wish to see that Hill Top and its contents, as arranged by Beatrix herself or at her direction, be preserved by the Trust as a 'permanent "memorial"' together with all the furniture, pictures, original drawings, and 'everything she was most interested in . . .' William had never seen some of her original drawings until they were taken out of their packages from behind the geyser in the bathroom at Castle Cottage. He stipulated in his own will that the drawings for Beatrix's books should also 'if possible remain at Hill Top and be displayed for all', and so they were for almost forty years. After that they were moved for conservation purposes to a new gallery in Hawkshead created out of William's former law offices. Ironically, it fell to the National Trust agent Bruce Thompson, who had never been invited to Hill Top during Beatrix's lifetime, to arrange for the house to be open to the public. And so it remains, drawing millions of pilgrims from all over the world.[7]

Beatrix left all of her royalties and copyrights, shares and debentures in Frederick Warne and Company to William during his lifetime and then to Norman Warne's nephew Frederick Warne Stephens. These were later ceded to the publishing company.

It had always been Beatrix's intent that her portfolios of fungi watercolour drawings, beautifully tied up with ribbon, be offered to the Armitt Library in Ambleside. These beautifully accurate botanical drawings reveal the evolution of her scientific enquiries. They are still studied today for their scientific content. Typically, Beatrix directed, 'if they accept drawings I want them to accept books'. Those included Coates's life of her mentor Charles McIntosh and her treasured Stevenson volumes on fungi classification.[8]

Rudderless and exhausted, William Heelis entered the Paley Crest Nursing Home in York in April 1945, hoping to recover his strength and eventually return to Sawrey. From there he sent wages to the farm tenants, asked for progress reports, and remained the ever-vigilant manager of his wife's largesse. He died in early August 1945, barely eighteen months after Beatrix. In that time he had carried out her wishes impeccably, endured the inevitable preparation of a biography, and negotiated her complicated bequest to the National Trust for Places of Historic Interest or Natural Beauty.[9]

In February 1944 the National Trust announced the 'Greatest Ever Lakeland Gift'. The properties given in the Heelis Bequest added over 4,300 acres to the National Trust's holdings in the Lake District and included forty separate conveyances, and sixty individual properties. There were fifteen farms, scores of cottages, several houses and more than 500 acres of woods. The properties were scattered into all the Lake counties, Cumberland, Westmorland and Lancashire. With characteristic foresight Beatrix had also provided that £5,000 be put in trust for improving these properties or adding to them. It was part of the insightful stewardship of a practical 'amateur' land agent, who knew better than most the high cost of preservation. This bequest was augmented by William's own gift of farms and property in 1945.[10]

The National Trust secretary, Donald Mathews, wrote to William immediately on learning of Beatrix's death. He called her a 'many-sided genius' who 'by her own splendid example . . . demonstrated her understanding of the problems of preservation in the Lake District and how they were linked to those of successful sheep farming'. Even before knowing all the details of her bequest, Trust officials were aware of its importance to the preservation of the Lake District. Beatrix Heelis had not only bought important farms, scenic lands, forests and houses, but by strategic acquisition she had purchased particularly vulnerable and threatened areas. Remarkably, her purchases ensured that the valley-heads would be protected at both Troutbeck and Eskdale.[11]

As a farmer and breeder of Herdwick sheep, the primary aim of her stewardship was the preservation of a culture of hill farming and sheep stocks. Her will specifically declared that 'the landlord's sheep stocks on my Fell Farms shall continue to be maintained of the pure Herdwick breed' and that the sheep stocks on Troutbeck farm should consist of 750 ewes, 250 gimmer twinters, and 175 gimmer hogs. William's will mandated specific numbers of heath-going sheep at Tilberthwaite as well. In addition, Beatrix specifically forbade hunting by otter hounds and harriers on the whole of her Troutbeck property.[12]

Writing about her gift to the National Trust in March 1944, Bruce Thompson identified the unique character of Beatrix Potter Heelis's stewardship. 'No other woman', he wrote, 'was so knowledgeable about the local breed and method of farming, both of which are unusual.' In his view, if the National Trust could continue to maintain her success at both, there could not be a more 'appropriate memorial to a practical benefactor'. Beatrix understood only too well that 'times change', but with her bequest she attempted to ensure that the culture of hill farming and of hefted sheep would 'as far as possible' continue. These were the key words in her will and they expressed her pragmatic intention that the National Trust would 'so far as possible let and manage the same on the same lines as previously let and managed' during her lifetime. While she understood, as Rawnsley had before her, that the Trust was the 'only salvation for the Lake District', she also knew it was a fallible human institution. 'Things of a passing day', she once called it. As a far-sighted benefactor, she tried her best to ensure the continuation of a vulnerable landscape and culture. Because of her stewardship, more gifts flowed to the National Trust after the end of the Second World War. In 1951 the perimeters of the Lake District National Park were designated. It was an idea debated since Canon Rawnsley's time, and one regarded with considerable scepticism by Beatrix. As it happened, all of the Heelises' bequests were encompassed within it.[13]

Beatrix's stipulation that those little grey Herdwicks remain on her fell farms has turned out to be a challenging legacy for tenant hill farmers, who for over half a century have struggled to make a living from their coarse fleeces and only mildly popular meat. Sustainability has been difficult to achieve. Subsidies based on total numbers of livestock and changing agricultural policies have encouraged the keeping of more stock than is environmentally sustainable. Many hill areas have become too heavily grazed, and farmers continue to struggle to retain viable businesses. Balancing the demands of fell farmers, tourists, wildlife and forests has become increasingly difficult, as Beatrix knew it would.

In the spring of 2001 Lakeland sheep, including Herdwicks, were decimated by an epidemic of foot-and-mouth disease of unprecedented proportions. Hundreds of farms were affected, vaccination was too slow in coming, and millions of sheep were lost. By then Lakeland had become in many ways an artifact or more appropriately a 'cultural landscape', with a unique blend of nature and nurture that required the most imaginative management to flourish in an age of increasing globalization.[14]

Beatrix's legacy was severely tested in 2005 when, despite nationwide opposition, High Yewdale, one of Beatrix Heelis's prized Monk Coniston farms, was broken up by the National Trust on the grounds that it was no longer economically viable under new subsidy rules. The dismemberment of the farm was precipitated by the retirement of the Trust tenant, whose father Beatrix herself had persuaded to come and manage High Yewdale in the 1930s. The farm's enclosed land was divided among three neighbouring farms, and its prizewinning fell flock of hefted Herdwicks moved to another Trust-owned farm. The decision elicited local outrage. Many complained that the National Trust had violated the terms of Beatrix's bequest to keep her farms tenanted and managed, 'so far as is possible', in the same manner as she had in her lifetime.[15]

Sadly, High Yewdale's fate is probably not unique. Such policy threatens the survival of every Trust-owned hill farm in the Lake District and undermines the aspirations of other public-spirited benefactors. Whether or not 'hill farming faces a rapid and unmanaged collapse', as one Trust report claimed, it is certain that Beatrix Heelis's desire to protect and preserve a distinctive culture will continue to be a challenging obligation. But it cannot be debated that the future of public stewardship in the Lake District requires more, rather than less, of the kind of imaginative vision that Beatrix brought to it.[16]

Beatrix Potter brought nature back into the English imagination with her books and her illustrations. She wrote most of them at a time when nature was viewed as something of little value, when the plunder of nature was more popular than its preservation. After her marriage in 1913 the emphasis of her imaginative work shifted more and more away from literature towards the land and the animals it sustained. Beatrix cared about the old ways, and about what was necessary to live simply in nature.

Imagination is the precursor to policy, the precondition to action. Imagination, like wonder, allows us to value something. Imagination allowed Beatrix Potter to value the natural world and to share the treasures she found in the Lake District and its culture. As a far-sighted businesswoman she understood that their preservation was inherently linked to the success of fell farming.

Beatrix Heelis's stewardship created a singular moment in the recovery of nature in the twentieth century; a paradigm of environmental awakening. Her brusque exterior notwithstanding, Beatrix did care what others thought of her and how her legacy would be regarded. She had already won a place in the hearts of children nearly the world over. With her early desire to do something useful with her life, she had written books and drawn pictures that will forever conjure nature for millions of big and little children. Through her passionate and imaginative stewardship of the land, she challenged others to think about preservation, not just of a few farms or fells, but of a regional ecology, of a distinct farming culture, and of a particular breed of nimble-footed grey sheep.

Notes

Abbreviations

Manuscript Collections

BPG	Beatrix Potter Gallery, The Hawkshead and Beatrix Potter Property, N T
BPS	Beatrix Potter Society, London (Archives on loan to V&A)
CCP	Cotsen Children's Library, Princeton University
CRO/B	Cumbria Records Office, Barrow-in-Furness
CRO/C	Cumbria Records Office, Carlisle
CRO/K	Cumbria Records Office, Kendal
FLP	Free Library of Philadelphia
FWA	Frederick Warne Archives, London
LDM@TA	Lakes Discovery Museum @ The Armitt, Ambleside. The name has recently been changed to The Armitt Collection
NT	The National Trust
PC	Private Collection
V&A	Victoria and Albert Museum, London

Published Works

ABP	Beatrix Potter, *The Art of Beatrix Potter*, selected and arranged by Leslie Linder and W. A. Herring (1955; second edition, 1972; except where noted, all citations are from second edition)
ASC	Judy Taylor, *Beatrix Potter: Artist, Storyteller and Countrywoman* (1986; revised edition, 2002)
BPA	Beatrix Potter, *Beatrix Potter's Americans: Selected Letters*, edited by Jane Crowell Morse (1982)
BP/AW	Judy Taylor, Joyce Irene Whalley, Anne Stevenson Hobbs

and Elizabeth Battrick, *Beatrix Potter, 1866–1943: The Artist and Her World* (1987)

BP Journal   Beatrix Potter, *The Journal of Beatrix Potter, 1881–1897*, transcribed from her code writings by Leslie Linder (1966; revised edition, 1989)

BP's Art   Beatrix Potter, *Beatrix Potter's Art: Paintings and Drawings*, edited by Anne Stevenson Hobbs (1989)

BPSN   *Beatrix Potter Society Newsletter*

BPS Studies   *Beatrix Potter Society Studies*

BP/V&A   Anne Stevenson Hobbs and Joyce Irene Whalley, *Beatrix Potter: The V&A Collection* (1985)

DIDJ   Beatrix Potter, *Dear Ivy, Dear June: Letters from Beatrix Potter*, edited by Margaret Crawford Maloney (1977)

ELCL   Beatrix Potter, *The Choyce Letters: Beatrix Potter to Louie Choyce, 1916–1943*, edited by Judy Taylor (1994)

HD   Beatrix Potter, *A Holiday Diary: With a Short History of the Warne Family*, edited and written by Judy Taylor (1996)

HWBP   *A History of the Writings of Beatrix Potter*, edited by Leslie Linder (1981, revised edition 1987)

Letters   Beatrix Potter, *Beatrix Potter's Letters*, selected by Judy Taylor (1989)

LTC   Beatrix Potter, *Letters to Children from Beatrix Potter*, edited by Judy Taylor (1992)

ML   Beatrix Potter, *Beatrix Potter's Farming Friendship: Lake District Letters to Joseph Moscrop, 1926–1943*, edited by Judy Taylor (1998)

MY   Margaret Lane, *The Magic Years of Beatrix Potter* (1978)

Notes, RBG   Mary Noble, 'Beatrix Potter, Naturalist & Mycologist and Charles McIntosh, the "Perthshire Naturalist"', *Notes from the Royal Botanic Garden Edinburgh*, 44/3 (1987), 607–27

TBP   Margaret Lane, *The Tale of Beatrix Potter* (1946)

TMH   John Heelis, *The Tale of Mrs William Heelis – Beatrix Potter* (1999)

TNR   Judy Taylor, *That Naughty Rabbit: Beatrix Potter and Peter Rabbit* (2002)

VN   Eileen Jay, Mary Noble and Anne Stevenson Hobbs, *A Victorian Naturalist: Beatrix Potter's Drawings from the Armitt Collection* (1992)

Beatrix Potter and Her Correspondents

ACM	Anne Carroll Moore
ALW	Amelia 'Millie' Warne
AMK	Alexander McKay
BLT	Bruce L. Thompson
BMM	Bertha Mahony Miller
BP	Beatrix Potter
BPH	Beatrix Potter Heelis
CC	Caroline (Hutton) Clark
CJW	Carl J. Weber
CMI	Charles McIntosh
DB	Delmar Banner
DH	Daisy Hammond
DMM	Donald M. Matheson
ELC	Eleanor 'Louie' Choyce
EN	Esther Nicholson
FC	Fanny Cooper
FW	Fruing Warne
GN	Grace Nicholson
GPC	Mary-Abigail (Gail) Parsons Coolidge
GW	George Walker
HDR	Hardwicke Drummond Rawnsley
HPC	Henry P. Coolidge
HW	Harold Warne
JDV	Josefina de Vasconcellos
JM	Joseph Moscrop
MFHP	Marian Frazer Harris Perry
NDW	Norman Dalziel Warne
NNH	Nancy Nicholson Hudson
SHH	Samuel H. Hamer

Prologue: Ownership

1. BPH to ALW, 8 November 1918, FWA. *Westmorland Gazette*, 8 November 1918.

2. BP to HW, 10 October 1905, *Letters*. BP to HW, 2 October 1905, FWA/V&A.

3. *BP Journal* (19 August 1882), 20–21. H. S. Cowper, *Hawkshead* (1899). Bruce L. Thompson, *The Lake District and the National Trust* (1946), 154–7. Although BP distinguishes her postal address as Near Sawrey, she refers to the village simply as Sawrey.

4. *BP Journal* (29 September 1885), 275.

5. Ibid. (21 September 1895), 403. See for example the painting *Harvest Scene, Esthwaite Water, c.* 1895, V&A, and *From the Garden at Ees Wyke, looking toward Esthwaite Water*, June 1911, FWA. *BP Journal* (15 July–17 November 1896), 427–35.

6. Ibid. (28 July 1896), 427.

7. F. T. Wright to The Caretaker [Mrs Ludbrook], Hill Top, 27 March 1951, NT.

8. *MY*, 94; *HWBP*, 168. BP to NDW, 11 December 1904, *Letters*, 111.

9. *BP Journal* (17 November 1896), 433. Thompson, *The Lake District and the National Trust*, 1–7. Wordsworth's description of the scenery of the lakes, (1835) includes the phrase 'district of the Lakes' and the term 'Lakeland'.

1 Roots

1. Beatrix Potter (Heelis), biographical profile provided to the *Horn Book* editors in November 1942 for a *Horn Book* publication, *Illustrators of Children's Books 1744–1945*, ed. Bertha Mahony and others (1947). Part of this profile is published in *BPA*, 213.

2. 'Roots of the Peter Rabbit Tales', *The Horn Book* (May 1929); *BPA*, 207–9. Unitarianism is a denomination within the English Dissenting or free-church tradition which rejects the doctrine of the Trinity. Never large in numbers, and particularly prevalent in the Midlands and North of England, Unitarians were disproportionately represented among the new entrepreneurial segments of society and in scientific, literary and

academic circles, and were particularly identified with political liberalism.

3. *BPA*, 207–8.

4. Ibid.

5. J. Mordaunt Crook, *The Rise of the Nouveaux Riches* (1999), 1–32.

6. Quoted in J. G. Hurst, *Edmund Potter and Dinting Vale* (1948), 6. J. Scott, J. H. Smith and D. Winterbottom, *Glossop Dale, Manor and Borough* (1973), 57–73. Edmund Potter, 'Calico Printing as an Art Manufacturer' (1852, in Manchester Central Library Archives), 49; 'Edmund Potter & Co. Ltd.', Derbyshire Record Office. In her journal for December 1894 (*BP Journal*, 368), Beatrix incorrectly reports that the pattern was 'a poker and tongs crossed, black on a blue ground'.

7. Under an Act of 1753, in force until 1836, all Dissenters were required to be married in the Church of England. Hurst, *Edmund Potter*, 2–7. Glynis Reeve (Greenman), *A North Country Lass* (privately published [Glossop], 2001); Eileen Jay, *Beatrix Potter's Manchester Roots* (1994): The children of Edmund and Jessy in birth order were: Edmund Crompton, Clara, Rupert, Walter, William, Mary and Lucy.

8. Hurst, *Edmund Potter*, 12. Rowena Godfrey, 'A Genial Man: Edmund Potter and his Calico Printing Work', *BPS Studies*, 11 (2005), 21–34.

9. Scott, Smith and Winterbottom, *Glossop Dale*, 59. Reeve, *A North Country Lass*, 4.

10. Reeve, *A North Country Lass*, 4. Hurst, *Edmund Potter*, 28–30: Edmund Potter, *Picture of a Manufacturing District* (1856) remains a valuable statistical portrait of a Victorian mill town. Raymond V. Holt, *The Unitarian Contribution to Social Progress in England* (1952), 196–209. E. Potter, 'The Strike: A Letter to the Working Classes', and 'Letter to Rev. Charles Richson in reply to opinions on "Trade Schools as necessary to promote national education"', in *Pamphlets published by Edmund Potter* (Manchester, 1831–55); Manchester Local Studies Library, Manchester.

11. He was a reporter for the jury on the exhibits of printing and dyeing, and entered exhibits displaying the progress of machine-printed fabrics. Obituary, *Inquirer* (3 November 1883). Edmund Potter, 'Schools of Art', in *Pamphlets*. Potter helped organize the Art Treasures Exhibition at Manchester in 1857; Robert H. Kargon, *Science in Victorian Manchester* (1977), 16–19. Edmund Potter, 'Remarks on Education', at the opening of the Unitarian Chapel in Glossop, 12 June 1875, *Inquirer*, 19 June 1875.

12. Manchester College, founded in 1786 for the sons of Dissenters, had

removed to York early in the nineteenth century, but returned to Manchester for a second period during which it was officially Manchester New College. It had several more reiterations, becoming Manchester College Oxford in 1889. Its most recent incarnation is as Harris-Manchester College. Edmund served on the Board of Regents and sent all four sons to Manchester New College. For simplicity I refer to the college that Rupert attended as Manchester College. During his time, Manchester's degrees were awarded by University College London. Hurst, *Edmund Potter*, 72–9. E. Potter, *Pamphlets*.

13. 'Memories of Camfield Place', *c.* 1891, *BP Journal*, 444.

14. Ibid. 447. Until rather recently Camfield Place was the home of Barbara Cartland, the romance writer. Still owned by the Cartland family today, it has been only slightly altered from when Beatrix used to lie happily in Bedroom number 4 with its well-loved green bed hangings. Probated will of Edmund Potter, 17 January 1884, Principal Probate Registry. This amount is distinct from real property, which is excluded from probate valuations. (The equivalent amount in US currency is $2,143,700 in 2003.) Probated values are taken from the calendars in the Probate Department of the Principal Registry, Family Division. Modern equivalents, rounded off, are derived from John J. McCusker, 'Comparing the Purchasing Power of Money in Great Britain from 1264 to Any Other Year . . .', www.Oanda.com/convert/fxhistory. Crompton Potter died just six months before his father in 1883. Walter died in 1871, and William, who never married, died of typhoid in 1873. All three Potter daughters survived: Clara, never married, continued to live at Queen's Gate, Mary married Edwin Wrigley, a successful paper manufacturer from Bury, and Lucy became the wife of the noted chemist Sir Henry Roscoe.

15. Background on the Leech family is from family obituaries in *Inquirer* and *Christian Life*, from Samuel Hill, *Bygone Stalybridge* (1907), 223–8, and *A History of the Mansions of Manufacturers*, n.d., Manchester Central Library Archives. Interview with Christine Clough of The Friends of Gorse Hall, May 2000. Enid Bassom, 'Profile: Gorse Hall', *BPSN*, 76 (April 2000), 5–6. Reeve, *A North Country Lass*, 5–7.

16. Obituary of John Leech, *Christian Reformer*, 17 (1861), 320. Obituary of Mrs Leech, *Christian Life* (12 January 1884), 21–2. The overlap between the two families in their Unitarian associations is quite striking both intellectually and socially; Royal Manchester Institute, lists of

subscribers, Manchester Central Library Archives; *History of the Royal Manchester Institute*, 1881. Manchester Central Library Archives. *BP Journal* (5 May 1884), 83.

17. Beatrix always refers to the Burton home as 'Gwaynynog' but it is now spelled 'Gwaenynog'. The equivalent amount in 2003 would be $954,000. M. Harvey to the author, 21 April 2003. Probated will of Harriet Burton, 10 June 1905, Principal Probate Registry. John and Jane Leech, the two elder Leech children, are buried at Gee Cross near the Potter crypt. The senior Leeches are buried at Dukinfield. The younger John Leech had a daughter, Ethel, who married Sir William Hyde Parker, from a family with naval connections, and subsequently lived at Melford Hall.

18. 'Northern Notes', *Inquirer* (30 July 1966), 5; 'Stalybridge', *Inquirer* (26 February 1870), 138. Jack Bredbury, *The Foundation of the Staly-bridge Unitarian Church and Sunday School and the Connection of Their Origins with the Leech Family* (2001), 1–4.

19. *BP Journal* (28 March 1884), 79. 'Northern Notes', *Inquirer* (30 July 1966), 5.

20. 'Mrs Leech', *Christian Life* (12 January 1884), 21. Revd J. Grant Bird, *Stalybridge Reporter* (11 January 1884). Bird's comments on Leech's benevolence are extraordinary, as he was a clergyman of the Church of England. 'London Diary', *Inquirer* (6 August 1966), 3, (13 August 1966), 3. *BP Journal* (6 January 1884, 30 March 1884), 62, 80.

21. Rupert Potter to Edmund Potter, 1846, V&A.

22. V. D. Davis, *A History of Manchester College* (1932), 105–9, 119–20. 'Mr Rupert Potter', *Inquirer* (16 May 1914). Beatrix recalls her father's respect for Martineau's character and conscience in 1884; *BP Journal* (19 November 1884), 118.

23. Rupert later collected some thirty pen-and-ink drawings by the illustrator Randolph Caldecott, while Crompton amassed an important collection of modern British painters and valuable Chinese enamels and porcelains. *BP Journal* (19 March 1884), 76 and note. Edmund promoted photography at the Manchester Exhibition and very likely owned a camera. The youngest Potter child, Lucy, took up photography early, taking a competent portrait of her father in 1859.

24. David Wykes, 'Sons and Subscribers: Lay Support and The College', in Barbara Smith (ed.), *Truth, Liberty, Religion: Essays Celebrating Two Hundred Years of Manchester College* (1986), 32–77.

25. *Records of the Honourable Society of Lincoln's Inn* (II), Admissions, 1896. *The Black Books*, V, Lincoln's Inn, 1968. The Law List (1858). *Men-at-the-Bar: A Biographical Hand-List* (1885). *The Black Books*, VI, Book XLVI, p. 334, Lincoln's Inn, 2001. In 1934 Beatrix acknowledged her father's esteem for Lincoln's Inn when she gave the Society a portrait of another of their famous members, Henry Peter Brougham, Baron Brougham and Vaux, a north-country man who had been much admired by the Crompton and Potter families. The portrait of Brougham was painted by S. Gambardella, much admired by Millais, and had place of honour in the Potter dining room; G. F. Holborn to the author, 12 February 2003. *BP Journal* (30 January 1884, 9 April 1885), 67, 144.

26. *ASC*, 15. Rupert Potter Sketchbook, V&A.

27. The Law List (1858), 87. Rupert Potter, *A Few Observations upon Lord Westbury's Bill to facilitate the proof of title to, and the conveyance of Real Estates* (1862). R. M. Jackson, *The Machinery of Justice in England* (4th edition, 1964).

28. In the 1867 case in question, Rupert appeared as English junior to a Scottish advocate in a Scottish appeal to the Judicial Committee of the Privy Council. The case of *Dunlop* v. *Johnston* concerned the effect of a husband's subsequent bankruptcy on his wife's post-nuptial settlement. In order to appear in a case before the Council, Rupert would have had to have achieved some standing. *Dunlop* v. *Johnston* (2 April 1876), Law Reports, Scotch and Divorce Appeal Cases before the House of Lords, vol. 1, sess. 1866–9, 109–17. The appeal was denied.

29. *TBP*, 15–16; *MY*, 16–17. Margaret Lane's interpretation was based largely on the lack of obvious case records and the memory of Dora Roscoe, daughter of Rupert's youngest sister Lucy. Dora would have been too young to remember much about her uncle's legal practice and its specialized nature would have been beyond her knowledge. Last Will and Testament of Edmund Potter, 1883, 17 January 1884, Principal Probate Registry. Last will and testament of Clara Potter, 19 January 1906, Principal Probate Registry. Rupert was the sole executor of Clara's estate.

30. Lord Justice James (Sir William Milbourne James) was a friend and legal associate, and Sir Louis Mallet, a neighbour in Bolton Gardens, was an authority on free trade, who had just been made the Permanent Under-Secretary of State for India. James was a member of the Reform Club and had been Vice-Chancellor of the Court of Chancery. Potter and Mallet were also related by the marriage of Mallet's son and Rupert's

niece, Margaret Roscoe, the daughter of his youngest sister Lucy. Information on the mechanics of election supplied by the Athenaeum Club; 'Certificate of Candidate for Ballot, 4590', 27 April 1874, Athenaeum Archive, Ballot Books.

31. Helen's sister Elizabeth and Walter Potter died in 1867 and 1871 respectively, leaving two children, Edmund and Edith. On the Leech marriage settlement, see BP to Edith Potter Gaddum, 8 June 1923, *Letters*, 281–2. Barbara Caine, *Destined to be Wives* (1986), 1–11. The lack of evidence has forced interpreters to rely primarily on two sources, neither particularly objective: Beatrix's own comments in her journal and later in letters about her mother's behaviour, personality and activities; and the family photographic record created by Rupert Potter. Helen's opinions of her marriage, family life, children, and domestic and social responsibilities, in so far as we have record of them, are second-hand. There were two sides to Helen's story but regrettably only one is available.

32. Bredbury, *The Foundation*, 4, 6–7. *HWBP*, 295. BPH to AMK, 13 July 1938, *Letters*, 39. Joyce Irene Whalley, *BPSN*, 84 (April 2002), 19.

33. Leech–Potter wedding quilt, 8 August 1863. Blickling Textile Conservation Studio, Blickling, Norfolk; NT; Pam Lancaster, 'A Wedding Gift', *BPSN*, 101 (July 2006), 8–9.

34. Bredbury, *The Foundation*, 2–4. *Inquirer* (30 July 1966), 5.

35. Caine, *Destined to be Wives*, 5–8.

36. Potter Family Album, 'Helen Potter, 1873', BPG. The bone structure of the jaw in Helen's photographs and in a later caricature drawn by Beatrix suggest this conclusion; BP's caricature of her mother, V&A.

37. Census of 1881. Rupert bought the mews at numbers 4 and 11 for his household staff.

38. *ASC*, 17. 'Births', *The Times* (30 July 1866). Biographical profile, *BPA*, 213.

2 Exposures

1. Margaret Lane, Potter's first biographer, embellished her account with such architectural detail, either to reinforce her view that Potter had endured a sad and solitary childhood as a virtual prisoner in her parents' home, or because she incorrectly assumed its existence; 'at the barred third-floor windows of the second house, there was stationed day after

day a little girl who had leisure and solitude enough for the most prolonged study', *TBP*, 13. The idea of virtual imprisonment was later repeated by Lane in *MY*, 12, and passed into accepted truth. See especially Marcus Crouch, *Beatrix Potter* (1960); Maurice Sendak, *Caldecott & Company: Notes on Books and Pictures* (1988); Alexander Grinstein, *The Remarkable Beatrix Potter* (1995); Alison Lurie, *Don't Tell the Grown-ups: Subversive Children's Literature* (1990), 90–98; and Ruth K. MacDonald, *Beatrix Potter* (1986). In a recent memoir of Potter, *She was Loved: Memories of Beatrix Potter* (2003), Josefina de Vasconcellos (Josefina Banner) carried on the view that Potter's parents were insensitive and unloving, and her 'nursery was Her prison'. Judy Taylor was the first to challenge this interpretation, offering a more sophisticated understanding of Victorian family life in her 1986 biography *Beatrix Potter: Artist, Storyteller and Countrywoman*. Lane, who in real life was the Countess of Huntingdon, was a writer of exceptional descriptive power. But neither Rupert Potter's several photographs of number 2 and the surrounding houses nor Beatrix's paintings from the nursery window indicate the existence of any bars.

2. 'Memories of Camfield Place', *c.* 1891, *BP Journal*, 444, 449.

3. *BP Journal* (2 April 1884), 81.

4. 'Memories of Camfield Place', 444–5.

5. Edmund Potter rented Kinnaird House from 1859 to 1862, and possibly earlier. Sir Henry Enfield Roscoe, *The Life and Experiences of Sir H. E. Roscoe, DCL, LLD, FRS, written by Himself* (1906). Rupert Potter rented Tulliemet from Alexander Duncan, who was tenanted there in the 1870s; Records from the Collection at Blair Castle, Perthshire. J. Marle Bassett, 'Beatrix Potter's Perthshire "Home"', *Highlander* (July/August 1997); 19–22.

6. Edmund was friendly with Sir Curtis Miranda Lampson, the promoter of the Atlantic cable and telegraph, who rented Dalguise House 1861–3 and no doubt suggested it as a possible holiday house for Rupert. John Steuart was Master of the Supreme Court in Cape Town, South Africa, during the years the Potters rented the house. A rather ghastly beaux-arts tower was added to the house in 1885, changing its appearance dramatically. David C. Duncan, 'The Significance of Dalguise for Beatrix Potter', *BPS Studies*, 11 (2005), 18–34. *BP Journal*, 104, nn. 15, 16.

7. BP to Rupert Potter, n.d., *Letters*, 11; Rupert Potter to BP, 1874, V&A.

8. *BP Journal* (8 May 1884), 85.

9. Quoted in *BP Journal* (14 June 1884), 93, n. 32. Barbara Brill, *William Gaskell, 1805–1884* (1984), 115–16. 'John Bright in the Highlands', *Pall Mall Gazette* (2 April 1889), is based upon an interview with Rupert Potter and a show of his photographs of Bright. W. Gaskell to BP, 23 August 1877, V&A.

10. W. J. Eggeling, *Millais and Dunkeld: The Story of Millais' Landscapes* (1982), 5–18. Records from the Collection at Blair Castle, Perthshire. See also Phyllis Rose, *Parallel Lives: Five Victorian Marriages* (1984). M. Harvey, 'Rupert Potter and Millais', *Creative Camera* (February 1973), 62–3.

11. *BP Journal* (1 September 1892), 261–2.

12. Census of 1871. 'Memories of Camfield Place', *BP Journal*, 446. This spelling of the nurse's surname is taken from the 1871 census, and from the spelling on one of the cards from her in 'Beatrix Potter's Victorian Scrap Album, 1872–1878', a collection of 84 cards given to her by various family members; CCP. BP to FW, 3 January 1912, PC. BP, 'Roots', *BPA*, 207.

13. *BP Journal* (8 May 1884), 85.

14. Julia Briggs, 'Women Writers and Writing for Children: From Sarah Fielding to E. Nesbit', in Gillian Avery and Julia Briggs (eds.), *Children and Their Books* (1989), 221–41; Norma Clark, 'The Cursed Barbauld Crew: Women Writers and Writing for Children in the Late Eighteenth Century', in Mary Hilton, Morag Styles and Victor Watson (eds.), *Opening the Nursery Door* (1997), 91–103; Anne Stevenson Hobbs, 'Beatrix Potter's Writings: Some Literary and Linguistic Influences – with a Scottish Slant', *BPS Studies*, 3 (1989), 28–40; *BP/AW*, 35–40. John Goldthwaite, *The Natural History of Make-Believe* (1966), 59–73. BP to the Children's Librarian (Katherine Watson), Denver Public Library, 19 November 1930, Denver Public Library, Denver, Colorado. Harriet Beecher Stowe's novel was published in 1852 in a pirated version, and one children's edition was illustrated by George Cruikshank. *BP Journal* (20 August 1896), 430. BP to Helen Dean Fish, *Letters*, 369: BP, 'Roots', *BPA*, 208.

15. Joyce Irene Whalley, 'Beatrix Potter before "Peter Rabbit": Her Art Work', *BPS Studies*, 3 (1989), 22–7. Miscellaneous drawings by Beatrix Potter 1874–9; Linder Bequest, V&A. See *BP/V&A*. 'Corner of the School Room', 26 November 1885, in *ABP*, 34. The specimen cabinet was recently discovered among the belongings of Bertram's wife's family.

16. Rupert and Helen were President and Patroness of the Club; minutes of the Annual General Meeting of the Dalguise Curling Club, Easter Dalguise, 20 October, 18 November 1874.

17. Vere Henry Lewis Foster (1819–1900) was a prolific producer of copybooks used to teach handwriting as well as drawing. They were first published by Blackie, now owned by Frederick Warne, and were widely used by schools in the last half of the nineteenth century. A sketch of antique Roman charioteers and rearing horses on the back of a card she sent to Beatrix indicates that Helen too enjoyed sketching from the copybooks. Beatrix wrote this on one of Rupert Potter's drawings of birds done about 1872 or 1873; NT.

18. *ABP*, 2, 38: Joyce Irene Whalley to author, 25 May 2001, 17 March 2002. Vere Foster Manuals, various series, *BP/V&A*. Helen Beatrix Potter, *Narcissus; Foxgloves and periwinkle 1876, BP/V&A*. Transfer prints, *BP/V&A*. Anne Stevenson Hobbs, 'Context and Content: Working on Beatrix Potter's Art', *BPS Studies*, 9 (2001), 28–43.

19. 'Impressions of Mrs Hugh Blackburn', *BP Journal* (5 June 1891), 215–16. Mrs Hugh Blackburn, *Birds Drawn from Nature* (1868).

20. *Blackburn's Birds*, edited by Rob Fairley (1993), 14–15. In Potter's 1894 illustrations for *Little Red Riding Hood*, Blackburn's even earlier work, *The Cat's Tale* (1870), is an obvious influence. The late Dr Mary Noble argued persuasively that Potter modelled Jemima Puddle-duck, at least in name if not ornithological behaviour, on Jemima Blackburn.

21. Anne Lundin, *Victorian Horizons: The Reception of the Picture Books of Walter Crane, Randolph Caldecott and Kate Greenaway* (2001), 2–17. Percy Muir, *Victorian Illustrated Books* (1971), 21. Perry Nodelman, *Words about Pictures: The Narrative Art of Children's Books* (1988). F. J. Harvey Darton, *Children's Books in England: Five Centuries of Social Life*, third edition, edited by Brian Alderson (1982), 277. J. H. Plumb, 'New World for Children', in Neil McKendrick, John Brewer and J. H. Plumb (eds.), *The Birth of a Consumer Society* (1982), 286–315. William Henley, 'Randolph Caldecott', *Art Journal* (July 1881), 212. Anne Carroll Moore, 'Kate Greenaway and Randolph Caldecott', in Arthur King and A. F. Stuart, *The House of Warne* (1965), 18–29.

22. Mary Louisa Stewart Molesworth (1839–1921) was the daughter of a businessman and grew up in Manchester. She wrote both fantasy and moral stories, and some of her children talked in baby language. BP to Helen Dean Fish, 8 December 1934, *Letters*, 369. Joyce Irene Whalley,

'Beatrix Potter and the Illustration of Children's Books', *BPS Studies*, 8 (1999), 69–81.

23. Joyce Irene Whalley, 'The Young Artist and Early Influences', in *BP/AW*, 35–40. Ruari McLean, 'Children's Books During the Childhood of Beatrix Potter', *BPS Studies*, 3 (1989), 8–14. *BP Journal* (8 December 1883), 59. BP to ACM, 17 January 1940, *BPA*. Warne & Co. were the English agent for *St. Nicholas* magazine.

24. BP to Helen Dean Fish, 8 December 1934, *Letters*, 369. Hobbs, *BPS Studies*, 9 (2001), 29. [The editors,] 'Beatrix Potter and Lewis Carroll', *BPSN*, 70 (October 1998), 14–15.

25. BP to Mrs Ramsay Duff, 13 July 1943, *BPA*. BP, 'Roots', *BPA*, 208. Percy Muir, *English Children's Books, 1600–1900* (1954), 86–92. Dale Schafer, 'How Beatrix Potter's Childhood Reading Influenced her Writing Style', *BPS Studies*, 8 (1999), 91–103. BP to FW, 3 January 1912, PC. See also Laura C. Stevenson's discussion in 'A Vogue for Little Books: *The Tale of Peter Rabbit* and its Contemporary Competitors', BPS *Studies* 10 (2003), 11–27. Ivy Trent of the Cotsen Children's Library, Los Angeles, called my attention to the inventory of the Leech library at Gorse Hall: sale catalogue, Gorse Hall, Stalybridge (July 1885); CCP. BP to Denver Children's Librarian, 19 November 1930, Denver Public Library. Whalley, *BPS Studies*, 8 (1999), 94. Hobbs, *BPS Studies*, 9 (2001), 28.

26. BP, 'Roots', *BPA*, 208.

27. Before going on a Continental tour of Italy, Germany and Austria in 1871 Rupert had adopted the dry plate process. Helen tried her hand with the camera as well. Photograph album, *Marseilles, Genoa, & Pisa*, Cotsen Occasional Press (1998) contains some of their European tour photographs; CCP. Other albums are in the BPG. In 'John Bright in the Highlands', Rupert refers to his photographs of his distinguished guests.

28. The earliest prints date from 1865 when he was at Lochgair in Argyllshire on holiday. Potter contributed to the Annual Exhibitions of 1885, 1886 and 1889. See *Marseilles, Genoa & Pisa*, CCP.

29. Helen Potter to BP, 12 February n.d., PC. It was thought that Rupert's health benefited from the sea air, and in the 1880s and 1890s they chose the south coast for spring holidays.

30. *ASC*, illustration on p. 21. Vere Foster Drawing Books, V&A. Hobbs, *BPS Studies*, 9 (2001), 35.

31. BP, 'Roots', *BPA*, 208: BPH to MFHP, 4 October 1934, *BPA*.

32. BP, 'Roots', *BPA*, 208. BPH to Mrs Ramsay Duff, 13 July 1943, *BPA*: 'I have *not* been a greedy person; perhaps it is because my own upbringing was so spartan . . .'

33. *BP Journal* (3 October 1892), 279.

34. This study of animal anatomy was an expression of the Victorian passion for natural history. It was also common practice among artists, who needed to understand the body structure of the creatures they painted.

35. *BP Journal* (20–21 September 1893), 54. *ASC*, 32–3. The extant letters to their children, and the nurturing of their interests and talents, are expressive of the Potters' affection for their children. A similar conclusion is offered by Elaine R. Jacobsen's essay, 'Americans Look at Beatrix Potter', *BPS Studies*, 7 (1997), 75–92, which considers other evidence.

36. *BP Journal* (13 August 1896), 429.

37. *TBP*, 24, 27. Invitation list, Monday, 21 June 1875, FWA. Postal Directory, Local Studies Library, Kensington Library, London. For example, John Charles Wilson, from Oxford, was a house guest on the evening of the census of 1871.

38. Census of 1871, 1881, 1891. *BP Journal* (30 May 1885), 150.

39. *BP Journal* (5 February 1893), 311.

40. Ibid., 311–12. Census of 1881. Mary Rosalind Paget was a distinguished social reformer, nurse and midwife. She was made Dame in 1935. See *DIDJ*, introduction, pp. vii–ix.

41. *BP Journal* (5 February 1893), 312.

42. *BP/AW*, 50. *BP Journal* (25 December 1884), 123; (21–31 December 1895), 412. BP to Ivy Steel, 30 December 1929, *DIDJ*. Rupert chose to celebrate St Valentine's Day instead, but even this remarkable keeping of the old Puritan tradition was inconsistent. See 'Beatrix Potter's Victorian Scrap Album, 1872–1878', CCP, and Eric Hobsbawn and Terence Ranger (eds.), *The Invention of Tradition* (1983). There are additional cards sent to Bertram at BPG.

43. *BP Journal* (30 September 1884), 107–8. The influence of Unitarianism on Potter's intellectual outlook has been neglected by scholars, but its cultural influence is central to her emotional and intellectual perspective. M. Daphne Kutzer, *Beatrix Potter: Writing in Code* (2003), 16–18, supports this view.

44. *BP Journal* (23 February 1896), 418. Her rather outspoken views at this time were modified in later life. She was known to enjoy Anglican

services, but seems to have preferred the Quaker meeting above all others. *Inquirer* (20 August 1966), 3. Obituary of Rupert Potter, *Inquirer*, (1914). James Ballantyne, 'Origins of Essex Church, Notting Hill Gate, London', *Transactions of the Unitarian Historical Society*, 7 (1939–42), 130–38.

45. BP, 'Roots', *BPA*, 208–9.

46. Between 1875 and 1878 a Miss Madeline Davidson was briefly in charge. She appears in one of Rupert's photographs at Dalguise in 1876, when Beatrix was about ten. Miss Hammond oversaw most of her education. Her given name is unknown and 'Florrie', perhaps for 'Florence', is a conjecture taken from a later reference.

47. *BP Journal* (21 June 1883), 48; (17 July 1883), 49.

48. Ann Bermingham, *Learning to Draw: Studies in the Cultural History of a Polite and Useful Art* (2000), 212–24.

49. BP to Miss (Kate) Wyatt, 27 November 1920, *Letters*, 266.

50. *BP's Art*, 7–23, 30; see fig. 5, 'Early rabbit at rest, 1880'. *TNR*, 14–20.

51. Whalley, *BPS Studies*, 8 (1999), 74–5.

52. Science and Art Form No. 213, February 1880; Art Form No. 899, May 1881; Examination in Second Grade Drawing at South Kensington, 21 May 1880; 17 June 1881. Science and Art Department of the Committee of Council on Education, CCP. *BP Journal* (28 May 1883), 47.

53. Ibid. (25 June 1884), 94; (13 August 1896), 429.

54. Lady Eastlake, the former Elizabeth Rigby, was herself a distinguished author and translator of German and Russian art history and criticism. Sir Charles Eastlake had much influence on Rupert, in addition to sponsoring him for membership of the Athenaeum. Rupert sought Lady Eastlake's advice on matters of education for both his children.

55. *BP Journal* (21 November 1883), 56–7.

56. Ibid. (24 November 1883), 57–8.

57. Ibid. (29 November 1883), 58; (5 December 1883), 58–9; (10 June 1882), 17–19.

58. Dianne Sachko MacLeod, *Art and the Victorian Middle Class: Money and the Making of Cultural Identity* (1996), 267–325.

59. *BP Journal* (8, 9 February 1884), 67–8. Eventually Rupert owned eight from this series, framing them all together, and over time owned about thirty illustrations. *BP's Art*, 12: *BP/AW*, 45. BP to Jacqueline Overton, 7 April 1942, *Letters*, 441. BP to NDW, 15 July 1902, *Letters*, 64. *BP Journal* (15 December 1883), 60.

60. Ibid. (15 November 1884), 117; (13 January 1883), 28, 30.
61. Ibid. 28–31. *BP's Art*, 80–81. Irene Whalley, 'The Young Artist and Early Influences', in *BP/AW*, 40. Waterford, a watercolour artist of considerable talent, did a series of biblical scenes and illustrations of the lives of good children. Bonheur was famous for her realistic painting of wild animals.
62. *BP Journal* (note of 1886 to entry of 13 January 1883), 31; (3 March 1883), 32. The note indicates that until 1883 Beatrix had been exposed only to contemporary British paintings and drawings, and only rarely to the work of Renaissance and Reformation artists. She was 16, not 17 at the time of the Old Masters exhibition.

3 Transitions

1. *BP Journal* (25 April 1883), 39; Leslie Linder, 'The Code Writing', ibid., pp. xvii–xxiii. The extant journal begins on 4 November 1881 when she was 15, but there is evidence that she began her code writing at least a year earlier, and destroyed those pages at later reading, judging them unworthy. The last entry in the journal is dated 31 January 1897, some fifteen years later, when she was 30. In between there are some 200,000 words. There was no 'title' given to the scraps of paper found by her executors in various chests at Hill Top after Potter's death. Potter's observations were not always written daily. Some were written days, even weeks after the events they describe.
2. BP to CC, 15 November 1943, NT.
3. *BP Journal* (15 November 1884), 117; ibid., appendix B. Leslie Linder, 'Beatrix Potter's Code Writing', *The Horn Book*, 39/2 (April 1963), 141–54. In 1958 Potter collector and bibliophile Leslie Linder broke her code after years of effort. After more years of painstaking transcription, he published her journal in 1966. This edition omitted a number of passages at the request of Potter's executors. They were restored in the 1989 edition.
4. Maurice Sendak, 'Beatrix Potter/1', in his *Caldecott & Company: Notes on Books and Pictures* (1988), 64. This essay first appeared in *Publisher's Weekly* (11 July 1966).
5. See Susan Denyer, *At Home with Beatrix Potter: The Creator of Peter Rabbit* (2000), 8, 36.

6. *BP Journal* (8 May 1884), 84–5; (20 April 1882, 11 May 1882), 15, 16.

7. Ibid. (10, 21 July 1882), 20–21. 'John Bright in the Highlands', *Pall Mall Gazette*, 7501 (2 April 1889), 2.

8. *BP Journal* (10, 21 July 1882), 20–21. Ian Gordon, 'A History of Wray Castle' (n.d.). Bruce L. Thompson, *The Lake District and the National Trust* (1946), 132–3.

9. Gordon, 'A History'. Rawnsley set up a mission in Bristol to the poor, and while there was instrumental in preserving a fourteenth-century church tower. However, his unorthodox methods provoked the church hierarchy and he was dismissed from the parish; Rosalind Rawnsley, 'HDR – A Lover of His Fellow Men', *Cumbria*, 37 (October 1987), 409–11.

10. Elizabeth Battrick, '*The Most Active Volcano in Europe*': Canon Hardwicke Drummond Rawnsley (1995). John Simpson, '*The Most Active Volcano in Europe*': *A Short Life of Canon Hardwicke Drummond Rawnsley, Vicar of Crosthwaite, Keswick 1883–1917* (n.d.), 3–7. Alan Hankinson, 'Canon Hardwicke Drummond Rawnsley', *Cumbrian Life*, 30 (September/October 1993), 25–7.

11. H. A. L. Rice, 'The Happy Warrior', in his *Lake Country Portraits* (1967), 122–42. Christopher Hanson-Smith, 'Beatrix Potter and the National Trust', *BPS Studies*, 1 (1985), 5. Rawnsley published nearly forty books.

12. Eleanor F. Rawnsley, *Canon Rawnsley: An Account of His Life* (1923), quoting from Robert Somervell, 48.

13. *BP Journal* (9 October 1882), 24. Rawnsley, *Canon Rawnsley*, 47.

14. Bruce L. Thompson, 'The Guardian of the Lakes' (*c.* 1971), CRO/K. 'The Proposed Permanent Lake District Defence Society', May 1883, CRO/K. Records of the Lake District Defence Society, correspondence regarding the Braithwaite & Buttermere Railway Bill, CRO/C.

15. Simpson, '*The Most Active* . . .', 5.

16. BP to Rupert Potter, 3 April 1883 from Ilfracombe, *Letters*, 12–13. Rupert joined the family later in the week, having been again to Brighton where his brother, Edmund Crompton, was seriously ill.

17. *BP Journal* (18, 25 April 1883), 38, 39, 40.

18. Ibid. (17 July 1883), 49.

19. Rupert had been Crompton's executor, but a codicil in 1883 replaced him with John Bagshaw, a partner in the Edmund Potter Company. This was a practical consideration.

20. *BP Journal* (15 May 1883), 45. Crompton left an estate valued at

£113,714. His art collection fetched £32,558 the following year, while his magnificent collection of *cloisonné* ware, 'containing some of the finest specimens to be found in England', brought an additional £5,117. 16s. But much of that went to pay the debt for his share of the company.

21. *BP Journal* (2–6 May 1883), 45. Obituaries of E. Crompton Potter, *Manchester Guardian* (7 May 1883), 5, (12 May 1883), 7; *Inquirer* (12 May 1883), 300.

22. Probated will of Edmund Crompton Potter, 23 August 1883. Third codicil of E. Crompton Potter, 23 April 1883. *BP Journal* (15 May 1883), 45.

23. Ibid. (28 July 1883), 49.

24. Ibid. (4, 20 September 1883), 54; (2 August 1883), 50.

25. Ibid. (30 October 1883), 55; (5 November 1883), 56.

26. 'Mr Edmund Potter, FRS', *Christian Life* (3 November 1883), 530.

27. Will of Edmund Potter, November 1881, probated 17 January 1884. The estate was complicated by the funds owed to Edmund by Crompton for his partnership in the Dinting Vale printworks, a debt that contributed to his widow's later penury. Rupert received additional money at the death of his mother when her will was probated in 1892, but a larger sum passed down to him at his sister Clara's death in 1905. Michael Harvey notes correctly that Rupert's increased wealth made no perceptible change in the family's conservative life style.

28. *BP Journal* (12 June 1884), 93.

29. Ibid. (12, 14 June 1884), 93–4.

30. Henry Enfield Roscoe, *The Life and Experiences of Sir H. E. Roscoe, DCL, LLD, FRS, written by Himself* (1906), 370; Roscoe had recently been knighted for his contributions to chemistry and scientific education. *BP Journal* (2 January 1885), 124–5. This was one of the passages that the Heelis executors objected to and which was removed in the initial publication of the journal. Before Edmund's death, Beatrix had written witheringly, 'privately I think the boy has certainly several loose screws in his system'; ibid. 122.

31. *BP Journal* (5 July 1884), 98.

32. Ibid. (20 April 1884), 82; (8 December 1883), 59; (18 March 1884), 75.

33. Ibid. (12, 23, 26 October 1884), 109; (13, 25 December 1884), 122–3.

34. Alexander Grinstein, *The Remarkable Beatrix Potter* (1995), 22–32. Grinstein, among other psychoanalysts, suggests her depression was caused by 'low self-esteem'.

35. *BP Journal* (28 March 1884), 79.

36. Ibid. (31 March, 2, 3 April 1884), 80–81.

37. Ibid. (8, 19 May 1884), 84, 87.

38. Ibid. (8 May 1884), 85.

39. Ibid. (26 May 1884), 89.

40. Ibid. (28 June 1884), 96; (28 July 1884), 104. Bertram's uncle, William Leech, had a well-known drinking problem and died of it in 1887.

41. Ibid. (16 July, 1 August 1884), 100, 104; (4 October 1884), 109. The property, like nearby Hatfield House, was owned by Lord Salisbury. See *A Scottish Garden in June from Nature, ca. 1882, From the drawing-room window at Camfield Place, 1884* and *From the terrace at Camfield Place, December 1884, BP's Art*, plates 12, 14.

42. *BP Journal* (27 May 1884), 90; (10 June 1884), 93.

43. Ibid. (25 June 1884), 94; (8 July 1884), 99; (30 January 1884), 66; (19 February 1885), 131. Millais's portrait was intended for the Hall of Christ Church, Oxford, where it still hangs. Michael I. Wilson, 'The Potters and Photography', Linder Lecture, 17 May 2000, BPS. Michael Harvey to author, 25 September 2003. The only other Potter photograph known to have been made into a carte-de-visite was his portrait of John Bright, now in the National Portrait Gallery collection.

44. *BP Journal* (16 July 1884), 100; (7 March 1886), 192; (15 March 1895) 138.

45. Ibid. (19 December 1884), 122; (29 January 1886), 173. M. Harvey, 'Rupert Potter and Millais', *Creative Camera* (February 1973), 62–3.

46. *BP Journal* (4 October 1884), 109.

47. Ibid. (28 November 1884), 120–21; (9 November 1885), 159–60; (6 May 1885), 146. *BP's Art*, 7–15.

48. *BP Journal* (20 March 1885), 141–2.

49. Ibid. (3 June 1885), 151. The original of *The Private Secretary* was a play by the German Gustav von Moser. It featured Beerbohm Tree in the lead, but Hawtrey replaced him with W. S. Penley and the play became a great success, running until 1886, rivalling the popularity of *Charley's Aunt*.

50. Ibid. (9 November 1885), 159–60; (6 May 1885), 146.

51. Ibid. (5 May 1884), 83; (28 March 1885), 143–4.

52. Ibid. (29 May 1885), 149.

53. Ibid. (30 May 1885), 150; (18 June 1885), 152–3.

54. Ibid. (10 July 1885), 154. *ASC*, 43. *LTC*, 12–13. The Moore children

in birth order were Noel, Eric, Marjorie, Winifrede (Freda), Norah, Joan, Hilda and Beatrix.

55. *BP Journal* (7 September 1885), 156. The Potters would spend nine summers at Lingholm between 1885 and 1907.

56. *BP Journal* (7 September, 13 October 1885), 156, 158, 159.

57. Ibid. (9, 12, 17 February 1886), 179, 182, 193.

58. Ibid. (24, 27 November 1885), 163–4. Roscoe was defeated in the following General Election of 1886.

59. *BP Journal* (23 February 1886), 183–8. Robert H. Kargon, *Science in Victorian Manchester* (1977), 204–12. Roscoe, 363. Lucy's photograph was titled *The Fisherman* and is reproduced prominently in Roscoe, *Life and Experiences*.

60. *BP Journal* (31 December 1885), 168.

61. Ibid. (December 1886), 201; (end of June 1887), 204.

62. This was the only indication that Rupert now had more expendable income. There were 520 boys listed in 1887. Bertram entered Hodgsonsites House for Oration Quarter, Autumn 1886, and left after Long Quarter, Spring 1887, before he sat for any exams. *Carthusian* (December 1918), 252. M. Mardell, Archivist, Charterhouse, Surrey, letters to the author, 3, 5 September 2003. *BP Journal* (1 April 1887), 203; (Summer 1887), 204. Beatrix reports he had 'pleurisy' but one suspects that Bertram's respiratory distress was fabricated at best, and at worst related to alcohol abuse. M. Mardell to author, 10 September 2003. 'Medical Statistics Summary and Report', April 1887, Charterhouse.

63. *BP Journal* (16 September 1884), 106. Bertram Potter to BP, 12 October? 1886, V&A.

64. *BP Journal* (25 February 1886), 188. *BP's Art*, 37–9.

65. Ibid. (18 October 1886), 202.

66. Frances Burney (1752–1840), *The Early Diary of Frances Burney* (1890). Burney's diaries were first published between 1842 and 1846. Pat Rogers, in *The Oxford Dictionary of National Biography* (2004). Grinstein, *The Remarkable Beatrix Potter*, 39–42. *BP Journal* (May 1890), 211–14.

67. *ASC*, 51. Graham Murphy, *Founders of the National Trust* (1987), 79–80. Murphy repeats here the story that Noel Rawnsley believed Beatrix Potter was the love of his father's life; a view which is appealing, but almost certainly wishful thinking. The Potters were at Lingholm in 1885, 1887 and 1888.

68. *BP Journal* (May 1890), 212.

69. Ibid. 213. *BP/AW*, 49–51. Bertram sent a postcard from Paris dated September 1889. It is not known how long he was away or with whom he travelled.

70. *BP Journal* (May 1890), 214. This account of her first publishing success is written to 'Esther'; *TNR*, 20–21.

71. *ASC*, 52. *A Happy Pair* is undated and is extremely rare. Potter only sold her drawings to this and one other publisher, Ernest Nister, to illustrate the work of another author.

72. Frederick Warne & Company to BP, 12 November 1891, FWA.

73. Obituary, 'Mrs Jessy Potter', *Inquirer* (12 September 1891), n.p. It is especially notable that the obituary was titled with her given name.

74. 'Memories of Camfield Place', *c.* 1891, *BP Journal*, 444; (2 July 1884), 96.

4 Experiments

1. *BP Journal* (29 October 1892), 305. Charles McIntosh of Inver (1839–1922); the correct spelling of 'McIntosh' has latterly been much debated, but all the evidence confirms 'McIntosh'.

2. Essential to understanding the relationship of women to science and natural history in nineteenth-century England are Barbara T. Gates, *Kindred Nature: Victorian and Edwardian Women Embrace the Living World* (1998); her anthology of women's writing and illustration, *In Nature's Name: An Anthology of Women's Writing and Illustration, 1780–1930* (2002), and Barbara T. Gates and Ann B. Shteir, *Natural Eloquence: Women Reinscribe Science* (1997). The best analysis of this 'craze' for natural history and of women's participation and exclusion is Lynn Barber, *The Heyday of Natural History* (1980), 125–38.

3. P[hilip] H[enry] Gosse's popular works on natural history included many fine illustrations and drawings. The Potters would have known his other books, especially *A Naturalist's Rambles on the Devonshire Coast* (1853) or *Tenby: A Sea-side Holiday* (1856), which delighted readers with vivid descriptions of the minutest things. As a young person Beatrix had 'borrowed' the volumes of F. O. Morris's *A Natural History of British Moths: Accurately Delineating Every Known Species* (1872) from her father's library, and had copied many of them.

4. See Anne Stevenson Hobbs, 'Flora and Fauna, Fungi and Fossils',

71–94, and Joyce Irene Whalley, 'Introduction', in *BP/AW*, 7–8. Hobbs's critical evaluation in *VN*, 139–81, is particularly helpful.

5. John Sowerby and C. Pierpoint Johnson, *British Wild Flowers* (1882); inscribed volume dated 12 October 1884, Beatrix Potter Collection, Daito Bunka University, Tokyo.

6. 'Letter to the Times' (1888), *BP Journal*, 206. The letter fragment is one of two entries for that year. This is the first extant 'letter to the editor', a writing habit she was to continue all her life. *HWBP*, 390–92.

7. The journal was published 1865–93; Cooke was editor 1872–93. Cooke drew his fungi sections one step behind the main drawing, a practice Beatrix did not employ until later. It chronicled the immense popular interest and participation in natural history during the later nineteenth century. See *VN*, 141.

8. See Robert McCracken, 'Beatrix Potter, Scientific Illustrator', *Antiques*, 149/6 (June 1996), 868–77.

9. Two extant watercolours of 1887 are *Stropharia aeruginosa*, or verdigris toadstool, 12 October 1887, and *Clitocybe geotropa*, 27 October 1887. They are part of the Beatrix Potter Collection of fungi paintings Beatrix bequeathed to the Armitt Trust Library, Ambleside. The Library is now part of the Lakes Discovery Museum @ The Armitt (hereafter cited as LDM@TA). Mary Noble, 'Beatrix Potter and Charles McIntosh, Naturalists', *VN*, 60–61.

10. Rupert Potter to CMI, 3 March 1887. M. Noble to the author, 16 July 2000.

11. *BP Journal* (28, 29 July 1892), 248–9.

12. Ibid. (27–9 July 1892), 247–9; (9 September 1892), 264. Cuthbert Graham, 'Beatrix Potter's Birnam in Code Diary', *Perthshire Advertizer* (1966). Clippings file, Dunkeld Cathedral Archives.

13. *BP Journal* (4 August 1892), 251.

14. Ibid. (1 August 1892), 250.

15. Ibid. (12 September 1892), 266.

16. Ibid. (28, 30 July 1892), 248–9. Nister had a London office at 24 Bride Street; *ABP*. Leslie Linder, 'Summary of Fungi drawing by year', Linder Archive, V&A. Linder's meticulous summary shows six fungi paintings for 1892.

17. *BP Journal* (29 October 1892), 305, 306–7. Beatrix had been up to Inver to see Kitty MacDonald, even sitting outside Charlie's humble house

on a bench. Colin Gibson, 'The Postman Naturalist' (1999), Dunkeld Cathedral Archives.

18. To play the cello, he used the edge of his injured hand in place of fingers to slide up and down the fingerboard; he also used the same technique to play the bass notes on the organ. 'Charles Mackintosh', in J. Murray Neil, 'The Scots Fiddle: Tunes, Tales & Traditions of the North-East and Central Highlands', unpublished MS (1998), PC.

19. Gibson, 'The Postman Naturalist', 118–22. Henry Coates, *A Perthshire Naturalist: Charles Macintosh of Inver* (1923), 96–140. Coates, a student of McIntosh's, argues that he was ahead of his time in such important botanical areas as identifying the larch canker disease, understanding ecological relationships, and concern for environmental destruction. McIntosh died in 1922 at the age of 83.

20. John Clegg, *Beatrix Potter: Artist, Storyteller and Scientist* (1989), 8–9. Interviews with Dr Mary Noble, 10, 16 April 2000. Noble, an expert in plant pathology and a passionate Potter scholar, died in July 2002. The Stevenson volumes are now in the Perth Museum. *BP Journal*, 306, n. 78.

21. Ibid. (29 October 1892), 305–6.

22. Ibid. 305.

23. Ibid. Mary Noble, 'Beatrix Potter and Charles McIntosh, Naturalists', *VN*, 62–5, and 'Beatrix Potter and Her Funguses', *BPS Studies*, 1 (1985), 41–6. Noble discovered the sketchbook with the initials 'HP' on the spine along with the correspondence between Beatrix and Charlie. The watercolours from that sketchbook are now at the Perth Museum. Mary Noble to W. P. K. Findlay, 7 July 1978, BPS.

24. *BP Journal* (29 October 1892), 306. Potter's tone throughout her journal account of their initial meeting is somewhat condescending, not of McIntosh's knowledge, but about his strange appearance and lack of social grace.

25. BP to CMI, 10 December 1892. The Dunkeld correspondence, consisting of three letters from Rupert Potter, eleven from Beatrix, and two from McIntosh, is in the National Library of Scotland and was published by Mary Noble, 'Beatrix Potter, Naturalist & Mycologist and Charles McIntosh, the "Perthshire Naturalist"', *Notes from the Royal Botanic Garden Edinburgh*, 44/3(1987), 607–27 (hereafter cited as *Notes, RBG*). Copies of the correspondence are in the Royal Botanic Garden Library, Edinburgh. Beatrix produced at least two drawings of every

specimen, sending one to McIntosh and keeping the other herself. The drawings she sent to McIntosh eventually came to the Perth Museum and Art Gallery. None of them are signed, and they remained unidentified until Noble authenticated them. See M. A. Taylor and R. H. Rodger (eds.), *A Fascinating Acquaintance: Charles McIntosh and Beatrix Potter* (2003). Copies of correspondence are at the Perth Museum and Art Gallery, and at LDM@TA.

26. The objectionable fungus is the common stinkhorn, *Phallus impudicus*.

27. Carla Yanni, *Nature's Museum: Victorian Science and the Architecture of Display* (2000), 3–43. The museum and not the laboratory was the central institution of Victorian science. BP to CMI (undated, 1893); partial letter in *Notes, RBG*. VN, 80–84.

28. *BP Journal* (1893), 310. In sharp contrast to the detailed account of her activities Beatrix had kept the previous summer, her journal for most of 1893 is blank. The records of ownership, lease and sublease of Eastwood to the Potters for 1893 are in the Blair Castle Archives, Perthshire. Atholl McGregor rented Eastwood from the Duke from 1882 to 1899. His sublet to Potter for the summer is confirmed by O. C. Lewis, Rector of Dunkeld Cathedral, to Leslie Linder, 1 March 1970; V&A. The name McGregor was a common one in the area. David Duncan to the author, 14 April 2003.

29. The fungus *Strobilomyces strobilaceus*, which has returned to its original name, is still rare in Scotland. One drawing of the fresh specimen is in LDM@TA and one is at the Perth Museum. The dried one which she painted first, discovered only in 1988, was given to the Perth Museum by Mrs Joan Duke, widow of the executor of Beatrix Heelis's estate. The dried specimen is dated 'Aug 11 Eastwood, Drummond Wood Crieff 1889'. This particular fungus dries exceedingly well, enabling Potter to paint it quite adequately after its return to McIntosh; Dr Roy Watling to the author, 18 January 2004; Robin Rodger, Curator, Perth Museum and Art Gallery. A postcard from John Stevenson is in McIntosh's papers verifying the identification in 1893. Stevenson noted the 1893 find in a holograph in his book. Mary Noble, 'Beatrix Potter, Mycologist', *BPSN*, 2 (March 1981). *VN*, 72–3. Elizabeth Battrick, *Beatrix Potter: The Unknown Years* (1999), 13.

30. *HWBP*, 110. *TNR*, 22–3.

31. It is also interesting that by 1893 the Moore family consisted of four children: two boys and two girls. Beatrix claimed as an old woman that

she had no one in particular in mind when she created Mr McGregor and never knew anyone by that name, but she had obviously forgotten. She may also have been reluctant to identify McIntosh as her model since the naturalist was anything but a crass villain. McIntosh credits John McGregor, late forester to the Duke of Atholl, in his article on the larch disease, 'Notes by a Naturalist Round Dunkeld', *Transactions of the Perthshire Society of Natural Science*, 2/6 (1887–8), so it was a name Potter would have heard around Eastwood. Peter Parker, 'Gardening with Beatrix Potter', *BPS Studies*, 10 (2003), 98–9, argues that McGregor was definitely working class and not an Edwardian gentleman; I concur. Beatrix made her own artistic adjustments to fit the story. BP to Noel Moore, 4 September 1893, FWA.

32. BP to Eric Moore, 5 September 1893, CCP. Judy Taylor to the author, 8 August 2003. Correspondence with Ivy Trent, Cotsen Children's Library, formerly in Los Angeles.

33. BP to CMI, 19 November 1893, *Notes*, RBG, 619, n. 14. BP to CMI (n.d., *c.* November 1893), *VN*, 80–82. Roy Watling to the author, 16 February 2004.

34. CMI to BP, 10 January 1894, *Notes*, RBG. This letter was found in a copy of Henry Coates's biography of McIntosh, *A Perthshire Naturalist*, which Beatrix gave the Armitt Trust along with other volumes in her library. Very likely she had kept the letter since 1894 because of his excellent instructions. This is one of only two extant letters from McIntosh to Potter.

35. *VN*, 94. See Mary Noble and Roy Watling, 'Cup Fungus or Basidiomycete, and Potterism', *Bulletin of the British Mycological Society* 20 (1986), 45–7, and W. P. K. Findlay, *Wayside and Woodland Fungi* (1967), where fifty-nine of Potter's fungi drawings are published.

36. There may have been more than seventy-three paintings, but these are the extant number.

37. BP to CMI, 1894, *Notes*, RGB, n. 21. Leslie Linder, 'Summary of Fungi drawings by year', Linder Archive, V&A: 50 drawings in 1894, 23 drawings in 1895. *BP Journal* (10 October 1894), 363–4.

38. Ibid. (14 March 1893), 314–16.

39. Crompton Hutton was related to Richard Holt Hutton, an important Unitarian editor and reviewer, who graduated ahead of Rupert at Manchester College and was a James Martineau acolyte.

40. *BP Journal* (12 June 1894), 319, and n. 2, regarding a 1956 letter from Caroline Hutton Clark.

41. Ibid. (1894), 322. See Peter Hollindale, 'Beatrix Potter and Natural History', *BPS Studies* 9 (2001), 65. Hollindale argues that Potter was above all an 'empirical observer of immediate natural phenomena'.

42. *BP Journal* (1894), 320, 324.

43. Ibid. (12 June 1894 and ff.), 320–26.

44. Mary Hutton became a well-regarded geologist, specializing in fossil sponges; Brian G. Gardiner, 'Beatrix Potter's Fossils and Her Interest in Geology', *Linnean*, 16/1 (January 2000), 31–47.

45. Letter to Eric Moore, 28 March 1894; letter to Noel Moore, 29 March 1894, CCP.

46. Archivist, Charterhouse, Surrey, correspondence with the author, September–October 2003. Archives of the Athenaeum, 'Walter Bertram Potter, Supporters Sheet', entry 13 May 1890; Sir James Caird, MP, and Sir John E. Millais were his proposers. Bertram Potter to BP, 6 September 1889, postmarked Paris, V&A. The only unexplained discrepancy is that the records from Magdalen College list Bertram as coming up from Charterhouse; while those at Charterhouse clearly show he withdrew in 1887. Robin Darwall-Smith, Archivist, Magdalen College, Oxford to the author, 25 July 2003; *Alumni Oxonienses: The Historical Register of the University of Oxford* (1900), 812.

47. *BP Journal* (29 July 1894), 330.

48. BP to Eric Moore, 13 September 1894, CCP.

49. *BP Journal* (6, 23 August 1894), 333, 337, 338. Inside Beatrix's copy of Geikie's *Outlines of Geology* (1888), inscribed 'July 1894', were three sheets of her pen-and-ink drawings of fossilized fish with notations on each as to their identification through reference to Hugh Miller's popular book *The Old Red Sandstone* (1841). There was also a photograph of an archaeological dig at Glacier Garden, Lucerne, taken and signed 'WB Potter', but not dated, by Bertram that same summer. See Barber, *Heyday*, 225–38.

50. See the Beatrix Potter Collection, LDM@TA. *BP Journal* (14 September, 1894), 346; (26 July 1894), 329; (3, 6, 10 October 1894), 358–62.

51. Ibid. (18 August 1894), 337–8; (10, 20 September 1894), 344, 350; (1 October 1894), 356.

52. Ibid. (20, 25 September 1894), 350, 354.

53. CMI to BP, n.d., *Notes*, *RBG*, 614. *BP Journal* (5 October 1894), 356–7, 360.

54. Ibid. (27 September 1894), 356. Beatrix thought the bites might be from spiders but probably they were ticks, which are still common in the Borders. BP to Eric Moore, 15 September 1894, CCP.

55. *BP Journal* (13 September 1894), 346; (11 September 1894), 344–5; (10 October 1894), 364.

56. Ibid. (2, 10 October 1894), 357, 363.

57. Ibid. (10 October 1894), 364–5; (11 November 1895), 408; (16 January 1896), 417.

58. Eileen Jay and Jenny Hall, *A Tale of London Past: Beatrix Potter's Archaeological Paintings from the Armitt Collection* (1990). The archaeological drawings are part of the Potter collection at LDM@TA and were given by Beatrix in April 1935 together with two sketch maps and her notes on their provenance. Sadly, the original artefacts have disappeared.

59. Eileen Jay, 'Beatrix Potter's Archaeology', *VN*, 49–54. *VN*, 153. Ruskin noted the similarities between the Pre-Raphaelite approach to natural detail and natural history studies: Lynn L. Merrill, 'Natural History', in Sally Mitchell (ed.), *Victorian Britain: An Encyclopedia* (1988), 530–32. BP gave her copy of Henry W. Acland and John Ruskin, *The Oxford Museum* (1859), a work which argues that all art and decoration follow from forms in nature, to the LDM@TA in 1935. Dr S. T. Chapman, 'The Other Beatrix Potter', *Westmorland Gazette* (10 October 1986). *ABP*, 6.

60. *BP Journal* (26, 27 April 1895), 383; (27, 30 April 1896), 421–2. Jay, 'Beatrix Potter's Archaeology', 16–17.

61. *BP Journal* (23 November 1895), 410; (9, 13 July 1895), 389, 390; (25 April 1896), 421. Lynn M. Merrill, *The Romance of Victorian Natural History* (1989), 65–74.

62. *BP Journal* (27, 30 April 1896), 421–2. *BP/AW*, 91–4. Hollindale, 'Beatrix Potter and Natural History', 61.

63. Caroline Anne Martineau (1843–1902) was the author of *Aunt Rachel's Letters about Water and Air* (1871) and *Easy Lessons on Heat* (1880). Constance and Caroline were the daughters of Richard Martineau, a well-to-do brewer and philanthropist and a cousin to Rupert's mentor James and his sister, the writer and reformer, Harriet; *Pedigree of the Martineau Family*, Archives of Manchester College, Oxford University. *BP Journal* (19 November 1884), 118.

64. Emma Cons (1838–1912) had also worked as a stained-glass restorer for John Ruskin. Both Cons and Martineau knew H. D. Rawnsley from their work with Hill. Octavia Hill, together with Rawnsley and Robert Hunter, was a founder of the National Trust in 1895. Morley Memorial College was renamed simply Morley College. Judi Leighton, 'Emma Cons', in *The Oxford Dictionary of National Biography* (2004). Nancy Boyd, *Three Victorian Women Who Changed Their World* (1982), 60–82.

65. *BP Journal* (7 January 1896), 415; (23 March 1896), 420; (23 November 1896), 410.

66. A third drawing seems to have been a 'trial run' by the publisher, of miscellaneous items: a moth, an old pottery pitcher, a caterpillar, an enlarged section of an insect leg and foot, an eland's head, two rabbits and several fungi sketches. All are signed 'H. B. Potter ad. nat. del. Copyright'; V&A.

67. *BP Journal* (3 November 1895), 408.

68. Flower (1831–99) was Director of the museum from 1884 to 1898. *BP Journal* (17 May 1896), 422–3, 425. Gardiner, 'Beatrix Potter's Fossils', 38.

69. Henry Woodward (1832–1921) was an eminent naturalist and a vertebrate and invertebrate palaeontologist who created the catalogue for the British Museum's fossils. Gardiner, 'Beatrix Potter's Fossils', 45, suggests that Beatrix might have assisted Gertrude in illustrating some of Woodward's articles for the Palaeontological Society, but I have found no evidence. *BP Journal* (13 July 1895), 391. An indication that the Potters and Woodwards knew one another also comes from Richard Hough, 'The Tailors of Gloucester', *Signal*, 42 (September 1983), 150–55. The Woodwards, however, were not Unitarians.

70. Gertrude Woodward (1861–1939), Alice Woodward (1862–1951). There is no specific reference to Alice Woodward in Potter's journal, but it is impossible to imagine that both Alice and Gertrude did not encourage her ambition to write and illustrate a 'booklet' for children. 'Alice Bolingbroke Woodward Illustrated Work. Chronological Listing', Natural History Library, Natural History Museum, London.

71. Robert E. Mack to BP, 25 May 1894; BP to Ernest Nister (Robert E. Mack), 2 June 1894; Robert E. Mack to BP, 4 June 1894, *HWBP*, 176–7. *BP/AW*, 126–7. *ASC*, 66. The full title is *Comical Customers at the New Stores of Comical Rhymes and Stories* (1884).

72. *BP Journal* (14 December 1895), 411.

73. BP to CMI, *c.* Summer 1895; CMI to BP, *c.* 1895; BP to CMI, 20 August 1896; in *Notes RBG*.

5 Discoveries

1. The Pleasure Garden had been open to the public ever since Kew's rescue from decades of neglect in the 1840s. But the admission of the 'pleasure seekers' to other parts of the garden, except in a limited way, was hotly debated for decades. Ray Desmond, *Kew: The Royal Botanic Gardens* (1995), 223–38; Richard Drayton, *Nature's Government: Science, Imperial Britain and the 'Improvement' of the World* (2000), 243–8.

2. Desmond, *Kew*, pp. xiii–xvi, 268; William Thiselton-Dyer, 'A Historical Account of Kew to 1841', *Kew Bulletin*, 60 (1891), 279–327; Lucile H. Brockway, *Science and Colonial Expansion: The Role of the British Royal Botanic Gardens. Studies in Social Discontinuity* (1979), 58–67, 75; Drayton, *Nature's Government*, 244–7; Peter Alter, *The Reluctant Patron: Science and the State in Britain, 1850–1920* (1987).

3. Desmond, *Kew*, 268, 249–50; 252–67; Drayton, *Nature's Government*, 238–45; Paul Lawrence Farber, *Finding Order in Nature: The Naturalist Tradition from Linnaeus to E. O. Wilson* (2000), 96.

4. W. B. Turrill, *The Royal Botanic Gardens, Kew* (1959), 25. This volume, written by a member of the Kew staff, dismisses Thiselton-Dyer's administrative accomplishments and castigates his rigid personality and his unpopularity with his staff. Drayton, *Nature's Government*, 221–48, is crucial to understanding just how powerful a scientist Thiselton-Dyer became. Desmond, *Kew*, 282–3. Thiselton-Dyer's decision to hire women at Kew was considered advanced.

5. David Elliston Allen, *The Botanists: A History of the Botanical Society of the British Isles through a Hundred and Fifty Years* (1986), 4–24. The Botanical Society of the British Isles was founded in 1836 in response to the estrangement of many botanists from the Linnean. The latter encompassed botany and zoology while the Botanical Society was exclusively botanical.

6. Even those papers which were selected for publication could be delayed for months or years, given the high cost of publication and the Society's budget. A. T. Gage and W. T. Stearn, *A Bicentenary History of the*

Linnean Society of London (1988), 88–93, 149–58. The Linnean Society had one of the most rigid protocols of any learned societies. It was not until 1829 that members were offered coffee and cake at meetings. David Elliston Allen, *The Naturalist in Britain: A Social History* (1976), 151–6. See especially David Elliston Allen (ed.), *Naturalists and Society: The Culture of Natural History in Britain, 1700–1900* (2001); Brockway, *Science and Colonial Expansion*, 69–92. By comparison, the Royal Zoological Society admitted women from its incorporation in 1829, and the Royal Entomological Society did so in 1833. The woman responsible for opening admission of women to the Linnean was herself blackballed because of her efforts. But by this time the Linnean had been eclipsed by the other societies in its leadership of the new botany; Gage and Stearn, 89.

7. D. E. Allen, 'The Early Professional in British Natural History', in Alwyne Wheeler and James H. Price (eds.), *From Linnaeus to Darwin: Commentaries on the History of Biology and Geology* (1985), 1–12; Leslie M. Crossley, 'The Professionalization of Science in Victorian Britain', Ph.D. diss. (University of New South Wales, 1980); Gerald L. Geison, *Michael Foster and the Cambridge School of Physiology* (1978), 4–9. Lynn Barber, *The Heyday of Natural History* (1980), 286–96; Lynn L. Merrill, *The Romance of Victorian Natural History* (1989), 3–49. Allen, *The Botanists*, 161–74. Farber, *Finding Order in Nature* 33–4, 96–9. Barbara Gates, *Kindred Nature* (2001), 83–4. Gillian Beer, *Open Fields: Science in Cultural Encounter* (1996), 160. Dorinda Outram, 'New Spaces in Natural History', N. Jardine, J. A. Secord and E. C. Spray (eds.), *Cultures of Natural History* (1996), 249–65.

8. The best work on women in botany is Ann B. Shteir, *Cultivating Women, Cultivating Science: Flora's Daughters and Botany in England 1760–1860* (1996), 208–224.

9. Anyone wishing to come to Kew in the morning hours before 1898 had to be a bona-fide botanist armed with testimonials from 'two respectable households'; Desmond, *Kew*, 232–8.

10. Annie Lorraine Smith became an authority on lichens and was among the first women admitted to membership in the Linnean Society in 1905. *BP Journal* (7 January 1896), 415; (11 February 1896), 417–18.

11. William Roscoe was a Renaissance scholar, the author of *The Life of Lorenzo de' Medici* (1795) and *The Life and Pontificate of Leo the Tenth* (1805). He was also Member of Parliament for Liverpool, and went

bankrupt after a run on his bank in 1820; William Roscoe, *Life of William Roscoe*, 2 vols. (1833). Margaret Roscoe, Henry's aunt, was also a highly regarded botanical artist who published an important volume, *Floral Illustrations of the Seasons* (1829–31). Sale catalogue for Gorse Hall, Stalybridge, contents of Gorse Hall, 1895, V&A.

12. In 1895 Henry's eldest daughter, Margaret Roscoe, married Charles Mallet, the nephew of Sir Louis Mallet, the Potters' next-door neighbour in Bolton Gardens; marriage certificate 11 July 1895, Essex Church, The Mall, Kensington. *BP Journal* (11 July 1895), 389; (3 October 1895), 406; (2 February 1896), 417; (27 February 1896), 419.

13. Ibid. (21–3 March 1896), 419–20. The painting *Witches' Butter* and the microscopic drawings done at Woodcote are in the Beatrix Potter Collection, LDM@TA. *VN*, 140. The Roscoes began renting Woodcote in 1892. After he lost his re-election bid in 1895, they spent more time in the country. Dora Roscoe, *Lucy Roscoe: A Memoir* (1911).

14. *BP Journal* (19 May 1896), 423–4. It is unclear whether she went to Kew on the 19th or the 20th.

15. Ibid. Biographic information from Desmond, *Kew*, 425–36.

16. *BP Journal* (19 May 1896), 423–4.

17. Ibid.

18. Ibid. 424.

19. Ibid. Thiselton-Dyer (1843–1928) was ten years younger than Roscoe, but Beatrix must have thought him older because of his authoritarian manner.

20. Ibid. (13 June 1896), 425.

21. BP to CMI, 20 August 1896, *Notes*, *RBG*. Robert Peck, 'Beatrix Potter, Scientific Illustrator', *Antiques* (1996) 868–77. *BP/AW*, 90. *BP Journal* (13 June 1896), 425.

22. Ibid. (23 July 1896), 426. Lakefield had been built in 1742 as a retreat for a Lancashire mill owner.

23. Ibid. (26 August 1896), 430. These drawings of the *peẓiẓas* and nearly as many *boletes* are part of the Beatrix Potter Collection at LDM@TA.

24. *BP Journal* (31 August 1897), 431.

25. She was also carefully documenting her theories by photographs as well as drawing. The close association between photography and botanical art was part of the drive among Victorian naturalists to convey nature as accurately as possible. On 9 October 1896 she made several photo-

graphs of a polypore on an elm log at Putney Park, the nearby home of the other branch of her Hutton cousins. Photographs, V&A. *BP Journal* (17 November 1896), 435.

26. Ibid. (n.d. 1896), 436.

27. Ibid.

28. Ibid. (18 November 1896), 436. While Potter uses the term 'slip', I have substituted 'slide' for clarity. She appears to have done her microscopic work in the kitchen at Bolton Gardens and made her slides there as well. Tap water was probably the most common medium used for germination, but the formula found among her drawings is for a nutrient solution consisting of a base of sugar water with trace metals, nitrous ammonia and acid tartrate. She could have let the slides dry and rehydrated them when she wanted. John Clegg speculates that she used the 'hanging drop' technique, in which a small quantity of nutrient solution is dropped onto a microscope slide, with or without a concave well; John Clegg, *Beatrix Potter: Artist, Storyteller and Scientist* (1989), 12. Formula courtesy of Beatrix Potter Collection, LDM@TA.

29. *BP Journal* (18 November 1896), 436.

30. Ibid. (20, 30 November 1896), 437. Lunt was the co-author of Roscoe's text *Elementary Lessons in Chemistry* (1866). By the 1890s typewriters were widely available in London. Petri dishes had been invented and would have been in use in Lunt's laboratory. There is at least one drawing of moss germination done in a Petri dish in 1898 in the Beatrix Potter Collection at the LDM@TA.

31. BP to W. Thiselton-Dyer, 3 December 1896, director's correspondence, vol. 99/7, Royal Botanic Gardens, Kew; reprinted in *Letters*, 38.

32. Roscoe did his post-graduate work with Bunsen in 1853 and always boasted the superiority of German science.

33. *BP Journal* (3 December 1896), 437. Most scholars assume her parents either inhibited or actively thwarted her scientific efforts; see, for example, M. Daphne Kutzer, *Beatrix Potter: Writing in Code* (2003), 8.

34. Ibid.

35. Tom Wakeford, *Liaisons of Life* (2001), 24–5. Although Wakeford has confused some facts surrounding the evolution of Beatrix's scientific paper, his readable book is invaluable for understanding the basic science of symbiosis, the physiology of lichens and the real importance of Potter's work.

36. *BP Journal* (7 December 1896), 438. Ward (1854–1906), who had

studied at Owens College, Manchester, during Roscoe's tenure, was at Cambridge from 1895 to 1906 and specialized in plant pathology.

37. Ibid.

38. Ibid. (11 December 1896), 438–9.

39. Ibid.

40. Ibid.

41. Ibid. (25 December 1896), 440; (26 December 1896), 440. Contemporary mycologists have applauded Beatrix for this charming and quite accurate metaphor, since this particular jelly fungus 'weeps' and literally becomes liquid; a truly unstable plant. See Mary Noble, 'Beatrix Potter and Her Funguses', *BPS Studies*, 1 (1985), 44.

42. *BP Journal* (25 December 1896), 440. This latter statement has reinforced the view that Beatrix would have kept this paper along with her other fungi drawings and that its singular absence is the result of loss or destruction after her death.

43. Ibid. (29 December 1896), 440. I do not read this statement as an indictment of her parents' attitude towards science, but as a humorous remark. BP to CMI, 22 January 1897. McIntosh's paper on the larch disease was read before the Perthshire Society of Natural Science on 10 February 1898 and published as 'Notes by a Naturalist Round Dunkeld', *Transactions of the Perthshire Society of Natural Science*, 2/6 (1897–8), 1–3; *Notes*, *RBG* and n. 50. McIntosh's letter to Beatrix about the larch disease was written between 12 and 22 January 1897. Beatrix's microscopic drawing of the larch canker, *Lachnellula willkommii*, is in the Beatrix Potter Collection, LDM@TA.

44. *BP Journal* (30 December 1896), 441.

45. Ibid. (26 December 1896), 440.

46. *BP Journal* (9, 31 January 1897), 442. Ward's response to her theories is unknown. Evidence for her visit to Cambridge appeared recently in a letter to Noel Moore. Beatrix writes that she 'went to Cambridge last Friday, it was so wet in the country'. BP to Noel Moore, 13 February 1897, PC.

47. BP to CMI, 12 January 1897, *Notes*, *RBG*.

48. BP to CMI, 22 January 1897, *Notes*, *RBG*; see especially nn. 49–51. McIntosh, 'Notes by a Naturalist'. In this brief paper on the larch disease McIntosh makes the important connection between the outbreak of the disease, the appearance of insect-feeding birds, and abatement of the aphis plague. He presented it on 10 February 1898.

49. *BP Journal* (9, 24, 28, 31 January 1897), 442–3.

50. Extant drawings of the germination of spores drawn every six hours at 600 × are in the Beatrix Potter Collection at the LDM@TA. *BP/ AW*, 90.

51. BP to CMI, 22 February 1897, *Notes, RBG*.

52. W. P. K. Findlay, *Wayside and Woodland Fungi* (1967). Sheet number 30 shows green alga cells and fungus/lichen including *Aspergillus, Cladosporum, Penicillium and Mucor*, LDM@TA. BP to CMI, 22 February 1897, *Notes, RBG*. Roy Watling, 'Helen Beatrix Potter', *The Linnean: Newspaper and Proceedings of the Linnean Society*, 16/1 (January 2000), 26–8. Watling points out in a later article that her paper was based on the sprouting of the spores of the agarics. Gage and Stearn, *Bicentenary History*, 155–6. Leslie Linder to C. W. Stephens, 31 January 1964. Minutes of Council Meeting, Linnean Society, 21 March 1897.

53. Roy Watling, 'But if . . . Helen B. Potter's Year of Anxiety!', in Armitt Papers, LDM@TA (1997), 39. Minutes of the Linnean Society General Membership Meeting, 1 April 1897. Gage and Stearn, *Bicentenary History*, 149.

54. Minutes of the Council Meeting of the Linnean Society, 8 April 1897; Proceedings of the Linnean Society, November 1896–June 1897, 11.

55. BP to CMI, 21 September 1897 (unfinished), *Notes, RBG*. W. P. K. Findlay to Mary Noble, 17 July 1978, BPS. Findlay also casts doubt on whether some of the germinating spores were really basidiospores, and argues further that the professionals would have dismissed Beatrix's discoveries simply because they had not observed them for themselves. See also his memo to Noble, 'Beatrix Potter's paper'.

56. Leslie Linder to John Clegg, 6 July 1964, V&A; Linder to C. W. Stephens, 31 January 1984, V&A; Linder, 'Summary of Fungi Drawings, 1897 – 40, 1898 – 20', BP to CMI, 21 September 1897 (unfinished), *Notes, RBG*.

57. Every scholar since her death has searched for it. There is no record of the paper at Kew, or in the private papers of the other principals: Massee, Thiselton-Dyer, Roscoe, Ward or McIntosh. Leslie Linder, who would surely have discovered it if it were extant, concluded that it was burnt along with other papers before he had access to them; Linder to John Clegg, 9 September 1964; to Naomi Gilpatrick, 13 March 1972, V&A; Naomi Gilpatrick, 'The Secret Life of Beatrix Potter',

Natural History, 81 (October 1972), 38–41, 88–97. It is unlikely that Potter destroyed it herself. *VN*, 101, 107–23.

58. *TBP*, 33–4. *MY*, 40, 47–8. Alexander Grinstein, *The Remarkable Beatrix Potter* (1995), 42–3. Both Lane and Grinstein argue that BP was 'bitterly angry' and depressed by the Linnean experience. Thomas O. Brady, General Secretary, Linnean Society, 20 January 1964; Watling, 'But if . . .', 39; Gage and Stearn, *Bicentenary History*, 149, 155–9, 219; John Clegg, 'The Lake District, Natural History and Beatrix Potter', *BPS Studies* 2 (1986), 11–14; Roy Watling, 'Beatrix Potter as a Mycologist before Peter Rabbit and Friends', Linnean Society, London (24 April 1997). 'Apology to end tale of Beatrix botanist', *The Times*, 24 April 1997; Sandra Barrick, 'We were wrong about Beatrix . . .', *Daily Telegraph* (17 February 1997). The executive secretary of the Linnean Society publicly acknowledged that Potter had been 'treated scurvily' by members of the Society. Without her paper to judge, nothing more can be accurately claimed for Potter's hypothesis. However, the evidence from her journal and extant drawings demonstrate that she was the first to succeed in germinating spores of basidiomycetes in Britain, and the first in Britain to argue for the symbiotic nature of lichens, preceded only by Schwendener in Switzerland. Not a bad record for an amateur.

59. BP to CMI, 22 January 1897, *Notes*, *RBG*; BP to Walter Gaddum, 6 March 1897, in *LTC*, 100. Massee published prolifically and by 1911 had embraced the lichen hypothesis, but there is no evidence he did any further research on germination.

60. Shteir, *Cultivating Women*, 11–31, 208–27, 233–7. Shteir raises the question of why Potter apparently did not know the work of Anna Maria Hussey, who painted fungi showing the sections a step back. Gates, *Kindred Nature*, 83–6; Roy MacLeod and Russell Moseley, *Days of Judgement: Science, Examinations and the Organization of Knowledge in Late Victorian England* (1982), 75–106; Allen, *The Botanists*, 161–71.

61. BP to Henry Coates, *c.* 1923, quoted in M. A. Taylor and R. H. Rodger (eds.), *A Fascinating Acquaintance: Charles McIntosh and Beatrix Potter* (2003), 21, 28. BP wrote to McIntosh's biographer in 1922: 'He was a keen observer and a first-rate field naturalist fifty years ago, and the kind of student who would continue to learn through a long life': Henry Coates, *A Perthshire Naturalist: Charles McIntosh of Inver* (1923), 210–31. McIntosh, 'Notes . . .' McIntosh continued to make important contri-

butions to mycology, geology and ecology, particularly with his research on fungal pathogens. He recorded thirteen species of fungi new to Britain, of which four were new to science. Watling, 'But if . . .', 40; Findlay, *Wayside*, 25; Catherine Golden, 'Beatrix Potter: Naturalist Artist', *Women's Art Journal*, 11/1 (1990), 16–20.

62. BP to the writer of a letter published in *The Times*, c. November 1930, 'about toads', BPG; William Thiselton-Dyer to Henry Roscoe, 13 May 1900. English Manuscript 963.23, John Rylands Library; Sir Henry Enfield Roscoe, *The Life and Experiences of Sir H. E. Roscoe, DCL, LLD, FRS, written by Himself* (1906); Drayton, *Nature's Government*, 240–43. By the end of Thiselton-Dyer's tenure Kew had in fact become what he boasted it would – 'the botanical centre of the world'.

63. 'A Dream of Toasted Cheese', 1899, PC; reproduced in Roscoe, *Life and Experiences*, 243; *BP/AW*, 85–6.

64. *BP/AW*, 54–70. Ivy Trent to the author, 6–7 August 2001.

65. *BP Journal* (17 November 1896), 435.

6 Fantasies

1. *ABP*, 219–31; *The Day's News*, c. 1892; *BP/AW*, 56; *BP's Art*, 66. BP to Kate Wyatt, 27 November 1920, FLP.

2. Joyce Irene Whalley, 'Beatrix Potter before "Peter Rabbit": Her Art Work', *BPS Studies*, 3 (1989), 22–7. *BP Journal* (16 September 1884), 107. Peter Hollindale, 'Uncle Remus and Beatrix Potter', unpublished lecture to the Beatrix Potter Society, AGM (March 2003), 2, BPS. Hobbs, 'Beatrix Potter's Writings: Some Literary and Linguistic Influences – With a Scottish Slant', *BPS Studies*, 3 (1989), 32–4.

3. The sequel, *Nights with Uncle Remus*, appeared about 1884 in England. The best-known illustrations are by A. B. Frost, originally published in *Uncle Remus and His Friends* (1892). His illustrations for *Songs and Sayings* did not appear until 1895. Potter would not have known these until she had begun her own versions. John Goldthwaite, *The Natural History of Make-Believe* (1966), 254–88, argues that Potter was singularly influenced by *Uncle Remus*. *BP/AW*, 66–9.

4. Judy Taylor, *LTC*, has offered the definitive collection of extant Potter letters to children as of 1992; since then other letters have come to light. In 2004 Lloyd Cotsen published his collection in facsimile letters in *The*

Beatrix Potter Collection of Lloyd Cotsen (CCP). BP to Frida (*sic*) Moore, 26 January 1900; to Marjorie Moore, 13 March 1900, *LTC*, 64–7; BP to Noel Moore, 24 April 1900, CCP.

5. *BP Journal* (20 August 1892), 255–6. BP to Noel Moore, 21 August 1892, CCP; BP to Eric Moore, 21 August 1892, CCP.

6. BP to Eric Moore, 28 March 1894, CCP; BP to Noel Moore, 13 February 1897, CCP; BP to Noel Moore, 27 February 1897; BP to Molly Gaddum, 6 March 1897, *LTC*.

7. *BP Journal* (16 April 1895), 377–8; BP to Noel Moore, 21 April 1895, CCP. This is one of the few picture letters which illustrate something she has already described in her journal.

8. BP to Eric Moore, 5 September 1895, CCP.

9. BP to Noel Moore, 10 April 1895, CCP. This letter also tells about sea birds and how they catch fish. BP to Noel Moore, 7 August 1896, *LTC*.

10. BP to Noel Moore, 26 August 1897, *LTC*; BP to Noel Moore, 14 June 1897, 5 October 1898, CCP.

11. BP to Noel Moore, 30 March 1898, PC.

12. Remark attributed to Bertram Potter; see Liz Taylor, 'The Tale of Bertram Potter', *Weekend Scotsman* (11 November 1978), 7. Gillian Avery, 'Beatrix Potter and Social Comedy', *Rylands University of Manchester Bulletin*, 76/3 (Autumn 1994), 185–9.

13. *BP Journal* (3, 11 November 1895), 408, 411; (2 February 1896), 417; (3 December 1897), 437.

14. R. K. Webb, 'The Background: English Unitarians in the Nineteenth Century', in Leonard Smith (ed.), *Unitarian to the Core: Unitarian College Manchester, 1854–2004* (2004), 1–30; N. G. Annan, 'The Intellectual Aristocracy', in J. H. Plumb (ed.), *Studies in Social History* (1955), 241–87.

15. *BP Journal* (June 1894), 320.

16. The honorary title was conferred for all these activities to better his 'flock', in the community and in the diocese, and he was always addressed as 'Canon' Rawnsley. In 1909 he was made a residentiary canon at Carlisle and thereafter was required to spend three months in residence; the rest of the year he served at Crosthwaite. See John Simpson, *'The Most Active Volcano in Europe': A Short Life of Canon Hardwicke Drummond Rawnsley, Vicar of Crosthwaite, Keswick 1883–1917* (n.d.), 16.

17. Rawnsley and Hill had worked together in London before Rawnsley

was ordained and it was Hill who sent him to recuperate in Ambleside in the Lake District when he suffered a breakdown of health. Rawnsley married Hill's friend Edith Fletcher, whom he had met in Ambleside. Gillian Darley, *Octavia Hill: A Life* (1990); Nancy Boyd, *Three Victorian Women Who Changed Their World: Josephine Butler, Octavia Hill, and Florence Nightingale* (1982); Graham Murphy, *Founders of the National Trust* (1987), 44–68, 69–100. Robert Hunter (1844–1913), a solicitor to the Post Office, served as treasurer of the NT. Hill (1838–1912) never held a Trust office, but served on the executive committee until her death and took the lead in all the early acquisitions. Both Hill and Hunter were enthusiastic visitors to the Lake District.

18. Christopher Hanson-Smith, 'Beatrix Potter and the National Trust', *BPS Studies*, 1 (1985), 6. Life Members were a special category of more expensive memberships. Rupert's membership proves his regard for the Trust's mission and confidence in Rawnsley's leadership. As early as 1904 it was suggested that the English Lake District be nationalized. In 1907 the National Trust was registered under a special Act of Parliament.

19. W. R. Mitchell, *Beatrix Potter: Her Life in the Lake District* (1998), 24–6; Eleanor F. Rawnsley, *Canon Rawnsley: An Account of His Life*, (1923), 107–16; Elizabeth Battrick, 'Canon Rawnsley and The National Trust', *BPS Studies* 7 (1997), 33; H. A. L. Rice, *Lake Country Portraits* (1967), 122–43.

20. S. D. Dodgson and Noel Rawnsley, circular letter, Herdwick Sheep Association, 4 September 1899, PC.

21. 'Moral Rhymes for the Young' was reprinted in Canon T. B. A. Saunders (ed.), *Prelates and People of the Lake Counties* (1948), 72. The original publication date is unknown, as the British Library did not catalogue children's books at that time. Rawnsley, *Canon Rawnsley*, 346–70. *ASC*, 69.

22. *ABP*, 75; *BP's Art*, 106–7. *Rain*, August 1898. Wynne Bartlett and Joyce Irene Whalley, *Beatrix Potter's Derwentwater* (1995), 49–59, 78–85. *The Derwentwater Sketchbook*, *1909*, facsimile (1984), with commentary by Wynne Bartlett and Joyce Irene Whalley; original at BPG.

23. BP to Marjorie Moore, 26 January 1900, *LTC*, 64–5.

24. *TNR*, 26–30. Ruth K. MacDonald, *Beatrix Potter* (1986), 26–7.

25. BP to Marjorie Moore, 13 March 1900, *LTC*, 66–7. It is in this charming letter, the original of which is in the Pierpont Morgan Library, New

York, that she describes and sketches the Reading Room, telling Marjorie: 'Next time Miss Potter goes to the British Museum she will take some Keating's powder! It is very odd there should be fleas in books!'

26. *TNR*, 32. Laura C. Stevenson, 'A Vogue for Little Books': *The Tale of Peter Rabbit* and its Contemporary Competitors', in *BPS Studies*, 10 (2003), 11–27. Stevenson speculates that Nister was one of the 'Grub Street' publishers that Potter talks of arguing with. BP to Freda Moore, 24 April 1900, PC.

27. Stevenson, 'A Vogue . . .', 22–4. Golliwog books were written by Ruth Upton and illustrated by her daughter, Florence.

28. Ibid. 20–22. BP to BMM, *BPA*; BP to ACM, 12 December 1925, *BPA*, 8–9.

29. Stevenson, 'A Vogue . . .', 21–2. *TNR*, 32–3.

30. BP, 'Roots', *BPA*, 208. *TNR*, 36, 33. 'Conversation with Miss Norah C. Moore, 17 December 1987', PC. There is some suggestion that Rupert contributed to her initial effort, but more likely, he aided her private efforts later.

31. Beatrix Potter and Canon H. Rawnsley, *Peter Rabbit's Other Tale*, reprinted by The Beatrix Potter Society (1989). Stevenson, 'A Vogue . . .', 22–3. BP to Messrs Warne & Co., 11 September 1901, *Letters*, 55.

32. F. Warne & Co. to Canon Rawnsley, 18 September 1901, FWA.

33. *TNR*, 34–6. Arthur King and A. F. Stuart, *The House of Warne: One Hundred Years of Publishing* (1965), 28–36. F. Warne & Co. to Canon Rawnsley, 18 September 1901, FWA. Laura C. Stevenson to the author, 23 October 2002.

34. Stevenson, 'A Vogue . . .', 11–17.

35. Henry Brooke, *Leslie Brooke and Johnny Crow* (1982), 36–8; Stevenson, 'A Vogue . . .', 23–4. Stevenson makes clear that while Potter's book was revolutionary in concept, Warne were receptive, in part because of the intensely competitive market for small picture books at just that time. *TNR*, 34, 36. Leslie Brooke would publish his own picture book, *Johnny Crow's Garden*, in 1903. *ASC*, 74.

36. King and Stuart, *House of Warne*, 1–15, 30–31. Ironically, Potter's fungi drawings were published in Step's Wayside and Woodland series in 1967.

37. Ibid. 13–15, 29–30. *ASC*, 74–8. Norman Dalziel Warne was born 6 July 1868. He was the youngest of eight children, but only three sons

survived to adulthood. 'Fruing' was their mother Louisa Jane Warne's maiden name.

38. BP to F. Warne & Co., 18 December 1901, *Letters*, 56–7.

39. BP to NDW, 22 May 1902, *Letters*, 62.

40. *HWBP*, 110. *TNR*, 43. BP to F. Warne & Co., 18 December 1901, *Letters*, 56.

41. BP to Mrs Hollins, 17 December 1901, FLP. BP to Miss Whitehead, 7 February 1902, PC. BP to F. Warne & Co., 19 January 1902, *Letters*, 59.

42. BP to NDW, 30 April, 2 May 1902, *Letters*, 60–61. *TNR*, 46–7.

43. Taylor, 'The Tale of Bertram Potter', 6.

44. Marriage certificate, 20 November 1902. Author interviews with Liz Taylor, Melrose, Scotland, 14 April 2000; with Reita Wilson, Hawick, Scotland, 15 April 2000; with Helen Jackson, Perth, Scotland, 10 April 2000.

45. Certificate of candidate for ballot, no. 8292, Monday, 30 April 1906; supporters' sheet, Archives of the Athenaeum Club. Liz Taylor believes that Beatrix was told or found out about his marriage after a year or so, and sympathized with the couple, but it could have been much later. See Taylor, 'Bertram Potter and the Scottish Borders', *BPS Studies*, 2 (1986), 43–6.

46. BP to NDW, 8 May 1902, *Letters*, 62. The first printing was made up in two bindings, cloth and paper. *TNR*, 47–9; *ASC*, 76. BP to NDW, 17 August 1902, *Letters*, 61–2.

47. *TNR*, 48, 52–3. Potter's final contract, signed in June 1902, called for a royalty of 1s. 4d. The first printing of 3,000 copies were without royalty, and some others, the sixth edition for example, were at a slightly higher rate. At a very conservative estimate, from October 1902 to October 1904 Potter earned approximately £438 on *Peter Rabbit* in addition to the £40 she had made from sales of the private editions. BP to NDW, 9 November 1903, *Letters*, 82.

48. BP, 'Roots,' *BPA*, 209. BP to BMM, 25 November 1940, *BPA*.

49. Peter Hollindale, 'Animal Stories since Beatrix Potter and her Influence on the Genre', *BPS Studies*, 8 (1999), 25–31; Peter Parker, 'The Gardens of Beatrix Potter', *Hortus*, 30 (Summer 1994), 106–5; Parker, 'Gardening with Beatrix Potter', *BPS Studies*, 9 (2001), 96–109; Catherine Golden, 'Beatrix Potter Naturalist Artist', *Women's Art Journal*, 11/1 (Spring/Summer 1990), 16–20; Hollindale, 'Beatrix Potter and

Natural History', *BPS Studies*, 9 (2001), 54–66. *BP Journal* (28 May 1895), 387.

50. The critical literature on *The Tale of Peter Rabbit*, the other 'Little Books', and on Potter's art is immense: see Select Bibliography. Leslie Linder, 'A View of Miss Potter's Art in Writing and Illustrating Books' (n.d. *c.* 1970), FWA.

51. Frederick Warne & Company catalogue, 1902–3, 9, FWA. In their catalogue, *The Tale of Peter Rabbit* was added by hand to the list (January 1903, 115). Elizabeth Booth, unpublished lecture to the Beatrix Potter Society (July 2000).

7 Ideas

1. BP to Norah Moore, 25 July 1901, *LTC*, 71–6; BP to Noel Moore, 26 August 1897, *LTC*, 49–50. Whalley, *BPS Studies*, 3 (1989), 26. Red squirrels, *Sciurus vulgarus*, now rare, were still abundant in the Lake District when Potter was writing this story.

2. BP to Norah Moore, 25 July 1901, *LTC*, 71–6; BP to Freda Moore, Christmas 1901, *LTC*, 76; Winifrede (Freda) Allen to William Heelis, 22 February 1944, PC.

3. Keith Clark, *Beatrix Potter's Gloucester* (1988), 12–20.

4. *HWBP*, 111–13. *ASC*, 80. Clark, *Beatrix Potter's Gloucester*, 15–16.

5. Ibid. Beatrix Potter, MS, 'The Tailor of Gloucester', Rare Book Collection, FLP. This is the opening line of the published version, set in the Regency period. Paduasoy is a corded silk fabric.

6. *HWBP*, 113–14. *TBP*, 52.

7. BP to NDW, 15, 21, 28 July 1902, *Letters*, 64–6.

8. BP to NDW, 6 November 1902, FWA.

9. BP to NDW, 6, 22 November, 1 December 1902, FWA; 17 December 1902, *Letters*, 69.

10. BP to Mrs Wicksteed, 17 January 1903, V&A. To this old family friend Beatrix reported that, although her father has occasional bouts of lumbago, 'his health has been better as he gets older'. BP to Angela, Denis and Clare Mackail, 1 January 1903, quoted in Margot Strickland, *Angela Thirkell: Portrait of a Lady Novelist* (1977). Beatrix was already getting 'fan' mail from other children.

11. A good example of the genre of natural history writing is the work

of the English-born wildlife writer and Boy Scout leader Ernest Thompson Seton. Ruth K. MacDonald, *Beatrix Potter* (1986), 68. Potter's anthropomorphism borrows from that of Charles Darwin's observations, which tended to see animal life and human affairs as permeable one with the other. Eileen Crist, *Images of Animals: Anthropomorphism and Animal Mind* (1999), 7, 80–84.

12. BP, Photographs of Old Brown's oak tree, 1903, BPG.

13. Judy Taylor, 'The Tale of Peter Rabbit', in *BP/AW*, 111–15; Mac-Donald, *Beatrix Potter*, 67–70; Margaret Blount, *Animal Land: The Creatures of Children's Fiction* (1975), 136–7; Gillian Avery, 'Beatrix Potter and Social Comedy', *Rylands University of Manchester Bulletin*, 76 (Autumn 1994), 190–94.

14. BP to NDW, 5 February 1903, *Letters*, 70; 8 February 1903, FWA.

15. *HWBP*, 118; the story of Beatrix in the Museum was told to Linder by Mrs Susan Ludbrook, the first curator of Hill Top. BP to NDW, 27 March 1903, FWA. Oliver Garnett, *Melford Hall Suffolk: A National Trust Guide* (2005).

16. *HWBP*, 138–40. BP to NDW, 21 March 1903, *Letters*, 72–3.

17. BP to BMM, 20 November 1942, *BPA*. The objection was Norman Warne's.

18. *HWBP*, 117. BP to NDW, 30 April, 15 December 1903, *Letters*, 74, 84. The squirrel was manufactured by Farnell and Company. In order to have secured US copyright for *The Tale of Peter Rabbit*, Warne would have had to apply for it on the same day as the book was published in the UK. Even if that had occurred, it is unlikely that copyright could have been secured because the book had been privately published, even though the two versions were quite different. The Copyright Reform Act of 1891 allowed for a flourishing business in US piracies. Interview with James J. Barnes, Columbus, Ohio, 10 August 2004, and James J. Barnes, *Authors, Publishers and Politicians* (1974).

19. BP to NDW, 20 August 1903, *Letters*, 80; BP to NDW, 8 September 1903, FWA.

20. BP to Lady Mary Isabel Warren, 23 December 1919, *Letters*, 260; Avery, 'Beatrix Potter and Social Comedy', 185–8. Beatrix's impression should be revised in the light of at least the first year's royalty comparison, as the *Tailor* paid her more than *Squirrel Nutkin*.

21. *HWBP*, 121.

22. 'The Tailor of Gloucester, A Xmas Fairy Tale', *Tailor & Cutter*, 39

(24 December 1903), 779, reprinted in *BPSN*, 31 (December 1988–January 1989), 9–10.

23. BP to NDW, 8 July 1903, *Letters*, 77.
24. BP to HW, 14 July 1903, *Letters*, 78; *ASC*, 88–9.
25. BP to HW, 15 July 1903, *Letters*, 79.
26. Ibid. ; BP to HW, 28 July 1903, FWA.
27. BP to NDW, undated, September 1903, *Letters*, 81. Wynne K. Bartlett and Joyce Irene Whalley, *Beatrix Potter's Derwentwater*, 65–71. 'Derwentwater Sketchbook', BPG.
28. BP to HW, 6 November 1903, *Letters*, 82; BP to NDW, 9 November 1903, *Letters*, 82–3. *ASC*, 91–2. BP to NDW, 2 December 1903, quoted in *HWBP*, 149; BP to NDW, 15 December 1903, *Letters*, 84.

8 Realities

1. Bedford Square, named for the ducal family who were once ground landlords of Bloomsbury, is no longer predominantly residential; most of the houses are now used as offices.
2. Various correspondence between Winifred Warne and Margaret Lane, c. 1944–5; *TBP*, 58–9; *ASC*, 90–91; *HD*, 67–76.
3. NDW to Jennie Stephens, 15 January 1899, Warne Family Papers, FWA. *ASC*, 87, 90.
4. *ASC*, 91. Photographs, Warne Family Papers, FWA.
5. BP to NDW, 15, 10 December 1903, *Letters*, 83–4, 85.
6. BP to NDW, 15 December 1903, *Letters*, 84. *TNR*, 59–60. Patent Office Registration No. 423888, FWA.
7. *TNR*, 60; Camilla Hallinan, *The Ultimate Peter Rabbit* (2002), 32–3. A limited edition of 2,500 dolls following her copyright design was finally produced in 1993.
8. BP to NDW, 29 April 1904, *Letters*, 93–4; BP to NDW, 22 November (1904?), *Letters*, 109.
9. BP to NDW, 23 October 1904, 22 November (1904?), 30 January 1905, 27 February 1905, *Letters*, 105, 109, 112, 114. Sanderson's eventually published the wallpaper frieze.
10. BP to NDW, 7 December 1904, *Letters*, 110–11.
11. BP to NDW, 23, 25 October, 7 December 1904, *Letters*, 105, 110–11. *TNR*, 61–2.

12. BP to NDW, 15 December 1903, *Letters*, 84. Beatrix had named her mice 'Tom Thumb' and 'Hunca Munca' after the hero and heroine of Henry Fielding's eighteenth-century comedy *Tom Thumb the Great*. *MY*, 123–4. *Johnny Crow's Garden* (1903) was the first in a series by Brooke featuring comic doggerel verse.

13. BP to NDW, 1 January 1904, *Letters*, 84–5.

14. BP to NDW, 12 February 1904, *Letters*, 85.

15. BP to NDW, 18 February 1904, *Letters*, 86.

16. BP to NDW, 24 February 1904, *Letters*, 88.

17. BP to NDW, 12 February, 1 March, 20 April 1904, *Letters*, 85, 88, 93; BP to NDW, 20 April 1904. The photograph of the doll's house is reproduced in *ASC*, 94. Judy Taylor, interview with Winifred Warne Boultbee, 1990: Boultbee's memories are drawn from three different interviews: 1971, 1983 and 1990.

18. BP to NDW, 15 March 1904, *Letters*, 90.

19. BP to NDW, 3 March 1904, *Letters*, 89. In 1910 Beatrix commented to Millie Warne, 'What games there seem to be with the suffragettes! It is very silly work'; 19 November 1910, FWA.

20. BP to Miss Sharpley, 18 April 1904, PC; Sharpley and the other members are unidentified. BP to NDW, 10, 19 April 1904, *Letters*, 92.

21. BP to NDW, 21 February 1904, 8 June 1904, *Letters*, 87, 95.

22. *HWBP*, 72–87.

23. In *LTC*, Judy Taylor reproduces all the miniature letters that were known in 1992; see especially pp. 9, 84–93, 138–45, 166–9.

24. *LTC*, 110–13; *HWBP*, 72–87. Leslie Linder bought many of these miniature letters for his collection.

25. BP to NDW, 16 June 1904, *Letters*, 95–6.

26. BP to NDW, 11 December 1904, *Letters*, 111.

27. *BP/AW*, 119. *LTC*, 78–9. BP to NDW, 12 September 1904, *Letters*, 103.

28. *ASC*, 95. *Times Literary Supplement* (28 October 1904). BP to NDW, 2 November 1904, *Letters*, 106. Another 10,000 copies of *Two Bad Mice* were also printed. In the first two months Beatrix earned approximately £156 on *Benjamin Bunny* and she earned the same amount from *Two Bad Mice* in the first three months.

29. *HWBP*, 85–6. These miniature letters are almost perfunctory and tell more about Beatrix's activities than her characters.

30. Ruth K. MacDonald, *Beatrix Potter* (1986), 32–8; M. Daphne Kutzer, *Beatrix Potter: Writing in Code* (2003), 49–50.

31. *BP Journal* (30 October 1892), 306–7.

32. *BP's Art*, 138–43. *BP/AW*, 116–18.

33. BP to NDW, 14 September 1904; *Letters*, 104; MacDonald, *Beatrix Potter*, 72–5; Kutzer, *Beatrix Potter: Writing in Code*, 65–76. Kutzer argues Potter's personal and domestic rebellion as well as her hostility towards the working classes and class agitation are the underlying themes of *Two Bad Mice*.

34. See BP to Frida (*sic*) Moore, 26 January 1900, *HWBP*, 38–41, 149–50. *LTC*, 64–5. The more refined mice of Freda's picture letter from Winchelsea reappear instead in *Appley Dapply's Nursery Rhymes*.

35. BP to NDW, 25 September 1904, FWA. 'The Tale of Two Bad Mice', *Bookman*, Christmas 1904.

36. See Elizabeth Logan, 'The Tale of Two Bad Mice, an Author and an Editor', in *Miscellany Britannica: A Collection of Essays Based on Primary Material for the Study of Modern Britain in Stanford University Library Collections* (1998), 50–63. Logan makes the point that Norman Warne was an exceptional critic and encouraged Potter to create her own style of expression. *MY*, 109.

37. BP to NDW, 6 August, 14 September 1904, *Letters*, 98, 103–4.

38. See *Beatrix Potter's Nursery Rhyme Book* (2000), 18–19. BP to FW, 12 October 1920, *Letters*, 263. *BP's Art*, 114. BP to NDW, 14 September 1904, *Letters*, 103–4. The two Pricklepins in the V&A collection are probably of two different hedgehogs. At least one Pricklepin was Mrs Tiggy-winkle's 'Uncle'. See *HWBP*, 229, and 'The Tale of Kitty-in-Boots', unpublished; *HWBP*, 223.

39. BP to NDW, 2 July 1905, *Letters*, 121. *BP Journal* (1 August 1892), 250. BP, inscription to Lucie Carr, Christmas 1901, *LTC*, 106–7.

40. *HWBP*, 155. In a small exercise book found at Hill Top which Linder believed to be the earliest manuscript of the tale, Beatrix had written 'Made at Lingholm, Sept. 01, told to cousin Stephanie at Melford, Nov. 01 – written down Nov. 02. There are no pictures, it is a good one to tell.'

41. Wynne K. Bartlett and Joyce Irene Whalley, *Beatrix Potter's Derwentwater* (1995), 95–101.

42. Beatrix Potter, *The Derwentwater Sketchbook, 1909*, facsimile (1984), 23, 58–9; Beatrix Potter, *The Tale of Mrs. Tiggy-Winkle*. (Warne, 2002), 40. Lambs' ears are cut in identifiable markings to indicate what farm they belong to. These markings are a matter of tradition and great

importance, as they identify property. Each year a sheep's coat is also given certain smit marks for similar purposes. It is these marks that Beatrix refers to in the story.

43. *LTC*, 106–10. *Beatrix Potter's Nursery Rhyme Book*, 10.
44. BP to NDW, 20 October 1904, 12 September 1904, *Letters*, 104, 103. 'Sept 19th '04, The Greta, Near Portinscale, Keswick, H. B. P.' *Letters*, 429; *HWBP*, 156.
45. BP to NDW, 2 November 1904, *Letters*, 106.
46. BP to NDW, 12 November 1904, *Letters*, 107.
47. BP to NDW, 17 November 1904, *Letters*, 108.
48. BP to NDW, 12 November 1904, *Letters*, 107.
49. BP to NDW, 5 December 1904, *Letters*, 109.
50. BP to NDW, 3 February 1905, *Letters*, 112–13.
51. BP to NDW, 27 February 1905, *Letters*, 114.
52. BP to Hugh Bridgeman, 5 March 1905, PC.

9 Losses

1. BP to NDW, 26 March 1905, *Letters*, 115. *HWBP*, 168–70.
2. BP to NDW, 11, 13 April 1905, FWA. *HWBP*, 170.
3. A patty-pan is a small round or scalloped tin pan used to bake pasties and some other small meat or fruit pies. As an empty tin it is commonly put upside down inside a larger pie to prevent the top crust from collapsing. In the story Duchess uses the patty-pan in this manner.
4. BP to FW, 21 May 1905, *Letters*, 115.
5. *HWBP*, 168–9, 170–71; NDW to BP, 25 May 1905, V&A. At some point Norman decided that *Tiggy-Winkle* would be produced in the same small format as *Peter Rabbit* and there was a sudden flurry to find a companion in that format, whereas *The Pie* would be in the larger one.
6. BP to NDW, 6, 8, 26 June 1905, *Letters*, 119–20, 121.
7. BP to NDW, 18 June 1905, FWA.
8. BP to NDW, 8, 20 June 1905, *Letters*, 119–20.
9. Ibid.
10. BP to NDW, 26 June 1905, *Letters*, 121.
11. BP to NDW, 2, 4 July 1905, *Letters*, 121, 122.
12. Ibid. *HWBP*, 158.

13. *HD*, 11–12.

14. BP to NDW, 21 July 1905, *Letters*, 122.

15. The letter is missing and doubtless destroyed, as is Beatrix's response, if she ever made one in writing. Margaret Lane and Leslie Linder both assume that Beatrix was in Wales when she received Warne's letter of proposal, but there is clear evidence that she received it in London. The date comes from a letter Beatrix wrote to Millie Warne seven months later, on 1 February 1906, *Letters*, 139.

16. *TBP*, 68–9. Lane quotes from a missing letter from BP to Caroline Hutton.

17. Ibid.

18. *Kelly's Directory* shows that a Miss Hammond resided at 51 Minster Road, West Hampstead, in July 1905. Since Florrie Hammond accompanied Beatrix to the Warne office the next day, Beatrix must have spent the night. BP to HW, 30 July 1905, *Letters*, 124. Winifred Warne Boultbee, 'Some Personal Recollection . . .', *The Horn Book* (1971), 587–8.

19. BP to HW, 30 July 1905, *Letters*, 124.

20. Watercolours dated at Amersham; see *ABP*, 82–3. See Lane's account in the 1985 revision of *TBP*, 83–5. Evidence of the gift to Norman comes from BP to ALW, 15 July, 1917, CCP. Anne Stevenson Hobbs and Joyce Irene Whalley, *Beatrix Potter: V&A Collection*, items 974–6. *BP/AW*, 61.

21. Diary of Edith Warne/Stephens, 1905, Warne/Stephens Archive, FWA.

22. *HD* (1905).

23. Ibid. 49.

24. Louisa Jane Warne to Jennie Stephens, 20 August 1905, Warne/Stephens Archive, FWA.

25. Edith Stephens, *Immortelles*, 25 August 1905. Warne/Stephens Archive, FWA. Last will and testament of Norman Dalziel Warne, 25 August 1905, probated 7 December 1905. He left an estate valued at £14,014. Certified death certificate: lymphatic leucoeythaemia, 2½ months.

26. *HD* (1905). BP to ALW, 14 February 1906, CCP, mentions that she attended the funeral.

27. *HD* (1905). It is possible the letter could have been from Millie Warne, though it is doubtful that she would have been in any state to write. The walking stick and thrashing refers to the proverb Beatrix and

Norman had enjoyed: 'a spaniel, a woman, and a walnut tree – the more you beat them – the better they be.'

28. Ibid. 52–3, 139.
29. Judy Taylor, interview with David Henry Beckett, Kendal, 13 November 1989, PC. BP to ALW, 23 December 1905, in *HD* (1905). In this letter she comments on how young and serene Norman looked compared to her elderly aunt Clara Potter, who died at the age of 74 just before Christmas 1905.
30. BP to ALW, 1 February 1906, *Letters*, 139. Norman's death was publicly announced by the firm of Frederick Warne & Co. on black bordered notices dated 1 September 1905.
31. BP to HW, 5 September 1905, *Letters*, 125–6.
32. Ibid.
33. BP to Winifred Warne, 6 September 1905, *LTC*, 120–21.
34. BP to Winifred Warne, 6 September 1905, *Letters*, 127–30; BP to Mary Warne, 26 September 1905, *Letters*, 131–2; BP to ALW, 23 December 1905, in *HD*.
35. Last will and testament of Harriet Burton, 2 April 1904. Probated estate of Harriet Burton, 10 June 1905, Principal Probate Registry, London. The net value of Harriet's personal property was £31,170, a large sum for a married woman. Although Beatrix is not named as a specific legatee, private bequests were the privilege of Harriet's husband and their two sons as executors. After reviewing the Potter–Leech family wills, I am convinced that Harriet Leech Burton of Gwaynynog either left instructions for a private bequest to her niece, or Frederick Burton (Uncle Fred) took it upon himself to make it. Beatrix subsequently used this legacy as part of the purchase price of Hill Top Farm. Lane also identifies 'Aunt Burton' as the source of the 'legacy from an Aunt' (*MY*, 140).

10 Stories

1. Potter's purchase of Hill Top Farm has been disputed both as to date and source of the monies used.
2. It has been assumed that Potter's parents disapproved of her purchase of Hill Top. There is little evidence to support this. The fact that the legacy came through her mother's sister and that her father's solicitors acted as agents suggests that she was encouraged to invest in land. While they

were not prepared for her spending much time in Lancashire, the Potters knew she was making this purchase before Norman Warne's death.

3. Property deeds and conveyance, Hill Top Farm, 15 November 1905; conveyance to Frederic Fowkes, 25 September 1905; John Howson, vendor, Frederic Fowkes, purchaser. Fowkes's signature was witnessed in Sawrey. Arnold Greenwood & Sons of Kendal acted for both Fowkes and Howson. Fowkes signed the deed in Sawrey; Potter received her deeds from her father's solicitors, Braikenridge & Edwards, in London following completion on 25 November 1905. There is no indication of who witnessed for Potter. There is no evidence that any other solicitors were involved in the sale or purchase. Pertinent documents are from BPG and CRO/K.

4. Hand-drawn plans of Buckle Yeat Croft copied by BP from deed and conveyance of 11 December 1905, BPG. Her notes on these drawings indicate those boundaries which were not clearly defined and about which she was justly concerned. Contracts for sale and purchase had been exchanged and became binding on 30 October. Potter was thus allowed access to the farmhouse and was contracting for its management, alteration and improvement; J. R. Cawood to the author, 6 February 2002. Fowkes had made a profit of £1,430 ($6,964) on the sale of Hill Top Farm to Potter. The Croft conveyance was also arranged through Braikenridge & Edwards in London; J. R. Cawood to the author, 27 March 2003. The purchase united the two fields, but Potter never owned a tiny parcel that ran along the road, shown on the deed plans as 'Winfell' and owned by J. Wright.

5. Cannon was most likely appointed by Henry Preston's executors to manage the farm until a new buyer was found, and had been there since February 1905. BP to HW, 2 October 1905, FWA.

6. BP to ALW, 14 October 1905, *Letters*, 134. Her hope that Millie could visit her at Hill Top illustrates how vital their friendship was to her. Millie made at least one visit to Hill Top before April 1906.

7. Ibid. Susan Denyer, *At Home with Beatrix Potter: The Creator of Peter Rabbit* (2000), 26–9, 48, 89–91; Judy Taylor, *Beatrix Potter and Hill Top* (1989), 6–7. Henry B. Preston and his family had farmed Hill Top since 1855 at least. Preston died on 16 February 1905 and the farm then came up for sale. Kendal Library, newspaper files, Census records and Cumbria Genealogical Society suggest he owned the farm and was not

a tenant and that his family had owned the farm for several generations; Susan Wittig Albert to the author, 10 December 2003.

8. *ASC*, 107–8. Denyer, *At Home*, 29.

9. Ibid. Sketch of Hill Top by Beatrix Potter, *c.* 1905, BPG.

10. Probated will of Clara Potter, 6 January 1906, Principal Probate Registry. BP to ALW, 14 February 1906, CCP.

11. BP to ALW, 5 April 1906, *Letters*, 140. The style of 'cottage gardening' practised by Gertrude Jekyll was immensely popular at this time and her influence is seen at Hill Top.

12. Ibid.

13. Ibid. BP to ALW, ? April (Thursday evening) 1906, FWA; BP to Winifred Warne, 14 April 1906, CCP.

14. BP to Eric Moore, 5 September 1893, CCP. *HWBP*, 175–8.

15. *BP/AW*, 126–9. Ruth K. MacDonald, *Beatrix Potter* (1986), 96–8.

16. John R. Clark Hall, *A Concise Anglo-Saxon Dictionary* (1969). Other sources show the name as 'Sawrayes' in the sixteenth century, meaning the 'muddy place', before becoming 'Narr Sawrey' in 1656. Moss Eccles was also known as 'Moss Heckel'.

17. Catherine J. Golden, 'Beatrix Potter: Naturalist Artist', *Women's Art Journal*, 11/1 (1990), 16–20; 'Natural Companions: Text and Illustration in the Work of Beatrix Potter', *BPS Studies*, 8 (1999), 50–68; Humphrey Carpenter, 'Excessively Impertinent Bunnies: The Subversive Element in Beatrix Potter', in Gillian Avery and Julia Briggs (eds.), *Children and Their Books* (1989), 271–98. See also Susan Wittig Albert, *The Tale of Hill Top Farm* (2004).

18. *BP/AW*, 129–30. BP to ALW, 18 July 1906, *Letters*, 141. MacDonald, *Beatrix Potter*, 50–52. *HWBP*, 183–4.

19. BP to ALW, 18 July, 5 August (?) 1906, *Letters*, 141–3.

20. BP to ALW, 5 August (?) 1906, *Letters*, 142–3; 17 August 1906, PC. In the extant correspondence Beatrix never refers to Fruing and Mary's son, Norman, by his given name.

21. BP to ALW, 27 August 1906, FLP.

22. Ibid.; BP to ALW, 6, 30 September 1906, *Letters*, 143, 146.

23. BP to ALW, n.d. (summer 1906), FLP; BP to ALW, 30 September, 4, 12 October 1906, *Letters*, 147–9; Denyer, *At Home*, 94–103. She also kept the mock orange bush that grew against the warm wall between Hill Top and Tower Bank Arms. Elizabeth Battrick, *Beatrix Potter*

Gardener, exhibition text, Armitt Museum, Ambleside, 2004; Peter Parker, 'The Gardens of Beatrix Potter', *Hortus*, 30 (Summer 1994), 106–15, identifies many of the flowers that feature in Potter's fictional gardens, many of which were planted at Hill Top.

24. BP to ALW, 30 September 1906, *Letters*, 147.

25. Ibid.; BP to ALW, 12 October 1906, *Letters*, 149.

26. BP to ALW, 4 October 1906, *Letters*, 147–8.

27. BP to ALW, 4, 12 October 1906, *Letters*, 148–9.

28. BP to ALW, 26 December 1906, PC.

29. *The Roly-Poly Pudding* was published in a larger format to provide greater opportunity for details of the house and garden. The book was reduced in size, and the title was changed to *The Tale of Samuel Whiskers* in 1926.

30. Marcus Crouch, *Beatrix Potter* (1960), 36–8.

31. *MY*, 153–5; *BP/AW*, 131–3; MacDonald, *Beatrix Potter*, 98–104; *HWBP*, 185–6.

32. BP to Louie Warne, 8 July 1907, *Letters*, 152. *HWBP*, 268–9. BP to HW, 17 August 1908, 15 December 1908, *Letters*, 161, 165–6.

33. BP to Louie Warne, 6 July 1907, *LTC*, 123; BP to ALW, 30 August 1907, PC.

34. BP to ALW, 30 August 1907, PC; BP to ALW, 6 October 1907, *Letters*, 154–5.

35. BP to ALW, 6 October 1907, *Letters*, 154–5; BP to Louie Warne, 8 July 1907, *Letters*, 152. Denyer, *At Home*, 30. BP to Louisa Ferguson, 26 February 1908, *LTC*, 132–5.

36. BP to HW, 24 August, 13 September 1907, *Letters*, 153, 154.

37. BP to ALW, 2 January 1908, *Letters*, 156; BP to HW, 18 January, 27 February 1908, *Letters*, 157–8; 22 April 1908, FWA.

38. BP to ALW, 26 April 1908, FLP.

39. Interview with Dr Mary Noble, 10, 16 April 2000. Potter was influenced by Blackburn's painting, particularly admiring her young herring gull and the hoodie crow. Jemima Blackburn, *Blackburn's Birds*, ed. Rob Farley (1993), 9–16. Blackburn died barely a year after the Potter book was published.

40. Jane Gardam, 'Some Wasps in the Marmalade', reprinted in Judy Taylor, *'So I Shall Tell You a Story . . .': Encounters with Beatrix Potter* (1993), 82. A pudding at this period could mean a meat dish rather than a dessert.

41. *HWBP*, 191–4. MacDonald, *Beatrix Potter*, 104–10.

42. BP to HW, 18 November 1908, *Letters*, 164; BP to William Warner, 11 August 1908, PC.

43. BP to HW, 17 November, 15 December 1908, 9 January 1909, *Letters*, 164, 166, 168; 5 January, 10 March 1909, FWA.

44. BP to HW, 22, 23 April, 30 June, 15 July 1910, *Letters*, 179–80, 182.

45. *HWBP/AW*, 139–40; *HWBP*, 195–6, 350–59; Tim Longville, 'Return to Mr McGregor's Garden', *Country Life* (5 September 2002), 144–5. 'Llewellyn's Well' in *HWPB*, 357. On the manuscript Potter wrote, 'Made and part written at Gwaynynog, Denbigh.'

46. Beatrix was at Gwaynynog in early June and again in late July 1911. 'The Fairy in the Oak', written about the same time, begins with the description of the kitchen garden at Gwaynynog. *HWBP*, 350–56.

47. BP to ALW, 8 (?) April 1909, FWA.

11 Diversions

1. BP to HW, 14 June 1909, FWA. Records of Beatrix Potter merchandise, 1903–28, compiled by Elizabeth Booth, FWA. Brian Alderson, '"All the Little Side Shows": Beatrix Potter Among the Tradesmen', in Judy Taylor (ed.), *So Shall I Tell You A Story . . .: Encounters with Beatrix Potter* (1993), 154–67.

2. William Hopes Heelis, the senior partner and father of William Dickenson, died in 1900; *TMH*, 32–4. *ASC*, 128–30. From John and Thomas Rigg, 22 acres of pasture and woodland, 1 December 1908: Schedule of Beatrix Heelis's land conveyances, 15 November 1905–11 November 1943, BPS.

3. Deed to Castle Farm, NT. Potter bought Castle Farm from Mary Ann Hawkrigg, Richard Hartley and a mortgagee, William Long. Hartley was related to the Revd Samuel Hartley, who had once had an ownership stake in Buckle Yeat Croft: Schedule of Beatrix Heelis's land conveyances, 15 November 1905–11 November 1943, BPS. *TBP*, 96. *ASC*, 127–30.

4. The inscription in the exercise book reads, 'Ginger and Pickles. With love to Louie from Aunt Beatrix, Christmas, 1908.'

5. Broad Leys was owned by a wealthy Manchester merchant called Milne, one of the founders of Kendal, Milne & Company, retailers and clothiers with shops in the Lake District as well as Manchester.

6. BP to ALW, 17 November 1909, *Letters*, 171–2. *The Tale of Ginger and Pickles*, reviewed in *Bookman* (Christmas 1909). BP to HW, 16 August, 11 September 1909, *Letters*, 169, 170; BP to Louisa Ferguson, 8 January 1910, *LTC*, 135.

7. BP to Mrs Bunkle, 16 December 1909, BPS.

8. BP to HW, 11 September, 9, 19 October 1909, FWA; BP to ALW, 16 September 1909, FWA. Bracken, a ubiquitous fern, now an invasive pest plant, was used as winter bedding for cattle.

9. BP to ALW, 17 November 1909, *Letters*, 171–2; BP to ALW, 23 December 1909, PC.

10. BP to HW, 20 December 1909, *Letters*, 172.

11. BP to HW, 14 June 1909, FWA; BP to HW, 22 April 1910, *Letters*, 179. *TBP*, 94. The first general election began on 15 January. A second election was required in December 1910.

12. At this period the labels Conservative, Tory and Unionist are used interchangeably. The term Unionist grew out of the split in the Liberal Party in 1886 over the issue of Irish Home Rule. In 1910 the term refers to those Conservatives owing their allegiance to Joseph Chamberlain. BP to Louisa Ferguson, 8 January 1910, *LTC*, 135. *TBP*, 91–4. BP, leaflet against free trade, March 1910, printed by Martin, Hood & Larkin, London, BPG.

13. BP to Edmund Evans, 11 January 1910, V&A. A verse she had written was printed below the doll. See *HWBP*, 399. E. E. Williams had declared in his book *Made in Germany* (1896), 'the Industrial Supremacy of Great Britain . . . is fast turning into a myth.' It initiated a concerted anti-German campaign in Britain and increased protectionist sentiment ultimately reflected in the general elections. Andrew Marrison, *British Business and Protection, 1903–1932* (1996), 19–46.

14. BP, 'The Shortage of Horses', printed and published by Edmund Evans, Ltd., London. See *HWBP*, 401–7. BP to Messrs Edmund Evans, 28 February, 8 March 1910, *Letters*, 175–6. Miss Hammond, 'Florrie', lived with her niece Margaret, known as Daisy. Leslie Linder surmises that it was Daisy, not the elder Florrie, who helped with the campaign. One other leaflet concerned international copyright restrictions and elicited some responses from printers suffering from inadequate protection.

15. General election 1910 (January): Liberals 275, Unionists, 273, Labour, 40, Irish Nationalists, 82, giving a majority for a Parliament Bill and

Home Rule. Beatrix had been asked to address a meeting on the subject of tariff reform by a 'leading Kendal tradesman' but 'had no difficulty resisting the temptation!' BP to HW, 20 January 1910, *Letters*, 175.

16. BP to ALW, 20 July 1910, FWA; BP to ALW, 23 August 1910, *Letters*, 183.

17. Ibid.

18. Rupert Potter to Miss Moore, 17 October 1910, CCP. A second printing of 10,000 copies was made in November 1910.

19. BP to ALW, 9 October 1910, *Letters*, 185. *TBP*, 89.

20. BP to ALW, 19 November 1910, FWA. William Rollinson, *Life and Tradition in the Lake District* (1974, revised 1981), 189–92. F. B. Smith, *The People's Health, 1830–1910* (1979), 195–226. Like thousands of others, Beatrix found it difficult to avoid germs, especially upper respiratory illness, in the soot, smog and poor hygienic conditions of London.

21. BP to Mrs Carr, 1 January 1911, V&A.

22. When *Timmy Tiptoes* was published the grey squirrel had not become a major pest to British agriculture, nor had it yet extended its range to drive out the native red squirrel.

23. In 1907 Beatrix had described her farm animals at Hill Top in a letter to Louie Warne with the idea of making a painting book and planned one out following her letter. *BP/AW*, 144–5. BP to Louie Warne, 8 July 1907, *LTC*, 124. *HWBP*, 270–71. BP to HW, 12 July 1911, FWA.

24. BP to FW, 9 August 1911, *Letters*, 188.

25. BP to ALW, 4 February 1911, FWA.

26. Bruce L. Thompson, typescript of deeds which later came into possession of the National Trust, 27 November 1947, NT. Conveyance, 28 February 1911, Baines to H. B. Potter.

27. BP to ALW, 6 April 1911, FLP; BP to ALW, 18 June 1911, PC; BP to HW, 14 June 1911, FWA.

28. BP to ALW, 3 September 1911, FLP.

29. BP to Louie Warne, 12 August 1911, *LTC*, 128–9.

30. BP, draft letter, 'Grandmotherly legislation', *Letters*, 190–91.

31. BP to ALW, 13 December 1911, *Letters*, 192; BP to Robert Burn and to Barbara Ruxton, two letters, both 13 December 1911, *LTC*, 155–6.

32. BP to ALW, 13 December 1911, *Letters*, 191.

33. Beatrix Potter, 'Letter to the Editor', *Country Life* (13 January 1912), 74.

34. H. D. Rawnsley, 'Hydro-aeroplanes on Windermere', *The Times*,

4 January 1912; BP, 'A Further Protest', *The Times*, 11 January 1912; 'The Hydroplane on Windermere', *The Times*, 12 January 1912; 'The Question of the Ferry', *The Times*, 19 January 1912; E. W. Wakefield, 'Reply to Canon Rawnsley', *The Times*, 11 January 1912.

35. 'Hydro-Aeroplanes on Windermere', *The Times*, 18 January 1912. BP to HW, 27 January 1912, *Letters*, 195. BP, 'Hydroplanes on Windermere', *The Times*, 29 August 1912. BP to ALW, 22 August 1912, *Letters*, 199. Only on letters published by *Country Life* did she sign as 'Beatrix Potter'.

36. BP to HW, 27 January, 3 February, 4 April 1912, *Letters*, 195–7.

37. BP to HW, 3 February 1912, *Letters*, 196. Jack Bredbury, *The Foundation of the Stalybridge Unitarian Church and Sunday School and the Connection of Their Origins with the Leech Family* (2001). *Inquirer* (13 August 1966), 3.

38. BP to HW, 20, 21 November 1911, *Letters*, 189–90; BP to FC, 11 December 1911, NT.

39. BP to ALW, 1 April 1912, PC; BP to HW, 4 April 1912, *Letters*, 196; BP to HW, 11 July 1912, FWA. In November Beatrix was asked to judge at one of the local farm shows, this one, of 'trussed poultry', a further indication of her increased involvement in the community. BP to HW, 11 November 1912, PC. *MY*, 172.

40. BP to HW, 11 June 1912, *Letters*, 197; BP to ALW, 19 June 1912, FWA.

41. *HWBP*, 210. BP to HW, 14 July 1912, *Letters*, 198.

42. It was not until after Beatrix wrote *Mr. Tod* that scientists came to believe that badgers seemed susceptible to bovine tuberculosis and could transmit the disease to cattle, making them unpopular with farmers. Potter later opposed badger digging and baiting.

43. BP to Harold Botcherby, 17 February 1913, *Letters*, 202. It was the fox who smelled and whose earth required the housekeeping.

44. BP to ALW, 22 August 1912, *Letters*, 199. Either Rupert or Beatrix photographed Joan and Norah with the chicks at the farm; photograph, FWA.

45. BP to ALW, 22 August 1912, *Letters*, 199.

46. Ibid. *MY*, 173.

12 Satisfactions

1. There are no extant letters between William Heelis and Beatrix Potter during these years, though Margaret Lane had access to some immediately after Potter's death; *TBP*, 96–101. *ASC*, 130–32. BP to ALW, 26 April 1908, FLP.

2. *TMH*, 2, 14–42.

3. BP to HW, 9 October 1912, *Letters*, 200.

4. *ASC*, 130. *TBP*, 97–8. *MY*, 172. The clearest sense of the chronology of her engagement comes from Beatrix's first extant letter to her Crompton cousin Fanny Cooper, 9 October 1913, NT.

5. BP to HW, 3, 7 March 1913, *Letters*, 203.

6. BP to HW, 7, 8, 19 April 1913, *Letters*, 203–5.

7. BP to HW, 29 April 1913, *Letters*, 207.

8. Sawrey House Estate conveyance documents, 30 December 1913, NT; Schedule of Beatrix Heelis's land conveyances, 15 November 1905–11 November 1943, BPS.

9. Clark is quoted in *TBP*, 98.

10. BP to ALW, 17 May 1913, PC. In this letter, which is in private hands and has not been fully transcribed, Beatrix tells Millie how ill she has been, that Bertram is in London, and that she feels 'now suddenly better'. Liz Taylor, 'The Tale of Bertram Potter', *Weekend Scotsman* (11 November 1978), 6, and 'Bertram Potter and the Scottish Borders', *BPS Studies*, 2 (1986), 43–6. *ASC*, 13. *TBP*, 97.

11. In 1986 Mary Noble visited Mary Potter's mother's family in Hawick and learned that the Huttons of Hawick, whose niece Mary was, had a long connection with Birnam and Atholl, owned land there and had built the house the Potters rented in 1892; Mary Noble to John Clegg, 21 October 1986, PC. It is unclear if the proper terminology is 'wine merchant' or 'tavern keeper'.

12. BP to HW, 4 June 1913, *Letters*, 208; BP to E. Wilfred Evans, 10 July 1913, *Letters*, 208.

13. BP to ALW, 4 July 1913, FWA. One of the most contentious issues was whether the Potters would have to give up their London home if she married Heelis. Beatrix argued that there was no reason for her father to live in London any longer and that she could manage their care if they too moved to the Lake District.

14. BP to FC, 9 October 1913, NT; BP to HW, 25 July 1913, *Letters*, 210.

15. *HWBP*, 213–14. BP to Andrew Fayle, 22 January 1910, *LTC*, 141. BP to Joy (surname unknown), 26 September 1913, PC.

16. The signpost appears both on the last page and in the frontispiece, suggesting that Potter saw it as symbolic of her choices for happiness and a country life. *HWBP*, 213–17; Ruth K. MacDonald, *Beatrix Potter* (1986), 122–7. *BP/AW*, 148–52. Peter Hollindale, 'These Piglets Fled Away', *Signal* (May 1994), 141–8.

17. *HWBP*, 213–17. *BP/AW*, 148–52; MacDonald, *Beatrix Potter*, 120–27. *ASC*, 134. BP to Gertrude Woodward, 24 September 1913, *Letters*, 213. *The Tale of Pigling Bland*, copy dedicated to William, 27 October 1913, LDM@TA. BP to Margaret Hough, 4 November 1913, *LTC*, 170.

18. BP to HW, 13 September 1913; BP to Gertrude Woodward, 24 September 1913, *Letters*, 210, 213. Thomas Haygarth Baines to Helen Beatrix Heelis, 30 December 1913. The 66 acres of the Sawrey House Estate included Moss Heckle (Eccles) Intake and part of the Tarn; see Schedule of Beatrix Heelis's conveyances, BPS.

19. BP to FC, 9 October 1913, NT.

20. Ibid. See Anthony Wohl, 'Unfit for Human Habitation', in H. J. Dyos and Michael Wolff (eds.), *The Victorian City*, 2 vols. (1973), vol. ii, pp. 603–24, and his *Endangered Lives: Public Health in Victorian Britain* (1983), 1–9, 136–7. These essays on hygiene and disease make it clear why Beatrix was so often ill when she returned to London.

21. BP to FC, 9 October 1913, NT; BP to Gertrude Woodward, 24 September 1913, *Letters*, 212.

22. *St Mary Abbots: The Parish Church of Kensington* (1992).

23. *TMH*, 3. A studio photograph by C. E. Fry & Sons of Gloucester Terrace, South Kensington, undated, was taken with Beatrix seated on an elaborate chair and William perched beside her. She appears to be wearing the same blouse and skirt as in the photograph taken on 14 October. Beatrix sent a copy of a photograph to Millie Warne saying that it was 'taken on my wedding day, but nobody likes it, the side of the face seems puffed out' – a description corresponding to the studio photograph cited above. Beatrix Heelis (hereafter cited as BPH) to ALW, 7 November 1913, FWA.

24. Interview with David Henry Beckett by Judy Taylor, 13 November 1989, and with Elizabeth Battrick, 11 May 1990, Hawkshead. The officiating curate, called to perform a mid-week ceremony, was not the

notable Somerset Edward Pennefather, the incumbent Vicar. Heelis–
Potter certified copy of marriage register, 15 October 1913, St Mary
Abbots Parish Register, London.

25. Judy Taylor, interview with Beatrix Moore, *c.* December 1985, quoted
in *ASC*, 134. *TMH*, 2–4. Once married, Beatrix was insistent that she
be addressed only by her married name.

26. Heelis–Potter, marriage notice, *The Times*, 18 October 1913. The same
notice was printed in the *Westmorland Gazette*.

27. BPH to ALW, 21 October 1913, FLP.

13 Partnerships

1. BPH to ALW, 3 November 1913, FLP; BPH to Mrs Martin,
28 October 1913, *Letters*, 213.

2. BPH to ALW, 7 November 1913, FWA.

3. BPH to Edith Gaddum, 6 November 1913; BPH to ALW, 3 November
1913, FLP; BPH to ALW, 7 November 1913, FWA.

4. BPH to ALW, 23 December 1913, 15 April 1913, PC; BPH to Barbara
Ruxton, 6 November, 31 December 1913, *LTC*, 152–4, 160.

5. BPH to ALW, 15 April 1914, PC. Millie had sent Beatrix a gift of a
handsome card case and was forwarding another belated wedding gift.
BPH to ALW, 23 December 1913, PC. *TMH*, 24–7.

6. The tarn was created sometime around the turn of the century by
damming the lower end of the beck which drained the higher moss.
BPH's portion of the tarn was the smaller part. The individual closes
are listed in the Assent created after BPH's death. Conveyance deed of
30 December 1913, NT; descriptions refer to plot numbers on the 1914
Ordnance Survey map.

7. BPH to ALW, 12 March 1914, PC; BPH to HW, 20 March 1914,
Letters, 217.

8. BPH to HW, 9 May 1914, *Letters*, 217–18. Sir Alfred Downing Fripp
(1865–1930), certified death certificate, Rupert Potter, 8 May 1914,
General Register Office.

9. BPH to ALW, 19 May 1915, PC.

10. Conversion to 2002 equivalency from 'The History of Money',
www.ex.ac.uk. The third codicil was made on 11 December 1913 when
Miss Hammond was still living. 'Rupert Potter, deceased. Lists of shares

debentures of companies, stocks or funds, stock funds and bonds of foreign countries, dependencies and colonies'; 'Debts due at the death'; material from executors of the estate, July 1914, BPS. BPH to HW, 3 August 1914, *Letters*, 219.

11. 'Beatrix Potter's Housekeeper Looks Back on Life at Sawrey', *Westmorland Gazette* (29 July 1966). Mary Agnes Rogerson (Mrs Thomas) had been overseeing both properties before Potter's marriage. BPH to Barbara Ruxton, 31 December 1913, *LTC*, 160.

12. The other stories were 'Pace Eggers', 'Mole Catcher's Burying', and 'Carrier's Bob', a tragic but true story of a faithful dog being run over by a cart, which the editor did not think 'happy'; *HWBP*, 376–83.

13. BPH to HW, 23 February 1914, 20 March 1914, *Letters*, 216, 217; BPH to HW, 21 March 1914, quoted in *HWBP*, 218.

14. BPH to ALW, 19 May 1914, PC; BPH to HW, 10 June 1914, FWA; BPH to HW, 12 July 1914, *Letters*, 218.

15. Sue Beckett, Judy Taylor and Elizabeth Battrick, 'David Henry Beckett's Recollections of Beatrix Potter's Family', interview, n.d. January 2002, NT; BPH to ALW, 11 September 1914, FLP.

16. Rupert's estate could not be entirely cleared until the two mews properties were disposed of a decade later. Jackson-Stops & Staff, Estate Agents, circular, 'Lindeth Howe, Windermere, Westmorland'; BPH to HW, 18 May 1915, *Letters*, 221.

17. BPH to ALW, 11 September 1914, FLP. Information on Bertram's military status is from *ASC*, 136, but unconfirmed. Pamela Horn, *The Changing Countryside in Victorian and Edwardian England and Wales* (1984), 226–42.

18. BPH to ALW, 21 December 1915; BPH to FW, 18 (?) December 1915, FWA.

19. BPH to HW, 3 August 1914, *Letters*, 219; BPH to HW, 8 May 1915, FWA; BPH to HW, 18 May 1915, *Letters*, 221.

20. BPH to FW, 18 (?) December 1915, *Letters*, 221–2.

21. Ibid.

22. BPH to ALW, 21 December 1915, FWA.

23. David B. Grigg, *English Agriculture: An Historical Perspective* (1989), 40–58. *Times* report cited Pamela Horn, *Rural Life in England in the First World War* (1984), 114–39. The WNLS was unsuccessful, but its successor, the Women's Land Army, placed about 23,000 women on the land.

24. BPH to Augusta Burn, 10 January 1916, PC.

25. BPH (A Woman Farmer), 'Women on the Land', 10 March 1916; *The Times* (13 March 1916).

26. Eleanor L. Choyce, 'Louie' (1876–1963); her initial reply is lost. Selwyn Goodacre, 'Beatrix Potter Writes to *The Times*', *BPSN*, 8 (15 January 1985). *TBP*, 101–3. BPH to ELC, 15 March 1916, *ELCL*.

27. Nigel Gee, Introduction, *ELCL. LTC*, 177–8.

28. ELC to Mrs Choyce, 25 May 1916, *ELCL*; quote from *TBP* (letter now lost), 134–5.

29. BPH to Denys Lowson, 3 October 1916, *LTC*, 178.

30. BPH to ALW, 10 January 1916, PC; BPH to ALW, 15 December 1916, *Letters*, 228–9.

31. BPH to HDR, 5 February 1917, *Letters*, 230.

32. Rawnsley's son Noel was the source of this view; *ASC*, 151. Graham Murphy, *Founders of the National Trust* (1987), 52, repeats the notion. Speculation increased when Eleanor's 1923 biography of her husband contained no mention of his friendship with the Potter family or with Beatrix, nor any of their common endeavours; Eleanor F. Rawnsley, *Canon Rawnsley: An Account of His Life* (1923).

33. BPH to ALW, 15 December 1916, FWA; BPH to HW, 19 December 1916, *Letters*, 229.

34. Eileen Jay, 'Beatrix Potter and the Armitt Collection', *VN*, 39. BPH to Frederic Fowkes, 19 November, 1 December 1914, n.d. 1916, PC.

35. BPH to Frederic Fowkes, 19 November, 1 December 1914, n.d. 1916, PC; BP to HDR, 27 August 1913, NT.

36. Esther Nicholson (1899–1984) became a teacher and emigrated to New Zealand leaving a legacy of educational good will. Nancy Nicholson Hudson (1909–2007), became a Norland nurse (infant and children's nanny), married Hugh Hudson in 1965 and returned to a farm in Kirkby Thore.

37. BPH to GN, 18 March 1917, PC.

38. Esther was most likely able to attend St Katharine's because of Beatrix's beneficence.

39. BPH to GN, 10(?), 11 August 1916, V&A. Judy Taylor to the author, 21 October 2004. The story of the visit was told by NNH to Taylor in an interview in 1990 and is recounted in *LTC*, 172 and in *TMH*, 75–7. BPH to NNH, Christmas 1916, in a ring binder, V&A.

40. BP, 'The Fairy in the Oak', *c.* 1911, text in *HWBP*, 351–6. She recalls

the great oak at Camfield, which was described in the Doomsday Book. *HWBP*, 'Oaks', 'Acorns' and 'Of Timber', 393–4. These are unfinished fragments intended as letters to *Country Life* or *The Field*.

41. BPH to HW, 12 August 1916, *Letters*, 227.

42. Ibid. For Ernest A. Aris (1882–1963), I am indebted to correspondence with Dudley Chignall and to his MS 'The Man who Drew for Beatrix Potter – Ernest Aris' (2004). Emma Laws on the exhibit 'Ernest Aris: Beatrix Potter's "second string"', *BPSN*, 94 (October 2004).

43. BPH to Ernest A. Aris, quoted in Dudley Chignall, 'The Man who Drew . . .', ch. 3: 'An Artlessly Conceited Little Bounder', V&A. Ernest A. Aris to BPH, 18 September 1916, V&A. *HWBP*, 240–41. BPH to NNH, September (1917?), V&A. Sketches are in the V&A. NNH to Leslie Linder, 9 August 1966, V&A. William's fear proved well founded. Aris appropriated the oakman characters after the war in books published under the pseudonym Dan Crow.

44. BPH to FW, 10 November 1917, *Letters*, 239.

45. Ibid. Ernest Aris to BPH, 21 November 1917. Chignall, 'The Man who Drew . . .', ch. 3.

46. BPH to FW, 13 November 1917, *Letters*, 240; BPH to Ernest Aris, 23 November 1917 (draft), *Letters*, 241.

47. BPH to HW, 12 June 1916, ?end of February 1917, *Letters*, 225, 231.

48. BPH to GN, 18 March 1917, PC. Andrew O. Hagan, *The End of British Farming* (2001), 31–3; Grigg, *English Agriculture*, 50–58. BPH to HW, 19 March 1917, *Letters*, 231–2.

49. Ibid.

14 Salvages

1. *The Times* (3 April 1917), 3.

2. BPH to ALW, 5 April 1917, FWA.

3. Ibid.

4. *The Times* (11 April 1917), 3; (27 April 1917), 3. See also Alexander Grinstein, *The Remarkable Beatrix Potter* (1995), 228–31.

5. *ASC*, 138, 139–40. BPH to FW, 30 April 1917, *Letters*, 233–4.

6. BPH to FW, 28 June 1917, *Letters*, 235. In the end it was sold to a neighbour and eventually lost.

7. Ibid.; BPH to ALW, 5 July 1917, FWA.

8. BPH to FW, 21, 28 June 1917, *Letters*, 234–6. *ASC*, 140–41. *HWBP*, 225–8, 430–31. The first printing of *Appley Dapply* was 20,000 copies, and the second 15,000; Frederick Warne & Co. catalogue, January 1918, FWA.

9. BPH to FW, 4 May 1918, *Letters*, 247.

10. The Frederick Warne Archives hold dozens of fascinating notes from Potter to HW and FW during the period 1905–28 giving her opinions on licences and products. Elizabeth Booth, 'Beatrix Potter's Early Merchandise, 1903–1928', FWA. BPH to FW, ? September 1917, FWA; BPH to FW, 17 October 1917, *Letters*, 238.

11. Ibid.

12. BPH to FW, 1 September 1917, *Letters*, 236–7; BPH to NNH, ? September 1917, V&A.

13. BPH to FW, 3 September 1917, *Letters*, 237. E. Booth, inventory, FWA.

14. BPH to GN, 7, 23, 30 August 1917, V&A.

15. BPH to NNH, Monday, ?September 1917, V&A.

16. BPH to GN, 7 August 1917, 11 August 1916 (?), V&A; BPH to NNH, 15 September 1917, V&A.

17. BPH to GN, 29 March 1918, V&A.

18. BPH to EN, 2 April 1918, *LTC*, 24.

19. BPH to Tom Harding, 21 December 1917, *LTC*, 80. She enclosed a copy of *Appley Dapply*. BPH to FW, 1 February 1918, *Letters*, 245.

20. BPH to FW, 26 February 1918, FWA.

21. BPH to FW, 18 March 1918, *Letters*, 246.

22. BPH to FW, 4, 6 May 1918, *Letters*, 247–8. Scafell is a peak of 978 metres in the Wasdale fells, approached from Langdale or Borrowdale.

23. *HWBP*, 'The Tale of Johnny Town-Mouse', 243–4. There were at least two Mary Rogersons of Sawrey. One owned Duchess, the Pomeranian, the other, her daughter-in-law, was the Heelises' housekeeper after 1911. The Mrs Rogerson of Eeswyke appears to be the one who owned the dogs and who is drawn. *BP/AW*, 156–7. One critic calls the tale 'an unusually strident argument on the virtues of country living' and wonders if Potter intended it to justify her retreat from active publication and public life, a comment which ignores the reality of Potter's life at the time; Ruth K. MacDonald, *Beatrix Potter* (1986), 78–81.

24. Quote from *Bookman* in FW to BPH, 31 December 1918, FWA.

25. BPH to ALW, 30 June 1918, BPS.

26. 'General Disposition & Settlement of Walter Bertram Potter, Ashyburn,

Ancrum, 1918' (the will was signed 8 October 1915), PC. Liz Taylor, 'Bertram Potter and the Scottish Borders', *BPS Studies* 2 (1986), 43–6; and 'The Tale of Bertram Potter', *Weekend Scotsman* (11 November 1978), 6; interview with Liz Taylor, Melrose, Scotland, 4 April 2000. Certificate of Death, Ancrum, 1918. Bertram died on 22 June 1918 at 7.30 a.m. Witnessed by Robert Robertson, a neighbour and sometime farmhand; BPH to FW, 2 July 1918, *Letters*, 250.

27. BPH to HDR, 13 September 1918, *Letters*, 251.

28. BPH to EN, 16 July 1918, *LTC*, 75.

29. BPH to NNH, 2 October 1918, V&A.

30. BPH to ALW, 8 November 1918, FWA.

15 Opportunities

1. BPH to ELC, 1924 June 17, *ELCL*.

2. Melvyn Bragg, *Land of the Lakes* (1983), 79–83. BPH to FC, 14 December 1925, NT; BPH to Ivy Steel, 27 November 1924, *DIDJ*. Interview with Bruce Logan, n.d., CRO/K.

3. J. D. Marshall and John K. Walton, *The Lake Counties from 1830 to the Mid-Twentieth Century: A Study in Regional Change* (1981), 55–66; David B. Grigg, *English Agriculture: An Historical Perspective* (1989), 53–86; Alun Howkins, *Reshaping Rural England: A Social History, 1850–1925* (1991), 222–75. BPH to Ivy Steel, 27 November 1924, *DIDJ*; BPH to FC, 14 December 1925, NT; BPH to Kate Wyatt, 15 November 1920, FLP. See E. M. Cleland, 'How Peter Rabbit's Creator Nearly Became a Canadian', *Toronto Globe & Mail* (4 February 1956), reprinted in Judy Taylor, *'So I Shall Tell You a Story . . .': Encounters with Beatrix Potter* (1993), 40–43.

4. The new firm was registered on 25 May 1919. They offered, and Potter approved, a combination of cash and debentures to repay their debts. BPH to FW, 10 April 1919, *Letters*, 256; BPH to FW, 17 May 1919, FWA. *Letters*, 257n.

5. FW to BPH, 19 May 1919; BPH to FW, 23, 29 May 1919, FWA. *The Tale of the Faithful Dove* was published posthumously in 1955.

6. *HWBP*, 245. BPH to FW, 29 May 1919, *Letters*, 257–8.

7. BPH to FW, 5 August, 3 November 1919, *Letters*, 258–9.

8. BPH to FW, 11 March, 7 May, 12 October 1920, *Letters*, 261, 263.

HWBP, 246: BPH to Kate Wyatt, 15 November 1920, *Letters*, 264.

9. BPH to FW, 28 February 1919, *Letters*, 254; BPH to FW, 6 February 1922, FWA; BPH to FC, 27 December 1924, NT.

10. BPH to NHH, 8 November 1919, V&A; BPH to Edith Gaddum, 13 February 1922, PC; BPH to FW, 6 February 1922, FWA.

11. William Rathbone VI, Mrs Paget's brother, founded district nursing in 1858 and established a training school modelled directly on Florence Nightingale's system. In 1887 the successful District Nursing Association had been granted royal patronage as Queen Victoria's Jubilee Institute for Nurses, hence the term Queen's Nurse for someone who had been trained in that system. *BP Journal* (5 February 1893), 312. Rosalind Paget (1855–1948) was named DBE in 1935. Gwen Hardy, *William Rathbone and the Early History of District Nursing* (1981), 4–7; June Hannam, 'Rosalind Paget: Class, Gender and the Midwives Act', *History of Nursing Society Journal*, 5 (1994–5), 133–49.

12. Canon Thomas Henry Irving was Vicar at St Michael and All Angels in Hawkshead from 1909 to 1927. Initially £92 6s. was promised in annual subscriptions, and £270 in endowments, much of that amount contributed anonymously by Beatrix. *Ambleside, Brathay & Hawkshead Parish Magazine* (June, August, September, December 1919), LDM@TA. Susan Ludbrook, 'The Foundation of the Hawkshead District Nursing Association', 3 February 1988, V&A. Barbara Crossley, *The Other Ambleside* (2000), 70–72. *TBP*, 158–9. BPH to GN, 1 December 1919, 16 September 1920, V&A.

13. BPH to GN, 11 August 1922, V&A. Miscellaneous letters about purchase of Hanniken cottage from Jas. Walker, courtesy of Eileen Jay. *Ambleside, Brathay & Hawkshead Parish Magazine* (February 1920), LDM@TA.

14. BPH to Mrs Edwards, 11 February 1924, PC. *Ambleside, Hawkshead and Brathay Parish Magazine* (September 1924), LDM@TA. Transcripts, 'District Nursing', Ambleside Oral History Group, Ambleside Library.

15. Elizabeth Battrick, 'Mrs Heelis Settles In', *BPS Studies*, 4 (1990), 36–45, and *The Real World of Beatrix Potter* (1987), 35–8; author interview with E. Battrick, 14 July 2000. *Ambleside, Hawkshead, Wray and Brathay Parish Magazine* (1925), LDM@TA. BPH to FC, 14 December 1925, NT.

16. BPH to GN, 6 June 1922, V&A; BPH to ELC, 19 September, 13 December 1922, 2 May 1923, 16 October 1925, *ELCL*; BPH to FW,

8–9 January 1926, *Letters*, 294; BPH to Nora Burt, 5 June 1932, NT.

17. *TMH*, 31–2. *Hawkshead Parish Magazine*, April 1920, May 1921, LDM@TA.

18. Elisabeth Holbrook, 'Camping at Sawrey', *BPSN*, 73 (July 1999), 13–14. Interview with Margery Stevenson, Windermere, 22 October 2000. Judy Taylor, interview with Joy Brownlow, Windermere, 3 July 1985. BPH to Joy Brownlow, 13 August 1943.

19. 'Peter Rabbit and the Guides at Troutbeck Park, May 31, 1928', Chorlton-cum-Hardy Company Log Book, May 1928. BPH to Joy Brownlow, December 1929. Album compiled by Cynthia Forbes, Cumbria South Guide Association. Log of the 1st Chorlton-cum-Hardy Guide and Ranger camp, Hawkshead, Ambleside, 17–25 May 1929, BPG. *ASC*, 166. Susan Benson, *Guiding: The Magazine of Girl Guiding, UK*, CRO/B; Girlguiding Collection, CRO/B.

20. BPH to Nora Burt, 5 June 1931, NT.

21. BPH to Margery McKay, 22 September 1930, PC.

22. BPH to Kitty Holdsworth, 5 July 1928, 11 March 1935, Girl Guide Association, CRO/B; BPH to MFHP, 10 February 1928, BPA.

23. *TMH*, 50–58; Willow Taylor, *Through the Pages of My Life*, edited by Judy Taylor (2000), 23–38.

24. BPH to FW, 9 January 1924, *Letters*, 284; FW to BPH, 25 January 1924, FWA.

25. BPH to FW, 19 June 1924; BPH to Miss L. C. Smythe, June 1924; L. C. Smythe to BPH, 30 June, 13 November 1924; BPH to FW, 2 July, 8 August, 24 October 1924, FWA. Copies of the extant Christmas cards are in the V&A and BPG. These drawings, in contrast to the familiar book illustrations, are practically unknown. Edwin Mullins, 'The Unknown Beatrix Potter', *Weekend Telegraph*, 92 (1 July 1966), 22–7.

26. BPH to FW, 22 January 1924, *Letters*, 285.

27. Beatrice Potter Webb's Christian names were 'Martha Beatrice'. The article in the *Sunday Herald*, entitled 'Spite before Honour', was written by Sir J. Foster Fraser. The retraction did not stop the error from being repeated in the *Evening Standard*, the *Daily Dispatch* and again as late as 1927.

28. See Beatrice Webb, *My Apprenticeship* (1926). Webb was eight years older than Heelis. Margaret Cole, *Beatrice Webb* (1946) and Deborah Epstein Nord, *The Apprenticeship of Beatrice Webb* (1985). BPH to FW, 6 February 1924, *Letters*, 286.

29. BPH to FW, 17 June 1921, *Letters*, 269. Owen (1858–1939) preferred the biblical spelling of her name, but changed it often; Beatrix is inconsistent. BPH to MFHP, 17 November 1933, 15 December 1935, *BPA*. Jane Morse, 'Beatrix Potter's American Neighbour, Rebecca Owen', *BPS Studies*, 7 (1997), 52–9; Jane Morse, 'Beatrix Potter and Rebeccah Owen', *BPSN*, 13 (June 1984), 5–6; 18 (October 1985), 4–5; Carl J. Weber, *Hardy and the Lady from Madison Square* (1952), 3–29. The first American visitor to Hill Top was Charles G. Y. King, a watercolourist and photographer, who called in May 1913, stayed for tea, famously photographed Beatrix in the doorway at Hill Top and also took a favourite photo of Beatrix and Kep. BPH to C. G. Y. King, 27 May 1913, PC. Kenneth Hecht to Editors, *Smithsonian Magazine* (March 1989) and to Jane Morse, 24 March 1989, courtesy of Jane Morse.

30. BPH to ACM, 24 June 1921, *Letters*, 270; Anne Carroll Moore, 'An Appreciation', in *ABP* (1955 edition), p. xvi.

31. Ibid., pp. xviii–xx; *BPA*, pp. ix, 3.

32. BPH to FW, 5 August 1921, *Letters*, 271.

33. BPH to FW, 10 May 1922 (?), *Letters*, 276; BPH to ELC, 13 December 1922, *ELCL*.

34. BPH to 'Nicholas', 22 October 1922, *BPA*; *LTC*, 148–51.

35. William Lusk Webster Field, Headmaster, Milton Academy 1917–42. Author, interview with Herbert G. Stokinger, Milton, Mass., 5 May 2002; *BPA*, pp. ix–x, 5–7.

36. A brief author profile was published in *Realms of Gold* (1929), a reference guide on children's authors and children's literature published under the auspices of *The Horn Book*. The rest of it appeared as '"Roots" of the Peter Rabbit Tales', *The Horn Book*, 5 (May 1929), 69–72. BPH copies her text in a letter to ACM, 12 December 1925, for approval. See *BPA*, 8–9. BMM to Margaret Lane, 25 September 1944, Simmons College Archive. Lolly Robinson, 'Beatrix Potter's American Friends', *BPS Studies*, 11 (2005), 70–82. The Bookshop for Boys and Girls was supported by the Women's Educational and Industrial Union (WEIU), founded in 1876 as a mission to help young women of humble origin become economically independent, and was affiliated with what later became Simmons College. Mahony had worked for the WEIU since 1906. The WEIU, known as the Women's Union, still exists today.

37. BPH to DH, 17 June 1920, 19 April 1922, 18 July 1924, PC. Daisy Hammond was a beneficiary of Rupert Potter's will.

16 Legacies

1. Hardwicke D. Rawnsley, 'A Crack about Herdwick Sheep', in his *By Fell and Dale at the English Lakes* (1911).

2. W. J. Malden, *British Sheep and Shepherding* (1915), 6–18, 59–61, 82–8. Malden's book remains the definitive book on the subject of British breeds and breeding in the early twentieth century. C. Hanson-Smith, 'The Herdwick Sheep of Cumbria', *BPS Studies*, 2 (1986), 47–9.

3. The Herdwick Sheep Association was ignored by R. H. Lamb, *Herdwick: Past and Present. A History of the Breed* (1936), 30–32, and H. D. and Noel Rawnsley's involvement in its formation has been similarly undocumented and subject to misinterpretation. I am indebted to Eddie McDonough for sharing his extensive knowledge of the literature of Herdwick sheep and shepherding, and for copies of the documents cited below. Letter from S. D. Dodgson and Noel Rawnsley, 4 September 1899, proposing a Herdwick Sheep Association; 'Report of the First Preliminary Meeting. Herdwick Sheep Association, September 6, 1899', reprinted from the *Keswick Guardian*; letter from Noel Rawnsley, Herdwick Sheep Association, Crosthwaite, Keswick, to W. Barnes 3(?), 8 October 1899, PC. Dodgson was elected president of the Herdwick Sheep Breeders' Association (HSBA) in 1916.

4. Rawnsley, 'A Crack about Herdwick Sheep', 47–54. Beatrix's membership in the HSBA was a direct result of her purchase of Troutbeck Park. Records of the HSBA show that, as one of only a few female members, she attended five annual meetings between 1924 and 1943. But this does not reflect the number of local meetings she attended. See Geoff Brown, 'Herdwick Sheep', HSBA leaflet, 2002.

5. Conveyance of Troutbeck Park Estate, Windermere, Westmorland, between John Mason, Stella Lockhart Hamilton and Alexander Cairns Hamilton (mortgagees) and the Troutbeck Park Green Slate Company Limited and Helen Beatrix Heelis, purchaser (1,875 acres, 1 rod and 16 perches), NT. A schedule of properties conveyed to the National Trust is in BPS.

6. *BP Journal* (7 August 1895), 391; BPH to Bruce Logan, 14 October 1924, BPG. She enclosed a cheque for £2 saying if there was any left over to give it 'to the hounds, with my compliments and thanks!'; BPH, 'The Lonely Hills', *The Horn Book* (May 1942), 156.

7. The Leake family were tenants, not owners, of Troutbeck Park Farm. BPH to SHH, 26 July 1926, *Letters*, 298.

8. The 1923 will is not extant. However, the same proviso appears in her will of 31 March 1939. The huts were not built in Mickelden, and the Trust purchased Bridge House on the beck side of Rydal Road.

9. BPH to SHH, 31 January, 2, 3, 5 February 1925, 13 February, 18 March 1926, NT.

10. BPH to SHH, 26 June 1926, *Letters*, 296–8.

11. Ibid.

12. Ibid.

13. Malden, *British Sheep*, 202, 216–18; Jane Upton and Dennis Soden, *An Introduction to Keeping Sheep* (1996), 74–103; Christopher Hanson-Smith, 'The Fell Farmer's Year', *ML*, 28–33. The liver fluke parasite has several intermediate hosts, but water snails, *Lymnaea columella*, which act as a vector by enabling it to complete its life cycle, are the most common. Modern ecological remedies include encouraging flocks of ducks which feed on the water snail, but boluses and drenches are still common. Success depends upon how entrenched the worm is in the sheep's liver. 'Rotten' animals are usually slaughtered.

14. BPH to JM, 14 June 1926, *ML*. Yellows or *icterus* in dogs is a liver disease usually caused by a bacterial or viral infection or sometimes toxic plants. Veterinary medicine in the 1930s was unable to determine the cause or to treat it successfully.

15. BPH to SHH, 26 June 1926, *Letters*, 296–7. The cupboard and table are still in the Troutbeck farmhouse. Interview with Gordon Tyson, Troutbeck Park Farm, 30 September 2001.

16. Susan Denyer, *At Home with Beatrix Potter: The Creator of Peter Rabbit* (2000), 124.

17. By tradition, fell farms that were tenanted passed on to the new owner a 'landlord's flock' of hefted sheep, part of the valuation of the farm when it was sold. Valley farms carry only so many sheep, and each heaf carries only a certain number of sheep. Farmers take care to see that no more than the right number are allowed up to the fell. William Rollinson, *Life and Tradition in the Lake District* (1974, revised 1981), 87–96; BPH to SHH, 26 June 1926, *Letters*, 296–7. W. R. Mitchell, 'Where Sheep Farming Stays in the Family', *Cumbria Magazine* (November 1997), 39–41.

18. Transcript of an interview by Elizabeth Battrick, 'Recollections of Tom

Storey', Sawrey, 1985. Hereafter cited as Storey, 'Recollections'; N T. Elizabeth Battrick, *The Real World of Beatrix Potter* (1987), 38–46, 'Mrs Heelis Settles In', *BPS Studies*, 4 (1990), 40–42.

19. Storey, 'Recollections'; Battrick, 'Mrs Heelis Settles In', 41. Storey's interview discusses both the new capsule cure for fluke as well as an injection used against the 'drop', or hypomagnesaemia, a disease caused by a sudden deficiency of magnesium. The injection of 100 ml. of calcium borogluconate in several sites could revive an animal.

20. Joseph Moscrop (1885?–1966). The Moscrop correspondence was initially deposited at CRO/C in 1967 by Joseph's brother Richard Moscrop's son, Robert, augmented by his niece Rosalind. The National Trust now owns all the letters but one. All the letters are published as *Beatrix Potter's Farming Friendship* (*ML*). The Carlisle Record Office still holds Joseph's correspondence with Richard, as well as Richard's farm accounts, recipes and spelling books.

21. Rosalind Moscrop, 'Joseph Moscrop', *ML*; BPH to JM, 13 January 1928, *ML*. Frank W. Garnett, *Westmorland Agriculture: 1800–1900* (1912), 90–91; David B. Grigg, *English Agriculture: A Social History, 1850–1925* (1991), 47–60. Whitsuntide or Whitsun is the seventh Sunday after Easter.

22. It appears that Beatrix negotiated her own agreements with Moscrop and her other Troutbeck shepherds. While William kept the books, he had no idea about Beatrix's management style or her insight into how and whom to pay. BPH's letters to JM during the Second World War are particularly revealing of these subtle negotiations and her skill at them.

23. BPH to JM, 14 June 1926, 12 April 1927, 25 June 1927, 2 April 1927, *ML*.

24. BPH to JM, 13 January 1928, *ML*. Ted Wood may well have been the shepherd first charged with instituting Scottish methods of sheep raising at Troutbeck, an effort ridiculed by the locals and abandoned by Storey. See W. R. Mitchell, *Beatrix Potter: Her Life in the Lake District* (1998). Sheep show catalogues from 1919 to 1925 indicate that she won no prizes in that period but she entered sheep at Hawkshead, Keswick and Windermere every year. For the 1921 Hawkshead show, Beatrix and William were members of the show committee, indicating the level of her interest. Collection of Heelis sheep show catalogues, 1919–36, LDM@TA.

25. Storey, 'Recollections'. The smit mark for Troutbeck Park was a red 'pop' on the left hind shoulder. Smit marks in black or red or blue, and lug marks, various cuts on the ear, follow ancient usage of each farm and were recorded in a flock book and maintained by the various breed societies. Ownership of the smit mark follows the farm, not the farmer.

26. Storey, 'Recollections'. Phyllis Arkle, *The Real Sawrey* (n.d.), 19–21. *Hawkshead Sheep Show Catalogue*, 6 September 1927, LDM@TA. Second prize in the Best of Group of Herdwicks went to John Gregg, now farming in Langdale.

27. Storey, 'Recollections'.

28. Liz Taylor, 'The Tale of Bertram Potter', *Weekend Scotsman* (11 November 1978), 7.

29. Storey, 'Recollections'. R. H. Lamb, *Herdwicks Past and Present: A Study of the Breed* (1936), 16–20. Interviews with Eddie McDonough (various dates).

30. Mitchell, *Beatrix Potter*, 82–94; Storey, 'Recollections'. This may have been the sheep's head in a very bold 'experimental style and vivid palette', item 204 in *BP's Art*.

31. W. R. Mitchell, *Letters from the Lakes* (1995), 89–93.

32. Malden, *British Sheep*, 201–39; Upton and Soden, *An Introduction*, 77–85. BPH to Samuel Cunningham, unknown date, quoted in *TBP*, 150.

33. BPH to HPC, 28 June 1928, *Letters*, 311; BPH to JM, 13, 15, 18 January 1928, *ML*.

34. BPH to GW, 28 December 1929, *BPS*. William joined her in interviewing the Walkers. There are important letters from Lucy Walker (George Walker's wife) to Joseph, and from Margaret Lane to Joseph. The Walker letters are the property of BPS.

35. BPH to JM, 9 January 1929, 4, 11 April 1929, *ML*.

36. JM to Richard Moscrop, 7, 16, 29 May 1929, CRO/C; BPH to Ivy Steel, 12 August 1929, *DIDJ*. Mitchell, *Beatrix Potter*, 88–92.

37. Storey, 'Recollections'.

38. BPH to AMK, 13 September 1929, *BPA*; Agricultural Fair Catalogues, Penrith, Gosforth District, Keswick, Cockermouth, 1930, 1931, 1932, 1933, LDM@TA.

39. Agriculture Fair Catalogues, Ennerdale, Keswick, Loweswater, Eskdale, 1929, 1930, 1931, LDM@TA. BPH to Ivy Hunt, 21 October 1930, *DIDJ*. W. R. Mitchell, 'One Woman and Her Sheep', *Yorkshire Post* (30 March 2001).

40. BPH to ELC, 28 August 1937, *ELCL*.

41. BPH to Ivy Steel, August 5, 1935, *DIDJ*. Keswick Sheep Show, 4 September 1935; special prizes, Loweswater & Brakenthwaite Sheep Show, 12 September 1935, LDM@TA. BPH to Betty Harris Stevens, 4 September 1930, *BPA*.

42. Mitchell, *Letters from the Lakes*, 91–3; Mitchell, *Beatrix Potter*, 86–105. There are many versions of her shepherd's recollections, some in print, and some from oral interviews, and many points of disagreement.

17 Americans

1. BPH to FW, 21 November 1924, FWA. *Letters*, 291 and n. *ASC*, 164–6. During his 1924 visit Charles Hopkinson painted a landscape featuring Beatrix's houses called *Far Sawrey*. In 1907 he painted *HHR Meets Peter Rabbit on the Path*. His daughter Isabella (Halstead) remembers the visit. Isabella Halstead to Leslie Linder, 4 December 1968, V&A.

2. BPH to FW, 21 November 1924, FWA; 28 October 1926, 13 January 1927, *Letters*, 299, 300.

3. Bruce L. Thompson, *The National Trust for Places of Historic Interest or Natural Beauty* (1949), 118.

4. BPH to BMM, 20 May 1927, *Letters*, 304. Receipts from the sale are missing. Some drawings appear to have been of other subjects than Peter Rabbit. Rose Kennedy (mother of President Kennedy) is thought to have purchased nine drawings, one for each of her children.

5. Ibid. 'Peter Rabbit and His Homelands', *The Horn Book* (August 1927), 18–19. Barbara Bader, 'Peter Says Please', *The Horn Book* (March April 1999), 119–22. BPH to MFHP, 30 November 1927, 10 February 1928, *BPA*.

6. 'Biographical Sketch of Marian Frazer Harris Perry by her niece, Elizabeth H. Stevens', n.d., courtesy of Mrs Nonya Wright.

7. Beatrix was born in July 1866, Marian Perry in December. Her father, James Smith Harris, was an astronomer, topographer, civil engineer and surveyor who worked on the Northwest Boundary Survey in 1857. Her mother, Delia Brodhead, was the daughter of the President of the New York Stock Exchange. The Revd James DeWolfe Perry was a descendant of the naval explorer Commodore Matthew C. Perry

(1794–1858), who initiated the opening of Japan to the West in the mid-nineteenth century. Interview with Mrs Nonya Wright, 14 April 2005, Berwyn, Pa. 'Obituary, Very Rev. James DeWolfe Perry, Jr', *New York Times* (21 May 1927), 27. Marian Perry died in 1960. *BPA* details the history of this friendship.

8. BPH to MFHP, 17 February, 25 April 1929, *BPA*.

9. Henry P. Coolidge (1914–99), 'Notes on Meeting Beatrix Potter', Lecture at the Boston Museum of Fine Arts, 1977. Coolidge to Judy Taylor Hough, 30 October 1990, *LTC*, 210–14. 'Obituary. Henry Parsons Coolidge', *Lincoln Journal* (14 January 1999); obituary, *Boston Globe* (13 January 1999). Interview with Judith Coolidge Jones, 17 May 2005. Mary-Abigail ('Gail') Parsons Coolidge was the daughter of a Unitarian family from Kennebunk, Maine and New York City. At the time of this visit Gail Coolidge was a director of the WEIU.

10. BPH to GPC, 15 September 1927, *BPA*.

11. *LTC*, 212.

12. Coolidge, 'Notes on Meeting Beatrix Potter'. Henry P. had finished his studies at Belmont Hill School near Boston and went to Phillips Exeter Academy in New Hampshire. He entered Harvard College in 1933, earning two degrees in English. He served as Instructor in English there and at Tufts University.

13. Ibid. See *BPA*, illustrations 132, 135, 143; *LTC*, 212. It is impossible to know exactly which drawings Beatrix gave Henry P. on this visit except for the ones she dated on the picture. She generously gave him others on subsequent visits. *HWBP*, 203. BPH to BMM, 11 October 1940, *BPA*.

14. BPH to GPC, 21 September 1927, *BPA*; Coolidge, 'Notes on Meeting Beatrix Potter'.

15. BPH to GPC, 21 September 1927, *BPA*.

16. BPH to GPC, 30 September 1927, *BPA*.

17. Ibid.

18. Henry P. wrote an account of his visit to Hill Top and Beatrix Potter which Mahony published as 'A Visit to Beatrix Potter', *The Horn Book* (February 1928), 48–50.

19. These stories would become part of *The Fairy Caravan* (1929).

20. BPH to HPC, 28 June 1928, *BPA*.

21. BPH to HPC, 10 December 1928, *BPA*. 'Birds' Place' and 'Over the

Hills and Far Away' were sent to Henry P. 'Birds' Place' was a part of Edmund Potter's property at Camfield Place near Essenden in Hertfordshire. The *Almanac* was published in September 1928.

22. BPH to Mrs Charles Hopkinson, 12 December 1927, *Letters*, 309. Alexander McKay (1886–1953) and his brother James inherited their father's distinguished Philadelphia publishing firm in 1918 and established their children's list by buying Street and Smith's extensive line of children's books, among others. There is evidence that sometime in the mid-1930s, Alexander McKay bought an Altemus piracy of *The Tale of Peter Rabbit*, published about 1907, when Altemus went out of business. The title appears for sale in the David McKay catalogue for 1935. There is no indication that Beatrix, Frederick Warne & Co. or *The Horn Book* was ever aware of this offering. It appears McKay waited to include it in his catalogue until he was fairly certain Beatrix would not publish more books in the USA. Obituary, Alexander McKay, *New York Times* (5 September 1953). John Tebbel, *A History of Book Publishing in the United States*, 2 vols. (1975), vol. ii, pp. 421–3.

23. *ASC*, 165. Stephens was a double relation: brother to Fruing's wife Mary and the stepson of Fruing's sister Edith. He was thus Fruing's step-nephew as well as his brother-in-law.

24. Ibid. *BP Journal* (16 April 1885), 146; (24 August 1895), 397.

25. BPH to HPC, 28, 29 June 1928, *BPA*.

26. Ibid. Beatrix Potter, 'Over the Hills and Far Away', *The Horn Book* (February 1929), 3–10; Beatrix Potter, *The Fairy Caravan* (London, 1929). Mary Hutton to BPH, 21 November 1929, NT.

27. Willow Taylor, *Through the Pages of My Life*, edited by Judy Taylor (2000), 76–7. Willow grew up at Tower Bank, the inn next door to Hill Top, where her parents were the innkeepers. She became Curator of Hill Top in 1971, serving until 1985 and volunteering thereafter.

28. 'Inventory of the Household Furnishings of No. 2 Bolton Gardens, 1914'. BPH to ELC, 26 April 1924, *ELCL*; BPH to FC, 27 December 1924, NT; BPH to MFHP, 13 July 1936, *BPA*.

29. The SPAB was founded in 1877 by William Morris. Many of the Pre-Raphaelite painters whom Beatrix admired were early members. BPH to MFHP, 10 February 1928, *BPA*; Philip Venning to Enid Bassom, 16 September 1998, BPS.

30. BPH to GN, 17 October 1928, V&A; BPH to GPC, 20 November 1928, *BPA*. Jack Heelis was the youngest child of William's brother,

Thomas Heelis, the Rector of Crosthwaite, and Ada. After nearly five years they moved to a place below Belmount. *TMH*, 39–41.

31. BPH to GPC, 20 November 1928, *BPA*. Copy of contract between Mrs H. B. Heelis and David McKay for US book rights in 'The Caravan Stories', 19 December 1928, BPS. Royalty began at 10 per cent and went to 15 per cent after 20,000 copies. There was an additional 6 per cent on supplementary reading editions. BPS. BPH to AMK, 18 January, 28 March 1929, *BPA*.

32. BPH to AMK, 28 February, 30 June, 28 July 1929, *BPA*.

33. BPH to AMK, 28 March, 11 October 1929, *BPA*. *HWBP*, 292–4, 431. McKay was not above publishing Potter piracies only six years later.

34. BPH to AMK, 23 August, 11 October 1929; BPH to HPC, 27 October 1929, *BPA*.

35. BPH to AMK, 31 October 1929, *BPA*: Alice M. Jordan, 'The Fairy Caravan by Beatrix Potter', *The Horn Book* (November 1929), 9–11. Jordan was a friend and colleague of Bertha Mahony at the time she opened the Bookshop. Later Jordan became editor of the book review section. Helen Chrystie, reviewing it in *Saturday Review of Literature*, thought it 'a bit of a jumble', but called the sketches 'inexhaustibly delightful'. The *New York Herald Tribune* reviewer applauded the 'beauty and poetry of the tale', along with the 'neat economy of phrase that made the earlier books such a delight to read aloud to children' (Helen Chrystie, 'Two Hemispheres', *Saturday Review of Literature* (16 November 1929), 430; Marcia Dalphin, 'Beatrix Potter's World', *New York Herald Tribune* (17 November 1929), 7).

36. BPH to GPC, 9 December 1929, *BPA*.

37. Storey, 'Recollections'. BPH to JM, 15 January 1931, *ML*.

38. BPH to AMK, 20 February 1929, *Letters*, 313; BPH to AMK, 31 October 1929; BPH to GPC, 9 December 1929, *BPA*; BPH to HPC, 1 January 1930, *BPA*. Karen J. Lightner, 'The Fairy Caravan "Explained"', *BPS Studies*, 7 (1997), 60–74, gives an explanation of the 'explains'. Many versions exist. The 'explains' were so vital to appreciating the book that they were later published as part of the endmatter. A list of Potter's 'explains' was published in *HWPB*, 296–305. Bruce L. Thompson also made some corrections and additions which add to the identification of places and her meaning; see BLT papers, CRO/K.

39. BPH to AMK, 17 December 1929, *BPA*. *HWBP*, 256–8. An early

version of the story comes from a letter to her father from Ilfracombe in 1883. *ASC*, 171. BPH to BMM, 24 November 1941, *BPA*.

40. BPH to AMK, 21 June, 8, 15 July, 9 September 1930, *BPA. HWBP*, 257. Copy of contract between Mrs H. B. Heelis and David McKay for the US book rights in *The Tale of Little Pig Robinson*, 7 February 1930, BPS. McKay offered the same percentage scale of royalties as *The Fairy Caravan*, as well as an advance of £200. BPS.

41. BPH to AMK, 9 September 1930, *BPA. HWBP*, 256–62. Ruth K. MacDonald, *Beatrix Potter* (1986), 83–6. Some critics have suggested that Potter realized her last writings were inferior, which was why she offered them to American publishers. Neither Stephens at Warne's or McKay gave *Little Pig Robinson* the kind of critical response which might have improved the tale.

42. BPH to AMK, 15 July 1930, *BPA*.

18 Ventures

1. BPH to HPC, 27 October 1929, *Letters*, 321.

2. BPH to SHH, 20 October 1929, NT.

3. BPH to SHH, 28 October 1929, *Letters*, 323. Tarn Hows was even then one of the most visited spots in Lakeland. The Brathay is the river which flows down from Elterwater into Windermere.

4. Ibid.

5. Conveyance documents, Monk Coniston Estate, 1930, NT; BPH to SHH, 29 May 1930, NT. Bruce L. Thompson, *The Lake District and the National Trust* (1946), 142–52 for a description of the Monk Coniston properties. Marshall's holdings included High and Low Yewdale, Yew Tree, High and Low Tilberthwaite, Stang End, Boon Crag, High Arnside and Rose Plantation.

6. BPH to SHH, 21, 17 October 1929, NT.

7. BPH to SHH, 29 May 1930, NT. Beatrix learned after the fact that Marshall signed a letter of intent with the Forestry Commission, but they could not act upon it until the Commission meeting in November 1929.

8. BPH to SHH, October 21, 1929. NT.

9. BPH to SHH, 23, 24, 25, 26 October 1929, NT.

10. BPH to SHH, 25, 27, 30 October 1929, NT.

11. BPH to SHH, 28, 30 October 1929, NT.

12. BPH to SHH, 31 December 1930, NT; BPH to BLT, 23 July 1932, NT.

13. BPH to SHH, 17 November, 12, 21 December 1929, NT.

14. Each of these parcels was described, numbered and coordinated with the number on the 1914 Ordnance Survey Map, along with the area in acres to the third decimal place; NT. 'The Schedule of Beatrix Heelis's Land Conveyances, 15 November 1905–11 November 1943', BPS.

15. John Bailey, 'Preserving the Lakes: A Generous Offer', *The Times*, 15 February 1930.

16. BPH to SHH, 27 May 1930, NT. Miss Holt belonged to a Unitarian family from Liverpool who had made a fortune in shipping.

17. BPH to SHH, 2, 27 March, 29 April 1930, 17, 26 January, 25 February 1931, NT. Beatrix Heelis's Farm Accounts, 1938–1943, BPS. BPH to SHH, 27 February 1931, *Letters*, 342–3.

18. BPH to SHH, 20 July 1932, *Letters*, 348; BPH to BLT, 23 July 1932, *Letters*, 349. It is likely that Beatrix also anonymously gave High Tarn Hows Cottage, which was held back from the main sale of Monk Coniston. Beatrix was anxious to secure it for the Trust and gave it to them as a gift in 1931. Sometime later she decided to make another anonymous gift of Thwaite Farm, which bordered Coniston Water and was already surrounded by Trust property. Her requested anonymity, however, was breached when her gift was mistakenly published in the Trust's annual report for 1932 – an error that annoyed her exceedingly.

19. BPH to SHH, 14 September 1930, NT; BPH to Ivy Steel, 21 October 1930, *DIDJ*; BPH to CC, 13 December 1930, PC; BPH to Helen Dean Fish, 19 September 1930, *BPA*.

20. BPH to SHH, 16, 17, 20 October 1929, NT. The Heelises urged the suitability of a retired naval man, having Lieutenant-Commander Kenneth Duke, the husband of Beatrix's second cousin, Stephanie Hyde Parker, specifically in mind. Samuel Hamer retired as secretary at the end of 1934 and was succeeded by Donald MacLeod Matheson.

21. BPH to BLT, 27 February 1931, NT. Thompson's important survey was published as *National Trust Properties in the Lake District* (*c.* 1933). In 1932 Thompson became Northern Area Representative, the first full-time Trust staff member named anywhere in the country. He was responsible for all the Trust's properties in the Lake District *other* than Monk Coniston.

22. BPH to MFHP, 14 December 1930, *BPA*; BPH to SHH, 8 October 1930, *Letters*, 334; BPH to CC, 13 December 1930, *Letters*, 335–6.

23. BPH to John Bailey, 15 February 1930, *Letters*, 329.

24. BPH to NNH, 5 May 1931, V&A; BPH to June Steel, 2 June 1931, *DIDJ*.

25. Lucy Walker to JM, 15 January 1932, Walker Letters, BPS. Lucy had written earlier of their concern for their employer's health, much run down in caring for her mother.

26. BPH to JM, 23 January 1932, *ML*. Elizabeth Battrick, 'Some Thoughts on Beatrix Potter's Books', *BPSN*, 79 (January 2001), 12–13.

27. BPH to NNH, 5 June 1932; BPH to AMK, 18 December 1932, *Letters*, 352.

28. Certificate of death, Helen Potter, 20 December 1932, County of Westmorland; William was listed as being present at the time of death. See, for example, BPH to HPC, 14 December 1933, *BPA*.

29. BPH to Eleanor Rawnsley, n.d. 1933, quoted in *TBP*, 138.

30. Gross estate, probated: £69,105. Helen's wealth was primarily in bonds and securities that derived from Rupert's estate; Family Division, High Court of Justice, Rupert Potter's Trust, W. B. Potter, deceased. Haddon & Turnbull, Hawick to Wm. Heelis, 2 May 1933, BPS.

31. 'Helen Potter', *Inquirer*, 31 December 1932; 'Death of Bowness Nonagenarian', *Westmorland Gazette*, 24 December 1932. BPH to JM, 31 January 1933, *ML*.

32. Lindeth Howe was sold in March 1933. At the public auction of household contents, Beatrix and William purchased nine items for £22.19s. Circular for the Sale of Lindeth Howe, Storrs Park, Windermere, William J. McVey, 'Public Auction of contents of Lindeth Howe, March 23 & 24, 1933', BPS; bill of sale, Wm. McVey, Auction of Household Contents of Lindeth Howe, BPS.

33. BPH to SHH, telegram, 23 February 1933; BPH to SHH, 23 February, 5 March 1933, *Letters*, 355–7.

34. BPH to CC, 8 April 1934, *Letters*, 361; BPH to Thomas Stoddart, 15 March 1934, PC. She supplied coal and firewood from old fencing, and helped Tommy get a good dog, also supplying dogfood as she did for the dogs at Troutbeck. Beatrix now personally managed three tenanted farms: Hill Top, Troutbeck Park, and the Tilberthwaites, which included Holme Ground and were managed as one property.

35. BPH to Mrs John B. Capper, *c.* 20 November 1930, NT. It is not

known whether she sent the letter, but it would appear she had every intention of doing so. See Letters, *The Times*, 19 November 1930. 'Musical Toads' appeared in *The Times*, 8 November 1930.

36. BPH to Mrs John B. Capper, *c.* 20 November 1930, NT.

37. BPH to SHH, 7 November 1930, NT.

38. 'Wasted Land' is addressed 'Sir', and was written after 1930. 'Oaks', 'Acorns' and 'Of Timber' refer specifically to farms she managed for the Trust at Monk Coniston. All fragments seem written in response to newspaper articles. Reprinted in *HWBP*, 392–5; all in V&A.

39. Inventory of Hill Top Farm, BPG. BPH to ELC, *c.* 1925, *ELCL*. Lists of furniture, BPH to Mrs Thomas Stoddart, n.d. 1934; BPH to Mrs Stoddart, 14 March 1934, PC.

40. Susan Denyer, *At Home with Beatrix Potter: The Creator of Peter Rabbit* (2000), 52–68; and 'Beatrix Potter and the Decorative Arts', *BPS Studies*, 7 (1997), 39–52. BPH to BMM, 11 October 1940, *BPA*. A Windsor chair painted dark green or black is one of the rarest and most valuable examples of this style. Julie Cole, 'Educated Eye: The Windsor Chair', *Southern Accents* (July–August 2005), 72.

41. Alison Smithson, 'Beatrix Potter's Places', *Studio International*, 201 (1988), 20–21 (first published 1967); Graham Murphy, *Founders of the National Trust* (1987), 88–90. BPH to BMM, 13 December 1934, *BPA*. Vivienne Woolf, 'At Home with Samuel Whiskers', *Country Life* (5 December 1991), 13–15.

42. BPH to SHH, 28 November 1932, *Letters*, 350. BPH, 'Yew Tree Farm, Coniston. July 8, 1932', BPG. Powys was SPAB secretary from 1911 until his death in 1936.

43. When the last tenant left in May 1932 Beatrix wrote to Hamer about the 'splendid [Herdwick] sheepstock' at Yew Tree, and urged the purchase of a landlord's flock hoping to make it into a Herdwick stock farm. This was a fight with the Trust that she eventually lost. BPH to SHH, 12, 30 May, 19 July 1932, NT.

44. The autographed letters were put into a large wooden framed case under glass. BPH to MFHP, 18 October 1933, *BPA*. The exact meaning of 'smush' is unknown, but her meaning is clear from the context. BPH, drawing of Yew Tree Farm, Coniston, 8 July 1932, BPG. BPH to Eleanor Rawnsley, 24 October 1934, *Letters*, 367.

45. BPH to BMM, 13 December 1934, *BPA*. Photograph provided to author courtesy of Mrs Jean Birkett, Yew Tree Farm, Coniston. Tourists

and teas returned to Yew Tree Farm in 2004 when the current Trust tenants revived the tea shop. Terry Fletcher, 'Tea with Beatrix Potter', *Cumbria Magazine* (September 2004), 22–3.

46. BPH to BMM, 13 December 1934, *BPA*. William Miller was the owner of the W. F. Whitney Company. Bertha Mahony continued to use her maiden name professionally, and I refer to her hereafter as both Mahony and Miller.

47. Woolf, 'At Home with Samuel Whiskers,' 5–7; Susan Denyer, 'Beatrix Potter and the Decorative Arts', 46–51. BPH to BMM, 13 December 1934, *BPA*.

48. Fragment, on old oak furniture and decoration, n.d., NT. This fragment comes from her reading of Lockwood and, while it was not written to any particular correspondent, she used it as the basis of her letter to Bertha. Clearly she had in mind some further use. BPH to BMM, 11 October 1940, *BPA*. The text is different from that illustrated in Denyer's book, suggesting there are several versions of her notes. Denyer, *At Home*, 53, 70.

49. BPH to NNH, 18 December 1933, V&A; BPH to SHH, 26 January 1933, NT; BPH to CC, 19 December 1933, *Letters*, 360; BPH to Nora Burt, 30 December 1933, NT. Fanny Cooper was married to a physician, Dr Charles Cooper; after Fanny's death in late 1933, BPH continued to correspond with her husband. BPH to Charles Cooper, 28 January 1934, NT.

50. BPH to JM, 30 January, 26 March 1934, *ML*; BPH to ELC, 12 April 1934, *ELCL*.

51. BPH to MFHP, 31 August 1934, *BPA*; BPH to CC, 19 December 1933, 8 April 1934, *Letters*, 360–61; BPH to Ivy Steel, 5 August 1935, *DIDJ*.

52. BPH to CC, 8 April 1934, *Letters*, 361. Incomplete letter intended for *Country Life*, c. 1932, on spoiling the Coniston Valley, V&A.

53. BPH to unknown correspondent, on spoiling the Coniston Valley, c. 1937, V&A; BPH to ACM, 17 April, 18 December 1937, *BPA*; BPH to GN, 28 November 1937, V&A.

54. BPH to Editors, *Country Life*, 14 November 1937, CCP; 'Letters', *Country Life*, 27 November 1937. BPH wrote to the editors again to be sure that her letter would be published; BPH to Editors, 14 November 1937, CCP.

55. Harvey May, *BPSN*, 88 (April 2003), 26.

19 Passages

1. BPH to CC, 15 February 1937, NT.

2. Edith Potter Gaddum (1863–1937) was Beatrix's double first cousin. Beatrix was particularly fond of William Gaddum, who was a trustee for her mother and for herself. BPH to GN, 31 January 1936, V&A.

3. Ibid. There is an unconfirmed tale that she could not get the buttons of her dress undone and so slept in it until Mrs Rogerson arrived the next morning.

4. BPH to NNH, 17 December 1936, V&A; BPH to Celia Edwards, 19, 21 October 1937, PC; BPH to GN, 28 November 1937, V&A. During the war Nurse Heaton went about on her bicycle to conserve petrol. Documents of the Nursing Trust (established as the governing board of the Hawkshead, Wray and Sawrey Nursing Charity), which were once in the possession of the firm of Gately and Heelis, have been lost.

5. BPH to NB, 30 March, 18 December 1935, NT; BPH to Dr Henderson, 10 February 1931, NT; BPH to Mary Wilkinson, 19 September 1930, FLP.

6. John Heelis, 'On William Heelis', 11 August 1985, PC. *ASC*, 183. [Mary Agnes Rogerson,] 'Beatrix Potter's Housekeeper Looks Back on Life at Sawrey', *Westmorland Gazette* (29 July 1966). Storey, 'Recollections'.

7. ASC, 183. Elizabeth Battrick, 'Some Thoughts on Beatrix Potter's Books', *BPSN*, 79 (January 2001), 13.

8. BPH to MFHP, 1 March, 13 July 1936; *BPH* to Betty Harris Stevens, 13 July 1936, *BPA*. Beatrix herself is inconsistent with the spelling of the dogs' names.

9. BPH to Ivy Steel, 14 April 1936, *DIDJ*; BPH to Miss Dobson, 26 October 1936, PC.

10. BPH to Betty Harris Stevens, 4 September 1930, *BPA*. Betty married Richard K. Stevens in April 1931. Mrs Stevens's reminiscence, Beatrix Potter Colloquium, FLP, 1966.

11. BPH to Ivy Steel, 20 January, 14 April 1936, *DIDJ*.

12. BPH to Ivy Steel, 1 June 1936, *DIDJ*; BPH to Dick and Betty Stevens, 10 September 1936, *BPA*. *LTC*, 193–7. BPH to Ivy Steel, 27 August 1936; BPH to June Steel, 20 September 1936, *DIDJ*. BPH's letters to

Ivy continued until September 1943. Beatrix's letters are in the Toronto Public Library as part of the Osborne and Lillian H. Smith Collections.

13. BPH to child friends in Denver, 12 July 1936, Denver Public Library. *ASC*, 185. See *LTC*, 15. Noel Moore (1887–1969) retired from the London mission in 1955 and lived near his brother Eric, serving as chaplain to an Anglican convent for mentally retarded girls. His career in the Church, however, was marred by a conviction for paedophilia in 1951, although he was permitted to serve as Vicar to St Mary's Church, Buxted, East Sussex, after four years in prison. 'Child Abuse Shame of Boy Inspired Peter Rabbit', *Mail on Sunday*, 28 May 2006, 51. Selwyn Goodacre, 'Beatrix Potter and the Moores', *BPS Studies*, 11 (2005), 60–69.

14. These included: Busk Farm, Dale End, Penny Hill Farm, Low Oxenfell Farm, the Elterwater closes and Great Intake. Conveyance schedule and description of Heelis Properties, 1943, BPS. Bruce L. Thompson, *The Lake District and the National Trust* (1946), 140–52, 173–5.

15. Delmar Banner (1896–1983). BPH to DB, 4 October 1936, V&A.

16. Josefina's given name was sometimes Anglicized as 'Josephina', a spelling which Beatrix occasionally uses. The chronology of their friendship is difficult to untangle as both Delmar and Josefina published memoirs of their friendship with Potter. Delmar published an 'Appreciation' in *The Times* (30 December 1943), and another, 'Memories of Beatrix Potter', *Nineteenth Century and After*, 140 (October 1946), 230–32. From the poetic style of both pieces, however, it is likely that Josefina was the primary author, as Delmar's style was extremely pedantic. Both contain similar phrasing to interviews Josefina gave to W. R. Mitchell and other Lakeland historians. In a reprinted edition of Banner's 'Memories of Beatrix Potter', *'So I Shall Tell You a Story . . .': Encounters with Beatrix Potter* (1993), 44–50, Judy Taylor included excerpts from a letter from Josefina Banner to Margaret Lane. Margaret Lewis, *Josefina de Vasconcellos: Her Life and Art* (2002), 53–67. BPH to DB, 8, 23 September, 4 October 1936, V&A. Josefina's manuscript 'Posted at Sawrey, selections from letters set in a Patchwork', V&A, written about 1961, was considered by C. W. Stephens at Warne's and by Leslie Linder, but proved unsuitable for publication. Josefina de Vasconcellos, *She was Loved: Memories of Beatrix Potter* (2003) contains some of the same material and was published when she was 98. She died in July 2005 at the age of 100.

17. BPH to DB, 8, 14 September 1936, V&A. Lewis, *Josefina de Vasconcellos*, 53–64.

18. Ibid. 69–71. BPH to DB, 23 September, 11, 13 October 1936, V&A. The Banners subsequently rented Heathwaite Farm. In 1939 they finally were able to buy an old Cumbrian farmhouse called The Bield in Little Langdale, where Beatrix visited them. It was a perfect spot with a spectacular view of Little Langdale Tarn, Pike of Blisco, and the high fells.

19. Elizabeth Battrick, transcript, 'Recollections of Josefina de Vasconcellos,' 4 April 1990, Ambleside, NT. Hereafter cited as JDV, 'Recollections'. Lewis, *Josefina de Vasconcellos*, 9, 42–65. There are many, sometimes conflicting, versions of this initial meeting because Josefina was interviewed so many times that story has become part of the mythology of both women.

20. JDV, 'Recollections'. Delmar Banner's portrait of Beatrix Potter, painted in 1938, shows her in similar apparel, though the tweed coat she was wearing in 1936 was probably made of coarser Herdwick wool than the lovat coat he painted. Delmar Banner, 'Memories of Beatrix Potter' (1946). BPH to DB and 'Pig-wig' Banner, 1 December 1936, V&A.

21. Banner, 'Memories', in Taylor, *'So I Shall Tell You a Story . . .'*, 40.

22. BPH to DB, 7 October 1937, V&A.

23. Ibid.; BPH to JDV, 28 February 1938, V&A. Lewis, *Josefina de Vasconcellos*, 81. Banner's portrait hung at Hill Top until after William Heelis's death in 1945. In 1948 Banner presented it to the National Portrait Gallery, London.

24. Lewis's biography details the isolation of Josefina's married life and the triumphs of her artistic one. JDV, 'Posted at Sawrey'. W. R. Mitchell, 'Encounters with Beatrix Potter', *Cumbria Magazine* (June 1986), 161–4, and *Beatrix Potter: Her Life in the Lake District* (1998), 94–7.

25. BPH to ELC, 31 January 1937, *ELCL*.

26. BPH to ELC, 31 January, 22 April 1937, *ELCL*; BPH to NNH, 5 March, 4 April, 19 May 1937, V&A.

27. BPH to JM, 25 February 1937, *ML*.

28. Galloways are polled, meaning hornless, but were not always so. Beatrix commented on hornless cattle in Scotland in the 1880s. Patricia Pruitt, 'Galloway Cattle', *Breeds of Livestock* (1997).

29. BPH to CC, 15 February 1937, NT; BPH to JM, 25 February 1937,

ML. Moscrop's brother Richard raised cattle and Beatrix frequently asked Joseph to consult with him about prices at the big Scottish fair at Road Head, or at dispersal sales where she sometimes bought cattle.

30. Annual valuation of farming stock, implements, etc. at Hill Top, Troutbeck Park Farm, Tilberthwaite Farm for 1937, 1939, BPS.

31. BPH to JM, 10 February, 2, 20 March 1938, *ML*; C. S. Forrester to BPH, 15 April 1938, PC.

32. John Hammond, Jr., I. L. Mason and T. J. Robinson, *Hammond's Farm Animals* (1940, 1971), 79–90.

33. BPH to DMM, 22 April 1936, *Letters*, 377.

34. Thompson was born 24 February 1907 in Bowness and died at Troutbeck at the age of 70 on 10 March 1977; obituary, *Westmorland Gazette*, 18 March 1977. Bruce L. Thompson, *National Trust Properties in the Lake District* (*c.* 1933). Thompson was appointed land agent in 1936 but did not take over Monk Coniston until January 1937. *Letters*, 316n. Interview with Eileen Jay, historian, trustee, and past president of the Armitt Trust Library, Rogerground, Hawkshead, November 2001 and following.

35. Eileen Jay to the author, 25 November 2001. The Rigg family had made a fortune when the railways reached Windermere, and in the coach trade that followed. In 1939 Thompson was named honorary librarian of the Armitt. Thompson was active in the Troutbeck parish and, after 1936 frequently worshipped at the simple Jesus church in Troutbeck Valley where Beatrix sometimes attended.

36. BPH to Bruce Logan, 14 October 1924, 4 October 1935, PC. Storey, 'Recollections'. Papers of Bruce Logan Thompson, CRO/K: Eileen Jay, *The Armitt Story, Ambleside* (1998), 59–62. Thompson also served as president of the Fell Pony Society after the Second World War. After Thompson retired as land agent, about 1946, he published the first history of the National Trust in the Lake District, a distinguished work of local history and culture that still remains authoritative. A later anthology, *The Prose of Lakeland* (1954), published by Warne's, follows the style of Rawnsley's collections of Lakeland writers and writing. Included in Thompson's volume is a selection from Potter's *The Fairy Caravan*, a work which he admired for its depiction of the local countryside and on which he left extensive notes.

37. BPH to DMM, 22 April 1936, *Letters*, 377.

38. Ibid. The Trust's portion included Low Hallgarth Farm, Yew Tree

Farm, with part of High Yewdale Farm, land on Holme Fell, Tarn
Hows, including Rose Castle Cottage and High and Low Tilberthwaite
and Holme Ground farms, which Beatrix had rented back from the
Trust in 1934 and managed as one property. After 1937 she was merely
another Trust tenant – a status that was not well suited to her style or
temperament.

The following Coniston farms are those BPH continued to own and
manage herself: High and Low Yewdale, including grazing rights on
Coniston Fell and a flock of 378 sheep, Far End Farm, High Park Farm,
Stang End Farm, including cottages and woodlands, and High and Low
Oxenfell Farm, its woodlands and cottages.

39. BPH to BLT, 8 May, 26 June, 20, 22 July 1937, NT; BLT to DMM,
    31 October 1939, NT; BPH to BLT, 4, 13, 14, 28 January 1937, NT.
40. BPH to BLT, 11, 17 January 1938, NT.
41. BPH to BLT, 2 February 1938, NT.
42. BPH to DMM, 9 May 1938, NT.
43. BPH to DMM, 3, 9, 11, 18 May 1938, NT; DMM to BPH, 20 May
    1938, NT.
44. BPH to DMM, 17 October 1939, NT.
45. BPH to BLT, 2 October 1939; BPH to DMM, 17, 21 October 1939,
    NT. Beatrix corrected Matheson, telling him she did not say 'Thompson
    was unsatisfactory as the Trust's representative,' only that 'he shows
    no judgement in dealing with trees and woods at Coniston'.
46. Her letters to the Estates Committee are not extant, nor is Matheson's
    first letter to Thompson, warning that fresh trouble was brewing at
    Monk Coniston; *Letters*, 410n.
47. DMM to BLT, 30 October 1939; DMM to BPH, 30 October 1939;
    BLT to DMM, 31 October 1939, NT.
48. BPH to ELC, 9 December 1939, *ELCL*.
49. Schedule of Heelis Properties, 1943. 'Dwelling house and premises
    known as Belmount Hall with woods and fields near Hawkshead',
    28 August 1937, BPS. BPH to CC, 18 March 1939, *Letters*, 396–7. Carl
    Weber, *Hardy and the Lady from Madison Square* (1952), 241.
50. BPH to MFHP, 14 December 1937, *BPA*; BPH to CC, 18 March
    1939, *Letters*, 396.
51. BPH to MFHP, 4 October 1938; BPH to ACM, 17 November 1938,
    BPA.
52. BPH to DH, November 1938, V&A.

53. BPH to DH, 31 October, 7 November 1938, V&A; BPH to June Steel, 26 November 1938, *DIDJ*; BPH to ACM, 17 November 1938, *BPA*; BPH to NNH, 30 November 1938, V&A. A caruncle is caused by the prolapse of the epithelial lining of the urethra through the external urethral opening. The tissues heap up and bleed severely. The condition was treated by surgical excision and cautery, but the results of such procedures were rarely satisfactory. Ann Coleville to the author, 11 January 2002.

54. BPH to BMM, 11 December 1938, *BPA*.

55. BPH to MFHP, 13 December 1938, *BPA*; BPH to CC, 15 February 1937, *Letters*, 384–5.

20 Challenges

1. BPH to CC, 18 March 1939, *Letters*, 396–7; BPH to JM, 23 January 1939, *ML*.

2. BPH to MFHP, 3 July, 24 August 1939, *BPA*.

3. BPH to NNH, 15 April, 6 December 1931, BPS.

4. BPH to NNH, 26 February 1933, BPS; BPH to DH, February 1939, *Letters*, 395; BPH to Hettie Douglas, 31 March 1939, *Letters*, 402. *TMH*, 38–9.

5. BPH to JM, 24 March 1939, *ML*; BPH to Nora Burt, 29 March 1939, NT; BPH to MFHP, 30 March 1939, *BPA*.

6. Handwritten will of Beatrix Heelis, together with handwritten list of legacies, 31 March 1939, BPS. BPH to Nora Burt, 29 March 1939, NT; BPH to DMM, 31 March 1939; DMM to BLT, 3 April 1939; William Heelis to BLT, 4 April 1939, NT; BPH to ACM, 13 April 1939, *BPA*.

7. BPH to DH and Cecily Mills, 30 March 1939, *Letters*, 398–9.

8. BPH to MFHP, 30 March 1939, *BPA*.

9. BPH to ACM, 30 March 1939, *BPA*.

10. BPH to DH, 16? April 1939, *Letters*, 403; BPH to ACM, 13 April 1939, *BPA;* Arthur Alexander Gemmell (1892–1960), the son of a prominent Liverpool gynaecologist, had a distinguished career. His progression up the professional ranks was unusually rapid, and it is likely that his surgical experience in gynaecology was somewhat limited because of it. He was considered a superb clinician and prospered, becoming President of the Royal College of Obstetricians and Gynae-

cologists (1952–5) and was knighted in 1955. He performed a subtotal, rather than a complete, hysterectomy in 1939, leaving the cervix intact, which then could develop cancer. The fact that he used a mid-line abdominal incision, which was common practice, rather than a Pfannenstiel's or transverse incision, meant there was a greater risk of the incision bursting, which unfortunately was exactly what happened. Ann Coleville, John F. Nunn and Dr Harold Francis, once Gemmell's colleague at Liverpool, contributed to my understanding of the medical science and procedures used in 1939. The interpretation of the material they have shared is my own.

11. BPH to CC, 5 June 1939, NT.

12. BPH to MFHP, 3 July 1939, *BPA*; Lucy Walker to JM, 21 July 1939, BPS.

13. BPH to MFHP, 3 July 1939, *BPA*; BPH to ELC, 19 July 1939, *ELCL*; BPH to Cecily Mills, July 1939; BPH to Nora Burt, 28 July 1939, NT.

14. BPH to ELC, 10 May 1939, *ELCL*; BPH to DH, 7 November 1938, V&A.

15. BPH to ELC, 10 May 1939, *ELCL*; BPH to Nora Burt, 28 July 1939, NT.

16. BPH to ELC, 10 May 1939, *ELCL*.

17. BPH to ELC, 9 December 1939, *ELCL*; BPH to Ivy Steel, 11 October 1939, *DIDJ*.

18. BPH to ELC, 9 December 1939, *ELCL*. BPH to June Steel, 11 October 1939, *DIDJ*; BPH to Mrs Charles Hopkinson, 3 November 1939, *BPA*. At the end of August women and children were evacuated from London, and were sent to 'safe' communities away from the large cities. Evacuees could be from the next town, or from many miles away. Homeowners with extra rooms in their houses or extra buildings could be ordered to take them in.

19. Ibid.; BPH to GN, 20 December 1939, V&A; BPH to Nora Burt, 4 January 1940, NT; BPH to JM, 9 January 1940, *ML*.

20. BPH to ACM, 25 May 1940, *BPA*. The Hyde Parkers included two adults, two children and a nanny. Beatrix's first mention of their residence at Hill Top is June 1940.

21. Ulla Hyde Parker, *Cousin Beatie: A Memory of Beatrix Potter* (1981), 34–8. *ASC*, 193–4. The Hyde Parkers occupied Hill Top until May 1941 when they were able to move back to Suffolk. Melford Hall, however, remained an army bivouac, and was badly damaged by

military occupation as well as by fire in 1942. Ulla Hyde Parker's reminiscences contain a number of arresting personal insights, but are factually inaccurate. BPH to MFHP, 29 June, 14 August 1940, *BPA*.

22. BPH to ACM, 25 May 1940, *BPA*.
23. BPH to Stephanie and Ken Duke, 28 May 1940, PC; BPH to Betty Stevens, 25 May 1940, *BPA*.
24. BPH to ACM, 5, 25 June 1940; BPH to MFHP, 13, 29 June 1940, *BPA*.
25. BPH to MFHP, 11 July 1940, 24 July 1940, *BPA*.
26. BPH to MFHP, 24 July 1940, *BPA*.
27. BPH to MFHP, 13 June 1940; BPH to BMM, 30 July 1940, *BPA*.
28. BPH to BMM, 13 December 1934, *BPA*. Quoted in Judy Taylor, *So I Shall Tell You a Story . . .: Encounters with Beatrix Potter* (1993), 32.
29. BPH to MFHP, 13 December 1933, 4 February 1935, *BPA*. Graham Greene, 'Beatrix Potter: A Critical Estimate', *London Mercury* (1933), reprinted in Sheila Egoff *et al.*, *Only Connect: Readings on Children's Literature* (1980), 265 and in Taylor, '*So I Shall Tell*', 24–32. When this essay was reprinted in his *Collected Essays* in 1969 Greene revealed that Beatrix had written an 'acid letter' in which she had 'denied any emotional disturbance' at the time; Taylor, 32. Beatrix's letter to Greene, if extant, has never been published. Grinstein, *The Remarkable Beatrix Potter* (1995), 197–206, explores Potter's feelings of aggression in *Mr Tod* along the same psychoanalytical lines.
30. BPH to BMM, 13 December 1934, 30 July 1940, *BPA*. Nancy Dean was BMM's step-granddaughter, and she remembers how she loved hearing the 'Caravan' stories read aloud to her; interview with Nancy Dean Kingman, 5 November 2005.
31. BPH to Nancy Dean, 30 July 1940, *BPA*. This letter and BP's revised biographical statement are also published as part of Miller's *Horn Book* article.
32. BPH to BMM, 11 October, 25 November 1940, *BPA*; Bertha Mahony Miller, 'Beatrix Potter and Her Nursery Classics', *The Horn Book* (May 1941), 230–38.
33. BPH to BMM, 25 November 1940, *Letters*, 422–3. In this recollection she claimed not to know how she chose the name 'McGregor'.
34. BPH to BMM, 30 July 1940; 24 November 1941, *BPA*. *HWBP*, 328n.
35. Sally Benson was a composite of several old countrywomen Beatrix had known and admired. She had heard their stories through the district nurse who called on them in their infirm years.

36. BPH to BMM, 25 November 1940, *BPA*. Beatrix Potter, 'Wag-by-Wa'', in *HWBP*, 332–5. Potter gives the title as 'Wag-by-the-Wall' in a letter to BMM, 28 August 1943. The MS version, the only one remaining out of private hands, has few changes from Linder's version. *Horn Book* Records, Simmons College Archive.

37. BPH to NNH, 8 August 1940, PC; BPH to MFHP, 14 August 1940, *BPA*.

38. BPH to Betty Stevens, 19 September 1940, *BPA*; BPH to BMM, *BPA*, 213. Bolton Gardens was destroyed on 10 October 1940. It is now, quite fittingly, the site of the Bousfield Primary School. *ASC*, 212.

39. BPH to JM, 5 December 1940, *ML*.

40. BPH to MFHP, 24 December 1940. *BPA*; BPH to JM, 18 January 1941, *ML*.

41. BPH to Ivy Steel, 16 November 1940, *DIDJ*; BPH to BMM, 24 November 1941, *BPA*.

42. BPH to NNH, 15 February 1941, V&A; BPH to Arthur Stephens, 23 February, 19 April 1941, *Letters*, 424, 427.

43. BPH to ELC, 8 May 1941, *ELCL*. Choyce was still at Hill Top for Christmas 1942, but gone by late spring 1943. She worked washing dishes for the evacuees. BPH to NNH, 1 November 1941, V&A.

44. BPH to JM, 18 January, 21, 23, 24, 27 June 1941, *ML*.

45. BPH to Ivy Steel, 16 November 1940, 12 November 1941, 23 March 1941, *DIDJ*.

46. The USA declared war on Japan on 8 December and against Germany and Italy on 11 December 1941. BPH to BMM, 28 December 1941, *BPA*; BPH to Ivy Steel, 12 November 1941, *DIDJ*.

47. BPH to BMM, 24 November 1941, *BPA*; Bertha E. Mahony, 'Beatrix Potter in Letters', *The Horn Book* (May 1944), 223.

48. BPH to BMM, 17, 18 February 1942, *BPA*. The stories as originally sent included characters from *The Fairy Caravan* who have a tea party at High Buildings, which Beatrix cut out of the final version of 'Wag-by-the-Wall'.

49. Ibid.; BPH to BMM, 19 March 1942, *BPA*.

50. BPH to GPC, 12 February 1942, *BPA*; BPH to BMM, 18 June 1942, *BPA*.

21 Reflections

1. BPH to ACM, 31 January 1942, *BPA*; BPH to GC, 12 February 1942, *BPA*; BPH to CJW, 16 September, 2 November, 3 December 1940; 6 July, 23 September 1941; 21 March 1942, Colby College Archives. The last extant letter to Weber was written on 20 May 1942 and contains lengthy quotations from Hardy's letters. Shipments were completed in 1946 by the executors of the Heelis estate.

2. BPH to J. K. Stone, 19 August 1939, 5 June 1940, *Letters*, 406, 416. Stone wrote about his visit to Sawrey in an article, 'The Immortal world of Jemima Puddle-duck', *Christchurch Star* (n.d. 1969).

3. *ASC*, 199–201. BPH to Reginald Hart, 24 October 1942, *Letters*, 452–3; BPH to Ivy Steel, 3 January 1942, *DIDJ*; BPH to Hettie Douglas, 14 January 1942, *Letters*, 435; BPH to Reginald Hart, 16 November 1942, PC. Taylor, 'Alison Hart', *LTC*, 226–7. BPH to BMM, 18, 23, 28 August 1943, *BPA*. For Christmas 1942, Beatrix sent Alison a story called 'The Chinese Umbrella' about her pekes, Miss Choyce and her lost umbrella with a duck's head handle. She made a slightly different version as a present for Miss Choyce. See *LTC* for both versions.

4. BPH to Samuel Cunningham, *TBP* (rev. 1985), 138.

5. Ibid. 150, 154, 157, 163. Cunningham died on 23 August 1946.

6. BPH to Arthur Stephens, 14 May 1942, *Letters*, 445.

7. BPH to BMM, 23 March 1942, *BPA*, letter published in 'The Hunt Breakfast' section of *The Horn Book* (May–June 1942), 130.

8. Beatrix Potter, 'The Lonely Hills', *The Horn Book* (May–June 1942) 153–6. 'The Lonely Hills' was part of the first manuscript booklet that comprised a longer version of 'Wag-by-Wall' and 'The Solitary Mouse', probably written about 1929, but it could also have come from an earlier copybook as a suppressed chapter of *The Fairy Caravan*. *HWBP*, 310, 319–21. BPH to BMM, 17 February 1942, 6 April 1942, *BPA*.

9. BPH to BMM, 13 July 1942, *BPA*.

10. 'So penicillium has arrived . . .' is a sheet torn from a notebook and found in one of Beatrix's sketchbooks after her death. In 1944 William Heelis gave it to Margaret Lane, who gave it and the 1875 sketchbook to Leslie Linder. It is now part of the Linder Bequest, V&A. The late Dr Mary Noble transcribed Beatrix's handwritten note, and made interlinear comments on the probable mould species she referred to.

There are at least five watercolour drawings of fungi in which Beatrix notes the presence of *penicillium* in the collection at LDM@TA, including her 1896 drawing of the witches' butter, *Tremella intumescens*, at Woodcote.

11. Penicillin's antibacterial properties were noted by John Burdon-Sanderson and John Tyndall, and in the 1880s by Louis Pasteur and Joseph Lister. Its bacterial antagonism was undoubtedly of great interest to Beatrix and Henry Roscoe. Penicillin's modern application was discovered in 1928 by Dr Alexander Fleming at St Mary's Hospital, Paddington. Fleming published his findings in an article in the *British Journal of Experimental Pathology*, 10 (1929), 226–36. His discovery was not sufficiently pursued or widely publicized. In 1939 Dr Howard Florey began intensive research at Oxford University. It is unlikely that Beatrix knew anything about Fleming's early article. Her note more likely dates to 1942–3, when she undoubtedly read a leader in *The Times* (27 August 1942) which drew attention to the new drug, and followed the subsequent dispute over whether Fleming or Florey should be given credit for its discovery. Her reference to 'forty years earlier' would be to 1902–3 when she was still doing mycological research. I am grateful to Dr Kevin Brown, Trust Archivist & Alexander Fleming Laboratory Museum Curator, St Mary's NHS Trust, London, for his help in dating this fragment. Ronald Hare, *The Birth of Penicillin* (1970), 105–69; Council of the Pharmaceutical Society of Great Britain, *Antibiotics* (1952), 1–5.

12. BPH to Ivy Steel, 17 July 1942, *DIDJ*; Girl Guide Log Book, 5 August 1940; Skylark Guide Log Book, 5–6, August 1940, Girlguiding, Cumbria South Archives, CRO/B: Judy Taylor, interview with Miss Joy Brownlow, 3 July 1985, quoted in *ASC*, 202.

13. Windermere, Ambleside, Hawkshead Guide Log Book, 28 July 1943, Cumbria South Archives, CRO/B.

14. BPH to Joy Brownlow, 30 July, 13 August 1943, Girlguiding, Cumbria South Archives, CRO/C; BPH to Arthur Stephens, 30 July 1943, FWA.

15. BPH to MFHP, 18 November 1942; BPH to GPC, 19 November 1942, *BPA*.

16. BPH to BMM, 18 August 1943, *BPA*; BPH to JM, April 1943, *ML*; BPH to C. S. Forrester, 25 January, 11 March 1943, BPS. In April Beatrix purchased The Lodge, a house, cottage and various outbuildings

in Hawkshead and an adjoining field known as 'Ewan Meadow', from William Heelis and John Heelis. In November she bought Low and High Loanthwaite Farms, and additional land, about eighty acres, near Hawkshead, and in December she contracted for the purchase of Tower Bank House, with all outbuildings, parrocks and intakes, nearly fifty acres, in Sawrey. That conveyance was made posthumously on 5 April 1944. Heelis Schedule of Conveyances, BPS.

17. BPH to Charlie Cooper, 18 August 1943, NT.

18. BPH to JM, 12 March 1943, *ML*. GW to JM, 15 January 1943, Walker Letters, BPS. Lucy Walker died of cancer in June 1944.

19. Beatrix was elected president for 1944, but did not live to take office. She had often been in the 'chair' at various local meetings. R. H. Lamb's history (1936) makes no mention of Mrs Heelis, or her contributions to Herdwick breeding. For other reasons Lamb also ignores Rawnsley's role in preserving the breed as well as his son Noel's early organizational efforts. BPH to BMM, 18 August 1943, *BPA*; BPH to JM, April 1943, *ML*. Bob Orrell, 'A Breed Apart', *Cumbria Magazine*, 55/6 (September 2005), 30.

20. BPH to ELC, 26 May, 29 June, 16 August 1943, *ELCL*; BPH to NNH, 2 February 1943, BPS.

21. BPH to Ivy Steel, 2 September 1943, *DIDJ*; BPH to Tommy Stoddart, 6 September, 4 October, and two undated, 1943, PC; BPH to George Wilson, 13 October 1943, *Letters*, 460.

22. BPH to BMM, 5 November 1943, *BPA*.

23. BPH to Celia Edwards, 10 November 1943, PC.

24. BPH to MFHP, 13 November 1943; BPH to ACM, 30 November 1943, *BPA*; BPH to GW, 20, 26 November 1943, BPS.

25. BPH to ELC, 30 November 1943, *ELCL*. Beatrix gave the archaeological drawings of the Roman and post-Roman objects found in the Bucklesbury excavations to the Armitt Trust Library in 1935 after consulting with Herbert Bell and touring the Roman camp at Borrans Field. Beatrix Potter Collection, LDM@TA. Jay, *The Armitt Story, Ambleside* (1998), 42–3.

26. BPH to CC, 15 November 1943, NT.

27. BPH to JM, 13 December 1943, *ML*. Tom Storey, 'Recollections', NT: Storey died in March 1986 at the age of 90.

28. BPH to FC, 27 December 1924, NT. Certificate of death, Helen Beatrix Heelis, 22 December 1943; cause of death is given as 'acute bronchitis,

myocarditis, and carcinoma of the uterus'. It was signed by Dr A. Brownlee.

Epilogue: Stewardship

1. 'Register of Cremations Carried out by Corporation of Blackpool at the Crematorium at Carleton', William Heelis and a required witness, Jos. Walker, JP, signed the register as applicants for cremation which was carried out on 24 December 1943. The ashes were delivered to William Heelis, but there is an obvious error in the date on the Register as it reads 21 December 1943. It is possible that the ashes could have been delivered on the 24th but not likely, as it was Christmas Eve. Liz Bienias, Cameteries & Crematorium Officer at Carleton, suspects the correct date is closer to 27 December. Will of William Heelis, undated holograph draft, sent to George Heelis, (*c.* 1944); probated 8 November 1945, Principal Probate Registry. William's gross estate was revised at £91,684. 14*s*. 6*d*.; BPS. Joan Duke, 'Tom Storey', *BPSN*, 21 (June 1986), 1.

2. Will of Helen Beatrix Heelis, 2 March 1944, Principal Probate Registry. She had signed the will, dictated to William, on 31 March 1939.

3. William Heelis to George Heelis, 3 January 1944, BPS; William Heelis to DMM, 10 January 1944, NT. Enid Bassom, 'The National Trust and Beatrix Potter', *BPSN*, 59 (January 1996), 7.

4. Lucy May Walker, funeral notice, 3 January 1945, CRO/C. GW to JM, 16 November 1944, *ML*; William Heelis to JM, February 1944, *ML*.

5. William Heelis to Dr Cooper, 23 February 1944, NT; CC to William Heelis, 6 January, 18 March 1944, CCP.

6. William Heelis to MFHP, 3 April 1944, *BPA*. Beatrix Potter, 'Wag-by-Wall', *The Horn Book* (May–June 1944); contract for US copyright, 28 August 1944, BPS.

7. B. L. Thompson, 'Recollections of Beatrix Potter', n.d. (*c.* 1952), CRO/K. The NT tries to limit visitors to 80,000 per year. Liz Hunter to the author, 19 September 2004.

8. Holograph notes dictated by BPH, Instructions for Disposition of Personal Property, BPS.

9. William Heelis to GW, 27 May 1945, BPS.

10. 'Mrs Heelis' Bequest to the National Trust, Greatest Ever Lakeland

Gift', *The News*, 19 February 1944, FWA. Will of Helen Beatrix Heelis.

11. DMM to William Heelis, 23 December 1944, NT.

12. Will of Helen Beatrix Heelis; will of William Heelis.

13. B. L. Thompson, 'Beatrix Potter's Gift to the Public', *Country Life* (3 March 1944), 370–71. BPH to SHH, 30 December 1930: H. B. Heelis, '"The Lake District as a National Park", or a "National Park in the Lake District?"', letter to *The Times* (?), 17 December 1938, BPS.

14. Sir Martin Holdgate, 'The Ecology of Lakeland, Past, Present and Future', *Cumbrian Wildlife* (August 2001), 10–13.

15. Terry Fletcher, 'Furore at NT over Farm Break-up', *Cumbria Magazine*, 55/8 (November 2005), 22–5.

16. 'Hill Farming is Facing Collapse, Warns Trust', *Westmorland Gazette* (8 July 2005), 3. Bob Orrell, 'Rocket Goes up', *Cumbria Magazine*, 55/9 (December 2005), 33.

Select Bibliography

Books by Beatrix Potter
(published by Frederick Warne, unless otherwise noted)

1901	*The Tale of Peter Rabbit* (privately printed)
1902	*The Tale of Peter Rabbit*
1902	*The Tailor of Gloucester* (privately printed)
1903	*The Tale of Squirrel Nutkin*
1903	*The Tailor of Gloucester*
1904	*The Tale of Benjamin Bunny*
1904	*The Tale of Two Bad Mice*
1905	*The Tale of Mrs. Tiggy-Winkle*
1905	*The Tale of The Pie and The Patty-Pan*
1906	*The Tale of Mr. Jeremy Fisher*
1906	*The Story of A Fierce Bad Rabbit*
1906	*The Story of Miss Moppet*
1907	*The Tale of Tom Kitten*
1908	*The Tale of Jemima Puddle-Duck*
1908	*The Roly-Poly Pudding*; later renamed *The Tale of Samuel Whiskers*
1909	*The Tale of the Flopsy Bunnies*
1909	*The Tale of Ginger and Pickles*
1910	*The Tale of Mrs. Tittlemouse*
1911	*Peter Rabbit's Painting Book*
1911	*The Tale of Timmy Tiptoes*
1912	*The Tale of Mr. Tod*
1913	*The Tale of Pigling Bland*
1917	*Tom Kitten's Painting Book*
1917	*Appley Dapply's Nursery Rhymes*
1918	*The Tale of Johnny Town-Mouse*
1922	*Cecily Parsley's Nursery Rhymes*

1925   *Jemima Puddle-Duck's Painting Book*

1928   *Peter Rabbit's Almanac for 1929*

1929   *The Fairy Caravan* (David McKay, Philadelphia)

1929   *The Fairy Caravan* (privately printed)

1930   *The Tale of Little Pig Robinson* (David McKay, Philadelphia, and Frederick Warne)

1932   *Sister Anne*, with illustrations by Katharine Sturges (David McKay, Philadelphia)

1944   *Wag-by-Wall* (The Horn Book, Boston)

Editions of Beatrix Potter's Work

Potter, Beatrix, *The Art of Beatrix Potter*, selected and arranged by Leslie Linder and W. A. Herring (London: Frederick Warne, 1955; second edition, 1972).

—— *Beatrix Potter Artist & Illustrator, paintings and drawings selected by Anne Stevenson Hobbs* (London: Frederick Warne, 2005).

—— *The Beatrix Potter Collection of Lloyd Cotsen* (Los Angeles: Cotsen Occasional Press, 2004).

—— *Beatrix Potter's Americans: Selected Letters*, edited by Jane Crowell Morse (Boston: Horn Book, 1982).

—— *Beatrix Potter's Art: Paintings and Drawings*, edited by Anne Stevenson Hobbs (London: Frederick Warne, 1989).

—— *Beatrix Potter's Farming Friendship: Lake District Letters to Joseph Moscrop, 1926–1943*, edited by Judy Taylor (London: Beatrix Potter Society, 1998).

—— *Beatrix Potter's Letters*, selected by Judy Taylor (London: Frederick Warne, 1989).

—— *The Choyce Letters: Beatrix Potter to Louie Choyce, 1916–1943*, edited by Judy Taylor (London: Beatrix Potter Society, 1994).

—— *Dear Ivy, Dear June: Letters from Beatrix Potter*, edited by Margaret Crawford Maloney (Toronto: Toronto Public Library, 1977).

—— *The Derwentwater Sketchbook, 1903*, facsimile (London: Frederick Warne, 1984).

—— *A History of the Writings of Beatrix Potter*, edited by Leslie Linder (London: Frederick Warne, 1981, revised edition, 1987).

—— *A Holiday Diary: With a Short History of the Warne Family*, edited and written by Judy Taylor (London: Beatrix Potter Society, 1996).

—— *The Journal of Beatrix Potter, 1881–1897*, transcribed from her code writings by Leslie Linder (London: Frederick Warne, 1966; revised edition, 1989).

—— *Letters to Children from Beatrix Potter*, edited by Judy Taylor (London: Frederick Warne, 1992).

Biography and Criticism

Albert, Susan Wittig, *The Cottage Tales of Beatrix Potter: The Tale of Hill Top Farm; The Tale of Holly How; The Tale of Cuckoo Brow Wood* (New York: Berkley, 2004, 2005, 2006).

Avery, Gillian, 'Beatrix Potter and Social Comedy', *Rylands University of Manchester Bulletin*, 76/3 (Autumn 1994), 185–200.

Bartlett, Wynne K., and Whalley, Joyce Irene, *Beatrix Potter's Derwentwater* (London: Frederick Warne, 1988; revised edition: Leading Edge, 1995).

Battrick, Elizabeth, *Beatrix Potter: The Unknown Years* (London: Armitt Library & Museum Centre; F. Warne & Co., 1999).

—— *The Real World of Beatrix Potter* (Norwich: National Trust and Jarrold Publishing, 1987).

Beatrix Potter Society Studies, i–xi (London: Beatrix Potter Society, 1984–2005).

Clark, Keith, *Beatrix Potter's Gloucester* (London: Frederick Warne, 1988).

Clegg, John, *Beatrix Potter: Artist, Storyteller and Scientist* (Torquay: Torquay Natural History Society, 1989).

Crouch, Marcus, *Beatrix Potter* (London: Bodley Head, 1960).

Denyer, Susan, *At Home with Beatrix Potter: The Creator of Peter Rabbit* (New York: Harry Abrams, 2000).

—— *Beatrix Potter and Her Farms* (London: National Trust, 1992).

Grinstein, Alexander, *The Remarkable Beatrix Potter* (Madison: International Universities Press, 1995).

Heelis, John, *The Tale of Mrs William Heelis – Beatrix Potter* (Phoenix Mill: Sutton Publishing, 1999).

Hobbs, Anne Stevenson, and Whalley, Joyce Irene, *Beatrix Potter: The V&A Collection* (London: Victoria and Albert Museum and Frederick Warne, 1985).

Hurst, John G., *Edmund Potter and Dinting Vale* (Manchester: Edmund Potter and Company, 1948).

Jay, Eileen, Noble, Mary, and Hobbs, Anne Stevenson, *A Victorian Naturalist: Beatrix Potter's Drawings from the Armitt Collection* (London: Frederick Warne, 1992).

King, Arthur, and Stuart, A. F., *The House of Warne: One Hundred Years of Publishing* (London: Frederick Warne, 1965).

Kutzer, M. Daphne, *Beatrix Potter: Writing in Code* (New York: Routledge, 2003).

Lane, Margaret, *Purely for Pleasure* (New York: Alfred Knopf, 1967).

—— *The Magic Years of Beatrix Potter* (London: Frederick Warne, 1978).

—— *The Tale of Beatrix Potter* (London: Frederick Warne, 1946; revised edition 1985).

MacDonald, Ruth K., *Beatrix Potter* (Boston: Twayne Publishers, 1986).

Parker, Peter, 'The Gardens of Beatrix Potter', *Hortus*, 30 (Summer 1994), 106–15.

Peck, Robert McCracken, 'Beatrix Potter, Scientific Illustrator', *Antiques*, 149/6 (June 1996), 868–77.

—— 'The Tale before Peter Rabbit', *International Wildlife*, 20 (Jan.–Feb. 1990), 42–5.

Potter, Edmund, *Picture of a Manufacturing District* (London: James Ridgeway, 1856).

Quinby, Jane, *Beatrix Potter: A Bibliographical Check List* (Stroud: Ian Hodgkins & Co., 1999).

Smithson, Alison, 'Beatrix Potter's Places', *Architectural Design* (Dec. 1967), 89–90.

Taylor, Judy, *Beatrix Potter: Artist, Storyteller and Countrywoman* (London: Frederick Warne, 1986; revised edition, 2002).

—— *Beatrix Potter and Hawkshead* (London: National Trust, 1988).

—— *Beatrix Potter and Hill Top* (London: National Trust, 1989).

—— *That Naughty Rabbit: Beatrix Potter and Peter Rabbit* (London: Frederick Warne, 2002).

—— (ed.), *'So I Shall Tell You a Story . . .': Encounters with Beatrix Potter* (London: Frederick Warne, 1993).

Taylor, Judy, Whalley, Joyce Irene, Hobbs, Anne Stevenson, and Battrick, Elizabeth, *Beatrix Potter, 1866–1943: The Artist and Her World* (London: Frederick Warne and National Trust, 1987).

Taylor, Liz, 'The Tale of Bertram Potter', *Weekend Scotsman* (11 Nov. 1978), 6–7.

Taylor, Willow, *Through the Pages of My Life*, edited by Judy Taylor (London: Beatrix Potter Society, 2000).

Agriculture

Bingham, Roger, *From Fell & Field: A History of the Westmorland County Show, 1799–1999* (Milnthorpe, Cumbria: Cicerone Press, 1999).

Denyer, Susan, *Herdwick Sheep Farming* (London: National Trust, 1993).

Grigg, David B., *English Agriculture: An Historical Perspective* (New York: Basil Blackwell, 1989).

Howkins, Alun, *Reshaping Rural England: A Social History, 1850–1925* (London: HarperCollins Academic, 1991).

Humber, R. D., *Game Cock & Countryman*, with illustrations by John Roberts (London: Cassell, 1966).

Lamb, R. H., *Herdwicks Past and Present: A Study of the Breed* (Penrith: Herald Print Company, 1936, revised 1997).

O'Hagan, Andrew, *The End of British Farming* (London: Profile Books, 2001).

Orrell, Bob, 'A Breed Apart', *Cumbria*, 55/6 (Sept. 2005), 30.

Upton, Jane, and Soden, Dennis, *An Introduction to Keeping Sheep* (Ipswich: Farming Press, 1996).

Whetham, Edith H., *Agrarian History of England and Wales*, vol. viii: *1914–1939*, edited by H. P. R. Finberg and Joan Thirsk (Cambridge: Cambridge University Press, 1978).

Children's Literature, Art and Photography

Alderson, Brian, *Sing a Song for Sixpence: The English Picture Book Tradition and Randolph Caldecott* (Cambridge: Cambridge University Press, 1986).

Avery, Gillian, and Briggs, Julia (eds.), *Children and Their Books* (Oxford: Clarendon Press, 1989).

Barnes, Martin, *Benjamin Bucknell Turner: Rural England through a Victorian Lens* (London: V&A Publications, 2001).

Beatrix Potter's Peter Rabbit: A Children's Classic at 100, edited by Margaret Mackey (Lanham, Md.: Scarecrow Press, 2002).

Bermingham, Ann, *Learning to Draw: Studies in the Cultural History of a Polite and Useful Art* (New Haven: Yale University Press, 2000).

Blount, Margaret, *Animal Land: The Creatures of Children's Fiction* (New York: William Morrow & Company, 1975).

Brooke, Henry, *Leslie Brooke and Johnny Crow* (London: Frederick Warne, 1982).

Brooke, L. Leslie, *Johnny Crow's Garden* (London: Frederick Warne, 1903).

Butler, Marilyn, *Maria Edgeworth: A Literary Biography* (Oxford: Clarendon Press, 1972).

Chignall, Dudley, 'The Man Who Drew for Beatrix Potter – Ernest Aris' (unpublished manuscript, 2004).

Crist, Eileen, *Images of Animals: Anthropomorphism and Animal Mind* (Philadelphia: Temple University Press, 1999).

Darcy, Cornelius P., *The Encouragement of the Fine Arts in Lancashire* (Manchester: Manchester University Press, 1976).

Darton, F. J. Harvey, *Children's Books in England: Five Centuries of Social Life*, third edition, edited by Brian Alderson (Cambridge: Cambridge University Press, 1982).

Golden, Catherine J., 'Beatrix Potter: Naturalist Artist', *Women's Art Journal*, 11/1 (1990), 16–20.

—— (ed.), *Book Illustrated: Text, Image and Culture, 1770–1930* (New Castle, Del.: Oak Knoll Press, 2000).

Goldthwaite, John, *The Natural History of Make-Believe* (New York: Oxford University Press, 1966).

Harvey, Michael, 'Rupert Potter: 'A Victorian Amateur Photographer' (unpublished manuscript, 1979).

—— 'Rupert Potter and Millais', *Creative Camera*, 104 (Feb. 1973), 62–3.

—— 'Ruskin, the Pre-Raphaelites and Photography', Parts 1 & 2, *British Journal of Photography*, 120 (16 March 1973), 234–8; (23 March 1973), 268–72.

Henley, William, 'Randolph Caldecott', *Art Journal* (July 1881), 212.

Hewison, Robert, Warrell, Ian, and Wildman, Stephen, *Ruskin, Turner and the Pre-Raphaelites* (London: Tate Gallery, 2000), 11–19.

Hilton, Mary, Styles, Morag, and Watson, Victor (eds.), *Opening the Nursery Door: Reading, Writing and Childhood, 1600–1900* (London: Routledge, 1997).

Lundin, Anne, *Victorian Horizons: The Reception of the Picture Books of Walter Crane, Randolph Caldecott and Kate Greenaway* (Lanham, Md.: Scarecrow Press, 2001).

MacLeod, Dianne Sachko, *Art and the Victorian Middle Class: Money and the Making of Cultural Identity* (New York: Cambridge University Press, 1996).

Mahony, Bertha E., Lattimer, Louise Payson, and Folmsbee, Beulah (eds.), *Illustrators of Children's Books 1744–1945* (Boston: The Horn Book, 1947).

Muir, Percy, *Children's Books of Yesterday: A Catalogue of an Exhibition Held at 7 Albemarle Street, London, During May 1946* (Detroit: Singing Tree Press, 1970).

—— *Victorian Illustrated Books* (London, 1971).

Paul, Lissa, 'Beatrix Potter and John Everett Millais: Reproductive Technologies and Coolhunting', in Margaret Mackey (ed.), *Beatrix Potter's Peter Rabbit: A Children's Classic at 100* (Lanham, Md.: Scarecrow Press, 2002), 53–75.

Sale, Roger, *Fairy Tales and After: From Snow White to E. B. White* (Cambridge, Mass.: Harvard University Press, 1978).

Scott, Carole, 'Clothed in Nature or Nature Clothed: Dress as Metaphor in the Illustrations of Beatrix Potter and C. M. Barker', *Children's Literature*, 22 (1994), 70–89.

Sendak, Maurice, *Caldecott & Company: Notes on Books and Pictures* (New York: Farrar, Straus, and Giroux, 1988).

Stemp, Robin, 'The Seeing Eye', *Artist* (March 1990), 38–40.

Tucker, Nicholas, 'Fairy Tales and the Early Opponents in Deference of Mrs Trimmer', in Hilton, Styles and Watson (eds.), *Opening the Nursery Door*, 104–16.

—— (ed.), *Suitable for Children? Controversies in Children's Literature* (Berkeley: UCLA Press, 1976).

Contemporaries

Boyd, Nancy, *Three Victorian Women Who Changed Their World: Josephine Butler, Octavia Hill, and Florence Nightingale* (New York: Oxford University Press, 1982).

Brill, Barbara, *William Gaskell 1805–1884: A Portrait* (Manchester: Manchester Literary and Philosophical Society, 1984).

Darley, Gillian, *Octavia Hill: A Life* (London: Constable, 1990).

Fairley, Rob (ed.), *Blackburn's Birds: The Paintings of Jemima Blackburn* (Edinburgh: Canongate, 1993).

Hardy, Gwen, *William Rathbone and the Early History of District Nursing* (Ormskirk: G.W.&A. Hesketh, 1981).

Ponsonby, Laura, *Marianne North at Kew Gardens* (Exeter: Webb & Brower, 1954).

Roscoe, Sir Henry Enfield, *The Life and Experiences of Sir H. E. Roscoe, DCL, LLD, FRS, written by Himself* (London: MacMillan and Co., 1906).

Webb, Beatrice, *My Apprenticeship* (New York: Longmans, Green and Co., 1926).

Weber, Carl J., *Hardy and the Lady from Madison Square* (Port Washington, NY: Kennikat Press, 1952).

Environmental History

Anker, Peder, *Imperial Ecology: Environmental Order in the British Empire, 1895–1945* (Cambridge, Mass.: Harvard University Press, 2001).

Evans, David, *A History of Nature Conservation in Britain* (London: Routledge, 1992).

McGaffey, Beth Ann Knight, 'The Three Founders of the British Conservation Movement, 1865–1895: Robert Preston, Octavia Hill, Hardwicke Drummond Rawnsley', Ph.D. diss. (Texas Christian University, 1978).

Mackenzie, John M., *The Empire of Nature: Hunting Conservation and British Imperialism* (Manchester: Manchester University Press, 1988).

Sheail, John, *An Environmental History of Twentieth-century Britain* (New York: Palgrave, 2002).

Smout, T. C., *Nature Contested: Environmental History in Scotland and Northern England since 1600* (Edinburgh: Edinburgh University Press, 2000).

The Lake District

Battrick, Elizabeth, *'The Most Active Volcano in Europe': Canon Hardwicke Drummond Rawnsley* (Keswick: National Trust, 1995).

Bragg, Melvyn, *Land of the Lakes* (London: Hodder & Stoughton, 1983).

Brunskill, R. W., *Vernacular Architecture of the Lake Counties* (London: Faber, 1987).

Davies, Hunter, *A Walk Around the Lakes* (London: Weidenfeld & Nicolson, 1979).

—— *Beatrix Potter's Lakeland* (London: Frederick Warne, 1988).

Denyer, Susan, and Martin, Janet (eds.), *A Century in the Lake District* (London: National Trust, 1995).

Gambles, Robert, *Out of the Forest: The Natural World and the Place-Names of Cumbria* (Kendal: Laverock Books, 1989).

Halliday, Geoffrey, *A Flora of Cumbria* (Lancaster: University of Lancaster, Centre for North-West Regional Studies, 1997).

Hervy, G. A. K., and Barnes, J. A. G., *Natural History of the Lake District* (London: Frederick Warne, 1970).

Hunt, Irvine, *Lakeland Yesterday*, vol. i (Otley: Smith Settle, 2002).

Jay, Eileen, *The Armitt Story, Ambleside* (Kendal: Loughrigg Press, 1998).

Marshall, J. D., and Walton, John K., *The Lake Counties from 1830 to the Mid-Twentieth Century: A Study in Regional Change* (Manchester: Manchester University Press, 1981).

Mitchell, W. R., *Beatrix Potter: Her Life in the Lake District* (Settle: Castleberg, 1998).

—— *Changing Lakeland* (Kendal: Dalesman Press, 1989).

—— *How They Lived in the Lake District* (Settle: Castleberg, 2002).

—— *Lakeland Dalesfolk* (Kendal: Dalesman Publishing Company, 1983).

—— *Letters from the Lakes* (Settle: Castleberg, 1995).

Murphy, Graham, *Founders of the National Trust* (London: Christopher Helm, 1987).

Rawnsley, Eleanor F., *Canon Rawnsley: An Account of His Life* (Glasgow: Maclehose, Jackson, 1923).

Rawnsley, Revd Hardwicke Drummond, *By Fell and Dale at the English Lakes* (Glasgow: James MacLehose & Sons, 1911).

—— 'Moral Rhymes for the Young', in T. B. A. Saunders (ed.), *Prelates and People of the Lake Counties* (Kendal: no publisher, 1948).

Rawnsley, Rosalind, 'HDR – A Lover of His Fellow Men', *Cumbria*, 37 (October 1987), 409–11.

Rollinson, William, *History of Cumberland and Westmorland* (London: Phillimore & Company, 1978).

—— *Life and Tradition in the Lake District*, foreword by Melvyn Bragg (Kendal: Dalesman Publishing Co., 1974; revised, 1981).

Simpson, John, *'The Most Active Volcano in Europe': A Short Life of Canon Hardwicke Drummond Rawnsley, Vicar of Crosthwaite, Keswick 1883–1917* (Keswick: no publisher, n.d.).

Thompson, Bruce L., 'Beatrix Potter's Gift to the Public', *Country Life* (3 March 1944), 370–71.

Thompson, Bruce L., *The Lake District and the National Trust* (Kendal: Titus Wilson & Sons, 1946).

—— (compiler), 'The National Trust for Places of Historic Interest or Natural Beauty' (Kendal: Cumbria Record Office, *c.* 1949).

Walton, John K., 'Canon Rawnsley and the English Lake District', *Armitt Library Journal*, 1 (1998), 1–17.

Winchester, Angus J. L., *The Harvest of the Hills* (Edinburgh: University of Edinburgh Press, 2000).

Mycology, Palaeontology and Archaeology

Coates, Henry, *A Perthshire Naturalist: Charles McIntosh of Inver* (London: T. Fisher Unwin, 1923).

Findlay, W. P. K., *Wayside and Woodland Fungi* (London: Frederick Warne, 1967).

Gardiner, Brian, 'Beatrix Potter's Fossils and Her Interest in Geology', *The Linnean*, 16/1 (Jan. 2000), 31–47.

Gibson, Colin, 'The Perthshire Naturalist', *Scots Magazine*, 97/2 (1972), 117–25.

Gilpatrick, Naomi, 'The Secret Life of Beatrix Potter', *Natural History Magazine*, 81 (Oct. 1972), 38–41, 88–97.

Jay, Eileen, *A Tale of London Past: Beatrix Potter's Archaeological Paintings from the Armitt Collection* (London: Frederick Warne for the Armitt Trust, 1990).

Noble, Mary, 'Beatrix Potter: Mycologist and Biorecorder', *Journal of the Scottish Wildlife Trust*, 17/3 (Sept. 1981), 15–18.

—— 'Beatrix Potter, Naturalist & Mycologist and Charles McIntosh, the "Perthshire Naturalist"', *Notes from the Royal Botanic Garden Edinburgh*, 44/3 (1987), 607–27.

—— 'The Old Man of the Woods', *Beatrix Potter Society Newsletter*, 31 (December 1988–January 1989), 5–6.

—— and Watling, Roy, 'Cup-fungus or Basidiomycete, and Potterism', *Bulletin of the British Mycological Society*, 20 (1986), 145–7.

Taylor, M. A., and Rodger, R. H. (eds.), *A Fascinating Acquaintance: Charles Mcintosh and Beatrix Potter* (Perth: Perth Museum & Art Gallery, 2003).

Wakeford, Tom, *Liaisons of Life* (New York: John Wiley & Sons, 2001).

Watling, Roy, 'Beatrix Potter as a Mycologist: The Period before Peter

Rabbit and Friends', lecture (London: The Linnean Society, 24 April 1997).

—— 'But if . . . Helen B. Potter's Year of Anxiety!', *Armitt Library Journal* (1997).

—— 'Helen Beatrix Potter', *The Linnean: Newsletter and Proceedings of the Linnean Society of London*, 16/1 (Jan. 2000), 24–31.

—— 'The Role of the Amateur in Mycology – What Would We Do without Them?', *Mycroscience*, 39 (1998), 513–22.

Religion: Unitarians and Quakers

Ballantyne, J. C., 'Origins of Essex Church, Notting Hill Gate, London', *Transactions of the Unitarian Historical Society*, 7 (1939–42), 130–38.

Bredbury, Jack, *The Foundation of the Stalybridge Unitarian Church and Sunday School and the Connection of Their Origins with the Leech Family* (Stalybridge: Ken and Sue Howard, 2001).

Davis, V. D., *A History of Manchester College* (London: George Allen & Unwin, 1932).

Haakonssen, Knud (ed.), *Enlightenment and Religion: Rational Dissent in Eighteenth-Century Britain* (Cambridge: Cambridge University Press, 1996).

Watt, Ruth, *Gender, Power and the Unitarians in England, 1760–1860* (New York: Longman, 1998).

R. K. Webb, 'The Background: English Unitarianism in the Nineteenth Century', in Leonard Smith (ed.), *Unitarian to the Core: Unitarian College Manchester, 1854–2004* (Manchester: Unitarian College, 2004).

—— 'The Faith of Nineteenth-Century Unitarians: A Curious Incident', in Richard Helmstadter and Bernard Lightman (eds.), *Victorian Faith in Crisis: Essays on Continuity and Change in Nineteenth-Century Religious Belief* (Stanford, Calif.: Stanford University Press, 1990), 126–49.

—— 'The Limits of Religious Liberty', in Richard Helmstadter (ed.), *Freedom and Religion in the Nineteenth Century* (Stanford, Calif.: Stanford University Press, 1997), 120–49.

—— 'The Unitarian Background', in Barbara Smith (ed.), *Truth, Liberty, Religion: Essays Celebrating Two Hundred Years of Manchester College* (Oxford: Manchester College, 1986), 3–29.

Wykes, David, 'Sons and Subscribers: Lay Support and the College', in Barbara Smith (ed.), *Truth, Liberty, Religion: Essays Celebrating Two*

Hundred Years of Manchester College (Oxford: Manchester College, 1986), 32–77.

Science and Natural History

Allen, David Elliston, *The Botanists: A History of the Botanical Society of the British Isles through a Hundred and Fifty Years* (Winchester: St Paul's Bibliographies, 1986).

—— 'The Early Professional in British Natural History', in Alwyne Wheeler and James H. Price (eds.), *From Linnaeus to Darwin: Commentaries on the History of Biology and Geology* (Society for the History of Natural History, 1985), 1–12.

—— *The Naturalist in Britain: A Social History* (London: Allen Lane, 1976).

—— (ed.), *Naturalists and Society: The Culture of Natural History in Britain, 1700–1900* (Burlington, Vt.: Ashgate Publishing Company, 2001).

Alter, Peter, *The Reluctant Patron: Science and the State in Britain, 1850–1920* (Oxford: Oxford University Press, 1987).

Barber, Lynn, *The Heyday of Natural History* (Garden City, NY: Doubleday & Co., 1980).

Blunt, Wilfrid, *The Ark in the Park: The Zoo in the Nineteenth Century* (London: Hamish Hamilton, 1976).

Brockway, Lucile H., *Science and Colonial Expansion: The Role of the British Royal Botanic Gardens. Studies in Social Discontinuity* (Oxford: Oxford University Press, 1990).

Desmond, Ray, *Kew: The History of the Royal Botanic Gardens* (Kew: Harvill Press, 1995).

Drayton, Richard, *Nature's Government: Science, Imperial Britain and the Improvement of the World* (New Haven: Yale University Press, 2000).

Farber, Paul Lawrence, *Finding Order in Nature: The Naturalist Tradition from Linnaeus to E. O. Wilson* (Baltimore: Johns Hopkins University, 2000).

Gage, A. T., and Stearn, W. T., *A Bicentenary History of the Linnean Society of London* (London: Academic Press, 1988).

Gosse, P. H., *Evenings at the Microscope* (1859).

Jardine, N., Secord, J. A., and Spray, E. C. (eds.), *Cultures of Natural History* (Cambridge: Cambridge University Press, 1996).

Kargon, Robert H., *Science in Victorian Manchester* (Baltimore: Johns Hopkins University Press, 1977).

Knoepflmacher, U. C., and Tennyson, G. B. (eds.), *Nature and the Victorian Imagination* (Berkeley: University of California Press, 1977).

Mackenzie, J. (ed.), *Imperialism and the Natural World* (Manchester: University of Manchester Press, 1990).

MacLeod, Roy, and Moseley, Russell (eds.), 'Fathers and Daughters: Reflections on Women, Science and Victorian Cambridge', *History of Education*, 8/4 (1979), 325.

Merrill, Lynn L., *The Romance of Victorian Natural History* (Oxford: Oxford University Press, 1989).

Outram, Dorinda, 'New Spaces in Natural History', in N. Jardine, J. A. Secord and E. C. Spray (eds.), *Cultures of Natural History* (Cambridge: Cambridge University Press, 1996), 249–65.

Peterson, M. Jeanne, *The Medical Profession in Mid-Victorian London* (Berkeley: University of California, 1978).

Porter, Roy, 'Gentlemen and Geology: The Emergence of a Scientific Career, 1660–1920', *Historical Journal*, 21 (1978), 809–36.

Ritvo, Harriet, *The Animal Estate: The English and Other Creatures in the Victorian Age* (Cambridge, Mass.: Harvard University Press, 1987).

Shteir, Ann B., *Cultivating Women, Cultivating Science: Flora's Daughters and Botany in England, 1760–1860* (Baltimore: Johns Hopkins University Press, 1996).

Yanni, Carla, *Nature's Museums: Victorian Science and the Architecture of Display* (Baltimore: Johns Hopkins University Press, 2000).

Women

Bland, Lucy, *Banishing the Beast: English Feminism and Sexual Morality, 1885–1914* (Harmondsworth: Penguin Books, 1995).

Boyd, Nancy, *Three Victorian Women Who Changed Their World* (New York: Oxford University Press, 1982).

Dyhouse, Carol, *Girls Growing Up in Late Victorian and Edwardian England* (London: Routledge & Kegan Paul, 1981).

Gates, Barbara T. (ed.), *In Nature's Name: An Anthology of Women's Writing and Illustration, 1780–1930* (Chicago: University of Chicago Press, 2002).

—— *Kindred Nature: Victorian and Edwardian Women Embrace the Living World* (Chicago: University of Chicago Press, 1998).

Gates, Barbara T., and Shteir, Ann B. (eds.), *Natural Eloquence: Women Reinscribe Science* (Madison: University of Wisconsin Press, 1997).

Gleadle, Kathryn, *The Early Feminists: Radical Unitarians and the Emergence of the Women's Rights Movements, 1831–1851* (New York: St Martin's Press, 1998).

Griffin, Susan, *Women and Nature: The Roaring Inside Her* (New York: Harper and Row, 1978).

Horn, Pamela, *Victorian Countrywomen* (Oxford: Basil Blackwell, 1991).

Laslett, Barbara, Kohlstedt, Sally Gregory, Longino, Helen, and Hammonds, Evelynn (eds.), *Gender and Scientific Authority* (Chicago: University of Chicago Press, 1996).

Levine, Philippa, *Feminist Lives in Victorian England: Private Roles and Public Commitment* (Oxford: Basil Blackwell, 1990).

Nord, Deborah Epstein, *The Apprenticeship of Beatrice Webb* (Amherst: University of Massachusetts Press, 1985).

Peterson, M. Jeanne, *Family, Love and Work in the Lives of Victorian Gentlewomen* (Bloomington: Indiana University Press, 1989).

Rose, Phyllis, *Parallel Lives: Five Victorian Marriages* (London: Chatto & Windus, 1984).

Sheffield, Suzanne Le-May, *Revealing New Worlds: Three Victorian Women Naturalists* (London: Routledge, 2001).

Vicinus, Martha (ed.), *Suffer and Be Still: Women in the Victorian Age* (Bloomington: Indiana University Press, 1972).

Index

In the subheadings of this index, Beatrix Potter's name is abbreviated to BP. Her paintings and publications are entered under their titles, as are anonymous publications; all other works are entered under their originators. Subjects appearing in the notes section are indexed only where a note includes information not directly concerning the subject under discussion at the associated point in the main text.